Lecture Notes in Computer Science   801

Edited by G. Goos and J. Hartmanis

Advisory Board: W. Brauer   D. Gries   J. Stoer

Jan-Olof Eklundh (Ed.)

Computer Vision — ECCV '94

Third European Conference on Computer Vision
Stockholm, Sweden, May 2–6, 1994
Proceedings, Volume II

Springer-Verlag
Berlin Heidelberg New York
London Paris Tokyo
Hong Kong Barcelona
Budapest

Jan-Olof Eklundh (Ed.)

Computer Vision – ECCV '94

Third European Conference on Computer Vision
Stockholm, Sweden, May 2-6, 1994
Proceedings, Volume II

Springer-Verlag
Berlin Heidelberg New York
London Paris Tokyo
Hong Kong Barcelona
Budapest

Series Editors

Gerhard Goos
Universität Karlsruhe
Postfach 69 80
Vincenz-Priessnitz-Straße 1
D-76131 Karlsruhe, Germany

Juris Hartmanis
Cornell University
Department of Computer Science
4130 Upson Hall
Ithaca, NY 14853, USA

Volume Editor

Jan-Olof Eklundh
Department of Numerical Analysis and Computer Science
Royal Institute of Technology
S-10044 Stockholm, Sweden

CR Subject Classification (1991): I.3, I.5, I.2.9-10, I.4

ISBN 3-540-57957-5 Springer-Verlag Berlin Heidelberg New York
ISBN 0-387-57957-5 Springer-Verlag New York Berlin Heidelberg

CIP data applied for

This work is subject to copyright. All rights are reserved, whether the whole or part
of the material is concerned, specifically the rights of translation, reprinting, re-use
of illustrations, recitation, broadcasting, reproduction on microfilms or in any other
way, and storage in data banks. Duplication of this publication or parts thereof is
permitted only under the provisions of the German Copyright Law of September 9,
1965, in its current version, and permission for use must always be obtained from
Springer-Verlag. Violations are liable for prosecution under the German Copyright
Law.

© Springer-Verlag Berlin Heidelberg 1994
Printed in Germany

Typesetting: Camera-ready by author
SPIN: 10131081   45/3140-543210 - Printed on acid-free paper

Conference Chairman
Jan-Olof Eklundh   Royal Institute of Technology, Stockholm

Conference Board
M. Brady	Oxford University
B. Buxton	GEC Hirst Research Center
O. Faugeras	INRIA, Sophia-Antipolis
G. Granlund	Linköping University
D. Hogg	Leeds University
J. Mayhew	Sheffield University
R. Mohr	INPG, Grenoble
H. Nagel	IITB, Karlsruhe
B. Neumann	Hamburg University
G. Sandini	University of Genova
V. Torre	University of Genova

Program Committee
N. Ayache	INRIA, Sophia-Antipolis
R. Bajcsy	University of Pennsylvania
A. Blake	Oxford University
P. Bouthemy	IRISA, Rennes
H. Burkhard	University of Hamburg-Harburg
H. Buxton	University of Sussex, Brighton
S. Carlsson	Royal Institute of Technology, Stockholm
A. Casals	University of Barcelona
J. Crowley	INPG, Grenoble
R. Deriche	INRIA, Sophia-Antipolis
E. Dickmanns	Universität der Bundeswehr, Munich
W. Enkelmann	IITB, Karlsruhe
E. Granum	Aalborg University
I. Gurevitch	Russian Academy of Science, Moscow
R. Horaud	INPG, Grenoble
L. Kirousis	University of Patras
H. Knutsson	Linköping University
J. Koenderink	Utrecht State University
S. Peleg	The Hebrew University of Jerusalem
J. Porrill	Sheffield University
W. von Seelen	Bochum University
G. Sparr	Lund University
G. Sullivan	University of Reading
M. Tistarelli	University of Genova
S. Tsuji	Osaka University
D. Vernon	Trinity College, Dublin
A. Verri	University of Genova
A. Zisserman	Oxford University

Foreword

The European Conference on Computer Vision (ECCV) has since it was first arranged in 1990 established itself as a major event in this exciting and very active field of research. It has therefore been both a challenge and an honor for me to arrange the 3rd ECCV in Stockholm, May 2–6, 1994.

This two-volume proceedings collects the 115 papers accepted for presentation at the conference. Selecting them from over 300 submissions of excellent quality has been extremely difficult. I would like to extend my deep gratitude to my friends in the program committee for performing this task under very tight time constraints. In my view, the outcome of this work is a well balanced conference reflecting the state-of-the-art in computer vision in an excellent way.

I would also like to ask those who might perceive imperfection in how their contributions were treated to understand how difficult such a process is. In fact, so many high quality papers were submitted that acceptance was guided more by the wish to keep the single track conference than by some absolute measure of quality.

Arranging the conference and its scientific program has been possible only through extensive efforts by many more people than those in the program committee. I thank all the others who have helped us with reviewing the papers, whose names you can find listed on pages VII and VIII of volume I of this proceedings. I also thank all the members of my research group, the Computational Vision and Active Perception Laboratory (CVAP) at KTH, for their help. Especially I would like to thank Stefan Carlsson, Jonas Gårding and Birgit Ekberg, who have been instrumental in the work with arranging the program and this book. Giulio Sandini, who chaired ECCV 92 has provided invaluable help and advice at all stages of the work.

Finally, I wish to thank KTH and its President Janne Carlsson, The National Swedish Board for Technical and Industrial Development (NUTEK) and The European Vision Society for supporting the conference.

Stockholm, February 1994,   Jan-Olof Eklundh

Contents

Segmentation and Restoration

Illumination

Shading and Colour

Motion Segmentation

Feature-Extraction

Registration and Reconstruction

Geometry and Invariants

Author Index 483

Contents of Volume I

Motion Segmentation and Tracking

Ego-Motion and 3D Recovery

Recognition I

Shape Modelling

Shape Estimation

Geometry and Shape II

Calibration and Multiple Views

Recognition II

Stereo and Calibration

Active Vision I

Active Object Recognition Integrating Attention and Viewpoint Control*

Sven J. Dickinson,¹ Henrik I. Christensen,²
John Tsotsos,¹ and Göran Olofsson³

¹ Dept. of Computer Science, University of Toronto,
6 King's College Rd., Toronto, Ontario, Canada M5S 1A4
² Laboratory of Image Analysis,
Aalborg University, DK-9220 Aalborg, Denmark
³ Computational Vision and Active Perception Laboratory,
Royal Institute of Technology, S-100 44 Stockholm, Sweden

Abstract. We present an active object recognition strategy which combines the use of an attention mechanism for focusing the search for a 3-D object in a 2-D image, with a viewpoint control strategy for disambiguating recovered object features. The attention mechanism consists of a probabilistic search through a hierarchy of predicted feature observations, taking objects into a set of regions classified according to the shape of their bounding contours. If the features recovered during the attention phase do not provide a unique mapping to the 3-D object recognized, the probabilistic feature hierarchy can be used to guide the camera to a new viewpoint from where the object can be unambiguously...

1. Introduction

An important aspect of active vision is the use of an attention mechanism to decide where in the image to search for a particular object[14][15]. Template matching schemes which move an object template throughout the image order are a common mechanism since all positions in the image are treated equally. However, any recognition scheme that preprocesses the image to extract some set of features provides a basis for a top-down mechanism. Assuming that the recovered image features correspond to model features, object search can be performed at those locations in the image where the features are recovered.

For an attention mechanism to be effective, the features must be inexpensive to recover (low entropy). The recovered features are common to every object

* The authors gratefully acknowledge the assistance of Lars Olsson, Göran Anliot, James Maclean, Sean Culhane, Winky Wai, Yiming Ye, and Feng Lu in the implementation of this work. Henrik Christensen and Göran Olofsson would like to acknowledge funding support from ... BOT project based at the University of ... and Intelligent Systems, a Network of Centres ... of Canada. Tsotsos is the CP/Unesco Chair of the Canadian Institute for Advanced Research.

Active Object Recognition Integrating Attention and Viewpoint Control*

Sven J. Dickinson[1], Henrik I. Christensen[2],
John Tsotsos[1], and Göran Olofsson[3]

[1] Dept. of Computer Science, University of Toronto
6 King's College Rd., Toronto, Ontario, Canada M5S 1A4
[2] Laboratory of Image Analysis, IES
Aalborg University, DK-9220 Aalborg, Denmark
[3] Computational Vision and Active Perception Laboratory
Royal Institute of Technology, S-100 44 Stockholm, Sweden

Abstract. We present an active object recognition strategy which combines the use of an attention mechanism for focusing the search for a 3-D object in a 2-D image, with a viewpoint control strategy for disambiguating recovered object features. The attention mechanism consists of a probabilistic search through a hierarchy of predicted feature observations, taking objects into a set of regions classified according to the shapes of their bounding contours. If the features recovered during the attention phase do not provide a unique mapping to the 3-D object being searched, the probabilistic feature hierarchy can be used to guide the camera to a new viewpoint from where the object can be disambiguated.

1 Introduction

An important aspect of active vision is the use of an attentional mechanism to decide where in the image to search for a particular object [14]. Template matching schemes which move an object template throughout the image offer no attention mechanism since all positions in the image are treated equally. However, any recognition scheme that preprocesses the image to extract some set of features provides a basis for an attention mechanism. Assuming that the recovered image features correspond to model features, object search can be performed at those locations in the image where the features are recovered.

For an attention mechanism to be effective, the features must be distinguishing, i.e., have low entropy. If the recovered features are common to every object

---

* The authors gratefully acknowledge the assistance of Lars Olsson, Gene Amdur, James Maclean, Sean Culhane, Winky Wai, Yiming Ye, and Feng Lu in the implementation of this work. Henrik Christensen and Göran Olofsson would like to acknowledge funding support from EP-7108-VAP "Vision as Process". The PLAYBOT project, based at the University of Toronto, is part of the Institute for Robotics ad Intelligent Systems, a Network of Centers of Excllence funded by the Government of Canada. Tsotsos is the CP-Unitel Fellow of the Canadian Institute for Advanced Research.

being searched, they offer little in the way of focusing a search for an object. This is typical in object recognition systems which match simple image features like corners or zeroes of curvature to model features, e.g., [10, 5, 8]. Although invariant to viewpoint, there may be an abundance of such features in the image, leading to a combinatorial explosion in the number of possible correspondences between image and model features that must be verified. In the first part of this paper, we will argue that regions, characterized by the shapes of their bounding contours, provide a more effective attention mechanism than simple linear features. We go on to present a Bayesian attention mechanism which maps objects into volumetric parts, maps volumetric parts into aspects, and maps aspects to component faces. Face predictions are then matched to recovered regions with a goodness-of-fit providing an ordering of the search locations.

In the second part of this paper, we extend our object representation for attention to support active viewpoint control. We will introduce a representation, called the *aspect prediction graph*, which is based on the aspect graph. Given an ambiguous view of an object, the representation will first tell us if there is a view of the object which is more discriminating. If so, the representation will tell us in which direction we should move the camera to encounter that view. Finally, the representation will tell us what visual events (the appearance or disappearance of features on the object) we can expect to encounter while moving the camera to the new viewpoint.

2 Attention

2.1 Review of the Object Representation

To demonstrate our approach to attention, we have selected an object representation similar to that used by Biederman [1], in which the Cartesian product of contrastive shape properties gives rise to a set of volumetric primitives called geons. For our investigation, we have chosen three properties including cross-section shape, axis shape, and cross-section size variation (Dickinson, Pentland, and Rosenfeld [3]). The cartesian product of the dichotomous and trichotomous values of these properties give rise to the set of ten volumes illustrated in Figure 1; to construct objects, the volumes are simply attached to one another.

Traditional aspect graph representations of 3-D objects model an entire object with a set of aspects, each defining a topologically distinct view of an object in terms of its visible surfaces (Koenderink and van Doorn [7]). Our approach differs in that we use aspects to represent the (typically small) set of volumetric part classes from which each object in our database is constructed, rather than representing an entire object directly. The representation, called the *aspect hierarchy*, consists of three levels, including of the set of *aspects* that model the chosen volumes, the set of component *faces* of the aspects, and the set of *boundary groups* representing all subsets of contours bounding the faces. The ambiguous mappings between the levels of the aspect hierarchy were originally captured in a set of upward conditional probabilities (Dickinson et al. [3]), mapping boundary

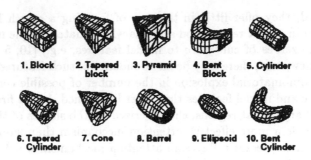

Fig. 1. The Ten Modeling Primitives

groups to faces, faces to aspects, and aspects to volumes.[4] However, for the attention mechanism described in this paper, the aspect hierarchy was augmented to include the downward conditional probabilities mapping volumes to aspects, aspects to faces, and faces to boundary groups. Figure 2 illustrates a portion of the augmented aspect hierarchy.

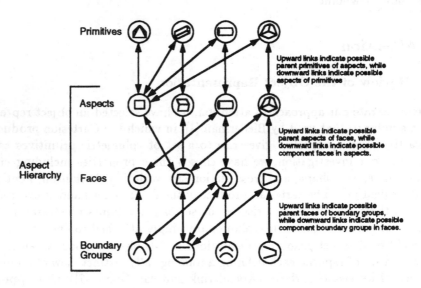

Fig. 2. The Augmented Aspect Hierarchy

2.2 A Case for Focusing on Regions

Given the various levels of the augmented aspect hierarchy, the question arises: At which recovered features from the image do we focus our search for a particular object? Many CAD-based recognition systems advocate extracting simple features like corners, high curvature points, or zeroes of curvature. Although robustly recoverable from the image, there may be many such features in the image offering marginal utility for directing a search. Such features are analogous to the boundary group level of features in the augmented aspect hierarchy. By examining the conditional probabilities in the augmented aspect hierarchy, we can compare the relative utility of boundary groups and faces in inferring the identity of a volumetric part.[5]

To compare the utility of boundary groups versus faces in recovering volumes, we will use the conditional probabilities captured in the augmented aspect hierarchy to define a measure of *average inferencing uncertainty*, or the degree to which uncertainty remains in volume identity given a recovered boundary group or face. More formally, we define average inferencing uncertainty for boundary groups, U_{Avg}^{BG}, and for recovered faces, U_{Avg}^{F}, as follows:[6]

$$U_{Avg}^{BG} = -\frac{1}{N_{BG}} \sum_{i=1}^{N_{BG}} \sum_{j=1}^{N_V} Pr(V_j \mid BG_i) \log Pr(V_j \mid BG_i) \qquad (1)$$

$$U_{Avg}^{F} = -\frac{1}{N_{FA}} \sum_{i=1}^{N_F} \sum_{j=1}^{N_V} Pr(V_j \mid F_i) \log Pr(V_j \mid F_i) \qquad (2)$$

where:

N_{BG} = number of boundary groups in the augmented aspect hierarchy
N_{FA} = number of faces in the augmented aspect hierarchy
N_V = number of volumes in the augmented aspect hierarchy

The average inferencing uncertainty for faces is 0.23 while that for boundary groups is 0.74. Clearly, faces offer a more powerful focus feature for the recovery of volumetric parts than do the simpler features that make up the boundary groups. However, this advantage is only realizable if the cost of extracting the two types of features is comparable. By using simple region segmentation techniques whose complexity is comparable to common edge detection techniques, we can avoid the complexity of grouping lines into faces. We can accommodate the segmentation errors associated with a cheap region grower by using partial information to intelligently guide viewpoint control to improve the interpretation.

---

[5] Since aspect recovery first requires the recovery of component faces, we will examine the choice between recovering simple contour-based features (boundary groups) and regions (faces).

[6] We have suppressed the zero-probability terms in this and remaining expressions for notational simplicity.

2.3 Focus of Attention

Our attention mechanism will exploit the augmented aspect hierarchy to map target objects down to target faces which, in turn, will be compared to image faces recovered during preprocessing. In selecting which recovered face to focus our attention on, we utilize a decision theoretic approach using a Baysian framework. A similar approach was reported by Levitt et al. [9], who use Baysian networks for both model representation and description of recovered image features. Specifically, they use Baysian networks for both data aggregation and selection of actions and feature detectors based on expected utility. The approach is thus centered around the use of a Baysian approach to integration and control. Similar techniques have also been reported by Rimey and Brown [13], and Jensen et al. [6], where both regions of interest and feature detectors are selected according to utility/cost strategies.

To select a region of interest, i.e., attend to a particular face, the augmented aspect hierarchy may be considered as a Baysian network, allowing us to utilize decision theory as described, for example, by Pearl [12]. To apply such a strategy, it is necessary to define both utility and cost measures. The utility function, U, specifies the power of a given feature at one level of the augmented aspect hierarchy, e.g., volumes, aspects, faces, and boundary groups, to discriminate a feature at a higher level. The cost function, C, specifies the cost of extracting a particular feature. The subsequent planning is then aimed at optimizing the benefit, $\max B(U, C)$; profit, e.g., $utility - cost$, is often maximized in this step.

For the system described in this paper, the face recovery algorithm was chosen to support a simple implementation on a Datacube image processor. From an input image, our bottom-up processing step yields a *face topology graph*, in which nodes encode the possible face interpretations of segmented image regions, and arcs encode region adjacency. For a given node, the face interpretations are ranked in decreasing order of probability; for details on face recovery, see [11]. Since the cost of face recovery is assumed to be constant and equal for all types of faces, the selection of which face to consider next should simply optimize the utility function.

Given a target object, $object_T$, the first step is to choose a target volume, $volume_T$, to search for. Next, given a target volume, $volume_T$, we choose a target aspect, $aspect_T$, to search for. Finally, given a target aspect, $aspect_T$, we choose a target face, $face_T$, to search for. Given a target face, $face_T$, we then examine the face topology graph for labeled faces which match $face_T$. If there is more than one, they are ranked in descending order according to their probabilities.

The above top-down sequence of predictions represents a best-first search of a tree defined by each object; the root of the tree represents the target object, while the leaf nodes of the tree represent target faces. The target volume subtrees for each object tree are independent of the object database and can be specified at compile time. The branching factor at a given node in any object tree can be reduced by specifying a probability (or utility) threshold on a prediction. The heuristic we use to guide the search is based on the power of an object's features, e.g., volumes, aspects, and faces, to identify the object. For example, to determine how discriminative a particular volume, $volume_i$, is in identifying the target object, $object_T$, we use the following function:

$$D(volume_i, object_T) = \frac{Pr(object_T | volume_i)}{\sum_j Pr(object_j | volume_i)} * Pr(volume_i) \qquad (3)$$

The numerator specifies how discriminative $volume_i$ is for $object_T$, while the ratio specifies the "voting power" of $volume_i$ for the object of interest. $Pr(object_i | volume_j)$, for any given i and j, is computed directly from the contents of the object database. The last term specifies the likelihood of finding the volume, and is included to discourage the selection of a volume which is highly discriminative but very unlikely. The $Pr(volume)$ may be calculated as follows:

$$Pr(volume_i) = \sum_k (Pr(volume_i | object_k) * Pr(object_k)) \qquad (4)$$

where $Pr(volume_i | object_k)$, for any given i and k, is computed directly from the object database, and $Pr(object_k)$ represents a priori knowledge of scene content. $D(aspect_i, volume_T)$ and $D(face_i, aspect_T)$ are defined in an analagous fashion.

When we descend the search tree to a given target face, we search for matching face candidates in the face topology graph. We focus our attention on the best face matching the target face, and proceed to verify the object. If a target face, target aspect, or target volume cannot be verified, the search algorithm backtracks, applying the above utility functions to remaining faces, aspects, and volumes in the search tree.

2.4 Verification

Verification is the process by which we move from a matched target face node in the search tree back up to an object. Once we have a matched face leaf node, our next step is to verify its parent (target) aspect [3]. This entails searching the vicinity of the target face for faces whose labels and configuration match the target aspect using an interpretation tree search (Grimson and Lozano-Pérez [4]). Note that the resulting verified aspect has a score associated with it which can be compared to a score threshold to terminate the search from a particular target face. The score of a recovered aspect is calculated as follows:

$$AspectScore = \frac{1}{N} \sum_{k=1}^{N} Pr(Face_k) * \frac{Length(BG_k)}{Length(Region_k)} \qquad (5)$$

where: N is the number of faces in model aspect, $Length(BG_k)$ is the length of boundary group, and $Length(Region_k)$ is the perimeter of the region. Note that if the region boundary graph recovered for the shape exactly matches some face in the augmented aspect hierarchy, its probability will be 1.0 and the length of its boundary group will be the perimeter of the entire region. The score of a volume is calculated as follows:

$$VolumeScore = AspectScore * Pr(ModelVolume | ModelAspect) \qquad (6)$$

where:

$Pr(ModelVolume|ModelAspect)$ = probability of volume given aspect
(from the augmented aspect hierarchy)

Once a target aspect is found, we then proceed up the tree one level to the target volume, defining a mapping between the faces in the target aspect and the surfaces on the target volume. Moving back one level to the object, we must then decide whether or not we have enough information confirming the target object. If so, the recognition process is complete. If not, we must then decide which volume to search for next. If we choose a volume which is connected to a volume we have already verified, we can move back down its branch in the tree and, when matching its target faces to image faces, consider only those image faces that are topologically adjacent to the faces belonging to the verified volume.

3 Viewpoint Control

Through segmentation errors, occlusion, or "accidental viewpoint" [7], a recovered aspect may be ambiguous. By extending our object representation, we can use the recovered aspect to drive the sensor to a new position from which the object's part can be disambiguated. The extended representation, called the *aspect prediction graph*, tells us which of the volume's aspects represents a "better" view of the volume, how the camera should be moved in order to achieve this view, and what visual events can be expected as the camera is moved.

The aspect prediction graph (APG) is derived from two sources: an aspect graph and the augmented aspect hierarchy. The APG is a more efficient version of the aspect graph in which topologically equivalent nodes are grouped regardless of whether their faces map to different surfaces on the object. For example, the APG encodes 3 aspects for a block (volume 1 in Figure 1) while an aspect graph encodes 26 aspects. Next, the APG specifies the visual events in terms of which faces appear/disappear when moving from one aspect to another. Furthermore, the position of such a face appearance/disappearance from a source aspect to a target aspect is specified with respect to particular contours of faces in the source aspect (event contours). Moreover, the transition between two nodes (aspects) encodes the direction(s) relative to the event contours that one must move in the image plane in order to observe the visual event. Finally, the APG borrows from the augmented aspect hierarchy both the $Pr(volume|aspect)$ and $Pr(aspect|volume)$ conditional probabilities, and assigns them to the nodes in the APG.

To illustrate the above concepts, Figure 3 presents the APG for the block volume, illustrating the three possible aspects of the block. Between every two nodes (aspects) in the aspect prediction graph are a pair of directed arcs. The directed arc between aspect 1 and aspect 2 in Figure 3(a) is expanded in Figure 3(b). From aspect 1 in Figure 3(a), there are three ways to move to a view

---

[7] The probability of an "accidental viewpoint" is actually quite significant, as was shown in [15].

in which aspect 2 will be visible. Movement relative to contours 0 and 1 on face 2 will cause a visual event in which face 2 disappears at contour 1 on face 0 and at contour 3 on face 1. Or, movement relative to contours 0 and 1 on face 0 will cause a visual event in which face 0 will disappear at contour 0 on face 1 and contour 0 on face 2. Finally, movement relative to contours 0 and 3 on face 1 will cause a visual event in which face 1 will disappear at contour 0 on face 0 and contour 1 on face 2.

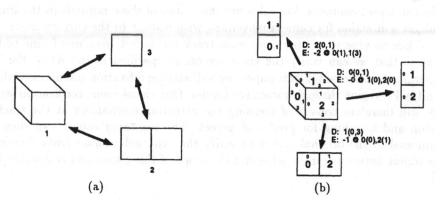

(a)   (b)

Fig. 3. (a) Aspect Prediction Graph (APG) for Volume 1 (Block) (b) APG Transitions from Aspect 1 to Aspect 2

It should be noted that in the augmented aspect hierarchy, each aspect has an indexing of its component faces, and each component face has a similar indexing of its bounding contours. By referring to the normals of such well-defined contours in a recovered aspect, we can qualitatively specify direction rules with respect to an aspect-centered coordinate system. The direction of view change is hence specified as a vector sum of the normals to particular contours of the recovered aspect corresponding to the current APG aspect.[8] The face events are also defined with respect to these specified contours. For example, we can predict along which contour in the current aspect a new face will appear or disappear when moving towards a new aspect.

Using the attention mechanism described earlier in section 2.3, the search for an object includes a search for its component volumes. Each recovered volume is characterized by the aspect in which it is viewed. For a given aspect of a volume, we can use the volume to aspect mappings in the augmented aspect hierarchy to determine which aspects (if any) are more probable (or stable) than the current one, by maintaining an ordered list of aspects for each volume, ranked in decreasing order of their downward conditional probabilities. Conversely, if we have an ambiguous aspect whose mapping to the hypothesized volume is weak, we can use the aspect to volume mappings in the augmented aspect hierarchy to determine which aspects offer a less ambiguous mapping to that volume. These

---

[8] For concave and convex curve segments, the normal at the midpoint is used.

aspects, ranked in decreasing order of their upward conditional probabilities, offer an effective means of disambiguating a given view of a volume.

When we want to move the camera in a direction to get a "better" view, we first check the APG to see which aspects (neighboring nodes) can be reached from the current aspect (node). The probabilities associated with the APG nodes tell us to which aspect to move in order to achieve a more likely view of the volume or to disambiguate it. The arc to this "best" neighbor node encodes the view change direction (in the image plane) in terms of a function of the normals of selected aspect contours. We calculate the values of these normals in the image and get a direction for camera movement with respect to the current aspect.

While moving the camera, we must track the aspect from one frame to the next so that we can verify the visual events as specified in the APG. For the experiments described in this paper, we will assume a fixation mechanism which can track a region through successive frames. Our visual event verification strategy will therefore consist of focusing the attention mechanism at the tracked region and searching for predicted aspect. The recovered aspect can then be compared to the original aspect to verify the expected visual events. Tracking the object between frames is beyond the scope of this paper and is described in [2].

4 Results

We test the attention and viewpoint control strategies in the context of a multi-disciplinary research effort exploring active vision in the domain of robotic aids for the handicapped (PLAYBOT). Through a touch-screen interface, a child can instruct a mobile robot vision system to identify, localize, and manipulate 3-D objects in its environment. To support simple manipulation of the objects, the domain of objects that the system can visually identify consists of the ten volumetric shapes outlined in Figure 1[9]; more complex objects, modeled as constructions of the ten shapes, will be supported in the future. In the following results, the images were acquired using the stereo head at the CVAP Laboratory at KTH, Stockholm. Only one camera was used to acquire images and during viewpoint control, the camera was fixated on the object.

In Figure 4, we present the results of applying the attention mechanism to a scene containing single-volume objects. Moving top to bottom and left to right, the first image shows the results of the region segmentation step; recall that the face topology graph constructed from the region topology graph is the input to the attention mechanism. The next three images show the three best instances of the block viewed in its most likely aspect containing three faces. The faces in the aspect are highlighted in the image; only those contours (boundary group) used in defining the face are highlighted in the face.

Using this measure, the first three volumes received the score of 1.0, 1.0, and 0.86, respectively. The next three images show the best three instances of the

---

[9] Each of the ten objects is assumed to be equally likely.

second most likely aspect containing two faces; each recovered aspect received the score of 0.48. Continuing, the next two images show the best two instances of the least likely aspect containing one face; each recovered aspect received the score of 0.22. The last three images show the highest-scoring instances of the tapered block (0.79), the cylinder (0.27), and the barrel (0.46), respectively. Due to noise and occlusion, only certain portions of each shape were recovered. In the case of the barrel, region undersegmentation results in the recovered aspect being incorrectly oriented with the visible end assumed to be occluded at the bottom.

In Figure 5, we show the result of the attention mechanism as it searches for a block (first image) and a cylinder (third image). The block is recovered in its second most likely aspect which is ambiguous (common to volumes 1 and 4), while the cylinder is recovered in its second most likely aspect which is ambiguous (common to volumes 1, 2, 3, 4, 5, and 10). Guided by the aspect prediction graph, the camera is moved to the left in each case and the attention scheme is guided to disambiguate the volume by searching for its most likely aspect, as is shown in the second and fourth images.

5 Conclusions

In examining the balance between recovery and verification, we have clearly moved towards recovery. Recovering more discriminating features facilitates an effective attention mechanism based on the viewing probabilities in the aspect hierarchy. However, there is a cost in attempting to recover more complex features (in our case, a set of regions and their bounding shapes). Our solution to this problem is to pass along this cost to a dynamic sensor. We assume that some relatively unoccluded, fronto-parallel surfaces will project into regions that can be quickly and cheaply extracted using simple region segmentation techniques. We use this recovered partial information to intelligently guide the sensor to a position where the object can be disambiguated. The aspect hierarchy, and its extension to the aspect prediction graph, provides a unifying representation for the active vision problems of attention and viewpoint control.

References

1. I. Biederman. Human image understanding: Recent research and a theory. *Computer Vision, Graphics, and Image Processing*, 32:29–73, 1985.
2. S. Dickinson, P. Jasiobedzki, H. Christensen, and G. Olofsson. Qualitative tracking of 3-D objects using active contour networks. In *Proceedings, CVPR '94*, Seattle, June 1994.
3. S. Dickinson, A. Pentland, and A. Rosenfeld. 3-D shape recovery using distributed aspect matching. *IEEE Transactions on Pattern Analysis and Machine Intelligence*, 14(2):174–198, 1992.
4. W. Grimson and T. Lozano-Pérez. Model-based recognition and localization from sparse range or tactile data. *International Journal of Robotics Research*, 3(3):3–35, 1984.

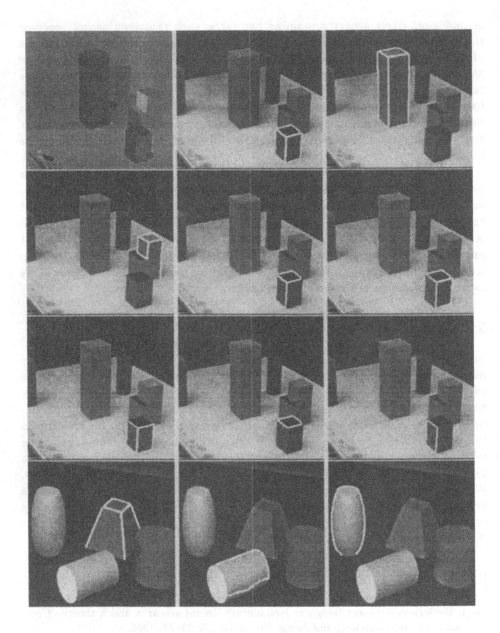

Fig. 4. Demonstration of the Attention Mechanism. The top three rows show the results of searching for Volume 1 in Figure 1. The last row shows the results of searching for Volumes 2, 5, and 8. (see text for explanation)

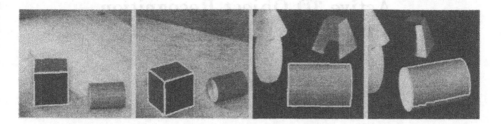

Fig. 5. Moving the Sensor to Disambiguate Recovered Volumes

5. D. Huttenlocher and S. Ullman. Recognizing solid objects by alignment with an image. *International Journal of Computer Vision*, 5(2):195–212, 1990.
6. F. Jensen, H. Christensen, and J. Nielsen. Baysian methods for interpretation and control in multiagent vision systems. In K. Bowyer, editor, *SPIE Applications of AI X: Machine Vision and Robotics*, volume 1708, pages 536–548, Orlando, FL, April 1992.
7. J. Koenderink and A. van Doorn. The internal representation of solid shape with respect to vision. *Biological Cybernetics*, 32:211–216, 1979.
8. Y. Lamdan, J. Schwartz, and H. Wolfson. On recognition of 3-D objects from 2-D images. In *Proceedings, IEEE International Conference on Robotics and Automation*, pages 1407–1413, Philadelphia, PA, 1988.
9. T. Levitt, J. Agosta, and T. Binford. Model based influence diagrams for machine vision. In M. Herion, R. Shacter, L. Kanal, and J. lemmer, editors, *Uncertainty in Artificial Intelligence 5*, volume 10 of *Machine Intelligence and Pattern Recognition Series*, pages 371–388. North Holland, 1990.
10. D. Lowe. *Perceptual Organization and Visual Recognition*. Kluwer Academic Publishers, Norwell, MA, 1985.
11. D. Metaxas and S. Dickinson. Integration of quantitative and qualitative techniques for deformable model fitting from orthographic, perspective, and stereo projections. In *Proceedings, Fourth International Conference on Computer Vision (ICCV)*, Berlin, May 1993.
12. J. Pearl. *Probabilistic Reasoning in Intelligent Systems*. Morgan Kaufmann Publishers, Inc., 1987.
13. R. Rimey and C. Brown. Where to look next using a bayes net: Incorporating geometric relations. In G. Sandini, editor, *European Conference on Computer Vision (ECCV)*, volume 588 of *Lecture Notes in Computer Science*, pages 542–550. Springer Verlag, May 1992.
14. J. Tsotsos. On the relative complexity of active vs passive visual search. *International Journal of Computer Vision*, 7(2):127–141, 1992.
15. D. Wilkes, S. Dickinson, and J. Tsotsos. Quantitative modeling of view degeneracy. In *Proceedings, 8th Scandinavian Conference on Image Analysis*, University of Tromsø, Norway, May 1993.

Active 3D Object Recognition using 3D Affine Invariants

Sven Vinther and Roberto Cipolla

Department of Engineering, University of Cambridge, Cambridge CB2 1PZ, England

Abstract. We evaluate the power of 3D affine invariants in an object recognition scheme. These invariants are actively estimated by Kalman filtering the data obtained from real-time tracking of image features through a sequence of images. Object information is stored and retrieved in a hash table using the invariants as stable indices. Recognition takes place when significant evidence for a particular shape has been found from the table. Results with real data are presented, and the noise problems arising due to the *weak* perspective approximation and corner localisation errors are discussed. Preliminary results for extending this method to multiple object recognition in cluttered scenes are also presented.

1 Introduction

Central to any object recognition scheme are issues of model representation, feature extraction and feature matching. An extensive survey describing current methods of object representation and matching can by found in [1]. A number of different working recognition schemes have been proposed for simple 3D objects. Lowe [2] presents a 3D object recognition system which uses a single image, *perceptual groupings* and viewpoint consistency constraints to detect 3D objects from 2D data. Alignment [3] uses a minimal set of features to calculate the model-to-image transformation, which is then verified using back-projection of model edges. Other approaches make use of 3D data extracted with a range finder or computed from multiple calibrated views. An example is the approach by Grimson and Lozano-Perez [4] which operates by examining all hypotheses between segmented range data and model surfaces, and efficiently discarding inconsistent ones by using local constraints. An alternative approach involves *geometric invariants* [5].

2 Geometric Invariants

Geometric invariants are properties of image features which do not change under a variety of transformations. Those properties which are invariant under rigid 3D transformations and perspective or *weak* perspective projection, are particularly attractive in computer vision tasks such as 3D object recognition, since they allow an efficient object representation which can be used in shape indexing. A well-known example of invariance under perspective projection is the *cross-ratio* of four points on a line. In this paper we evaluate the power of 3D affine invariants in a 3D object recognition scheme.

Lecture Notes in Computer Science, Vol. 801
Jan-Olof Eklundh (Ed.)

Weak Perspective Throughout this paper the *weak* perspective assumption
will be made about the projection of the 3D object into the image plane. *Weak*
perspective is a good approximation of full perspective when the distance from
object to camera, is much greater than the extent of the object (a ratio greater
than 10:1) [6]. The use of this approximation means the transformation of a
3D object from world coordinates (X_w, Y_w, Z_w) to image points (u, v), which
consists of a combination of rigid motions and the *weak* perspective projection,
can be represented by the general 3D affine transformation matrix shown in (1).

$$\begin{bmatrix} su \\ sv \\ s \end{bmatrix} = \begin{bmatrix} t_{11} & t_{12} & t_{13} & t_{14} \\ t_{21} & t_{22} & t_{23} & t_{24} \\ 0 & 0 & 0 & t_{34} \end{bmatrix} \begin{bmatrix} X_w \\ Y_w \\ Z_w \\ 1 \end{bmatrix} \tag{1}$$

2.1 3D Affine Invariants

The objects to be recognised are represented by point sets denoting the position
of the object vertices. By creating a 3D basis (figure 1) using four of these points,
it is possible to define the position of any other point $\mathbf{X_4}$ by a linear combination
of the basis vectors with the appropriate coefficients (2).

$$\mathbf{X_4} = \mathbf{X_0} + \alpha\mathbf{E_1} + \beta\mathbf{E_2} + \gamma\mathbf{E_3} \tag{2}$$

These coefficients (α, β, γ) are in fact invariant under any 3D affine transformation (1) [7, 8], and we will refer to them as 3D *affine* invariants. The affine
invariants contain a description of the 3D structure of the object, up to a 3D
affine transformation. Since the effect of the intrinsic camera parameters on
projection can be absorbed into the affine transformation, affine invariants are
unchanged by these aswell, with the benefit to the recognition system that no
extensive calibration is required. The recovery of the 3D affine invariants from
an unconstrained 2D image is not possible [9], unless some external prior information about the model is available (*e.g.* shape symmetry [10]). However the
extraction of the 3D affine invariants becomes fairly simple from multiple images
with known point correspondence [5, 11]. In this paper we estimate the affine invariants by Kalman filtering the data obtained from real-time tracking of image
features through a sequence of images. This has the advantages of reducing the
uncertainty in the invariant estimate and it avoids the correspondence problem
present with stereo image pairs.

3 Object Model Acquisition and Recognition

A preliminary task for any object recognition system is the reliable extraction
of features from raw intensity images. We wish to detect corners in the image
which relate to the projections of object vertices (as in [3]). These vertices are
tracked through a sequence of images, and a Kalman Filter is used to optimally
estimate the invariants from the stream of data. The feature extraction and
tracking processes are described in greater detail in [11]. The next task is to
match the invariants extracted from the image data with those computed from

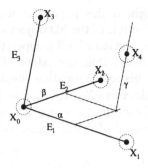

Fig. 1. Affine Basis.

a 3D model. Instead of calculating all the invariants for each 3D object model at recognition time, the information can be precomputed and stored in a database off-line. This greatly speeds up the final recognition process at the cost of extra storage space. Geometric hashing [13] is used to implement this data storage.

3.1 Optimal Estimation of the Invariants and their Uncertainty

The most important stage in the recognition scheme is the accurate estimation of the 3D affine invariants. This goal is achieved by using a Kalman filter to integrate data from multiple views, and optimally estimate the invariant coefficients α, β, γ. In addition the Kalman filter returns the uncertainty of the invariant estimates, in terms of estimate variances.

Estimate Uncertainty There are a number of factors which will affect the uncertainty of the 3D affine invariant estimate. Firstly the amount of noise expected in the track data needs to be considered. This will depend on the accuracy of point localisation by the corner detector, and will probably vary in different imaging environments. Its value can either be measured from test data or estimated, and input into the observation noise matrix of the Kalman Filter.

Secondly the 3D basis geometry will affect the sensitivity of the invariants to noise. If the basis is formed from 3D points which are nearly coplanar the resulting equations will become ill-conditioned, and thus provide noise sensitive estimates. The object rotation between the initial and final image will also affect how well-conditioned the equations are, in a similar fashion to the stereo camera baseline. The effect of the basis geometry is reflected in the variance returned by the Kalman Filter, and during recognition it may be necessary to try several different bases in order to find one which gives well-conditioned equations. This can be implemented by running several Kalman filters on the track data in parallel, each using a different set of points as the basis and selecting the invariants from the one with least uncertainty.

Finally some perspective distortion of the data will also occur, although we have assumed none is present in the computation of the affine invariants. The effect of this distortion is nonlinear, and it depends on the object pose relative to the camera, which is unknown. The size of this error will depend on the accuracy of the weak perspective approximation.

Estimates using Real Data Figure 2a shows an image of the initial position of the object we aim to recognise, and a second image of its final position after it has been rotated on the turntable. Several important features have been superimposed onto this second image. These include:

The basis which defines the affine coordinate frame on the object. It is shown as three white lines marked E_1, E_2, E_3. In this case the basis is orthogonal in 3D space, and should form a good basis for computing the invariants.

The track data for each detected point appears as a black line. During tracking one of the points was lost and is marked as such.

Labelled points (pt1-pt4) are the four points for which the Kalman Filter will estimate invariant affine coordinates.

The graphs of figure 2b show the Kalman filter estimates of the invariants for the data from figure 2a. These estimates are continuously updated as more track data is input into the Kalman Filter, such that the estimate of the invariants improves and the uncertainty is reduced. The graphs have an initial transient stage due to the initialisation of the filter with zeros.

Rather than just tracking the object through an arbitrary range of viewpoints, it is preferable to *actively* be able to decide at which point to stop tracking (*i.e.* at which point the invariant estimates reach an acceptable accuracy). This can be achieved by examining the uncertainty covariance matrix and innovation returned by the Kalman Filter [12].

3.2 Geometric Hashing

The geometric hashing approach to 2D model-based object recognition was proposed by Lamdan, Schwartz and Wolfson [13]. In this approach geometric invariants are used as a simple and stable index into a hash table. We expand on their idea and have a 3D index, $H(\alpha, \beta, \gamma)$, with each indexed location in the hash table storing information about the object used to create the invariant, the points used to form the basis and the point referenced in that basis. A large amount of pre-computation is performed on the model library to create the hash table, but since this can be done off-line it will not affect recognition speed. Invariants are calculated for all permutations of basis and points and data stored in the hash table.

An obvious problem when creating the hash table is the large quantity of data present. If an object has N_v vertices, there are $N_b = N_v!/(N_v - 4)!$ possible bases ($O(N_v^4)$), and $N_{invs} = N_b(N_v - 4)$ associated invariant sets. This problem needs to be addressed by pruning away bases, and this can be done by only selecting those bases which are well conditioned, using structural information about the object, and eliminating permutations of the same basis points. This is discussed in more detail in [12].

The effect of the uncertainty of the invariant estimates on indexing performance needs to be considered in geometric hashing, and error analysis of the uncertainty can be found in [14, 12]. The most basic information gained from this analysis is that larger invariants have larger noise components. In order to

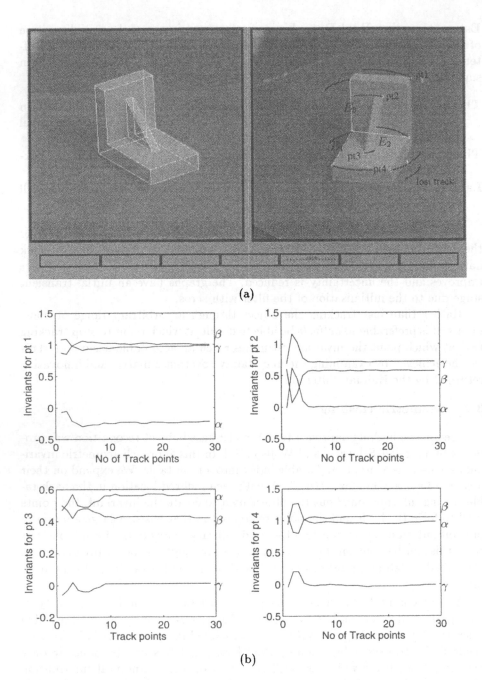

(a)

(b)

Fig. 2. (a) Image with track data and basis superimposed. (b) Kalman Filter Outputs for 4 points in this basis. The estimate is continuously updated as more track data is input into the Kalman Filter.

compensate for this the hash table can be constructed in such a way that bins become larger for larger invariant values. The discrete nature of the bins also means some invariants lie at the limit of a bin. This problem is alleviated by searching not only the indexed bin but also its immediate neighbour. The exact implementation of this indexing is described in detail in [12].

Direct Model Acquisition from Scenes In some circumstances it may be advantageous to compile the object hash table directly from real scenes. The attraction of such an approach is that the features used in database formation and recognition are similar, since the same feature extraction process is used in both cases. Unpredictable effects such as corner detectability in the images which is unavailable in a CAD model, now form an integral part of model formation. The implementation of this scheme involves combining the results from several image sequences, in order to average out any errors in the invariants and to give an indication of likely variations. In this way complete coverage of the shape is also ensured. The approach can be viewed as having a training set for database formation, and the later recognition providing a test set. The problem with such an approach is that more human interaction is required in the form of matching points in the different sequences.

The Recognition Process Once the invariants have been estimated for a particular basis, the recognition process is completed as follows.

1. For each invariant set (α, β, γ) index into the hash table. For every (Object,Basis) grouping which appears in the associated bin register a vote in a recognition tree [12]. The recognition tree provides a fast way of accumulating votes for an (object, basis) group. In order to account for uncertainty in the 3D invariant estimate, examine not just the indexed bin but also local surrounding ones.

2. If a grouping (Object,Basis) scores a large number of votes, then this object is possibly present in the scene.

3. Compute the transformation (1) between matched model and real data points. A minimum of four points are required to calculate this transformation. At least five point matches (usually more) are available, so least squares minimisation is used to find a solution. Verify that the least squares solution to the transformation projects all model points satisfactorily to their matched image points.

4. Transform the edges of the model according to this transformation. Verify how close the projected edges lie to scene edges, if there is good correlation then the object has been recognised. A model that has been successfully projected onto the image is shown in figure 2a. Failure to match the edges requires the process to be restarted with a different basis.

Overall recognition time depends on two factors. At present the most time is spent tracking features and this will be very hardware dependent. After that estimation of invariants, indexing and backprojection is very fast but will depend on how many bases need to be tried before recognition is successful. With the simple polyhedral objects recognition is usually achieved with the first basis choice.

4 Working in Cluttered Scenes

The basic 3-dimensional object recognition system has been demonstrated to work for simple polyhedral objects, when there is an accurately localised set of corner points, from which the affine basis can be formed. Although the system can cope with some noisy points by selecting random bases until a successful one is found, this is clearly a simplistic approach which will fail in environments with many false points or where points lie on several different objects. Some information on how sets of points are interrelated is required, and *perceptual groupings* [15] provide us with a means of finding such relations.

Perceptual Groupings using Multiple Views A strong cue for grouping points which belong to the same object is connectivity between the points. However a number of problems occur with this simple inter-connectivity in cluttered scenes. Junctions of lines (where points are located in the image) are formed not only by a single object's geometry, but also when objects start occluding each other, occluding themselves or shadows start appearing (figure 4), and in a simple perceptual grouping scheme, these unwanted points can wrongly link up groups of points on different objects.

In fact these unwanted points usually correspond to T-junctions of lines which can fairly easily be detected and removed, separating the groups. Unfortunately in certain circumstances geometric junctions can align accidentally in such a way that they also resemble T-junctions. This latter type of T-junction will only be a transient effect however, and therefore important information can be gained from the *multiple views* available in our recognition system to distinguish between types of T-junctions. By tracking the *stability* of a junction through a series of views we are able to determine its significance. Junctions formed by shadows for example tend to be quite unstable and will disappear in new views, whereas T-junctions caused by occlusion will remain T-junctions. Figures 4 and 5 show examples of the same junctions seen in different views.

An *active perceptual grouping* scheme is therefore proposed based on the concept that *a useful perceptual grouping is one that remains stable through several different viewpoints.* The first image is used to initialise groupings, and subsequent views are used to update groupings.

Example Perceptual grouping based on point interconnectedness is performed on figure 4, creating a graph structure linking all the points in the scene. In order to separate the point sets belonging to the two objects, we wish to remove junction figure 4b, which is caused by occlusion and forms a T-junction. However removing all T-junctions also removes useful points like figure 4c. Information from a new view (figure 5), allows us to distinguish between types of T-junction, so we can remove junction figure 4b but not figure 4c.

The use of a single grouping cue often leads to the formation of many small disparate groups of features, because the segmentation procedure failed to locate a linking *corner* or *edge*. Additional cues must be employed: for polyhedral objects, parallelism of edges, or proximity of points can be applied. Here again information from multiple views can be combined to give a better idea of grouping than a single image can. Figure 3 shows objects recognised using this multiple view perceptual grouping method.

5 Conclusions

The use of invariants for object recognition is clearly very appealing. They allow a single object description for many different viewpoints, and therefore provide a simple index into a shape table. A crucial requirement for any 3D object representation is that it be robust to occlusion and missing data, effects which are likely to arise in real images. Affine invariants provide such a representation since they can be evaluated for any set of just five points. More visible points simply improve the noise tolerance of the system. A common problem with many existing 3D model based object recognition systems such as Alignment [3], is that a single model is tested against the scene at a time, which can greatly reduce performance when the database contains many different objects. Geometric hashing on the other hand allows one to check against all models stored simultaneously, speeding up the recognition.

The two main problems with this approach to 3D object recognition lie firstly in the exponential growth of the hash table, a problem that has only partly been addressed [12]. It is probable that more complex features than simple corner points are required to satisfactorily solve this problem. Secondly in the difficulty of selecting four points to form a basis, which all lie on the same object and match model points. This problem is especially highlighted in cluttered scenes. Some hopeful results have been achieved using simple perceptual groupings from multiple views, but as yet it is unknown how well this will work for complex objects.

References

1. R.T. Chin and C.R. Dyer. Model-Based Recognition in Robot Vision. *ACM Computing Surveys*, 18(1):67–108, 1986.
2. D.G. Lowe. The viewpoint consistency constraint. *Int. Journal of Computer Vision*, 1:57–72, 1987.
3. D.P. Huttenlocher and S. Ullman. Recognising solid objects by alignment with an image. *Int. Journal of Computer Vision*, 5(2):195–212, 1990.
4. W.E.L. Grimson and T. Lozano-Perez. Localising Overlapping Parts by Searching the Interpretation Tree. *IEEE Trans. Pattern Analysis and Machine Intell.*, 9(4):469–482, 1987.
5. J.L. Mundy and A.Zissermann editors. *Geometric Invariance in Computer Vision*. MIT Press, 1992.
6. L.G. Roberts. Machine perception of three - dimensional solids. In J.T. Tippet, editor, *Optical and Electro-optical Information Processing*. MIT Press, 1965.
7. J.J. Koenderink and A.J. van Doorn. Affine structure from motion. *J. Opt. Soc. America*, 8(2):377–385, 1991.
8. D. Weinshall. Model-Based Invariants for 3-D Vision. *Int. Journal of Computer Vision*, 10(1):27–42, 1993.

9. J. B. Burns, R. S. Weiss, and E. M. Riseman. View variation of point-set and line-segment features. *IEEE Transactions on Pattern Analysis and Machine Intelligence*, 15(1):51–68, January 1993.

10. R. Fawcett, A. Zisserman, and M. Brady. Extracting structure from an affine view of a 3D point set with one or two bilateral symmetries. In *Proceedings of the British Machine Vision Conference*, pages 349–358, Guildford, 1993.

11. S. Vinther and R. Cipolla. Towards 3D object model acquisition and recognition using 3D affine invariants. In *Proc. British Machine Vision Conference 1993*, pages 369–378, 1993.

12. S. Vinther and R. Cipolla. Active 3D object recognition using 3D affine invariants. Technical Report CUED / F - INFENG / TR164, Dept. of Engineering, University of Cambridge, 1994.

13. Y. Lamdan, J.T. Schwartz, and H.J. Wolfson. Affine Invariant Model-Based Object Recognition. *IEEE Trans. on Robotics and Automation*, 6(5):578–589, 1990.

14. W.E. Grimson, D.P. Huttenlocher, and D. Jacobs. A study of affine matching with bounded sensor error. In *Proc. 2rd European Conf. on Computer Vision*, 1992.

15. D.G. Lowe. Three dimensional object recognition from single two-dimensional images. *Artificial Intelligence*, 31:355–395, 1987.

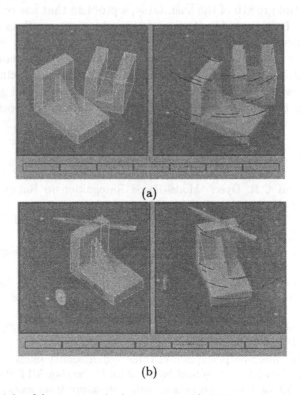

(a)

(b)

Fig. 3. a) Multiple objects recognised in a scene. b) Object recognised in a cluttered scene. T-junctions are removed using multiple view information.

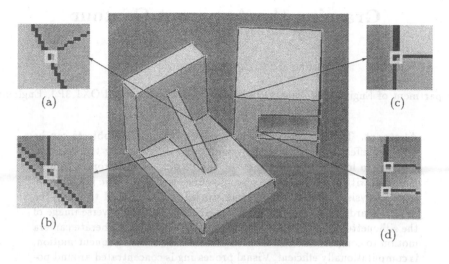

Fig. 4. A Variety of T-junctions caused by: (a) self-occlusion (b) occlusion (c) accidental alignment (d) shadows

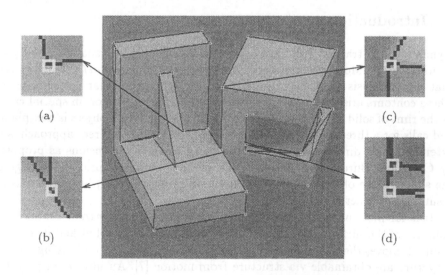

Fig. 5. The T-junctions as seen from a different viewpoint. In particular (b) has remained a stable T-junction, making it likely it was caused by occlusion. (c) which was caused by accidental alignment is no longer a T-junction. By tracking the *stability* of a junction through a whole series of views we are able to determine how it affects the perceptual groupings.

Grasping the Apparent Contour

Michael J. Taylor and Andrew Blake

Department of Engineering Science, University of Oxford, Oxford OX1 3PJ, England.

Abstract. Two fingered grasps of *a priori* unknown 3D objects can be achieved effectively using active vision. Real-time contour tracking can be used to localise the silhouette of the object, viewed from a camera mounted with a gripper, on a moving robot arm. Geometric information from analysis of motion around one vantage point is used to guide the robot towards a new vantage point from which the *rim* (inverse image of the silhouette) admits a more stable grasp. This use of deliberate camera motion to compute the best direction for the robot's subsequent motion, is computationally efficient. Visual processing is concentrated around potential grasp points and costly global reconstruction of an entire surface is avoided. The computation is shown to be robust, both theoretically, owing to a connection with visual parallax, and in computational experiments.

1 Introduction

Dynamic curve-trackers [10] have proved to be effective in visually guided path planning [2, 3]. More recently, they have been used in a *symmetry-based* system that uses analysis of visual symmetry [5] for grasping planar contours [8, 4]. These contours arise either as the outlines of laminar objects or, in special cases, as the rims of solid objects. More generally, the rim of a solid object is non-planar and calls for a three-dimensional extension of the theory. A direct approach is to extend the two dimensional symmetry theory to three dimensions as proposed by Chen and Burdick [6]. However this requires complete prior knowledge of the shape of the object surface, obtainable in principle [1, 7], but an unnatural assumption for active vision.

It is far more natural to assume initially that only an *apparent contour* (silhouette) of the surface is visible and that, shortly after the robot and its camera begin to move, the shape of the corresponding rim and the underlying surface curvature are obtainable via structure from motion [7]. An initial grasp on the rim can be chosen by applying the planar, symmetry-based algorithm to the apparent contour to obtain *apparent antipodal grasps*. Then the computed surface curvature at these initial grasp points can be used, it will be shown, to determine an optimum direction of motion for the robot. While the robot moves, the apparent contour deforms continuously as the rim moves over the surface. Grasp points are tracked, again using computed curvature, around the rim, in such a way that the stability of the planned grasp improves — the coefficient of friction required for grasping decreases progressively to arrive at a more stable grasp (figure 6).

Lecture Notes in Computer Science, Vol. 801
Jan-Olof Eklundh (Ed.)

It emerges, in the development of the theory, that there is a felicitous dependence of the computed robot trajectory on motion parallax. It is known that computation of three-dimensional structure via parallax [11, 12] is robust to uncertainty in viewpoint motion, and this principle extends to computation of surface curvature [7]. Parallax can be inconvenient to measure in practice because of the need to find suitable adjacent surface features and measure their motion. In the case of grasp computation however it can be shown that the positions of the two fingers constitute suitable adjacent features. Purely *relative* measurement of the displacement of the apparent contour at the finger-positions is sufficient to determine the robot trajectory.

2 Two-dimensional analysis

In order to introduce the viewpoint-motion theory, it is useful to explain it first in two dimensions. The earlier symmetry-based theory [4] was two-dimensional in the sense that it was restricted to planar objects; it involves object geometry but not viewpoint motion. Here, the object is taken to be planar in a plane containing the viewpoint (figure 1), and this is the basis for a simple form of the theory. It is an adaptation of the two-dimensional theory of Giblin and Weiss [9] for analysis of deformation of the apparent contour under viewpoint-motion. Optimal conditions for grasping occur when $\mathbf{R}\cdot\mathbf{v} = 0$ in figure 1 so that that the required coefficient of friction for equilibrium is zero. The viewpoint can approach this condition by moving transversely to the line of sight in a direction chosen to reduce the relative depth $\Delta\lambda = |\mathbf{R}\cdot\mathbf{v}|$ of the two grasp points on the apparent contour.

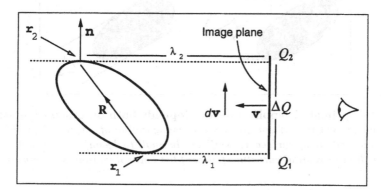

Fig. 1. Two-dimensional viewpoint-motion for grasp-planning. *Potential finger positions* $\mathbf{r}_1$ *and* $\mathbf{r}_2$ *on the apparent contour are imaged orthographically to* Q_1 *and* Q_2. *Their separation in the image is* ΔQ. *The viewing direction is defined by the unit vector* $\mathbf{v}$. *The rate of change of the relative depth determines what motion the viewpoint should make.*

The appropriate direction of motion is the one in which $\Delta\lambda(\mathrm{d}\Delta\lambda/\mathrm{d}v) < 0$ where

$$\frac{\mathrm{d}\Delta\lambda}{\mathrm{d}v} = \Delta Q - (\rho_1 + \rho_2) \tag{1}$$

and ρ_1, ρ_2 are radii of surface curvature along the lines of sight at the finger positions $\mathbf{r}_1, \mathbf{r}_2$. The direction of motion depends both on radii of curvature and on the diameter ΔQ of the grasp, and this is illustrated in figure 2. Alternatively, in terms of image measurables, and their temporal derivatives,

$$\frac{\mathrm{d}\Delta\lambda}{\mathrm{d}v} = -\frac{\mathrm{d}^2\Delta Q}{\mathrm{d}v^2},$$

(2)

the relative acceleration of the projection of the two image points or *rate of parallax* [7]. It is because ρ_1, ρ_2 occur only as a sum , $\rho_1 + \rho_2$, that the computed direction of motion is purely a function of image parallax. The fact that the image normals $\mathbf{n}_1, \mathbf{n}_2$ are opposed leads to cancellation of error due to motion uncertainty in the term $\rho_1 + \rho_2$.

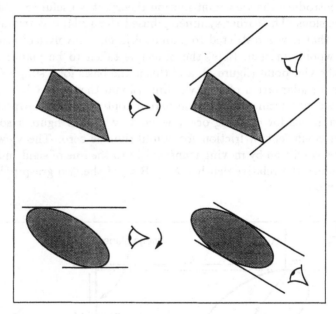

Fig. 2. The optimal viewpoint motion depends both on grasp diameter and on surface curvature. *When, for a given configuration of fingers, the radii of curvature of the underlying surface are sufficiently small (polygon) the optimal motion is upward; with large radii of curvature (ellipse) the optimal motion is downward.*

3   Three-dimensional viewpoint-motion theory

The full theory, presented in this section, incorporates as special cases the two planar theories described already. An apparent antipodal grasp is found initially via the planar symmetry-based theory. A generalised version of the planar viewpoint-motion theory determines the optimal motion of the viewpoint, a direction in the plane orthogonal to the line of sight. As the viewpoint moves, the finger positions must be *tracked* around the apparent contour, in order to maintain the condition for apparent antipodal grasp.

3.1 Optimal camera motion

An optimal viewpoint motion is defined to be one that decreases the square $\epsilon = (\Delta\lambda)^2$ of the relative depth most rapidly, that is, descending the gradient $\nabla\epsilon$ with respect to change in the viewpoint $\mathbf{v}$. Expressed in the basis $\{\mathbf{n}_2, \mathbf{t}_2, \mathbf{v}\}$ (figure 3), it can be shown that:

$$\nabla\epsilon = 2\Delta\lambda \begin{bmatrix} \Delta Q - \left(\rho_v^{(1)} + \rho_v^{(2)}\right) + E_n \\ E_t \\ 0 \end{bmatrix} \tag{3}$$

where ΔQ is the grasp diameter (figure 1) and $\rho_v^{(i)}$ denotes radius of surface curvature along each line of sight. The vector given by (3) corresponds to the change in viewing direction that increases ϵ most (see the appendix for more details concerning its derivation). Optimal viewpoint motion is now taken to be in the direction of $-\nabla\epsilon$. The normal component of $\nabla\epsilon$, which is the first component of the vector in (3) includes a term from the 2D theory (1) plus an

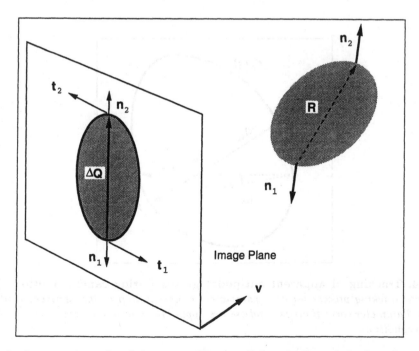

Fig. 3. Apparent antipodal grasp. *The parallel projection of the boundary of a convex object showing the 3D configuration of two finger positions on the surface in an apparent antipodal grasp. Clearly both fingers lie on the rim, and also* $\mathbf{R}$, $\mathbf{n}_1$, $\mathbf{n}_2$ *and* $\Delta\mathbf{Q}$ *are coplanar.*

additional term E_n. The tangential component in (3) is E_t which, of course, appears only in the 3D theory. Both E_n and E_t are functions of the curvature of the apparent contours in the image and of the angles that the rim makes with the viewing direction. For instance, when the rim runs perpendicular to the viewing direction at both fingers, E_n and E_t are both zero and (3) reduces to the 2D case. It should be emphasised that curvatures *along* the line of sight appear in (3) *only* in the expression that also appears in the 2D theory, which has already been shown to be equal to the rate of parallax. This means that the computed 3D optimal viewpoint motion is a *robust* quantity.

3.2   Tracking apparent antipodal grasps

In order to maintain the apparent antipodal grasp condition, as the viewpoint moves, the vectors n_1, n_2 and R (figure 3) must be kept coplanar. This calls for a continuous tracking process in which, as the viewpoint moves and the rim itself deforms, the planned finger positions slip around the rim. Once the initial apparent antipodal grasp has been found [4], tracking can then be defined as a continuous process in which the speed of the images of the fingers around the apparent contour are specified, so that finger motion is "geared" to viewpoint motion. The tracking process is well-defined provided that the local map between motions of the camera and motions of the points on the surface is not degenerate.

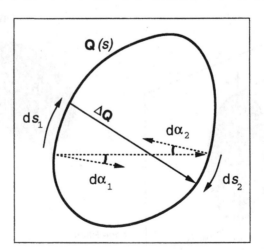

Fig. 4. Tracking of apparent antipodal grasps during camera motion. *The contour tracking process yields a parametric representation of the apparent contour* $Q(s)$. *Parameter corrections* ds_1 *and* ds_2 *are applied to maintain the apparent antipodal grasp condition.*

An expression is required that specifies an infinitesimal change in the position of the apparent antipodal grasp on the apparent contour subject to viewpoint motion. When a camera undergoes an infinitesimal motion, the image motion corresponding to rigid world motion is determined by the constraint that image motion must lie along epipolar lines [7]. However to maintain the apparent antipodal grasp condition, the images of the finger positions move non-rigidly. The additional non-rigid component of motion, in terms of the parameter s of the apparent contour, can be shown to be:

$$\begin{pmatrix} \mathrm{d}s_1 \\ \mathrm{d}s_2 \end{pmatrix} = D \begin{pmatrix} \rho_1 \left(\rho_2 - \Delta Q \right) & -\rho_1 \rho_2 \\ -\rho_1 \rho_2 & \rho_2 \left(\rho_1 - \Delta Q \right) \end{pmatrix} \begin{pmatrix} \mathrm{d}\alpha_1 \\ \mathrm{d}\alpha_2 \end{pmatrix} \qquad (4)$$

where ρ_i are the radii of curvature of the apparent contour in the image at the finger positions, $\Delta Q = |\Delta \mathbf{Q}|$, angles α_i are defined in figure 4 and $D = 1/\left(\Delta Q - \rho_1 - \rho_2 \right)$.

4 Implementation

Figure 5 shows a view of a potato from a general initial viewpoint such as the one seen in figure 6a. The robot proceeds by first calculating the positions of all

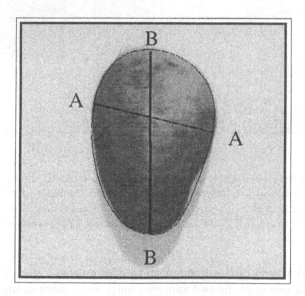

Fig. 5. Apparent antipodal grasps on the apparent contour of a potato.
From the viewpoint shown in figure 6a, grasp A is found to have approximately zero relative depth and grasp B is found to have a significant relative depth, so A is the more favourable grasp.

the apparent antipodal grasps from the apparent contour. In this example there are two, marked A and B. The relative depth of each grasp is then measured. To do this, the robot makes small translational motions of the camera along the line

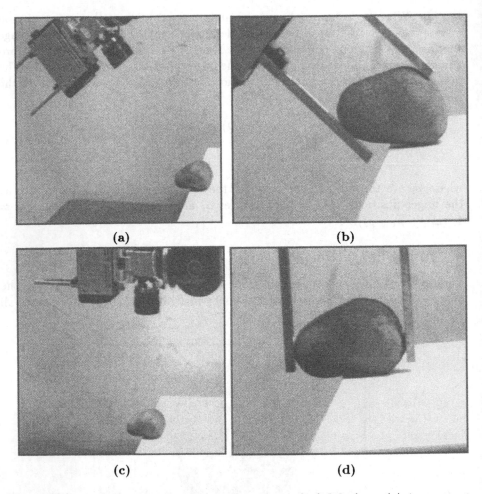

Fig. 6. Using relative depth to move to a more fruitful view. *(a) An* ADEPT-1 *robot with camera and parallel jaw is directed towards the potato from an initial viewpoint, from which it plans the apparent antipodal grasp labelled B in figure 5. This is an unfavourable grasp (b). (c,d) as (a,b) but for a more favourable grasp, seen from a new vantage point.*

of the normal of each of the apparent antipodal grasps. Figure 7 shows how the relative displacement of the two apparent antipodal points changes with camera position for both A and B. In the situation shown, the robot would execute grasp A. However, from a generic initial configuration, none of the apparent antipodal grasps need have zero relative depth, so it is reasonable to choose the one with the smallest relative depth and track that over changing viewpoint. Rather than extracting the geometric quantities in (3) from the derivatives of image measurements to calculate $\nabla\epsilon$, it is preferable, practically, to estimate the local value of $\nabla\epsilon$. This can be done by measuring the relative depth of the apparent antipodal points at the current viewpoint, and at four other viewpoints displaced perpendicular to the viewing direction, spanning the set of possible

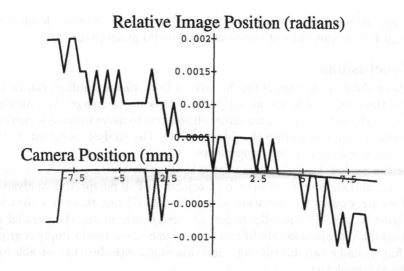

Fig. 7. Measuring depth difference. *The gradient of the graphs shown is a practical measure of parallax from which relative depth can be determined. Grasps A (in grey) and B (in black) from figure 5 generate the graphs shown. Regression over a baseline of 18mm, sampled at 60 points, leads to computed relative depths of 1.2±1.5mm and 19.7±1.5mm respectively, so clearly grasp A is the more favourable. The dominant source of noise in the measurements is due to pixel quantisation errors.*

locally optimal camera motions. With reference to figure 5 and figure 6a, the robot estimates the local relative depth gradient of grasp B by measuring the relative depth at 80mm displacements along t_1, t_2, n_1 and n_2 respectively (figure 3). $\nabla \epsilon$ can be estimated from the values in table 1. It can be seen that the relative depth is clearly moving towards zero with movement in the n_2 direction. The rate of change of relative depth with respect to motion in the tangential direction is below the noise level. In this way the camera is able to move iteratively, in

Camera displacement (mm)	Relative depth (mm)
0	19.7±1.5
+80n_2	14.1±1.5
+80n_1	23.2±1.5
+80t_2	19.6±1.5
+80t_1	20.0±1.5

Table 1. Measurement of the gradient of the relative depth of grip B in figure 5.

short steps, to the overhead position (figure 6c) where the relative depth is zero and grasp B is a true, three-dimensional, antipodal grasp (figure 6d).

5 Conclusions

It has been shown how relative depth, derived from visual parallax, can be used to assess the quality of apparent antipodal grasps in the image. An analysis of geometry of the surface and its curvature shows how to move towards a viewpoint from which an improved grasp should be visible. The analysis is robust, both in theory, and practically in our experiments.

The theory has been developed for orthographic viewing and it is natural to consider an extension to perspective projection. Full perspective analysis has been done previously for curvature along the rim [7] but there is a drawback in applying it here. The parallel fingers of our gripper match the parallel rays in orthographic projection. Modification for perspective would imply a gripper whose fingers had a variable tilt angle and this would introduce undesirable extra mechanical complexity.

The measurement of the local gradient of the relative depth of these points from image quantities was shown to be sufficiently reliable for guiding the camera to better view points.

Acknowledgements

The financial support of the SERC and the EEC Esprit programme is gratefully acknowledged. Discussions with A. Nairac, P.J.Giblin, A.Zisserman, J.M.Brady and A. McLean were most valuable.

References

1. C. Bard, C. Bellier, G. Vercelli, C. Laugier, J. Troccaz, and B. Triggs. Integrating grasp planning and vision based reconstruction techniques to achieve autonomous manipulation tasks involving a robot arm equipped with a dextrous hand. *Submitted to Int. Journal of Robotics Research*, 1993.
2. A. Blake. Computational modelling of hand-eye coordination. *Phil. Trans. R. Soc*, 337:351–360, 1992.
3. A. Blake, J.M. Brady, R. Cipolla, Z. Xie, and A. Zisserman. Visual navigation around curved obstacles. In *Proc. IEEE Int. Conf. Robotics and Automation*, volume 3, pages 2490–2499, 1991.
4. A. Blake and M.J. Taylor. Planning planar grasps of smooth contours. In *Proc. Int. Conf. Robotics and Automation*, pages 834–839, 1993.
5. J.M. Brady and H. Asada. Smooth Local Symmetries and their Implementation. *Int. Journal of Robotics Research*, 3(3), 1984.
6. I-M. Chen and J.W. Burdick. Finding antipodal point grasps on irregularly shaped objects. In *IEEE Proc. Robotics and Automation*, pages 2278–2283, 1992.
7. R. Cipolla and A. Blake. Surface shape from the deformation of apparent contours. *Int. Journal of Computer Vision*, 9(2):83–112, November 1992.
8. B. Faverjon and J. Ponce. On computing two-finger force-closure grasps of curved 2d objects. In *Proc. IEEE Int. Conf. Robotics and Automation*, volume 3, pages 424–429, 1991.

9. P. Giblin and R. Weiss. Reconstruction of surfaces from profiles. In *Proc. 1st Int. Conf. on Computer Vision*, pages 136–144, London, 1987.
10. M. Kass, A. Witkin, and D. Terzopoulos. Snakes:active contour models. In *Proc. 1st Int. Conf. on Computer Vision*, pages 259–268, 1987.
11. J.J. Koenderink and A.J. Van Doorn. Invariant properties of the motion parallax field due to the movement of rigid bodies relative to an observer. *Optica Acta*, 22(9):773–791, 1975.
12. H.C. Longuet-Higgins and K. Pradzny. The interpretation of a moving retinal image. *Proc. R. Soc. Lond.*, B208:385–397, 1980.
13. Barrett O'Neill. *Elementary Differential Geometry*. Academic Press, 1966.

A   Further details on the gradient of the relative depth

The quantity we wish to minimise with respect to change in viewing direction $\mathbf{v}$ is

$$\epsilon = (\Delta\lambda)^2 = (\mathbf{R}{\cdot}\mathbf{v})^2 \tag{5}$$

and $d\epsilon$ depends on $\mathbf{v}$, $\mathbf{n}_i$ and $\mathbf{r}_i$:

$$d\epsilon = \nabla_v\epsilon\, d\mathbf{v} + \nabla_x\epsilon\, d\mathbf{x}, \tag{6}$$

where $d\mathbf{x} = (d\mathbf{r}_1, d\mathbf{r}_2, d\mathbf{n}_1, d\mathbf{n}_2)^{\mathrm{T}}$. Now $d\mathbf{x}$ is constrained such that

$$\mathbf{n}_1{\cdot}\mathbf{v} = 0 \ \text{ and } \ \mathbf{n}_2{\cdot}\mathbf{v} = 0, \tag{7}$$

the conditions satisfied by all points on the contour generator, and by

$$(\mathbf{n}_1 \wedge \mathbf{R}){\cdot}\mathbf{v} = 0 \ \text{ and } \ (\mathbf{n}_2 \wedge \mathbf{R}){\cdot}\mathbf{v} = 0, \tag{8}$$

the conditions for an apparent antipodal grasp in the image, that $\mathbf{R}$, $\mathbf{n}_1$, $\mathbf{n}_2$ and $\mathbf{v}$ are coplanar. Two subsidiary constraints on $d\mathbf{x}$, first that $d\mathbf{r}_i{\cdot}\mathbf{n}_i = 0$, stating that local motion of $\mathbf{r}_i$ is restricted to the tangent plane at the point, and secondly $d\mathbf{n}_i - W_i(d\mathbf{r}_i) = 0$, where W_i is the shape operator [13]. These four constraints can be combined in a vector equation $d\mathbf{g} = 0$ and so

$$d\mathbf{g} = \nabla_v\mathbf{g}\, d\mathbf{v} + \nabla_x\mathbf{g}\, d\mathbf{x} = 0 \tag{9}$$

Rearranging, we get

$$d\mathbf{x} = -\left(\nabla_x\mathbf{g}\right)^{-1}\nabla_v\mathbf{g}\, d\mathbf{v}, \tag{10}$$

so we can write, from (6)

$$\nabla\epsilon = \left(\nabla_v\epsilon - \nabla_x\epsilon\left(\nabla_x\mathbf{g}\right)^{-1}\nabla_v\mathbf{g}\right)d\mathbf{v} \tag{11}$$

which can be evaluated to give (3).

Visual Tracking of High DOF Articulated Structures: an Application to Human Hand Tracking

James M. Rehg[1] and Takeo Kanade[2]

[1] Carnegie Mellon University, Department of Electrical and Computer Engineering, Pittsburgh PA 15213, jimr@cs.cmu.edu
[2] Carnegie Mellon University, The Robotics Institute, Pittsburgh PA 15213, tk@cs.cmu.edu

Abstract. Passive sensing of human hand and limb motion is important for a wide range of applications from human-computer interaction to athletic performance measurement. High degree of freedom articulated mechanisms like the human hand are difficult to track because of their large state space and complex image appearance. This article describes a model-based hand tracking system, called DigitEyes, that can recover the state of a 27 DOF hand model from ordinary gray scale images at speeds of up to 10 Hz.

1 Introduction

Sensing of human hand and limb motion is important in applications from Human-Computer Interaction (HCI) to athletic performance measurement. Current commercially available solutions are invasive, and require the user to don gloves [15] or wear targets [8]. This paper describes a noninvasive visual hand tracking system, called DigitEyes. We have demonstrated hand tracking at speeds of up to 10 Hz using line and point features extracted from gray scale images of unadorned, unmarked hands.

Most previous real-time visual 3D tracking work has addressed objects with 6 or 7 spatial degrees of freedom (DOF)[5, 7]. We present tracking results for branched kinematic chains with as many as 27 DOF (in the case of a human hand model). We show that simple, useful features can be extracted from natural images of the human hand. While difficult problems still remain in tracking through occlusions and across complicated backgrounds, these results demonstrate the potential of vision-based human motion sensing.

This paper has two parts. First, we describe the 3D visual tracking problem for objects with kinematic chains. Second, we show experimental results of tracking a 27 DOF hand model using two cameras.

2 The Articulated Mechanism Tracking Problem

Visual tracking is a sequential estimation problem: given an image sequence, recover the time-varying state of the world [5, 7, 14]. The solution has three basic components: state model, feature measurement, and state estimation. The state model specifies a mapping from a state space, which characterizes all possible spatial configurations of the mechanism, to a feature space. For the hand, the state space encodes the pose of the palm (seven states for quaternion rotation and translation) and the joint angles of the fingers (four states per finger, five for the thumb), and is mapped to a set of image lines and points by the state model. A state estimate is calculated for each image by inverting the model to obtain the state vector that best fits the measured features. Features for the unmarked hand consist of finger link and tip occluding edges, which are extracted by local image operators.

Articulated mechanisms are more difficult to track than a single rigid object for two reasons: their state space is larger and their appearance is more complicated. First, the state space must represent additional kinematic DOFs not present in the single-object case, and the resulting estimation problem is more expensive computationally. In addition, kinematic singularities are introduced that are not present in the six DOF case. Singularities arise when a small change in a given state has no effect on the image features. They are currently dealt with by stabilizing the estimation algorithm. Second, high DOF mechanisms produce complex image patterns as their DOFs are exercised. People exploit this observation in making shapes from shadows cast by their hands.

To reduce the complexity of the hand motion, we employ a high image acquisition rate (10-15 Hz depending on the model) which limits the change in the hand state, and therefore image feature location, between frames. As a result, state estimation and feature measurement are *local*, rather than global, search problems. In the state space, we exploit this locality by linearizing the nonlinear state model around the previous estimate. The resulting linear estimation problem produces state corrections which are integrated over time to yield an estimated state trajectory. In the image, the projection of the previous estimate through the state model yields coordinate frames for feature extraction. We currently assume that the closest available feature is the correct match, which limits our system to scenes without occlusions or complicated backgrounds.

Previous work on tracking general articulated objects includes [14, 10, 9]. In [14], Yamamoto and Koshikawa describe a system for human body tracking using kinematic and geometric models. They give an example of tracking a single human arm and torso using optical flow features. Pentland and Horowitz [10] give an example of tracking the motion of a human figure using optical flow and an articulated deformable model. A much earlier system by O'Rourke and Badler [9] analyzed human body motion using constraint propagation.

In addition to the work on general articulated object tracking, several authors have developed specialized techniques for visual human motion analysis. This previous work differs from ours in two ways. First, markers or gloves are often used to simplify motion analysis [4]. Second, analysis is typically restricted to a subset of the total hand motion, such as a set of gestures [2] or rigid motion of the palm [1]. In [4], Dorner describes a system for interpreting American Sign Language from image sequences of a single hand. Dorner's system uses the full set of the hand's DOFs, and employs a glove with colored markers to simplify feature extraction. Darrell and Pentland describe a system for learning and recognizing dynamic hand gestures in [2]. Their approach avoids the problems of hand modeling, but doesn't address 3D tracking. In other hand-specific work, Kang and Ikeuchi describe a range sensor-based approach to hand pose estimation [6], used in their Assembly Plan from Observation system. See [11] for a more extensive bibliography.

In order to apply the DigitEyes system to specific applications, such as HCI, two practical requirements must be met. First, the kinematics and geometry of the target hand must be known in advance, so that a state model can be constructed. Second, before local hand tracking can begin, the initial configuration of the hand must be known. We achieve this in practice by requiring the subject to place their hand in a certain pose and location to initiate tracking. A 3D mouse interface based on visual hand tracking is presented in [11].

In the sections that follow, we describe the DigitEyes articulated object tracking system in more detail, along with the specific modeling choices required for hand tracking.

3 State Model for Articulated Mechanisms

The state model encodes all possible mechanism configurations and their corresponding image feature patterns as a two-part mapping between state and feature spaces. The first part is a kinematic model which captures all possible spatial link positions, while the second part is a feature model which describes the image appearance of each link shape.

3.1 Kinematic Models: Application to the Human Hand

We model kinematic chains, like the finger, with the Denavit-Hartenburg (DH) representation, which is widely used in robotics [13]. Since feature models require geometric information not captured in the kinematics, the DH description of each link is augmented with an additional transform from the link frame to a *shape frame*, which describes the position of the visible link geometry in space. A solid model in the shape frame generates features through projection into the image.

We model the hand as a collection of 16 rigid bodies: 3 individual finger links (called phalanges) for each of the five digits, and a palm. From a kinematic viewpoint, the hand consists of multi-branched kinematic chains attached to a six DOF base. We make several simplifying assumptions in modeling the hand kinematics. First, we assume that each of the four fingers of the hand are planar mechanisms with four degrees of freedom (DOF). The abduction DOF moves the plane of the finger relative to the palm, while the remaining 3 DOF determine the finger's configuration within the plane. Fig. 1 illustrates the planar finger model. Each finger has an *anchor point*, which is the position of its base joint center in the frame of the palm, which is assumed to be rigid. The base joint is the one farthest (kinematically) from the finger tip. We use a four parameter

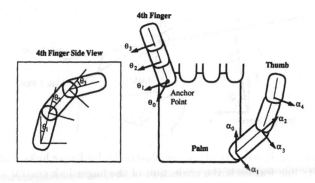

Fig. 1. Kinematic models, illustrated for fourth finger and thumb. The arrows illustrate the joint axes for each link in the chain.

quaternion representation of the palm pose, which eliminates rotational singularities at the cost of a redundant parameter. The total hand pose is described by a 28 dimensional state vector.

The thumb is the most difficult digit to model, due to its great dexterity and intricate kinematics. We currently employ the thumb model used in Rijpkema and Girard's grasp modeling system [12] (see Fig. 1). They were able to obtain realistic animations of human grasps using a five DOF model. DH parameters for the first author's right hand, used in the experiments, can be found in [11].

Real fingers deviate from our modeling assumptions in three ways. First, most fingers deviate slightly from planarity. This deviation could be modeled with additional kinematic transforms, but we have found the planar approximation to be adequate in practice. Second, the last two joints of the finger, counting from the palm outwards, are driven by the same tendon and are not capable of independent actuation. It is simpler to model the DOF explicitly, however, than to model the complicated angular relationship between the two joints. The third and most significant modeling error is change in the anchor points during motion. We have modeled the palm as a rigid body, but in reality it can flex. In gripping a baseball, for example, the palm will conform to its surface, causing the anchor points to deviate from their rest position by tens of millimeters. Fortunately, for free motions of the hand in space, the deviation seems to be small enough to be tolerated by our system.

The modeling framework we employ is general. To track an arbitrary articulated structure, one simply needs its DH parameters and a set of shape models that describe its visual appearance. Within the subproblem of hand tracking, this allows us to develop a suite of hand models whose DOFs are tailored to specific applications.

3.2 Feature Models: Description of Hand Images

The output of the hand state model is a set of features consisting of lines and points generated by the projection of the hand model into the image plane.

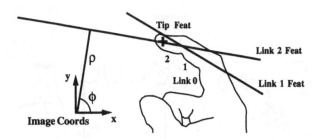

Fig. 2. Features used in hand tracking are illustrated for finger links 1 and 2, and the tip. Each infinite line feature is the projection of the finger link central axis.

Each finger link, modeled by a cylinder, generates a pair of lines in the image corresponding to its occlusion boundaries. The bisector of these lines, which contains the projection of the cylinder central axis, is used as the link feature. The link feature vector $[a\, b\, \rho]$ gives the parameters of the line equation $ax + by - \rho = 0$. Using the central axis line as the link feature eliminates the need to model the cylinder radius or the slope of the pair of lines relative to the central axis, which is often significant near the finger tips. We use the entire line because the endpoints are difficult to measure in practice. Fig. 2 shows two link feature lines extracted from the first two links of a finger.

Each finger tip, modeled by a hemisphere, generates a point feature by projection of the center into the image. The finger tip feature vector $[x\, y]$ gives the tip position in image coordinates, as illustrated in Fig. 2. The total hand appearance is described by a $(3m + 2n)$-dimensional vector, made up of link and tip features, where m and n are the number of finger links and tips, respectively, in the model.

Other feature choices for hand tracking are possible, but the occlusion contours are the most powerful cue. Hand albedo tends to be uniform, making it difficult to use correlation features. Shading is potentially valuable, but the complicated illuminance and self-shadowing of the hand make it difficult to use.

4   Feature Measurement: Detection of Finger Links and Tips

Local image-based trackers are used to measure hand features. These trackers are the projections of the spatial hand geometry into the image plane, and they serve to localize and simplify feature extraction. A finger link tracker, drawn as a "T"-shape, is depicted along with its measured line feature in Fig. 3. The stem of the "T" is the projection of the cylinder center axis into the image. The image sampling rate ensures that the true feature location is near the projected tracker.

Once the link tracker has been positioned, line features are extracted by sampling the image in slices perpendicular to the central axis. For each slice, the derivative of the 1D image profile is computed. Peaks in the derivative with the

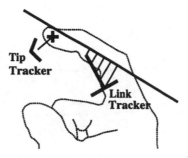

Fig. 3. Image trackers, detected features, and residuals for a link and a tip are shown using the image from Fig. 2. Slashed lines denote the link residual error between the T-shaped tracker and its extracted line measurement. Similarly, the tip tracker (carat shape) is connected to its point feature (cross) by a residual vector.

correct sign correspond to the intersection of the slice with the finger silhouette. The extracted intensity profile and peak locations for a single slice are illustrated in Fig. 4. Line fitting to each set of two or more detected intersections gives a measurement of the projected link axis. If only one silhouette line is detected for a given link, the cylinder radius can be used to extrapolate the axis line location. Currently, the length of the slices (search window) is fixed by hand. Finger tip positions are measured through a similar procedure.

Using local trackers and sampling along lines in the image reduces the pixel processing requirements of feature measurement, permitting fast tracking.

5 State Estimation for Articulated Mechanisms

State estimation proceeds by making incremental state corrections between frames. One cycle of the estimation algorithm goes as follows: The current state esti-mate is used to predict feature locations in the next frame and position feature trackers. After image acquisition and feature extraction, measured and predicted feature values are compared to produce a state correction, which is added to the current estimate to obtain a new state estimate. The difference between mea-sured and predicted states is modeled by a residual vector, and the state correc-tion is obtained by minimizing its magnitude squared. A high image sampling rate allows us to linearize the nonlinear mapping from state to features around an operating point, which is recomputed at each frame, to obtain a linear least squares problem in the model Jacobian. The following subsections describe the residual model and estimation algorithm in detail.

5.1 Residual Model: Link and Tip Image Alignment

The tip residual measures the Euclidean distance in the image between predicted (c_i) and measured (t_i) tip positions. The residual for the ith tip feature is a

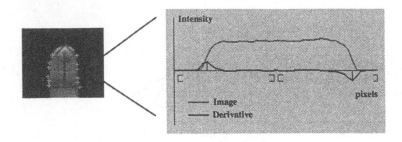

Fig. 4. A single link tracker is shown along with its detected boundary points. One slice through the finger image of a finger is also depicted. Peaks in the derivative give the edge locations.

vector in the image plane defined by

$$v_i(q) = c_i(q) - t_i \ , \tag{1}$$

where c_i is the projection of the tip center into the image as a function of the hand state.

The link residual is a scalar that measures the deviation of the projected cylinder axis from the measured feature line. It is illustrated for a single finger link in Fig. 3. The residual at a point along the axis equals the perpendicular distance to the feature line. We incorporate the orthographic camera model into the residual equation by setting $m = [a\, b\, 0]^t$ and writing

$$l_i(q) \ = \ m^t p_i(q) - \rho \ , \tag{2}$$

where $p_i(q)$ is the 3D position of a point on the cylinder link in camera coordinates, and $[a\, b\, \rho]$ are the line feature parameters. The total link residual consists of one or more point residuals along the cylinder axis (at the base and tip), each given by (2). Note that both residuals are linear in the model point positions.

The feature residuals for each link and tip in the model are concatenated into a single residual vector, $R(q)$. If the magnitude of the residual vector is zero, the hand model is perfectly aligned with the image data.

5.2 Estimation Algorithm: Nonlinear Least Squares

The state correction is obtained from the residual vector by minimizing $H(q) = \frac{1}{2} \| R(q) \|^2$. We employ the Levenburg-Marquardt (LM) algorithm for nonlinear least squares problems [3]. The source of nonlinearity in the state model for articulated mechanisms is trigonometric terms in the forward kinematic model. The other source of nonlinearity, inverse depth coefficients in the perspective camera model, is absent in our orthographic formulation.

Let $R(q_j)$ be the residual vector for image j. The LM state update equation is given by

$$q_{j+1} = q_j - [J_j^t J_j + S]^{-1} J_j^t R_j \ , \tag{3}$$

where $\mathbf{J}_j$ is the Jacobian matrix for the residual $\mathbf{R}_j$, both of which are evaluated at $\mathbf{q}_j$. $\mathbf{S}$ is a constant diagonal conditioning matrix used to stabilize the least squares solution. $\mathbf{J}_j$ is formed from the link and tip residual Jacobians. The same basic approach was used by Lowe in his rigid body tracking system [7].

In the remainder of this section, we derive the link Jacobian and discuss its computation. The tip Jacobian derivation proceeds identically, and can be found in [11]. To calculate the link Jacobian we differentiate (2) with respect to the state vector, obtaining

$$\frac{\partial l_i(\mathbf{q})}{\partial \mathbf{q}} = \mathbf{m}^t \frac{\partial \mathbf{p}_i(\mathbf{q})}{\partial \mathbf{q}} . \tag{4}$$

The above gradient vector for link i is one row of the total Jacobian matrix. Geometrically, it is formed by projecting the *kinematic Jacobian* for points on the link, $\partial \mathbf{p}_i(\mathbf{q})/\partial \mathbf{q}$, in the direction of the feature edge normal.

The kinematic Jacobian in (4) is composed of terms of the form $\partial \mathbf{p}_i/\partial \mathbf{q}_j$, which arise frequently in robot control. As a result, these Jacobian entries can be obtained directly from the model kinematics by means of some standard formulas (see [13], Chapter 5). There are three types of Jacobians, corresponding to joint rotation, spatial translation, and spatial rotation DOFs. All points must be expressed in the frame of the camera producing the measurements. For a revolute (rotational) DOF joint $\mathbf{q}_j$ we have

$$\frac{\partial \mathbf{p}_i}{\partial \mathbf{q}_j} = \mathbf{w}_j \times (\mathbf{p}_i - \mathbf{d}_c^j) , \tag{5}$$

where $\mathbf{w}_j$ is the rotation axis for joint j expressed in the camera frame, and $\mathbf{d}_c^j$ is the position of the joint j frame in camera coords. There will be a similar calculation for *each* camera being used to produce measurements.

The Jacobian calculation for the palm DOFs must reflect the fact that palm motion takes place with respect to the world coordinate frame, but must be expressed in the camera frame. We obtain the rotation and translation components:

$$\frac{\partial \mathbf{p}_i}{\partial \mathbf{v}} = \mathbf{R}_c^w \quad \text{and} \quad \frac{\partial \mathbf{p}_i}{\partial \mathbf{q}_j} = [\mathbf{R}_c^w \mathbf{J}_w]_j \times \mathbf{p}_i , \tag{6}$$

where $\mathbf{v}$ is the palm velocity with respect to the world frame and $\mathbf{q}_j$ is a component of the quaternion specifying palm rotation. In addition, $\mathbf{R}_c^w$ is the camera to world rotation and $\mathbf{J}_w$ is a Jacobian mapping quaternion velocity to angular velocity, with $[\cdot]_j$ denoting the jth column of a matrix.

5.3 Tracking with Multiple Cameras

The tracking framework presented above generalizes easily to more than one camera. When multiple cameras are used, the residual vectors from each camera are concatenated to form a single global residual vector. This formulation can exploit partial observations. If a finger link is visible in one view but not in the another due to occlusion, the single view measurement is still incorporated into the residual, and therefore the estimate.

6 Experimental Results: Hand Tracking With Two Cameras

The DigitEyes system was used to track a full 27 DOF hand model, using two camera image sequences. Because the hand motion must avoid occlusions for successful tracking, the available range of travel is not large. It is sufficient, however, to demonstrate recovery of articulated DOFs in conjunction with palm motion. Figure 5 (at the end of the paper) shows sample images, trackers, and features from both cameras at three points along a 200 frame sequence. The two cameras are set up about a foot and a half apart with optical centers verging near the middle of the tracking area. Fig. 6 shows the estimated model configurations corresponding to the sample points. In the left column, the estimated model is rendered from the viewpoint of the first camera. In the right column, it is shown from an arbitrary viewpoint, demonstrating the 3D nature of our tracking result. The estimated state trajectories for the entire sequence are given in Figs. 7 and 8.

Direct measurement of tracker accuracy is difficult due to the lack of ground truth data. We plan to use a Polhemus sensor to measure the accuracy of the 6 DOF palm state estimate. Obtaining ground truth measurements for joint angles is much more difficult. One possible solution is to wear an invasive sensor, like the DataGlove, to obtain a baseline measurement. By fitting the DataGlove inside a larger unmarked glove, the effect of the external finger sensors on the feature extraction can be minimized.

7 Implementation Details

The DigitEyes system is built around a special board for real-time image processing, called IC40. Each IC40 board contains a 68040 CPU, 5 MB of dual-ported RAM, a digitizer, and a video generator. The key feature of this board is its ability to deliver digitized images to processor memory at video rate with no computational overhead. This removes an important bottleneck in most workstation-based tracking systems. Ordinary C code can be compiled and down-loaded to the board for execution.

In the multicamera implementation, there is an IC40 board for each camera. The total computation is divided into two parts: feature extraction and state estimation. Feature extraction is done in parallel by each board, then the extracted features are passed over the VME bus to a Sun workstation, which combines them and solves the resulting least squares problem to obtain a state estimate. Estimated states are passed over the Ethernet to a Silicon Graphics Indigo 2 workstation for model rendering and display.

8 Conclusion

We have presented a visual tracking framework for high DOF articulated mechanisms, and its implementation in a tracking system called DigitEyes. We have demonstrated real-time hand tracking of a 27 DOF hand model using two cameras. We will extend this basic work in two ways. First, we will modify our feature extraction process to handle occlusions and complicated backgrounds. Second, we will analyze the observability requirements of articulated object tracking and address the question of camera placement.

References

1. A. Blake, R. Curwen, and A. Zisserman. A framework for spatiotemporal control in the tracking of visual contours. *Int. J. Computer Vision*, 11(2):127–145, 1993.
2. T. Darrell and A. Pentland. Space-time gestures. In *Looking at People Workshop*, Chambery, France, 1993.
3. J. Dennis and R. Schnabel. *Numerical Methods for Unconstrained Optimization and Nonlinear Equations*. Prentice-Hall, Englewood Cliffs, NJ, 1983.
4. B. Dorner. Hand shape identification and tracking for sign language interpretation. In *Looking at People Workshop*, Chambery, France, 1993.
5. D. Gennery. Visual tracking of known three-dimensional objects. *Int. J. Computer Vision*, 7(3):243–270, 1992.
6. S. B. Kang and K. Ikeuchi. Grasp recognition using the contact web. In *Proc. IEEE/RSJ Int. Conf. on Int. Robots and Sys.*, Raleigh, NC, 1992.
7. D. Lowe. Robust model-based motion tracking through the integration of search and estimation. *Int. J. Computer Vision*, 8(2):113–122, 1992.
8. R. Mann and E. Antonsson. Gait analysis– precise, rapid, automatic, 3-d position and orientation kinematics and dynamics. *BULLETIN of the Hospital for Joint Diseases Orthopaedic Institute*, XLIII(2):137–146, 1983.
9. J. O'Rourke and N. Badler. Model-based image analysis of human motion using constraint propagation. *IEEE Trans. Pattern Analysis and Machine Intelligence*, 2(6):522–536, 1980.
10. A. Pentland and B. Horowitz. Recovery of nonrigid motion and structure. *IEEE Trans. Pattern Analysis and Machine Intelligence*, 13(7):730–742, 1991.
11. J. Rehg and T. Kanade. Digiteyes: Vision-based human hand tracking. Technical Report CMU-CS-TR-93-220, Carnegie Mellon Univ. School of Comp. Sci., 1993.
12. H. Rijpkema and M. Girard. Computer animation of knowledge-based human grasping. *Computer Graphics*, 25(4):339–348, 1991.
13. M. Spong. *Robot Dynamics and Control*. John Wiley and Sons, 1989.
14. M. Yamamoto and K. Koshikawa. Human motion analysis based on a robot arm model. In *IEEE Conf. Comput. Vis. and Pattern Rec.*, pages 664–665, 1991.
15. T. Zimmerman, J. Lanier, C. Blanchard, S. Bryson, and Y. Harvill. A hand gesture interface device. In *Proc. Human Factors in Comp. Sys. and Graphics Interface (CHI+GI'87)*, pages 189–192, Toronto, Canada, 1987.

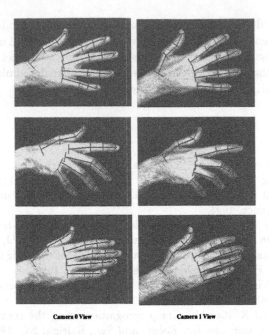

Fig. 5. Three pairs of hand images from the continuous motion estimate plotted in Figs. 7 and 8. Each stereo pair was obtained automatically during tracking by storing every fiftieth image set to disk. The samples correspond to frames 49, 99, and 149.

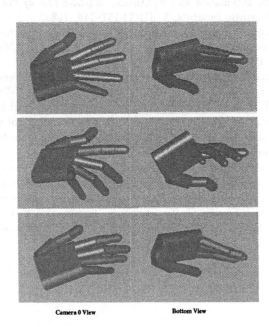

Fig. 6. Estimated hand state for the image samples in Fig. 5, rendered from the Camera 0 viewpoint (left) and a viewpoint underneath the hand (right).

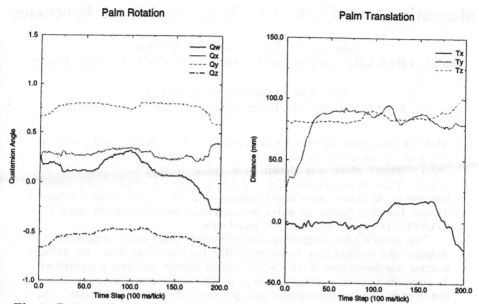

Fig. 7. Estimated palm rotation and translation for motion sequence of entire hand. Q_w-Q_z are the quaternion components of rotation, while T_x-T_z are the translation. The sequence lasted 20 seconds.

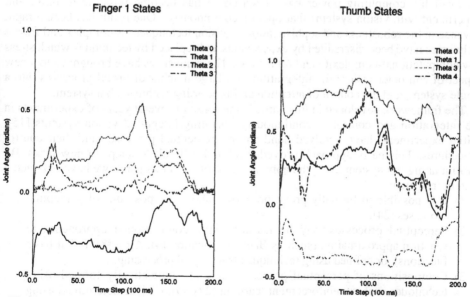

Fig. 8. Estimated joint angles for the first finger and thumb. The other three fingers are similar to the first. Refer to Fig. 1 for variable definitions.

Integration and Control of Reactive Visual Processes[1]

James L. Crowley and Jean Marc Bedrune
IMAG - LIFIA, I.N.P. Grenoble, 46 Ave Félix Viallet, 38031 Grenoble, France

Morten Bekker and Michael Schneider
L.I.A. Aalborg University, Fr. Bajers Vej 7, DK-9220 Aalborg, Denmark

Abstract This paper describes a new approach to the integration and control of continuously operating visual processes. Visual processes are expressed as transformations which map signals from virtual sensors into commands for devices. These transformations define reactive processes which tightly couple perception and action. Such transformations may be used to control robotic devices, including fixation an active binocular head, as well as the to select and control the processes which interpret visual data.

This method takes inspiration from so-called "behavioural" approaches to mobility and manipulation. However, unlike most previous work, we define reactive transformations at the level of virtual sensors and device controllers. This permits a system to integrate a large number of perceptual processes and to dynamically compose sequences of such processes to perform visual tasks. The transition between visual processes is mediated by signals from a supervisory controller as well as signals obtained from perception. This method offers the possibility of constructing vision systems with large numbers of visual abilities in a manner which is both scalable and learnable.

1. Introduction

As available computing power has increased, it has become possible to build and experiment with vision systems that operate continuously. One result has been a rapid advance in the robustness and sophistication of vision techniques, as complex and fragile techniques have been discredited by experiments and replaced by techniques which stress low computational-complexity and robustness. These advances have brought us to a new aspect of computer vision: the integration of a large number of visual processes into a single system, and the control of attention and processing within such a system.

The framework developed in this paper is the result of several years of experiments in the integration and control of continuously operating integrated vision systems [15]. Initial experiments have involved hand-coding perceptual processes and their control procedures. This early approach proved rigid and difficult to adapt to new tasks. By reformulating our system using the approach described in this paper we have obtained a system in which:

1) It is possible to formally prove properties about compositions of perceptual processes [24].
2) Perceptual processes may be learned using connectionist approaches to function approximation (such as Back-propagation [4], ART [8], radial basis functions), or defined using techniques from signal processing.
3) Compositions of perceptual processes may be automatically formed using techniques such as reinforcement learning [27], [9], [19], or determined using rule based planning techniques.

This approach is inspired by an approach to mobile robotics often referred to as

[1]Funded by the CEC DG III, ESPRIT Basic Research project EP 7108 Vision as Process

"Behavioural" [5]. The notion of a reactive behaviour has been shown to provide a compact and general formalism for such tasks as grasping and haptic exploration [26], autonomous vehicle driving [23], and navigation [11].

Criticisms of this "behavioural" approach to robotics contend that

1) Inhibition based control regimes, such as subsumption [5], are inadequate for constructing complex systems,
2) Perception without intermediate representations are subject to an exponential explosion in computational cost.
3) The concept of "goal" is fundamental to systems which must perform useful tasks in changing environment.

Our experience confirms these criticisms. However, reactive transformations may be used with control regimes other than subsumption. Indeed a number of researchers are beginning to look at the use of other forms of composition of primitive reactive transformations [22]. Furthermore, this approach opens the possibility of techniques for learning compositions of robot behaviours [27] through such techniques as reinforcement learning. With regard to the second criticism, it is possible to base the perceptual space on functions computed from internal representations of the world. Such an approach permits the complexity reduction benefits of intermediate representations [28]. Furthermore, goals may be included as intermediate representation.

The framework we propose is related to the work of Kosecka and Bajcsy [20] on the use of state transition networks formalised as a Discrete Event Dynamics Systems (DEDS) notation [24]. In their approach, composite reactive transformations are hand crafted and expressed in a formal tool in order to prove properties about such compositions. We have approached the problem from a view point of obtaining a framework in which the composition of transformations can be controlled by a rule-based planning system. Furthermore, we believe that this approach opens the possibility of acquiring both visual processes and their composition using connectionist approaches to machine learning.

A crucial problem in a continuously operating vision system is dealing with the very large quantity of ambiguous and noisy data provided by cameras. An often overlooked property of the human visual system is that the perceptual processes are serial and highly restrictive about what data is processed at each instant. The human visual system can be seen as a pipeline of filters for eliminating unnecessary information. Even before the visual data arrives at the retina, it is restricted to a narrow depth of field by the optics of the eye. The region of the world perceived is even more severely filtered by simple processes which restrict attention to the horopter (those parts of the world which project to the same location in the stereo retinas). The horopter is moved dynamically around the scene by saccadic movements of the eyes, limiting the perception at each instant to a narrow slice of the world. The primary role of binocular vision thus seem to be separation of figure and ground, and not 3D reconstruction. Active vision systems take inspiration from this "filtering" principle to limit the amount of data which must be attended to in order to provide a response within a fixed delay.

Active vision may be defined as "Control of cameras and control of processing to aid the observation of the world". A number of researchers have provided demonstrations of systems which perform simple visual tasks in real time using this principle [2], [3], [6], [17], [21], [22]. However, in each case the system was limited to demonstrating the advantages which active control brought to a particular visual process. Little has been done on the problem of extending an active approach to all levels of the vision system. This paper addresses this problem with a framework for integration and control of visual behaviuors based on reactive transformations.

2. Reactive Visual Process

In order to place our framework on a solid foundation, this section presents definitions of reactive visual processes and their components. These definitions are then used in section 3 to develop a framework for integration and control of visual processes. Examples of these concepts are presented in section 4.

2.1 Perceptual Spaces

Perceptual systems make observations of the external world through perceptual organs or "transducers". We define a transducer as an organ which provides a digitized measure of some property of the world from a region of space during an interval of time. The result is a digital signal which may be a scalar, a vector, an image, or even a vector of images. This measured property partially reflects the "state" of the external world. For example, the composition of the lenses, retina, camera electronics and digitizer which provide images to a machine vision system constitutes a transducer. The resulting signal has as many dimensions as pixels in the image.

Brooks has argued [5] that robotic systems can be composed of reactive behaviours which map directly from transducers to actuators. While such an approach is possible, it does not scale well to non-trivial processes. In order to go beyond the purely reactive behaviours of insect-like systems, it is necessary to reduce computational complexity by introducing intermediate processing. This intermediate processing may involve fusing signals acquired at different times to construct an intermediate description (or estimate) of the state of the external world, (a local model). Such an intermediate description can provide input for a large number of visual processes with a minimum of computations.

Let us define an <u>intermediate representations</u> as a collection of properties, $R_i(t)$. Among the intermediate representations, we include such things as the current systems goals and information from long term memory. This provides a way to include the system goals within a reactive visual process. We define a <u>virtual sensor</u> to be a digitized time sampled function, $S_i(t)$, which is computed on a subset of the set of transducers $T_i(t)$ and intermediate representations $R_i(t)$. Examples of virtual sensors include a bank of space-time Gabor filters applied to an image sequence [29], perceptual grouping procedures applied to a gradient image, and the current goal for a mobile robot expressed as a position relative to the robot.

A <u>perceptual space</u> is a vector space defined by a set of virtual sensors. Thus a perception, $P_k(t)$, is a vector in a perceptual space.

$$P_k(t) = \{S_1(t), S_2(t), \dots, S_n(t)\}$$

An important role of virtual sensors is to reduce the number of dimensions required for a perceptual space.

A <u>perceptual signal</u> is a signal which is created when a perception occurs within a pre-defined region of a perceptual space. Perceptual signals are used to signal a change in state within a visual process. This change in state may be planned or unexpected.

2.2 Action Spaces

A symmetry exists between perception and action. Each of the concepts defined above for perception has a counterpart in action. The counterpart of a transducer is an <u>actuator</u>. An actuator applies a change to the state of the external world. An actuator interprets a command, $A_i(t)$, which we will define to be a time sampled, digitized signal. Thus we group the motor controller, power amplifier, motor and mechanical system together as an actuator. A command may be a scalar, a vector, or have any number of dimensions.

Each actuator operates in its own coordinate space. It is often preferable to specify actions in coordinates which relate to the device or to the external world. We define a device controller as an interpreter which transforms commands from a "virtual" device to the real actuators. A device controller interprets a time sampled digitized signal, $D_i(t)$. A parameter may be a scalar or a vector and provides a reference signal for the device controller. A common example of a device controller is the Cartesian arm controller which is standard for most robot manipulators. Other examples include a vehicle controller for a robotic vehicle [16] and the a Cartesian head controller for a binocular head [14].

A composition of parameters for device controllers and/or actuators forms an action space [4]. A command is a vector of parameters in an action space.

$$C(t) = \{D_1(t)...D_n(t)\}$$

2.3 Behaviours: From perception to action.

Using the above definitions, the behaviour of a reactive process is defined as a transformation from a perceptual space to an action space.

Reactive Process: $C(t) \leftarrow B_i(P_k(t))$

A large variety of techniques exist for defining such transformations. The classical approach is to use a PID controller. A modern control theory approach involves applying a controller based on a Kalman filter, lattice filter, of alpha-beta tracker. The use of fuzzy control is rapidly gaining popularity [25]. A large number of systems have recently been built using various artificial neural network approaches such as ART [8] and back propagation [23]. By defining reactive visual processes using virtual sensors, it becomes possible for such processes to exploit local models of the environment. Thus it is possible to take advantage of the reduction in complexity made possible by clever use of intermediate representations.

2.4 Predictions: From action to perception

In order to select the appropriate action, it is useful for a supervisory system to be able to predict the effect that an action will have on the external world. Predicting the effect of an action is equivalent to predicting the change in a perception from an action. We define a prediction as a transformation from an action space to perceptual space.

$$P_k(t+\Delta T) \leftarrow P_i(C(t))$$

As with a reactive visual process, a prediction may be defined by any number of techniques.

3 Selection and Control of Visual Processes

The subsumption architecture [5] posits the use of a simple hierarchy of processes using inhibition as a control mechanism. Such a mechanism assumes that the tasks of the system do not change. Efforts to construct such systems with more than a few "behaviours" soon leads to problems of which process should inhibit which and when. As an alternative, we propose to construct systems with a large repertoire of possible reactive visual processes (or behaviours or modes or controllers) and to use a supervisory controller to select the appropriate process based on current circumstances and goals.

3.1 Supervisory Control of Reactive Processes

The supervisory controller and its relation to the repertoire of visual processes is illustrated in figure 1. This figure shows a set of possible processes (B_1 through B_6) set up to receive their perceptual data from a set of virtual sensors and to produce commands for a set of device controllers. The currently active processes (shown as dark ellipses) are selected by the supervisory controller based on perceptual signals and current goals. Any conflicts in the commands issued by the processes are resolved by the device controllers.

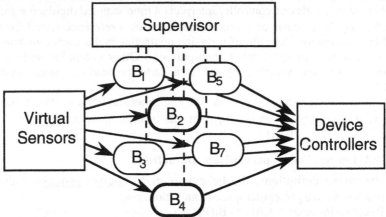

Figure 1 . A Supervisory controller selects and controls the sequencing of perceptual processes. Multiple processes can be active at the same time. Arrows indicate flow of data, dashed lines indicate control, the highlighted ellipses are currently active.

A number of techniques are available to organise the supervisory controller. The most natural of these appears to be to organise the processes as a network of states, where each state corresponds to a set of reactive processes with associated control parameters. For each state, a set of possible next states can be selected based on both the current goals (or sub-goals) and on perceptual signals. Multiples states can be active at the same time, and transitions to states can be conditioned on unexpected events, such as detection of an impending collision, or the presence of a human master.

A state network approach provides a number of advantages.

- Networks can be abstracted by collapsing sub-networks into "super-states" to form a more abstract network. In this way, a system can reason hierarchically about its actions, reducing complexity.
- The same visual process (or sets of visual processes) with different parameters can be represented by different states.
- Formal methods exist to prove properties about such state transition networks.

Such an approach also makes it possible for planning techniques to be used in the design of state transitions networks, and provides an approach for control of plan execution. In this way, a mission may be specified as a sequence of tasks to be accomplished [12]. Each task can be translated into sub-goals expressed in terms of desired world state. The system can then select a sequence of reactive processes which may be applied at the current world state to transform the world to the desired state.

This approach also opens new problems. One such problem is the transition between reactive processes. It is relatively easy to construct pairs of reactive processes which drive the system back and forth between a transition and thus generate an oscillation. Even when there is no oscillation, care must be taken at the transition between reactive processes to avoid [18].

3.2 Selection and Sequencing by Signals

The Supervisory control problem for reactive processes can be expressed as <u>selection</u> and sequencing. Selection is the process of determining which reactive processes can next be executed. Sequencing determines when to make the transition to the next process. From the point of view of the reactive process, both selection and sequencing are controlled by signals. A <u>signal</u> triggers a change of reactive process. The value of the signal serves to select the next process, while the time of arrival of the signal serves to determine when the transition occurs.

We distinguish two kinds of signals: <u>command</u> signals and <u>perceptual</u> signals. Command signals flow from the supervisory controller to the reactive processes. These may be divided into two sub-classes: <u>unconditional</u> commands and <u>conditional</u> commands. An unconditional command orders an immediate transition to the new reactive process. A conditional command enables a transition to a new reactive process at the reception of an appropriate perceptual signal. In this way the delay in communications between the supervisor and the reactive controller can be avoided in the actual transition. A set of conditional commands can enable a set of possible reflex-level reactions to uncontrollable events. The state transition, whether conditional or unconditional, should be accompanied by an acknowledgement to the supervisor.

Perceptual signals are generated by a form of reactive process and are used to change the current set of reactive processes. Perceptual signals can be used to trigger the transition of reactive processes from external events with a minimum of delay. They can also be used as watch-dogs which enable the system to quickly react to uncontrollable events.

4 Example: A System for Detection, Fixation and Tracking

To illustrate our approach, we describe a minimal system designed as a composition of four reactive visual processes for detection, fixation and tracking. This example illustrates how a system composed of reactive visual processes can be designed to attend to dynamic events, including events which occur unexpectedly.

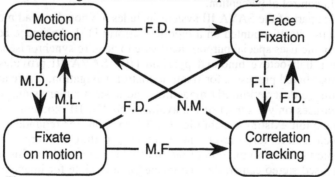

Figure 2. The State transition network for the demonstration.

4.1 Attending to motion and while watching for faces.

The state transition network which describes the demonstration is shown in figure 2. The basic task of our demonstration is to watch for motion, and when motion is detected, to maintain a 3D fixation on the thing that moved. In its initial state, the system is looking for motion within the binocular visual field. If motion is detected by either camera, the system attempts to fixate the center of gravity of the motion using both cameras. Such fixation is servoed in 2D but provides an estimate of the fixation point in 3D head centered coordinates. When a region of motion is centered in both visual fields, the system switches to a mode in which a correlation tracker is used to hold the 3D fixation point on the object which is found in the center of the image. If fixation on the object is broken, the system reverts to the motion detection state. A face detection process operates in parallel with these processes. If a face is detected in either visual field, the system switches its fixation to the face. If the face correlation is lost, the system reverts to correlation tracking on the "form" found where the face was present (usually the human's head). In this way, a person can turn his back to the robot and walk away and the robot will follow.

4.2 Implementation in the SAVA III Test-bed

This example uses the SAVA III distributed vision test-bed [15]. SAVA III provides an infrastructure for experiments in continuously operating vision. The SAVA system is composed of a number of individual modules connected by a message passing facility implemented using sockets. Each SAVA module is constructed within an interpreter (CLIPS 5.1) which provides a lisp-like syntax for functions, rules and objects. This interpreter acts as a scheduler, a message interpreter and an interpreter for rule-based "demons".

Each module contains a collection of procedures which concern a data structure. A small set of rules provide a scheduler which calls the selected procedures in a cyclic manner. Because the scheduler is interpreted, the set of procedures and their parameters can be changed dynamically. Between each procedure call, the interpreter reads and interprets any messages received from the other modules. Such messages are typically used to interrogate local data structures, or to define the processing within a module. The SAVA modules send and receive messages encoded as ASCII strings using a mail box facility. The first word of each message is a function which is interpreted by the CLIPS interpreter using lisp-like "eval" function. The "build" command in CLIPS makes it possible to define a new message type with a message from another module. Using an interpreter for control and communications between modules has greatly accelerated experiments in control of perception.

The robotics part of the SAVA III system includes a binocular head mounted on a 6-axis manipulator, itself mounted on a mobile platform [13]. An image acquisition and processing module uses special purpose hardware to acquire synchronised stereo images and compute a half-octave binomial pyramid [10]. SAVA III provides independent modules as distributed processes for fixation control, navigation, image acquisition and processing, image description, 3D modeling, and system supervision. This particular demonstration uses only a subset of the available SAVA III modules. The system has been able to exploit existing capabilities for 3D fixation, for redundant control of the head and vehicle, and for reflex level control of focus, aperture and vergence.

Figure 3 shows the configuration of modules which are used for this demonstration. Two synchronised stereo cameras are connected to a module for image acquisition and processing. This module responds to requests from the system supervisor and from the fixation control module. The fixation control module contains state variables for the current 3D fixation point, and for 2D fixation points for each camera. Messages from the supervisor set the desired value for these fixations. Fixation control interprets the fixation command to generate commands to the 10-degree of freedom head-body system. If maintaining fixation requires movement by the vehicle, fixation control can send messages to the navigation system to perform the necessary movements. A synchronization module provides a global time reference so that all data and commands can be time-stamped. This time stamp is used to produce timing diagrams to illustrate the execution speeds of the modules as their processes change.

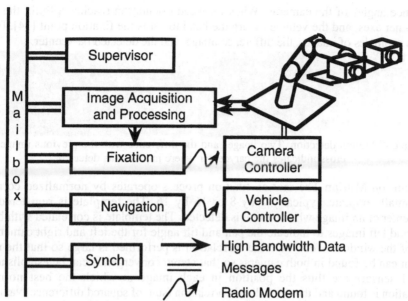

Figure 3 Configuration of demonstration system within the SAVA III Vision test-bed.

4.3 Vocabulary of Visual Processes

The visual processes which make up this demonstration include motion detection, fixation, face detection and tracking. Each of these processes depends on an image processing procedure executed by the image acquisition and processing module, and commanded by the fixation module. For each process we identify the virtual sensors and the device level commands that are generated, and describe the transformation from perceptual space to action space

Motion Detection: The motion detection process is based on the energy in a temporal derivative of the images. The process relies on virtual sensor values:
Virtual Sensors:
M: The sum of squared difference of successive images
C_x, C_y: The barycenter of squared difference image.
The action space for this process is the pan and tilt directions for the camera:
Action Space:
α, ϕ Pan and tilt angle to bring barycenter of motion to the center of image.

The motion detection process is implemented as a sum of squared difference of successive images followed by a calculation of the barycenter of local energy. The input images are selected from one of the levels of a binomial pyramid [10]. The pyramid an important reduction in communication and computation. An re-sampled image size of 64 x 64, corresponding to smoothing by a binomial filter ($\sigma = 4$) is used for the experiments described below. A difference image is computed from the previous image and then squared. If the sum of the squared difference is below a threshold, the process signals no motion. Otherwise, the barycenter is computed for the squared difference image. The row and column values of the barycenter, and the sum of squared difference constitute the virtual sensor for this first reactive behaviour.

The pan and tilt values are specified to the fixation controller. The fixation controller uses the sum of the pan angles to set the head orientation ϕ_4 and the difference to set the vergence angles of the cameras. When the head orientation reaches a limit, the system uses other axes, and the vehicle to turn the head towards the fixation point [14]. Figure 4 shows examples of images, the difference image, and the detected barycenter.

Figure 4. Motion detection. Two images and the difference with the previous image . The cross indicates the barycenter where motion was detected.

Fixation on Motion The motion fixation process operates by normalized correlation of a small template, typically 8 by 8 or 16 by 16. The template is registered at the barycenter of an image when motion is detected. The template is correlated with both the right and left images to indicate the pan and tilt angle for the left and right cameras. The area of the window over which the correlation is performed is large so that the moving pattern can be found in both cameras so that stereo convergence can be established. The virtual sensors are thus the position in each image at which the best normalized correlation is found and the normalized correlation (sum of squared difference) values.

Virtual Sensors:

D_r, D_l: Best normalized correlation scores for left and right images.

x_r, y_r: Image position of best correlation score in right image.

x_l, y_l: Image position of best correlation score in left image.

The action space is the pan and tilt angle required to bring the best correlation positions to the center of the left and right images.

Action Space:

α_r, ϕ_r Pan and tilt angle to bring correlation to center of right image.

α_l, ϕ_l Pan and tilt angle to bring correlation to center of left image.

Conversion of the pan and tilt angles to a 3D fixation point is performed by the fixation control module.

Tracking Fixation: Once the form is centered in both images, it is possible to reduce the search region, resulting in a gain in processing speed. The system moves to a tracking behaviour in which the virtual sensors are of the same nature as motion fixation, except that the search region is much smaller and at higher resolution. We have recently begun experiments in which the search region is a parameter of the delay since the last cycle of fixation.

Face Detection Face Detection is a back-ground signal detection process, programmed as a demon. Face detection operates by normalized correlation of a small (16 by 16) average face image with several levels of the Gaussian pyramid. The average face image has been formed by acquiring a number of face images of laboratory members with a neutral background, normalising their position and orientation, and then computing an average image. Detection of a face constitutes a perceptual signal which moves the system to the face fixation process. In face fixation, the virtual sensors are the row and column positions of the best correlation of the average face in the left and right images, and the sum of squared difference between the face window and each image at this best correlation value.

Virtual Sensors:

D_{fr}, D_{fl}:   Best normalized correlation scores for left and right images.

x_{fr}, y_{fr}:　　　Image position of best correlation score in right image.
x_{fl}, y_{fl}:　　　Image position of best correlation score in left image.
The action space is the pan and tilt angle required to bring the face position to the center of each image.

Action Space:

α, ϕ　Pan and tilt angle to bring face to center of image.

The set of perceptual signals and their definitions are as follows.

F.D.　　　The <u>face</u> <u>detection</u> signal is given by a threshold on normalized correlation (SSD) with the average face.

M.D.　　　M<u>otion</u> <u>detected</u> is signaled by the sum of the squared temporal difference greater than a threshold.

M.F.　　　The <u>motion</u> <u>fixated</u> signal is triggered when the motion field is within 16 pixels of the center of both images.

F.L.　　　A <u>face</u> <u>lost</u> signal is detected when the best normalized correlation (sum of squared differences) of the average face with both images falls above a threshold.

N.M.　　　The <u>no</u> <u>motion</u> signal is triggered when the tracked window has not moved by more than n pixels in last m images

M.L.　　　A <u>motion</u> <u>lost</u> signal occurs in motion fixation if the motion signal (sum of squared temporal difference) falls above a threshold.

4.4 Systems Execution

Timing diagrams have proven to be a useful tool for debugging visual behaviours. Each module contains a synchronised clock. At the start of each cycle, the module retrieves the time that has elapsed since the start of the last cycle. This value is appended to a list which is output to a file at the end of execution.

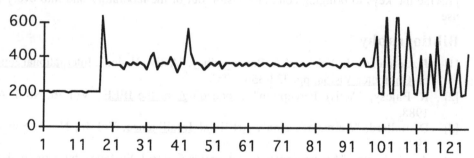

Figure 4. Timing diagram for image acquisition and processing from a typical tracking session. Vertical axis is milliseconds. The horizontal axis is the cycle number.

Figure 4 illustrates timing in the image acquisition and processing module during a typical tracking session using 64 by 64 images. The vertical axis is cycle time measured in milliseconds, while the horizontal axis is the cycle number. The motion detection demon is invoked near cycle number 17, causing the cycle time to rise from 200 milliseconds to 360 milliseconds. At cycle number 101, the demon detected motion and sent a signal to engage the fixation process. During fixation, the cycle times oscillate between 500 milliseconds and 200 milliseconds. The 500 millisecond cycle occurs when a command has been received to compute correlation with the template in both images. A 200 millisecond cycle occurs when no command is received, and only image acquisition and pyramid computation are performed. At cycle 111, fixation is achieved and the tracking demon is invoked. During tracking, the module requires around 400 milliseconds to determine the correlation.

5 Conclusions

Vision systems which can not dynamically control acquisition and processing are limited to a small number of task in a fixed environment. In order to integrate more than a few visual behaviours, an approach is required which permits data and processing to be dynamically selected in response to system goals and external events. This paper presents such an approach based on the concept of reactive vision processes.

The use of reactive processes for robotics has generally been restricted to transformations from sensor signals to motor commands. In order to overcome limitations imposed by the complexity of perception we define the reactive transformation on virtual sensors which may include local modeling systems, long term memory and even system goals. Commands are generated to device level controllers which integrate such commands with proprioceptive signals, and resolve contradictory commands. Formulating a continuously operating vision system in terms of such reactive processes permits the system to be scalable and to adapt to a changing and unpredictable environment.

This new approach to vision systems opens new problems, including techniques for
- Analysing the stability of compositions of reactive transformations.
- Learning reactive controllers and prediction functions for reactive processes.
- Learning to detect perceptual signals which are relevant to control.
- Learning the composition of visual processes to form perceptual "skills".

The tight coupling of vision and action and the introduction of learnable techniques may provide the keys to bringing computer vision out of the laboratory and into every-day use.

Bibliography

[1]   J. Aloimonos, I. Weiss and A. Bandopadhay, "Active Vision", International Journal on Computer Vision, pp. 333-356, 1987.

[2]   R. Bajcsy, "Active Perception", Proceedings of the IEEE , Vol 76, No 8, Aug. 1988.

[3]   D. Ballard, "Animate Vision", Artificial Intelligence, Vol 48, No. 1, February 1991.

[4]   A. G. Barto, "An approach to Learning Control Surfaces by Connectionist Systems", in M. Arbib and A. Hanson, Vision, Brain and Cooperative Computation, MIT Press, Cambridge MA 1987.

[5]   R. A. Brooks, "A Robust Layered Control System for a Mobile Robot, IEEE Journal of Robotics and Automation, RA-2(1) March 1986.

[6]   C. Brown, "Prediction and Cooperation in Gaze Control", Biological Cyber 63, 90.

[7]   K. Brunnström, "Active Exploration of Static Scenes", Doctoral Dissertation, KTH - Royal School of Technology, Stockholm Sweden, 1993.

[8]   Carpenter G. A. "Neural network models for pattern recognition and associate memory", Neural Networks, Vol 2, 1989.

[9]   D. Chapman and L. P. Kaelbling, "Learning from Delayed Reinforcement in a Complex Domain", Proc. of the IJCAI, 1991.

[10] A. Chehikian and J. L. Crowley, "Fast Computation of Optimal Semi-Octave Pyramids", 7th S.C.I.A., Aalborg, August 1991.

[11] Robot Learning, Edited by J. Connell and S. Mahadevan, Kluwer Academic Publishers, Boston, 1993.

[12] Crowley, J. L., "Coordination of Action and Perception in a Surveillance Robot", IEEE Expert, Vol 2(4), pp 32-43 Winter 1987, (Also appeared in IJCAI-87).

[13] Crowley, J. L. "Towards Continuously Operating Integrated Vision Systems for Robotics Applications", SCIA-91, Seventh Scandinavian Conference on Image Analysis, Aalborg, August 91.

[14] Crowley, J. L., P. Bobet and M. Mesrabi, "Camera Control for a Active Camera Head", Pattern Recognition and Artificial Intelligence, Vol 7, No. 1, January 1993.

[15] Crowley, J. L.and H. I. Christensen, Vision as Process. Springer Verlag Basic Research Series, to appear 1993.

[16] Crowley, J. L. and P. Reignier, "Asynchronous Control of Rotation and Translation for a Robot Vehicle", Robotics and Autonmous Systems, Vol 10, No. 1, Jan. 1993.

[17] Eklundh, J. O. and K.Pahlavan, "A head-eye system: Analysis and Design.", CVGIP, 56:1. 1993.

[18] J. A. Coelho and R. A. Grupen, "Constructing Effective Multifingered Grasp Controllers", 1994 IEEE Conf. on Robotics and Automation, 1994.

[19] L. P. Kaelbling Learning in Embedded Systems, MIT Press, Cambridge Mass, 93.

[20] J. Kosecka and R. Bajcsy, "Discrete Event Systems for Autonomous Mobile Agents", Intelligent Robotic Systems, '93, Zakopane, 1993 (also to appear in Robotics and Autonomous Systems, 12(3) March 94.

[21] Krotkov, E., "Focusing", International Journal of Computer Vision, 1, 1987.

[22] Krotkov, E., Henriksen, K. and Kories, R., "Stereo Ranging from Verging Cameras", IEEE Trans on PAMI, Vol 12, No. 12, pp. 1200-1205, December 1990.

[23] D. A. Pomerlau, "Neural Network Based Autonomous Navigation", in Vision and Navigation, C. Thorpe (ed)., Kluwer Academic Publishers, Boston, 1990.

[24] P. J. Ramadge and W. M Wonham, "The Control of Discrete Event Systems", Proceedings of the IEEE, 77(1), January 1989.

[25] P. Reignier, "Fuzzy Logic Techniques for Mobile Robot Obstacle Avoidance", Intelligent Robotic Systems, '93, Zakopane, 1993 (also in Robotics and Autonomous Systems, 12(3) March 94.

[26] K. Souccar, M. Huber, and J. A. Coelho, "Sequencing Contollers - Experiments in Auronomous Reaching and Grasping", 1994 IEEE Conference on Robotics and Automation, May 1994.

[27] R. S. Sutton, "Integrated Architectures for Learning, Planning and Reacting Based on Approximating Dynamic Programming", in Proceedings of the 7th Int. Conf. on Machine Learning, June 1990.

[28] J.K. Tsotsos, "Representational Axes and Temporal Co-operative Processes, In: Vision", Brain and Co-operative Computation, (Eds.) M.A. Arbib & A.R. Hanson, MIT Press, Cambridge, Mass, pp. 361-418, 1987.

[29] Westelius, C. J., H. Knutsson, and G. H. Granlund, "Focus of Attention Control", SCIA-91, Seventh Scandinavian Conference on Image Analysis, Aalborg, Aug. 91.

Motion and Structure

Motion Estimation on the Essential Manifold*

Stefano Soatto,¹ Ruggero Frezza,² Pietro Perona¹,²

¹ California Institute of Technology 116-81, Pasadena, CA 91125, soatto@caltech.edu
² Università di Padova, Dipartimento di Elettronica ed Informatica, Padova, Italy

Abstract. We introduce a novel perspective for viewing the ego-motion reconstruction problem as the estimation of the state of a dynamical system having an implicit measurement constraint and unknown inputs. Such a system happens to be "linear", but it is defined on a space (the "Essential Manifold") which is not a linear (vector) space.

We propose two recursive schemes for performing the estimation task: the first consists in "flattening the space" and solving a nonlinear estimation problem on the flat (Euclidean) space. The second consists in viewing the system as embedded in a larger euclidean space, and solving at each step a linear estimation problem on the linear space, followed by a "projection" onto the Essential Manifold.

Both schemes produce motion estimates together with the joint second order statistics of the estimation error which can be used by any "structure from motion" module which incorporates motion error [18, 23 in...

Experiments are presented with real and synthetic image sequences.

1 Introduction

A camera on a human agent - moving inside a static scene. The objects populating the ambient space are projected onto the CCD surface (or the retina), and their projection changes in time as the camera moves. The "visual motion" problem consists of reconstructing the in time of the camera's ego-motion and the "structure" of the topology of the scene.

Euler representation, it is and the set of ...
some frame instance, the on moving with the camera, a
$X = [\; x_1, \; x_2 \;]^T \in \mathbb{R}^3$ the coordinates of the point in a moving and we have $x = [\; x_1, \;]^T$. As the camera moves between two time-instants with rotation R and translation T, the coordinates relative to the rigid motion stand:

$$ X(t+1) = V(t+1) X(t) \quad (1) $$

* Research funded by the California Institute of Technology CISE grant WATIM (91-0900), an AT&T Foundation Special Purpose grant. P.P. and ... ASI (Italian Space Agency). P.P. grateful to ... the Italian Space Agency for ... Mathematical Sciences at Cambridge. We thank ... who participated as part of this research.

Motion Estimation on the Essential Manifold*

Stefano Soatto[1], Ruggero Frezza[2], Pietro Perona[1,2]

[1] California Institute of Technology 116-81, Pasadena–CA 91125, soatto@caltech.edu
[2] Università di Padova, Dipartimento di Elettronica ed Informatica, Padova–Italy

Abstract. We introduce a novel perspective for viewing the "ego-motion reconstruction" problem as the estimation of the state of a dynamical system having an implicit measurement constraint and unknown inputs. Such a system happens to be "linear", but it is defined on a space (the "Essential Manifold") which is not a linear (vector) space.

We propose two recursive schemes for performing the estimation task: the first consists in *"flattening the space"* and solving a nonlinear estimation problem on the flat (euclidean) space. The second consists in viewing the system as embedded in a larger euclidean space, and solving at each step a *linear estimation* problem on a *linear* space, followed by a *"projection"* onto the Essential Manifold.

Both schemes output motion estimates together with the joint second order statistics of the estimation error, which can be used by any "structure from motion" module which incorporates motion error [18, 22] in order to estimate 3D scene structure.

Experiments are presented with real and synthetic image sequences.

1 Introduction

A camera (or a human eye) is moving inside a static scene. The objects populating the ambient space are projected onto the CCD surface (or the retina), and their projection changes in time as the camera moves. The "visual motion" problem consists of reconstructing the motion of the camera ("ego-motion") and the "structure" of the scene from its time-varying projection.

A simple representation of the "structure" of a scene is obtained from the position of a (finite) set of salient "feature" points in 3D space with respect to some reference frame, for example the one moving with the viewer. We call $\mathbf{X}^i = \begin{bmatrix} X \ Y \ Z \end{bmatrix}_i^T \in \mathbb{R}^3$ the coordinates of the ith point in a cartesian frame, and we let $i = 1 \ldots N$. As the camera moves between two discrete time instants, with rotation R and translation T, the coordinates change according to the rigid motion constraint:

$$\mathbf{X}^i(t+1) = R(t)\mathbf{X}^i(t) + T(t) \quad \forall i = 1 \ldots N, \tag{1}$$

* Research funded by the California Institute of Technology, ONR grant N00014-93-1-0990, an AT&T Foundation Special Purpose grant and the ASI-RS-103 grant from the Italian Space Agency. P.P. gratefully acknowledges the Newton Institute for Mathematical Sciences of Cambridge, UK, where he conducted part of this research.

where $T \in \mathbf{R}^3$ and $R \in SO(3)$ —the group of Special Orthogonal (rotation) matrices. We model the camera as an ideal perspective projection of the euclidean space onto the real-projective plane [2, 16] (pinhole camera):

$$\pi : \mathbf{R}^3 \to \mathbf{R}P^2 \qquad \mathbf{X} \mapsto \pi(\mathbf{X}) \doteq \begin{bmatrix} x & y & 1 \end{bmatrix}^T = \mathbf{x} \doteq \begin{bmatrix} \frac{X}{Z} & \frac{Y}{Z} & 1 \end{bmatrix}^T . \qquad (2)$$

In [20] we show how visual motion can be formulated as a combined "inversion-estimation" or "identification-estimation" task for the dynamical model (1)-(2). However, due to the "driftless" structure of the model, any inverse system is essentially *instantaneous*, and hence it does not exploit the benefits of recursiveness in terms of noise rejection and computational efficiency. Using the trick of "dynamic extension" [9] we show how the visual motion task can be transformed into the estimation of the state of a nonlinear system with unknown inputs, which in the estimation process are viewed as disturbances. A fundamental issue in deriving a state estimator (observer) is of course *observability*, which for linear systems is a necessary and sufficient condition for having an estimation error with spectrally assignable dynamics. For nonlinear systems the issue is more subtle [9, 12]; however, at least "local weak observability" is required in order to be able to state sufficient conditions for the existence of an observer with linear and spectrally assignable error dynamics. Other traditional state estimation techniques, such as the Extended Kalman Filter (EKF) [11, 10] are based upon the linearization of the model about the current trajectory.
The model which derives from (1)-(2) has the peculiarity of not only having a linearization which is not observable, but of also being non-"locally weakly observable". Hence, for the local linearization-based methods, it is not possible to derive sufficient conditions for convergence [19]. However, we show that, *once motion is estimated*, structure is linearly observable in the model (1)-(2), and therefore standard techniques, such as the EKF, can be used effectively for *structure estimation* [14, 18, 22]. Therefore the representation described by (1) and (2), though being the very simplest one can imagine, is not the most appropriate for motion estimation.

The recent literature proposes a variety of techniques for recovering structure and/or motion recursively [3, 14, 8, 7, 1, 18, 22], all of them based essentially on the same basic model (1)-(2), which in fact *defines* the visual motion problem for feature-points in the euclidean 3D space[3]. In particular, among those dealing with both structure and motion estimation, [1] is based on an extended model with motion added to the state space, the structure referred to the observer's reference at time 0 and a more general camera model. In [18] motion is recovered from 2 frames and fed to a model similar to (1)-(2), hence at each step motion is considered known and it does not exploit a dynamical model, as in [14]. In [22] motion is computed instantaneously as in [18], and then inserted it into the state dynamics with a model similar to the one used in [1].

---

[3] We have described a "viewer-centered" representation of the visual motion problem. "Object-centered" representations are essentially equivalent to the previous up to a diffeomorphism, therefore we will not make a distinction between the two.

This work is motivated by the fundamental limitations of the model (1)-(2), and presents a new dynamic model for motion estimation which is globally observable [4]. In section 2 we introduce and describe the Essential Manifold, in sections 3 and 4 we show how motion can be represented and estimated on the Essential Manifold. We introduce then the two approaches for performing the estimation task, which are unified within the new representation. In section 5 we address some special cases and possible generalizations. Finally in section 6 we show some experiments on real and synthetic image sequences.

2 The Essential Space

2.1 Rigid motion and the Essential Constraint

Suppose the correspondence of N feature points is given between time t and $t + 1$, while the viewer has moved of (T, R). It is immediate to see (fig. 1 left) that the vector $\mathbf{X}$, describing the coordinates of the generic point at time t, the corresponding vector $\mathbf{X}'$ at time $t + 1$, and T are coplanar, and therefore their triple product is zero [13]. This is also true with $\mathbf{x}$ in place of $\mathbf{X}$, since the two represent the same projective point. When expressed with respect to a common reference, for example that at time t, the coplanarity condition is written as $\mathbf{x}'^{T}_{i} R(T \wedge \mathbf{x}_i) = 0 \ \forall \ i \ = \ 1 \ldots N$. Once more than 8 correspondent points in general position are given [13, 15, 6, 16], the above constraint is also sufficient to characterize rigid motions up to a finite number of solutions. The operator $T\wedge$ belongs to $so(3)$ —the algebra of skew symmetric matrices; following the notation of Longuet-Higgins [13] we define $\mathbf{Q} \doteq RS \doteq RT\wedge$ so that the above coplanarity condition, which we call the "Essential Constraint", becomes

$$\mathbf{x}'^{T}_{i} \mathbf{Q} \mathbf{x}_i = 0 \ ; \ \forall i = 1 \ldots N. \tag{3}$$

Since the constraint is linear in $\mathbf{Q}$, it can be written as $\chi(\mathbf{x}'(t), \mathbf{x}(t))\mathbf{q}(t) = 0$; χ is an $N \times 9$ matrix whose generic row is $[x_1 x'_1 \ x_2 x'_1 \ x'_1 \ x_1 x'_2 \ x_2 x'_2 \ x'_2 \ x_1 \ x_2 \ 1]$, and $\mathbf{q}$ is a nine-vector obtained by stacking the columns of $\mathbf{Q}$. We will occasionally use the (improper) notation $\chi \mathbf{Q} \doteq \chi \mathbf{q}$, confusing $\mathbf{Q}$ and $\mathbf{q}$.

2.2 The Essential Manifold

We have seen that a rigid motion can be encoded using the Essential Constraint (3) based on the 3×3 matrix $\mathbf{Q} \doteq R(T\wedge) \subset \mathbf{R}^9$. Since we can reconstruct translation only up to a scale factor, we can restrict $\mathbf{Q}$ to belong to $\mathbf{R}P^8$ — the real projective space of dimension 8— or impose the norm of translation to be unitary. We will address later the case $T = 0$. The matrix $\mathbf{Q}$ belongs to the set $\tilde{E} \doteq \{RS | R \in SO(3), S \in so(3)\} \cap \mathbf{R}P^8$ which we call the *Essential*

---

[4] The maximal dimension of the observability codistribution of the basic model is reached after four levels of Lie-differentiation. Therefore in order to recover the observable components of the state-space it is necessary to perform a number of error-prone operations. The model that we will introduce has the advantage of being globally observable with only one level of differentiation [19].

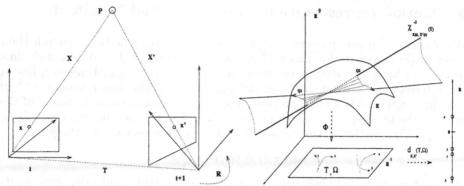

Fig. 1. *(Left) The Essential Constraint. (Right) Structure of the motion problem on the Essential Space*

Space; it encodes rigid motion in a more compact way than $SE(3)$ —the Special Euclidean group of rigid motions— the price being that we loose the smooth group structure. However, a slight modification of the Essential Space proves to have the structure of a topological manifold of class at least C_0 [20]. Consider the map

$$\Phi : E \rightarrow \mathbf{S}^2 \times \mathbf{R}^3 \sim \mathbf{R}^5 \qquad \mathbf{Q} \mapsto \begin{bmatrix} T \\ \Omega \end{bmatrix} = \begin{bmatrix} \pm V_{.3} \\ U R_Z(\pm \frac{\pi}{2}) V^T \end{bmatrix} \qquad (4)$$

where U, V are defined by the Singular Value Decomposition (SVD) of $\mathbf{Q} \doteq U \Sigma V^T$, $V_{.3}$ denotes the third column of V and $R_Z(\frac{\pi}{2})$ is a rotation of $\frac{\pi}{2}$ about the Z axis. T, Ω denote the local coordinates[5] of $\mathbf{Q}$; T is represented in spherical coordinates and Ω is the rotation 3-vector corresponding to the 3×3 rotation matrix $U R_Z(\frac{\pi}{2}) V^T$ via the Rodrigues' formulae [17]. The map Φ defines the local coordinates of the Essential Manifold modulo a sign in the direction of translation and in the rotation angle of R_Z. This ambiguity can be resolved by imposing that the observed points are in front of the viewer [13]. Consider one of the four local counterparts of $\mathbf{Q} \in E$, and the triangulation map $d_{x,x'}$: $E \rightarrow \mathbf{R}^{1+1}$, $d_{x,x'}(\mathbf{Q}) = [Z, Z']^T$ which gives depth of each point as a function of its projections and the motion parameters. We redefine the Essential Space as $E \doteq \tilde{E} \cap d_{x,x'}^{-1}(\mathbf{R}_+^2)^N$, or

$$E \doteq \{RS | R \in SO(3), S \doteq T\wedge \in so(3), \|T\| = 1, d_{x^i, x'^i}(RS) > 0 \; \forall i = 1 \ldots N\}.$$

Now it is easy to see that Φ, restricted to E, locally qualifies as a homeomorphism. The inverse map is simply $\Phi^{-1}(\Omega, T) = e^{(\Omega\wedge)}(T\wedge)$, which is smooth. E also has the structure of an algebraic variety [15], which we will not discuss in this paper.

---

[5] There is an abuse of notation: T indicates both the translation between two frames and the translation part of the canonical (screw) coordinates of motion. We allow such an ambiguity since the two are equivalent up to a diffeomorphism [17].

3 Motion representation on the Essential Manifold

We observe N points moving in space under some rigid motion through their noisy projections onto the image plane: $\mathbf{x}_i(t) + n_i(t)$; $i = 1 \ldots N$. At each time instant we have a constraint in the form $\chi \mathbf{q}(t) \doteq -\tilde{n} \cong 0$, and hence $\mathbf{q}$ lies at the intersection between the Essential Manifold and the linear variety $\chi^{-1}(0)$ (see fig. 1 right). $\tilde{n}$ is a noise process which can be characterized in terms of the noise in the image-plane measurements n_i [20]. As time goes by, the point $\mathbf{Q}(t)$, corresponding to the actual motion, describes a trajectory on E satisfying

$$\mathbf{Q}(t + 1) \doteq \mathbf{Q}(t) + n_{\mathbf{Q}}(t).$$

The last equation is in fact just a *definition* of the right-hand side, since we do not know $n_{\mathbf{Q}}(t)$. If we want to make use of such a model for estimating $\mathbf{Q}$ we have to make some assumptions. For now we will consider it as a discrete time dynamical model for $\mathbf{Q}$ on the Essential Manifold, having *unknown* inputs. If we accompany it with the Essential Constraint, we get

$$\begin{cases} \mathbf{Q}(t + 1) = \mathbf{Q}(t) + n_{\mathbf{Q}}(t) \ ; \ \mathbf{Q} \in E \\ 0 = \chi \mathbf{Q}(t) + \tilde{n}(t). \end{cases} \quad (*)$$

This shows that motion estimation can be viewed as state estimation of a dynamical system defined on a topological manifold and having an implicit measurement constraint and unknown inputs. As it can be seen the system is "linear" (both the state equation and the Essential Constraint are linear in $\mathbf{Q}$), but the word "linear" is not appropriate in this context, since E is not a linear space.

4 Recursive estimation on the Essential Space

The first approach for performing the estimation task consists in composing $(*)$ with the local coordinates chart Φ defined in (4), ending up with a *nonlinear* dynamical model for motion in the *linear* space $\mathbf{R}^5$. At this point we have to make some assumptions about motion: if we do not have any dynamical model available, we may assume a statistical model. In particular we will assume that motion is a *first order random walk in $\mathbf{R}^5$ lifted to the Essential Manifold* (see fig. 2 left). The task is now to estimate the state of a nonlinear system driven by white, zero-mean gaussian noise. This will be done using a variation of the traditional EKF for systems with implicit measurement constraints, which we call the Implicit Extended Kalman Filter (IEKF).

In the second approach we change the model for motion: in particular we assume motion to be a *first order random walk in $\mathbf{R}^9$ projected onto the Essential Manifold* (see fig. 2 left). We will see that this leads to a method for estimating motion via solving at each step a *linear estimation* problem in the linear embedding space $\mathbf{R}^9$ and then "projecting" the estimate onto the Essential Manifold (see fig. 2 right). The notion of projection onto the Essential Manifold will be made clear later.

It is very important to understand that these are *modeling assumptions* and can be validated only a posteriori. In general we observe that the first method

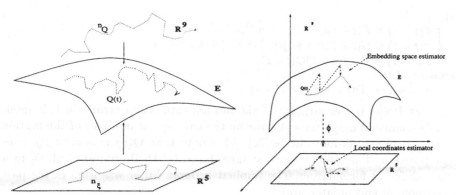

Fig. 2. *(Left) Model of motion as a random walk in $\mathbb{R}^5$ lifted to the manifold or as a random walk in $\mathbb{R}^9$ projected onto the manifold. (Right) Estimation on the Essential Space*

solves a strongly nonlinear problem with techniques based upon linearizing the system about the current reference trajectory. The update of the second method does not involve linearization, while it imposes the constraint of belonging to the Essential Manifold in a weaker way. The next two sections are devoted to describing these two techniques which produce, together with the motion estimates, the variance of the estimation error, which is to be used by the subsequent modules of the structure and motion estimation scheme [22].

4.1 Local coordinates estimator

Compose the model (*) with the map Φ defined in (4). Call $\xi \doteq [T, \Omega]^T \in \mathbb{R}^5$ the local coordinates of $\mathbf{Q}$. Then the system becomes

$$\begin{cases} \xi(t+1) = \xi(t) + n_\xi(t) \; ; \; \xi(t_0) = \xi_0 \\ 0 = \chi\mathbf{Q}(\xi(t)) + \tilde{n}(t). \end{cases} \quad (**)$$

We model motion as a first order random walk, i.e. $n_\xi(t) \in \mathcal{N}(0, R_{n_\xi})$ for some R_{n_ξ} which is referred to as variance of the model error. While the above assumption is arbitrary and can be validated only a posteriori, it is often safe to assume that the noise in the measurements $n_i(t)$ is a white zero-mean gaussian process. The second order statistics of $\tilde{n}$ can be inferred from n_i, as it has been done in [20]. Now (**) is in a form suitable for using an IEKF. A derivation of the IEKF is reported in [20]: it is based upon the fact that the variational model about the best current trajectory is linear and *explicit*, so that a linear update equation can be derived and a pseudo-innovation process can be defined. Finally call $C \doteq \left(\frac{\partial \chi \mathbf{q}}{\partial \xi}\right)$ and $D \doteq \left(\frac{\partial \chi \mathbf{q}}{\partial \mathbf{X}}\right)$, we have

Prediction step :
$$\begin{cases} \hat{\xi}(t+1|t) = \hat{\xi}(t|t) \; ; \; \hat{\xi}(0|0) = \xi_0 \\ P(t+1|t) = P(t|t) + R_{n_\xi} \; ; \; P(0|0) = P_0 \end{cases}$$
Update step :
$$\begin{cases} \hat{\xi}(t+1|t+1) = \hat{\xi}(t+1|t) - L(t+1)\chi\mathbf{Q}(\hat{\xi}(t+1|t)) \\ P(t+1|t+1) = \Gamma(t+1)P(t+1|t)\Gamma^T(t+1) + L(t+1)R_{\tilde{n}}(t+1)L^T(t+1) \end{cases}$$

Gain :
$$\begin{cases} L(t+1) = P(t+1|t)C^T(t+1)\Lambda^{-1}(t+1) \\ \Lambda(t+1) = C(t+1)P(t+1|t)C^T(t+1) + R_{\tilde{n}}(t+1) \\ \Gamma(t+1) = I - L(t+1)C(t+1) \end{cases}$$

Variance of $\tilde{n}$:
$$\left\{ R_{\tilde{n}}(t+1) = D(t+1)R_{\mathbf{x}}D^T(t+1) \right.$$

Note that $P(t|t)$ is the variance of the motion estimation error which is modeled as variance of measurement error by the subsequent modules of the motion and structure estimation scheme [22]. Also note that $Q(\xi)$ is a strongly non-linear function. This model was first introduced by Di Bernardo et al. [5] in a slightly different formulation. The Implicit Kalman Filter was used in the past by Darmon [4] and in later works.

4.2 The Essential Estimator in the embedding space

Suppose that motion, instead of being a random walk in $\mathbf{R}^5$, is represented on the Essential Manifold as the "projection" of a random walk through $\mathbf{R}^9$ (see fig. 2 left). The "projection" onto E is defined as follows:

$$pr_{<E>} : \mathbf{R}^{3\times3} \to E$$

$$M \mapsto U\text{diag}\{1,1,0\}V^T$$

where $U, V \in \mathbf{R}^{3\times3}$ are defined by the SVD of $M \doteq U\Sigma V^T$. The fact that this operator maps onto the Essential Manifold is a standard result [15] and is proved in [20]. Note that the projection minimizes the Frobenius norm and the 2-norm of the distance of a point in $\mathbf{R}^{3\times3}$ from the Essential Manifold. Now define the operator $\oplus$ that takes two elements in $\mathbf{R}^{3\times3}$, sums them and then projects the result onto the Essential Manifold:

$$\oplus : \mathbf{R}^{3\times3} \times \mathbf{R}^{3\times3} \to E$$

$$M_1, M_2 \mapsto \mathbf{Q} = pr_{<E>}(M_1 + M_2)$$

where the symbol $+$ is the usual sum in $\mathbf{R}^{3\times3}$. With the above definitions our model for motion becomes simply

$$\mathbf{Q}(t+1) = \mathbf{Q}(t) \oplus n_{\mathbf{Q}}(t)$$

where n_Q is modeled as a white zero-mean gaussian noise in $\mathbf{R}^9$ with variance R_{n_Q}. If we couple the above equation with the lower part of $(*)$, we have again a dynamical model on an euclidean space driven by white gaussian noise. Note that the final model is precisely $(*)$ with $\oplus$ in place of $+$ and the constraint $\mathbf{Q} \in E$ released. The Essential Estimator is the least variance filter for such a model, and corresponds to a linear Kalman filter update in the embedding space, followed by a projection onto the Essential Manifold (see fig. 2 right). Note that in principle the gain could be precomputed offline, for each possible configuration of motion and feature positions.

Prediction step :
$$\begin{cases} \hat{\mathbf{q}}(t+1|t) = \hat{\mathbf{q}}(t|t) \; ; \; \hat{\mathbf{q}}(0|0) = \mathbf{q}_0 \\ P(t+1|t) = P(t|t) + R_{n_Q} \; ; \; P(0|0) = P_0 \end{cases}$$

Update step :
$$\begin{cases} \hat{q}(t+1|t+1) = \hat{q}(t+1|t) \oplus L(t+1)\chi(t)\hat{q}(t+1|t) \\ P(t+1|t+1) = \Gamma(t+1)P(t+1|t)\Gamma^T(t+1) + L(t+1)R_{\tilde{n}}(t+1)L^T(t+1) \end{cases}$$

Gain :
$$\begin{cases} L(t+1) = -P(t+1|t)\chi^T(t)\Lambda^{-1}(t+1) \\ \Lambda(t+1) = \chi(t)P(t+1|t)\chi^T(t) + R_{\tilde{n}}(t+1) \\ \Gamma(t+1) = I - L(t+1)\chi(t) \\ R_{\tilde{n}}(t+1) = D(t+1)R_{\mathbf{x}}D^T(t+1) \end{cases}$$

5 Special cases and generalizations

Singular case: what if we observe less than 8 points? − Suppose we are in the situation $N(t) < 8$ for some (possibly all) t. Then the Essential Constraint will have a preimage which is a whole subspace, and its intersection with the Essential Manifold (see fig. 1 right) will no longer be two points on E. However, suppose we move under constant (or "slowly varying") velocity; at each time instant we get a new Essential Constraint, whose preimage intersects the Essential Manifold in a new variety. The intersection of these varieties eventually comes to a single point on the Essential Manifold, when the viewer does not move on a quadric containing all the visible points [19]. It is interesting to note that extended observations of *one only point* are sufficient to determine ego-motion.

Zero-translation case − The above schemes were described under the standing assumption of non-zero translation. When translation is zero there is no parallax, and we are not able to perceive depth. The Essential Constraint is undetermined, however we can still recover rotation and hence update the previous estimate of structure correctly. In fact, due to noise in the measurements of $\mathbf{x}_i, \mathbf{x}'_i$, there will be always a small translation compatible (in least squares sense) with the observed points. This translation is automatically scaled to norm one by the algorithm. This allows us to recover the correct rotation and scales depth by the inverse norm of the true translation. If we keep track of the scale factor, as described below, we can update the current estimate of structure and recover translation within the correct scale. This procedure has proved successful, as we show in the experimental section.

Recovery of the scale factor − The Essential filters recover translation only up to a scale factor. However, once some scale information is available *at one step* it can be propagated across time allowing recovery of motion and structure within the correct scale. This has been tested in the simulations by adding the scale factor in the filter dynamics with a random walk model.

On-line camera calibration − In introducing our algorithms we have described the camera as a simple static map from $\mathbb{R}^3$ to $\mathbb{R}P^2$. The model for the camera may be made more general [6, 16], time-varying, and inserted into the state dynamics with a statistical model, as we have done for motion. As long as the resulting model preserves observability properties, this will allow us to recover camera calibration together with relative orientation. Azarbayejani et al. [1] include the camera focal length in the standard formulation (1)-(2).

Segmentation and detection of outliers − The Essential models are peculiar in that they do not represent structure explicitly in the state, which allows varying the feature set at each time [21]. However, the innovation process of the filters is a measure of how far *each point* is from the current rigid-motion interpretation. At each time instant it is possible to compare each component of the innovation with the variance of the prediction at the previous time and reject all points that do not fall within a threshold. The Essential filters have proved useful in building a scheme for 3D transparent motion-based segmentation, which is reported in [21].

6 Experimental assessment

We have tested the described algorithms on a variety of motion and structure configurations. We report the simulations performed on the same data sets of [22]. These consist of views of a cloud of points under a discontinuous motion with singular regions (zero-translation and non-zero rotation). Gaussian noise with 1 pixel std has been added to the measurements. Simulations have been performed with a variable number of points down to 1 point for constant velocity motion, and show consistent performance. Tuning has been performed within an order of magnitude. See [20] for details.

The local coordinates estimator − In fig. 3 we show the three components of translational and rotational velocity as estimated by the local coordinates estimator. Convergence is reached in less than 20 steps. Initialization is performed with one step of the traditional Longuet-Higgins algorithm [13]. The computational cost of one iteration os of about 300 Kflops for 20 points. Note that if we have some dynamical model available for motion, we can easily insert it into the state model.

The Essential Estimator in the embedding space − When the estimated state is brought to local coordinates we have estimates for rotation and translation (see fig. 4). It is noted that the homeomorphism Φ can have singularities due to noise when the last eigenspace is changed with one of the other two. This causes the spikes observed in the estimates of motion. However, note that there is no transient to recover, since *the errors do not occur in the estimation step, but in trasferring to local coordinates*. The switching can be avoided by a higher level control on the continuity of the singular values. The computational cost amounts to circa 41 Kflops per step for 20 points. We report the mean of the estimation error of the two schemes, in order to show the absence of estimation biases, and the standard deviation to compare the performance. The results are summarized in the following table:

Scheme	T_X (m, std)10^{-3}	T_Y	T_Z	Ω_X	Ω_Y	Ω_Z	Flops	Conv.
Local	(.2,.4)	(-1.5, 4.8)	(.2, .4)	(.8, 2.2)	(.2, .2)	(-.2, .8)	300K	15 steps
Embedding	(.0397, .1)	(1.7, 1.3)	(.2, .1)	(-.8, .4)	(.004, .2)	(-.0016, .4)	41K	50 steps

Experiments on real image sequences − We have tested our schemes on a sequence of 10 images of the rocket scene (see fig. 5). There are 22 feature points

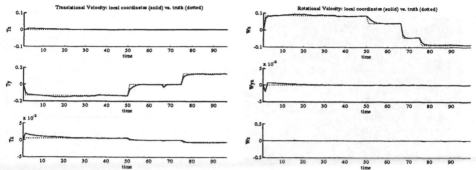

Fig. 3. *(Left) Components of translational velocity as estimated by the local coordinates estimator. The ground truth is shown in dotted lines. (Right) Rotational velocity.*

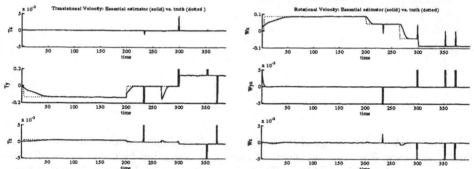

Fig. 4. *(Left) Components of translational velocity as estimated by the Essential estimator. Note the spikes due to the local coordinates transformation. Note also that they do not affect convergence since they do not occur in the estimation process, but while transferring to local coordinates. (Right) Rotational velocity.*

visible, and the standard deviation of the error on the image plane is about one pixel. The local coordinates estimator has a transient of about 20 steps to converge from any initial condition. Hence we have run it starting from zero, and used the final estimate as initial condition for a new run, the results of which are reported in figure 5. We did not perform any ad hoc tuning, and the setting was the same as that used in the simulation experiments. As it can be seen, the estimates are within 5% error, and the final estimate is less than 1% off the true motion. In this experiment we have used the true norm of translation as scaling factor. We have also run experiments in which the scale factor was calculated by updating the estimate of the distance between the two closest features, as in the simulation experiments. In this case convergence is slower, and the innovation norm reaches regime in about 20-25 steps (three runs over the sequence).

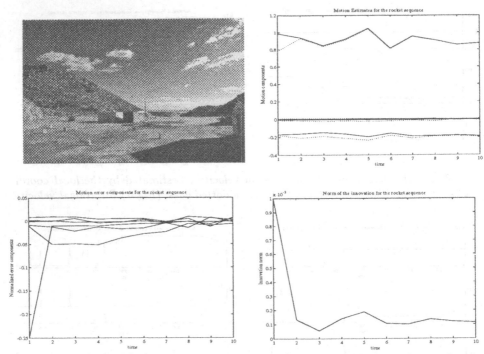

Fig. 5. *(Top-Left) One image of the rocket scene. (Top-Right) Motion estimates for the rocket sequence: The six components of motion as estimated by the local coordinates estimator are showed in solid lines. The corresponding ground truth is in dotted lines. (Bottom-Left) Error in the motion estimates for the rocket sequence. All components are within 5% of the true motion. (Bottom-Right) Norm of the pseudo-innovation process of the local estimator for the rocket scene. Convergence is reached in less than 10+5 steps.*

7 Conclusions

We have presented a novel perspective for viewing motion estimation. This has resulted in two different approaches for solving the motion problem which are cast in a common framework. Each scheme has its own personality, the filter in the embedding space being faster and more geometrically appealing, the local coordinates estimator being more flexible and robust. The schemes are based on a globally observable model and enjoy common features such as recursiveness, allowing us to exploit at each time all previous calculations, and noise rejection from exploiting redundancy. They all benefit from independence from structure estimation, which allows us to deal easily with a variable number of points and feature sets. Hence we do not need to track specific features through time, and we can deal easily with occlusion and presence of outliers.

Both schemes produce, together with an estimate of motion, the second order statistics of the estimation error.

The approaches can be interpreted as an extension of the Longuet-Higgins' algorithm [13] to infinite baseline, and the observability analysis as a generalization of N-points M-frames theorems. The schemes work for any number of points provided that enough frames are viewed. Possible extensions include on-line estimation of the camera model.

Acknowledgements

We wish to thank Prof. Giorgio Picci for his constant support and advice, Prof. J.K. Åström for discussions on implicit Kalman filtering, Prof. Richard Murray, Prof. Shankar Sastry and Andrea Mennucci for many useful suggestions. We also thank John Oliensis and J. Inigo Thomas for providing the rocket sequence.

References

1. Azarbayejani, A., Horowitz, B., and Pentland, A. Recursive estimation of structure and motion using relative orientation constraints. *Proc. CVPR* (New York, 1993).
2. Boothby, W. *Introduction to Differentiable Manifolds and Riemannian Geometry*. Academic Press, 1986.
3. Broida, T., and Chellappa, R. Estimating the kinematics and structure of a rigid object from a sequence of monocular frames. *IEEE Trans. Pattern Anal. Mach. Intell.* (1991).
4. Darmon. A recursive method to apply the hough transform to a set of moving objects. *Proc. IEEE, CH 1746 7/82* (1982).
5. Di-Bernardo, E., Toniutti, L., Frezza, R., and Picci, G. Stima del moto dell'osservatore e della struttura della scena mediante visione monoculare. *Tesi di Laurea–Università di Padova* (1993).
6. Faugeras, O. *Three dimensional vision, a geometric viewpoint*. MIT Press, 1993.
7. Gennery, D. Tracking known 3-dimensional object. In *Proc. AAAI 2nd Natl. Conf. Artif. Intell.* (Pittsburg, PA, 1982), pp. 13–17.
8. Heel, J. Direct estimation of structure and motion from multiple frames. *AI Memo 1190, MIT AI Lab* (March 1990).
9. Isidori, A. *Nonlinear Control Systems*. Springer Verlag, 1989.
10. Jazwinski, A. *Stochastic Processes and Filtering Theory*. Academic Press, 1970.
11. Kalman, R. A new approach to linear filtering and prediction problems. *Trans. of the ASME-Journal of basic engineering. 35-45* (1960).
12. Krener, A. J., and Respondek, W. Nonlinear observers with linearizable error dynamics. *SIAM J. Control Optim. vol. 23 (2)* (1985).
13. Longuet-Higgins, H. C. A computer algorithm for reconstructing a scene from two projections. *Nature 293* (1981), 133–135.
14. Matthies, L., Szelisky, R., and Kanade, T. Kalman filter-based algorithms for estimating depth from image sequences. *Int. J. of computer vision* (1989).
15. Maybank, S. *Theory of reconstruction from image motion*, vol. 28 of *Information Sciences*. Springer-Verlag, 1992.
16. Mundy, J., and Zisserman, A., Eds. *Geometric invariance in computer vision*. MIT Press, Cambridge, Mass., 1992.
17. Murray, R., Li, Z., and Sastry, S. *A Mathematical Introduction to Robotic Manipulation*. Preprint, 1993.
18. Oliensis, J., and Inigo-Thomas, J. Recursive multi-frame structure from motion incorporating motion error. *Proc. DARPA Image Understanding Workshop* (1992).
19. Soatto, S. Observability of rigid motion under perspective projection with application to visual motion estimation. *Technical Report CIT-CDS 94-001, California Institute of Technology* (1994).
20. Soatto, S., Frezza, R., and Perona, P. Recursive motion estimation on the essential manifold. *Technical Report CIT-CDS 93-021 and CIT-CNS 32/93, California Institute of Technology* (1993).
21. Soatto, S., and Perona, P. Three dimensional transparent structure segmentation and multiple 3d motion estimation from monocular perspective image sequences. *Technical Report CIT-CDS 93-022, California Institute of Technology* (1993).
22. Soatto, S., Perona, P., Frezza, R., and Picci, G. Recursive motion and structure estimation with complete error characterization. In *Proc. IEEE Comput. Soc. Conf. Comput. Vision and Pattern Recogn.* (New York, June 1993), pp. 428–433.

Motion From Point Matches Using Affine Epipolar Geometry

Larry S. Shapiro, Andrew Zisserman and Michael Brady

Robotics Research Group, Department of Engineering Science,
Oxford University, Parks Road, Oxford, OX1 3PJ.

Abstract. Algorithms to perform point–based motion estimation under orthographic and scaled orthographic projection abound in the literature. A key limitation of many existing algorithms is that they rely on the selection of a minimal point set to define a "local coordinate frame". This approach is extremely sensitive to errors and noise, and forfeits the advantages of using the full data set. Furthermore, attention is seldom paid to the statistical performance of the algorithms. We present a new framework that caters for errors and noise, and allows *all* available features to be used, without the need to select a frame explicitly. This theory is derived in the context of the *affine camera,* which generalises the orthographic, scaled orthographic and para–perspective models. We define the affine epipolar geometry for two such cameras, giving the fundamental matrix in this case and discussing its noise resistant computation. The two–view rigid motion parameters (the scale factor between views, projection of the 3D axis of rotation and cyclotorsion angle) are then determined *directly* from the epipolar geometry. Optimal estimates are obtained over time by means of a linear Kalman filter, and results are presented on real data.

1 Introduction

Orthographic and scaled orthographic projection are widely used in computer vision to model the imaging process [1, 3, 5, 7, 9, 10, 21, 22, 23]. They provide a good approximation to the perspective projection model when the field of view is small and the variation in depth of the scene along the line of sight is small compared to its average distance from the camera [20]. More importantly, they expose the ambiguities that arise when perspective effects diminish. In such cases, it is not only *advantageous* to use these simplified models but also *advisable* to do so, for by explicitly incorporating these ambiguities into the algorithm, one avoids computing parameters that are inherently ill–conditioned [7]. This paper investigates the motion estimation problem in the context of the *affine camera,* which generalises the orthographic, scaled orthographic and para–perspective models (see [18]).

Many existing point–based motion algorithms are of limited practical use because the inevitable presence of noise is often ignored [10, 12], unreasonable demands are often made on prior processing (e.g. a suitable perceptual frame must first be selected) [10], special case motions are often assumed (e.g. no rotation about a fixed axis) [8, 9], and some algorithms require batch processing rather than the more natural sequential processing [21]. The tool we employ to redress these

Lecture Notes in Computer Science, Vol. 801
Jan-Olof Eklundh (Ed.)

shortcomings is *affine epipolar geometry*. The epipolar constraint is well–known in the stereo literature, and has also been used in motion applications under perspective and projective viewing to establish motion correspondence, recover the translation direction and compute rigid motion [6, 12]. By contrast, *affine* epipolar geometry has seldom been used for motion estimation (though see [9, 10]).

Section 2 defines the epipolar geometry of the affine camera and derives its special fundamental matrix; no camera calibration is needed at this juncture. To obtain a reliable solution for these parameters, we evaluate three least squares algorithms based on image distances, and determine that a 4D linear method performs best. The utilisation of *all* available points (rather than just a minimum set) not only improves the accuracy of the solution (by providing immunity to noise and enabling detection of outliers), but also obviates the need to *select* a minimal point set. Section 3 relates the affine epipolar geometry to the rigid motion parameters, and formalises Koenderink and van Doorn's novel motion representation [10]. Using two views, we compute scale, cyclotorsion and the projected axis *directly* from the epipolar geometry, requiring only the aspect ratio. Our n–point framework subsumes the results for minimum configurations. For the multiple view case, we define a linear Kalman filter to determine optimal two–view estimates. Unlike some previous point–based structure and motion schemes (e.g. [4]), we do not assign an individual Kalman filter to each 3D feature; this liberates us from having to track individual 3D points through multiple views, so points can appear and disappear at will.

2 Affine epipolar geometry

2.1 Affine and weak perspective cameras

A camera projects a 3D world point $\mathbf{X} = (X, Y, Z)^\top$ into a 2D image point $\mathbf{x} = (x, y)^\top$. The *weak perspective* (or *scaled orthographic*) camera has the form

$$\mathbf{x} = \frac{f}{Z_{ave}^c} \begin{bmatrix} \xi \mathbf{R}_1^\top \\ \mathbf{R}_2^\top \end{bmatrix} \mathbf{X} + \begin{bmatrix} t_x \\ t_y \end{bmatrix} = \mathbf{M}_{wp} \mathbf{X} + \mathbf{t}_{wp}, \tag{1}$$

where $\mathbf{M}_{wp}$ is a 2×3 matrix whose rows are the scaled rows of a rotation matrix $\mathbf{R} = [R_{ij}]$, and $\mathbf{t}_{wp} = (t_x, t_y)^\top$ is a 2–vector (the projection of the origin of the world coordinate frame, $\mathbf{X} = 0$). This equation is derived by approximating the depth Z_i^c of each individual point i (measured along the line of sight in the camera frame) by the average distance of the object from the camera, Z_{ave}^c. The camera is "calibrated" when its intrinsic parameters are known, namely the camera aspect ratio ξ and focal length f.

The *affine camera* has the same form as Equation (1) but has no constraints on the matrix elements. It is written as

$$\mathbf{x} = \mathbf{M}\mathbf{X} + \mathbf{t}, \tag{2}$$

where $\mathbf{M}$ is a general 2×3 matrix and $\mathbf{t}$ a general 2–vector. The affine camera has eight degrees of freedom and corresponds to a projective camera with its optical centre on the plane at infinity [14]. Consequently, *all projection rays are parallel,* and lines that are parallel in the world remain parallel in the image. The affine camera covers: (i) a 3D *affine* transformation between world and camera coordinate systems; (ii) parallel projection onto the image plane; and (iii) a 2D affine transformation of the image. It therefore generalises the weak perspective model in two ways: *non-rigid* deformation of the object is permitted (due to the 3D *affine* transformation) and calibration is unnecessary (unlike in Equation (1)).

Consider an affine stereo pair. A 3D world point $\mathbf{X}_i$ is projected by an affine camera $\{\mathbf{M}, \mathbf{t}\}$ to an image point $\mathbf{x}_i = \mathbf{M}\mathbf{X}_i + \mathbf{t}$, and the scene moves according to $\mathbf{X}'_i = \mathbf{A}\mathbf{X}_i + \mathbf{D}$, where $\mathbf{X}'_i$ is the new world position, $\mathbf{A}$ a 3×3 matrix and $\mathbf{D}$ a 3-vector. This *motion transformation* encodes relative motion between the camera and the world as a 3D affine transformation (12 degrees of freedom). The new world point projects to

$$\mathbf{x}'_i = \mathbf{M}\mathbf{X}'_i + \mathbf{t} = \mathbf{M}\left(\mathbf{A}\mathbf{X}_i + \mathbf{D}\right) + \mathbf{t} = \mathbf{M}\mathbf{A}\mathbf{X}_i + (\mathbf{M}\mathbf{D} + \mathbf{t}) = \mathbf{M}'\,\mathbf{X}_i + \mathbf{t}', \quad (3)$$

which can be interpreted as a second affine camera $\{\mathbf{M}', \mathbf{t}'\}$ observing the original scene, where $\{\mathbf{M}', \mathbf{t}'\}$ accounts for changes in both the extrinsic and intrinsic camera parameters.

2.2 The affine epipolar line and fundamental matrix

The concept of an epipolar line is well known in the stereo and motion literature. For an affine camera, the epipolar lines are all parallel, since the projection rays are parallel and the affine camera preserves parallelism. Thus, the epipoles lie at infinity in the image planes. An implicit form of the epipolar line is derived by eliminating the world coordinates (X_i, Y_i, Z_i) from Equations (2) and (3), giving a single equation in the *image measurables*:

$$\boxed{a\,x'_i + b\,y'_i + c\,x_i + d\,y_i + e = 0} \quad (4)$$

This *affine epipolar constraint equation* [24] is a *linear* equation in the unknown constants $a \ldots e$, which depend only on the camera and motion parameters, not structure. Only the ratios of $a \ldots e$ can be computed, so Equation (4) has only four independent degrees of freedom. Solving this equation does not require a calibrated camera, since an affine camera model has been used throughout. This equation may also be expressed in the form of a *fundamental matrix* $\mathbf{F}_A$,

$$\mathbf{p}'^{\mathsf{T}} \mathbf{F}_A\, \mathbf{p} = \begin{bmatrix} x'_i\ y'_i\ 1 \end{bmatrix} \begin{bmatrix} 0\ 0\ a \\ 0\ 0\ b \\ c\ d\ e \end{bmatrix} \begin{bmatrix} x_i \\ y_i \\ 1 \end{bmatrix} = 0, \quad (5)$$

where $\mathbf{p}' = (x', y', 1)^{\mathsf{T}}$ and $\mathbf{p} = (x, y, 1)^{\mathsf{T}}$ are homogeneous image vectors. The matrix $\mathbf{F}_A$ has maximum rank two. The epipolar lines corresponding to $\mathbf{p}$ and $\mathbf{p}'$ are $\mathbf{u}' = \mathbf{F}_A\mathbf{p}$ and $\mathbf{u} = \mathbf{F}_A^{\mathsf{T}}\mathbf{p}'$ respectively, where $\mathbf{u} = (u_1, u_2, u_3)^{\mathsf{T}}$ represents the line $u_1 x + u_2 y + u_3 = 0$. The form of $\mathbf{F}_A$ in Equation (5) is a special case of the general 3×3 fundamental matrix $\mathbf{F}$ used in stereo and motion algorithms (e.g. [13]). Equation (4) can also be written as $\mathbf{r}_i^{\mathsf{T}}\mathbf{n} + e = 0$, where $\mathbf{r}_i = (x'_i, y'_i, x_i, y_i)^{\mathsf{T}}$ and $\mathbf{n} = (a, b, c, d)^{\mathsf{T}}$. Here, $\mathbf{n}$ is the normal to a 4D hyperplane and when $\mathbf{r}_i$ is noisy,

$|\mathbf{r}_i\mathsf{T}\mathbf{n}+e|\,/\,|\mathbf{n}|$ is the 4D perpendicular distance from $\mathbf{r}_i$ to this hyperplane. For the following, $\bar{\mathbf{r}}$ will denote the centroid of the 4-vectors $\{\mathbf{r}_i\}$ and $\mathbf{v}_i$ the centred points $\mathbf{v}_i = \mathbf{r}_i - \bar{\mathbf{r}}$. Note that $\mathbf{n}_1 = (c,d)^\mathsf{T}$ and $\mathbf{n}_2 = (a,b)^\mathsf{T}$ are the 2D normals to the epipolars in I_1 and I_2 respectively (Figure 1).

2.3 Solving the epipolar equation

Equation (4) is defined up to a scale factor, so only four point correspondences are needed to solve for the four independent unknowns (conditions for *existence* of a solution are discussed in [19]). When n correspondences are available $(n > 4)$, it is advantageous to use *all* n points, since this improves the accuracy of the solution, allows detection of (and hence provides immunity to) outliers, and obviates the need to select a minimal point set. The presence of "noise" (i.e. corner localisation/measurement error) in the overdetermined system means that the points won't lie exactly on their epipolar lines (Figure 1), and an appropriate minimisation is required. The perpendicular distance D_i' between $\mathbf{x}_i'$ and its associated epipolar line in I_2 is $D_i' = (\mathbf{r}_i^\mathsf{T}\mathbf{n}+e)/\sqrt{a^2+b^2}$; the counterpart distance in I_1 is $D_i = (\mathbf{r}_i^\mathsf{T}\mathbf{n}+e)/\sqrt{c^2+d^2}$.

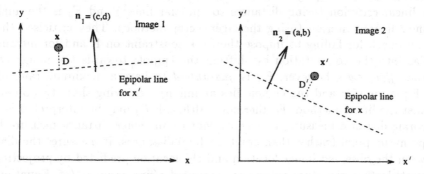

Fig. 1. *The normals to the epipolar lines are* $\mathbf{n}_1$ *and* $\mathbf{n}_2$. *Noise displaces a point* $\mathbf{x}'$ *in* I_2 *from the epipolar line associated with its counterpart* $\mathbf{x}$ *by perpendicular distance* D'. *A similar displacement by* D *occurs in* I_1.

We examine the following three minimum variance cost functions which involve the epipolar parameters, and differ in the image distances minimised:

$$E_1(\mathbf{n},e) = \left(\frac{1}{a^2+b^2}+\frac{1}{c^2+d^2}\right)\sum_{i=0}^{n-1}(ax_i'+by_i'+cx_i+dy_i+e)^2 \qquad (6)$$

$$E_2(\mathbf{n},e) = \frac{1}{a^2+b^2}\sum_{i=0}^{n-1}(ax_i'+by_i'+cx_i+dy_i+e)^2 \qquad (7)$$

$$E_3(\mathbf{n},e) = \frac{1}{a^2+b^2+c^2+d^2}\sum_{i=0}^{n-1}(ax_i'+by_i'+cx_i+dy_i+e)^2 \qquad (8)$$

All three functions minimise the sum of squares of a perpendicular distance measure, all are *scale-invariant* (i.e. if $\{\mathbf{n},e\}$ is a solution, then so is $\{k\mathbf{n},ke\}$ where k

is a non–zero scalar), and all can be minimised over e directly (giving $e = -\mathbf{n}^\top \bar{\mathbf{r}}$).

Discussion The three abovementioned functions all involve image distances; this is important since the observations are made in the image and the system noise originates there [7]. We assess these cost functions in terms of accuracy and complexity, and show that E_3 is superior to E_1 and E_2 in several respects.

Cost function E_1 sums the squared perpendicular image distances over I_1 and I_2, i.e. $E_1 = \sum_{i=0}^{n-1} D_i^2 + (D_i')^2$. The solution satisfies a system of non–linear simultaneous equations and requires non–linear minimisation. Cost function E_2 sums the squared perpendicular distances in a single image, e.g. $E_2 = \sum_i (D_i')^2$ (for I_2). The solution involves a 2D eigenvector equation. Cost function E_3 sums the squared 4D perpendicular distances between the concatenated image points and the 4D fitted hyperplane, i.e. $E_3 = \sum_i (\mathbf{r}_i \cdot \mathbf{n} + e)^2 / |\mathbf{n}|^2$. This is classic linear least squares, or *orthogonal regression.* The solution satisfies the eigenvector equation $\mathbf{W}\,\mathbf{n} = \lambda_1\,\mathbf{n}$, where $\mathbf{W} = \sum \mathbf{v}_i\,\mathbf{v}_i^\top$ and $\mathbf{n}$ is the unit eigenvector corresponding to the minimum eigenvalue λ_1.

Faugeras et al. [13] evaluated candidate cost functions for computing the fundamental matrix $\mathbf{F}$ of a *projective* camera; E_1 is the affine analogue of their favoured non–linear criterion (using distances to epipolar lines[1]) and E_3 is the analogue of their linear criterion (using the eigenvector method). They criticised the linear approach for failing to impose the rank constraint on $\mathbf{F}$ and for introducing a bias into the computation by shifting the epipole towards the image centre. In the *affine* case, however, $\mathbf{F}_A$ is *guaranteed* to have a maximum rank of two (cf. Equation (5)) and the epipole lies at infinity, removing these two objections against the linear method. Furthermore, although E_3 may be interpreted as a 4D algebraic distance measure, it is equivalent to an *image* distance measure based on point–to–point (rather than point–to–line) distances. It measures the distance between the observed image location and the location predicted by projecting the computed affine structure using the computed affine cameras (cf. Equations (2) and (3)), that is,

$$E_{TK} = \sum_{i=0}^{n-1} |\mathbf{x}_i - \mathbf{M}\mathbf{X}_i - \mathbf{t}|^2 + \sum_{i=0}^{n-1} |\mathbf{x}_i' - \mathbf{M}'\mathbf{X}_i - \mathbf{t}'|^2 \ . \tag{9}$$

Reid [16] showed Equation (9) to be the cost function minimised by Tomasi and Kanade [21]. We have shown further [19] that after differentiating E_{TK} with respect to $\mathbf{t}$, $\mathbf{t}'$ and $\mathbf{X}_i$ and resubstituting, E_3 obtains. It is sensible to minimise E_{TK} since it involves the exact number of degrees of freedom in the system, namely $\mathbf{t}$, $\mathbf{t}'$, $\mathbf{M}$, $\mathbf{M}'$ and $\mathbf{X}_i$. Thus, E_3 is optimal with respect to both the structure $\mathbf{X}_i$ and the camera parameters $\{\mathbf{M}, \mathbf{t}\}$ and $\{\mathbf{M}', \mathbf{t}'\}$.

It can be shown that E_2 is the affine version of the expression minimised by Harris [7]. This approach has several drawbacks, the most important being that by only minimising the noise in *one* image, the errors are unevenly distributed between I_1 and I_2: a set of epipolars which fits one image well, may not do likewise

---

[1] They also weighted each point by its inverse distance to the epipole; for the affine case, the epipole lies at infinity so all points are weighted equally.

in the other image, leading to discrepancies in the epipolar geometry [13]. The E_2 method is therefore unattractive.

Noise model The noise characteristics of linear least squares solutions (such as E_3) were analysed in [17]. Suppose each data point r_i is perturbed by independent, isotropic, additive, Gaussian noise δr_i. The noise has zero mean ($E\{\delta r_i\} = 0$) with variance σ^2, so $E\{\delta r_i \delta r_j^\top\} = \delta_{ij}\sigma^2 I_4$, where δ_{ij} is the Kronecker delta function and I_4 the 4×4 identity matrix. The noise in r_i induces an error δv_i in the centred data point v_i, which propagates through to the solution n. The eigenvalues of W, $\{\lambda_1, \ldots, \lambda_4\}$, are arranged in increasing order with corresponding eigenvectors $\{u_1, u_2, u_3, u_4\}$. The eigenvector corresponding to the minimum eigenvalue, u_1, gives the solution vector n. The covariance matrix for n is [17]

$$\Lambda_n = [\Lambda_{ij}] = E\{\delta n \, \delta n^\top\} = \sigma^2 \sum_{k=2}^{4}(u_k \, u_k^\top)/\lambda_k. \tag{10}$$

This matrix provides a confidence measure in the parameters of the epipolar fit. Furthermore, it facilitates the rejection of *outliers*, "rogue observations" which plague data analysis techniques such as linear least squares regression. Removing these outliers is crucial since an analysis based on the contaminated data set distorts the underlying parameters. This is another reason for using all available points, since outliers cannot be identified using minimal point sets. We employ the eigenvalue–based regression diagnostic of Shapiro and Brady [17].

Results Figure 2 shows two sequences, one with a camera moving in a static world and the other with an object moving relative to a stationary camera. Corner features were extracted and tracked over time (using the scheme in [19]), and outliers removed. Figure 2 shows the computed epipolar lines. The mean perpendicular distances between each corner and its epipolar line are 0.76 and 0.49 for the two sequences respectively; the epipolar lines are thus typically within pixel accuracy (on 256×256 images) and so provide effective constraints for correspondence.

Figure 2(e) illustrates the advantage of using *all* available points when computing epipolar geometry. A synthetic scene with 63 points (no outliers) had its 256×256 images corrupted by independent, isotropic, Gaussian noise ($\sigma = 0.6$ pixels). Subsets of the data comprising p points (where p varied from 4 to 63) were randomly selected and a fit $\{n, e\}$ computed using this subset. The E_1 distance was then calculated for the whole point set, summing the squared perpendicular image distances from each point to its computed epipolar line. For each value of p, 500 experiments were performed. The median distance and the standard deviation of the distances are shown for each value of p. Both decrease as p increases, showing that the use of more points leads not only to better fits but also to more consistent ones.

3   Rigid motion: two views

It is well–known that two distinct views of four non–coplanar, rigid points generate a one–parameter family of structure and motion solutions under parallel projection [3, 9, 10]. This section shows how to compute the partial two–view motion solution *directly* from the affine epipolar geometry.

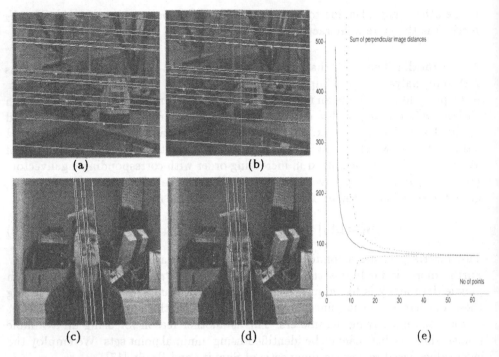

Fig. 2. Corner points with associated affine epipolar lines: (a)(b) The camera moves (every 10th line shown); (c)(d) The object moves (every 2nd line shown); (e) Improvement in the epipolar geometry as the number of points increases. The solid line shows median perpendicular distance between points and their epipolar lines and the dotted line shows the standard deviation (1σ level).

3.1 Previous work

Harris [7] used a weak perspective camera and the Euler angle representation to solve for rotation angles over two frames. The weak perspective form of E_2, whose shortcomings were outlined in Section 2.3, was minimised and shown to be *independent* of the turn angle out of the plane, illustrating the bas–relief ambiguity. No confidence estimates in the solution were provided, and only the projected axis was interpreted (not the cyclotorsion angle or scale). Koenderink and van Doorn [10] solved for the scale factor and the projections of the axes of rotation by observing a chosen local coordinate frame comprising 4 non–coplanar world points. Our scheme retains the underlying principles of their approach, but uses *all* available points and obviates the need to first define an affine basis. Lee and Huang [11] independently described the same technique as that of Koenderink and van Doorn.

Huang and Lee [9] assumed orthographic projection and proposed a linear algorithm to solve the equation $R_{23}\Delta x' - R_{13}\Delta y' + R_{32}\Delta x - R_{31}\Delta y = 0$ (a special case of the form given later in Equation (11)). Hu and Ahuja [8] criticised this approach, noting that the equation has only *two* independent unknowns, since $R_{13}^2 + R_{23}^2 = R_{31}^2 + R_{32}^2 = 1 - R_{33}^2$. Our formulation has *three* independent unknowns since we also cater for the scale factor s, making a linear solution valid.

None of the above authors [8, 9] noted that the projections of the axis of rotation could be found directly from R_{13}, R_{23}, R_{31} and R_{32}. Huang and Lee [9] deduced that two views yield a one–parameter family of motion (and structure) solutions, since R_{13}, R_{23}, R_{31} and R_{32} could only be recovered up to a scale factor.

3.2 Weak perspective epipolar geometry

Rigidity is imposed on the world motion parameters $\{\mathbf{A}, \mathbf{D}\}$ by requiring $\mathbf{A}$ to be a rotation matrix $\mathbf{R}$. This reduces the degrees of freedom in the motion parameters from 12 to 6. The use of *relative image coordinates* (or "difference vectors") cancels out translation effects, where the Δ notation denotes registration with respect to a designated reference point.

Three rotational degrees of freedom then remain. Since solving for $\mathbf{R}$ requires the measurement of angles (which are not affine invariants), it is necessary to use *weak perspective* cameras, $\mathbf{M}_{wp}$ and $\mathbf{M}'_{wp}$ (cf. Equation (1)). We introduce the scale factor $s = Z^c_{ave}/Z^{c'}_{ave}$ ($s > 1$ for a "looming" object) and define scaled depth $\Delta z_i = f \Delta Z^c_i / Z^c_{ave}$. The aspect ratios ξ and ξ' must be known in order to compute angles, and the ratio of focal lengths f/f' must be known (or unity if unknown) in order to determine scale. No other calibration parameters are needed. The rigid motion, difference–vector form of the affine epipolar constraint equation (Equation (4)) is then

$$\boxed{R_{23}\Delta x' - R_{13}\Delta y' + sR_{32}\Delta x - sR_{31}\Delta y = 0} \qquad (11)$$

This equation generalises the pure orthographic forms ($s = 1$) derived by Huang and Lee [9] and used in [8]. There are only three independent degrees of freedom in Equation (11), since only the ratios of the coefficients may be computed; we show these to be the scale factor s and two rotation angles.

There are various ways to parameterise rotation angles, the most popular being Euler angles and the angle–axis form. Koenderink and van Doorn [10] introduced a novel rotation representation (which we term *KvD* and show in [19] to be a variant of Euler angles), and presented a geometric analysis of it. We formalise their representation algebraically to illustrate its advantages. In *KvD*, a rotation matrix $\mathbf{R}$ is decomposed into two parts, $\mathbf{R} = \mathbf{R}_\rho \mathbf{R}_\theta$. First, there is a rotation $\mathbf{R}_\theta$ in the image plane through angle θ (i.e., about the line of sight). This is followed by a rotation $\mathbf{R}_\rho$ through an angle ρ about a unit axis Φ lying in a plane parallel to the image plane and angled at ϕ to the positive X axis, i.e., a pure rotation *out of* the image plane. We write $\Phi = (\cos \phi, \sin \phi)^\mathsf{T}$.

The *KvD* representation has three main advantages. First, rotation about the optic axis provides no new information about structure, and it therefore makes sense to first remove this "useless" component. Second, it explicitly captures the depth–turn (or *bas–relief*) ambiguity in a way that the more popular angle–axis form doesn't – an advantage of Euler forms in general [7]. Third, it is elegant in that two views enable us to completely solve for two rotation angles (ϕ and θ), with the third (ρ) parameterising the remaining family of solutions. This contrasts with the angle–axis form, for which only one angle is obtained from two views, the two remaining angles satisfying a non–linear constraint equation [3]. The disadvantage of *KvD* is that the physical interpretation of rotation occurring about a single 3D axis is lost.

3.3   Solving for s, ϕ and θ

We now solve for the scale factor (s), the projection of the axis of rotation (ϕ) and the cyclotorsion angle (θ) directly from the affine epipolar geometry. Substituting the KvD expressions for R_{ij} into the epipolar constraint of Equation (11) gives

$$\boxed{\sin \rho \left[\cos \phi\, \Delta x_i' + \sin \phi\, \Delta y_i' - s \cos(\phi - \theta)\, \Delta x_i - s \sin(\phi - \theta)\, \Delta y_i \right] = 0} \qquad (12)$$

It is evident from Equation (12) that s, θ and ϕ can be computed directly from the affine epipolar geometry, because the difference vector form of Equation (4) is

$$a \Delta x_i' + b \Delta y_i' + c \Delta x_i + d \Delta y_i = 0,$$

and a direct comparison with Equation (12) yields

$$\tan \phi = b/a, \quad \tan(\phi - \theta) = d/c \quad \text{and} \quad s^2 = (c^2 + d^2)/(a^2 + b^2), \qquad (13)$$

with $s > 0$ (by definition). This illustrates, for instance, that *the projection of the axis of rotation Φ is perpendicular to the epipolar lines.* (Recall from Figure 1, for instance, that $\mathbf{n}_2 = (a, b)^{\mathsf{T}}$ is the normal to the epipolar line in I_2.) Equation (12) also shows immediately that Equation (11) has only *two* independent rotation parameters, θ and ϕ, because the angle ρ cancels out (provided it is non–zero). If $\rho = 0°$, there is no rotation *out of* the image plane and Φ is obviously undefined, so this technique cannot be used. Equation (12) is therefore more informative than Equation (11) since it identifies explicitly what quantities can be computed, and under what circumstances.

Error model and Kalman filter We now compute noise models for s, ϕ and θ, each of which is a non–linear function of $\mathbf{n}$. Given the covariance matrix $\Lambda_{\mathbf{n}}$ from Equation (10), the task is to compute the means and variances of s, ϕ and θ. Let the true (i.e. noise–free) value of $\mathbf{n}$ be $\tilde{\mathbf{n}}$, with $\mathbf{n} = (n_1, n_2, n_3, n_4)^{\mathsf{T}}$. The noise perturbation of $\tilde{\mathbf{n}}$ is $\delta \mathbf{n}$, so $\mathbf{n} = \tilde{\mathbf{n}} + \delta \mathbf{n}$. The diagonal elements of $\Lambda_{\mathbf{n}}$ define the variances of δn_i while the off–diagonal elements define the covariances. The Taylor series for a function $q(\tilde{\mathbf{n}})$ expanded about $\mathbf{n}$ is

$$q(\tilde{\mathbf{n}}) = q(\mathbf{n} - \delta \mathbf{n}) = q(\mathbf{n}) - \sum_{i=1}^{4} \frac{\partial q(\mathbf{n})}{\partial \tilde{n}_i}\, \delta n_i + \frac{1}{2} \sum_{i=1}^{4} \sum_{j=1}^{4} \frac{\partial^2 q(\mathbf{n})}{\partial \tilde{n}_i\, \partial \tilde{n}_j}\, \delta n_i\, \delta n_j - \cdots$$

We ignore terms above second order, assume that $\partial^2 q/\partial n_i\, \partial n_j = \partial^2 q/\partial n_j\, \partial n_i$, and note that $E\{\delta \mathbf{n}\} = 0$ and $E\{\tilde{\mathbf{n}}\} = \tilde{\mathbf{n}}$. The estimate of q is in general biased, since $E\{q(\mathbf{n})\} = q(\tilde{\mathbf{n}}) - B$, with the bias term $B = \frac{1}{2} \sum_{i=1}^{4} \sum_{j=1}^{4} \frac{\partial^2 q(\mathbf{n})}{\partial \tilde{n}_i\, \partial \tilde{n}_j}\, \Lambda_{ij}$. Expressions for the variance and covariances of q can then be derived, and these provide confidence regions for the two–frame motion parameters.

Physical objects have inertia and it is sensible to exploit this temporal continuity to improve the motion estimates. We achieve this by means of a linear discrete–time Kalman filter [2], a popular framework for weighting observations and predictions. We estimate s, ϕ and θ, employing a constant position model ($\dot{s} = \dot{\phi} = \dot{\theta} = 0$). The state vector is $(s, \phi, \theta)^{\mathsf{T}}$ with state transition matrix $\mathbf{I}_3$. We observe s, ϕ and $\phi - \theta$, giving the observation vector $(s + B_s, \phi + B_\phi, \phi - \theta + B_{\phi-\theta})^{\mathsf{T}}$, where B_i are the relevant bias terms.

Results Figure 3 shows a subject shaking his head. The true axis is unknown, but it is approximately vertical and the results are qualitatively correct. Figure 4 shows the algorithm running on the images and corner data of Harris [7], where a car rotates on a turn–table about a known fixed axis. There is no scale change between views, and the fiducial axis is 10° off the vertical. Figure 4(a) graphs the successive two–frame estimates of the projected axis angle together with the computed errors, which serve as the filter input. Our unfiltered solution (using E_3) is identical to the Harris values (obtained using E_2); this will always be true when the scale s is unity (see Shapiro et al. [18]). The error estimates correctly bound the true parameter values (which lie within the computed 95% error bounds). The filtered output is shown in Figure 4(b) with the Kalman filter's 95% confidence intervals. The solution is clearly smoother (and more reliable) after filtering.

Fig. 3. *A shaking head, where the true axis is roughly vertical. The computed axis is drawn through the image centre in both black and white to enhance contrast.*

4 Conclusions

We have proposed a new framework, based on the affine camera and its epipolar geometry, for computing motion from point features viewed under parallel projection. This framework accounts for the major theoretical results pertaining to this problem [3, 7, 9, 11, 21, 22], including partial solutions, ambiguities and degeneracies [18]. The affine camera enables the identification of necessary camera calibration parameters, and the facility to use all available points both ensures robustness to noise and obviates the need to choose a local coordinate frame. Noise models provide confidence estimates in the computed parameters, and the processing of successive frame–pairs permits straightforward extension to long sequences in sequential mode.

Acknowledgements. We are grateful for financial support from the ORS Award, the Foundation for Research Development (RSA) and Esprit BRA VIVA. We have had fruitful discussions with Paul Beardsley, Andrew Blake, Phil McLauchlan, Ian Reid and Phil Torr (RRG) along with Richard Hartley and Joe Mundy (GE). Chris Harris kindly supplied his images and corner points.

References

1. J.Y. Aloimonos, "Perspective approximations", *Image and Vision Computing*, Vol. 8, No. 3, August 1990, pp. 179–192.

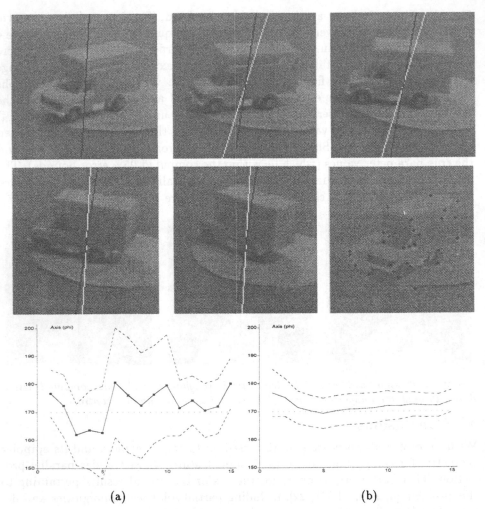

Fig. 4. The Harris truck sequence [7] (every second image). The unfiltered (white) and filtered (black) axes are superimposed. The final image shows a typical set of corner points. The graphs plot the solutions over the whole sequence: solid lines show computed values, dotted lines show "true" values, and dashed lines show 95% confidence intervals: (a) Our two–frame solution (circles) coincides with that of Harris (crosses); (b) The improved filtered values (dashed lines show 95% confidence levels).

2. Y. Bar–Shalom and T.E. Fortmann, *Tracking and data association*, Academic Press Inc., USA, 1988.
3. B.M. Bennett, D.D. Hoffman, J.E. Nicola and C. Prakash, "Structure from two orthographic views of rigid motion", *Journal of Optical Society of America*, Vol. 6, No. 7, July 1989, pp. 1052–1069.
4. D. Charnley, C. Harris, M. Pike, E. Sparks and M. Stephens, "The DROID 3D vision system: algorithms for geometric integration", Plessey Research, Roke Manor, Technical Note 72/88/N488U, Dec. 1988.
5. R. Cipolla, Y. Okamoto and Y. Kuno, "Robust structure from motion using motion parallax", *International Conference on Computer Vision (ICCV'4)*, Berlin, May 1993, pp. 374–382.

6. O.D. Faugeras, "What can be seen in three dimensions with an uncalibrated stereo rig?" in G. Sandini (ed.), *Proceedings European Conference on Computer Vision* (ECCV–92), 1992, pp. 563–578.

7. C. Harris, "Structure–from–motion under orthographic projection", *First European Conference on Computer Vision* (ECCV–90), 1990, pp. 118–123.

8. X. Hu and N. Ahuja, "Motion estimation under orthographic projection", *IEEE Transactions on Robotics and Automation*, Vol. 7, No. 6, pp. 848–853, 1991.

9. T.S. Huang and C.H. Lee, "Motion and structure from orthographic projections", *IEEE Trans. Pattern Anal. Machine Intell.*, Vol. PAMI–11, No. 5, pp. 536–40, 1989.

10. J.J. Koenderink and A.J. van Doorn, "Affine structure from motion", *Journal of Optical Society of America*, Vol. 8, No. 2, Feb 1991, pp. 377-385.

11. C. Lee and T. Huang, "Finding point correspondences and determining motion of a rigid object from two weak perspective views", *Computer Vision, Graphics and Image Processing*, Vol. 52, 1990, pp. 309–327.

12. H.C. Longuet–Higgins, "A computer algorithm for reconstructing a scene from two projections", *Nature*, Vol. 293, 1981, pp. 133–135.

13. Q–T. Luong, R. Deriche, O. Faugeras and T. Papadopoulo, "On determining the fundamental matrix: analysis of different methods and experimental results", Tech. Report 1894, INRIA (Sophia Antipolis), April 1993.

14. J.L. Mundy and A. Zisserman (eds), *Geometric Invariance in Computer Vision*, MIT Press, USA, 1992.

15. L. Quan and R. Mohr, "Towards structure from motion for linear features through reference points", *IEEE Workshop on Visual Motion*, New Jersey, 1991.

16. I.D. Reid, "The SVD minimizes image distance", Oxford University Robotics Research Group Internal Memo, Sept. 1993.

17. L.S. Shapiro and J.M. Brady, "Rejecting outliers and estimating errors in an orthogonal regression framework", to appear in *Philosophical Transactions of the Royal Society*, 1994.

18. L.S. Shapiro, *Affine Analysis of Image Sequences*, PhD thesis, Dept. Engineering Science, Oxford University, 1993.

19. L.S. Shapiro, A. Zisserman and M. Brady, "Motion from point matches using affine epipolar geometry", to appear in *International Journal of Computer Vision*.

20. D.W. Thompson and J.L. Mundy, "Three dimensional model matching from an unconstrained viewpoint" in *IEEE Conference on Robotics and Automation*, Raleigh, NC, 1987, pp. 208–220.

21. C. Tomasi and T. Kanade, "Shape and motion from image streams under orthography: a factorization method", *International Journal of Computer Vision*, Vol. 9, No. 2, Nov 1992, pp. 137–154.

22. S. Ullman, *The Interpretation of Visual Motion*, MIT Press, USA, 1979.

23. G. Xu, E. Nishimura and S. Tsuji, "Image correspondence and segmentation by epipolar lines: Theory, Algorithm and Applications", Technical Report, Dept. Systems Engineering, Osaka University, July 1993.

24. A. Zisserman, *Notes on geometric invariance in vision: BMVC'92 tutorial*, Leeds, Sept 1992.

Navigation using Affine Structure from Motion

P.A. Beardsley, A. Zisserman and D.W. Murray

Robotics Group, Dept of Eng Science, University of Oxford, Oxford OX1 3PJ, UK.
tel: +44-865 273154 fax: +44-865 273908 email: [pab,az,dwm]@robots.ox.ac.uk

Abstract. A structure from motion algorithm is described which recovers structure and camera position, modulo a projective ambiguity. Camera calibration is not required, and camera parameters such as focal length can be altered freely during motion. Unlike recent schemes which compute projective or affine structure using a batch process, the structure is updated sequentially over an image sequence. A specialisation of the algorithm to recover structure modulo an affine transformation is described. We demonstrate how the affine coordinate frame can be periodically updated to prevent drift over time.

Structure is recovered from image corners detected and matched automatically and reliably in image sequences. Results are shown for reference objects and indoor environments. Finally, the affine structure is used to construct free space maps enabling navigation through unstructured environments and avoidance of obstacles. The path planning involves only affine constructions. Examples are provided for real image sequences.

1 Introduction

The recovery of structure from motion (SFM) is a sufficiently mature field for several working systems to have been applied to the navigation of mobile vehicles [3, 4, 14]. Such systems recover 3D Euclidean structure and require a calibrated camera. More recently, researchers have investigated SFM when the camera is uncalibrated [9, 13] recovering structure modulo a projective ambiguity. These methods work in *batch* mode, determining structure and camera projection matrices from a complete sequence of images. In contrast, we devise and apply an algorithm which recovers projective structure by *sequential update*. The structure is obtained using matched corners in images from a camera moving in a static scene, and the work could fairly be described as a projective counterpart to the Euclidean system 'DROID' of Harris *et al* [3, 4]. Unlike DROID, camera calibration is not required. However, when partial or approximate calibration is available it is exploited to render "Quasi-Euclidean" structure i.e. structure within a small "projective skew" of the actual Euclidean structure.

The projective SFM scheme is specialised to produce affine structure by use of a result of Moons *et al* [10]. Extra invariants are available when the recovered structure is affine including ratios of lengths on parallel segments, ratios of areas on parallel planes, ratios of volumes, and centroids. The affine structure is applied to the task of path planning in an unstructured environment. A basic mechanism in classical path planning is to find a mid-point locus between obstacles. This is an affine, not Euclidean, construct - thus many of the techniques from path planning can be utilized when only affine rather than Euclidean structure is available. To demonstrate this, we navigate a camera held by a robot arm to a specified target, where the direct path to the target is occluded by unmodelled objects. The target is reached by incrementally determining free space regions from the affine structure as the robot moves, and path planning through these regions.

2 Camera models and projective representations

We introduce the camera models and notation used in the rest of the paper. These results are based mainly on [2, 7, 11]. Perspective projection from 3D projective space $\mathcal{P}^3$ to the image plane $\mathcal{P}^2$ is modelled by a 3×4 matrix P

$$\mathbf{x} = P\mathbf{X} \tag{1}$$

where $\mathbf{x} = (x, y, 1)^\top$ and $\mathbf{X} = (X, Y, Z, 1)^\top$ are homogeneous vectors. With homogeneous quantities, = indicates equality up to a non-zero scale factor. P can be partitioned as

$$P = (M| - Mt) \tag{2}$$

where $\mathbf{t}$ is the centre of projection, since the centre projects as $P(\mathbf{t}^\top, 1)^\top = 0$. This partitioning is valid provided the left 3×3 matrix M is not singular (i.e. the optical centre is not on the plane at infinity). In a Euclidean frame, P can be further decomposed as

$$P = K(R| - Rt) \tag{3}$$

where R and $\mathbf{t}$ are the rotation and translation of the camera in the Euclidean frame. K is a 3×3 matrix encoding the camera intrinsic parameters

$$K = \begin{pmatrix} \alpha_x & 0 & x_0 \\ 0 & \alpha_y & y_0 \\ 0 & 0 & 1 \end{pmatrix} \tag{4}$$

where α_x and α_y are the focal length measured in pixels along the x and y directions respectively, and (x_0, y_0) is the principal point.

For two cameras with $\mathbf{x}_1 = P_1\mathbf{X}$ and $\mathbf{x}_2 = P_2\mathbf{X}$, corresponding points in the two images satisfy the epipolar constraint

$$\mathbf{x}_2^\top F\mathbf{x}_1 = 0 \tag{5}$$

where F is the 3×3 *fundamental matrix*, with maximum rank 2. The epipolar line in image 2 corresponding to $\mathbf{x}_1$ is $\mathbf{l}_2 = F\mathbf{x}_1$, and similarly in image 1 corresponding to $\mathbf{x}_2$ is $\mathbf{l}_1 = F^\top\mathbf{x}_2$, where $\mathbf{l}_i$ are homogeneous vectors. Partitioning P_1 and P_2 as in equation (2) facilitates a number of equivalent representations of F

$$F = M_2^{-\top}[\mathbf{t}_1 - \mathbf{t}_2]_\times M_1^{-1} = [M_2(\mathbf{t}_1 - \mathbf{t}_2)]_\times M_2 M_1^{-1} = M_2^{-\top} M_1^\top [M_1(\mathbf{t}_1 - \mathbf{t}_2)]_\times \tag{6}$$

where the notation $[\mathbf{v}]_\times$ is the vector product represented as a matrix

$$[\mathbf{v}]_\times = \begin{pmatrix} 0 & -v_z & v_y \\ v_z & 0 & -v_x \\ -v_y & v_x & 0 \end{pmatrix}$$

Under a 3D projective transformation, $\mathbf{X}' = \mathbf{HX}$, where $\mathbf{H}$ is a non-singular 4×4 matrix, a camera matrix $\mathbf{P}$ is transformed to $\mathbf{P}' = \mathbf{PH}^{-1}$ since

$$\mathbf{x}_i = \mathbf{P}'\mathbf{X}' = \mathbf{PH}^{-1}\mathbf{HX} = \mathbf{PX} \tag{7}$$

In the following, a canonical camera matrix $\mathbf{P}_1 = (\mathbf{I}|\mathbf{0})$ will be used, where $\mathbf{I}$ is the 3×3 identity. This can always be achieved by setting $\mathbf{H}^{-1}$ in equation (7) to be

$$\mathbf{H}^{-1} = \begin{pmatrix} \mathbf{M}_1^{-1} & \mathbf{t}_1 \\ \mathbf{0}^{\top} & 1 \end{pmatrix}$$

3 Projective Structure From Motion

Corner correspondences between images are used to recover the position of 3D points and the optical centre up to a projectivity of $\mathcal{P}^3$ i.e. if $\mathbf{X}_E = (X, Y, Z, 1)^{\top}$ is a homogeneous vector representing the Euclidean position (X, Y, Z) of a point then the recovered position is $\mathbf{X} = \mathbf{HX}_E$ where $\mathbf{H}$ is a non-singular 4×4 matrix which is unknown but the same for all points.

3.1 Frame initialisation

Previous methods for projective reconstruction from two or more images [2, 9] have selected a five point basis from the 3D points. The problem with this procedure is that if one of the points is poorly localised in an image, the accuracy of the entire reconstruction degrades. Instead, we follow more closely the approach of Hartley [6] and utilise *all* point matches to determine the projective frame, by specifying the perspective projection matrices $\mathbf{P}_1$ and $\mathbf{P}_2$ for two images.

$\mathbf{P}_1$ is chosen to have the canonical form $\mathbf{P}_1 = (\mathbf{I}|\mathbf{0})$ (Section 2). The fundamental matrix $\mathbf{F}$ is obtained from corner matches (Section 3.3) and decomposed as the matrix product $\mathbf{F} = -[\mathbf{M}_2\mathbf{t}_2]_{\times}\mathbf{M}_2 = [\mathbf{s}]_{\times}\mathbf{M}_2$ (equation (6)). It can be shown that the most general form of $\mathbf{P}_2$ which is consistent with $\mathbf{P}_1$ and $\mathbf{F}$ is $\mathbf{P}_2 = [\mathbf{M}_2+\mathbf{a}^{\top}\mathbf{s}|b\mathbf{s}]$ where $\mathbf{a}$ is a 3-vector and b a scalar i.e. there are 4 DOF in $\mathbf{P}_2$ (plus the usual homogeneous scale factor). In the absence of any other information, values for $\mathbf{a}$ and b are arbitrary. However, if partial or approximate intrinsic parameters or ego-motion are available then this information is utilised, firstly by using natural camera measurements i.e. an image corner at pixel position (u, v) is assigned homogeneous coordinates $\mathbf{x} = ((u - x_0)/\alpha_x, (v - y_0)/\alpha_y, 1)^{\top}$ where $\alpha_x, \alpha_y, (x_0, y_0)$ are defined in equation (4), and secondly by choosing $\mathbf{P}_2$ (setting the 4 DOF) so that $\mathbf{P}_2 = (\mathbf{R}| - \mathbf{Rt})$ where $\mathbf{R}$ and $\mathbf{t}$ are the approximate rotation and translation of the camera. This produces a "Quasi-Euclidean" frame i.e. a frame which is exactly Euclidean if the intrinsic parameters and ego-motion are exact, but subject to a projective skew otherwise.

3.2 3D point initialisation and update

The 3D coordinates of scene points and optical centres are computed in the projective coordinate frame as in [2]. The camera centre $\mathbf{C}_i = (\mathbf{t}_i^{\top}, 1)^{\top}$ associated with $\mathbf{P}_i = (\mathbf{M}_i| - \mathbf{M}_i\mathbf{t}_i)$ is determined from $\mathbf{P}_i\mathbf{C}_i = 0$. The 3D coordinates of a point $\mathbf{X}$ which projects to $\mathbf{x}_1$ in image 1 by $\mathbf{P}_1$ and $\mathbf{x}_2$ in image 2 by $\mathbf{P}_2$ are found, as in conventional stereo, by intersecting backprojected rays. The ray for a point $\mathbf{x}_i$ in image i is given by $\alpha \mathbf{C}_i + \beta \mathbf{X}_i^\infty$, where $\mathbf{X}_i^\infty = \mathbf{M}_i^{-1}\mathbf{x}_i$ is the ray's intersection with the plane at infinity. In practice the reconstructed rays from the two cameras will be skew so $\mathbf{X}$ is determined as the midpoint of the perpendicular between the rays. Such an approach would not be justified in an arbitrary projective frame because "mid-point" and "perpendicularity" are not projective invariants. However, the estimate is good in a Quasi-Euclidean frame.

Update of 3D point coordinates involves two stages - *(1)* use of matches between corners in I_n (image n) which have associated 3D coordinates and corners in I_{n+1} to compute the perspective projection matrix for I_{n+1}, *(2)* update of 3D point coordinates with an Iterated Extended Kalman Filter (IEKF). A separate IEKF is run on each 3D point - the state vector is the point's non-homogeneous 3D coordinates, the observation vector is the point's non-homogeneous image coordinates, and the observation equation is the standard projection equation (1) expressed in non-homogeneous form. In the usual way, a covariance matrix is produced and updated in association with each state vector.

3.3 Implementation

Image corners are extracted to sub-pixel accuracy using [5]. Correspondence matching is carried out automatically, without any information about camera motion, as a three stage process:

Unguided matching: the aim is to obtain a small number of reliable seed matches, then to compute $\mathbf{F}$ and $\mathbf{P}$ which are used to guide further matching. Given a corner at position (x, y) in the first image, the search for a match is centred on (x, y) in the second image, and the strength of candidate matches is measured by cross-correlation. The threshold for match acceptance is deliberately conservative to minimise incorrect matches.

Use of epipolar geometry: the seed matches are used to compute $\mathbf{F}$ by an iterative linear process - at each iteration, matches are weighted according to their agreement with the current estimate of $\mathbf{F}$; at the final iteration, outlying matches are removed altogether and marked as unmatched (see also [8]). The estimated $\mathbf{F}$ is used to generate epipolar lines, and the search for a correspondence for an unmatched corner can be restricted to a band about its epipolar line.

Use of projected structure: corners in I_n (image n) which have associated 3D coordinates and which are matched to corners in I_{n+1} provide a correspondence between 3D points and the image corners in I_{n+1}. Hence, it is possible to compute the perspective projection matrix for I_{n+1}, and we employ an iterative process similar to the one used for $\mathbf{F}$. Once $\mathbf{P}$ has been found, it is used to project unmatched 3D points onto I_{n+1}, and the search area for a corner's match is confined to a circle around the projected point.

The final set of matches is used to recompute $\mathbf{F}$ and $\mathbf{P}$, firstly using the linear methods above, and then employing a non-linear method which minimises an error based on image plane distance, rather than algebraic distance as in the linear case. In addition, $\mathbf{rank(F)} = 2$ is enforced in the non-linear case, which cannot be done in the linear computation [2].

System parameters such as search radii and match strength thresholds which are used in the above processing are supplied as *a priori* values at the start of the sequence and are then updated at the end of the frame according to the current matching statistics. Typically the number of corners in a 512×512 image of an indoor scene is about 300, the number of seed matches is about 100, and the final number of matches is about 200-250.

3.4 Results

The experimental setup is a camera mounted on a robot arm, moving in a horizontal plane and rotating around a vertical axis. Figure 1 shows a reference object made of two perpendicular Tsai calibration grids. Recovered structure is assessed by *(1)* measuring projective invariants, and *(2)* transforming to a Euclidean coordinate frame to measure Euclidean invariants.

Fig. 1. *First and last images from a sequence of the reference object.*

Four equally spaced collinear points have a cross-ratio of 4/3. Thirty-two such cross-ratios are computed for the reference object at each frame, and the results plotted in Figure 2. The recovered structure shows monotonic improvement.

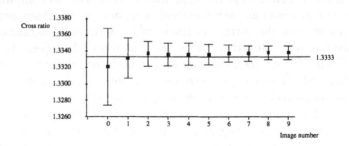

Fig. 2. *Mean value and one sigma standard deviation for cross ratios (actual value 4/3) computed from the recovered projective structure, against frame number.*

Transformation of the structure into a Euclidean frame requires the coordinates of five or more points in the projective and Euclidean frames [12], where direct physical measurement on the reference object is carried out to obtain the Euclidean positions. See Figures 3 and 4.

Measurements on the structure are given in Table 1. The collinearity measure $L = \sqrt{\sigma_y^2 + \sigma_z^2}/\sigma_x$ and the coplanarity measure $P = \sigma_z/\sqrt{\sigma_x^2 + \sigma_y^2}$ for a selected

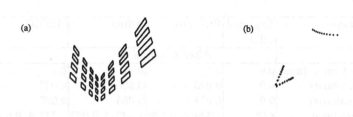

(a)   (b)

Fig. 3. (a) *Structure of the reference object in an arbitrary projective frame - copla-narity and collinearity are preserved as expected, but the structure is projectively skewed along one plane, and the angle between the two planes is less than 90° (connectivity has been added to the point structure for illustration).* (b) *Plan view of the computed struc-ture viewed edge-on along the planes of the reference object (lower left) and showing the computed camera positions (upper right) in the arbitrary projective frame. Compare with the plan view after transformation to the Euclidean frame in Figure 4.*

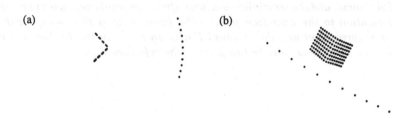

(a)   (b)

Fig. 4. (a) *Plan view of the reference object structure and camera motion transformed to a Euclidean frame - at left is the reference object with its planes edge-on, and at right the arc of dots shows successive camera positions in a circle.* (b) *View from behind the arc of camera positions.*

set of 3D points are obtained by using Singular Value Decomposition to obtain the principal axes of the set's spatial distribution together with the variance σ_{xyz} of point positions along each axis. A straight line has $L = 0$ and a perfect plane has $P = 0$. The table also includes a comparison with a local implementation of the DROID system [3, 4] which computes Euclidean structure directly. The results indicate that there is no significant difference between the quality of the projective and Euclidean systems, even though no camera calibration is employed in the projective case.

Section 3.1 introduced the Quasi-Euclidean frame which is obtained using approximate knowledge of the camera intrinsic parameters and ego-motion. Ex-periments in [1] investigate the effect of varying the estimates of the intrinsic parameters, and show that numerical instabilities causing degradation in the computed structure only arise with *extreme* projective frames which are far from Euclidean. Figure 5 shows results in a Quasi-Euclidean frame for an indoor scene.

Measure	Expected value	Projective	Affine	DROID
		After 2 frames		
Point error (mm)	0.0	0.5	0.7	0.7
Collinearity	0.0	0.003	0.005	0.006
Coplanarity	0.0	0.004	0.006	0.007
Cross-ratio	4/3	1.332 ± 0.006	1.333 ± 0.003	1.332 ± 0.005
Distance ratio	1.0	0.999 ± 0.012	1.002 ± 0.009	1.000 ± 0.013
		After 20 frames		
Point error (mm)	0.0	0.4	0.4	0.5
Collinearity	0.0	0.002	0.002	0.004
Coplanarity	0.0	0.002	0.003	0.004
Cross-ratio	4/3	1.333 ± 0.002	1.333 ± 0.001	1.333 ± 0.002
Distance ratio	1.0	1.000 ± 0.004	1.000 ± 0.006	0.999 ± 0.007

Table 1. *For the projective structure, the cross-ratio measurement was made before transformation to the Euclidean frame, and the remaining measures after. For the affine structure, the cross-ratio and ratio measurements were made before transformation to the Euclidean frame, and the remaining measures after. 128 points were used to compute the transformation to the Euclidean frame. The point error is the average distance between a measured point and the veridical Euclidean point, in the Euclidean frame. Coplanarity is a mean value for the two faces of the reference object.*

4   Affine Structure From Motion

The objective of the affine SFM processing is to recover the 3D position of scene points and the optical centre up to an *affine* transformation of three-space, i.e. if $X_E = (X, Y, Z, 1)^\top$ is a homogeneous vector representing the Euclidean position (X, Y, Z) of a point, then the recovered position is $X = H_A X_E$ where H_A is an affine transformation which is unknown but the same for all points,

$$H_A = \begin{bmatrix} A & T \\ 0^\top & 1 \end{bmatrix} \tag{8}$$

with A a non-singular 3×3 matrix and T a general 3-vector.

Moons *et al* [10] have shown that affine structure can be obtained from a perspective camera undergoing pure translational motion with fixed internal parameters. We capitalise on this observation, using a single pure translation to determine the plane at infinity π_∞ in the current projective coordinate frame. Subsequently, we make occasional pure translational motions to update the plane at infinity in case of drift over time. Measurement of π_∞ follows from the lemma [1]:

> Given two camera matrices $P_1 = (I|0)$ and $P_2 = (M|t^*)$ for identical cameras related by a pure translation, then $M = kI + t^* v^\top$ where $\pi_\infty = (v^\top, 1)$ is the equation of the plane at infinity.

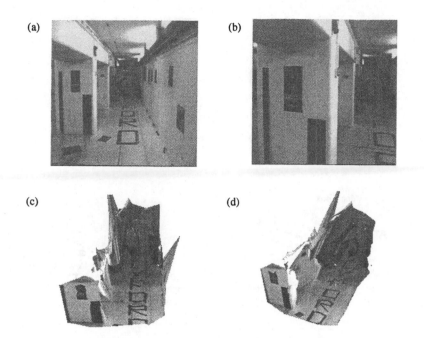

Fig. 5. (a),(b) *Example images taken during translation and rotation of an AGV (Autonomous Guided Vehicle) in a laboratory.* (c),(d) *Images constructed by mapping image intensity onto the computed 3D structure, and viewing from different positions. The mapping process is based on a Delaunay triangulation of the 2D image corners. The structure is in a quasi-Euclidean frame.*

We determine when $D = \lambda I - M$ drops rank to 1 as a function of λ; then $D = t^* v^\top$, and t^* is known, so it is possible to solve for v.

As well as updating the plane at infinity, the case of pure translation is exploited in determining the fundamental matrix. If the camera is undergoing pure translation and the intrinsic parameters are fixed, then equation (6) has the special form $F = M^{-\top}[t_1 - t_2]_\times M^{-1}$. Thus F is skew and has only two DOF. This reduces processing in the computation of F and leads to a more accurate result than the general case.

4.1 Results

Table 1 includes quantitative results for computed affine structure. Figure 6 shows results for an indoor sequence.

5 Navigation in Affine Space

The affine SFM scheme is utilised for navigation by incrementally computing free space regions, and planning paths through these regions in order to reach a specified target. For both the robot arm used in our experiments and an AGV, it is sufficient to project recovered affine structure onto the ground plane, and to compute free space and plan motions in 2D on this plane.

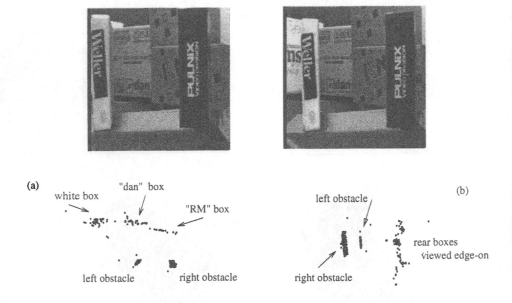

Fig. 6. *Two images from a sequence with structure recovered in a Quasi-Euclidean affine frame. (a) Plan view of recovered structure. (b) View from the right and to the rear of the obstacles. See the schematic plan view in Figure 8.*

At the most basic level the robot could be controlled by *servoing* alone i.e. with no calibration the robot could be driven to rotate until a distinguished affine feature such as a centroid is at the middle of the image. Instead we transform between the affine coordinate system and the robot Euclidean frame. Determining the transformation requires the coordinates of the camera centre in the affine frame and the robot Euclidean frame at a minimum of four non-coplanar positions. Once in the robot frame, projection to the ground plane is straightforward.

A limitation of the 3D structure consisting solely of points is that there is no representation of continuous surfaces and thus no notion of the free space between objects. We use a simple occlusion test to detect free space as illustrated in Figure 7. If a 3D point is visible continuously over a number of frames, then there is no occluding surface in the region defined by the 3D point and the moving optical centre. This free space region is projected onto the ground plane defining a free space triangle. If the triangle contains any other points from the projected structure, it is rejected. The free space map is the union of all accepted triangles.

Processing begins with a check on the free space map to determine whether there is an unobstructed route to the target. If an obstruction is present, a choice of alternative direction is made by selecting the free space "lobe" of largest area, and moving along its mid-line. As long as no obstruction is present, the camera

Fig. 7. *3D points projected onto the ground plane. The camera moves from C_1 to C_2. (a) Point P is visible continuously and C_1PC_2 does not contain any other projected points, so it is marked as free space. (b) Triangle C_1PC_2 is unacceptable as free space because of the presence of Q; however C_1QC_2 is accepted.*

moves in a straight line and two checks are carried out - firstly on time-to-contact measurements to detect potential collision in the forward direction; secondly on the line of sight to the target to detect whether the obstacle has been passed and an adjustment in the direction to the target can take place - the robot then proceeds to the target.

5.1 Results

Figure 8 is a schematic plan view of the experimental setup. Figure 9 shows plan views of the computed free space, and the projection of the structure onto the ground plane. The robot is unable to proceed directly to the target position because it would strike the left obstacle, so it moves first to the gap and then alters trajectory toward the target. Typical images from the sequence are shown in Figure 6.

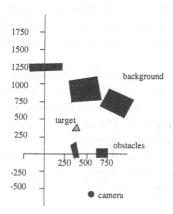

Fig. 8. *Plan view of the experimental layout (c.f. Figures 6 and 9). Axes in mm.*

6 Discussion of Implementation

Wide-angle lens: use of a wide angle lens leads to better camera localisation because rays to scene points have good divergence; it also makes it easier to fix

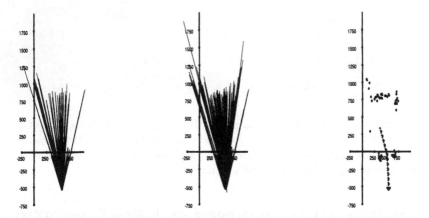

Fig. 9. *Plan view of free space (marked black) maps taken early and late in a sequence, with a consequent filling out of space in the later map. The right-hand figure shows the projection of 3D scene structure and camera motion (vertical line) onto the ground plane (c.f. the schematic plan view in Figure 8). Axes are labelled in mm.*

each new camera position in the ongoing coordinate frame because many points remain in view between images.

Forward motion: simple forward motion produces poor structure because rays from the camera to a scene point change angle slowly (*c.f.* the effect of a lateral motion) resulting in large error in the computed point position. To avoid this situation forward motion paths are "dithered" with lateral movements. Stereo would be of obvious benefit.

Computation of F : accuracy of epipolar computation (average distance of a corner from its epipolar line) is typically 0.4 pixels when using corner detection on indoor scenes, and 0.02 pixels when image points are located by line intersection on the reference object.

Sensitivity to outliers: empirically, the computation of F is less sensitive to the presence of mismatches than the computation of P, so F is always computed first and used to eliminate mismatches (Section 3.3).

Homogeneous coordinates: The arbitrary homogeneous component in a homogeneous vector is typically chosen as unity, e.g. an image corner (x, y) is represented as $(x, y, 1)$. Increased stability is achieved if the third component is chosen to be of the same order of magnitude as x and y (as in Section 3.1). The same considerations apply in $\mathcal{P}^3$.

7 Conclusion

The recovery of projective and affine structure is increasingly well-understood, but its use raises interesting problems about what can be achieved when Euclidean measurements are not available. We have demonstrated the recovery of projective and affine structure with an accuracy similar to a system using calibrated cameras, and applied the affine structure in path planning. The use of the translational motion constraint [10] to attain affine structure is part of a spectrum of possibilities for investigation, ranging from fully calibrated stereo heads through to cameras of unknown intrinsic parameters and motion. We have concentrated on the uncalibrated end of the spectrum but have introduced a mechanism, the Quasi-Euclidean frame, for incorporating poor or partial camera calibration in the structure computation.

This work was supported by SERC Grant No GR/H77668 and Esprit BRA VIVA. Thanks for helpful discussions with Richard Hartley, Jitendra Malik, John Mayhew, Joe Mundy, and to colleagues in the Robotics Research Group, particularly Andrew Blake, Mike Brady, Phil McLauchlan, Ian Reid, Larry Shapiro, and Phil Torr.

References

1. P.A. Beardsley, A.P. Zisserman, and D.W. Murray. Sequential update of projective and affine structure from motion. Technical report OUEL 2012/94, Dept of Eng Science, University of Oxford, 1994.
2. O.D. Faugeras. What can be seen in three dimensions with an uncalibrated stereo rig? In *Proc. 2nd European Conference on Computer Vision*, pages 563–578. Springer-Verlag, 1992.
3. C.G. Harris. Determination of ego-motion from matched points. In *Third Alvey Vision Conference*, pages 189–192, 1987.
4. C.G. Harris and J.M. Pike. 3D positional integration from image sequences. In *Third Alvey Vision Conference*, pages 233–236, 1987.
5. C.G. Harris and M. Stephens. A combined corner and edge detector. In *Fourth Alvey Vision Conference*, pages 147–151, 1988.
6. R. Hartley, R. Gupta, and T. Chang. Stereo from uncalibrated cameras. *Proc. Conference Computer Vision and Pattern Recognition*, 1992.
7. R.I. Hartley. Estimation of relative camera positions for uncalibrated cameras. In *Proc. 2nd European Conference on Computer Vision*, pages 579–587. Springer-Verlag, 1992.
8. Q.T. Luong, R. Deriche, O. Faugeras, and T. Papadopoulo. On determining the fundamental matrix. Technical report 1894, INRIA, Sophia-Antipolis, France, 1993.
9. R. Mohr, F. Veillon, and L. Quan. Relative 3D reconstruction using multiple uncalibrated images. *Proc. Conference Computer Vision and Pattern Recognition*, pages 543–548, 1993.
10. T. Moons, L. Van Gool, M. Van Diest, and A. Oosterlinck. Affine structure from perspective image pairs under relative translations between object and camera. Technical report KUL/ESAT/M12/9306, Departement Elektrotechniek, Katholieke Universiteit Leuven, 1993.
11. J.L. Mundy and A.P. Zisserman. *Geometric invariance in computer vision*. MIT Press, 1992.
12. J.G. Semple and G.T. Kneebone. *Algebraic projective geometry*. Oxford University Press, 1952.
13. R. Szeliski and S.B. Kang. Recovering 3D shape and motion from image streams using non-linear least squares. DEC technical report 93/3, DEC, 1993.
14. Z. Zhang and O. Faugeras. *3D Dynamic Scene Analysis*. Springer-Verlag, 1992.

A Paraperspective Factorization Method
for Shape and Motion Recovery

Conrad J. Poelman and Takeo Kanade

School of Computer Science, Carnegie Mellon University
5000 Forbes Avenue, Pittsburgh, PA 15213-3890
(Conrad.Poelman@cs.cmu.edu, tk@cs.cmu.edu)

Abstract. The factorization method, first developed by Tomasi and Kanade, recovers both the shape of an object and its motion from a sequence of images, using many images and tracking many feature points to obtain highly redundant feature position information. The method robustly processes the feature trajectory information using singular value decomposition (SVD), taking advantage of the linear algebraic properties of orthographic projection. However, an orthographic formulation limits the range of motions the method can accommodate. Paraperspective projection, first introduced by Ohta, is a projection model that closely approximates perspective projection by modelling several effects not modelled under orthographic projection, while retaining linear algebraic properties. We have developed a paraperspective factorization method that can be applied to a much wider range of motion scenarios, such as image sequences containing significant translational motion toward the camera or across the image. We present the results of several experiments which illustrate the method's performance in a wide range of situations, including an aerial image sequence of terrain taken from a low-altitude airplane.

1 Introduction

Recovering the geometry of a scene and the motion of the camera from a stream of images is an important task in a variety of applications, including navigation, robotic manipulation, and aerial cartography. While this is possible in principle, traditional methods have failed to produce reliable results in many situations [2].

Tomasi and Kanade [9][10] developed a robust and efficient method for accurately recovering the shape and motion of an object from a sequence of images, called the *factorization method*. It achieves its accuracy and robustness by applying a well-understood numerical computation, the singular value decomposition (SVD), to a large number of images and feature points, and by directly computing shape without computing the depth as an intermediate step. The method was tested on a variety of real and synthetic images, and was shown to perform well even for distant objects.

The Tomasi-Kanade factorization method, however, assumed an orthographic projection model, since it can be described by linear equations. The applicability of the method is therefore limited to image sequences created from certain types of camera motions. The orthographic model contains no notion of the distance from the camera to the object. As a result, shape reconstruction from image sequences containing large translations toward or away from the camera often produces deformed object shapes, as the method tries to explain the size differences in the images by creating size differences in the object. The method also supplies no estimation of translation along the camera's optical axis, which limits its usefulness for certain tasks.

There exist several perspective approximations which capture more of the effects of perspective projection while remaining linear. Scaled orthographic projection, sometimes referred to as "weak perspective" [4], accounts for the scaling effect of an object as it moves towards and away from the camera. Paraperspective projection, first introduced by Ohta [5] and named by Aloimonos [1], models the position effect (an object is viewed from different angles as it translates across the field of view) as well as the scaling effect.

In this paper, we present a factorization method based on the paraperspective projection model. The paraperspective factorization method is still fast, and robust with respect to noise. It can be applied to a wider realm of situations than the original factorization method, such as sequences containing significant depth translation or containing objects close to the camera, and can be used in applications where it is important to recover the distance to the object in each image, such as navigation.

We begin by describing our camera and world reference frames and introduce the mathematical notation that we use. We then present our paraperspective factorization method, followed by the results of several experiments using synthetic data which explore the method's performance. We conclude with the results of two experiments using real image sequences, which demonstrate the practicality of our system.

2 Problem Description

In a shape-from-motion problem, we are given a sequence of F images taken from a camera that is moving relative to an object. We locate P prominent feature points in the first image, and track these points from each image to the next, recording the coordinates (u_{fp}, v_{fp}) of each point p in each image f. Each feature point p that we track corresponds to a single world point, located at position s_p in some fixed world coordinate system. Each image f was taken at some camera orientation, which we describe by the orthonormal unit vectors i_f, j_f, and k_f, where i_f and j_f correspond to the x and y axes of the camera's image plane, and k_f points along the camera's line of sight. We describe the position of the camera in each frame f by the vector t_f indicating the camera's focal point. This formulation is illustrated in Fig. 1.

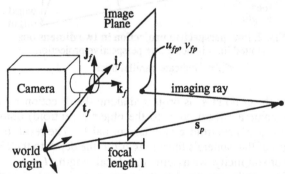

Fig. 1. Coordinate system

The result of the feature tracker is a set of P feature point coordinates (u_{fp}, v_{fp}) for each of the F frames of the image sequence. From this information, our goal is to estimate the shape of the object as $\hat{s}_p$ for each object point, and the motion of the camera as $\hat{i}_f$, $\hat{j}_f$, $\hat{k}_f$ and $\hat{t}_f$ for each frame in the sequence.

3 The Paraperspective Factorization Method

3.1 Paraperspective Projection

Paraperspective projection was first developed by Ohta [5] in order to solve a shape

99

from texture problem. It closely approximates perspective projection by modelling both the scaling effect (closer objects appear larger than distant ones) and the position effect (objects in the periphery of the image are viewed from a different angle than those near the center of projection [1]), while retaining the linear properties of orthographic projection. The paraperspective projection of an object onto an image, illustrated in Fig. 2, involves two steps.

1. An object point is projected along the direction of the line connecting the focal point of the camera to the object's centroid, onto a hypothetical image plane parallel to the real image plane and passing through the object's centroid.
2. The point is then projected onto the real image plane using perspective projection. Because the hypothetical plane is parallel to the real image plane, this is equivalent to simply scaling the point coordinates by the ratio of the camera focal length and the distance between the two planes.[1]

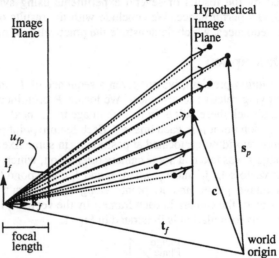

Fig. 2. Paraperspective projection in two dimensions
Dotted lines indicate true perspective projection
➤➤ indicate parallel lines.

In frame f, each object point s_p is projected along the direction $c - t_f$ (which is the direction from the camera's focal point to the object's centroid) onto the plane that passes through the object's centroid c and has normal k_f. The result of this projection is scaled by the ratio of the camera's focal length l to the depth to the object's centroid, $z_f = (c - t_f) \cdot k_f$. For simplicity, we assume unit focal length, $l = 1$.

Without loss of generality we simplify the mathematics by placing the world origin at the object's centroid c so that by definition

$$c = \frac{1}{P} \sum_{p=1}^{P} s_p = 0. \tag{1}$$

---

1. The scaled orthographic projection model (also known as "weak perspective") is similar to paraperspective projection, except that the direction of the initial projection in step 1 is parallel to the camera's optical axis rather than parallel to the line connecting the object's centroid to the camera's focal point. This model captures the scaling effect of perspective projection, but not the position effect. See [6] for details.

The equations for paraperspective projection using this formulation are

$$u_{fp} = \frac{1}{z_f} \{ \left[\mathbf{i}_f + \frac{\mathbf{i}_f \cdot \mathbf{t}_f}{z_f} \mathbf{k}_f \right] \cdot \mathbf{s}_p - (\mathbf{t}_f \cdot \mathbf{i}_f) \} \qquad v_{fp} = \frac{1}{z_f} \{ \left[\mathbf{j}_f + \frac{\mathbf{j}_f \cdot \mathbf{t}_f}{z_f} \mathbf{k}_f \right] \cdot \mathbf{s}_p - (\mathbf{t}_f \cdot \mathbf{j}_f) \} \qquad (2)$$

These equations appear much more complicated than the corresponding equations for orthographic projection, which are simply $u_{fp} = \mathbf{i}_f \cdot (\mathbf{s}_p - \mathbf{t}_f)$ and $v_{fp} = \mathbf{j}_f \cdot (\mathbf{s}_p - \mathbf{t}_f)$. However, both can be rewritten in the form

$$u_{fp} = \mathbf{m}_f \cdot \mathbf{s}_p + x_f \qquad v_{fp} = \mathbf{n}_f \cdot \mathbf{s}_p + y_f, \qquad (3)$$

although the corresponding definitions of x_f, y_f, $\mathbf{m}_f$, and $\mathbf{n}_f$ differ. In the orthographic case, $\mathbf{m}_f = \mathbf{i}_f$, $\mathbf{n}_f = \mathbf{j}_f$, $x_f = -\mathbf{i}_f \cdot \mathbf{t}_f$, and $y_f = -\mathbf{j}_f \cdot \mathbf{t}_f$. In the paraperspective case, the definitions are

$$z_f = -\mathbf{t}_f \cdot \mathbf{k}_f \qquad (4)$$

$$x_f = -\frac{\mathbf{t}_f \cdot \mathbf{i}_f}{z_f} \qquad y_f = -\frac{\mathbf{t}_f \cdot \mathbf{j}_f}{z_f} \qquad (5)$$

$$\mathbf{m}_f = \frac{\mathbf{i}_f - x_f \mathbf{k}_f}{z_f} \qquad \mathbf{n}_f = \frac{\mathbf{j}_f - y_f \mathbf{k}_f}{z_f} \qquad (6)$$

This similarity in the form of the projection equations enables us to perform the basic decomposition of the matrix in the same manner that Tomasi and Kanade did for the orthographic case, as is described in the following section.

3.2 Paraperspective Decomposition

We can combine (3), for all points p from 1 to P, and all frames f from 1 to F, into the single matrix equation

$$\begin{bmatrix} u_{11} & \cdots & u_{1P} \\ \cdots & \cdots & \cdots \\ u_{F1} & \cdots & u_{FP} \\ v_{11} & \cdots & v_{1P} \\ \cdots & \cdots & \cdots \\ v_{F1} & \cdots & v_{FP} \end{bmatrix} = \begin{bmatrix} \mathbf{m}_1 \\ \cdots \\ \mathbf{m}_F \\ \mathbf{n}_1 \\ \cdots \\ \mathbf{n}_F \end{bmatrix} \begin{bmatrix} \mathbf{s}_1 & \cdots & \mathbf{s}_P \end{bmatrix} + \begin{bmatrix} x_1 \\ \cdots \\ x_F \\ y_1 \\ \cdots \\ y_F \end{bmatrix} \begin{bmatrix} 1 & \cdots & 1 \end{bmatrix}, \qquad (7)$$

or in short

$$W = MS + T \begin{bmatrix} 1 & \cdots & 1 \end{bmatrix}. \qquad (8)$$

The $2F \times P$ matrix W, called the *measurement matrix*, collects all of the image measurements (u_{fp}, v_{fp}) such that each column of W contains all the observations for a single point, while each row contains the observed u- or v-coordinates for a single frame. M is the $2F \times 3$ motion matrix whose rows are the $\mathbf{m}_f$ and $\mathbf{n}_f$ vectors, S is the $3 \times P$ shape matrix whose columns are the $\mathbf{s}_p$ vectors, and T is the $2F \times 1$ translation vector.

Using (1) and (3) we can write

$$\sum_{p=1}^{P} u_{fp} = \sum_{p=1}^{P} (\mathbf{m}_f \cdot \mathbf{s}_p + x_f) = \mathbf{m}_f \cdot \sum_{p=1}^{P} \mathbf{s}_p + P x_f = P x_f$$
$$\sum_{p=1}^{P} v_{fp} = \sum_{p=1}^{P} (\mathbf{n}_f \cdot \mathbf{s}_p + y_f) = \mathbf{n}_f \cdot \sum_{p=1}^{P} \mathbf{s}_p + P y_f = P y_f \qquad (9)$$

Therefore we can compute x_f and y_f, which are the elements of the translation vector T, immediately from the image data as

$$x_f = \frac{1}{P} \sum_{p=1}^{P} u_{fp} \qquad y_f = \frac{1}{P} \sum_{p=1}^{P} v_{fp}. \qquad (10)$$

Once we know the translation vector T, we subtract it from W, giving the *registered measurement matrix*

$$W^* = W - T\begin{bmatrix} 1 & \dots & 1 \end{bmatrix} = MS. \tag{11}$$

Since W^* is the product of two matrices each of rank at most 3, W^* has rank at most 3, just as it did in the orthographic projection case. When noise is present, the rank of W^* will not be exactly 3, but by computing the SVD of W^* and only retaining the largest 3 singular values, we can factor it into

$$W^* = \hat{M}\hat{S}, \tag{12}$$

where $\hat{M}$ is a $2F \times 3$ matrix and $\hat{S}$ is a $3 \times P$ matrix. Using the SVD to perform this factorization guarantees that the product $\hat{M}\hat{S}$ is the best possible rank 3 approximation to W^*, in the sense that it minimizes the sum of squares difference between corresponding elements of W^* and $\hat{M}\hat{S}$.

3.3 Paraperspective Normalization

The decomposition of W^* into the product of $\hat{M}$ and $\hat{S}$ by (12) is only determined up to a linear transformation. Any non-singular 3×3 matrix A and its inverse could be inserted between $\hat{M}$ and $\hat{S}$, and their product would still equal W^*. Thus the actual motion and shape matrices are given by

$$M = \hat{M}A \qquad S = A^{-1}\hat{S}, \tag{13}$$

with the appropriate 3×3 invertible matrix A selected. The correct A is determined by observing that the rows of the motion matrix M (the $\mathbf{m}_f$ and $\mathbf{n}_f$ vectors) must be of a certain form. Taking advantage of the fact that $\mathbf{i}_f$, $\mathbf{j}_f$, and $\mathbf{k}_f$ are unit vectors, from (6) we observe that

$$|\mathbf{m}_f|^2 = \frac{1 + x_f^2}{z_f^2} \qquad |\mathbf{n}_f|^2 = \frac{1 + y_f^2}{z_f^2}. \tag{14}$$

We know the values of x_f and y_f from our initial registration step, but we do not know the value of the depth z_f. Thus we cannot impose individual constraints on the magnitudes of $\mathbf{m}_f$ and $\mathbf{n}_f$ as was done in the orthographic factorization method where we required that $\mathbf{m}_f$ and $\mathbf{n}_f$ each have unit magnitude. Instead we adopt the following set of constraints on the ratios of the magnitudes of $\mathbf{m}_f$ and $\mathbf{n}_f$.

$$\frac{|\mathbf{m}_f|^2}{1 + x_f^2} = \frac{|\mathbf{n}_f|^2}{1 + y_f^2} \qquad \left(= \frac{1}{z_f^2} \right). \tag{15}$$

There is also a constraint on the angle relationship of $\mathbf{m}_f$ and $\mathbf{n}_f$. From (6), and the knowledge that $\mathbf{i}_f$, $\mathbf{j}_f$, and $\mathbf{k}_f$ are orthogonal unit vectors,

$$\mathbf{m}_f \cdot \mathbf{n}_f = \frac{\mathbf{i}_f - x_f\mathbf{k}_f}{z_f} \cdot \frac{\mathbf{j}_f - y_f\mathbf{k}_f}{z_f} = \frac{x_f y_f}{z_f^2}. \tag{16}$$

The problem with this constraint is that, again, z_f is unknown. We could use either of the two values given in (15) for $1/z_f^2$, but in the presence of noisy input data the two will not be exactly equal, so we use the average of the two quantities. We choose the arithmetic mean over the geometric mean or some other measure in order to keep the solution of these constraints linear. Thus our second set of constraints is

$$\mathbf{m}_f \cdot \mathbf{n}_f = x_f y_f \frac{1}{2} \left(\frac{|\mathbf{m}_f|^2}{1 + x_f^2} + \frac{|\mathbf{n}_f|^2}{1 + y_f^2} \right). \tag{17}$$

This is the paraperspective version of the orthographic constraint that required that the dot product of $\mathbf{m}_f$ and $\mathbf{n}_f$ be zero.

Equations (15) and (17) are homogeneous constraints, which could be trivially satisfied by the solution $\forall f \; \mathbf{m}_f = \mathbf{n}_f = 0$, or $M = 0$. To avoid this solution, we impose the additional constraint

$$|\mathbf{m}_1| = 1. \tag{18}$$

This does not effect the final solution except by a scaling factor.

Equations (15), (17), and (18) give us $2F + 1$ equations, which are the paraperspective version of the *metric constraints*. We compute the 3×3 matrix A such that $M = \hat{M}A$ best satisfies these metric constraints in the least sum-of-squares error sense. This is a simple problem because the constraints are linear in the 6 unique elements of the symmetric 3×3 matrix $Q = A^T A$. Thus we compute Q by solving the overconstrained linear system of $2F + 1$ equations in 6 variables defined by the metric constraints, compute its Jacobi Transformation $Q = L \Lambda L^T$ (where Λ is the diagonal eigenvalue matrix), and as long as Q is positive definite, $A = (L \Lambda^{1/2})$.

3.4 Paraperspective Motion Recovery

Once the matrix A has been determined, we compute the shape matrix $S = A^{-1}\hat{S}$ and the motion matrix $M = \hat{M}A$. For each frame f, we now need to recover the camera orientation vectors $\hat{\mathbf{i}}_f$, $\hat{\mathbf{j}}_f$, and $\hat{\mathbf{k}}_f$, as well as the depth to the object z_f, from the vectors $\mathbf{m}_f$ and $\mathbf{n}_f$, which are the rows of M. From (6) we see that

$$\hat{\mathbf{i}}_f = z_f \mathbf{m}_f + x_f \hat{\mathbf{k}}_f \qquad \hat{\mathbf{j}}_f = z_f \mathbf{n}_f + y_f \hat{\mathbf{k}}_f. \tag{19}$$

Since the $\hat{\mathbf{i}}_f$, $\hat{\mathbf{j}}_f$, and $\hat{\mathbf{k}}_f$ produced must be orthonormal, they can be written as functions of only three rotational variables. We can then view the problem as, for each frame f, solving an overconstrained system of 6 equations (the expansion of (19) to each of its vector components) in 4 variables (the three rotational variables and z_f). These small systems of equations can be solved quickly and efficiently using any one of a variety of equation solving techniques. Due to the arbitrary world coordinate orientation, to obtain a unique solution we then rotate the computed shape and motion to align the world axes with the first frame's camera axes, so that $\hat{\mathbf{i}}_1 = \begin{bmatrix} 1 & 0 & 0 \end{bmatrix}^T$ and $\hat{\mathbf{j}}_1 = \begin{bmatrix} 0 & 1 & 0 \end{bmatrix}^T$.

All that remain to be computed are the translations for each frame. We calculate the depth z_f from (15). Once we know x_f, y_f, z_f, $\hat{\mathbf{i}}_f$, $\hat{\mathbf{j}}_f$, and $\hat{\mathbf{k}}_f$, we can calculate $\hat{\mathbf{t}}_f$ using (4) and (5).

4 Comparison of Methods using Synthetic Data

In this section we compare the performance of our new paraperspective factorization method with the previous orthographic factorization method. The comparison also includes a factorization method based on scaled orthographic projection, which models the scaling effect of perspective projection but not the position effect, in order to demonstrate the importance of modelling the position effect for objects at close range[1]. Our results show that the paraperspective factorization method is a vast improvement over the orthographic method, and underscore the importance of modelling both the scaling and position effects.

4.1 Data Generation

Each synthetic feature point sequence was created by moving a known unit-sized "object" (a set of 60 3D points) through a known motion sequence. The motion con-

---

1. The scaled orthographic factorization method is equivalent to using the paraperspective factorization method with the focal length of the camera set to infinity. It uses for metric constraints $|\mathbf{m}_f| = |\mathbf{n}_f|$, $\mathbf{m}_f \cdot \mathbf{n}_f = 0$, and $|\mathbf{m}_1| = 1$. See [6] for more details about this method.

sisted of 60 image frames of an object rotating through a total of 30 degrees each of roll, pitch, and yaw. The "object depth" (the distance from the camera's focal point to the front of the object) in the first frame was varied from 3 to 60 times the object size. In each sequence, the object translated across the field of view by a distance of one object size horizontally and vertically, and translated away from the camera by half its initial distance from the camera. Each "image" was created by perspectively projecting the 3D points onto the image plane, for each sequence choosing the largest focal length that would keep the object in the field of view throughout the sequence. The coordinates in the image plane were then perturbed by adding gaussian noise, to model tracking imprecision.

4.2 Error Measurement

We ran each of the three factorization methods on each synthetic sequence and measured the rotation error, shape error, X and Y offset error, and Z offset (depth) error. The errors shown are the root-mean-square (RMS) difference between the known shape or motion parameters and the measured values. Since the shape and translation are only recovered up to a scaling factor, we first scaled these results by the factor that minimized the RMS error. The term "offset" refers to the translational component of the motion as measured in the camera's coordinate frame rather than in world coordinates; the X offset is $\hat{t}_f \cdot \hat{i}_f$, the Y offset is $\hat{t}_f \cdot \hat{j}_f$, and the Z offset is $\hat{t}_f \cdot \hat{k}_f$. Note that the orthographic factorization method supplies no estimation of translation along the camera's optical axis, so the Z offset error could not be computed for that method.

4.3 Discussion of Results

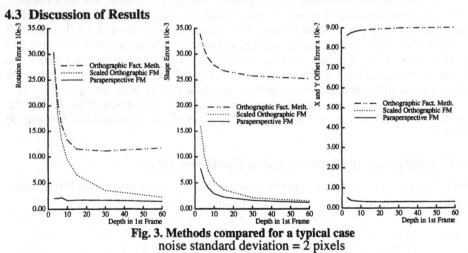

Fig. 3. Methods compared for a typical case
noise standard deviation = 2 pixels

Fig. 3 shows the average errors in the solutions computed by the various methods, as a functions of object depth in the first frame. We see that the paraperspective method performs significantly better than the orthographic factorization method regardless of depth, because orthography cannot model the scaling of the image that occurs due to the motion along the camera's optical axis. The figure also shows that the paraperspective method performs substantially better than the scaled orthographic method at close range, while the errors from the two methods are nearly the same when the object is distant. This confirms the importance of modelling the position effect when objects are near the camera.

In other experiments in which the object was centered in the image and there was no translation across the field of view, the paraperspective method and the scaled orthographic method performed equally well, as we would expect since such image sequences contain no position effects. Similarly, we found that when the object remained centered in the image and there was no depth translation, the orthographic factorization method performed very well, and the paraperspective factorization method provided no significant improvement since such sequences contain neither scaling effects nor position effects.

Our C implementation of the paraperspective factorization method required 20-24 seconds to solve a system of 60 frames and 60 points on a Sun 4/65, with most of this time spent computing the SVD of the measurement matrix.

4.4 Analysis of Paraperspective Method using Synthetic Data

Now that we have shown the advantages of the paraperspective factorization method over the previous method, we further analyze the performance of the paraperspective method to determine its behavior at various depths and its robustness with respect to noise. The synthetic sequences used in these experiments were created in the same manner as in the previous section, except that the standard deviation of the noise was varied from 0 to 4.0 pixels.

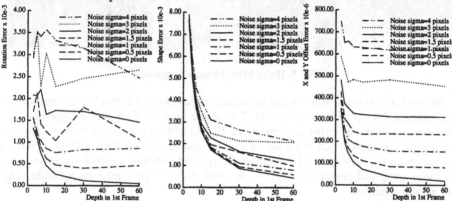

Fig. 4. Paraperspective shape and motion recovery by noise level

In Fig. 4, we see that at high depth values, the error in the solution is roughly proportional to the level of noise in the input, while at low depths the error is inversely related to the depth. This occurs because at low depths, perspective distortion of the object's shape is the primary source of error in the computed results. At higher depths, perspective distortion of the object's shape is negligible, and noise becomes the dominant cause of error in the results. For example, at a noise level of 1 pixel, the rotation and XY-offset errors are nearly invariant to the depth once the object is farther from the camera than 10 times the object size. The shape results, however, appear sensitive to perspective distortion even at depths of 30 or 60 times the object size. We also found that the error in the recovered depth to the object in each frame (Z offset error, not shown), was nearly proportional to both the noise level and the initial depth.

5 Shape and Motion Recovery from Real Image Sequences

We tested the paraperspective factorization method on two real image sequences - a laboratory experiment in which a small model building was imaged, and an aerial sequence taken from a low-altitude plane using a hand-held video camera. Both sequences contain significant perspective effects, due to translations along the optical axis and across the field of view. We implemented a system to automatically identify and track features, based on [10] and [3]. This tracker computes the position of a square feature window which minimizes the sum of the squares of the intensity difference over the feature window from one image to the next.

5.1 Hotel Model Sequence

A hotel model was imaged by a camera mounted on a computer-controlled movable platform. The camera motion included substantial translation away from the camera and across the field of view (see Fig. 5). The feature tracker automatically identified and tracked 197 points throughout the sequence of 181 images.

| Frame 1 | Frame 121 | Frame 151 |

Fig. 5. Hotel Model Image Sequence

We analyzed this sequence using both the paraperspective factorization method and the orthographic factorization method. The shape recovered by the orthographic factorization method was rather deformed (see Fig. 6) and the recovered motion incorrect, because the method could not account for the scaling and position effects which are prominent in the sequence. The paraperspective factorization method, however, models these effects of perspective projection, and therefore produced an accurate shape and accurate motion.

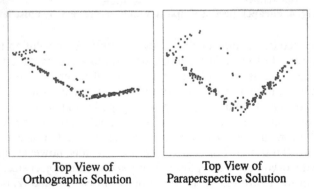

| Top View of Orthographic Solution | Top View of Paraperspective Solution |

Fig. 6. Comparison of Orthographic and Paraperspective Shape Results

Several features in the sequence were poorly tracked, and as a result their recovered 3D positions were incorrect. While they did not disrupt the overall solution greatly, we found that we could achieve improved results by automatically removing these features in the following manner. Using the recovered shape and motion, we computed the reconstructed measurement matrix W^{recon}, and then eliminated from W those features for which the average error between the elements of W and W^{recon} was more than twice the average such error. We then ran the shape and motion recovery again, using only the remaining 179 features. Eliminating the poorly tracked features decreased errors in the recovered rotation about the camera's x-axis in each frame by an average of 0.5 degrees, while the errors in the other rotation parameters were also slightly improved. The final rotation values are shown in Fig. 7, along with the values we measured using the camera platform. The computed rotation about the camera x-axis, y-axis, and z-axis was always within 0.29 degrees, 1.78 degrees, and 0.45 degrees of the measured rotation, respectively.

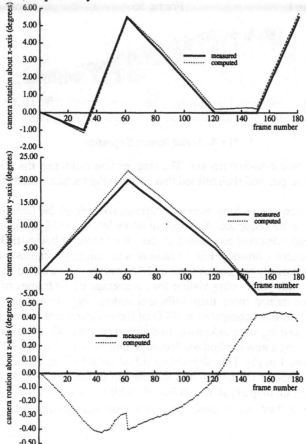

Fig. 7. Hotel Model Rotation Results

5.2 Aerial Image Sequence

An aerial image sequence was taken from a small airplane overflying a suburban Pittsburgh residential area adjacent to a steep, snowy valley, using a small hand-held video camera. The plane altered its altitude during the sequence and also varied its roll, pitch, and yaw slightly. Several images from the sequence are shown in Fig. 8.

Due to the bumpy motion of the plane and the instability of the hand-held camera, features often moved by as much as 30 pixels from one image to the next. The original feature tracker could not track motions of more than approximately 3 pixels, so we

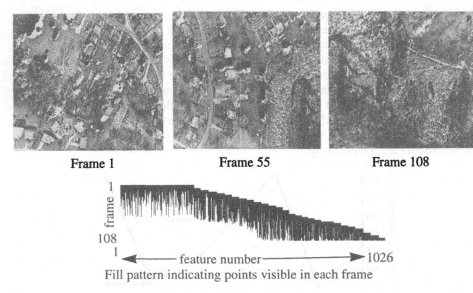

Fill pattern indicating points visible in each frame

Fig. 8. Aerial Image Sequence

implemented a coarse-to-fine tracker. The tracker first estimated the translation using low resolution images, and then refined that value using the same methods as the initial tracker.

The sequence covered a long sweep of terrain, so none of the features were visible throughout the entire sequence. As some features left the field of view, new features were automatically detected and added to the set of features being tracked. A vertical bar in the fill pattern (shown in Fig. 8) indicates the range of frames through which a feature was successfully tracked. A total of 1026 points were tracked in the 108 image sequence, with each point being visible for an average of 30 frames of the sequence. The data still contained more than sufficient redundancy to recover the shape and motion, but we could not compute the SVD of the measurement matrix since for some pairs (f, p), u_{fp} and v_{fp} were unknown. In order to accommodate the missing observations, we developed a new method for decomposing W into $W = \hat{M}\hat{S} + T$ without using the SVD, described in [6]. This slightly modified factorization method was then used to recover the shape of the terrain and the motion of the airplane. Two views of the reconstructed terrain map are shown in Fig. 9. While no ground-truth was available for the shape or the motion, we observed that the terrain was qualitatively correct, captur-

Fig. 9. Two Views of Reconstructed Terrain

ing the flat residential area and the steep hillside as well, and that the recovered positions of features on buildings were elevated from the surrounding terrain.

6 Conclusions

The principle that the measurement matrix has rank 3, as put forth by Tomasi and Kanade in [9], was dependent on the use of an orthographic projection model. We have shown in this paper that this important result also holds for the case of paraperspective projection, which closely approximates perspective projection. We have devised a paraperspective factorization method based on this model, which uses different metric constraints and motion recovery techniques, but retains many of the features of the original factorization method.

In image sequences in which the object being viewed translates significantly toward or away from the camera or across the camera's field of view, the paraperspective factorization method performs significantly better than the orthographic method. The paraperspective method requires that the camera's focal length and center of projection be known in order to accurately model the position effect. In cases in which these are not known, the scaled orthographic factorization method can still be used to model the scaling effect of image projection. Both methods also compute the relative distance from the camera to the object in each image and can accommodate missing or uncertain tracking data, which enables their use in a variety of applications.

7 Acknowledgments

The authors wish to thank Radu Jasinschi for pointing out the existence of the paraperspective projection model and suggesting its applicability to the factorization method. Additional thanks goes to Carlo Tomasi and Toshihiko Morita for their helpful and insightful comments.

8 References

1. John Y. Aloimonos, *Perspective Approximations*, Image and Vision Computing, 8(3):177-192, August 1990.
2. T. Broida, S. Chandrashekhar, and R. Chellappa, *Recursive 3-D Motion Estimation from a Monocular Image Sequence*, IEEE Transactions on Aerospace and Electronic Systems, 26(4):639-656, July 1990.
3. Bruce D. Lucas and Takeo Kanade, *An Iterative Image Registration Technique with an Application to Stereo Vision*, Proceedings of the 7th International Joint Conference on Artificial Intelligence, 1981.
4. Joseph L. Mundy and Andrew Zisserman, *Geometric Invariance in Computer Vision*, The MIT Press, 1992, p. 512.
5. Yu-ichi Ohta, Kiyoshi Maenobu, and Toshiyuki Sakai, *Obtaining Surface Orientation from Texels Under Perspective Projection*, Proceedings of the 7th International Joint Conference on Artificial Intelligence, pp. 746-751, August 1981.
6. Conrad J. Poelman and Takeo Kanade, *A Paraperspective Factorization Method for Shape and Motion Recovery*, Technical Report CMU-CS-93-219, Carnegie Mellon University, Pittsburgh, PA, December 1993.
7. William H. Press, Brian P. Flannery, Saul A. Teukolsky, and William T. Vetterling, Numerical Recipes in C: The Art of Scientific Computing, Cambridge University Press, 1988.
8. Camillo Taylor, David Kriegman, and P. Anandan, *Structure and Motion From Multiple Images: A Least Squares Approach*, IEEE Workshop on Visual Motion, pp. 242-248, October 1991.
9. Carlo Tomasi and Takeo Kanade, *Shape and Motion from Image Streams: a Factorization Method - 2. Point Features in 3D Motion*, Technical Report CMU-CS-91-105, Carnegie Mellon University, Pittsburgh, PA, January 1991.
10. Carlo Tomasi and Takeo Kanade, *Shape and Motion from Image Streams: a Factorization Method*, Technical Report CMU-CS-91-172, Carnegie Mellon University, Pittsburgh, PA, September 1991.
11. Roger Tsai and Thomas Huang, *Uniqueness and Estimation of Three-Dimensional Motion Parameters of Rigid Objects with Curved Surfaces*, IEEE Transactions on Pattern Analysis and Machine Intelligence, PAMI-6(1):13-27, January 1984.

Active Vision II

Active Camera Self-orientation using Dynamic Image Parameters

V. Sundareswaran, P. Bouthemy and F. Chaumette

IRISA / INRIA Rennes, Campus de Beaulieu,
35042 Rennes Cedex, France

Abstract. We are interested in the realization of active visual tasks, and we propose an innovative visual servoing method using parameters obtained from visual motion processing. In particular, we consider the task of dynamically aligning the optical axis of a translating camera with its unknown direction of translation, by controlling the orientation of the camera. Parameters of the 2D affine motion model are used. We show experimental results of this method implemented on a six d.o.f. robot arm carrying a camera on its end-effector.

1 Introduction

Combining active manipulation of the camera along with processing of visual motion could allow us to perform certain tasks in a more robust fashion. In general, the importance and advantages of active vision have been well-understood; in [6], it is shown that ill-posedness of certain problems can be eliminated by active perception. A system performing several active visual tasks, including closed-loop gaze-control (based on a differential analysis) for fixating on an object has been presented in [7]. Real-time responses that include saccades to moving regions of interest, using a transputer-based system has been demonstrated in [9]. A fixation method running in real-time on a head-eye system has been presented in [12]. Santos-Victor et. al. [8], and Coombs and Roberts [4] present methods to steer a camera between two walls, and to veer around obstacles, both methods being based on a simple analysis of the computed optic flow fields.

The work presented here is within the visual servoing formalism [5]. Visual servoing provides a framework to determine the control equations for camera motion to perform useful tasks. A strong motivation for the research described here is to explore the possibility of using visual information that is not simply a geometric feature, as has been done in visual servoing applications in the past [5]. The method described in this paper uses dynamic image parameters such as the coefficients in 2D affine motion model. Such a use of the dynamic image parameters is innovative, and it provides a starting point for other interesting closed-loop methods using these parameters. The use of the focus of expansion has already been investigated in [2] and [13].

The method presented here examines the possibility of controlling the orientation of a camera that is under motion due to an external agent such as the vehicle on which the camera is mounted. We consider a method to apply a control in order to align the optical axis of the camera with the direction of its unknown translation. We would simply refer to this process as the task of camera *alignment*. Such a reorientation would facilitate tasks to avoid obstacles and to perform other visual processing useful in navigation. For the purposes of this paper, we restrict ourselves to the pure translation situation, and hope that this will provide an initiative to solve the more general cases. In the section on experiments, we point out the errors that arise if external rotation is present and propose a way to successfully compensate for the errors.

2 Visual servoing using 2D affine motion parameters

The principle of visual servoing is to use visual information as observation in closed-loop control when the desired configuration can be described as a particular visual observation. More precisely, for a given vision-based task, we have to choose a set s of visual features suited for achieving the task (for example, the coordinates of an image point, the parameters of a selected line, etc). In order to obtain a control law based on s, we need to know the equations for the variation of s with respect to camera translational and rotational motion (T, Ω). In other words, we have to determine the matrix L described by the following equation:

$$\dot{\mathbf{s}} = L \begin{pmatrix} T \\ \Omega \end{pmatrix} \tag{1}$$

A *task function* $\mathbf{e} = M (\mathbf{s} - \mathbf{s}^*)$ can thus be defined where s is the measured visual features currently observed by the camera, $\mathbf{s}^*$ is the desired final configuration for s in the image, and M is a constant matrix which allows, for robustness issues, to take into account more visual features than necessary. Let us note that M can simply be chosen as the identity matrix when the number of the selected visual features is equal to the number of the camera d.o.f. controlled by the task.

The control problem thus appears as the regulation of the task function e to zero or, equivalently, as the minimization of $\|\mathbf{e}\|$ in the image by appropriate camera motion. If we would like the task function to decay exponentially towards zero, we get the control law

$$\begin{pmatrix} T \\ \Omega \end{pmatrix} = -\lambda \hat{L}^+ M^+ \mathbf{e}, \tag{2}$$

where $\lambda(>0)$ is the exponent that controls the speed of the decay, $\hat{L}^+$ and M^+ are the pseudo-inverses of $\hat{L}$ and M, $\hat{L}$ being a model of L. The convergence of the control law will be ensured under the sufficient condition [5]:

$$M L \hat{L}^+ M^+ > 0. \tag{3}$$

Usually, $\hat{L}$ is chosen as L^*, the value of L at convergence. Indeed, in that case, the positivity condition is valid around the desired configuration.

We begin by describing the parameters of the 2D affine motion model, and then derive a control law to achieve an alignment task using these parameters. We note here that two other recently proposed methods [8, 4] use motion information for the task of steering a camera between two walls.

The affine motion model is often useful. It is possible to derive expressions for the first-order parameters (affine parameters) assuming that an analytical surface is imaged (i.e., it is possible to describe the depth by a Taylor series expansion). It has been shown [10] that the affine parameters can be reliably estimated. Multiresolution methods for the estimation of the affine parameters [11] have proved to yield accurate values.

The optical flow equations, with translational velocity T (components U, V, W), and rotational velocity Ω (A, B, C), are

$$u(x, y) = \frac{1}{Z(x,y)}[-U + xW] + A[xy] - B[1 + x^2] + Cy,$$
$$v(x, y) = \frac{1}{Z(x,y)}[-V + yW] + A[1 + y^2] - B[xy] - Cx, \tag{4}$$

assuming unit focal length. Let the first-order approximation be

$$u(x, y) = a_1 + a_2 x + a_3 y, \quad v(x, y) = a_4 + a_5 x + a_6 y. \tag{5}$$

If we assume that the imaged surface has $Z = Z_0 + \gamma_1 X + \gamma_2 Y$ as the first-order approximation, from Eqns. (4), and (5), we get [1, 10]

$$
\begin{aligned}
a_1 &= -\frac{U}{Z_0} - B, & a_4 &= -\frac{V}{Z_0} + A, \\
a_2 &= \frac{1}{Z_0}(\gamma_1 U + W), & a_5 &= \frac{1}{Z_0}(\gamma_1 V) - C, \\
a_3 &= \frac{1}{Z_0}(\gamma_2 U) + C, & a_6 &= \frac{1}{Z_0}(\gamma_2 V + W).
\end{aligned} \tag{6}
$$

Our problem situation is when there is an unknown translational velocity T of the camera, for example due to the motion of the host vehicle. The task is to align the optical axis Z with the translation T by utilizing the free rotational parameters. Indeed, it is easy to see that the control of two rotational parameters (say, tilt A and pan B) is sufficient to align the optical axis with the translational direction We assume that acceleration, if present, manifests from time to time but not constantly. We further assume that the only rotational velocity arises due to the control action that is responsible for achieving the alignment.

Consider the two "parameters" $U_z = \frac{U}{Z_0}$ and $V_z = \frac{V}{Z_0}$. If we apply control in such a way to result in zero values for these variables, we will achieve the goal of setting the components U and V of the translational velocity to zero (the tacit assumption is that infinite depth does not occur). The derivatives of these parameters are given by

$$
\begin{pmatrix} \dot{U}_z \\ \dot{V}_z \end{pmatrix} = \begin{pmatrix} \frac{\dot{U}}{Z_0} - \frac{U}{Z_0}\frac{\dot{Z}_0}{Z_0} \\ \frac{\dot{V}}{Z_0} - \frac{V}{Z_0}\frac{\dot{Z}_0}{Z_0} \end{pmatrix}. \tag{7}
$$

The components of T, which remain constant in a global (world) coordinate system (during the time taken for the alignment), change however in the camera coordinate system because of the rotation of the camera axes. Since the rotational velocity is $\Omega = (A, B, C)$ about the three axes, the variation of T is simply the cross product $\dot{T} = -\Omega \times T$. Using this observation to substitute for $\dot{U}$ and $\dot{V}$ in Eqn. 7, and noting that $U_z = -a_1 - B$, $V_z = -a_4 + A$, we get

$$\begin{pmatrix} \dot{U}_z \\ \dot{V}_z \end{pmatrix} = \begin{pmatrix} 0 & -\frac{W}{Z_0} + \frac{\dot{Z}_0}{Z_0} \\ \frac{W}{Z_0} - \frac{\dot{Z}_0}{Z_0} & 0 \end{pmatrix} \begin{pmatrix} A \\ B \end{pmatrix} + \begin{pmatrix} C\frac{V}{Z_0} + a_1 \frac{\dot{Z}_0}{Z_0} \\ -C\frac{U}{Z_0} + a_4 \frac{\dot{Z}_0}{Z_0} \end{pmatrix}.$$

When the planar approximation to the viewed surface does not have a large angle of inclination with respect to the camera, we have

$$\frac{1}{\tau_c} = \frac{W}{Z_0} \approx -\frac{\dot{Z}_0}{Z_0} \approx \frac{a_2 + a_6}{2}, \tag{8}$$

where τ_c is used to denote the instantaneous *time-to-collision*. Furthermore, if we assume for simplicity that $C = 0$, we obtain, for an exponential decay of the task function, the following control law:

$$\begin{pmatrix} A \\ B \end{pmatrix} = \frac{1}{2} \begin{pmatrix} 0 & -\tau_c \\ \tau_c & 0 \end{pmatrix} \left(\lambda \begin{pmatrix} U_z \\ V_z \end{pmatrix} - \begin{pmatrix} \frac{a_1}{\tau_c} \\ \frac{a_4}{\tau_c} \end{pmatrix} \right). \tag{9}$$

Using the approximations (8), the positivity condition (3) is ensured when the task is realized. Convergence of the control law will thus be obtained if the initial configuration is *not too far* from convergence. Our experiments, wherein divergence was never observed, confirm that such approximations do not disturb the task behavior.

Let us finally note that the observations U_z and V_z are given by

$$U_z = -a_1 - B, \quad \text{and} \quad V_z = -a_4 + A, \tag{10}$$

where we use the previous measured values for A and B (under normal conditions, it is nothing but the control rotational velocity applied at the preceding instant). Other control strategies to perform the same task are described in [13] (using other combinations of the affine parameters or using the focus of expansion).

3   Alignment: experiments

The method based on the use of the parameters U_z and V_z has been implemented in a real system. Simulation experiments were also carried out on the other methods [13], but they are not detailed here for lack of space.

The camera with a field of view of about 35 degrees has been mounted on a six degrees-of-freedom cartesian robot (AFMA). The size of the images processed is 128 × 182 pixels. All the image processing and control velocity computations are carried out on the host (a Sun Sparc IPX) and the computed control is transmitted to the robot controller. The experiments were conducted indoors; a sample image can be seen in Fig. 1. The translational motion was towards the floor with cluttered objects; the floor was not fronto-planar, but with an average angle in the range 45-70 degrees between the floor surface and the optical axis.

For the image processing, the spatiotemporal derivatives of the (smoothed) intensity function are calculated using a simple procedure. The affine motion parameters are computed using a over-constrained set of equations by considering points from all over the image, thresholded by gradient magnitude to suppress contribution from relatively uniform regions where the estimates are noisy.

The robot is commanded to move the camera with a certain translational velocity. The control loop consists of the following steps which are repeated: obtain two successive images, compute the affine parameters of the flow field, compute the rotational velocity control required using the control law in Eqn. 9, and apply the control rotational velocity. Here, two different programs, one in which the control is applied for a finite duration and another in which the control is applied in a continuous manner, have been implemented. Each iteration took around three seconds.

The error plots from experiments using the two different implementations are shown in Fig. 1. The final error is 0.5 degrees for the implementation where the control is applied for a finite duration (discrete control), and for continuous control, the final error is 0.75 degrees. For the discrete control, while the two successive images are acquired, the control is withdrawn.

We restricted ourselves to the pure translation situation. It would be interesting to examine the general case where there is rotation also. We know that if there is external rotation, it could still be accommodated in the "pure translation" situation, with residual errors remaining as *lag*, which can be compensated for by estimating their effects and representing them using an additional term in the control law [3]. Furthermore, we assume that the affine approximation to the optical flow field is valid or at least sufficient for the task at hand. This is supported by several useful methods developed for scene motion recovery based on the affine approximation [1, 10]. Nevertheless, this approximation can fail for the entire image when there are objects located at very different depth in the scene, or moving objects of significant size. Motion-based segmentation of the image into regions [1] could be one possible solution, but far too complex to be implemented in such a closed-loop procedure. However, we have recently designed a multi-resolution robust estimation method which could cope with these situations [11].

The use of this task in aiding a qualitative method for motion detection is described in [2].

4 Conclusions

In this report, we have proposed a new active vision approach and showed how it can be performed by visual servoing methods using parameters derived from the motion information contained in a sequence of images. We presented the task of aligning the optical axis with the translational direction, and derived control equations for this task. The implementations on a real robot-camera configuration validate the methods and prove that it is possible to do motion information-based servoing at a reasonable frame-rate. We would like to stress in concluding that such innovative use of the dynamic image parameters can be expected to be fruitful in the approaches for various active vision tasks.

References

1. Bouthemy, P., François, E.: Motion segmentation and qualitative dynamic scene analysis from an image sequence. IJCV. **10-2** (1993) 157-182
2. Bouthemy P., Sundareswaran, V.: Qualitative motion detection with a mobile and active camera. Int. Conf. on Digital Signal Processing, Cyprus. (1993) 444-449
3. Chaumette, F., Santos, A.: Tracking a moving object by visual servoing. 12th World Congress IFAC, Sidney. **4** (1993) 409-414
4. Coombs, D., Roberts, K.: Centering behavior using peripheral vision. CVPR 93, New York. (1993) 440-445
5. Espiau, B., Chaumette, F., Rives, P.: A new approach to visual servoing in robotics. IEEE Trans. on Robotics and Automation. **8-3** (1992) 313-326
6. Fermüller, C., Aloimonos, Y.: The role of fixation in visual motion. IJCV. **11-2** (1993) 165-186
7. Grosso, E., Ballard, D.: Head-centered orientation strategies in animate vision. 4th ICCV, Berlin. (1993) 395-402
8. Santos-Victor, J., Sandini, G., Curotto, F., Garibaldi, S.: Divergent stereo for robot navigation: learning from bees. CVPR 93, New York. (1993) 434-439
9. Murray, D., McLauchlan, P., Reid, I., Sharkey, P.: Reactions to peripheral image motion using a head/eye platform. 4th ICCV, Berlin. (1993) 403-411
10. Negahdaripour, S., Lee, S.: Motion recovery from image sequences using only first order optical flow information. IJCV. **9-3** (1992) 163-184
11. Odobez, J.-M., Bouthemy, P.: Robust multiresolution estimation of parametric motion models applied to complex scenes. IRISA (1994) Report PI 788
12. Pahlavan, K., Uhlin, T., Eklundh, J.-O.: Dynamic fixation. 4th ICCV, Berlin, (1993) 412-419
13. Sundareswaran, V., Bouthemy, P., Chaumette, F.: Visual servoing using dynamic image parameters. IRISA (to appear 1994)

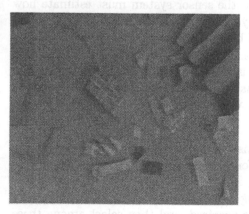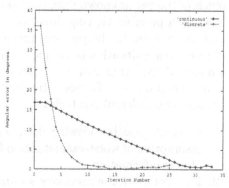

Fig. 1. On the left is a sample image from the sequence; on the right are the angular error plots for the experiment.

Planning the Optimal Set of Views Using the Max-Min Principle*

Jasna Maver, Aleš Leonardis, and Franc Solina

Computer Vision Laboratory, Faculty of Electrical Engineering and Computer Science
University of Ljubljana, Tržaška 25, 61001 Ljubljana, Slovenia
E-mail: Jasna.Maver@fer.uni-lj.si

Abstract. We present an approach to a typical task of active sensing, namely how to successively position the sensor in order to accomplish a given task. The approach is data driven since it is only the data that provides the information for planning the next views, and no a priori knowledge about the constituents of the scene is necessary. We applied our approach to the task of determining the 3-D coordinates of vertices of object silhouettes in the image under orthographic projection.

1 Introduction

It has long been realized that information obtained from a single viewpoint might not be sufficient for successfully accomplishing a task and that additional views are necessary [1,2,4,5,6].

In this paper we present an active sensor system which tends to accomplish a given task by acquiring a minimal number of images. The principle which guides the next-view planning is the *Max-Min principle*. The viewing direction from which the first image is acquired is arbitrary or predefined. To select the new viewing direction for image acquisition, the sensor system must estimate how much of the yet unknown data necessary to accomplish the task can be acquired from each possible viewing direction. This estimate is based only on the information acquired in the previous images. When there is insufficient information the worst-case situation is assumed. Thus for each viewing direction the minimal amount of data that can be obtained is anticipated, i.e., the utilization of the minimum principle. To select the best viewing direction for the next view we propose two different strategies:

1. From all possible viewing directions select the one which gives under the assumption of worst-case situation for the unknown data the maximal amount of new information.
2. First compute the necessary viewing directions from which all the necessary data to accomplish the task can be acquired, and then select among these viewing directions the one which maximizes the amount of new information.

---

* This research has been supported in part by The Ministry for Science and Technology of The Republic of Slovenia (Project P2-1122).

While the first strategy can be compared to a greedy algorithm which tries to obtain at each step the maximal information regardless of the final number of views, the second strategy with its look-a-head capability takes into account a more global view.

2 Geometry of the Viewer

The scene is defined in a rectangular coordinate system (X, Y, Z). The viewer's

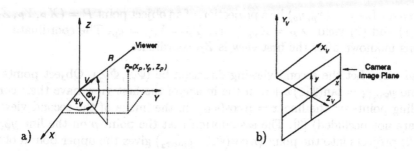

Fig. 1. (a) Viewing direction $\mathbf{V}$, (b) Camera image plane.

position is on a half sphere with radius R (Fig. 1(a)). The unit vector $\mathbf{V}$ pointing toward the viewer is given by $\mathbf{V}^T = [\cos \Psi_V \cos \Phi_V, \sin \Psi_V \cos \Phi_V, \sin \Phi_V]$. $\Psi_V \in [0, 2\pi)$ denotes the azimuth and $\Phi_V \in [0, \frac{\pi}{2}]$ the elevation. The viewer's coordinate system (X_V, Y_V, Z_V) is located in the center of the scene coordinate system. The coordinates of a point $P = (X_P, Y_P, Z_P)$ are in the viewer's coordinate system given as $(\mathbf{X}_V = \mathbf{Z} \times \mathbf{V}, \mathbf{X}_V \times \mathbf{Y}_V = \mathbf{V}, \mathbf{Z}_V = \mathbf{V})$

$$\begin{bmatrix} X_{V_P} \\ Y_{V_P} \\ Z_{V_P} \end{bmatrix} = \begin{bmatrix} -\sin \Psi_V & \cos \Psi_V & 0 \\ -\cos \Psi_V \sin \Phi_V & -\sin \Psi_V \sin \Phi_V & \cos \Phi_V \\ \cos \Psi_V \cos \Phi_V & \sin \Psi_V \cos \Phi_V & \sin \Phi_V \end{bmatrix} \begin{bmatrix} X_P \\ Y_P \\ Z_P \end{bmatrix} . \qquad (1)$$

The camera image plane is parallel to the viewer's X_V-Y_V plane where the image axes (x, y) are defined so as to be parallel to the axes (X_V, Y_V) (Fig. 1(b)). Z_V is orthogonal to the image plane. We assume that the imaging is performed under the orthographic projection:

$$x = X_V, \qquad y = Y_V . \qquad (2)$$

3 Task Definition

A set of objects lies on the horizontal base surface of the scene. Without loss of generality we can assume that the first image is acquired from the viewing direction $\mathbf{V}_1 = (0, 0, 1)$, i.e., $\Psi_{V_1} = -\frac{\pi}{2}, \Phi_{V_1} = \frac{\pi}{2}$. In the image obtained from the first viewing direction the vision system extracts the silhouettes of the objects[2].

---

[2] We assume that our vision system can distinguish whether an image point is a projection of the object or a projection of the support plane.

The task that we study can now be formulated as: *In the image of the first view determine the 3-D coordinates of the vertices on the detected silhouettes.*

4 Geometrical Information in the First two Views

To design an efficient algorithm we first have to answer the following two questions: 1. Which geometrical information of object points acquired in the image of the first view can be extracted from the image? 2. Which geometrical information can be obtained about these points from the second view?

First view: Let $p = (x_p, y_p)$ be a projection of an object point $P = (X_P, Y_P, Z_P)$. Eqs. (1) and (2) yield: $X_P = X_{V_P} = x_p$, $Y_P = Y_{V_P} = y_p$. The coordinate that remains unknown after the first view is Z_P coordinate.

Second view: Let the second viewing direction be (Ψ_{V_2}, Φ_{V_2}). Object points on the line $y_{\Psi_{V_2}, n} = \tan(\Psi_{V_2})x + n$ in the image of the first view have their corresponding points on the line $x = n\cos(\Psi_{V_2})$ in the image of the second view (if they are not occluded) [3]. The assumption that the point p on the line $y_{\Psi_{V_2}, n}$ (Fig. 2) projects into the point $(n\cos(\Psi_{V_2}), y_{max_2})$ gives the upper bound of the height of the scene at the location (X_P, Y_P). We denote the computed bound as Z_{max}. After the second view we know for each object point p its (X_P, Y_P) coordinates and the upper bound on its Z coordinate $Z_P \leq Z_{max}(X_P, Y_P)$.

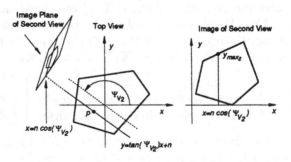

Fig. 2. Computation of Z_{max}.

5 Computation of Azimuth and Elevation Angle

From the first view we get (X, Y) coordinates of the vertices. All the following views are selected to determine their Z coordinates. Two conditions must be met to determine the Z coordinate of a vertex from the next view: 1. The vertex must not be occluded by any part of the scene. 2. The vertex must be uniquely determined in the image.

For each convex vertex v_i in the image of the first view we compute the set of possible viewing directions—the *azimuth angle* $\Psi(v_i)$ and for the selected azimuth the *elevation angle* $\Phi(v_i)$ [3] from which the viewer can uniquely determine 3-D coordinates of the vertex V_i.

Possible viewing directions for the second view: After the first view the height of the scene remains completely undetermined, therefore to compute $\Psi(v_i)$ and $\Phi(v_i)$ the following two assumptions are made for each azimuth value Ψ_{V_2}:

1. Vertex V_i is occluded if there is an object point on the line $y_{\Psi_{V_2},n}$ in the image of the first view in front of v_i relative to the viewer[3].
2. The corresponding point of v_i can not be uniquely determined if there is an object point on the line $y_{\Psi_{V_2},n}$ in the image of the first view behind v_i relative to the viewer.

Using these two assumptions we determine for each vertex v_i the minimal set of viewing directions. The slopes of the lines $y_{\Psi_{V_2},n}; n \in \Re, \Psi_{V_2} \in [0, 2\pi)$ which pass only through the vertex v_i define the set of all azimuth values—azimuth angle $\Psi(v_i)$. The elevation angle, which is equal for all vertices, is: $\Phi(v_i) = [0, \frac{\pi}{2})$ for any $\Psi_{V_2} \in \Psi(v_i)$. The point in the image of the second view corresponding to v_i is the point on the line $x = n \cos \Psi_{V_2}$ with the largest y coordinate [3].

Possible viewing directions for the third and all subsequent views: Knowing the Z_{max} coordinate (which is updated after each view) for each pair (X, Y) of the scene, we compute new azimuth and elevation angles for vertices v_i.

Let the two points p_1 and p_2 lie on the line $y_{\Psi_{p_1,p_2},n}$ in the image of the first view (Fig. 3). p_1 and p_2 are the projections of the surface points P_1 and P_2, respectively. Let the point P_1 be in front of the point P_2 relative to the viewer. The scene at the location (X_{P_1}, Y_{P_1}) can be occupied for $0 \leq Z \leq Z_{max}(X_{P_1}, Y_{P_1})$ and at the location (X_{P_2}, Y_{P_2}) for $0 \leq Z \leq Z_{max}(X_{P_2}, Y_{P_2})$.

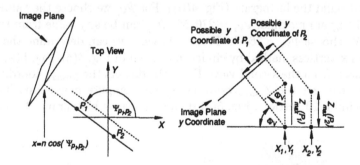

Fig. 3. Computation of the minimal viewing elevation.

The y coordinates of P_1 and P_2 lie on the intervals (Fig. 3):
$$y((X_{P_1}, Y_{P_1}, 0), \Psi_{p_1,p_2}, \Phi_V) \leq y_{p_1} \leq y((X_{P_1}, Y_{P_1}, Z_{max}(X_{P_1}, Y_{P_1})), \Psi_{p_1,p_2}, \Phi_V),$$
$$y((X_{P_2}, Y_{P_2}, 0), \Psi_{p_1,p_2}, \Phi_V) \leq y_{p_2} \leq y((X_{P_2}, Y_{P_2}, Z_{max}(X_{P_2}, Y_{P_2})), \Psi_{p_1,p_2}, \Phi_V),$$
respectively. The two intervals do not overlap if

$$\Phi_V > \arctan(\frac{Z_{max}(X_{P_1}, Y_{P_1})}{\sqrt{(Y_{P_1} - Y_{P_2})^2 + (X_{P_1} - X_{P_2})^2}}) = \Phi_{min}(p_1, p_2) \ . \qquad (3)$$

---

[3] v_i lies on the line $y_{\Psi_{V_2},n}$.

If p_2 is a vertex then for the viewing direction $(\Psi_{p_1,p_2}, \Phi_V > \Phi_{min}(p_1, p_2))$ the scene at the location (X_{P_1}, Y_{P_1}) does not occlude P_2. If p_1 is a vertex then for $(\Psi_{p_1,p_2}, \Phi_V > \Phi_{min}(p_1, p_2))$, we can distinguish the projection of P_1 from the projections of the points at (X_{P_2}, Y_{P_2}) [3]. Taking into account Z_{max} for each scene location the new azimuth and elevation angles can be computed.

6 Determining the Next Viewing Direction

For the next viewing direction we must determine the azimuth and the elevation value. The selection of azimuth has a dominant role.

First we build a histogram $\mathcal{H}(\psi)$ which shows the number of vertices that can be determined for any azimuth value $\psi \in [0, 2\pi)$.

One possible solution is to select as the next azimuth value the one from which the largest number of vertices can be determined, i.e., ψ for which $\mathcal{H}(\psi)$ has a global maximum. Another possible solution to the problem is first to analyze the histogram $\mathcal{H}(\psi)$ and find the necessary number of viewing directions from which we can compute the Z coordinate of all the vertices, and then select among them the one from which the largest number of vertices can be determined. Due to the lack of space the reader is referred to [3].

7 Experimental Results

A scene consists of two rectangloids and two pyramids. In the image of the first view (Fig. 4(a)) we locate 16 vertices. For each vertex we compute the azimuth angle and build the histogram (Fig. 4(b)). For Ψ_{V_2} we choose the value from one of the histogram maxima: $\Psi_{V_2} = 270, 5°$. Φ_{V_2} can be any value from the interval $[0, \frac{\pi}{2})$. We choose $\Phi_{V_2} = 76.5°$. From this view we can determine the Z coordinates of six vertices marked by circles, as shown in Fig. 4(c). Fig. 5(a) shows the image taken from the second view. Fig. 5(b) depicts the y_{max_2} coordinates from which we can get the Z_{max} coordinates. We compute new azimuth angles for the remaining 10 vertices. Fig. 5(c) depicts the new histogram. Two additional

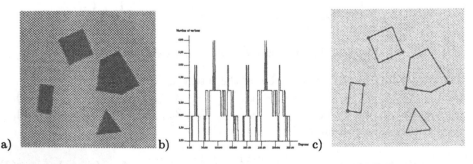

a) b) c)

Fig. 4. (a) Image of the scene taken from the first view, (b) Histogram showing the number of vertices for which the Z coordinate can be determined with respect to the azimuth value, (c) Six selected vertices.

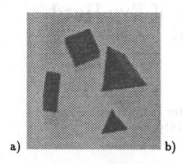 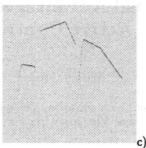 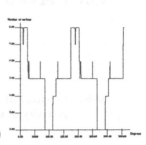

a) b) c)

Fig. 5. (a) The image of the scene taken from the second viewing direction, (b) y_{max_2} coordinates, (c) Histogram of remaining 10 vertices.

images must be acquired to accomplish the task: one azimuth value must be selected from the interval $(175°, 189°)$ or $(355°, 9°)$, another from the interval $(27°, 85°)$ or $(207°, 265°)$. We choose as the third azimuth value $\Psi_{V_3} = 2°$. For the vertices v_i which are selected by this azimuth we compute the minimal elevation $\Phi_{min}(v_i)$. Elevation must be $\Phi_{V_3} > \max_i(\Phi_{min}(v_i))$. We compute: $\Phi_{V_3} > 67°$.

8 Conclusion

In this paper we explored the issue of selecting the optimal set of views from which the viewer can determine the 3-D coordinates of convex vertices of objects silhouettes. However, the information acquired in the set of images is much richer—we also get the limits of the height of each object point in the scene, Z_{max}[4]. This information can be helpful in many robotic tasks to avoid collisions of robot arm with the objects in the scene. The method can also be extended to non-polyhedral scenes. In that case the foci of attention can be the convex parts of object silhouettes.

References

[1] J. Aloimonos and A. Bandyopadhyay, "Active Vision," In *Proc. of the IEEE 1 st Int. Conf. on Computer Vision*, pp. 35–54, June 1987.

[2] R. Bajcsy, "Active Perception", In *Proc. of the IEEE*, vol.76, no.8, pp. 996–1005, August 1988.

[3] J. Maver, *Planning the Next View Using the Max-Min Principle*, University of Ljubljana, Faculty of EE and CS, Tech. report LRV-93-4, 1993.

[4] J. Maver and R. Bajcsy, "Occlusions as a Guide for Planning the Next View," *IEEE Trans. on Pattern Anal. and Machine Intell.*, vol.15 no.5, pp. 417–433, 1993.

[5] D. Wilkes and J. K. Tsotsos, "Active Object Recognition," In *Proc. of the CVPR'92*, pp. 136–141, 1992

[6] J. Y. Zheng, F. Kishino, Q. Chen, and S. Tsuji, "Active Camera Controlling for Manipulation," In *Proc. of the CVPR'91*, pp. 413–418, 1991.

---

[4] That is true even though the point is occluded in all subsequent views.

On Perceptual Advantages of Eye-Head Active Control

Enrico Grosso

DIST, Department of Communication, Computer and System Sciences
University of Genoa, Via Opera Pia 11a, 16145 Genoa, Italy

Abstract. The paper presents a theoretical study on the perceptual advantages related to the active control of a binocular vision system. In particular the presentation focuses on the process of *improving perception*, a task strategically important in humans and many vertebrates. The analysis is based on an anthropomorphic system; the sensitivity of the transformation from world to camera coordinates is used as a cost function for driving the movements of the eye-head system. The control strategy obtained in this way allows to formally motivate, outside of a purely behavioral context, some relevant aspects of the biological vision like fixation, vergence and eye-head compensation.

Keywords: robot vision, eye-head coordination, vision based control.

1 Introduction

The development of new paradigms for vision [2, 1, 3] is gradually demonstrating the intimate relationship existing between vision and movement. In many cases visual perception can take advantage of an active movement of the visual system. On one hand, movement can be conceived as a strategy to simplify and improve the efficiency of computational processes, in relation to the fact that some essential parameters can be easily estimated, and ill posed vision problems become well posed for a moving observer [1, 8]. On the other hand, moving and interacting with the environment can be considered in a behavioral context as a key issue to solve problems and satisfy specific purposes [3, 7].

In this paper we show that active gaze control is important in relation to the possibility of *ameliorating perception*, despite noise and uncertainties in the system parameters. In other words, it is argued that basic visual behaviors, like for instance fixation, admit a simple explanation in term of perceptual robustness, besides common computational or behavioral interpretations. This robustness issue is of course very important if visual feedback is used to control the movements of a mechanical device [11, 5] and can be related to the criteria usually adopted designing robotic heads.

A formal analysis is presented for a binocular anthropomorphic system. The transformation from world to camera coordinates is investigated and the sensitivity of this transformation is evaluated, both in relation to static and dynamic information. It is demonstrated that fixation, vergence and compensatory movements of the head can sensibly improve spatial perception. The importance of fixation is furthermore analyzed in the case of perception of relative distances.

This research has been supported by the VAP - ESPRIT Basic Research Project.

2   Preliminaries

The anthropomorphic system considered in this paper is composed by a moving head and two moving cameras. Figure 1 shows the kinematic structure of the system and the position of the left, right and central (head) frames. A generic inertial reference frame is denoted by $< e >$.

The notation used throughout this paper is basically that used in [9, 10]. We

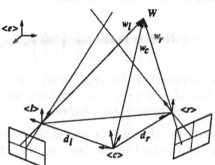

Fig. 1. Schematic representation of the head-eye reference frames.

Fig. 2. Schematic picture showing the effect of rotation and translation of the central system on the vergence angle.

denote by $^aw = (^ax, \, ^ay, \, ^az)^t$ the projection of the vector w in the frame $< a >$ and by ^b_aR the rotation matrix from the frame $< a >$ to the frame $< b >$.

Considering the pin hole model for the cameras [12] and denoting by (u, v) the image plane coordinates we can write:

$$\begin{cases} ^lx_l + \bar{u}_l \, ^lz_l = 0 \\ ^ly_l + \bar{v}_l \, ^lz_l = 0 \\ ^rx_r + \bar{u}_r \, ^rz_r = 0 \\ ^ry_r + \bar{v}_r \, ^rz_r = 0 \end{cases} \quad \begin{aligned} \bar{u}_l = \frac{u_l - u_{0l}}{\alpha_{ul}} \quad & \bar{v}_l = \frac{v_l - v_{0l}}{\alpha_{vl}} \\ \bar{u}_r = \frac{u_r - u_{0r}}{\alpha_{ur}} \quad & \bar{v}_r = \frac{v_r - v_{0r}}{\alpha_{vr}} \end{aligned} \tag{1}$$

where the indices l and r stand for left and right camera, respectively. The parameters α and u are usually called "intrinsic" because they define the internal structure of the cameras. Referring to figure 1, the position of a generic point W in space is given by:

$$\begin{aligned} ^lw_l &= \, ^l_cR \, ^cw_l = \, ^l_cR \, (\, ^cw_c - \, ^cd_l \,) \\ ^rw_r &= \, ^r_cR \, ^cw_r = \, ^r_cR \, (\, ^cw_c - \, ^cd_r \,) \end{aligned} \tag{2}$$

Vectors ^cd_l and ^cd_r define the position of the optical centers of the cameras with respect to the central frame $< c >$. They are usually referred, together with the rotation matrices ^l_cR and ^r_cR, as "extrinsic" parameters.

It is worth noting that the estimation of points and objects in the 3D space is an inverse problem typical in stereo vision [9]. This obviously depends on the model of the sensing system and on the uncertainties on the parameters of this model. However, it is very interesting to observe that stereo estimates are also *space dependent*. In other words, assuming different postures in space, the visual system can obtain different measures of the same physical quantity.

3 The Vision Problem

It is quite easy to show that equations (1) and (2) are sufficient to solve the inverse problem of locating a given point W with respect to the frame $< c >$ [9]. Assuming a perfect knowledge on both extrinsic and intrinsic parameters, we first define the matrices $J_l = \begin{bmatrix} 1 & 0 & \bar{u}_l \\ 0 & 1 & \bar{v}_l \end{bmatrix}$ and $J_r = \begin{bmatrix} 1 & 0 & \bar{u}_r \\ 0 & 1 & \bar{v}_r \end{bmatrix}$. Then, using equations (1) and (2), $^c w_c$ can be computed solving the following over-determined set of linear equations:

$$\begin{bmatrix} J_l & 0 \\ 0 & J_r \end{bmatrix} \begin{bmatrix} ^l_c R & 0 \\ 0 & ^r_c R \end{bmatrix} \begin{bmatrix} I_3 \\ I_3 \end{bmatrix} \, ^c w_c = \begin{bmatrix} J_l & 0 \\ 0 & J_r \end{bmatrix} \begin{bmatrix} ^l_c R & 0 \\ 0 & ^r_c R \end{bmatrix} \begin{bmatrix} ^c d_l \\ ^c d_r \end{bmatrix} \tag{3}$$

Remark 1 *It is straightforward to demonstrate that, for any bounded measurement, equation (3) always admits solution if and only if w_l and w_r are not parallel. The uniqueness of the solution derives from linear algebra.* □

Let us now assume to be able to measure the time derivatives of the terms in (1). Differentiating equations (1) and (2) and eliminating $^l \dot{w}_l$ and $^r \dot{w}_r$ we obtain:

$$\begin{bmatrix} -\frac{1}{^l z_l} J_l & 0 \\ 0 & -\frac{1}{^r z_r} J_r \end{bmatrix} \begin{bmatrix} ^l_c R & 0 \\ 0 & ^r_c R \end{bmatrix} \begin{bmatrix} I_3 \\ I_3 \end{bmatrix} \, ^c \dot{w}_c = \begin{bmatrix} \dot{\bar{u}}_l \\ \dot{\bar{v}}_l \\ \dot{\bar{u}}_r \\ \dot{\bar{v}}_r \end{bmatrix} +$$

$$\begin{bmatrix} -\frac{1}{^l z_l} J_l & 0 \\ 0 & -\frac{1}{^r z_r} J_r \end{bmatrix} \begin{bmatrix} ^l_c R & 0 \\ 0 & ^r_c R \end{bmatrix} \begin{bmatrix} C(^c w_c - ^c d_l) & 0 \\ 0 & C(^c w_c - ^c d_r) \end{bmatrix} \begin{bmatrix} ^l \Omega_l \\ ^r \Omega_r \end{bmatrix} \tag{4}$$

where Ω_l and Ω_r are the angular velocities of the frames $< l >$ and $< r >$, respectively, and $C(u)$ is the operational matrix of the vector product.

Remark 2 *Equations (3) and (4) represent our complete inverse model. They give an interesting example of the extent of the problem which involves a large number of parameters and position/velocity measures. In particular, it is clear that equation (4) depends upon the solution of equation (3), since there explicitly appears $^c w_c$.* □

4 Sensitivity Analysis

Both (3) and (4) are overdetermined sets of linear equations in the unknowns $^c w_c$ and $^c \dot{w}_c$. Since in practice noise and parameters uncertainties perturb the solution it is interesting to investigate the effect of these perturbations [6]. Consider first the system (3) and write it in the canonical form:

$$A \, B \, x = A \, b \tag{5}$$

$$A = \begin{bmatrix} J_l & 0 \\ 0 & J_r \end{bmatrix} \begin{bmatrix} ^l_c R & 0 \\ 0 & ^r_c R \end{bmatrix} \in \Re^{4x6} \quad B = \begin{bmatrix} I_3 \\ I_3 \end{bmatrix} \in \Re^{6x3} \quad b = \begin{bmatrix} ^c d_l \\ ^c d_r \end{bmatrix} \in \Re^6 \tag{6}$$

Assume that the system admits a solution x_0, that is $\| A \, B \, x_0 - A \, b = 0 \|$, and that this solution is unique. Then, following the rationale reported in [6] and provided that $\|\delta A\| \leq \frac{1}{2}\sigma_{min}(AB)$ the perturbation can be bounded by:

$$\frac{\|\delta x\|}{\|x_0\|} \leq \left\|(A\ B)^\dagger\right\| \|\delta A\| \left(\|B\| + \frac{\|b\|}{\|x_0\|}\right) + \left\|(A\ B)^\dagger\right\| \|A\| \frac{\|\delta b\|}{\|x_0\|} \quad (7)$$

Note that in the above equations $M^\dagger$ indicates the pseudo-inverse of the matrix M while $\sigma_{min}(M)$ denotes the minimum singular value.

Remark 3 *From the expression above we derive two important hints for the solution of the stereo vision problem. First of all it is important to minimize the effect of $\|b\|$ and $\|\delta b\|$ with respect to $\|x_0\|$. We will skip over a detailed analysis of this aspect but it is clear that the position of the central system can be constrained in this sense. Then, it is important to understand the structural properties of A, δA and $(A\ B)^\dagger$.* □

From a general point of view we have to consider three sources of uncertainty. The first is due to uncertainties in the intrinsic parameters and it obviously depends on the camera calibration procedure. In our analysis it appears in the matrices J_l and J_r and then in A. The second is due to uncertainties in the extrinsic parameters, essentially related to the mechanical calibration of the system. It appears in the matrices ${}^c_l R$ and ${}^c_r R$ and in the vectors ${}^c d_l$ and ${}^c d_r$. Finally we have to consider measurements errors hidden in J_l and J_r. Following sections will analyze in detail equation (7), describing the contribution of the various terms.

4.1 Explaining Fixation

Consider first the contribution of the term $\|\delta A\|$. We have immediately:

$$\|\delta A\| \leq \left\|\begin{matrix} J_l & 0 \\ 0 & J_r \end{matrix}\right\| \left\|\begin{matrix} \delta_c^l R & 0 \\ 0 & \delta_c^r R \end{matrix}\right\| + \left\|\begin{matrix} \delta J_l & 0 \\ 0 & \delta J_r \end{matrix}\right\| \doteq \|J\| \left\|\begin{matrix} \delta_c^l R & 0 \\ 0 & \delta_c^r R \end{matrix}\right\| + \|\delta J\| \quad (8)$$

The perturbation of the rotational components depends only on the calibration errors; this means that we have simply to compute the norm of the matrices J and δJ:

$$\|J\| = max\left(\sqrt{1 + (\bar{u}_l^2 + \bar{v}_l^2)}, \sqrt{1 + \left(\bar{u}_r^2 + \bar{v}_r^2\right)}\right)$$

$$\|\delta J\| = max\left(\sqrt{\delta\bar{u}_l^2 + \delta\bar{v}_l^2}, \sqrt{\delta\bar{u}_r^2 + \delta\bar{v}_r^2}\right)$$

Remark 4 *On the base of the above discussion we can affirm that for bounded calibration errors $\|\delta A\|$ is minimized by $\bar{u}_l = \bar{v}_l = \bar{u}_r = \bar{v}_r = 0$.*
The above result defines an important specification for the movements of the eyes. In fact it states that w_l and w_r must be preferably aligned with the optical axes of the cameras. In other words, fixation makes minimum the measurement error and, as a consequence, ameliorates 3D perception of the external world. □

It is worth noting that, due to the structure of the matrix A, we have immediately $\|A\| \leq \|J\|$. Then, the bound of $\|A\|$ is minimum under the same assumptions of remark 4.

4.2 Explaining vergence and head compensation

The term $\left\|(A\,B)^\dagger\right\|$ in equation (7) is very important because it has the effect of multiplying the perturbations on measures and system parameters. We have:

$$\left\|(A\,B)^\dagger\right\| = max_i \sqrt{\sigma_i\left((A\,B)^\dagger\,(A\,B)^{\dagger^t}\right)} = \left(min_i\sqrt{\sigma_i\,(B^t\,A^t A\,B)}\right)^{-1} \quad (9)$$

The minimization of expression (9) is based on linear algebra and can be found in [4]. We give here the main result, which depends on the relative rotation between the optical axes of the two cameras:

$$\sigma_{min}(B^t\,A^t A\,B) = 1 - |\cos\theta|$$

where, by definition, $\cos\theta = \frac{w_l \cdot w_r}{\|w_l\| \cdot \|w_r\|}$

Remark 5 *From equation (9) and the above result follows that the norm is minimized when $|\cos\theta|$ is minimum. This happens in particular in two cases:*

1. *Approaching the object while fixating; this implies a translational motion of the central system and makes the expression $|\cos\theta|$ decreasing.*
2. *Rotating the baseline, so as to bring the cameras in a symmetric position with respect to the target point (figure 2).* □

In summary, we can affirm that the analysis presented in this section demonstrates the importance of gaze control. From a more anthropomorphic perspective it explains two interesting behaviors. First of all it motivates *vergence movements*, in the sense that a symmetric movement of the eyes maintains the position at "minimum norm" once reached. Secondly, it explains compensatory movements of the head. These movements could be specifically devoted to maximize the vergence angle, independently from the fixation task performed by the eyes.

Remark 6 *Using equation (4) it is possible to demonstrate that also in the dynamic case good perception is guaranteed by using fixation. In other words, using a static vision system to deal with dynamic quantities is always a bad choice, independently from the ability of estimating intrinsic and extrinsic parameters. However, note that in the dynamic case it is impossible to derive a simple result on the vergence angle, equivalent to that presented in this section.* □

5 Measuring relative distances

In this section we briefly analyze the problem of estimating relative distances by using relative information on the image plain. Using the notation of section 4 and denoting by the indices 1 and 2 the quantities related to two different points in space we can write in canonical form:

$$A_1\,B\,x = A_1\,b \qquad\qquad A_2\,B\,(x + \Delta x) = A_2\,b$$

Denoting by ΔA the difference between A_2 and A_1 we obtain, by difference:

$$A_2\,B\,\Delta x = \Delta A\,(b - B\,x)$$

and, applying sensitivity analysis:

$$\frac{\|\delta\Delta x\|}{\|\Delta x_0\|} \leq \left\|(A_2\ B)^\dagger\right\| \left(f\left(\|\delta\Delta A\|,\ \|\Delta A\|\right) + \|\delta A_2\|\ \|B\|\right) \tag{10}$$

It is clear that a good observation strategy consists again in fixating one of the two points (the second one), minimizing $\left\|(A_2\ B)^\dagger\right\|$ and $\|\delta A_2\|$. The remaining terms (here generically denoted by f) depend on the relative quantities measured on the images and can be only marginally influenced by an active control of the eye-head system.

6 Conclusions

In this paper the problem of the coordinated movement of an eye-head system has been faced. The solution outlined is based on the fact that in an active system the position of the visual sensors can be controlled in order to gather optimal measurements, and this independently from the knowledge of the intrinsic and extrinsic parameters of the system itself. The analysis demonstrates the importance of fixation and eye-head compensation estimating dynamic quantities or relative distances between points in space.

References

1. J. Aloimonos, I. Weiss, and A. Bandyopadhyay. Active vision. *International Journal of Computer Vision*, 1(4):333–356, 1988.
2. R. K. Bajcsy. Active perception vs passive perception. In *Proc. Third IEEE Computer Society Workshop on Computer Vision: Representation and Control*, pages 13–16, Bellaire, MI, 1985.
3. D.H. Ballard and C. M. Brown. Principles of animate vision. *CVGIP*, 56(1):3–21, July 1992.
4. G. Cannata and E. Grosso. Active eye-head control. Technical Report LIRA-Lab TR-4-93, University of Genova, Genova, Italy, October 1993.
5. B. Espiau, F. Chaumette, and P. Rives. A new approach to visual servoing in robotics. *IEEE Transactions on Robotics and Automation*, 8(3):313–326, June 1992.
6. G. H. Golub and C. F. Van Loan. *Matrix Computations*. The John Hopkins University Press, Baltimore, USA, 1989.
7. E. Grosso and D.H. Ballard. Head-centered orientation strategies in animate vision. In *3rd Internatiional Conference on Computer Vision*, Berlin - Germany, 1993.
8. E. Grosso, M. Tistarelli, and G. Sandini. Active/dynamic stereo for navigation. In *Proc. of Second European Conference on Computer Vision*, S. Margherita Ligure, Italy, May 1992.
9. B. K. P. Horn. *Robot Vision*. MIT Press, Cambridge, USA, 1986.
10. A.J. Koivo. *Fundamentals of Robotic Manipulators*. Wiley, New York - NY, USA, 1989.
11. N.P. Papanikolopoulos, P.K. Khosla, and T.Kanade. Visual tracking of a moving target by a camera mounted on a robot: A combination of control and vision. *IEEE Trans. Robotics Automation*, 9(1):14–35, 1993.
12. G. Toscani and O.D. Faugeras. The calibration problem for stereo. In *IEEE Conference on Comp. Vision and Pattern Recognition*, Miami - FL, USA, 1986. IEEE Comp. Soc.

Matching and Registration

Improving Registration of 3-D Medical Images Using a Mechanical Based Method

Grégoire Malandain[1], Sara Fernández-Vidal[1] and Jean-Marie Rocchisani[2]

[1] INRIA - Project Epidaure - 2004 Route des Lucioles, BP 93
06902 Sophia Antipolis Cedex, France
[2] Hôpital Avicenne - Service de Médecine Nucléaire - 125 rue de Stalingrad
93000 Bobigny, France

Abstract. The registration of 3-D objects is an important problem in the medical imaging field. The problem arises with two images of the same modality taken from different positions or taken at different times (before and after an operation for example) or with two images of different modalities. We present a new method for computing the rigid transformation between two objects: we study the motion of a solid in a potential field instead of minimizing explicitly an energy. This article addresses a theoretical improvement of the method described in [1], some additional features like the undersampling of data or the multi-potentials approach. We present experimental results with real 3-D medical images.

1 Introduction

The rigid registration of 3-D objects is an important problem in medical imaging as well in computer vision, as it permits to put together multi-modal data (to combine anatomical and physiological information) or data acquired on separate occasions (to quantify an evolution of a pathology, or an observer motion).

Functions with respect to voxel intensity have been proposed to maximize a similarity index [2] or to minimize the variance of image ratio. Those techniques give good results for physiological imaging modalities (Single Photon Emission Computed Tomography (SPECT) or Positon Emitting Tomography (PET)) but have not been applied to others images.

External markers (points on a stereotaxic frame which can be viewed in several modalities) or internal landmarks (some particular anatomical points, like blood vessel bifurcations), have been widely studied. Each method has its own disadvantages. External markers need the patient to carry a stereotaxic frame between both acquisitions. Internal landmarks often need a manual detection, whose accuracy depends on image resolution.

A local matching, based on crest lines, is described in [3]. It is a feature based method more robust to noise, resolution and anatomical variations, but it works only for good quality and high resolution images.

Iterative methods provide an alternative to the above techniques. By pairing points of both sets to register [4] or computing the distance of a point of one set to the other [5], one may iteratively compute a transformation which minimize the distances of points of one set to the closest points of the other. This last class of methods requires that both objects to register are already segmented and that there exists a function to evaluate the closest point of one object (or the distance of one object) to a given point.

This paper presents such a general iterative method for the registration of 3-D objects. Its originality stems from its mechanical bases: instead of minimizing a potential energy with respect to transformation parameters, which is the common approach, we study the motion of a rigid object in a potential field.

2 Motion of a Solid in a Potential Field

The main idea of our approach is not to minimize explicitly an energy (based on the distance between both objects to register) but to study the motion of a solid ubject to a potential field: this motion derives from the force field generated by the potential field. Since we are looking for a rigid transformation, both objects to register may be considered as solids. We will use laws of mechanics in order to study the motion of one of them with respect to the other.

The parameters of the rigid transformation will be stored in the translation vector t and the rotation vector r. A first order evolution of the transformation parameters, as used in [1], is not rigorous enough: as a matter of fact, the first derivatives of t and r do not depend directly on forces that apply to the solid. We propose here a second order evolution of these parameters:

$$\begin{cases} t_{t+dt} = t_t + \dot{t}_t \, dt + \ddot{t}_t \, \frac{dt^2}{2} \\ r_{t+dt} = r_t + \dot{r}_t \, dt + \ddot{r}_t \, \frac{dt^2}{2} \end{cases} \tag{1}$$

where the dot and the double dot denote respectively the first and the second derivatives with respect to the time. In the following, we will first discuss the potential field generated by a static solid, denoted S_{sta}, and second present the equations governing the motion of a solid in a force field.

2.1 The Potential and the Force fields

The potential field, generated by a static solid S_{sta} in a given point M will be denoted by $p(M, S_{sta})$. We choose $p(M, S_{sta}) = \frac{(d(M, S_{sta}))^2}{2}$ where $d(M, S_{sta})$ is the distance of M to the closest point M_s of S_{sta}. If there is no ambiguity, we denote shortly $p(M, S_{sta})$ and $d(M, S_{sta})$ by $p(M)$ and $d(M)$.

The induced force field f_p has the general form $f_p(M) = -\nabla p(M)$, which leads here to $f_p(M) = -d(M)\nabla d(M)$ where ∇ is the gradient operator. The distance field $d(M)$ may be precomputed, approximately with chamfer distances [6] or rigorously [7].

Moreover, as we have the equality $d(M)\nabla d(M) = \overrightarrow{M_s M}$ if the function d is derivable in M, we may use either a distance field or an estimate of the closest point to compute the value of the force field in M.

2.2 Mechanical Theory Elements

Center of Mass and Inertia matrix. The center of mass G of a solid S can be computed by:

$$\int_{P \in S} P \, dm(P) = m(S) \, G \quad \text{with} \quad m(S) = \int_{P \in S} dm(P)$$

where $m(S)$ is the whole mass of S and $dm(P)$ is the elementary mass associated to any point $P \in S$.

The inertia matrix $\mathbf{J}(Q)$ of S with respect to a point Q is given by:

$$\mathbf{J}(Q) = \begin{bmatrix} \int_{P \in S}(y^2 + z^2)\, dm(P) & -\int_{P \in S} xy\, dm(P) & -\int_{P \in S} zx\, dm(P) \\ -\int_{P \in S} xy\, dm(P) & \int_{P \in S}(z^2 + x^2)\, dm(P) & -\int_{P \in S} yz\, dm(P) \\ -\int_{P \in S} zx\, dm(P) & -\int_{P \in S} yz\, dm(P) & \int_{P \in S}(x^2 + y^2)\, dm(P) \end{bmatrix}$$

where (x, y, z) are the coordinates of the vector $\overrightarrow{QP}$ in an orthonormal basis (X, Y, Z). The eigenvectors of this matrix give the principal axes of the solid S.

Kinematics. The velocity field of a solid S is described by the velocity of the center of mass G of S: $\mathbf{v}(G) = \dot{G}$, and the kinetic moment with respect to a point Q: $\sigma(Q) = \int_{P \in S} \overrightarrow{QP} \times \mathbf{v}(P)\, dm(P)$ where $\times$ is the vector product. Likewise, the acceleration field of S is described by the acceleration of G: $\gamma(G) = \ddot{G}$ and the dynamic moment with respect to Q: $\delta(Q) = \int_S \overrightarrow{QP} \times \gamma(P)\, dm(P)$.

When kinetic and dynamic moments are expressed with respect to G, we have the following equalities: $\sigma(G) = \mathbf{J}(G)\, \omega$, where ω is the angular velocity vector of the solid S, and $\delta(G) = \dot{\sigma}(G)$.

Force and Torque. If the solid S is submitted to a force field, like the one defined in Sect. 2.1, we are able to compute the whole force $\mathbf{f}$ and the torque $\mathbf{m}$ acting on it:

$$\mathbf{f} = \int_S \mathbf{f}_p(P)\, dv(P) \quad \text{and} \quad \mathbf{m}(Q) = \int_S \overrightarrow{QP} \times \mathbf{f}_p(P)\, dv(P)$$

where $dv(P)$ is the elementary volume associated to any point $P \in S$.

Newton's equation relates the linear acceleration of the center of mass G to the whole force acting on the solid S, whereas the Euler equation relates the dynamic moment to the torque acting on S.

2.3 Transformation Parameters

We will now relate the derivatives of $\mathbf{t}$ and $\mathbf{r}$ to kinematics elements. We express the rotation with respect to G, let P be in S, we have: $\overrightarrow{GP} = \mathbf{R}\,\overrightarrow{G_0 P_0}$ where $\mathbf{R}$ denotes the rotation matrix and indices 0 the points P and G at their initial positions at $t = 0$. The translation vector is then defined by: $\mathbf{t} = \overrightarrow{G_0 G}$.

Derivatives of the translation vector are obvious: $\dot{\mathbf{t}} = \mathbf{v}(G)$ and $\ddot{\mathbf{t}} = \gamma(G)$.

Derivatives of the rotation vector are more difficult to relate to kinematics elements. First, we estimate the derivative of the rotation matrix: $\dot{\mathbf{R}} = \mathbf{X}(\omega)\mathbf{R}$ where $\mathbf{X}(\omega)$ is the matrix associated with the vector product by ω.

In [8], Ayache has already established that the form of the derivative of the rotation matrix is: $\frac{d\mathbf{R}}{dq} = \mathbf{X}(\mathbf{s})\mathbf{R}$ with $\mathbf{s} = \mathbf{H}(\mathbf{r}) \frac{d\mathbf{r}}{dq}$ and

$$\mathbf{H}(\mathbf{r}) = \begin{bmatrix} h(\theta)\mathbf{r}_x^2 + f(\theta) & h(\theta)\mathbf{r}_x\mathbf{r}_y - g(\theta)\mathbf{r}_z & h(\theta)\mathbf{r}_x\mathbf{r}_z + g(\theta)\mathbf{r}_y \\ h(\theta)\mathbf{r}_x\mathbf{r}_y + g(\theta)\mathbf{r}_z & h(\theta)\mathbf{r}_y^2 + f(\theta) & h(\theta)\mathbf{r}_y\mathbf{r}_z - g(\theta)\mathbf{r}_x \\ h(\theta)\mathbf{r}_x\mathbf{r}_z - g(\theta)\mathbf{r}_y & h(\theta)\mathbf{r}_y\mathbf{r}_z + g(\theta)\mathbf{r}_x & h(\theta)\mathbf{r}_z^2 + f(\theta) \end{bmatrix}$$

$$\theta = \|\mathbf{r}\| \quad ; \quad f(\theta) = \frac{\sin\theta}{\theta} \quad ; \quad g(\theta) = \frac{1 - \cos\theta}{\theta^2} \quad ; \quad h(\theta) = \frac{1 - f(\theta)}{\theta^2} .$$

Then we get the first derivative of the rotation vector: $\dot{\mathbf{r}} = \mathbf{H}(\mathbf{r})^{-1}\omega$.
The second derivative of rotation vector is obtained by deriving the above equation, and we get:

$$\ddot{\mathbf{r}} = \mathbf{H}(\mathbf{r})^{-1} \left(\mathbf{J}(G)^{-1} \left[\delta(G) - \mathbf{X}(\omega)\,\sigma(G) \right] - \left[\dot{\mathbf{r}}^2\, h(\theta) + \frac{(\mathbf{r}.\dot{\mathbf{r}})^2}{\theta^2} [g(\theta) - 3h(\theta)] \right] \mathbf{r} \right.$$
$$\left. - (\mathbf{r}.\dot{\mathbf{r}})\left[2h(\theta) - g(\theta)\right] \dot{\mathbf{r}} - \frac{\mathbf{r}.\dot{\mathbf{r}}}{\theta^2} [f(\theta) - 2g(\theta)]\, \mathbf{r} \times \dot{\mathbf{r}} \right) .$$

3 Heuristic for a Potential Minimization

The motion of a solid in a potential field, deriving from (1) and other equations of Sect. 2 has no reason to lead to a minimum of potential. In fact, the whole system energy does not change and the system can not stop. By analogy, the motion looks like the one of a non damped pendulum. We present here a heuristic method to recover the potential minimum.

1. At time t, we compute the whole force $\mathbf{f}$ and the torque $\mathbf{m}(G)$ acting on S.
2. We compute the transformation parameters to reach the new position at time $t + dt$.
3. We compare the potential energies E_p at times t and $t + dt$:
   (a) If $E_{p,t+dt} < E_{p,t}$, the motion is always directed towards a minimum, we go to step 1 with $t = t + dt$.
   (b) If $E_{p,t+dt} \geq E_{p,t}$, we know that we passed a potential minimum.
      i. If the velocities at time t are not null, we set them to zero (i.e. we set the kinetic energy to zero at time t) and we go to step 2.
      ii. If the velocities at time t are already null, we look at smaller displacements by decreasing dt. If dt becomes too small, we stop the algorithm, else we go to step 2.

4 Improvements

Even though our algorithm converge to a local minimum of potential, it may or may not converge on the global minimum, i.e. the desired minimum. Consequently, we have to improve the robustness of the algorithm with respect to local minima and/or try different start positions in order to find the desired global minimum [4, 5].

Multi-Potentials Minimization. Iterative methods of matching are useful when we have not point-to-point correspondences between both objects to register. However, we can take advantage of the fact that, in the two objects, there are sets of points that have the same features (geometrical or topological properties): for instance, in case of complex 3-D objects made of surfaces, we may distinguish surface points from junction points [9].

We first classify points of both objects before the matching process. Each class of S_{sta} will generate a separate distance map. Points of the moving solid will be attracted by points of the same class: it means there is a different force field associated to each class of points.

Our experiments show that this multi-potentials minimization leads to a better accuracy of the results and allows some local minima to be avoided.

Undersampling of Data. If several start positions will be used to initiate the algorithm, the computational cost of the algorithm has to be decreased to be still efficient. A hierarchical approach addresses this particular problem.

To undersample the moving solid, a block of $e_x.e_y.e_z$ voxels from the initial image is collected. This block should be used to form a voxel in an undersampled image: if the block is non-empty, then the new voxel belongs to the undersampled moving solid. However, as we deals with mechanics, we provide an undersampling method adapted to our algorithm. We associate to the block a point with real coordinates (its center of mass) and an elementary mass equal to the sum of all elementary masses of the block. Thus, the whole mass and the center of mass of the undersampled points are the ones of the initial image. Moreover, we do not compute the inertia matrix of the undersampled points, but we keep the one of the initial image. Then, we make sure that the inertia parameters are preserved.

For the static solid, we have the choice between undersampling the initial image before computing a distance map and undersampling a distance map computed at the finest level. The first solution needs to compute a distance map at each level of the hierarchy, but makes sure to preserve a minimum when a resolution change occurs [5]. However, a minimum can be preserved by undersampling directly a distance map computed at the finest level: a block of $e_x.e_y.e_z$ voxels of the distance map is collected to form a voxel in the undersampled image, whose value is the minimum of the $e_x.e_y.e_z$ values of the block. Then, we have to compute only one distance map (at the finest level) and we can then deduce from it the distance maps at the coarser levels.

5 Conclusion

A 3-D registration algorithm has been described in this paper. its originality stems from its mechanical bases: instead of minimizing a potential energy with respect to transformation parameters, which is the common approach, we study the motion of a rigid object in a potential field.

Introducing a second order evolution of the transformation parameters leads to a considerable theoretical improvement of the method already described in [1].

Additional features, like multi-potentials minimization or undersampling of data, which take advantage of the mechanical nature of the algorithm, increase the robustness of the method: some local minima may be avoided, and several start positions may be tested by a hierarchical approach.

This method can be used to register any 3-D objects, if there exists a function to evaluate the closest point of one object (or the distance of one object) to a given point. We use it for registration between either mono-modality or multi-modalities images. Results on real images have shown the accuracy and the utility of the method (see Fig. 1).

Our future work will include a complete comparison of this method with some other matching algorithms, the study of the accuracy of the final registration and a bench test on several images.

136

Acknowledgment

This work was partially supported by Digital Equipment Corporation. We thank Dr. Jael Travère (Cyceron Center, CEA, Caen, France) for providing medical data.

References

1. G. Malandain and J.M. Rocchisani. Registration of 3-D medical images using a mechanical based method. In *EMBS satellite symposium on 3-D advanced image processing in medicine*, Rennes, France, November 2–4 1992. IEEE.
2. A. Venot, J.F. Lebruchec, and J.C. Roucayrol. A new class of similarity measures for robust image registration. *CVGIP*, 28:176–184, 1984.
3. J-P Thirion, O. Monga, S. Benayoun, A. Guéziec, and N. Ayache. Automatic registration of 3-D images using surface curvature. In *IEEE Int. Symp. on Optical Applied Science and Engineering*, San-Diego, July 1992.
4. P.J. Besl and N.D. McKay. A method for registration of 3-D shapes. *IEEE Transactions on Pattern Analysis and Machine Intelligence*, 14:239–256, February 1992.
5. G. Borgefors. Hierarchical chamfer matching: A parametric edge matching algorithm. *IEEE Transactions on PAMI*, 10(6):849–865, november 1988.
6. G. Borgefors. Distance transformations in digital images. *Computer Vision, Graphics, and Image Processing*, 34:344–371, 1986.
7. P.E. Danielsson. Euclidean distance mapping. *CGIP*, 14:227–248, 1980.
8. N. Ayache. *Artificial vision for mobile robots: stereo vision and multisensory perception*. MIT Press, 1991.
9. G. Malandain, G. Bertrand, and N. Ayache. Topological segmentation of discrete surfaces. *International Journal of Computer Vision*, 10(2):183–197, 1993.

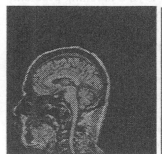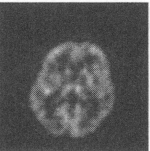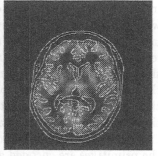

Fig. 1. From left to right: one slice of a 256x256x120 MRI brain image (the brain is extracted with morphological operators); one slice of a 256x256x7 PET image of the same brain; the same with anatomical edges, computed after registration.

Non-Iterative Contextual Correspondence Matching*

Bill Christmas, Josef Kittler and Maria Petrou

Department of Electronic and Electrical Engineering, University of Surrey

Abstract. In this paper, we develop a framework for the non-iterative matching of symbolic structures using contextual information. It is based on Bayesian reasoning and involves the explicit modelling of the binary relations between the objects. The difference between this and previously developed theories of the kind lies in the assumption that the binary relations used are derivable from the unary measurements that refer to individual objects. This leads to a non-iterative formula for probabilistic reasoning which is amenable to real-time implementation and produces good results. The theory is demonstrated using an application of automatic map registration.

1 Introduction

In machine vision, there are many ways of performing the important task of object recognition and matching. (For an extensive survey on 3D object recognition see [1].) One way of viewing object recognition is as a labelling problem, in which each object has to be assigned a label from a set of possible labels which form a sort of library or database of possible objects in the scene. The labeling should be done in accordance to measured attributes of individual objects, or parts of objects, in the scene and measurements concerning relationships between objects, and relevant knowledge which is encoded in the models of the label database. The problem of knowledge and measurement representation then arises. A very efficient way of dealing with it is the use of attribute relational graphs, in which image and model object primitives are represented by the nodes with the connecting arcs representing their relations. The properties of the primitives are encoded as the node attributes. The matching problem can be then formulated as one of attributed relational graph matching, for which many methods have been proposed. The early attempts, still widely popular, rely on graph search techniques with heuristic measures employed to reduce the inherently NP-complete problem to a manageable process. More recent are the efforts based on energy minimisation using simulated annealing, mean field theory or deterministic annealing, and relaxation labelling[7, 5, 2]. The latter approach in particular has the advantage that it converts the NP-complete problem into one

---

* This work was supported by IED and SERC, project number IED-1936, and by ESPRIT BRA project 7108. The aerial images were kindly provided by the Defence Research Agency, RSRE, UK.

of polynomial complexity. Recently [6] it was proposed that the explicit inclusion of binary relations in the formulation of the problem within the framework of probabilistic relaxation results in a very robust and relatively fast algorithm. However, no matter how efficient a probabilistic relaxation algorithm is, it is an iterative process, relying on a succession of updates of the probability values with which a label is assigned to a given object. This characteristic excludes any possibility of real time implementation.

In this paper, we propose an algorithm based on Bayesian reasoning, which is not iterative, and therefore achieves its objective very fast, in one pass only, and allows the possibility of a real time implementation. The idea of the algorithm stems from the observation that often the binary measurements which express the relationships between objects in the scene (and nodes in the attribute relational graphs) are derivable from the unary measurements which characterize individual objects. For example, if the relationship between two objects is expressed in terms of their relative orientation, the value of this binary measurement can be derived from the knowledge of the individual orientations of the objects involved, with respect to the same reference direction. Thus, in this paper, we assume that all the binary measurements involved in characterising relationships between pairs of objects are derivable from the unary measurements concerning the individual objects. Further, we assume that the binary measurements we are talking about are such that if we know the value of the binary measurement and the value of one of the unary measurements involved, the value of the other unary measurement can be uniquely derived.

2 Theoretical Framework for Object Labelling Using Bayesian Reasoning

In this section we express the general problem of shape matching in the framework of Bayesian probability theory, and illustrate how the resulting maximum a posteriori expression can be expressed in terms of known quantities. The complete derivation of the algorithm that follows may be found in [3].

We represent the nodes of the graph of the scene to be matched as a set of N objects $A = \{a_1, \ldots, a_N\}$. We then assign to each object a_i a label θ_i, which may take as its value any of the $M + 1$ model labels that form the set $\Omega = \{\omega_0, \omega_1, \ldots, \omega_M\}$, where ω_0 is the null label used to label objects for which no other label is appropriate. We use the notation ω_{θ_i} to indicate that we specifically wish to associate a model label with a particular scene label θ_i. We define two sets of indices, $N_0 \equiv \{1, \ldots, N\}$ and $N_i \equiv \{1, \ldots, i-1, i+1, \ldots, N\}$.

For each object a_i there are m_1 attributes, represented by unary measurements $\mathbf{x}_i = \{x_i^{(1)}, \ldots, x_i^{(m_1)}\}$. We use $\mathbf{x}_{i,i \in N_0}$ to denote the set $\{\mathbf{x}_1, \ldots, \mathbf{x}_N\}$. Similarly, for each pair of objects a_i and a_j we have a set of m_2 relations, represented by binary measurements $A_{ij} = \{A_{ij}^{(1)}, \ldots, A_{ij}^{(m_2)}\}$ which can be derived from the unary measurements $\mathbf{x}_i$ and $\mathbf{x}_j$. The abbreviation $A_{ij,j \in N_i} = \{A_{i1}, \ldots, A_{ii-1}, A_{ii+1}, \ldots, A_{iN}\}$ denotes all the binary measurements object a_i has with the other objects in the set. The same classes of unary and inferred binary measurements are also made on the model, to create the model graph: $\check{\mathbf{x}}_\alpha$ denotes the unary measurements of model label ω_α, and $\check{A}_{\alpha\beta}$ denotes the binary measurements between model labels ω_α and ω_β.

We invoke the Maximum A Posteriori (MAP) rule to state that the most appropriate label of object a_i is ω_{θ_i} given by:

$$P\left(\theta_i \leftarrow \omega_{\theta_i} \mid \mathbf{x}_{j,j\in N_0}, A_{ij,j\in N_i}\right) = \max_{\omega_\lambda \in \Omega} P\left(\theta_i \leftarrow \omega_\lambda \mid \mathbf{x}_{j,j\in N_0}, A_{ij,j\in N_i}\right) \quad (1)$$

In order to evaluate the terms in the right-hand side of this expression, we assume that the binary measurements can be entirely derived from the unary measurements. This contrasts with the assumption in [6] that the unary measurements are independent of the binary measurements. If we also assume that the unconditional match probabilities $P(\theta_i \leftarrow \omega_\alpha)$ are independent, then by repeated application of Bayes's rule and the theorem of total probability we can expand the expression on the right-hand size of (1) as follows:

$$P\left(\theta_i \leftarrow \omega_\lambda \mid \mathbf{x}_{j,j\in N_0}, A_{ij,j\in N_i}\right) = \frac{P\left(\theta_i \leftarrow \omega_\lambda\right) p\left(\mathbf{x}_i \mid \theta_i \leftarrow \omega_\lambda\right) Q_i\left(\omega_\lambda\right)}{\sum_{\omega_\alpha \in \Omega} \left\{P\left(\theta_i \leftarrow \omega_\alpha\right) p\left(\mathbf{x}_i \mid \theta_i \leftarrow \omega_\alpha\right) Q_i\left(\omega_\alpha\right)\right\}}$$

$$(2)$$

where

$$Q_i\left(\omega_{\theta_i}\right) = \prod_{j\in N_i} \sum_{\omega_\beta \in \Omega} p\left(A_{ij} \mid \theta_j \leftarrow \omega_\beta, \theta_i \leftarrow \omega_{\theta_i}\right) P\left(\theta_j \leftarrow \omega_\beta\right) \quad (3)$$

Thus the problem of labelling using the MAP rule can be solved as follows: we use (2) and (3) to calculate the a posteriori probabilities for all of the labellings of a node a_i, and then select the labelling that yields the maximum probability.

The quantity $Q_i\left(\omega_{\theta_i}\right)$ represents the support for the match $\theta_i \leftarrow \omega_{\theta_i}$ that is provided by all of the other matches that do not involve the scene node a_i. The density function $p\left(A_{ij} \mid \theta_j \leftarrow \omega_\beta, \theta_i \leftarrow \omega_{\theta_i}\right)$ plays the role of the compatibility coefficients used in many of the methods of probabilistic relaxation (e.g. [5, 7, 6]); that is, it quantifies the compatibility between the match $\theta_j \leftarrow \omega_\beta$ and a neighbouring match $\theta_i \leftarrow \omega_{\theta_i}$. We note however that, in spite of the similarity of the above formula to similar formulae of probabilistic relaxation approaches, the rule defined by (2) and (3) is not in a form that requires iterative implementation.

3 Evaluation of Terms in the MAP Formula

The evaluation of (2) and (3) requires the calculation of various match probabilities and density functions. The prior probabilities $P(\theta_i \leftarrow \omega_\alpha)$ are defined thus: we estimate the prior probability of the null label to be some value ζ, and the prior probabilities of all other labels are then set equal to each other.

In evaluating the density functions for the binary measurements, $p(A_{ij} \mid \theta_i \leftarrow \omega_\alpha, \theta_j \leftarrow \omega_\beta)$, we first consider the general case, in which neither a_i nor a_j is matched to the null label ω_0; in this case, because the density function is conditional on both matches, there is an associated model measurement $\check{A}_{\alpha\beta}$.

We assume that the noise in the binary measurements A_{ij} can be adequately approximated by a Gaussian:

$$p\left(A_{ij} \mid \theta_i \leftarrow \omega_\alpha, \theta_j \leftarrow \omega_\beta\right) = \mathcal{N}_{A_{ij}}\left(\breve{A}_{\alpha\beta}, \Sigma_2\right) \tag{4}$$

where Σ_2 is the covariance matrix for the binary measurements A_{ij}.

In the remaining cases, in which at least one out of a_i and a_j is matched to the null node, we assumed that they are uniformly distributed. Assuming each measurement $A_{ij}^{(k)}$ has a range of possible values whose width is $\rho^{(k)}$, and denoting the overall range of A_{ij} by $\mathcal{D}$, then

$$p\left(A_{ij} \mid \theta_i \leftarrow \omega_\alpha, \theta_j \leftarrow \omega_0\right) = \begin{cases} \dfrac{1}{\prod_{k=1}^{m_2} \rho^{(k)}} & \text{if } A_{ij} \in \mathcal{D}, \\ 0 & \text{otherwise} \end{cases} \tag{5}$$

We use a similar reasoning to determine density functions for the unary measurements.

4 Experimental Results

We applied the theory developed in the previous sections to two problems. The first was to match roads extracted from an aerial photograph with the corresponding roads in a digital map; the second was to match corresponding edges extracted from a stereo pair of images. In both applications we assume that the line segments that form the nodes have already been extracted. The unary measurements were: the absolute orientation and position of each line segment. The binary measurements were: the angle between line segments, and the direction and distance of the midpoint of one segment with respect to another.

The road-matching problem is illustrated in fig. 1. The black line segments in both images indicate the matched road segments. The white line segments in the image indicate road segments which could not be matched to the map, and were therefore matched to the null model node. The grey line segments in the map indicate road segments to which no image segments were matched. The black cross pointer on the map indicates where the centre of the scene lies on the map.

Fig. 2 shows a typical result of the matching of a stereo image pair. In this example the white lines in both images indicate matched segments, and the black lines are those that remained unmatched.

5 Discussion and Conclusions

We have developed a framework for non-iterative contextual correspondence matching for the matching of symbolic structures. The theory is based on two basic observations. In practical recognition problems we often do not consider higher than second-order relations between the objects (or parts of objects) involved in order to be able to perform the recognition task reliably. An example is the way humans identify regions on a large map: they usually consider the relative position and orientation of pairs of roads. The other observation concerns the way binary measurements are made in machine vision: they are usually derived from the unary measurements which have been made on the individual objects. By incorporating these two observations into the Bayesian theory of probability, we were able to derive a formula expressing the probability for each individual label assignment to an object, in terms of known functions only: the measurement error distributions and the modelling functions. The Maximum A Posteriori probability was then used to assign a label to each object. Thus we presented an algorithm which is non-iterative, allowing real-time one-pass implementation. Also it is parallelisable as each node can be treated by a separate processor independently from the treatment of the other nodes, since no result from one processor need be communicated to the others for the labelling to be completed. Further, the algorithm is very robust to errors and the presence (or absence) of parts of the objects to be identified due to the redundancy built into it by the explicit inclusion of the implied binary measurements. The ability to model these binary relations directly is a process that is reminiscent of the multiresolution approaches to image restoration [4], where the explicit inclusion of implicit relationships has been shown to produce better results in a much shorter time.

We have demonstrated our algorithm with two real problems, that of road network matching and stereo linear feature matching. For the applications we have assumed that the error in the binary measurements are Gaussian. We wish to stress however that if more accurate knowledge concerning the image noise and the measurement process is available, it can be very easily incorporated into our framework.

References

1. P.J. Besl and R.C. Jain. Three-dimensional object recognition. *Computing Surveys*, 17:75–145, 1985.
2. B. Bhanu and O.D. Faugeras. Shape matching of two-dimensional objects. *IEEE Trans. Pattern Analysis and Machine Intelligence*, 6:137–156, 1984.
3. W.J. Christmas., J. Kittler, and M. Petrou. Matching in computer vision using non-iterative contextual correspondence. Submitted to *Computer Vision, Graphics and Image Processing*.
4. B. Gidas. A renormalization group approach to image processing problems. *IEEE Trans. Pattern Analysis and Machine Intelligence*, 11:164–180, 1989.
5. R.A. Hummel and S.W. Zucker. On the foundations of relaxation labeling process. *IEEE Trans. Pattern Analysis and Machine Intelligence*, 5(3):267–286, May 1983.
6. J. Kittler, M. Petrou, and W.J. Christmas. Probabilistic relaxation for matching problems in computer vision. In *Proceedings of the Fourth International Conference on Computer Vision*, pages 666–673, Berlin, 1993.
7. A. Rosenfeld, R. Hummel, and S. Zucker. Scene labeling by relaxation operations. *IEEE Trans. Systems, Man, and Cybernetics*, 6:420–433, June 1976.

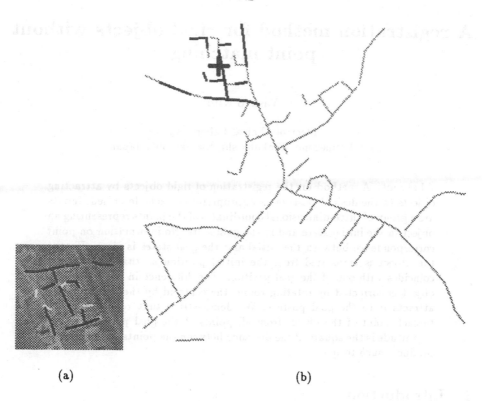

(a)   (b)

Fig. 1. Matching of road segments

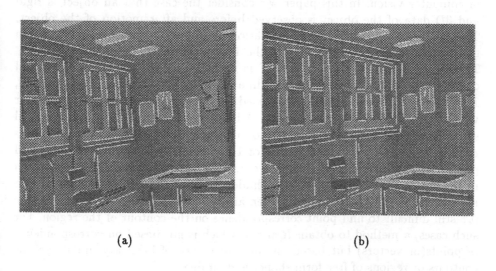

(a)   (b)

Fig. 2. Matching edge segments from a stereo pair of images

A registration method for rigid objects without point matching

Yasuyo Kita

Electrotechnical Laboratory
1-1-4 Umezono, Tsukuba-shi, Ibaraki, 305, Japan

Abstract. A method for the registration of rigid objects by attracting objects to the desired posture by appropriate forces is described. Inputs are a group of three-dimensional coordinates of the points representing an object in the initial state and in the goal state. No information on point correspondence between the initial and the goal states is given. Firstly, the object is translated from the initial position so that its centroid coincides with one of the goal position. The difference in posture of the object is corrected by rotating round the centroid by the torque which attracts it to the goal posture. We demonstrate that repulsive forces to each point of the object from all points at the goal posture, whose magnitude is the square of the distance between the points, satisfactorily produces such torque.

1 Introduction

Detecting the change in position and posture of objects which move in three-dimensional (from now, abbreviated as 3D) space is one of the important subjects of computer vision. In this paper, we consider the case that an object is rigid and 3D data of the object is observed before and after motion of the object. The change is represented by a translation matrix and a rotation matrix which transform the initial coordinates to the final ones in the form $X' = R * X + T$. Where, R is a rotation matrix, T is a translation matrix, X is the initial coordinates and X' is the final coordinates. As shown in some methods[1][2], R and T are generally calculated based on the correspondences of points or vectors (ex. normal vectors of surfaces) between the initial state and the final state. Since the number of possible correspondences of such simple elements usually becomes large, the selection of the correct pairs requires complicated processing. For example, if we observe color images with range data as shown in Fig. 1, the correspondence of the shadow region before and after the motion is relatively easy to find. However, even after that the correspondence is known, it's still difficult to find point correspondence on the contour of the region. For such cases, a method to obtain R and T which is not based on correspondence of points(or vectors) but based on correspondence of arbitrary units, such as contours or regions of free-form shape, is desirable.

One typical solution for this problem is based on moments[3][4]. In the method, however, not the exact but four possible rotation matrices are calculated and additional procedures are required to select the correct one from

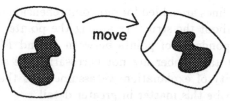

Fig. 1. Example that correspondence of points is very difficult to find, even though regions are known to correspond to each other.

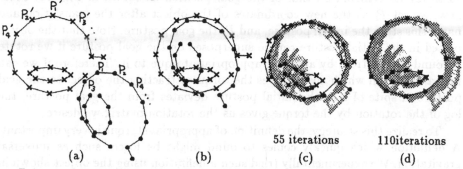

		55 iterations	110iterations
(a)	(b)	(c)	(d)

• Points at initial posture $P_i(x_i, y_i, z_i)$ × Points at goal posture $P_j'(x_j', y_j', z_j')$

Fig. 2. Convergence of object to goal posture

the four. Another defect in the method is that it can not detect the rotation matrix for the objects whose major and/or minor principle axis can not fixed, such as regular polyhedrons. Besides this, some other methods[5][6][7] are proposed for free-form shape matching using 3D data without the correspondence of any feature. These methods iteratively attracts observed data to model data so as to make the shortest distance between the two data as small as possible. Though these methods have advantage of allowing partial matching, they needs initial estimation of motion; if appropriate initial estimation is not given, these methods easily converge to wrong solution because of many local minima. In case that no initial estimation of rotation matrix is given, [5] needs try to start from 24 rotation matrices not to miss the global minimum.

In this paper, we propose a method to detect the rotation matrix which uses the physical rotation of the object when torque is applied to attract the object to the goal posture. Since the definition of the torque is devised not to produce many local minima, the object is stably converged to the goal posture from any posture whose angle of the rotation from the goal posture is within about $\pm\pi/2$ radian round any axis.

2 Outline of our method

In our method, an object is represented as a group of points because we want to treat arbitrary shape. Figure 2a shows an example(3D shape by combining a large and a small circles perpendicularly): initial state is represented with $P_i(x_i, y_i, z_i)$(i=1∼n, • in Fig. 2) and goal state is with $P_j'(x_j', y_j', z_j')$(j=1∼n, × in

Fig. 2). Though auxiliary lines are added for our comprehension of the 3D shape, no information is given about the structure among the points. No information is provided about correspondence of points between P_i and P_j'. Although the actual points and their total number are not necessarily the same before and after motion, for simplicity of explanation we assume that they are same. In subsection 3.3, we'll describe this matter in greater detail.

First, the object represented by P_i is translated from the initial position so as to lay its centroid on that of the goal position as shown in Fig. 2b. From now, we set P_i as the new coordinates of the object after the translation and name this state the initial posture, and P_j' the goal posture. Note that the object placed in the initial posture can be superposed on the goal posture if we rotate it round the centroid by applying appropriate torque to it. Therefore if we can find a definition which always gives the torque attracting the object to the goal posture in spite of how the initial posture deviates from the goal posture, the log of the rotation by the torque gives us the rotation matrix we desire.

To realize this strategy, the definition of appropriate torque is very important. A definition which quickly comes to mind might be forces such as universal gravitation. We experimentally tried such a definition using the object shown in Fig. 2. The attractive forces from all points of the goal posture are applied to each point of the object. The magnitude of the forces is defined to be inversely proportional to the square of the distance between the points (in the case where the distance=0, we define force=0). By rotating the object round the centroid with the torque caused by the forces, however, many local stable postures where the torque=0 were found besides the goal posture. Therefore, this definition is useful only when the difference between initial and goal postures is small. In the sense that this definition attracts the object mainly based on the distance between the closest points, it is similar to the other methods[5][6].

From the idea contrary to the above, a definition based on repulsive forces was experimentally tried and led to interesting results. If repulsive forces are applied to each point of the object from all points in the goal posture, whose magnitude is the square of the distance between the points, it was observed that the object is stably attracted to the goal posture when angle of the rotation from the goal posture is within about $\pm\pi/2$ radian round any axis. In the case when the initial posture is out of the range, the object converges to an opposite posture about the centroid.

The rotation of objects is calculated in a successive approximation way[1]. Figure 2c and 2d show the convergence process that object($\bullet$) follows as it is attracted in the goal posture($\times$). The gray lines show traces of the rotation process acting on the object. In this case, actual rotation is 90.0 degrees around the axis(0.641,0.299,0.707). By our method, 90.1 degrees around the axis(0.637,0.307,0.707) is obtained in a half second(SUN/SS10 workstation).

---

[1] The equation of motion is $I * d^2\theta/dt^2 + \gamma d\theta/dt = N$ (Here, I is the moment of inertia of the object, γ is viscous coefficient, and N is torque). If we assume that γ is negative with a large absolute value, the acceleration(first term of the equation) can be neglected; while $dt=1$, the object rotates by $d\theta = N/\gamma$.

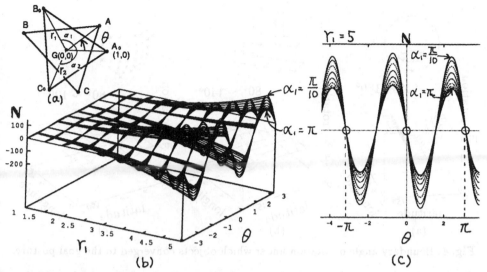

Fig. 3. Change of torque in case that objects composed of three points moves in a two dimensional polar coordinate system.

3 Performance characteristics

In this section, performance characteristics of the method are checked from several viewpoints.

3.1 Characteristics of stable posture

Let's analytically consider stable postures. Suppose that a repulsive force is applied from $P_1(r_1, \phi_1)$ to $P_2(r_2, \phi_2)$ in a polar coordinate system, whose magnitude is the square of the distance between the points. From the second cosine formula,
$|\mathbf{F}| = |\overline{P_1 P_2}|^2 = r_1^2 + r_2^2 - 2r_1 r_2 \cos\theta$.
Where, $\theta = \phi_2 - \phi_1$. From the sign formula, the torque caused by the force round the origin is:
$$|\mathbf{N}| = r_1 r_2 \sin\theta \sqrt{r_1^2 + r_2^2 - 2r_1 r_2 \cos\theta} \qquad (1)$$

When the object is placed in the goal posture, repulsive forces mutually arise between any pair among all points. From the equation (1), a pair of torques between any pair of points offset each other. As a result, the goal posture is a stable posture for any object consisting of arbitrary points.

Next, let's examine how torque changes as an object shifts from the goal posture by using simple objects, which are composed of three points in a 2D polar coordinate system. In order to represent a triangle with few parameters, we set the three points as shown in Fig. 3a. The origin is set at the centroid of the points; two points are A(1,0) and B(r_1, α_1); the remaining point C(r_2, α_2) is determined from these conditions. That is, the parameters r_2 and α_2 are a function of r_1 and α_1. The torque which is produced when the object is rotated by θ from the goal state(A(1,0),B(r_1, α_1),C(r_2, α_2)), is calculated using

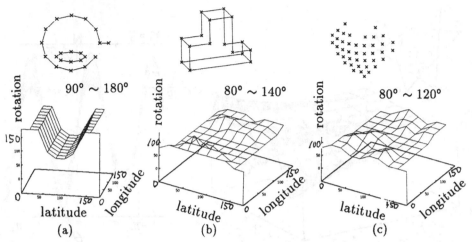

Fig. 4. Boundary angle of rotation under which objects converged to the goal posture.

the equation (1) as function of r_1, α_1 and θ. Figure 3b shows the results of fixing $\alpha_1 = m\pi/10(m=1\sim10)$. Figure 3c shows the profile at $r_1 = 5.0$. We notice that torque$= 0$ at $\theta=0$ and π and, in the near vicinity of the points, the torque has a sign opposite to the deviation from $\theta=0$ (or π). This brings back the object into $\theta=0$ (or π). As shown in the figures, these two states are the only stable states for most of triangles. Exceptions are triangles which are almost regular. In the cases of regular triangles, stable posture becomes 0, $2\pi/3$ and $4\pi/3$. Objects consisting of more than four points have not yet been analytically examined.

3.2 Experiments with various shape objects

We applied our method to various objects. The following phenomena are observed in most of objects. When angle of the rotation from the goal posture is within about $\pm\pi/2$ radian round an axis, objects converged to the goal posture. In the case when the initial posture is out of the range, objects can converge to a few other postures. Figure 4 shows boundary angle of rotation under which objects converged to the goal posture. In the figure, the direction of rotation axis is represented by latitude and longitude. Figure 4a is the boundary for the object we used in section 2. Figure 4b is one for a platform of honor represented by 14 points(vertices). Figure 4c is one for a heart painted on a curved surface, which is represented by 42 points selected at equal intervals.

The number of stable postures depends on the shape of objects. In the case of object in Fig. 4b and 4c, there are 4 stable postures, while the object in Fig. 4a has 2 stable postures. From experimental observation, the number of stable postures is expected not to become so high and is usually around 4.

Though the moment method[4] cannot treat objects whose major and/or minor principle can not fixed (ex. regular polihedrons), our method is also useful for such objects and the object becomes stable at one of overlapping postures, which is the closest to the initial posture.

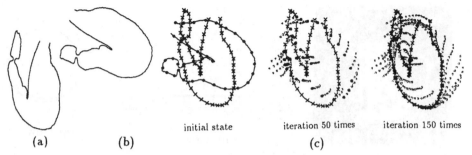

(a)   (b)   initial state   iteration 50 times   iteration 150 times

(c)

Fig. 5. Registration result in case that different representative points are selected before and after motion.

3.3 Influence of different representative points

Until now, we treated the same representative points before and after motion to examine the original characteristics of the attraction by the repulsive forces. Here, we show it is possible to select different representative points between the initial and goal states. Figure 5a and 5b show a curve in three-dimensional before and after motion. Originally, the line is represented by 1105 points. As shown in Fig. 5c, representative points are selected with different regular intervals, concretely, 55 points (every 20 points) from Fig. 5a and 33 points (every 33 points) from Fig. 5b. Figure 5c shows our method still can well register the object in the goal posture using different representative points. In this case, actual rotation is 60 degrees around the axis(0.492,0.0868,-0.866). By our method, 59.6 degrees around the axis(0.496,0.0867,-0.864) was obtained.

3.4 Experiment using data observed by range finder

In order to check practicality of the method, experiments were conducted on detection of position and posture of a mug observed by a laser range finder[8]. Figure 6a shows the mug we used for the experiment. The movement of the mug from the initial position and posture is calculated based on the 3D coordinates of the contours of the solid patterns on its surface: 6 *hiragana* characters ("て", "ら", "し", "や", "す" and "よ")[2]. Firstly, 3D data is observed at 6 canonical states of the mug, each of which is arranged to observe each pattern. A group of 3D coordinates of points on the contour of each pattern are detected and memorized as a canonical pattern. For example, the second canonical pattern is represented by 3D coordinates of 38 points(• in Fig. 6b). For each canonical state, the positions of the brim, the bottom and the handle of the mug are manually taught(lines in Fig. 6b).

After arbitrarily moving the mug, the new state of the mug is detected based on the pattern visible at each state. Figure 6c shows an example of observed 3D

---

[2] Generally, such a pattern is easily extracted than other edges because of stable contrast with its background. In our experiments, these patterns are detected as regions that lack 3D data, since the infrared laser of the range finder is not reflected from the black patterns.

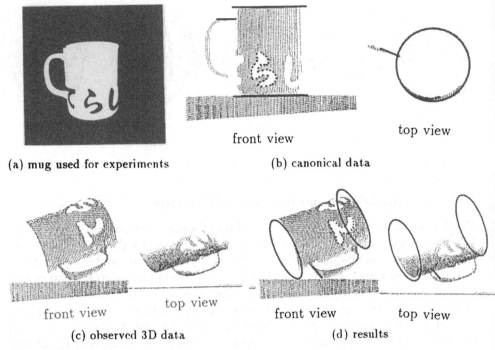

(a) mug used for experiments   (b) canonical data

(c) observed 3D data   (d) results

Fig. 6. Example of detection of position and posture of mug

data. Firstly, the possible regions for a pattern are selected and a group of 3D coordinates of points on the contour of each region are detected. By using the group as points representing the goal state, each canonical pattern is registered by the proposed method. The translation matrix and rotation matrix for the best matched pattern is selected for the movement of the mug. In case of Fig. 6c, pattern "て" was selected. In Fig. 6d, canonical 3D data transformed by the matrices are superposed on the observed data. It shows that the posture of the mug is well detected. For more than 10 experiments using different postures, our method gave similar results.

4 Conclusion

In this paper, a new simple method for registering rigid objects was described. In our method, the change in posture of an object is detected by simulating the rotation of the object when torque is applied to it so as to attract it to the goal posture. The strategy is realized based on the interesting property that repulsive forces from the goal posture stably produce an attractive torque.

One feature of our method is that the method does not need a point matching process and can use arbitrary shape, like contours or regions, as units of correspondence. This feature is useful since detecting characteristic points and finding point matching are often very difficult even in the case when correspondence of some part is easily found.

Even though the method uses iterative process to simulate rotation of objects, the processing time is short since one iteration is very simple and quick. The time increases proportionally to the square of the number of points representing objects and to the degree how much the initial posture shifts from the goal posture since the rotation is now simulated by unit degree(1 degree). When an object is represented by 20 points with 50 degrees shift from the goal posture, the object converges to the goal posture in a quarter second on a SUN/SS10 workstation. The computational time can be reduced, if we devise the numerical method to simulate the converging process. Though the time increases proportionally to the square of the number of points representing objects, our methods does not need dense points to get proper registration of objects as we see in section 3.3.

Additionally considering that the object converges to the goal posture when the shift from the goal posture is within about $\pm\pi/2$ radian round any axis, the method is expected to be useful for tracking an object which rotates quickly.

Acknowledgements   The author wishes to thank Dr. K. Fujimura for important advice, and Dr. K. Takase, Dr. F. Tomita and her colleagues of the Computer Vision Section, ETL for helpful discussions. For obtaining 3D data by the range finder, she is thankful to Mr. T. Yoshimi, Mr. T. Ueshiba and Mr. Y. Kawai. She is thankful to Dr. A. Zelinsky for his comments on English. She is grateful to Mr. N. Kita for all his help, especially for his effective advice.

References

1. O. D. Faugeras and M. Hebert: "The representation, recognition, and locating of 3D objects", *Int. J. Robotics Research*, Vol. 5, No. 3, pp. 27–52, 1986.
2. S. Umeyama, T. Kazvand and M. Hospital: "Recognition and positioning of three-dimensional objects by combining matchings of primitive local patterns", *Computer Vision, Graphics & Image Processing*, Vol. 44, No. 1, pp.58–76, 1988.
3. L. G. Brown: "A survey of image registration techniques", *ACM Computing Surveys*, Vol 24, No. 4, pp.325–376, 1992.
4. J. M. Galves and M. Canton: "Normalization and shape recognition of three-dimensional objects by 3D moments", *Pattern Recognition*, Vol. 26, No. 5, pp. 667–681, 1993.
5. P. J. Besl and N. D. Mckay: "A method for registration of 3D shapes", *IEEE Trans. on Pattern Analysis and Machine Intelligence*, PAMI-14, No.2, pp. 239–256, 1992.
6. L. Bruine, S. Lavallée, and R. Szeliski: "Using force fields derived from 3D distance maps for inferring the attitude of a 3D rigid object", In *Proc. of European Conference on Computer Vision '92*, pp.670–675, 1992.
7. T. Masuda and N. Yokoya: "Robust estimation of rigid motion parameters between a pair of range images", In *Proc. of The 8th Scandinavian Conference on Image Analysis*, pp. 499–506, 1993.
8. T. Yoshimi and M. Oshima: "Multi light sources range finder system", In *Proc. of IAPR workshop on CV*, pp. 245–248, 1988.

Non-parametric Local Transforms for Computing Visual Correspondence

Ramin Zabih[1] and John Woodfill[2]

[1] Computer Science Department, Cornell University, Ithaca NY 14853-7501, USA
[2] Interval Research Corporation, 1801-C Page Mill Road, Palo Alto CA 94304, USA

Abstract. We propose a new approach to the correspondence problem that makes use of non-parametric local transforms as the basis for correlation. Non-parametric local transforms rely on the relative ordering of local intensity values, and not on the intensity values themselves. Correlation using such transforms can tolerate a significant number of outliers. This can result in improved performance near object boundaries when compared with conventional methods such as normalized correlation. We introduce two non-parametric local transforms: the *rank transform*, which measures local intensity, and the *census transform*, which summarizes local image structure. We describe some properties of these transforms, and demonstrate their utility on both synthetic and real data.

1 Introduction

The correspondence problem is a fundamental problem in vision, as it forms the basis for stereo depth computation and most optical flow algorithms. Given two images of the same scene, a pixel in one image corresponds to a pixel in the other if both pixels are projections along lines of sight of the same physical scene element. If the two images are temporally consecutive, then computing correspondence determines motion. If the two images are spatially separated but simultaneous, then computing correspondence determines stereo depth. *Area-based* approaches to the correspondence problem [4] find a dense solution, usually by relying on some kind of statistical correlation between local intensity regions.

In this paper we propose a new area-based approach to the correspondence problem, based on non-parametric local transforms followed by correlation. We begin by motivating our approach, then show how non-parametric local transforms can be used to determine correspondence. In section 3 we introduce the *rank* and *census* transforms, and describe their properties. We give empirical evidence of the performance of our methods in section 4, using both natural and synthetic images. Finally, in section 5 we survey related work and discuss some planned extensions.

2 Non-parametric local transforms

Our approach to the correspondence problem is first to apply a local transform to the image, and then to use correlation. In this respect, our work is similar to that of Nishihara [12] and Seitz [14, 1]. Nishihara's transform is the sign bit of the image after convolution with a Laplacian, while Seitz's transform is the direction of the intensity gradient.

Most approaches to the correspondence problem have difficulty near discontinuities in disparity, which occur at the boundaries of objects. Near such a boundary, the pixels in a local region represent scene elements from two distinct instensity populations. Some of the pixels come from the object, and some from other parts of the scene. As a result, the local pixel distribution will in general be multimodal near a boundary. This poses a problem for many correspondence algorithms, such as normalized correlation [6].

Correspondence algorithms are usually based on standard statistical methods, which are best suited to a single population. Parametric measures, such as the mean or variance, do not behave well in the presence of distinct subpopulations, each with its own coherent parameters. This problem, which we will refer to as *factionalism*, is a major issue in computer vision, and has been addressed with a variety of methods, including robust statistics [2, 3], Markov Random Fields [5] and regularization [13].

The fundamental idea behind our approach is to define a local image transform that tolerates factionalism. Correspondence can be computed by transforming both images and then using correlation. For this approach to succeed, the transform must result in significant local variation within a given image; in addition, it must give similar results near corresponding points between the two images. (Marr and Nishihara [10] refer to these two properties as *sensitivity* and *stability*.) Finally, to handle stereo imagery, the transform should be invariant under changes in image gain and bias.

Our approach relies on local transforms based on non-parametric measures that are designed to tolerate factionalism. Non-parametric statistics [9] is distinguished by the use of ordering information among data, rather than the data values themselves. Non-parametric local transforms, which we introduced in [15], are local image transformations that rely on the relative ordering of intensities, and not on the intensity values themselves.

3   The rank transform and the census transform

We next describe two non-parametric local transforms. The first, called the *rank transform*, is a non-parametric measure of local intensity. The second, called the *census transform*, is a non-parametric summary of local spatial structure.

Let P be a pixel, $I(P)$ its intensity (usually an 8-bit integer), and $N(P)$ the set of pixels in some square neighborhood of diameter d surrounding P. All non-parametric transforms depend upon the comparative intensities of P versus the pixels in the neighborhood $N(P)$. The transforms we will discuss only depend on the sign of the comparison. Define $\xi(P, P')$ to be 1 if $I(P') < I(P)$ and 0 otherwise. The non-parametric local transforms depend solely on the set of pixel comparisons, which is the set of ordered pairs

$$\Xi(P) = \bigcup_{P' \in N(P)} (P', \xi(P, P')).$$

They differ in terms of their exact reliance on Ξ.

The first non-parametric local transform is called the *rank transform*, and is defined as the number of pixels in the local region whose intensity is less than the intensity of the center pixel. Formally, the rank transform $R(P)$ is

$$R(P) = \|\{ P' \in N(P) \mid I(P') < I(P) \}\|.$$

Note that $R(P)$ is not an intensity at all, but rather an integer in the range $\{0, \ldots, d^2 - 1\}$. This distinguishes the rank transform from other attempts to use non-parametric measures such as median filters, mode filters or rank filters [7]. To compute correspondence, we have used L_1 correlation (minimizing the sum of absolute values of differences) on the rank-transformed images.

The second non-parametric transform is named the *census transform*. $R_\tau(P)$ maps the local neighborhood surrounding a pixel P to a bit string representing the set of neighboring pixels whose intensity is less than that of P. Let $N(P) = P \oplus D$, where $\oplus$ is the Minkowski sum and D is a set of displacements, and let $\otimes$ denote concatenation. The census transform can then be specified,

$$R_\tau(P) = \bigotimes_{[i,j] \in D} \xi(P, P + [i, j]).$$

Two pixels of census transformed images are compared for similarity using the Hamming distance, i.e. the number of bits that differ in the two bit strings. To compute correspondence, we have minimized the Hamming distance after applying the census transform.

These local transforms rely solely upon the set of comparisons Ξ, and are therefore invariant under changes in gain or bias. The tolerance of these transforms for factionalism also results from their reliance upon Ξ. If a minority of pixels in a local neighborhood has a very different intensity distribution than the majority, only comparisons involving a member of the minority are affected. Such pixels do not make a contribution proportional to their intensity, but proportional to their number. This limited dependence on the minority's intensity values is a major distinction between our approach and parametric measures.

To illustrate the manner in which these transforms tolerate factionalism, consider a three-by-three region of an image whose intensities are

$$
\begin{array}{ccc}
127 & 127 & 129 \\
126 & 128 & 129 \\
127 & 131 & A
\end{array}
$$

for some value $0 \le A < 256$. Consider the effect on various parametric and non-parametric measures, computed at the center of this region, as A varies over its

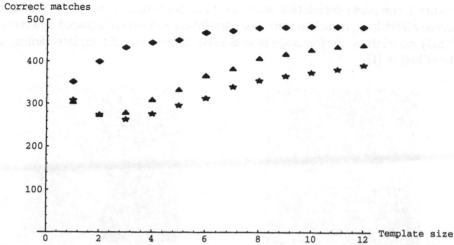

Fig. 1. Comparison of rank (◇), normalized (△) and SSD (⋆) correlation on Aschwanden data-set with salt-and-pepper noise

256 possible values. The mean[3] of this region varies from 114 to 142, while the variance ranges from 2 to 1823. These parametric measures exhibit continuous variation over a substantial range as A changes.

Non-parametric transforms are more stable, however. All the elements of Ξ except one will remain fixed as A changes. Ξ will be

$$\begin{matrix} 1 & 1 & 0 \\ 1 & & 0 \\ 1 & 0 & a \end{matrix}$$

where a is 1 if $A < 128$, and otherwise 0. The census transform simply results in the bits of Ξ in some canonical ordering, such as $\{1,1,0,1,0,1,0,a\}$. The rank transform will give 5 if $A < 128$, and otherwise 4.

This comparison shows the tolerance that non-parametric measures have for factionalism. A minority of pixels can have a very different value, but the effect on the rank and census transforms is limited by the size of the minority.

4 Empirical results

We have implemented these non-parametric local transforms, and have explored their behavior on both real and synthetic imagery. The motivation for our approach was to obtain better results near the edges of objects. We have obtained comparative results on synthetic data which show that our methods can outperform normalized correlation.

In [1], Aschwanden and Guggenbühl have described the performance of a number of area-based stereo algorithms under several different noise models.

---

[3] For convenience, we are rounding the actual values

Figure 1 compares correlation with the rank transform against two standard stereo algorithms, namely normalized correlation and sum of squared differences (SSD) correlation. Performance is measured as function of template radius, as described in [1].

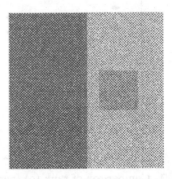

Fig. 2. Right and left random-dot stereograms

Fig. 3. Disparities from normalized correlation, rank and census transforms

Another way to compare correlation methods is with random dot imagery. Figure 2 shows a random dot stereogram of a square floating in front of a flat surface, on which there is a vertical intensity edge. The images are noise-free, but the intensities differ by fixed gain and bias.

Figure 3 shows the disparities computed from normalized correlation and from correlation with the rank and census transforms. There should only be 2 disparities in this scene: one for the background surface (which is at disparity 0), and one for the foreground square (which is at disparity 104). Notice the comparatively poor performance of normalized correlation near the edges, where it introduces spurious disparities. The performance of our approach can be seen by counting the pixels with incorrect disparities, as shown below.

Algorithm	Incorrect matches
Normalized	1385
Rank transform	609
Census transform	407

On this example, the non-parametric local transforms appear to exhibit better performance than normalized correlation.

The best evidence in favor of the non-parametric local transforms is their performance on real images. We have used the rank transform and the census transform on a number of different images to obtain stereo depth. Depth maps are shown with lighter shades indicating larger disparities and thus nearer scene elements. All the depth maps shown were generated with the same parameters (a transform radius of 7 pixels, and a correlation radius of 4 pixels).

Figure 4 shows a beam-splitter image of a puppet (Elmo from the television show "Sesame Street"). The depth results of the non-parametric local transforms are shown in figure 5. Figure 6 shows an image from a tree sequence[4] captured by moving a camera along a rail, and the depth results from the transforms.

5 Related work and planned extensions

The algorithms we describe are related to non-parametric measures of association, such as Spearman's correlation coefficient r_s or Kendall's τ. These are measures of association of paired data that are based upon comparisons. However, such measures are very expensive to compute, and do not capture the spatial structure of images.

Probably the most similar approach to ours is the work based on robust statistics [2, 11, 3]. Robust statistics differs from our approach in that they emphasize reducing the influence of outliers. Implicit in this work is the assumption that outliers are distributed randomly. However, at the edges of objects, factionalism produces outliers with consistent distributions. Our approach tolerates outliers with consistent distributions, and does not allow pixels from a small faction to contribute in a manner proportional to their intensity.

One limitation of the non-parametric transforms we have described is that the amount of information they associate with a pixel is not very large. We hope to address this shortcoming by combining a number of different non-parametric transforms into a vector of measures associated with a pixel. Ultimately, we would like to avoid the correlation phase altogether and simply match pixels according to a set of semi-independent measures, in a manner similar to that proposed by Kass [8].

Another limitation of our approach is that the local measures rely heavily upon the intensity of the center pixel. This has not been an issue in practice, but we propose to address it by doing comparisons from a local median intensity instead of $I(P)$. An additional idea we intend to pursue is to generalize Ξ, which currently uses the sign of the intensity differences. We plan to explore using higher-order differences, as well as the information contained in the total ordering of the local pixel intensities.

We are also interested in efficient algorithms for implementing such transforms. [15] describes a number of fast algorithms for computing the rank trans-

---

[4] The tree imagery appears courtesy of Harlyn Baker and Bob Bolles

form based on dynamic programming. We have recently implemented an approximation of the census transform on a Sun workstation, which produces stereo depth with 24 disparities on 640 by 240 images at 1–2 frames per second.

Acknowledgements

Portions of this work were done while the first author was at the Computer Science Department at Stanford University, supported by a fellowship from the Fannie and John Hertz Foundation. We wish to thank SRI for the use of their Connection Machine.

References

1. P. Aschwanden and W. Guggenbühl. Experimental results from a comparative study on correlation-type registration algorithms. In Förstner and Ruwiedel, editors, *Robust Computer Vision*, pages 268–289. Wichmann, 1993.
2. Paul Besl, Jeffrey Birch, and Layne Watson. Robust window operators. In *International Conference on Computer Vision*, pages 591–600, 1988.
3. Michael Black and P Anandan. A framework for the robust estimation of optical flow. In *International Conference on Computer Vision*, pages 231–236, 1993.
4. U. Dhond and J. Aggarwal. Structure from stereo — a review. *IEEE Transactions on Systems, Man and Cybernetics*, 19(6), 1989.
5. Stuart Geman and Donald Geman. Stochastic relaxation, gibbs distributions, and the bayesian restoration of images. *IEEE PAMI*, 6:721–741, 1984.
6. Marsha Jo Hanna. *Computer Matching of Areas in Stereo Images*. PhD thesis, Stanford, 1974.
7. R. Hodgson, D. Bailey, M. Naylor, A. Ng, and S. McNeill. Properties, implementations and applications of rank filters. *Journal of Image and Vision Computing*, 3(1):3–14, February 1985.
8. Michael Kass. Computing visual correspondence. *DARPA Image Understanding Proceedings*, pages 54–60, 1983.
9. E. L. Lehman. *Nonparametrics: statistical methods based on ranks*. Holden-Day, 1975.
10. David Marr and Keith Nishihara. Representation and recognition of the spatial organization of three-dimensional shapes. *Proceedings of the Royal Society of London B*, 200:269–294, 1978.
11. Peter Meer, Doron Mintz, Azriel Rosenfeld, and Dong Yoon Kim. Robust regression methods for computer vision: A review. *International Journal of Computer Vision*, 6(1):59–70, 1991.
12. H. Keith Nishihara. Practical real-time imaging stereo matcher. *Optical Engineering*, 23(5):536–545, Sept–Oct 1984.
13. Tomaso Poggio, Vincent Torre, and Christof Koch. Computational vision and regularization theory. *Nature*, 317:314–319, 1985.
14. Peter Seitz. Using local orientational information as image primitive for robust object recognition. *SPIE proceedings*, 1199:1630–1639, 1989.
15. Ramin Zabih. *Individuating Unknown Objects by Combining Motion and Stereo*. PhD thesis, Stanford University, 1994 (forthcoming).

158

Fig. 4. Elmo stereo pair from beam-splitter

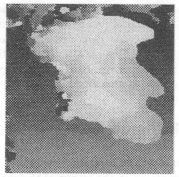

Fig. 5. Rank and census results on Elmo

Fig. 6. Tree image with rank and census correlation results

Measuring the Affine Transform Using Gaussian Filters

R. Manmatha *

Computer Science Department, University of Massachusetts, Amherst, MA-01003.
manmatha@cs.umass.edu

Abstract. Image deformations due to relative motion between an observer and an object may be used to infer 3-D structure. Up to first order these deformations can be written in terms of an affine transform. Here, a novel approach is adopted to measuring affine transforms which correctly handles the problem of corresponding deformed patches. The patches are filtered using gaussians and derivatives of gaussians. The problem of finding the affine transform is reduced to that of finding the appropriate deformed filter to use. The method is local and can handle arbitrarily large affine deformations. Experiments demonstrate that this technique can find scale changes and optical flow in situations where other methods fail.

1 Introduction

Changes in the relative orientation of a surface with respect to a camera cause deformations in the image of the surface. Deformations can be used to infer local surface geometry and depth from motion. Since a repeating texture pattern can be thought of as a pattern in motion, shape from texture can also be derived from deformations [5].

To first order, this deformation together with the image translation can be described using a six parameter affine transformation $(\mathbf{t}, \mathbf{A})$ where

$$r' = t + Ar \tag{1}$$

r' and r are the image coordinates related by an affine transform, t is a 2 by 1 vector representing the translation and **A** the 2 by 2 affine deformation matrix. The affine transform is useful because the image projections of a small planar patch from different viewpoints are well approximated by it [5].

In Figure (1) the image on the right is scaled 1.4 times the image on the left. Even if the centroids of the two image patches are matched accurately, measuring the affine transform is difficult since the sizes of every portion of the two images differ. This problem arises because traditional matching uses fixed correlation windows or filters. The correct way to approach this problem is to deform the correlation window or filter according to the image deformation.

---

* This research was supported by NSF grants CDA-8922572 and IRI-9113690. The author also thanks IBM Almaden Research Center which hosted him for 6 months.

This paper derives a computational scheme where gaussian and derivative of gaussian filters are used and the filters deformed according to the affine transformation. The resulting equations are solved by linearizing with respect to the affine parameters rather than the image coordinates. This allows the linearization point to be moved so that arbitrary affine transforms can be solved unlike traditional methods restricted to small affines. The method is local, applicable to arbitrary dimensions and can measure affine transforms in situations where other algorithms fail. For example, Werkhoven and Koenderink's algorithm [6] when run on the images in Figure (1) returns a scale factor of 1.16 while our algorithm does the matching correctly and therefore returns a scale factor of 1.41. For a review of related work see [5].

Fig. 1. Dollar Bill scaled 1.4 times

2 Deformation of Filters

The initial discussion will assume zero image translation; translation can be recovered as suggested in section 3. It is also assumed that shading and illumination effects can be ignored.

Notation Vectors will be represented by lowercase letters in boldface while matrices will be represented by uppercase letters in boldface.

Consider two Riemann-integrable functions F_1 and F_2 related by an affine transform i.e.

$$F_1(r) = F_2(Ar) \tag{2}$$

Define a generalized gaussian as

$$G(r, M) = \frac{1}{(2\pi)^{n/2} det(M)^{1/2}} exp(-\frac{r^T M^{-1} r}{2}) \tag{3}$$

where M is a symmetric positive semi-definite matrix. Then it may be shown that the output of F_1 filtered with a gaussian is equal to the output of F_2 filtered with a gaussian deformed by the affine transform (see [5] for details) i.e.

$$\int F_1(r) G(r, \sigma^2 I) dr = \int F_2(Ar) G(Ar, R\Sigma R^T) d(Ar) \tag{4}$$

where the integrals are taken from $-\infty$ to ∞. $\mathbf{R}$ is a rotation matrix and Σ a diagonal matrix with entries $(s_1\sigma)^2, (s_2\sigma)^2 ... (s_n\sigma)^2$ ($s_i \geq 0$) and $R\Sigma R^T = \sigma^2 AA^T$ (this follows from the fact that AA^T is a symmetric, positive semi-definite matrix).

Intuitively, (6) expresses the notion that the gaussian weighted average brightnesses must be equal, provided the gaussian is affine-transformed in the same manner as the function. The problem of recovering the affine parameters has been reduced to finding the deformation of a known function, the gaussian, rather than the unknown brightness functions. The equation is exact and is valid for arbitrary dimensions.

The level contours of the generalized gaussian are ellipsoids rather than spheres. The tilt of the ellipsoid is given by the rotation matrix while its eccentricity is given by the matrix Σ, which is a function of the scales along each dimension. The equation clearly shows that to recover affine transforms by filtering, one must deform the filter appropriately; a point ignored in previous work [1, 2, 6, 3]. The equation is local because the gaussians rapidly decay.

The integral may be interpreted as the result of convolving the function with a gaussian at the origin and will be written as

$$F_1 * G(r, \sigma^2 I) = F_2 * G(r_1, R\Sigma R^T) \qquad (5)$$

where $r_1 = Ar$. In the case of similarity transforms, $A = sR$ i.e. a scale change and a rotation, this reduces to,

$$F_1 * G(r, \sigma^2) = F_2 * G(r_1, (s\sigma)^2) \qquad (6)$$

Note that this equation is valid for an arbitrary rotation..

Similar equations may be written using derivative of gaussian filters (for details see [5]).

3 Solution for the Case of Similarity Transforms

To solve (6) requires finding a gaussian of the appropriate scale $s\sigma$ given σ. A brute force search through the space of scale changes is not desirable. Instead a more elegant solution is to linearize the gaussians with respect to σ. This gives an equation linear in the unknown α

$$F_1 * G(., (s\sigma)^2) \approx F_2 * G(., \sigma^2) + \alpha\sigma^2\nabla^2 F_2 * G(., \sigma^2) \qquad (7)$$

where $s = 1+\alpha$. The key notion here is that the *linearization is done with respect to σ and not the image coordinates*.

Equation (7) is not very stable if solved at a single scale. By using gaussians of several different scales σ_i the following linear least squares problem is obtained:

$$\Sigma_i \|F_1 * G(., \sigma_i^2) - F_2 * G(., \sigma_i^2) + \alpha\sigma_i^2 F_2 * \nabla^2 G(., \sigma_i^2)\|^2 \qquad (8)$$

and solved using Singular Value Decomposition (SVD).

The following σ_i (1.25,1.7677,2.5,3.5355,5.0) - spaced apart by half an octave - were found to work well. The corresponding filter widths were approximately $8 * \sigma_i$ (3,5,7,11,15,21,29,41)

Choosing a Different Operating Point: For large scale changes (say scale change ≥ 1.2) the recovered scale tends to be poor. This is because the Taylor series approximation is good only for small values of α. The advantage of linearizing the gaussian equations with respect to σ is that the linearization point can be shifted i.e. the right-hand side of (6) can be linearized with respect to a σ different from the one on the left-hand side (other methods linearize the function F or the gaussian with respect to r and are therefore constrained to measuring small affine transforms). Let the right-hand side of (7) be linearized around σ_j to give the following equation

$$F_1 * G(.,\sigma_i^2) \approx F_2 * G(.,\sigma_j^2) + \alpha'\sigma_j^2 F_2 * \nabla^2 G(.,\sigma_j^2) \qquad (9)$$

where $s = \sigma_j/\sigma_i(1 + \alpha')$. The strategy therefore is to pick different values of σ_j and solve (9) (or actually an overconstrained version of it). Each of these σ_j will result in a value of α'. The correct value of α' is that which is most consistent with the equations. By choosing the σ_j appropriately, it can be ensured that no new convolutions are required.

In principle, arbitrary scale changes can be recovered using this technique. In practice, most scale changes in motion and texture are ≤ 2.5 and therefore three operating points $(\sigma, 1.4\sigma, 2.0\sigma)$ should suffice.

Finding Image Translation: Image translation, i.e. optic flow can be recovered in the following manner. Let F_1 and F_2 be similarity transformed versions of each other (i.e. they differ by a scale change, a rotation and a translation). Assume that an estimate of the translation t_0 is available. Linearizing with respect to r and σ gives

$$F_1(r+t_0) * G(r,\sigma^2) - \delta t^T F_1(r+t_0) * G(r,\sigma^2) \approx F_2 * G(.,\sigma^2) + \alpha\sigma^2 F_2 * \nabla^2 G(.,\sigma^2)$$
$$(10)$$

which is again linear in both the scale and the residual translation δt. As before an overconstrained version of this equation using multiple scales is obtained and solved for the unknown parameters. Large scales are handled as before.

t_0 is obtained either by a local search or from a coarser level in a pyramid scheme, while δt is estimated from the equation (see [4] for details).

Note that since the gaussians are rotation invariant, the translation can be recovered for arbitrary rotations about an axis perpendicular to the image. No other scheme is able to do this.

3.1 Experimental Results

Experiments on synthetic images show that the affine transform can be recovered to within a few percent (see [5]).

Figure (2) illustrates the power of this algorithm. A random dot image is scaled by a factor of 1.1 and rotated around an axis perpendicular to the image by 30 deg. On the left is the flow produced by an SSD based pyramid scheme. Note that the algorithm fails quite dramatically because of the large rotation.

This occurs because for correct matching the template also needs to be rotated by the same angle. For small angles, the template rotation can be ignored but this cannot be done for large rotations. On the other hand the results of running the algorithm described here are shown on the right-hand side. The flow shown is clearly rotational. *Note that the flow has been computed at every point without fitting a global model.* To the best of our knowledge no other existing algorithm can compute the flow correctly in this situation A histogram of the of the recovered scale values peaks at 1.1 which is the correct value.

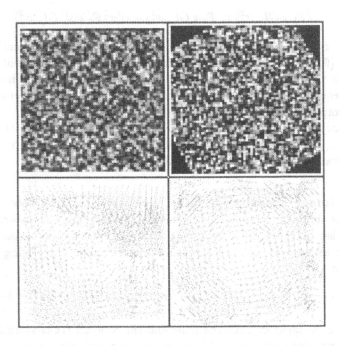

Fig. 2. Random Dot Sequence

Figure (1) shows a dollar bill scaled by 1.4. The algorithm correctly recovers the scale as 1.41. Other experiments with scaled and rotated versions of the dollar bill consistently show good recovery of scale within a few percent.

For other examples see [4].

4 Solving for the General Affine

The strategy adopted will be to first sample the space of scales and orientations to derive a finite set of filters. The gaussian equation is then linearized with respect to the scales and orientation about the elliptical filter closest to the right orientation and scales.

Recall that the gaussian weighted brightnesses are equal if

$$F_1 * G(r, \sigma^2 I) = F_2 * G(r_1, R(\theta + \phi)\Sigma' R^T(\theta + \phi)) \tag{11}$$

where F_2 is filtered with an elliptical gaussian of orientation $\theta + \phi$ and standard deviations $s_1\sigma_1$ and $s_2\sigma_2$. Linearizing the gaussian on the right with respect to σ_1, σ_2 and θ gives,

$$\begin{aligned} F_1 * G(r, \sigma^2 I) = {} & F_2 * G(r_1, R\Sigma R^T) + (s_1 - 1)\sigma_1{}^2 F_2 * G_{x'x'}(., R\Sigma R^T) \\ & + (s_2 - 1)\sigma_2{}^2 F_2 * G_{y'y'}(., R\Sigma R^T) \\ & + \phi[1/\sigma_2{}^2 - 1/\sigma_1{}^2] F_2 * G_{x'y'}(., R\Sigma R^T) \end{aligned} \tag{12}$$

where $G(., R\Sigma R^T)$ is a member of the sample set with sigma's σ_1, σ_2, $R = R(\theta)$ and $(x', y')^T = R(\theta)(x, y)^T$ i.e. (x',y') are the coordinate axes defined by the major and minor axes of the sample ellipse. Since θ is known, computing (x',y') and hence $G_{x'x'}$, $G_{x'y'}$ and $G_{y'y'}$ is straightforward. This is a good approximation if $(s_1 - 1)$, $(s_2 - 1)$ and ϕ are small.

In the case where σ_1/σ_2 this approximation may be rewritten so that elliptical gaussians are not needed and circular gaussians suffice.

Computing the matrix A: Now $AA^T = R\Sigma R^T$ is the SVD of AA^T. Also, note that $(A^T A)^{-1}$ can be recovered by interchanging the roles of F_1 and F_2 in (5), where $(A^T A)^{-1} = R_2{}^T \Sigma^{-1} R_2$ is the SVDto solve of $(A^T A)^{-1}$. Therefore $A = R\Sigma^{1/2} R_2$ (again using SVD). All the quantities on the right can be measured and hence **A** can be computed.

Acknowledgements: I wish to thank Harpreet Sawhney, John Oliensis and Al Hanson for comments and fruitful discussions.

References

1. J.R. Bergen, P. Anandan, K. J. Hanna, and R. Hingorani. Hierarchical model-based motion estimation. In *Proc. 2nd European Conference on Computer Vision*, pages 237–252, 1992.
2. M. Campani and A. Verri. Motion analysis from optical flow. *Computer Vision Graphics and Image Processing:Image Understanding*, 56(12):90–107, 1992.
3. D. G. Jones and J. Malik. A computational framework for determining stereo correspondence from a set of linear spatial filters. In *Proc. 2nd European Conference on Computer Vision*, pages 395–410, 1992.
4. R. Manmatha. Image matching under affine deformations. In *Invited Paper, Proc. of the 27nd Asilomar IEEE Conf. on Signals, Systems and Computers,*, 1993.
5. R. Manmatha and J. Oliensis. Measuring the affine transform – i: Scale and rotation. Technical Report Technical Report CMPSCI TR 92–74,University of Massachusetts at Amherst,MA,1992. Also in Proc. of the Darpa Image Understanding Workshop 1993.
6. P. Werkhoven and J. J. Koenderinck. Extraction of motion parallax structure in the visual system 1. *Biological Cybernetics*, 1990.

Extracting the Affine Transformation from Texture Moments

Jun Sato and Roberto Cipolla

Department of Engineering, University of Cambridge, Cambridge CB2 1PZ, England

Abstract. In this paper we propose a novel, efficient and geometrically intuitive method to compute the four components of an affine transformation from the change in simple statistics of images of texture. In particular we show how the changes in first, second and third moments of edge orientation and changes in density are directly related to the rotation (curl), scale (divergence) and deformation components of an affine transformation. A simple implementation is described which does not require point, edge or contour correspondences to be established. It is tested on a wide range of repetitive and non-repetitive visual textures which are neither isotropic nor homogeneous. As a demonstration of the power of this technique the estimated affine transforms are used as the first stage in shape from texture and structure from motion applications.

1 Introduction

The estimation of an affine transformation is often an integral part in structure from motion (or stereo) and shape from texture. In structure from motion relative motion between the viewer and scene induces distortion in image, and in small neighbourhoods this distortion can be described by an image translation and a four parameter *affine transformation* [6]. In shape from texture the distortion in an image of a surface with a repeated texture pattern can also be modelled by affine transformations [4, 9].

Many methods have been proposed to extract the affine transformations. The simplest method is based on the accurate extraction of points or lines and their correspondences. This requirement of correspondences becomes a non-trivial problem in densely textured images. Cipolla and Blake [3] presented a novel method to recover the affine transformation from image contours. Although this method did not require point or line correspondences the extraction and tracking of closed contours is also not always possible in richly textured images.

A large number of techniques have been developed which avoid the explicit correspondence of features. For small visual motions or distortions a common method is to estimate the affine transform from spatiotemporal gradients of image intensity [1]. The amount of visual motion allowed is limited by the smoothing scale factor. For estimating the *texture distortion* map Malik and Rosenholtz [9] have attempted to solve for the affine transformation in the fourier domain although this involves the choice of a suitable window and is computationally expensive. Under the assumptions of directional isotropy [10] it is

Lecture Notes in Computer Science, Vol. 801
Jan-Olof Eklundh (Ed.)

possible to estimate the surface orientation from the second moment matrix of image element orientations [5, 2]. Modifications of the second moment matrix which also exploit image intensity gradients have also been used [8]. However it is impossible to recover the affine transformation (four independent parameters) uniquely from the second moment matrix.

In this paper we propose a novel, efficient and geometrically intuitive method to compute the four components of an affine transformation from the change in simple statistics of the images of texture. A simple implementation is described which does not require correspondences to be established. It is tested on a wide range of repetitive and non-repetitive visual textures which are neither isotropic nor homogeneous. The estimated affine transform is also used in shape from texture and structure from motion applications.

2 Theoretical Framework

2.1 Decomposition of the Affine Transformation

Generally, an affine transformation, A, can be described by the product of an isotropic scale, S, and matrix, U, whose determinant is equal to one. Furthermore, the matrix, U, can be decomposed into a symmetric matrix, D, which we will call the geometric deformation and an asymmetric 2D rotation matrix, R. An affine matrix can thus be described with these three fundamental transformations:

$$A = S(s)R(\theta)D(\alpha, \mu) \tag{1}$$

where the isotropic scale, S, is specified by a scale parameter, s, and the rotation, R, is specified by an angle, θ. The deformation, D, is specified by an axis of deformation, μ, and a magnitude of deformation, α, and can be described using a rotation, $R(\mu)$, and symmetric matrix, $M(\alpha)$, whose eigenvalues are α and $\frac{1}{\alpha}$.

$$
\begin{aligned}
D(\alpha, \mu) &= R(\mu)M(\alpha)R^T(\mu) \\
&= \begin{bmatrix} \cos\mu & -\sin\mu \\ \sin\mu & \cos\mu \end{bmatrix} \begin{bmatrix} \alpha & 0 \\ 0 & \frac{1}{\alpha} \end{bmatrix} \begin{bmatrix} \cos\mu & \sin\mu \\ -\sin\mu & \cos\mu \end{bmatrix} \\
&= \begin{bmatrix} \frac{1}{\alpha}\sin^2\mu + \alpha\cos^2\mu & (\alpha - \frac{1}{\alpha})\sin\mu\cos\mu \\ (\alpha - \frac{1}{\alpha})\sin\mu\cos\mu & \alpha\sin^2\mu + \frac{1}{\alpha}\cos^2\mu \end{bmatrix}
\end{aligned} \tag{2}
$$

Deformation is equivalent to a pure shear which preserves area, i.e. an expansion by a factor, α, in the direction, μ, with a contraction by the same amount in a perpendicular direction.

2.2 Relationship between Changes in Image Orientation and the Affine Transformation

We now investigate the effect of these components of an affine transformation on the orientation of image detail. Consider an element of texture represented by an unit vector, $\mathbf{v}$, with orientation, φ. The affine transformation, A, transforms the vector, $\mathbf{v}$, into $\mathbf{v}'$ and changes its orientation by $\Delta\varphi$. The change in orientation, $\Delta\varphi$, can be written as the sum of two components: one due to rotation, θ, which changes the orientation of all elements equally and one due to deformation, $\Delta\varphi_d$.

$$\Delta\varphi = \theta + \Delta\varphi_d \tag{3}$$

$\Delta\varphi_d$, can be computed from the vector product $(\wedge)$ of $\mathbf{v}$ and the deformed vector, $\mathbf{v}'' = D(\alpha, \mu)\mathbf{v}$ as follows:

$$\begin{aligned}
\sin(\Delta\varphi_d) &= \frac{|\mathbf{v} \wedge \mathbf{v}''|}{|\mathbf{v}||\mathbf{v}''|} \\
&= \frac{\frac{1}{2}\left(\frac{1}{\alpha} - \alpha\right)\sin 2(\varphi - \mu)}{\sqrt{\frac{1}{\alpha^2}\sin^2(\varphi - \mu) + \alpha^2\cos^2(\varphi - \mu)}}
\end{aligned} \tag{4}$$

Note that the isotropic scale, S, does not affect orientation, while the change in orientation due to the deformation term depends on the initial orientation, φ, the axis of deformation, μ, and magnitude of deformation, α.

If the magnitude of deformation is small, the change in orientation can be described as follows from (3) and (4).

$$\Delta\varphi \simeq \theta + \frac{1}{2}\left(\frac{1}{\alpha} - \alpha\right)\sin 2(\varphi - \mu) \tag{5}$$

Koenderink and Van Doorn [7] derived a similar approximate equation for small displacements.

2.3 Texture Moments under Affine Transformation

In this section, we propose a novel method to calculate the four parameters of the affine transformation reliably without any correspondence of spatial image features using moments of the orientation and density of the texture. In previous work on shape from texture, the texture was often assumed either to be spatially homogeneous or isotropic in orientation, though such textures are limited in the real world. Here, we consider any visual pattern in the real world as a texture, and consider the change in the statistics of the visual texture under an affine transformation.

Consider the texture to have oriented elements with distribution, $f(\varphi)$, which will be changed to $f'(\varphi)$ by an affine transformation. From (5), the rotation term, R, changes the orientations of the texture elements equally. This means that rotation is related to a shift in the mean value of $f(\varphi)$ (i.e. the first moment of $f(\varphi)$), and does not affect higher moments. The deformation term, on the other hand, depends on the original orientation of the element and hence affects the variance of $f(\varphi)$ (i.e. the second moment). Furthermore because there is a term μ in the deformation term, we can infer that the changes in the distribution of orientation will not generally be symmetric about the mean of the orientations, (except for the case when $\mu = 0$) and hence the skewness of $f(\varphi)$ (i.e. the third moment) will be affected. Thus changes in first moment of orientation are related to the rotation, R, and the deformation, D. Changes to the second and third moments are only affected by D. Scale, S, affects the area of texture elements and their density, leaving orientations unaffected.

We show below how these simple geometrically intuitive relations can be used to directly recover the parameters of the affine transformation from changes in the density and orientation statistics of image textures.

From (5), an element with orientation, φ, is transformed into φ' such that:

$$\varphi' = \varphi + \theta + \lambda \sin 2(\varphi - \mu)$$
$$= \varphi + \theta + \lambda(\sin 2\varphi \cos 2\mu - \cos 2\varphi \sin 2\mu) \qquad (6)$$

where, λ is related to the magnitude term of the deformation by:

$$\lambda = \frac{1}{2}\left(\frac{1}{\alpha} - \alpha\right) \qquad (7)$$

The change in the first moment of $f(\varphi)$, ΔI_φ, in terms of the rotation, θ, axis, μ, and magnitude, λ, of the deformation is given by summing equation (6) for all elements.

$$\Delta I_\varphi = \lambda(I_{\sin 2\varphi} \cos 2\mu - I_{\cos 2\varphi} \sin 2\mu) + \theta \qquad (8)$$

where, $I_{\sin 2\varphi}$ and $I_{\cos 2\varphi}$ are the mean values of $\sin 2\varphi$ and $\cos 2\varphi$ respectively. If we assume that the deformation is small, that is $\lambda \ll 1$, then we can derive the relationships between the changes in second and third moments, $\Delta I_{\varphi\varphi}$, $\Delta I_{\varphi\varphi\varphi}$, and the rotation and deformation in closed form.

$$\Delta I_{\varphi\varphi} = 2\lambda(I_{\varphi \sin 2\varphi} \cos 2\mu - I_{\varphi \cos 2\varphi} \sin 2\mu) \qquad (9)$$
$$\Delta I_{\varphi\varphi\varphi} = 3\lambda(I_{\varphi^2 \sin 2\varphi} \cos 2\mu - I_{\varphi^2 \cos 2\varphi} \sin 2\mu) \qquad (10)$$

where $I_{\varphi \sin 2\varphi}$ and $I_{\varphi \cos 2\varphi}$ are the covariances between φ and $\sin 2\varphi$, and φ and $\cos 2\varphi$ respectively. $I_{\varphi^2 \sin 2\varphi}$ and $I_{\varphi^2 \cos 2\varphi}$ are third moments.

The rotation, θ, the axis of deformation, μ, and the magnitude of deformation, α, can be computed from:

$$\mu = \frac{1}{2} \tan^{-1}\left(\frac{M_1}{M_2}\right) \qquad (11)$$

$$\alpha = \frac{1}{2M_3}\left(\sqrt{M_1^2 + M_2^2 + 4M_3^2} - \sqrt{M_1^2 + M_2^2}\right) \qquad (12)$$

$$\theta = \Delta I_\varphi - \frac{1}{2M_3}\left(I_{\sin 2\varphi} M_2 - I_{\cos 2\varphi} M_1\right) \qquad (13)$$

where:

$$M_1 = 3\Delta I_{\varphi\varphi} I_{\varphi^2 \sin 2\varphi} - 2\Delta I_{\varphi\varphi\varphi} I_{\varphi \sin 2\varphi} \qquad (14)$$
$$M_2 = 3\Delta I_{\varphi\varphi} I_{\varphi^2 \cos 2\varphi} - 2\Delta I_{\varphi\varphi\varphi} I_{\varphi \cos 2\varphi} \qquad (15)$$
$$M_3 = 3\left(I_{\varphi^2 \cos 2\varphi} I_{\varphi \sin 2\varphi} - I_{\varphi^2 \sin 2\varphi} I_{\varphi \cos 2\varphi}\right) \qquad (16)$$

The special case where $M_3 = 0$ does not occur in practice. The change in scale, s, of the affine transformation can be obtained from the first moment of density or area of the texture elements [6, 3]. Having computed rotation, θ, the axis of deformation, μ, the magnitude of deformation, α, and the change in scale, s, we have recovered all four independent parameters of the affine transformation.

The properties of the proposed method are: (1) It does not require correspondence of individual image features. (2) This allows much greater interframe motions than spatio-temporal techniques. (3) The method relies on the comparison of statistics of the image patches. This therefore requires that corresponding areas of interest are identified. (4) The recovery of scale from the texture density assumes that the texture is homogeneous. If, instead, we can determine the changes in area of the texture elements [8], this assumption is no longer required.

3   Preliminary Results

In this section, we will present several results which show that this method does not need any assumptions like directional isotropy or spatial homogeneity to estimate the rotation and the deformation, though we need homogeneity of the texture to compute the scale component properly. Fig.1 shows the results from this method tested on a wide range of images. To demonstrate the accuracy of the extracted affine transform we have chosen to assume that the original images (upper most images in Fig.1) are of textures on a fronto-parallel plane and we use the affine transformation to estimate the new orientation of the plane assuming it is viewed under *weak* perspective (second row of images in Fig.1). The two ellipses in Fig.1 show that the estimated orientations are qualitatively good even with non-uniform textures. Table 1 compares the accuracy of this method quantitatively. The accuracy is seen to degrade when the texture in the image does not have preferred orientations. This was caused by filtering of orientation to avoid aliasing.

A second method for testing the accuracy of this method is to exploit the results in real applications.

Shape from Texture: For a repetitive texture on a curved surface the texture distortion in different directions is well modelled by an affine transform and the scale and deformation components of this affine transform can be used to recover the relative orientations and positions of the surface patches [9]. Fig.2 shows the result of using affine transforms by the method presented in this paper to recover the shape of a curved surface. The proposed method derives qualitatively good results, though there are some errors in the estimated orientations. These errors arise from (1) the difference in the sampling areas, (2) errors caused in the sampling of orientation, (3) the small deformation approximation used in the proposed method.

Qualitative Visual Navigation: In the next application, we will show how a moving observer can determine the object surface orientation and time to contact from the affine transformation estimated from texture moments. The relations between the motion parameters and the surface position and orientation were presented in [3, 6]. A translation along the optical axis towards the surface patch leads to a uniform expansion in the image. This determines the distance to the object which is conveniently expressed as a time to contact. A horizontal translation perpendicular to the visual direction results in image deformation with a magnitude determined by the slant and an axis determine by the tilt of the surface. In this case the axis of deformation bisects the tilt and direction of translation in the image. Table 2 shows the results of estimation of tilt angle of the surface and time to contact computed from Fig.3.

4 Conclusions

In this paper we have proposed a novel method to compute the four components of an affine transformation from the changes in moments of edge orientation and density. This method does not require point, edge or contour correspondences to be established, though the problem of selecting the area of interest still remains. It is extremely simple and efficient and the four parameters are linked to changes in orientation and texture density in a geometrically intuitive way.

Preliminary results have been presented and tested in simple applications exploiting the derived affine transformation. The estimated affine transformation has been of useful accuracy. However the sensitivity and error analysis as well as a quantitative comparison with other methods remain to be carried out.

References

1. P. Anandan. A computational framework and an algorithm for the measurement of visual motion. In *Int. Journal of Computer Vision*, pages 283–310, 1989.
2. A. Blake and C. Marinos. Shape from texture: estimation, isotropy and moments. *Artificial Intelligence*, 45:323–380, 1990.
3. R. Cipolla and A. Blake. Surface orientation and time to contact from image divergence and deformation. In G. Sandini, editor, *Proc. 2nd European Conference on Computer Vision*, pages 187–202. Springer–Verlag, 1992.
4. T. Kanade and J.R. Kender. Mapping image properties into shape constraints: Skewed symmetry, affine-transformable patterns, and the shape-from-texture paradigm. In J.Beck et al, editor, *Human and Machine Vision*, pages 237–257. Academic Press, NY, 1983.
5. K. Kanatani. Detection of surface orientation and motion from texture by a stereological technique. *Artificial Intelligence*, 23:213–237, 1984.
6. J.J. Koenderink. Optic flow. *Vision Research*, 26(1):161–179, 1986.
7. J.J. Koenderink and A.J. Van Doorn. Geometry of binocular vision and a model for stereopsis. *Biological Cybernetics*, 21:29–35, 1976.
8. T. Lindeberg and J. Garding. Shape from texture from a multi-scale perspective. *Proc. 4th Int. Conf. on Computer Vision*, pages 683–691, 1993.
9. J. Malik and R. Rosenholtz. A differential method for computing local shape-from-texture for planar and curved surfaces. *Proc. Conf. Computer Vision and Pattern Recognition*, pages 267–273, 1993.
10. A.P. Witkin. Recovering surface shape and orientation from texture. *Artificial Intelligence*, 17:17–45, 1981.

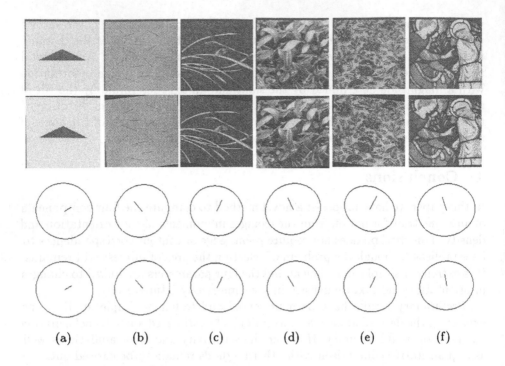

(a)   (b)   (c)   (d)   (e)   (f)

Fig. 1. Results of preliminary experiments. Examples of the images distorted by arbitrary affine transformations were processed by our affine transform from texture moments algorithm. Images in the first row and the second row are fronto-parallel images and transformed images respectively after changing the position and orientation of the plane viewed under *weak* perspective. The estimated orientations (upper ellipses) and true orientations (lower ellipses) of the transformed images are shown using normal vectors and oriented circles whose size and shape correspond to the scale change and distortion. Examples include (a) single triangle, (b) randomly oriented lines, (c) oriented grass, (d) leaves, (e) a cloth with texture and (f) stained glass as an example of a non-uniform texture.

Table 1. Accuracy of the surface parameters, scale, s, rotation, θ, tilt, τ, and slant, σ.

Images	True				Estimated			
	s	$\theta(°)$	$\tau(°)$	$\sigma(°)$	s	$\theta(°)$	$\tau(°)$	$\sigma(°)$
(a) triangle	1.0	0.0	30.0	15.0	1.0	0.0	30.0	15.0
(b) lines	1.0	-5.0	135.0	20.0	0.98	-3.8	133.0	25.1
(c) grass	0.95	5.0	60.0	25.0	0.95	5.1	60.3	24.8
(d) leaves	1.0	0.0	120.0	25.0	0.99	-2.7	117.0	25.8
(e) cloth	0.95	5.0	60.0	25.0	0.92	5.4	56.6	34.0
(f) stained glass	0.95	0.0	100.0	25.0	1.02	-2.3	112.3	26.9

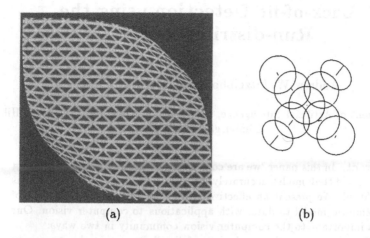

(a) (b)

Fig. 2. Shape from texture using the affine transform. Surface orientation of patches on a cylindrical object are estimated using the affine transform from texture moments. Estimated local orientations at each point are shown in (b) using oriented circles and their normal vectors.

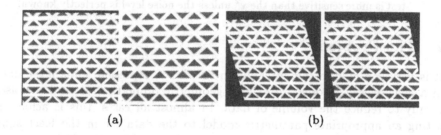

(a) (b)

Fig. 3. Two set of images are taken from a moving observer. Motion and optical direction are parallel in (a) and perpendicular in (b). The time to contact and the tilt angle of the surface recovered from the texture moments are shown in table 2.

Table 2. Tilt angle and time to contact. Scale, s, rotation, θ, axis and magnitude of the deformation, μ, α, recovered from the texture moments were used to compute the time to contact, t_c, in (a) and tilt angle of the surface, τ, in (b). Mean values and variances were estimated by changing the area of interest in each image.

Images		s	$\theta(^\circ)$	α	$\mu(^\circ)$	$\tau(^\circ)$	t_c
(a) **parallel**	True	1.20	0.0	1.0	-	-	10.0
	Estimated	1.19 ± 0.07	0.1 ± 0.1	1.01 ± 0.01	-	-	10.4 ± 3.2
perpen-	True	1.04	3.2	1.07	28	56	∞
(b) **dicular**	Estimated	1.03 ± 0.01	1.3 ± 0.1	1.07 ± 0.001	33 ± 2	66 ± 4	882 ± 496

Lack-of-fit Detection using the
Run-distribution Test

Andrew W. Fitzgibbon and Robert B. Fisher

Department of Artificial Intelligence, University of Edinburgh, 5 Forrest Hill,
Edinburgh EH1 2QL

Abstract. In this paper, we are concerned with the problem of deciding
whether a fitted model accurately describes the data to which it has
been fitted. We present an effective method of testing the lack-of-fit of
a parametric model to data, with applications to computer vision. Our
test is important to the computer vision community in two ways:

- We assume a broad enough class of distributions as to be essentially
  distribution independent.
- The test requires *no knowledge of the sensor noise level.*

We present results of experiments that compare the test with the standard χ^2 statistic. The experiments are designed to represent typical vision tasks, namely feature tracking and segmentation. We show that our
test is more sensitive than the χ^2 unless the noise level is perfectly known.

1   The Problem

It is very common in computer vision to wish to represent some large dataset
in a concise way in order to extract geometric properties, attenuate noise, or
simply to reduce the volume of data. In almost all cases, this is achieved by
fitting an appropriate parametric model to the data set in the least squares
sense. It is then vital to have some way of telling when the fit is wrong, and
the model is not 'appropriate' to the data. Simple least squares techniques [8]
assume the noise in the data to be strictly Gaussian of known variance, and
then use the χ^2 test to give an estimate of the probability that, under that
assumption, the data fits the model. Robust estimators [6] approach the problem
more directly, by effectively ignoring data points which do not fit the model.
Robust models are, however, even more expensive to fit than unbiased nonlinear
models. Our argument asserts that least squares is adequate for most purposes,
until its assumptions are violated. Of course it is precisely these boundaries, at
which the assumptions are violated, that are of most importance to the visual
process. Hence, a quick and effective test which identifies such errors will allow
a cheap estimator to be used on most of the signal, while the more expensive
techniques are held in reserve until the cheaper methods fail.

2   Goodness-of-fit Testing

We denote the data points to which the model is to be fitted by $\{\mathbf{x}_i\}_{i=1}^n$ and the
parameters of the model by $\{a_i\}_{i=1}^p$. We also assume that we have a distance

Lecture Notes in Computer Science, Vol. 801
Jan-Olof Eklundh (Ed.)

metric $D(\mathbf{a}, \mathbf{x})$ which measures the signed distance between a particular data point and the fitted model. The model fitting process is assumed to have found the value of $\mathbf{a}$ for which $\epsilon = \sum_{i=1}^{n} \phi(D(\mathbf{a}, \mathbf{x}_i))$ is minimized. The function $\phi(x)$ is an influence function, which for classical least squares is $\phi(x) = x^2$. We do not need to know the form of ϕ, simply that it must be symmetric or antisymmetric about $x = 0$. Having found the value $\mathbf{a}$, we can define the set of *residuals* $R = D(\mathbf{a}, \mathbf{x}_i)_{i=1}^{n}$. The task of lack-of-fit testing is to determine, based on the values of the residuals, whether it is unlikely that the model describes the data.

Chi Square Test: Whaite [11] provides an accessible summary of the chi-square testing technique. The basic assumption is that each observed point $\hat{\mathbf{x}}_i$ is the exact point corrupted by an isotropic zero-mean Gaussian noise process of variance σ^2. The disadvantages of the χ^2 test are well known: the Gaussian noise model has repeatedly proved unrealistic in computer vision and the noise variance is rarely known. Additionally, the test, depending on a linearization of the residual equation, fails in the presence of high noise (see Fig. 3c).

"RANSAC" Maximum Run Length Test: The "RANSAC" system of Fischler and Bolles [2] is the most similar test reported in the vision literature. Their system considers the *maximum* run length (see below) observed for a set of residuals. In our experiments, we have found this measure to be noise sensitive. In addition, we provide a possible extension to two dimensions.

3 Run-distribution Test

We now introduce our test, which we have called the run-distribution test. We describe the idea behind the test, the noise model which we assume, the actual test, and how it differs from similar tests in the literature.

The tests discussed above essentially extract one number from the set of residuals, and use that as a basis for discrimination. Instead we want to look at the set of residuals R, and decide whether that set is what we would expect, given data which is in concordance with both our parametric and noise models.

3.1 Motivation

We allow each point to be corrupted in each dimension by a scalar noise component sampled from a symmetric zero-median process plus an outlier process. Note that this is a very wide range of distributions, trivially including the normal distribution. Moreover, this particular type of distribution is common in computer vision. With such a distribution, the residuals after least-squares fitting will be similarly distributed. We can therefore detect outliers by quantifying the extent to which the *distribution* of the residuals matches our noise model.

We do this by creating the set $S = \text{sign}(R - \text{median}(R))$. By deleting the zeroes at the median from S, we now have a set whose elements may be represented as either + or -. Following von Mises [10, page 184] we define a *run*

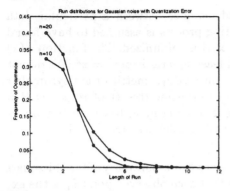

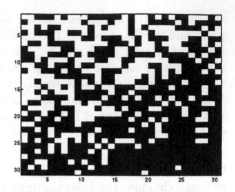

Fig. 1. Empirically derived distributions of run frequencies for two values of n, the number of data points.

Fig. 2. Example residuals sign map for a plane fit corrupted by several 10σ outliers clustered in the lower right corner.

as a sequence of one or more symbols of the same sign. For example the set $S = \{+-+++--+\}$ contains runs of lengths 1,1,3,2,1 respectively. Intuitively, we would expect that if the model fits well, there will be a large number of short runs, with long runs of positive or negative residuals indicating that the model has been biased.

This idea was used by Besl [1] to decide whether a model was of high enough order to describe the data. Besl also hints at the definition of an n dimensional run: We assume that there is some topology defining adjacency between different data points – commonly the points are defined on a grid, implicitly providing such a topology. A run is then a connected set of points with the same label, the 'length' of the run becoming the volume of the connected set. Again, with gridded data, this value will be an integral multiple of some constant. Figure 2 shows a two-dimensional example.

Measuring the likelihood of a particular distribution of runs is a problem that has been approached in the statistical literature [3, 5, 7]. In this paper, we compare the "actual" distribution to the observed distributions using a modified Kolmogorov-Smirnoff test.

3.2 Comparing the distributions

If we make a histogram $H(j)$ where bin j contains the number of runs of length j in the residuals, then the function $C(k) = \sum_{j=1}^{k} H(j)$ will approximate the cumulative distribution function. By comparing this function to the predicted cdf P given by a zero-median process (see Fig. 1), we can determine the extent to which the outlier process has corrupted the fit. Comparison of cdfs normally entails use of the Kolmogorov-Smirnoff test, where the likelihood is calculated from the known distribution of $D = \max |C_k - P(k)|$. However, this has the well-known disadvantage that the sample variance of D varies with k. Our alternative,

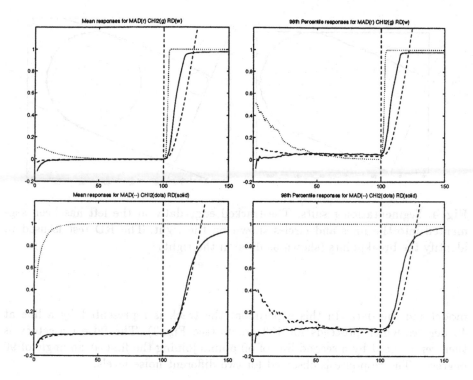

Fig. 3. Performance of the χ^2 (dots), MAD (dashes) and RD (solid) tests on the tracking task. See section 4 for details.

arrived at experimentally, was to calculate the weighted sum of distances $D = (\sum_{k=1}^{n}(P(k)-C_k)w_k)/\sum w_k$. In the experiments described below, the weighting function used was a simple quadratic $w_k = k^2$ chosen to give more importance to longer runs.

To enable use of the Kolmogorov-Smirnoff test, we must know the expected distribution of our measure. To this end we performed a Monte-Carlo simulation of the fitting process and recorded the results. We modelled the sensor noise process as a Gaussian plus quantization, which is an appropriate model for the laser range finder in use in our laboratory. The distributions are graphed in Fig. 1. See [4] for further details.

4 Experiment: Tracking

Here we consider the problem of tracking a point through time or space while maintaining an estimate of its trajectory. The tracking can often be foiled when one point passes in front of another and the program begins to follow the second point. The error may be detected by examining the fit between the trajectory

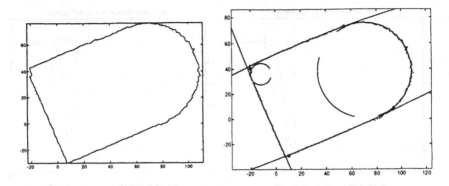

Fig. 4. Segmentation results. The tracked edge data on the left has been segmented into the lines and circles shown on the right. The RD test is used to identify the breakpoints (shown as dots on the right).

model and the data. In this experiment the track is represented by a line at 45 degrees which proceeds for 100 points (see **Fig. 3**). The false trajectory is then represented by a second line of 50 points joining the first at an angle of 90 degrees.[1] The response is observed for two different noise levels.

Discussion: The graphs of Fig. 3 may be interpreted as follows. To the left of the dotted vertical line, false rejections will occur if the response is high. To the right, low values imply false acceptances. A perfect test will be a step function going from 0 on the left to 1 on the right. The *sensitivity* of a test may be thought of as the slope of the response curve at the breakpoint. The greater the slope, the more likely the test will correctly reject outliers.

The top left graph, for the low noise case, shows all three tests performing well, particularly for large n. The χ^2, having been applied using the known noise variance shows the greatest sensitivity. Despite the tendency towards false rejections, as seen on the top right, a threshold of 0.95 will give excellent rejection. With the RD test, the low false rejection rate means that a much lower threshold will give similar results.

The real advantage of the RD test becomes apparent as noise is increased. The χ^2 test, with a slightly incorrect a priori noise model ($\sigma = 4$ rather than $\sigma = 5$) fails drastically, rejecting almost every point.

4.1   Segmentation

The test was applied to the problem of conic curve segmentation, with results as shown in Fig. 4. This experiment indicates the ability of the test to identify

---

[1] See [4] for a fuller description of experimental procedure.

subtle changes in model, at the C_2 discontinuity between line and circle for example. Curves were fitted to the 2D boundary of a 3D plane using Taubin's generalized eigenvector fit [9] and the RD test used to identify outliers. This model was chosen to be similar to that used by Whaite [11].

5 Conclusions and Current Work

We have introduced a new method of testing the hypothesis that some unknown data set is a noisy instance of a parametric model. Our method is superior to existing methods that make unrealistic assumptions about the noise characteristics of the input data. The method has $O(n)$ time and space complexity. Sensitivity to small deviations in the model is high, while the false rejection rate is extremely low, even when the data are heavily corrupted by noise. The major advantage of our test however is that there is no need to know the input noise level.

The 2D version of the test is still under development (see Fig. 2), but preliminary tests indicate similar performance to the 1D test. Using area as the equivalent to 'length' of a run may need to be changed to a fractal measure of slightly lower dimension. This is currently implemented by using morphological operators to approximate the dimensionality reduction, and then measuring areas.

References

1. P. J. Besl and R. C. Jain. Segmentation through variable-order surface fitting. *IEEE T-PAMI*, 10(2):167–192, March 1988.
2. R. C. Bolles and M. A. Fischler. A RANSAC-based approach to model fitting and its application to finding cylinders in range data. In *Proceedings, IJCAI*, pages 637–643, 1981.
3. K.A. Brownlee. *Statistical Theory and Methodology in Science and Engineering*. Wiley, 1960.
4. A. W. Fitzgibbon. Lack-of-fit detection using the run-distribution test. Technical report, University of Edinburgh, Dept. of A.I., 1994.
5. O. Kempthorne and L. Folks. *Probability, Statistics, and Data Analysis*. Iowa State University Press, Ames, Iowa 50010, 1971.
6. P. Meer, D. Mintz, A. Rosenfeld, and D.Y. Kim. Robust regression methods for computer vision: A review. *International Journal of Computer Vision*, 6(1):59–70, 1991.
7. A.M. Mood. The distribution theory of runs. *Ann. Math. Stat.*, 14:217–226, 1940.
8. W. H. Press et al. *Numerical Recipes*. Cambridge University Press, 2nd edition, 1992.
9. G. Taubin. Estimation of planar curves, surfaces and nonplanar space curves defined by implicit equations with applications to edge and range image segmentation. *IEEE T-PAMI*, 13(11):1115–1138, November 1991.
10. Richard von Mises. *Mathematical Theory of Probability and Statistics*. Academic Press, 1964.
11. P. Whaite and F. Ferrie. Active exploration: Knowing where we're wrong. In *Proceedings, ICCV*, 1993.

Disparity-Space Images and Large Occlusion Stereo

Stephen S. Intille and Aaron F. Bobick

Perceptual Computing Group
The Media Lab, Massachusetts Institute of Technology
20 Ames St., Cambridge MA 02139

Abstract. A new method for solving the stereo matching problem in the presence of large occlusion is presented. A data structure — the *disparity space image* — is defined in which we explicitly model the effects of occlusion regions on the stereo solution. We develop a dynamic programming algorithm that finds matches and occlusions simultaneously. We show that while some cost must be assigned to unmatched pixels, our algorithm's occlusion-cost sensitivity and algorithmic complexity can be significantly reduced when highly-reliable matches, or *ground control points*, are incorporated into the matching process. The use of ground control points eliminates both the need for biasing the process towards a smooth solution and the task of selecting critical prior probabilities describing image formation.

1 Introduction

Occluded regions are spatially coherent groups of pixels that can be seen in one image of a stereo pair but not in the other. These regions mark depth discontinuities and can be used to improve segmentation, motion analysis, and object identification processes, all of which must preserve object boundaries. There is psychophysical evidence that the human visual system uses geometrical occlusion relationships during binocular stereopsis[11] to reason about the spatial relationships between objects in the world. In this paper we present a stereo algorithm that does so as well.

Most stereo researchers have generally either ignored occlusion analysis or treated it as a secondary process that is postponed until matching is completed and smoothing is underway[6]. Consequently, occlusion regions are often a major source of error[3]. Stereo images of everyday scenes, such as people walking around a space, can contain contain disparity shifts and occlusion regions over eighty pixels wide[9] – much larger than occlusion regions found in typical stereo test imagery.

Our approach is to explicitly model occlusion edges and occlusion regions and to use them to drive the matching process. We develop a data structure which we will call the *disparity-space image* (DSI), and we use this data structure to develop a stereo algorithm that finds matches and occlusions *simultaneously*. We show that while some cost must be assigned to unmatched pixels, an algorithm's occlusion-cost sensitivity and algorithmic complexity can be significantly reduced

Lecture Notes in Computer Science, Vol. 801
Jan-Olof Eklundh (Ed.)

when highly-reliable matches, or *ground control points* (GCPs), are incorporated into the matching process.

Some previous stereo work has used the occlusion constraint explicitly in the matching process[1, 7, 5]. Our approach differs in that we use no additional criteria such as smoothness and intra and inter-scanline consistency since we use GCPs to eliminate sensitivity to occlusion costs.

2 The DSI Representation

The DSI is an explicit representation of matching space; it is related to figures that have appeared in previous work[4, 7, 13, 12]. We generate the DSI representation for i^{th} scanline in the following way: Select the ith scanline of the left and right images, s_i^L and s_i^R respectively, and slide them across one another one pixel at a time. At each step, the scanlines are subtracted and the result is entered as the next line in the DSI. The DSI representation stores the result of subtracting every pixel in s_i^L with every pixel s_i^R and maintains the spatial relationship between the matched points. As such, it may considered an *(x, disparity)* matching space, with x along the horizontal, and disparity along the vertical. Given two images I_L and I_R the value of the DSI is given:

$$\text{DSI}_i^R(x, d) = \begin{cases} I_R(x, i) - I_L(x + d, i) \\ \quad \text{when } 0 \leq (x + d) < N \end{cases} \tag{1}$$

where all other values are not defined and $0 \leq d < N$ and $0 \leq x < N$. The superscript of R on DSI^R indicates the right DSI. DSI_i^L is simply a negated, skewed version of the DSI_i^R.

The above definition generates a "full" DSI where there is no limit on disparity. By considering camera geometry and some maximum possible disparity shift, we can crop the representation. Further, to make the DSI more robust to effects of noise, we use correlation with a simplified version of adaptive windows[10] that preserves sharp boundaries at occlusion jumps in the DSI_i^L [9].

Figure 1-c shows the cropped, correlation DSI for a scanline through the middle of the test image pair shown in Figure 1-b. Near-zero values have been enhanced. Notice the characteristic streaking pattern that results from holding one scanline still and sliding the other scanline across. When a textured region on the left scanline slides across the corresponding region in the right scanline, a line of matches can be seen in the DSI_i^L. When two textureless matching regions slide across each other, a diamond-shaped region of near-zero matches can be observed. The more homogeneous the region is, the more distinct the resulting diamond shape will be. The correct path through DSI space can be easily seen as a dark line connecting block-like segments.

3 Occlusion Analysis and DSI Path Constraints

In a discrete formulation of the stereo matching problem, any region with non-constant disparity must have associated unmatched pixels. Any slope or disparity jump creates blocks of occluded pixels. Because of these occlusion regions, the matching zero path through the image cannot be continuous. The regions labeled

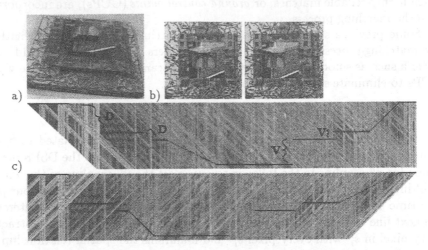

Fig. 1.: (a) A physical model of a sloping wedding cake, (b) a simulated image pair of the cake, (c) the enhanced, cropped DSI_i^L and DSI_i^R for one scan line.

"D" in Figure 1-c mark horizontal *gaps* in the enhanced zero line in DSI_i^L and DSI_i^R. The regions labeled "V" mark vertical jumps from disparity to disparity. These jumps correspond to left and right occlusion regions. We use this "occlusion constraint"[7] to restrict the type of matching path that can be recovered from each DSI_i^L. Each time an occluded region is proposed, the recovered path is forced to have the appropriate vertical or diagonal jump.

Nearly all stereo scenes obey the *ordering constraint* (or *monotonicity constraint* [7]): if object a is to the left of object b in the left image then a will be to the left of b in the right image. Thin objects with large matching disparities violate this rule, but they are rare. By assuming the ordering rule we can impose a second constraint on the disparity path through the DSI that significantly reduces the complexity of the path-finding problem. In the DSI_i^L, moving from left to right, diagonal jumps can only jump forward (down and across) and vertical jumps can only jump backwards (up). In the DSI_i^R the relationship is reversed: moving left to right diagonal jumps can only jump backwards and across and vertical jumps can only jump forwards (down). If this rule is broken the ordering constraint does not hold.

4 Finding the Best Path

Using the occlusion constraint and ordering constraint, the correct disparity path is highly constrained. From any location in the DSI_i^L, there are only three directions a path can take – a horizontal match, a diagonal occlusion, and a vertical occlusion. This observation allows us to develop a stereo algorithm that integrates matching and occlusion analysis into a single process.

Our algorithm for finding the best path through the DSI is formulated as a dynamic programming (DP) path-finding problem in $(x, disparity)$ space. We wish to find the minimum cost traversal through the DSI_i^L image when the occlusion constraints are imposed.

4.1 Dynamic Programming Constraints

The occlusion constraint and ordering constraint severely limit the direction the path can take from the path's current endpoint. If we base the decision of which path to choose at any pixel only upon the cost of each possible path we can take and not on any previous moves we have made, we satisfy the DP requirements and can use DP to find the optimal path.

Our DSI analysis led us to consider the occlusion problem in a "state-like" manner. As we traverse through the DSI image finding the optimal path, we can be in any of three states: *match (M), vertical occlusion (V), or diagonal occlusion (D)*. Figure 2 symbolically shows the legal transitions between each type of state. The path is further constrained at the edges of the DSI image, where several types of transitions may be invalid.

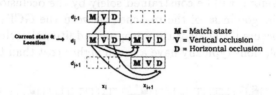

Fig. 2.: State diagram of moves the DP algorithm can choose through the DSI.

A cost is assigned to each pixel in the path depending upon the current state. We design our DP algorithm to *minimize* the cost of a path where the cost of a match is the value of the DSI_i^L pixel at the match point. The better the match, the lower the cost assessed. The algorithm will attempt to maximize the number of "good" matches in the final path. Since the algorithm will also propose unmatched points — occlusion regions — we need to assign a cost for unmatched pixels in the vertical or diagonal jumps. Otherwise the "best path" would be one that matches almost no pixels.

For the work presented here we chose a constant occlusion pixel cost. Without an additional constraint the algorithm is quite sensitive to this cost. In the next section we propose an alternative approach to reducing occlusion cost sensitivity that reduces complexity and does not artificially restrict the disparity path.

4.2 Ground Control Points

Unfortunately, slight variations in the occlusion pixel cost can change the globally minimum path through the DSI_i^L space, particularly with noisy data[5]. Because this cost is incurred for each proposed occluded pixel, the cost of a proposed occlusion region is linearly proportional to the width of the region.

In order to overcome this occlusion cost sensitivity, we need to impose another constraint in addition to the occlusion and ordering constraints. However, unlike previous approaches we do not want to bias the solution towards any generic property such as smoothness[7], inter-scanline consistency[12, 5], or intra-scanline "goodness"[5].

Instead, we use high confidence matching guesses: *Ground control points* (GCPs). These points are used to force the disparity path to make large disparity jumps that might otherwise have been avoided because of large occlusion costs.

Figure 3 illustrates this idea showing two GCPs and a number of possible paths between them. We note that regardless of which disparity path is chosen, the discrete lattice ensures that path-a, path-b, and path-c all require 6 occlusion pixels. Therefore, all three paths incur the same occlusion cost. Our algorithm will select the path that minimizes the cost of the proposed matches *independent of where occlusion breaks are proposed and the occlusion cost value.* If there is a single occlusion region between the GCPs in the original image, the path with the best matches is similar to path-a or path-b. On the other hand, if the region between the two GCPs is sloping gently, then a path like path-c, with tiny, interspersed occlusion jumps will be preferred. The path through *(x, disparity)* space, therefore, will be constrained solely by the occlusion and ordering constraints and the goodness of the matches between the GCPs. An exception to this situation occurs if the algorithm proposes additional occlusion regions as in path-d; such solutions typically have a much higher cost than the correct one.

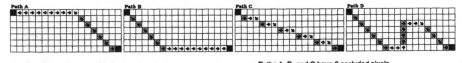

■ = Ground Control Point   ▨ = Occluded Pixel   Paths A, B, and C have 6 occluded pixels.
Path D has 14 occluded pixels.

Fig. 3.: Four possible paths through two GCPs.

4.3 Selecting and Enforcing GCPs

If we force the disparity path through GCPs, their selection must be highly reliable. We use several heuristic filters to identify GCPs before we begin the DP processing. The first heuristic requires that a control point be both the best left-to-right and best right-to-left match[8]. Second, to avoid spurious "good" matches in occlusion regions, we also require that control points have match value that is smaller than the occlusion cost. Finally, to further reduce the likelihood of a spurious match, we exclude any proposed GCPs that have no immediate neighbors that are also marked as GCPs.

Once we have a set of control points, we force our DP algorithm to choose a path through the points by assigning zero cost for matching with a control point and a very large cost to every other path through the control point's column. In the DSI_i^L, the path must pass through each column at some pixel in some state. By assigning a large cost to all paths and states in a column other than a match at the control point, we have guaranteed that the path will pass through the point.

An important feature of this approach of incorporating GCPs is that this method allows us to have more than one GCP per column. Instead of forcing

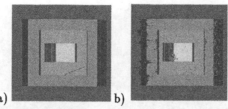

Fig. 4.: Results for the (a) noise-free and (b) noisy sloping wedding cake.

the path through one GCP, we force the path through one of a few GCPs. Even using multiple windows and left-to-right, right-to-left matching, it is still possible that we will label a GCP in error if only one per column is permitted. It is unlikely, however, that none of several proposed GCPs in a column will be the correct GCP. By allowing multiple GCPs per column, we have eliminated the risk of forcing the path through a point erroneously marked as high-confidence due image noise without increasing complexity or weakening the GCP constraint.

The use of GCPs reduces the complexity of the DP algorithm. With several GCPs the complexity can be less than 25% of the original problem[9].

5 Dynamic Programming Algorithm – Results

Input to our algorithm consists of a stereo pair. Epipolar lines are assumed to be known and corrected to correspond to horizontal scanlines. We assume that additive and multiplicative photometric bias between the left and right images is minimized, although the birch tree example shows our algorithm will work with significant additive differences.

The results generated by our algorithm for the noise-free sloping wedding cake are shown in Figure 4-a in the cyclopean view. The top layer of the cake has been shifted 84 pixels. Our algorithm found the occlusion breaks at the edge of each layer, indicated by black regions. Sloping regions have been recovered as a sloping region interspersed with tiny occlusion jumps. Since we have not used any smoothing or inter- or intra-scanline consistency, the solution in the sloping regions is governed only by the ground control points and the best matches in the region. Figure 4-b shows the results for the sloping wedding cake with noise (SNR = 18 dB). The algorithm still locates occlusion regions well.

Figure 5-a shows the "birch" image from the JISCT stereo test set[2]. The occlusion regions in this image are difficult to recover properly because of the skinny trees, some textureless regions, and a 15 percent brightness difference between images. The skinny trees make occlusion recovery particularly sensitive to occlusion cost when GCPs are not used, since there are relatively few good matches on each skinny tree compared with the size of the occlusion jumps to and from each tree. Figure 5-b shows the results of our algorithm *without* using GCPs. The occlusion cost prevented the path on most scanlines from jumping out to some of the trees. Figure 5-c shows the algorithm run with the same occlusion cost using GCPs. The occlusion regions around the trees are recovered reasonably well since GCPs on the tree surfaces eliminated the dependence on

Fig. 5.: (a) Image pair and results without (b) and with (c) GCPs.

the occlusion cost. The algorithm fails where the image is washed-out, the image is textureless, or where no GCPs were recovered on some trees.

Figure 6-a is the left image of a stereo image pair of some people. Figure 6-b shows the left image results obtained by the algorithm developed by Cox *et al.*[5]. The Cox algorithm is a similar DP procedure which uses inter-scanline consistency instead of GCPs to reduce sensitivity to occlusion cost. Figure 6-c shows our results on the same image. The Cox algorithm does a reasonably good job at finding the major occlusion regions, although many rather large, spurious occlusion regions are proposed. When the algorithm generates errors, the errors are more likely to propagate over adjacent lines, since inter-and intra-scanline consistency are used[5]. To be able to find the numerous occlusions, the Cox algorithm requires a relatively low occlusion cost, resulting in false occlusions. Our higher occlusion cost and use of GCPs finds the major occlusion regions cleanly. For example, the man's head is clearly recovered by our approach. The algorithm did not recover the occlusion created by the man's leg as well as hoped since it found no good control points on the bland wall between the legs. The wall behind the man was picked up well by our algorithm, and the structure of the people in the scene is quite good. Most importantly, *we did not use any smoothness or inter- and intra-scanline consistencies to generate these results.*

We should note that our algorithm does not perform well on images that only have short match regions interspersed with many disparity jumps. In such imagery our conservative method for selecting GCPs fails to provide enough constraint to recover the proper surface. However, the results on the birch imagery illustrate that in real imagery with many occlusion jumps, there are likely to be enough stable regions to drive the computation.

6 Summary

We have presented a stereo algorithm that incorporates the detection of occlusion regions directly into the matching process. We develop an dynamic programming solution that obeys the occlusion and ordering constraints to find a best path through the disparity space image. To eliminate sensitivity to occlusion cost

a)

b)

c)

Fig. 6.: (a) Left image. Results of (b) Cox *et al.* algorithm[5], and (c) our algorithm.

we use ground control points (GCPs)— high confidence matches. These points improve results, reduce complexity, and minimize dependence on occlusion cost without arbitrarily restricting the recovered solution.

References

1. P. Belhumeur. Bayesian models for reconstructing the scene geometry in a pair of stereo images. In *Proc. Info. Sciences Conf.*, Johns Hopkins University, 1993.
2. R. Bolles, H. Baker, and M. Hannah. The JISCT stereo evaluation. In *Proc. Image Understanding Workshop*, pages 263–274, 1993.
3. R.C. Bolles and J. Woodfill. Spatiotemporal consistency checking of passive range data. SRI Technical Report – to be published, SRI International, September 1993.
4. S.D. Cochran and G. Medioni. 3-d surface description from binocular stereo. *IEEE Trans. Patt. Analy. and Mach. Intell.*, 14(10):981–994, 1992.
5. I.J. Cox, S. Hingorani, B. Maggs, and S. Rao. Stereo without regularization. NEC Research Institute Report, NEC Research Institute, October 1992.
6. U.R. Dhond and J.K. Aggarwal. Structure from stereo – a review. *IEEE Trans. Sys., Man and Cyber.*, 19(6):1489–1510, 1989.
7. D. Geiger, B. Ladendorf, and A. Yuille. Occlusions and binocular stereo. In *Proc. European Conf. Comp. Vis.*, pages 425–433, 1992.
8. M.J. Hannah. A system for digital stereo image matching. *Photogrammetric Eng. and Remote Sensing*, 55(12):1765–1770, 1989.
9. S.S. Intille and A.F. Bobick. Disparity-space images and large occlusion stereo. MIT Media Lab Perceptual Computing Group Technical Report No. 220, Massachusetts Institute of Technology, October 1993.
10. T. Kanade and M. Okutomi. A stereo matching algorithm with an adaptive window: theory and experiment. In *Proc. Image Understanding Workshop*, pages 383–389, 1990.
11. K. Nakayama and S. Shimojo. Da Vinci stereopsis: depth and subjective occluding contours from unpaired image points. *Vision Research*, 30(11):1811–1825, 1990.
12. Y. Ohta and T. Kanade. Stereo by intra- and inter-scanline search using dynamic programming. *IEEE Trans. Patt. Analy. and Mach. Intell.*, 7:139–154, 1985.
13. Y. Yang, A. Yuille, and J. Lu. Local, global, and multilevel stereo matching. In *Proc. Comp. Vis. and Pattern Rec.*, 1993.

Registration of a Curve on a Surface Using Differential Properties

Alexis Gourdon, Nicholas Ayache

INRIA - Project Epidaure - 2004 Route des Lucioles, BP 93
06902 Sophia Antipolis Cedex, France.
Email : alexis.gourdon@sophia.inria.fr

Abstract. This article presents a new method to find the best rigid registration between a curve and a surface. It is possible to write a compatibility equation between a curve point and a surface point, which constrains completely the 6 parameters of the sought rigid displacement. This requires the local computation of third order differential quantities and leads to an algebraic equation of degree 16.

A second approach consists in considering pairs of curve and surface points. Then only first order differential are necessary to compute locally the parameters of the rigid displacement. Although computationally more expensive, the second approach is more robust, and can be accelerated with a preprocessing of the surface data.

To our knowledge, it is the first method which takes full advantage of local differential computations to register a curve on a surface.

1 Introduction

Finding the best spatial registration between a rigid curve and a rigid surface is an important problem in the medical field when a volume medical image must be registered either with a single cross-section acquired later with a CT-Scanner or MRI, or with a 3D curve acquired with a laser range finder on the external surface of a patient. Besl mentionned this problem in a paper on 3D registration [1], and Grimson presented recently an industrial application of this type but restricted to the recognition of cylinder objects [2].

The scope of our study is more general in that we do not restrict the shape of the observed surfaces or curves. In fact, although results are presented with planar curves, the developped formalism is valid also for general spatial curves and free form surfaces. On the other hand, we assume that it is possible to compute the differential properties of both the curve and the surface, either up to the third order (first approach), or at least up to the first order (second approach). Both are reasonable assumptions with high resolution medical volume images, where adequate spatial filtering allows for the extraction of anatomical surfaces and curves, with the computation of differential properties [3, 4, 5].

2 Registration Using one Point on Curve and Surface

2.1 Geometrical Constraints

At each point of a parametric curve, we can define an intrinsic orthonormal frame $(\mathbf{t}, \mathbf{n}, \mathbf{b})$ (the Frenet frame) and metric invariants (the curvature k and torsion τ). We can also build at each point of a parametric surface the two fundamental forms and infer from them an intrinsic orthonormal frame $(\mathbf{e_1}, \mathbf{e_2}, \mathbf{N})$ (the principal frame) and the two principal curvatures. $(k_1, k_2))$ [6]

When a curve lies on a surface, its tangent vector is in the tangent plane of the surface. We can then also construct a third intrinsic orthonormal frame $(\mathbf{t}, \mathbf{g}, \mathbf{N})$, called the Darboux frame. Thus, for each of these frames, we can express the derivatives of the frame along the curve with respect to the arc length s in the same frame (moving frame method) [6]. Using the relations between the Darboux frame and the Frenet frame or the principal frame we obtain:

$$k_n = k\cos\theta = \qquad k_1\cos^2\varphi + k_2\sin^2\varphi \qquad \text{(normal curvature)} \qquad (1)$$

$$k_g = k\sin\theta = \frac{1}{k_1 - k_2}\left(\frac{\partial k_1}{\partial e_2}\cos\varphi + \frac{\partial k_2}{\partial e_1}\sin\varphi\right) + \frac{d\varphi}{ds} \quad \text{(geodesic curvature)}^1 \quad (2)$$

$$\tau_g = \tau - \frac{d\theta}{ds} = \qquad (k_1 - k_2)\cos\varphi\sin\varphi \qquad \text{(geodesic torsion)} \qquad (3)$$

The knowledge of θ (angle betwen the normal to the curve and the normal to the surface) and φ (angle between the curve tangent and the principal direction e_1) characterizes the rotation between the Frenet frame and the principal frame.

For each point on the curve, we can compute its curvature k and its torsion τ and their derivatives with respect to the arc length s. Moreover, for each point of the surface the principal curvatures (k_1, k_2) and their derivatives along e_1 and e_2 can be computed. However k_n, k_g, τ_g, the two angles θ, φ and their derivatives with respect to s are unknown. In our problem, we have a model S of a surface and a curve α that we wish to register on S. For every point m of α and its homologous point M on the surface, every pair (θ, φ) which is solution of (1,2,3) gives us a unique registered Frenet frame. It is then easy to find the rotation of the Frenet frame and to infer the rigid transformation which maps m into M.

2.2 Determining the Angles θ and φ

The drawback of the system (1,2,3) where the unknown values are $(\theta(s), \varphi(s))$ is the presence of the derivatives of $(\theta(s), \varphi(s))$ with respect to s (except for (1)). Thus, in order to find (θ, φ) we must eliminate those derivatives. By derivating (1) with respect to s and using (2,3) and ^{2} we obtain:

$$\frac{1}{k}\frac{dk}{ds}k_n + k_g(3\tau_g - \tau) = \frac{\partial k_1}{\partial e_1}\cos^3\varphi + 3\frac{\partial k_1}{\partial e_2}\cos^2\varphi\sin\varphi + 3\frac{\partial k_2}{\partial e_1}\cos\varphi\sin^2\varphi + \frac{\partial k_2}{\partial e_2}\sin^3\varphi = C(\varphi)$$
$$(4)$$

Therefore we obtain one single algebraic equation in φ with

$$f(\varphi) = (k^2 - k_n^2(\varphi))(3\tau_g(\varphi) - \tau)^2 - (C(\varphi) - \frac{1}{k}\frac{dk}{ds}k_n(\varphi))^2 = 0 \qquad (5)$$

Since (5) is an algebraic equation of degree sixteen, there is no hope to find explicit roots for the general case, but classical methods may be used [7].

For each solution φ, (1) gives us $\cos\theta$; $\sin\theta$ is obtained by (2) and (4) .

2.3 Matching Algorithm

First at all we have to compute differential invariants in volume or planar images. The use of a Gaussian convolution filter transforms the digital 3D image into an infinitely differentiable function $I(x, y, z)$ [3, 5]. Then the implicit function theorem allows us to express the differential caracteristics of the iso-surface $I(x, y, z) = a$ as expressions of the derivatives of $I(x, y, z)$ [4].

Now we can describe our matching algorithm:

---

^{1} for each fonction $M\,(u, v)$ defined on the surface, $\frac{\partial M}{\partial e_1}(m) = \frac{dM}{dt}(m + te_1)$ for $(t = 0)$ is called the derivative of M with respect to e_1 in m.

^{2} for each function P of the coordinates of the surface (u, v), the derivative of the restriction of P on the curve may be written: $\frac{dP}{ds} = \frac{\partial P}{\partial e_1}\cos\varphi + \frac{\partial P}{\partial e_2}\sin\varphi$

1. For each remaining pair of points with one point on the curve and the other one on the surface, solve the equation for the angle φ. Then for each root:
   (a) Compute θ and determine the rigid transformation.
   (b) Apply the tranformation to the curve.
   (c) If a sufficient number of curve points lie at a distance of the surface smaller than a preset threshold, store the 6 parameters of the rigid transformation in a hash-table.
2. Repeat until at least one bucket of the hash-table contains a sufficient number of stored transfomations.

By applying the estimated transformation to the curve we can easily eliminate irrelevant transformations. However this last process requires the computation, for each point of the curve, of the closest point on the surface. This can be done by using octree-spline [8]. As soon as the initial guess is reasonably good, we can improve the registration by using an iterative method (see [9] for instance). Unfortunately, to find the initial guess, we have to compute third order derivatives on the curve and on the surface and solve an algebraic equation of high degree. This makes the method applicable to high quality data only. To address this last point, we present now a more expensive but more robust approach.

3 Registration Using pair of Points

3.1 Geometrical Constraints

The geometric constraints between a pair of points (a, b) on the curve α and its homologous pair of points (A, B) on the surface S require only first order differential invariants on the curve and surface.

Since the tangent to a curve lying on a surface is in the tangent plane of the surface and that the scalar product is invariant by a rigid transformation, the constraints between the pairs (a, b) et (A, B) can be written as:

$$\begin{cases} \| ab \| = \| \mathbf{AB} \| = d \\ \langle D(t_a)|\mathbf{N_A}\rangle = \langle D(t_b)|\mathbf{N_B}\rangle = 0 \end{cases} \text{ and } \begin{cases} \langle D(t_a)|\mathbf{AB}\rangle = \langle t_a|ab\rangle \\ \langle D(t_b)|\mathbf{AB}\rangle = \langle t_b|ab\rangle \end{cases}$$

D is the unknown displacement, (t_a, t_b) are the tangents to the curve in (a, b) and $(\mathbf{N_A}, \mathbf{N_B})$ are the normals to the surface in (A, B) homologous points of (a, b) by D. Writing $\langle \mathbf{N_A}|\mathbf{N_B}\rangle = \cos \Gamma$ and expressing $(D(t_a), D(t_b))$ in the bases of the tangent planes of the surface in (A, B) [3] we have:

$$\begin{cases} \sin \Gamma\, D(t_a) = \cos \alpha\, \mathbf{N_A} \wedge \mathbf{N_B} + \sin \alpha\, [\cos \Gamma \mathbf{N_A} - \mathbf{N_B}] \\ \sin \Gamma\, D(t_b) = \cos \beta\, \mathbf{N_A} \wedge \mathbf{N_B} + \sin \beta\, [\cos \Gamma \mathbf{N_B} - \mathbf{N_A}] \end{cases}$$

(α, β) are the angles between $(D(t_a), D(t_b))$ and $\mathbf{N_A} \wedge \mathbf{N_B}$.

By writing $\mathbf{AB}$ in the two bases and by computing the scalar products $\langle D(t_a)|\mathbf{AB}\rangle$ and $\langle D(t_b)|\mathbf{AB}\rangle$ we get two equations for the angles (α, β) of the form $A \cos \theta + B \sin \theta = C$ [4]. As the scalar product is invariant we can write: $\langle D(t_a)|D(t_b)\rangle = \langle t_a|t_b\rangle = \cos \gamma$. Thus we have one more equation:

$$\cos \alpha \cos \beta - \cos \Gamma \sin \alpha \sin \beta = \cos \gamma \tag{6}$$

Then by solving the equations verified by α and β and keep the roots which verify (6) we can find the rigid transformation which maps (a, b) on (A, B).

[3] when $\mathbf{N_A} \wedge \mathbf{N_B} \neq 0$
[4] An equation of the form $A \cos \theta + B \sin \theta = C$ has two roots if and only if $A^2 + B^2 \geq C^2$

3.2 Specific Situations

When $\sin \gamma = 0$ and $\sin \Gamma \neq 0$, (i.e. the tangent vectors in (a, b) are parallel). By using (6) we prove that (α, β) must be equal to 0 or π and that $(\mathbf{t_a}, \mathbf{t_b}, \mathbf{N_A} \wedge \mathbf{N_B})$ are proportional vectors. This can be seen in the following equation:

$$\lambda^2 = (\frac{\langle \mathbf{N_A} \wedge \mathbf{N_B} | \mathbf{AB} \rangle}{\sin \Gamma})^2 = \langle \mathbf{ab} | \mathbf{t_a} \rangle^2 = \langle \mathbf{ab} | \mathbf{t_b} \rangle^2 \qquad (7)$$

Thus in this particular case we have two invariants on the pair of curve points and on the pair of surface points : the intrinsic distance d and the quantity λ.

3.3 Registration Algorithm

Using the above-mentioned constraints, the matching algorithm is as follows:
1. for each pair of curve points and for each pair of surface points being at the same distance d:
   (a) find α and β and keep them if they satisfy (6) with a given accuracy ϵ.
   (b) Compute for each solution (α, β) the corresponding rigid transformation.
2. Then proceed the same way as in the first algorithm.

The main advantage of this algorithm with respect to the one based on the computation of φ comes from the use of first order differential invariants (curve tangents and surface normals), instead of the third order differential invariants.

However, this algorithm has a higher complexity: it is necessary to search for pairs of curve and scene points being at a similar distance of each other. A brute force algorithm leads to a combinatorial explosion, which is in $O(n^2 p^2)$.

The complexity can be decreased by reducing the number of pairs of curve points, i.e. selecting those being at a sufficiently large distance of each other. The surface can be preprocessed beforehand: pairs of surface points can be ordered by increasing distance d. Then, at recognition time, a given pair of curve points is compared to surface pairs of similar distance with a $O(\log(n^2))$ algorithm.

A further reduction in the number of such pairs can be easily obtained when dealing with planar and closed curves, by imposing parallel tangent vectors. In this case, as showed above, it is easy to compute 2 intrinsic invariants at each curve and scene point (d and λ computed with respect to curve point of same tangent vector). The number of pairs of curve points then reduces to $O(p)$, since for a given curve point there is a finite number of points on the curve with parallel tangents. Applying both strategies can reduce the recognition complexity to $O(p \log(n))$ for planar curves, and $O(p^2 \log(n))$ in the general case.

4 Experimental Results

4.1 Synthetic Examples

After the generation of synthetic volume images of a 3D object (Fig. 1), we extracted the object surface for a given iso-intensity value [4], and a curve in a randomly selected 2D cross-section, for the same iso-intensity value. The surface had about 7000 points while the curve had about 150 points.

Using the first approach, and using the proposed third order differential invariants, (5) yielded from 0 to 12 solutions for φ. By computing the derivatives analytically , the program returned for 90% of the curve points, the correct φ with an accuracy better than 5 degrees. When the derivatives were computed by local gaussian filtering this percentage was 75% of the curve points.

The second approach yielded a correct rigid transformation, for all our trials. In fact, we got additional solutions, which are quite reasonable due to the symmetries of the original object as can be seen in Fig. 1.

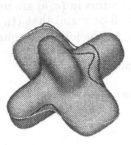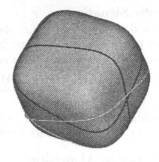

Fig. 1. Registrations on synthetic examples.

4.2 Real Data

We used a volume image of a skull acquired by an X-ray CT-Scan (provided by GE-MS), and we computed the iso-surface corresponding to the bone surface. In another image of the same skull in a different position, we extracted a single cross section and the iso-intensity contour corresponding again to the bone limit.

The algorithm using the second approach found the rigid transformation which superimposes the curve on the surface. As we knew that the cross section had been extracted grossly at the level of the orbits, we reduced the complexity of the matching algorithm by selecting only about 10 cross-sections of the first volume image of the skull, centered about the orbits and by taking the pairs of curve points whose inter-distance was larger than 75% of the curve diameter.

An iterative registration algorithm can improve the found solution. Typically, the initial solution is found with a tolerated distance of about 5 voxels between the transformed curve and the surface, and this distance can be decreased to 0.5 voxel after a few tens of iterations of the iterative closest point algorithm.

5 Conclusion

In this paper we have presented the differential constraints which can be exploited to register rigidly a curve on a surface. These constraints apply by considering either homologous points, which requires the computation of third order differential invariants and leads to a $O(np)$ algorithm, or homologous pairs of points between the curve and the surface, which brings about the computation of first order differential invariants and leads to a brute force complexity of $O(n^2p^2)$ algorithm. This last complexity can be significantly reduced, typically to $O(p \log(n))$ by applying additional constraints, in particular when the curve is planar and closed.

We presented results both with synthetic and real data, showing that only the second algorithm is robust enough in the presence of noise. Anyhow, the constraints used in the first algorithm can be used efficiently during the verification stage of the second algorithm, making the whole study useful in practice.

Aknowledgements

The authors wish to thank J.P. Thirion for his contribution of the general formulation of the problem, J. Feldmar for stimulating discussions, G. Medioni and also G. Malandain for their useful comments. This research was partially supported by Digital Equipment Corporation.

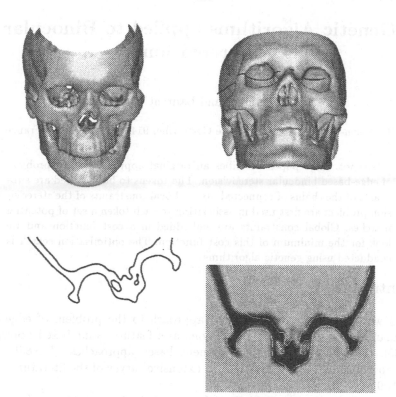

Fig. 2. Top: left: surface from the first CT scan; left: one particular fit. Bottom: left: curve from the second CT scan; right: the curve is superimposed on the interpolated cross section image.

References

1. P.J. Besl. *The Free-Form Surface Matching Problem (Machine Vision for 3-D Scenes).* H. Freeman, Ed., 1990.
2. W.E.L Grimson, T. Lozano-Pérez, N. Noble, and S.J. White. An automatic tube inspection system that finds cylinders in range data. In *Proceedings CVPR '93, New York City, NY.* IEEE, June 1993.
3. O. Monga, S. Benayoun, and O.D. Faugeras. Using partial derivatives of 3d images to extract typical surface features. In *Proceedings CVPR '92, Urbana Champaign, Illinois.* IEEE, July 1992.
4. Jean-Philippe Thirion and Alexis Gourdon. The 3D marching lines algorithm and its application to crest lines extraction. Technical Report 1672, INRIA, May 1992.
5. B.H. Romeny, L. Florack, A. Salden, and M. Viergever. Higher order differential structure of images. In H.H. Barrett and A.F. Gmitro, editors, *IPMI*, pages 77–93, Flagstaff, Arizona (USA), June 1993. Springer-Verlag.
6. M.P. Do Carmo. *Differential geometry of curves and surfaces.* Prentice Hall, 1976.
7. William H. Press, Brian P. Flannery, Saul A. Teukolsky, and William T. Vetterling. *Numerical Recipes in C, The Art of Scientific Computing.* Cambridge University Press, 1990.
8. Stéphane Lavallée, Richard Szeliski, and Lionel Brunie. Matching 3-d smooth surfaces with their 2-d projections using 3-d distance maps. In *SPIE, Geometric Methods in Computer Vision*, San Diego, Ca, July 1991.
9. P.J. Besl and N.D. McKay. A method for registration of 3-D shapes. *IEEE Transactions on PAMI*, 14(2), February 1992.

Genetic Algorithms applied to Binocular Stereovision

Régis Vaillant and Laurent Gueguen

Thomson-CSF LCR, Domaine de Corbeville, 91404 Orsay Cedex France

Abstract. This paper describes an original approach to the problem of edge-based binocular stereovision. The tokens to be matched are sub-chains of the chains of connected pixels. Local constraints of the stereovision problem are first used in associating to each token a set of potential matches. Global constraints are embedded in a cost function and we look for the minimum of this cost function. The optimisation search is conducted using genetic algorithms.

1 Introduction

In this work, we propose an original approach to the problem of edge-based binocular stereovision. Classical solutions are: feature point based approaches ([Gri85], [PMF85], [OK85]), line segment based approaches ([MN85]), curve based approaches ([BB89], [RF91]). An extensive survey of the literature is done in [DA89].

Here, we propose to use chains of connected edge points as tokens to be matched. The number of such features is relatively small (less than 300 in typical images). The matching process is implemented by first reducing the set of potential matches for each chain by using local constraints (epipolar constraint, disparity constraint, disparity gradient constraint and orientation of the gradient intensity constraint). In a following step, the solution of the matching problem is searched by using more global constraints. These constraints are embedded in a cost function and we look for a minimum of this cost function. This optimisation problem is solved using a genetic algorithm. The cost function evaluates the mapping from the set of features of the first image to the set of features of the second image and NIL. This problem reveals itself well adapted to the philosophy of the genetic algorithms. Using genetic algorithms, the optimisation of this function is done through a competition between different possible solutions to the problem of matching. This competition is assessed using the cost function. The different mappings are combined to form a new one using the cross-over operator. For example, in the ideal case of two mappings, one which is good for the upper part of the image but introduces errors for the lower part and the other which is only good for the lower part of the image are combined in such a way that the two good parts are joined in one new solution.

2 Binocular Stereovision

The problem of binocular stereovision is the reconstruction of the 3D coordinates of a number of points in a scene given two images obtained by cameras of known relative position and orientation. In this paper, we are more specifically interested by the correspondence problem. This problem has been widely studied and various constraints have been proposed.

The first and most important is the epipolar constraint (see [Fau93]). We simplify its use by first rectifying the images (see [HAL88]).

The edges of the images are extracted by classical techniques ([Der87]) and we form a set of chains of connected pixels for each image. We propose to divide each chains of pixels in sub-chains such that, in the rectified image, the ordinates of the pixels change monotically when we move from the beginning of the sub-chain to its end. Consequently, the intersection between an epipolar line and each sub-chains contains at most one point.

Individual constraints We now introduced a set of individual constraints. These constraints have to be verified for a match of a token of the first image with a token of the second image. By using them, we associate to each sub-chain ch_1 of the first image, a subset of the sub-chains of the second image which are potential matches for ch_1. These individual constraints are: the epipolar constraint, the disparity constraint, the disparity gradient constraint and orientation of the gradient of intensity. Details on the integration of these constraints are in [VG93].

Global Constraints The global constraints apply for the major part of the tokens of the scene. These constraints are the uniqueness constraint, the order constraint and the continuity constraint. These last two constraints are not always verified and it is not possible to build an algorithm which enforces them for all the tokens. So, we choose to impose these constraints to a solution of the matching problem globally and to look for the solutions among the mimima of a cost function. This function increases whenever some pair of matches violates one of the constraints. The cost function is a mapping σ from the set of valid solutions to $\mathbb{R}$. We call valid solutions the ones which respect the uniqueness constraint.

$$f(\sigma) = -\lambda_{match} f_{match}(\sigma) + \lambda_{order} f_{order}(\sigma) + \lambda_{dist} f_{dist}(\sigma) + \lambda_{angle} f_{angle}(\sigma)$$

- $f_{match}(\sigma)$ is the sum of the length of the matched sub-chains.
- $f_{order}(\sigma)$ is the sum of the length of the common part of the couples of matched chains which violate the order constraint.
- $f_{dist}(\sigma)$ and $f_{angle}(\sigma)$ evaluates the local continuity.

λ_{match}, λ_{order}, λ_{dist} and λ_{angle} are appropriate weighting coefficients.

3 Genetic Algorithms applied to Binocular Stereovision

The genetic algorithms mimic the mechanisms involved in natural selection to conduct a search through a given parameter space for the maximum/minimum of some objective function. Here, we will present the main features of the genetic algorithms. A detailed presentation can be found in [Gol89]. A point of the parameter space is called a chromosome. The algorithm maintains a population of N individuals which are represented by their chromosomes. It is rather different from the classical optimisation algorithms which maintains only one point in the search space. Operators are applied to the population and successive generation of the population are derived. These operators rely on probabilistic rules. The search for an optimal solution starts with a randomly generated population of chromosomes. The objective function f is estimated for each individual of the population. A new set of individuals, obtained by the application of the different operators, is the next generation. A stop criterion is tested. If it is decided to continue, the process for computing new generations is iterated.

Encoding of the Solutions We denote Ch_1 (resp. Ch_2) the set of sub-chains of connected pixels of the first image (resp. the second image) which vary monotically (see section 2). A valid solution σ of the matching problem associates to each element of Ch_1 one or zero element of Ch_2. For each element ch_1 of Ch_1, $\sigma(ch_1)$ must belong to the set of potential matches of ch_1 or be NIL (i.e. no match). Each element ch_2 of Ch_2 must be associated to at most one element of ch_1. This is the uniqueness constraint for the elements of Ch_2.

The description of an individual is an array which gives the number of the element of Ch_2 (or NIL) associated with each element of Ch_1. The elements of Ch_1 are introduced in the table according to a precise order defined by the position of their highest point in the image.

Selection The operator of selection chooses, among the N individuals of the population of the current generation, the elements which will be present in the next generation. The selection is based on the cost function.

Cross-Over This operator is used for mixing two individuals and deriving from them two new viable individuals. In accordance with the basic principle set out in [Gol89], a cut site is randomly chosen. It defines two sections on each individual. Two new individuals are derived by combining the opposing sections from the two initial individuals. Of course, the uniqueness constraint for the elements of Ch_2 is no longer necessarily respected and both new individuals must be corrected. The correction is done by scanning each individual from the first element to the cross-over site. For each element ch_1 of Ch_1, we test if the uniqueness constraint is respected for the element of Ch_2 which is associated to it. If it is not, we associate to ch_1 a randomly chosen element among the potential matches of ch_1. We restrict this choice to the elements which are not already used in this individual. If, the set of such elements is empty, no element is associated to ch_1.

Mutation A random site, which represents a sub-chain ch_1^i of Ch_1 is replaced randomly by one of the other potential matches of ch_1^i which are still free. If none is free, no element of Ch_2 is associated to ch_1^i. Processing like this, the result of the mutation is viable (respect the uniqueness constraint).

The Algorithm
Normal Algorithm

1. Initialization of a random population of viable individuals. An individual is randomly constructed by choosing successively for each element ch_1 of Ch_1 its associated element among the potential matches of ch_1 that are not already used. If none exists, no element is associated to ch_1. For this process, the elements of Ch_1 are scanned in random order. In this way, the individuals

built cover correctly the set of possible viable individuals.

2. Computation of the cost function associated with each individual and application of the selection operator. Application of the cross-over and the mutation.

3. While a stop criterion is false, goto 2.

The stop criterion that we have used is the total number of generations.

A Coarse to Fine Approach The proposed algorithm does not make any distinction between the most important structures that are a priori described by the longest sub-chains and the details which are described by shorter sub-chains. A solution to this problem is to use only the longest sub-chains at the beginning and progressively to insert the others. The number of genes of the individuals is increased. This operation is done simultaneously for all the individuals of the population. The insertion operation is a variant of the selection.

4 Experimental results and conclusion

Experimental results In this section, we show the results obtained using our algorithm. Figure 1.(a) shows the original doublet of images. Figure 1.(b) shows the extracted edges before rectification[1]. Figure 1.(c) shows the edges that have been matched by the algorithm. Figure 1.(d) shows the erroneous matches[2]. These results have been obtained by using the coarse to fine approach: the sub-chains are inserted progressively in the chromosome.

In these experiments, we have used the following parameters. number of individuals in the population: 100, probability of cross-over: 0.7, probability of mutation: 0.2, 2000 generations. The size of the population is increased by 20 every 200 generations. The computational time is directly proportional to the complexity of the cost function. In our case, the construction of a new generation needs several seconds.

The values of these parameters have not been thoroughly optimised. Only a few experiments have been done with different values. These experiments have shown that the results are quite insensitive to the precise values of the parameters. However, we think that some of these parameters, especially the increment of the population size and the number of generations with a fixed size could be set to decrease the computational time.

Conclusion In this article, we have presented an original approach to the edge-based stereovision problem. We propose to match sub-chains of connected edge pixels. The split of the chains in sub-chains is done using the epipolar constraint. This solution allowed us to operate on curved objects. We have first shown how we organized the specific constraints of the stereovision problem in such a way that finding a solution to the problem of matching is equivalent to a search for the minimum of a specific cost function. The cost function is

---

[1] For each sub-chain, we have only drawn a polygonal approximation of the part of the sub-chain which corresponds exactly to its match. This part is defined using the epipolar constraint.

[2] The classification between correct and incorrect matches has been made by hand.

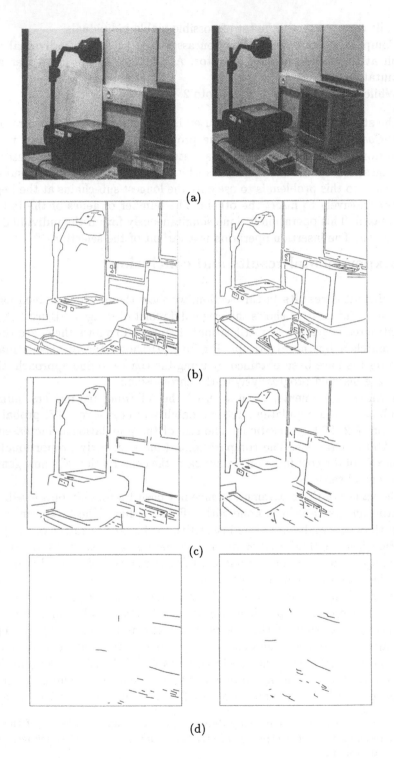

Fig. 1. (a) the original doublet of images and (b) the extracted edges, (c) the matched edges and (d) the erroneous matches

minimized using genetic algorithms. It is remarkable to notice that only a few modifications have been given to the classical operators of genetic algorithms. The operator of cross-over appeared to be remarkably adapted to the problem of stereovision, as two solutions which are not correct in the same parts of the image, could be merged in such a way that their correct parts are joined.

It is straight forward to combine a coarse to fine strategy with the genetic algorithms approach. In this article, we have proposed to integrate first the main features of the image in the cost function and to add successively the less important ones. Other strategies could be devised. A possible idea is to divide the image in several horizontal strips (three for examples) and to run the genetic algorithm independently for each of these strips. Afterwards, the obtained results are merged using a variant of the selection operator and the genetic algorithm is run another time on the resulting population. We hope that, by using these strategies, the global computation time will be reduced.

References

[BB89]   Andrew T. Brint and Michael Brady. Stereo Matching of Curves. In *International Advanced Robotics Programme*, October 1989.

[DA89]   Umesh D. Dhond and Jake K. Aggarwal. Structure from Stereo-A Review. *IEEE Transactions on Systems Man and Cybernetics*, 19:1489–1510, November/December 1989.

[Der87]   Rachid Deriche. Using Canny's Criteria to Derive an Optimal Edge Detector Recursively Implemented. In *The International Journal of Computer Vision*, volume 2, pages 15–20, April 1987.

[Fau93]   Olivier D. Faugeras. *Three-dimensional Computer Vision: a geometric viewpoint*. MIT Press, 1993.

[Gol89]   David E. Goldberg. *Genetic Algorithms in Search Optimization & Machine Learning*. Adison-Wesley, 1989.

[Gri85]   W.E.L. Grimson. Computational experiments with a feature based stereo algorithm. *IEEE Transactions on Pattern Analysis and Machine Intelligence*, 7, No 1:17–34, 1985.

[HAL88]   Charles Hansen, Nicolas Ayache, and Francis Lustman. Towards real-time trinocular stereo. In *Second International Conference on Computer Vision*, December 1988.

[MN85]   G. Medioni and R. Nevatia. Segment-based stereo matching. *Computer Vision Graphics and Image Processing*, pages 31:2–18, 1985.

[OK85]   Y. Ohta and T. Kanade. Stereo by Intra- and Inter-Scanline Search. *IEEE Transactions on Pattern Analysis and Machine Intelligence*, 7(2):139–154, 1985.

[PMF85]   S.B. Pollard, J.E.W. Mayhew, and J.P. Frisby. PMF: a Stereo Correspondance Algorithm using a Disparity Gradient Limit. *Perception*, 14:449–470, 1985.

[RF91]   Luc Robert and Olivier Faugeras. Curve-Based Stereo: Figural Continuity And Curvature. In *Computer Vision and Pattern Recognition*, 1991.

[VG93]   Régis Vaillant and Laurent Gueguen. Genetic algorithms applied to binocular stereovision. Technical Report ASRF-93-2, Thomson-CSF, L.C.R., September 1993.

Segmentation and
Restoration

Segmentation of echocardiographic images with Markov random fields

I. L. HERLIN, D. BEREZIAT, G. GIRAUDON, G. SCIVEN, C. GRAFFIGNE

INRIA, Rocquencourt
B.P. 105, 78153 Le Chesnay Cedex, France
INRIA Sophia-Antipolis
2004, route des Lucioles, B.P. 93
06902 Sophia-Antipolis Cedex, France
Laboratoire de Mathématiques, Université Paris XI
Centre d'Orsay — Bâtiment 425
91405 Orsay Cedex, France
Email: herlin@riemann.fr

Abstract. The aim of this work is to track specific anatomical structures in temporal sequences of echocardiographic images. This paper
presents a new spatio-temporal model and describes the relevant spatial
and temporal properties that must be taken into consideration to obtain
the best possible results. It is expressed within a Markov random field
framework and results are presented with different formulations of the
temporal properties.

Keywords: Segmentation, Markov Random Field, Stochastic Process, Medical
Images, Ultrasound

1. Introduction

In [HFG92], a model of spatial segmentation for cardiac cavities in ultrasound
images has been presented. This model supposes that grey level values of pixels inside the cavity follow a normal low perturbated by its constant mean
of grey level deviation. It supposes also that cavity's boundaries induce a
response having a high gradient norm, and that the boundary is smooth. This
model is sometimes insufficient and may provide inaccurate results, and we
found necessary to define an another model [HG93], that includes temporal properties in three different ways: in the first place, we include a temporal neighborhood; secondly we use, inside the segmentation process, the result obtained on
the previous image of the sequence, and thirdly we use a geometrical constraint
on the stability of the cavity's center of ... ... from this model presented some
limitations and drawbacks, and this paper defines a new spatio-temporal model
that takes two different types of information into consideration: the surface boundaries are moving slowly during the cardiac cycle or the initial values are moving
very little.

Segmentation of echocardiographic images with Markov random fields

I. L. HERLIN[1], D. BEREZIAT[1], G. GIRAUDON[2], C. NGUYEN[1],
C. GRAFFIGNE[3]

[1] INRIA, Rocquencourt
B.P. 105, 78153 Le Chesnay Cedex, France.
[2] INRIA Sophia-Antipolis
2004, route des Lucioles - B.P. 93
06902 Sophia Antipolis Cedex, France.
[3] Laboratoire de Mathématiques - Université Paris 11
Centre d'Orsay - Bâtiment 425
91405 Orsay Cedex, France.
Email: Isabelle.Herlin@inria.fr

Abstract. The aim of this work is to track specific anatomical structures in temporal sequences of echocardiographic images. This paper presents a new spatio-temporal model and describes the relevant spatial and temporal properties that must be taken into consideration to obtain the best possible results. It is expressed within a Markov random field framework and results are presented with different formulations of the temporal properties.

Keywords: Segmentation, Markov Random Field, Stochastic Process, Medical Images, Ultrasound.

1 Introduction

In [HNG92] a model of spatial segmentation for cardiac cavities in ultrasound images has been presented. This model supposes that grey level values of pixels, inside the cavity, follow a normal law parametrized by its constant mean and standard deviation. It supposes also that cavity's boundary includes a lot of points having a high gradient norm, and that the boundary is smooth. This model is sometimes insufficient and may produce inaccurate results; and we found necessary to define an another model [HG93], that includes temporal properties in three different ways: in the first place, we include a temporal neighborhood; secondly we use, inside the segmentation process, the result obtained on the previous image of the sequence; and thirdly we use a geometrical constraint on the stability of the cavity's center of mass. Again, this model presented some limitations and drawbacks, and this paper defines a new spatio-temporal model that takes two different types of motion into consideration: the cardiac boundaries are moving slowly during the cardiac cycle; the mitral valves are moving very fast.

Lecture Notes in Computer Science, Vol. 801
Jan-Olof Eklundh (Ed.)

Fig. 1 displays the echocardiographic video data and the cavity of interest in this study. These data were obtained on a VINGMED echograph from Henri Mondor Hospital, France (thanks to Gabriel Pelle). The sequence is 50 images and displays a cardiac cycle.

A major step in application of Gibbs fields or Markov fields to images viewed as two-dimensional arrays was D. and S. Geman's paper on image restoration [GG84]. The aim of the work presented here is non supervised segmentation based on a region growing algorithm [AG92], [Zuc76], and our paper is concerned with a special case of a region growing algorithm segmenting a cardiac cavity in ultrasound images.

2 Position of the problem

2.1 Description of the properties

This section is devoted to the description of the four main visual properties of a cardiac cavity scanned by ultrasound.

- homoneneity - The grey level values of the pixels inside the cavity are homogeneous. This property is translated into the following assumption: $\forall s \in C(x), im_s \sim \mathcal{N}(\mu_s, \sigma^2)$: the grey level value of each pixel of the cavity follows a normal law of local mean μ_s and constant standard deviation σ.
- smoothness - The second visual property concerns cavity's smoothness and boundary's smoothness. This property is expressed with an Ising model: the probability that a pixel is labelled 1, or -1, becomes higher if points in the neighborhood possess the same label.
- spatial gradient - The initial boundary of the cavity is attracted by high gradient norm values and the growing process must stop at the edge elements.
- temporal regularity - The result of segmentation presents a temporal regularity during the cardiac cycle.

2.2 Mathematical definition

We first define the following sets and variables:

- S denotes the set of pixels of the image; $\Gamma = \{0, \ldots, 255\}^{|S|}, \Omega = \{-1, 1\}^{|S|}$;
- $Im = (Im_s)_{s \in S}$ is a random variable defining the grey level values of the pixels. Its realization is $im = (im_s)_{s \in S} \in \Gamma$;
- $G = (G_s)_{s \in S}$ encodes the norm of the spatial gradient, $g = (g_s)_{s \in S} \in \Gamma$ and is obtained by Deriche's filter [Der87];
- $E = (E_s)_{s \in S}$ defines the edge process, $e = (e_s)_{s \in S} \in \Omega; e_s = 1 \iff s$ is an edge element;
- $X = (X_s)_{s \in S}$ defines the segmentation process: $x = (x_s)_{s \in S} \in \Omega$ and $x_s = 1 \iff s$ is inside the cavity; we denote by $C(x)$ the set of pixels inside this cavity;
- ν_s is the neighborhood of s (4-neighborhood);

 − $y = (im, g, e)$ denotes the observation. It is the result of process $Y = (Im, G, E)$; x^0 is an initial segmentation for the cavity, used at the beginning of the optimization process.

3 Spatial properties

These properties were studied and compared in [HNG92, HG93]. The property 1 defines the first term of the energy function, which is minimized during the optimization process:

$$U_1(x, y) = \sum_{x \in C(x)} \left(\left(\frac{im_s - \mu_s}{\sigma} \right)^2 - T \right), \tag{1}$$

T being defined by the normal law table for a chosen percentage (95% or 99%).
  Property 2 is expressed by an Ising Model and the second term of the energy function: $U_2(x) = -\alpha \sum_s x_s (\sum_{t \in \nu_s} x_t)$, α being a positive parameter.
  Property 3 is included in the definition of μ_s. This local mean must express the fact that the grey level values become lower (i.e. darker) in the region of the cardiac muscle, where the gradient norm has high value: $\mu_s = \mu_0 + kg_s(1 - e_s)$. k being negative, the value of μ_s is decreasing from the center to the cavity's boundary.

4 Temporal properties

In [HG93] we made use of temporal information in different ways:

 − To avoid escapes of the segmentation in the other cavity, when the mitral valve is open (see Fig. 1), we tried to add temporal properties and began with a first simple solution by adding a temporal neighborhood to the Ising model: $\nu'_s = \{\nu_s, s_{n-1}, s_{n+1}\}$ where ν_s is the spatial neighborhood and s_{n-1}, s_{n+1} are the pixels at same position than s on the previous image and on the next image of the sequence (n is the count of the studied image). The probability that a point is labelled 1 inside the cavity becomes higher if the pixel has the same label on the previous image or on the next image.
   This constraint is very strong and the segmentation result becomes too stable from an image to the next, as some modifications of the cavity are lost. On another hand, this temporal constraint is able to solve the problem of the opening of the mitral valve as shown on Fig. 2: the result of segmentation does not escape inside the other cavity.
 − We suppose also that the position of the center of mass is not varying from an image to the next. This constraint is global and we approximate it by adding an isotropic constraint on the distance between each pixel of the cavity and the center of mass of the reference cavity (its coordinates are (k_{ref}, l_{ref})):

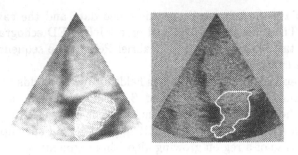

Fig. 1. Left: Echocardiographic video image and the studied cavity. **Right**: Mitral valves are opened: inaccuracy of segmentation

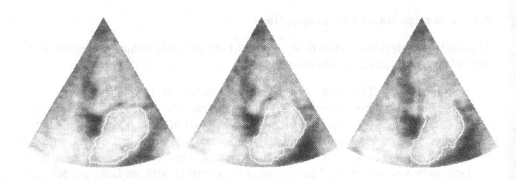

Fig. 2. Results of segmentation on three consecutive images of the sequence.

$$\gamma \sum_{s \in C(x)} [(k_s - k_{\text{ref}})^2 + (l_s - l_{\text{ref}})^2 - dm^2]$$ where (k_s, l_s) are the coordinates of s.

This energy term prevents a growing of the segmentation process in one particular direction. It avoids a penetration inside the other cavity if the mitral valve is open but, if pixels are nearer than dm, the label 1 is prefered.

In fact we need a temporal regularity constraint only in the region of the mitral valve because it is varying very fast.

In this region we have the following properties:

- the value of the spatial gradient (g_s) is low,
- the value of the temporal gradient (gt_s) is high.

At this point an energy term is added to help label -1 (outside the cavity) those pixels whose g_s term is low and gt_s high. In the same way all other configurations of g_s and gt_s help to label 1 (inside the cavity). In order to normalize the gradient

values we make use of two functions, $\phi_c(g_s)$ and $\Psi_{c'}(gt_s)$ with values in $[0, 1]$, such that $\phi_c(g_s) * \Phi_{c'}(gt_s)$ is maximum when g_s is low and gt_s is high.

These properties may be expressed by the global energy function:

$$U(x/y) = \sum_{s \in C(x)} \left[\left(\frac{im_s - \mu_s}{\sigma} \right)^2 - T \right] - \alpha \sum_{<s,t>} x_s x_t + \delta \sum_{s \in S} (\phi_c(g_s) * \Psi_{c'}(gt_s))$$

where ϕ_c and $\Psi_{c'}$ are two functions in $C^1(\mathbb{R}, [0, 1])$ satisfying:

- $\phi_c(0) = 1; \phi_c(c) = 1/2; \lim_{x \to \infty} \phi_c(x) = 0;$
- $\Psi_{c'}(0) = 0; \Psi_{c'}(c) = 1/2; \lim_{x \to \infty} \Psi_{c'}(x) = 1.$

ϕ_c is a thresholding function of the high values of the spatial gradient and $\Psi_{c'}$ is a thresholding function of the low values of the temporal gradient.

With such a modelling, a point is labelled as inside the cavity if $\left(\frac{im_s - \mu_s}{\sigma} \right)^2 \leq t_{\text{loc}}$, with: $t_{\text{loc}} = T + 2\alpha \sum_{t \in \nu_s} x_t - 2\delta \phi_c(g_s) * \Psi_{c'}(gt_s)$. Now t_{loc} becomes very low in the region of the mitral valve and the growing process will stop because we impose $x_s = -1$ (outside the cavity) when reaching this region. The thresholding functions include a weighting coefficient δ that must verify the following property: if $(\phi_c(g_s) \simeq 1)$ and $(\Psi_{c'}(gt_s) \simeq 1)$ (i.e. low spatial gradient and high temporal gradient) we want to ensure that $\left(\frac{im_s - \mu_s}{\sigma} \right)^2 > t_{\text{loc}}$.

We studied this model with the following choices for ϕ_c and $\Psi_{c'}$:

- $\phi_c(x) = \frac{1 - F(x/c)}{2}$, c is the mean of the norm of the spatial gradient,
- $\Psi_{c'}(x) = \frac{1 + F(x/c')}{2}$, c' is the mean of the norm of the temporal gradient,
- $F(x) = \frac{1 - x^a}{1 + x^a}, a > 1$. The value of a allows to adjust the slope of the functions. We choose $a = 2$.

With these choices, we tested the model and concluded that:

- The results obtained with this model is approximately accurate, even if the mitral valve is open, as is shown on Fig. 3 (left).
- Moreover, the result are more stable regarding to the iteration count of the ICM algorithm. This is illustrated on Fig. 3 where the result with 5, 10 or 20 iterations of ICM are displayed from left to right. On the image on the right, we can observe penetrations in the borders of the mitral valve because the segmentation algorithm works with pixels with high gradient norm values inside the cavity.

5 Conclusion

In this paper, we have compared different mathematical translations of spatio-temporal properties used for segmentation. We have seen that making use of a local temporal neighborhood is too restrictive and that a global geometric

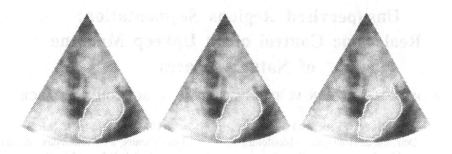

Fig. 3. Results of the model when the mitral valve is opened with 5, 10 and 20 ICM from left to right.

constraint on isotropy is accurate ; our final solution makes use of temporal gradient: this is a local constraint that takes into account all the images for recursive implementation. So we achieve the temporal tracking of a cardiac cavity during the cardiac cycle.

References

[AG92]   R. Azencott and C. Graffigne. Non supervised segmentation using multi-level markov random fields. In *Proceedings of the 11th International Conference on Pattern Recognition*, August 30-September 3 1992.

[Der87]   R. Deriche. Using Canny's criteria to derive a recursively implemented optimal edge detector. *International Journal of Computer Vision*, 1 (2), May 1987.

[GG84]   S. Geman and D. Geman. Stochastic relaxation, Gibbs distribution and the Bayesian restoration of images. *IEEE Transactions on Pattern Analysis and Machine Intelligence*, 6:712–741, 1984.

[HG93]   I. L. Herlin and G. Giraudon. Use of temporal information in a segmentation algorithm of ultrasound images. In *Proceedings of the conference on Computer Vision and Pattern Recognition*, New York, U.S.A., 15-17 June 1993.

[HNG92] I. Herlin, C. Nguyen, and C. Graffigne. Stochastic segmentation of ultrasound images. In *Proceedings of the 11th International Conference on Pattern Recognition*, August 30-September 3 1992.

[Zuc76]   S.W. Zucker. Region growing: Childhood and adolescence. *Computer Graphics and Image Processing*, (5):382–399, 1976.

Unsupervised Regions Segmentation:
Real Time Control of an Upkeep Machine
of Natural Spaces

M. DERRAS, C. DEBAIN, M. BERDUCAT
CEMAGREF
CLERMONT-FERRAND CENTRE
Domaine des Palaquins - Montoldre
03150 Varennes sur Allier, France
Tél.: 70 45 03 12   Téléfax : 70 45 19 46

P. BONTON, J. GALLICE
LASMEA,
U.R.A. 830 of the C.N.R.S.
Les Cézeaux, 24 Avenue des Landais
63177 Aubière cedex, France
Tél.: 73 40 72 63   Téléfax : 73 40 72 62

ABSTRACT.   An original image segmentation based on a Markovian modeling of a set of four parameters is presented. The application performed demonstrates the strength of an algorithm using texture analysis of natural scenes. A splitting limit is obtained which is going to become the basic primitive in order to hook up a mower robot. To obtain a real time application we also present a simple parallelization of the algorithm and a control servoing.

I INTRODUCTION

The aim of our project consists in the design of a help guidance system for an auto-propelled mower using texture analysis over 16x16 pixels dimension neighbourhoods : the texel [13]. A preliminary study [9] allowed, from a bibliographic research on reflectance physical properties of grass covers, the clearing of the most interesting zones of the electromagnetic spectrum for this application. So two parameters have been chosen using the co-occurrence matrices [7], [12], [13], [21] which re-transcribes the spatial distribution of grey level variations between neighbouring pixels of a region. To use the reflectance properties of the natural surfaces, two parameters issued from 16x16 pixel region histograms have been defined. These four descriptors, introduced in a relaxation process, are used to perform the segmentation of the image into regions. The first section of this paper deals with the development of an image segmentation method in homogeneous regions [15], [22]. However many data analysis methods [1], [14], [17] require, at different levels, an a priori choice which is incompatible with the application (element class number, comparison threshold). So the approach moved towards unsupervised segmentation methods. One of the solutions to the problem was brought by the Markov's field modelling [2], [6], [11], [19]. Moreover this segmentation has the advantage of being well adapted to the treatment of image sequences, because it offers the ability to take into account the result of the segmentation of the previous image. This is very important when the problem of motion is tackled, the final objective being a "real time" treatment. After a summary of the data and segmentation tool used, we develop our own contribution to the formulation of the problem. The second section explain the different steps of the process [10]. Then we develop the effective robot control by the use of a visual servoing [5], [16]. These algorithms are parallelized to permit a real time robot control. This parallelization leads to a pipeline architecture..

II - IMAGE SEGMENTATION

It is obvious that by increasing the number of descriptive elements, the choice of a different size of the sites or of the nature of the parameters have no influence on the following theory. This theory is supported on the example of the surface which corresponds to our application. The goal is to obtain homogeneous textured regions of natural surface images (grass cover).

Lecture Notes in Computer Science, Vol. 801
Jan-Olof Eklundh (Ed.)

II.1 - Solution with Markov's fields theory

The problem (labelling of distinct regions) lies in the fact that the image segmentation is only achieved from its different descriptive elements [8], [11]. Under a mathematic form, the problem is to maximize the a posteriori probability $P(X/Y)$, i.e. the probability of the searched object conditionally to the measures made [4]. X represent the result of the segmentation (field of labels) and Y represent the descriptive elements of the image. By applying Bayes's theorem, this a posteriori probability can be expressed by :

$$P(X/Y) = \frac{P(X).P(Y/X)}{P(Y)} \quad (1) \qquad P(X=\omega) = \left(\frac{1}{Z}\right).\exp\{-U(\omega)\} \quad \omega \in \Omega \quad (2)$$

Here $P(X)$ is the a posteriori probability of the field of labels. $P(Y/X)$ is the conditional probability of the measure in relation to one of the possible segmentations. It describes entirely the statistical relations existing between data and labels and $P(Y)$ is the probability to obtain an observation. It may easily be dropped as it doesn't depend on X [3]. Therefore, the image comes in the form of a data field that a label field must describe. The use of the Markov's fields theory permits to limit the effects of each element of the lattice representing the image to a local interaction between neighbouring sites. Then this first Bayes's equation must be expressed under another form more suitable for implementation. The Hammersley-Clifford theorem enables the use of Gibbs's distributions which are given by (2).
Here Z is a normalization constant and $U(\omega)$ an energy function. This distribution describes the stability of our system. ω is then a particular state of the system and Ω the set of possible states. Consequently, each terms of the equation (1) can be given under the form of a Gibbs's distribution. By using the natural logarithms of $P(X/Y)$ and $P(X)$, the expression can be reduced to $U(X/Y) = U(X) + U(Y/X)$ (3). The purpose is then to calculate $U(X)$ and $U(Y/X)$ to minimize the energy function $U(X/Y)$.

II.2 - Segmentation development

The implementation of the method of image segmentation by using the Markovian modelling have been inspired by the deterministic relaxation algorithm I.C.M. (Iterated Conditional Mode) [11]. For each site, the different possible values of the energy function are calculated and only the state corresponding to the minimal energy is retained. The two terms of the a posteriori energy function $U(X/Y)$ will be given by the a priori energy and the energy function related to the statistical relationships "data-labels".

II.2.1 - A priori energy

$U(X)$ is an a priori function. If the neighbourhood of a studied site is considered, the equation (4) can be defined which takes into account the neighbouring sites label where V_s is the neighbourhood of the studied site, A a weighting factor, V_c the potential assigned to the site e_s.

$$U(X) = \exp\left\{A.\left(\sum_{s \in V_s} V_c(e_s)\right)\right\} \quad (4) \qquad d^2(m, m') = \sum_{i=1}^{p}\left(\frac{K}{K_d}\right)\left(\frac{K_{im}}{K_s} - \frac{K_{im'}}{K_{s'}}\right)^2 \quad (5)$$

II.2.2 - Energy related to statistical relationships "data-labels"

A distance between each site and a general reference in the image (for example the region prototype) must be defined. The Euclidian one have been used but the well known difficulty of this distance is the effect of the variations of the amplitude of the considered elements on a statistic problem. That's the reason why the function

U(Y/X) (relation between data and labels) is given by the CHI-2 distance (5) between sites and region vectors (described by four parameters).

II.2.3 - Process description

The process breaks up into four steps. Nevertheless, one of the interests of this segmentation in an image sequence, is inherent in the use of the result issued from the previous image. An a priori information is take into account in the image segmentation. This constitutes the "dynamic" aspect, which consists in putting in relation the extracted data of the new image with the label field of the previous image. Obviously, it have been considered that there are few changes between two succiding images, and a noticeable gain of time is obtained for an equivalent efficiency segmentation.

The initialization step of the process, starts without knowing anything about the shape or the number of the different kinds of texture that can be found in an image. Consequently, the image is supposed to be composed of a single region at the beginning. The field of labels is therefore initialized at zero and a first cut-out is realized from the comparison of the local energy of each site with the value of the average global energy calculated on the entire image. A general reference P_I (H_I, E_I, M_I, Mo_I) constituted by elements which correspond to the averages of each descriptor on the whole of the image is used to calculate :

$$U_I(X/Y) = \left(\frac{1}{N}\right) \cdot \sum_{i=1}^{32} \sum_{j=1}^{32} \left\{ U_{ijPI}(Y/X) + U_{ij}(X) \right\} \quad (6)$$

Where H_I, E_I, M_I and Mo_I are the average values of homogeneity, entropy, local histogram mode and second order moment. P_I is the initial prototype. $U_{ijPI}(Y/X)$ represent the distance of the site *(ij)* to the prototype P_I. $U_{ij}(X)$ is the penalty function of the site *(ij)*. N is the site number defined in an image (here 1024) and $U_I(X/Y)$ is the global average energy function value of an image. For each site the local energy function is calculated by $U_{ij}(X/Y) = U_{ijPI}(Y/X) + U_{ij}(X)$ (7). $U_{ij}(X/Y)$ is then compared to $U_I(X/Y)$. If $U_{ij}(X/Y) \leq U_I(X/Y)$ the site *(ij)* is assumed to belong to the region zero and remains unchanged. Otherwise the label of the site *(ij)* is set to one (remember that all sites are initialized to zero).

At the end of the initialization, one region is obtained in the case of an homogeneous image, and two regions in other cases. The Initialization stabilization helps to suppress the very small regions and to redistribute the labels more regularly. The energy values in relation to the different labels are calculated and the state of each studied site is then modified according to the region giving the lowest energy. This step is repeated during several scans of the image, until there is no more change of labels. Step three and four which can be named "new textured class research" and "new class stabilization" are generalizations of the two first stages to all detected regions. The aim consists in detecting the presence of possible new regions inside those that have been defined by stages one and two (discontinuities are searched in these regions). As in step one, the average global energy values of each region are calculated as well as their prototype. If the segmentation provides k regions, a prototype P_k is obtained for each one as well as an average global energy value $U_k(X/Y)$. With these elements, we proceed as follows. The local energy values corresponding to the labels detected in the neighbourhood of the studied site are calculated. Only the lowest ones is kept. Then $U_{ijk}(X/Y)$ (local minimum energy value of the site *ij*, corresponding to the labelled region k) and $U_k(X/Y)$ (average global energy value of the labelled region k) are compared. If $U_{ijk}(X/Y) > U_k(X/Y)$ then the label of the site *(ij)* is set to a new value in the label field, otherwise its label remains unchanged. The process stops when the number of regions does not change any further.

III - APPLICATION : REAP LIMIT SEARCH

This theory has been applied to the search of the reap limit in an image in order to ensure the working of an upkeep mobile machine (a mower). We present one example of result of segmentation of grass surfaces.

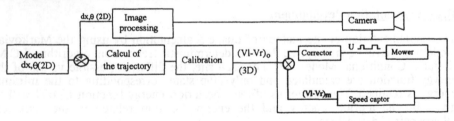

Picture n°1 : A turn of cut grass between two unmowed areas is detected.

In a dynamic use (image sequences), the Markov fields theory is entirely justified. The idea consists in using again, as an a priori information, the field of labels issued from the image segmentation at the time T to process the next image at the time $T + \Delta T$. The main purpose is to limit in one hand the computing time with a reactualization of the label field and, in the other hand, the errors of detection, because the changes between two successive images are supposed to be very slight. In the approach presented here, only the first image of the sequence is entirely processed (initialization step). Then, in order to improve the computing time, the segmentation is localised on an area of interest (half of the image) sufficient to ensure the future guidance of the upkeep machine. We must insist on the fact that luminance in natural scenes, vibrations of the engine, kind of grass, etc..., can not be controlled.

IV - MACHINE CONTROL [18, 20, 24]

Figure n°5 : Complete system.

The totality of the automation embedded on the robot is presented on the figure n°5. From these visual information and the computing time, the algorithm of control determines the trajectory. It calculates the order, that compared to real speeds, allows a numerical corrector to control the speed of the wheel. As the machine is moving to an average speed of 3 kilometres an hour, it makes slightly more than 80 centimeters in one second. So to obtain a periodicity of its control which should be compatible with its dynamics and to limit risks of interface losses in the image, we have developed a multi-processor architecture adapted to the chosen algorithms of image processing and control. The solution consists in sharing the algorithm in several tasks executed in parallel on three cards organized according to the model of the pipeline.

V- ARCHITECTURE AND PARALLELIZATION

In spite of the technological evolution of the microprocessors and especially of their

speed, it is necessary to realize a parallel approach of the algorithm on an adapted architecture to obtain a real time application. If its not a new parallelism approach [14] we can remark that the multiprocessor calculators and components (such as the transputers) have appeared too recently. Nonetheless few of these machines are available on the market. M.J. FLYNN [23] has proposed a classification of the parallel calculators in four groups based upon the nature of the instructions and the data stream. However, lots of other criteria exist which allow finer differentiation of the parallelization of the algorithms. These criteria depend often on the kind of memory use (shared or distributed) or the "grain" size (parallelization at the level of the instructions or at higher levels of groups of instructions).

In our case the knowledge of an a priori information (the previous image segmentation) and the algorithm parallelization permit us to reach our real time goal (230 ms average computing time per image). We have implemented an architecture composed by three VME microprocessors boards. The problem caused by such a pipeline construction consists in the repartition and the organization of all the concurrent tasks witch constitute the parallelized algorithm. Three tasks have been determined and attributed to each processor. To manage all the problems arising from by the shared resources between the different processors we have chosen the operating system OS9. Among all the different mechanisms of synchronization and communication between tasks offered by this environment we have particularily used the signals, the communication pipes and the data modules.

IV - CONCLUSION

The objective of this article was to demonstrate the important potential offered by the markovian modelling and above all its adaptability to face the various conditions of external scene. The method proposed here provides good results compared to the techniques using thresholds of comparison. The other advantage is the use of an a priori information which allows the solution of a part of the problems of the real time analysis of image sequences. The implementation of the application on a parallel architecture has permit to reduce the computing time to 230 ms. At last this approach can be extended to various kinds of agricultural tasks (harvesting for example). Although non formalised, the visual servoing approach of control seems to be similar the principle developed for the CRV of the manipulator robots. This theory is presently studied in our team. This paper describes an engine which actually runs at the CEMAGREF of Clermont-Ferrand. The complete architechture is embedded on the machine. The first tests carried out give satisfaction. A finer and deeper perfecting will increase the strength of the system.

REFERENCES

[1] - **S.C. Ahalt, A.K. Krishnamurthy, P. Chen, D.E. Melton**, "Competitive learning algorithm for vector quantization", Neural Networks, vol. 3, 1990, pp 277-290.

[2] - **M. Bernard, M. Sigelle**, "Champs de Gibbs et Champs markoviens", Télécom Paris, Département Images, Groupe Image, mai 1990.

[3] - **M. Berthod, G. Giraudon and J.P. Stromboni**, "Deterministic pseudo-annealing : optimization in Markov random fields. An application to pixel classification", Proceedings of the ECCV'92, second european conference on computer vision, Santa Margherita Ligure, Italy, (ed.) G. Sandini, may 1992, pp 67-71.

[4] - **R. Canals, P. Bonton**, "Segmentation spatio-temporelle : régularisation par champs markoviens", rapport interne au Laboratoire d'Electronique de l'Université Blaise-Pascal, Clermont II, avril 1991, 31 p.

[5] - **F. Chaumette**, "La commande référencée vision : une approche aux problèmes d'asservissements visuels en robotique", Thèse de doctorat de l'Université de Rennes, juillet 1990, 171 pages.

[6] - **Chaur Chin Chen, R.C. Dubes**, "Experiments in fitting discrete Markov random fields to texture", CVPR (Computer Vision and Pattern Recognition) 89, San-Diego, june 1989, pp 248-303.

[7] - **P.C. Chen, T. Pavlidis**, "Segmentation by texture using a cooccurence matrix and a split and merge algorithm", Computer Graphics and Image Processing, vol. 10, 1979, pp 172-182.

[8] - **H. Derin, H. Elliot**, "Modeling and segmentation of noisy and textured image using Gibbs random fields", IEEE Transactions on Pattern Analysis and Machine Intelligence, vol. PAMI-9, n°1, january 1987, pp 39-55.

[9] - **M. Derras, M. Berducat et P. Bonton**, "Vision guided mower for the upkeep of natural environment", Poceedings of the 1st International seminar of on-machine vision systems for the agricultural and bio-industries (3rd and 6th technical Sections of the CIGR), Montpellier, september 1991, 10 p.

[10] - **M. Derras, M. Berducat, P. Bonton, J. Gallice et R. Canals**, "Segmentation texturale originale appliquée au guidage visuel d'un engin d'entretien des espaces naturels", Quatorzième colloque sur le traitement du signal et des images, GRETSI, Juan-les-Pins, 13-16 septembre 1993, 4 pages.

[11] - **D. Genam, S. Genam, C. Graffigne, Ping Dong**, "Boundary detection by constrained optimization", IEEE Transaction on Pattern Analysis and Machine Intelligence, vol. 12, n°7, july 1990, pp 609-628.

[12] - **R.M. Haralick**, "Statistical and structural approches to texture", Proceeding of the IEEE, vol. 67, n°5, may 1979, pp 786-804.

[13] - **C.A. Harlow, M. Trivedi, R.W. Conners**, "Use of texture operators in segmentation", Optical Engineering, vol. 25, n°11, november 1986, pp 1200-1206.

[14] - **S.L. Horowitz and T. Pavlidis**, "Picture segmentation by a directed split and merge procedure", Proc. second international joint conference on Pattern Recognition, 1974, pp 424-433.

[15] - **O. Monga** "Segmentation d'images : où en sommes-nous ?", Rapport de recherche INRIA n°1216, avril 1990, 63 pages.

[16] - **R. Pissard-Gibollet et P. Rives**, "Asservissement visuel appliqué a un robot mobile : état de l'art et modélisation cinématique", Rapport de Recherche INRIA n°1577, unité de recherche de Sophia Antipolis, décembre 1991, 42 pages.

[17] - **M. Popovic, F. Chantemargue, R. Canals, P. Bonton**, "Several approaches to implement the merging step of the split and merge region segmentation", EUROGRAPHICS, Vienne, september 1991.

[18] - **C. Samson and K. Ait-Abderrahim**, "Mobile robot control part 1 : feedback control of nonholonomic wheeled cart in cartesian space", Rapport de Recherche INRIA n°1288, unité de recherche de Sophia Antipolis, octobre 1990, 50 pages.

[19] - **J.R. Sullins**, "Distributed learning of texture classification", Computer Vision, ECCV 90, Antibes 1990, pp 349-358.

[20] - **P. Tournassoud**, "Planification et contrôle en robotique : application aux robots mobiles et manipulateurs", Hermes, Paris 1992, 248 pages.

[21] - **R. Yokoyama, R.M. Haralick**, "Texture synthesis using a growth model", Computer Graphics and Image Processing, vol. 8, n°3, 1978, pp 369-381.

[22] - **S.W. Zucker**, "Region growing : childhood and adolescence", Computer graphics and Image processing, n°5, 1976, pp 382-399.

[23] - **M.J. Flynn**, "Some computer organization and their effectiveness", IEEE Transaction on Computer, vol. C21, n°9, september 1972, pp 948-960.

[24] - **N. Kehtarnavaz, N. C. Grisword, J. S. Lee**, "Visual control of an autonomous vehicle (BART) - The vehicle-following problem", IEEE Transaction on Vehicle Technologie, vol. 40, n°3, August 1991.

Synchronous Image restoration

Laurent Younes

CMLA-DIAM, Ecole Normale Supérieure de Cachan, 61 avenue du Président Wilson, 94 235 Cachan CEDEX.

Abstract. We analyse a class of random fields invariant by stochastic synchronous updating of all sites, subject to a generalized reversibility assumption. We give a formal definition and properties of the model, study the problem of posterior simulation, parameter estimation, and then present experimental results in image restoration.

1 Introduction.

We utilize in this work a new class of random fields on some given set of sites, which are invariant under the action of a transition probability which synchronously updates the states of all sites. We illustrate, with an issue of image restoration, the usefulness of these models, and their feasibility for practical applications.

We begin by a summary of the definition of p-periodic synchronous random fields. Let S be the finite set of sites, F a finite state space. The set of all configurations on S is F^S, and will be denoted by Ω_S (or Ω if no confusion is possible). A random field (r.f.) on S is a probability distribution on Ω.

Definition 1 *A synchronous kernel of order q is a family $\mathcal{P}$ of transition probabilities from Ω^q to F, denoted*

$$p_s(x(q), \ldots, x(1) \ ; \ y_s),$$

$(x(l) \in \Omega, \ l = 1, \ldots, q, \ y_s \in F)$.
We say that $\mathcal{P}$ is positive.

Definition 2 *If $\mathcal{P}$ is a synchronous kernel, its associated (synchronous) transition probability from Ω^q to Ω is*

$$P(x(q), \ldots, x(1) \ ; \ y) = \prod_{s \in S} p_s(x(q), \ldots, x(1) \ ; \ y_s).$$

It corresponds to a simultaneous updating of all sites according to the local transitions p_s.

For a function f defined on Ω^q, define

$$Pf(x(q), \ldots, x(1)) = \int f(x(q-1), \ldots, x(0)) P(x(q), \ldots, x(1) \ dx(0)). \tag{1}$$

Then, there exists a unique distribution $\bar{\pi}$ on Ω^q which satisfies :

$$\int Pf d\bar{\pi} = \int f d\bar{\pi} \tag{2}$$

for all f. We finally define a probability distribution on Ω, (rather than Ω^q), by

Definition 3 *We say that a law π on Ω is associated to the synchronous kernel $\mathcal{P}$ if π is one of the marginal distributions of $\bar{\pi}$, where $\bar{\pi}$ is defined in (2).*

It is easy to deduce from equation (2) that all the marginals of $\bar{\pi}$ are identical.
We now define p-periodicity :

Definition 4 *Let $p = q + 1$. The transition probability $P(x(q), \ldots, x(1) \ ; \ x(0))$ is p-periodic with respect to a distribution $\bar{\pi}$ on Ω^q if, for any functions $f_q, \ldots, f_0$ defined on Ω,*

$$\int f_q[x(q)] \ldots f_1[x(1)] P f_0[x(q), \ldots, x(1)] d\bar{\pi} = \int P f_q[x(q-1), \ldots, x(0)] f_{q-1}[x(q-1)] \ldots f_0[x(0)] d\bar{\pi} \tag{3}$$

In other terms, the compound distribution *on Ω^p, defined by*

$$\mu[x(q),\ldots,x(0)] = \bar{\pi}[x(q),\ldots,x(1)]P[x(q),\ldots,x(1) \ x(0)] \tag{4}$$

is invariant by circular permutation of $x(q),\ldots,x(0)$.

We shall say that a synchronous field is *p-periodic* if it is the marginal distribution of $\bar{\pi}$ (or μ) with respect to which P is p-periodic.

In *(younes 1993)*, the following characterization theorem is proved. We identify Ω^p with $\Omega_{S_1}\otimes\ldots\otimes\Omega_{S_p}$ where $S_i = S \times \{i\}$, $i = 1,\ldots,p$, are copies of S and add a new element to S, which can be considered as a "void site", and which we will denote by 0 ($0 \notin S$).

Theorem 1 *Let π be a probability measure on Ω. The following properties are equivalent :*

1. *π is a synchronous p-periodic r.f. associated to a positive synchronous kernel.*
2. *There exists a distribution μ on Ω^p such that*
   - i- *μ is invariant by circular permutation of the coordinates.*
   - ii- *For all $i = 1,\ldots,p$, the variables X_s, $s \in S_i$ are μ-conditionally independent given the other variables X_t, $t \notin S_i$.*
   - iii- *The conditional distribution*
     $$\mu(X_s \mid X_t, t \neq s)$$
     for $s \in S_i$ is positive.
   - iv- *π is the marginal distribution of μ over Ω_{S_1}.*

In that case, the associated synchronous kernel may be described as follows.

For each p-uple in $(S \cup \{0\})^p$, where 0 is the void site, of the kind $\bar{s} = (s_1,\ldots,s_p)$, there exists a function

$$h_{\bar{s}}[x(1),\ldots,x(p)] = h_{\bar{s}}[x_{s_1}(1),\ldots,x_{s_p}(p)]$$

defined on Ω^p, which only depends on variables $x_{s_k}(k)$ for indices k such that $s_k \neq 0$, such that $p_u[x(1),\ldots,x(q) ; x_u(p)]$ takes the form :

$$\exp\left\{ \sum_{\bar{s}=(s_1,\ldots,s_{p-1},u)} h_{\bar{s}}[x(1),\ldots,x(p)] \right\} Z_u[x(1),\ldots,x(p-1)]. \tag{5}$$

Moreover, the functions $h_{\bar{s}}$ are invariant by circular permutation of the indices, in the sense that, for any $x(1),\ldots,x(p)$,

$$h_{\bar{s}}[x(1),\ldots,x(p)] = h_{\bar{s}_r}[x(p),x(1),\ldots,x(p-1)],$$

where $\bar{s}_r = (s_p, s_1 \ldots, s_{p-1})$.

The p-step distribution μ can be expressed in terms of the functions $h_{\bar{s}}$:

$$\mu[x(1),\ldots,x(p)] = \frac{1}{Z}\exp\left\{ \sum_{\bar{s}} h_{\bar{s}}[x(1),\ldots,x(p)] \right\}. \tag{6}$$

We shall also refer to the following notion :

Definition 5 *A compound (or joint) partially synchronous distribution of order p is a Gibbs distribution μ on $\Omega_{\bar{S}}$ such that the variables X_s, $s \in S_i$ are μ-conditionally independent given the other variables X_t, $t \notin S_i$.*

If μ is a compound synchronous distribution, its marginal over $\Omega_{S_1} \equiv \Omega_S$ will be called a partially synchronous distribution of order p.

Remark. To sample from a partially synchronous distribution, one needs to sample from μ, which involves $p-1$ auxilliary variables, each of which being synchronously sampled conditionally to the others. The efficacy of such a parallel sampling therefore decreases when p is large.

From the preceding definition, we see that p-periodic fields are partially synchronous distributions associated to μ which is invariant by circular permutation of the coordinates. There is no such loss of efficiency in this case, since all auxilliary variables have the same marginals.

2 Synchronous sampling of a posterior distribution.

2.1 Sitewise degradation.

This issue can be considered as critical to measure the usefulness of a model for applications.

To formalize the situation, let Ω denote the configuration space of S, with state space F, and Ω' denote some other configuration space on some state space G. Assume that we are given a family of functions $(b_s, s \in S)$ from Ω to G, yielding a function b from Ω to Ω' defined by $b(x) = \xi$ with $\xi_s = b_s(x)$ for all s. In a statistical interpretation, Ω is the set of "original" configurations, and Ω' the set of "observed" configurations.

For a given probability distribution π on Ω, and a given configuration $\xi \in \Omega'$, we are concerned with the issue of sampling from the *posterior distribution* $\pi(\; . \; |\xi)$.

We shall consider the following important particular case in which the computation of ξ from x is performed coordinatewise, i.e. ξ_s only depends on x_s (so that b_s is a function from F to G). Examples in which this is satisfied are

- $F = G \times G'$ and only the G-component of x is observed (partial observations).
- Let $(x_s^0, s \in S)$ be an unobserved random field, and (ϵ_s) be a noise which is independent of x^0. Assume that x^0 and ϵ both follow a synchronous distribution, or more generally that the joint distribution of (x^0, ϵ) is synchronous. Assume finally that the observation takes the form : $\xi_s = b_s(x_s^0, \epsilon_s)$.

Proposition 1 *Assume that π is p-periodic and that for all s, $b_s(x) = b_s(x_s)$ only depends on x_s. Then, the posterior distribution $\pi(\; . \; |\xi)$. is partially synchronous of order p.*

This is not valid anymore when the condition $b_s(x) = b_s(x_s)$ is relaxed. Although this condition is true for a large range of applications, there remain some significant cases for which it is not satisfied. The most important among these, especially in the context of image restoration is the case of blurring. The next section addresses the case of linear blurring with additive Gaussian white noise.

2.2 Restoration of blurred pictures.

In this section, the state space F is no more finite, but equal to the real line $\mathbf{R}$. The random fields are assumed to have densities with respect to Lebesgue measure on Ω, which are given by the same kind of formulae as in the finite case, with the implicit integrability assumptions.

We assume that the observation is obtained through the equation

$$\xi_s = \sum_t \eta_{st} x_t + \epsilon_s, \tag{7}$$

where ϵ is some Gaussian white noise of variance σ^2, and η_{st} are the coefficients of a point-spread function around s. A particular case is when $\sigma^2 = 0$, in which the restoration problem reduces to deblurring the picture.

In order to restore the original picture from the observed ξ, the problem is still to devise an efficient sampling algorithm of the posterior distribution. The previous methods cannot be applied, unless $\eta_{st} = 0$ for $s \neq t$. The difficulty comes from the fact that, when expressing the energy of the conditional distribution of x given ξ, there appears a term $\sum(\xi_s - \sum_t \eta_{st} x_t)^2$, therefore yielding interactions between x_s and x_t for $t \neq s$. In the following proposition, we show how a very simple trick can be used to solve this problem.

Proposition 2 *Assume that π is p-periodic and that ξ is given by equation (7) above. Then, there exists a compound partially synchronous distribution μ, of order $p + 1$, of the kind*

$$\mu(z, \bar{z}, x(2), \ldots, x(p)),$$

such that the distribution of $(z + \bar{z})/2$ is $\pi(\; . \; |\xi)$.

Proof : Let $\mu_0[x(1), \ldots, x(p)]$ be the density of the p-step distribution associated to π ; it is of the kind

$$\exp[-Q(x(1), \ldots, x(p))]/Z,$$

Q being the associated energy function. To simplify notations, we set $x = x(1)$.

The energy function associated to the joint field $(x(1), \ldots, x(p), \xi)$ is

$$\frac{1}{2\sigma^2} \sum_s (\xi_s - \sum_t \eta_{st} x_t)^2 + Q(x, x(2), \ldots, x(p))$$

Introduce a new r.f., (u_s), which is Gaussian with energy $\frac{1}{2\sigma^2}(a \sum_s u_s^2 - \sum_s (\sum_t \eta_{st} u_t)^2)$, a being large enough for this quadratic form to be positive. Assume that u is independent of the other fields $(x(i), i = 1, \ldots, p$ and $\xi)$. After a simple transformation, the joint energy of $x, x(2), \ldots, x(p), \xi, u$ can be written

$$\frac{1}{2\sigma^2} \{ \sum_s [\xi_s - \sum_t \eta_{st}(x_t + u_t)][\xi_s - \sum_t \eta_{st}(x_t - u_t)] + a \sum_s u_s^2 \} + Q(x, x(2), \ldots, x(p))$$

It suffices now to set $z_t = x_t - u_t$ and $\bar{z}_t = x_t + u_t$. The distribution of z, $\bar{z}$, $x(2), \ldots, x(p)$ and ξ has for energy

$$\frac{1}{2\sigma^2} \{ \sum_s [\xi_s - \sum_t \eta_{st} z_t][\xi_s - \sum_t \eta_{st} \bar{z}_t] + \frac{a}{4} \sum_s (z_s - \bar{z}_s)^2 \} + Q((z + \bar{z})/2, x(2), \ldots, x(p)).$$

This provides the desired structure for the conditionnal distribution of z, $\bar{z}$, $x(2), \ldots, x(p)$ given ξ, which is the distribution μ we were looking for. □

3 Experiments.

We now present examples to illustrate the restoration of noisy pictures in this last case.

3.1 Modeling.

We include, as it is standard in image modeling, edge elements within the prior distribution and introduce two hidden fields, $(h_s, s \in S)$ and $(v_s, s \in S)$, with values in $\{0, 1\}$, respectively indicating the presence of a horizontal edge ($h_s = 1$) or vertical edge ($v_s = 1$). More precisely, if $s = (i, j)$ is the representation of s on the image grid, h_s indicates an edge between (i, j) and $(i - 1, j)$, and v_s between (i, j) and $(i, j - 1)$. To shorten notation, we set $(i - 1, j) = s.h$ and $(i, j - 1) = s.v$.

The prior distribution is therefore defined on the set of all configurations of (x, h, v). To model a synchronous r.f., we must introduce auxilliary fields $(y, \bar{h}, \bar{v})$, and model a compound distribution $\mu((x, h, v), (y, \bar{h}, \bar{v}))$ with the property that, given $(y, \bar{h}, \bar{v})$, all component $(x_s, h_s, v_s), s \in S$ are independent, and conversely ; we do not impose mutual independence of x_s, h_s and v_s. Up to a scaling factor, the density of this distribution μ is given by

$$\exp\{-\frac{1}{2\tau^2}[\, \delta \sum_s (x_s^2 + y_s^2) + \sum_s (x_s - y_s)^2 + \kappa \sum_s ((x_s - y_{s.v})^2 + (y_s - x_{s.v})^2 - 2\theta_0)(1 - v_s) \tag{8}$$

$$+\kappa \sum_s ((x_s - y_{s.h})^2 + (y_s - x_{s.h})^2 - 2\theta_0)(1 - h_s)\,] + Q(h, v, \bar{h}, \bar{v})\,\}$$

This density is with respect to the product of Lebesgue measures at each site for x_s and y_s variables, and counting measures on $\{0, 1\}$ for edge variables. The parameter δ is an arbitrary, very small number ensuring the integrability of the above expression. In fact, when we will be considering the posterior, for which this problem disappears, we will let δ tend to 0.

The second sum forces gray-level variables x_s and y_s to have values which are not too far apart. This allows us to interpret the third and fourth terms, which are weighted by a positive parameter κ, as terms forcing the differences of gray-level at neighboring pixels to be small unless an edge separates them. The parameter θ_0 appears like a threshold below which this difference should be in the absence of edge. For the experiments, we have heuristically fixed the values of τ, κ and θ_0. This is more or less made possible by the simplicity of this part of the model.

The "edge energy", Q, is quadratic in its variables. It has the form

$$Q(w^1, w^2, w^3, w^4) = \beta_0 \sum_{i,s} w_s^i \beta_1 \sum_1 w_s^i w_t^j + \ldots + \beta_k \sum_k w_s^i w_t^j \tag{9}$$

217

The sums $\sum_1, \ldots, \sum_k$ are made over specified families of indices i, s, j, t. For example, one of them represents self-relation (like the α parameter in the synchronous Ising model), and the sum is made over i, s, j, t such that $s = t$ and either $i = 1$ and $j = 3$ (horizontal edges) or $i = 2$ and $j = 4$ (vertical edges). Other contain interaction between adjacent aligned edge elements, of edge elements making a right angle, and so on. The constraint is that there may not be an interaction within (h, v) nor within $(\bar{h}, \bar{v})$, which means that one may not have $i = 1$ together with $j = 1$ or 2, nor $i = j = 2$, and similarly for 3 and 4. In our experiments, we used $k = 15$. It is clear that it is not possible to work with heuristics, nor by trial-and-error to set the value of such a number of parameters. This has been done with a help of a learning procedure which is summarized in remark R16.

Using the method given in Proposition 3, we introduce two additional auxilliary fields, z and $\bar{z}$, such that $x_s = (z_s + \bar{z}_s)/2$, and one obtains the distribution of $(z, \bar{z}, y, h, \bar{h}, v, \bar{v})$ given ξ.

This distribution can be sampled by iterating the following sequence of *synchronous* steps ; assume that a current configuration of $(z, \bar{z}, y, h, \bar{h}, v, \bar{v})$ is given. Then, a global updating of this configuration can be done by

1. Update z, given $\bar{z}, y, h, v$ and $\bar{h}, \bar{v}$ given h and v.
2. Set $x = (z + \bar{z})/2$
3. Update y given x, h, v.
4. Update h, v given $x, y, \bar{h}, \bar{v}$ and set $\bar{z} = z$.

We give some results of experiments in this context. The noise is Gaussian, additive, with variance 200, the image being coded in gray levels between 0 and 256. The blur is obtained through a 5 by 5 Gaussian filter given by $\eta_{st} = c . \exp(-\|s - t\|^2/2\zeta)$ if $\max(|s_1 - t_1|, |s_2 - t_2|) \le 2$, and 0 if not, c being a normalization ensuring that the sum of the η_{st} is 1.

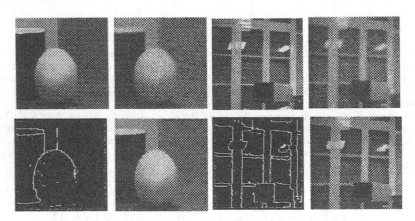

Fig. 1. Restoration : blurred pictures ($\zeta = 2$) with additive noise of variance 200 (Upper left : Original, upper right : Noisy, lower left : Estimated edges, lower right : restored picture).

References

J. Besag (1974) : Spatial Interaction and the Statistical Analysis of Lattice Systems. *J. of Roy. Stat. Soc.* B-36 pp 192-236.

D.A. Dawson (1975) : Synchronous and asynchronous reversible Markov systems *Canad. Math. Bull.* 17 633-649.

D. Geman (1991) :*Random Fields and Inverse Problems in Imaging*, In *Proceedings of the Ecole d'été de Saint-Flour*, Lecture Notes in Mathematics, Springer Verlag, New York.

D. and S. Geman (1984): Stochastic Relaxation, Gibbs Distribution and Bayesian Restoration of Images. *IEEE TPAMI.* Vol PAMI-6 pp 721-741.

O. Koslov and N. Vasilyev (1980) : Reversible Markov chains with local interactions. In *Multicomponent Random Systems*, R.L. Dobrushin and Ya. G. Sinai Editors. (Dekker New York). 415-469.

L. Younes (1993) : Synchronous Random Fields and Image restoration (preprint).

Parameterfree Information-Preserving Surface Restoration

Uwe Weidner*

Institut für Photogrammetrie
Nußallee 15 53115 Bonn
email: weidner@ipb.uni-bonn.de

Abstract. In this paper we present an algorithm for parameterfree information-preserving surface restoration. The algorithm is designed for 2.5D and 3D surfaces. The basic idea is to extract noise and signal properties of the data simultaneously by variance-component estimation and use this information for filtering. The variance-component estimation delivers information on how to weigh the influence of the data dependent term and the stabilizing term in regularization techniques, and therefore no parameter which controls this relation has to be set by the user.

1 Introduction

The first step for gaining a description of a 3D scene is the measurement of 3D point coordinates. During the data aqcuisition errors occur. These errors include systematic and random errors. The systematic errors can often be eliminated by calibrating the measurement equipment. Then the result of the measurement is a noisy discrete data set.

This data is the basis for the computation of the surface, on which the following first step of object recognition, i. e. feature extraction, is performed. Often features are related to some discontinuities in the data. Derivatives of the initial surface are commonly used for their extraction. The computation of these derivatives as well as the computation of the surface are ill-posed problems (c. f. [14]). These ill-posed problems have to be reformulated as well-posed problems.

Filters, surface approximations, or general regularization techniques are used to achieve this goal. Global techniques like linear filters or standard regularization (e.g. Tikhonov regularization) lead to a reduction of noise, but also affect the features and discontinuities, i. e. the information, by blurring the data. Therefore, the goal of surface restoration should be the regularization of the data including the suppression of noise with a minimal loss of information.

In this contribution we formulate filtering for regularization and noise suppression as a minimization problem which depends on local features based on an explicit physical and/or geometric model and the noise, and includes a procedure for estimating noise. Thus all parameters are estimated within a statistical framework. In this respect our approach differs significantly from other regularization techniques (cf. [13], [3], [7], [12]).

* supported by Deutsche Forschungsgemeinschaft SFB 350

The basic idea is to extract signal and noise properties from the data and use this information for the filtering of the data. The extraction of these properties is based on generic prior knowledge about the surface. This a priori knowledge also puts constraints on the data and is used for the regularization via the stabilizing function. If the data does not correspond to the a priori knowledge or the model respectively, the influence of regularization is weakened.

In our approach the function

$$F = \sum \frac{(z_i - \hat{z}_i)^2}{\sigma_z^2} + \sum \left(\frac{k_{1i}}{\sigma_{k_{1i}}}\right)^2 + \sum \left(\frac{k_{2i}}{\sigma_{k_{2i}}}\right)^2 \qquad (1)$$

is to be minimized. The principal curvatures k_1 and k_2 are used because they lead to a unique model surface and include directional information. Obviously the degree of regularization is made dependent on the variances of the data and of the true surface's smoothness. As both variances are derived from the data, this filter is a parameterfree information-preserving approach to surface restoration. The filter can be used for all applications in which surfaces are given by measured discrete points. The coordinates of these discrete points can be given either in a 3D coordinate sytem using arbitrary surface coordinates or in a 2.5D sensor coordinate system using a graph surface representation.

The kind of the input data is not really fixed and not only includes geometric surfaces, but may also represent the density distribution of a material. The only requirements of the data are that an interpretation of the data as a surface is possible, that the data is dense in order to have a sufficient redundancy, and, for ease of representation, that the data is regularly located on a grid given by arbitrary surface coordinates (u, v). Additionally, the data must have properties suited for regularization. Though our approach is more general, we restrict to using curvatures in our implementation.

In this paper we assume uncorrelated signal independent white Gaussian noise. This does not affect the presented approach as other knowledge about noise can be integrated easily in the estimation process via weights. Similarly, correlated noise could be taken into consideration.

The basic idea is to simultaneously estimate the variance of noise and of appropriate smoothness. Estimation techniques for the noise only (c. f. [9]) do not solve the problem we deal with, as they do not take the variance of smoothness into account. In [4] it is shown that noise and signal in observed autoregressive processes are seperable, using both Fourier analysis and variance-component estimation. Here, variance-components estimation is used for the estimation of signal and noise properties.

2 Algorithm

The algorithm is based on a geometric model. It is assumed that the expectations of the principal curvatures are zero, i. e. the surface can be locally approximated using planes. If the principal directions and the surface normals are known for the 3D representation, the principal curvatures can be computed by convolution. Those convolution kernels are gathered in the matrix of coefficients $\mathbf{X}$.

The information about a surface's curvature properties is fully contained in the Weingarten map or shape operator $\mathbf{W}$ (c. f. [2]). The eigenvalues of $\mathbf{W}^2 = \mathbf{W}\,\mathbf{W}$ are the squared eigenvalues of $\mathbf{W}$. The eigenvectors of $\mathbf{W}^2$ are equal to those of $\mathbf{W}$. We use the eigenvalues for estimating the local variance of the curvature of the surface.

The algorithm is based on the assumptions that

$$\mathbf{d} = \left(\mathbf{d}_1^T\ \mathbf{d}_2^T\ \mathbf{d}_3^T\right)^T = \mathbf{u} + \mathbf{n}, \quad E(\mathbf{d}) = \mathbf{u} \quad \text{and} \quad D(\mathbf{d}) = \sigma_d^2\,\mathbf{I} \quad (2)$$
$$\text{with} \quad \mathbf{d}_1 = \mathbf{x}(u,v) \quad \mathbf{d}_2 = \mathbf{y}(u,v) \quad \mathbf{d}_3 = \mathbf{z}(u,v)$$
$$E(\mathbf{k}_1) = 0,\ D(\mathbf{k}_1) = Diag(\sigma_{k1i}^2), \quad E(\mathbf{k}_2) = 0,\ D(\mathbf{k}_2) = Diag(\sigma_{k2i}^2)$$

where $Diag(p_i)$ denotes a diagonal matrix with entries p_i. If the surface normal and the principal directions are given, the following linear model with $m = 5$ groups of observations results (c. f. [6]):

$$E(\mathbf{y}) = \mathbf{X}\,\mathbf{u} \quad D(\mathbf{y}) = \sum_{i=1}^{5} \mathbf{V}_i\,\sigma_i^2 \quad (3)$$

$$\text{with} \quad \mathbf{X} = \left(\mathbf{X}_x^T\ \mathbf{X}_y^T\ \mathbf{X}_z^T\ \mathbf{X}_{k1}^T\ \mathbf{X}_{k2}^T\right)^T, \ \mathbf{y} = \left(\mathbf{d}_1^T\ \dots\ \mathbf{d}_5^T\right)^T, \ \mathbf{d}_4 = \mathbf{k}_1, \ \mathbf{d}_5 = \mathbf{k}_2$$

The matrix of coefficients, which describes the linear relation between the observations and the unknown parameters $\mathbf{u}$, splits into five submatrices, where the matrices $\mathbf{X}_x$, $\mathbf{X}_y$ and $\mathbf{X}_z$ are identity matrices and the rows of the matrices $\mathbf{X}_{k1}$ and $\mathbf{X}_{k2}$ contain the convolution kernels for the principal curvatures $\mathbf{k}_1$ and $\mathbf{k}_2$. The structure of $\mathbf{V}_i$ must be known in advance (c. f. [6]). Assuming independence of the observations and equal variances for the coordinates simplifies (3) to

$$E(\mathbf{y}) = \mathbf{X}\,\mathbf{u} \quad D(\mathbf{y}) = \sigma_d^2\mathbf{V}_d + \sigma_{k1}^2\mathbf{V}_{k1} + \sigma_{k2}^2\mathbf{V}_{k2} \quad (4)$$
$$\text{with} \quad \mathbf{V}_d = \sigma_d^2\,\mathbf{I}, \quad \mathbf{V}_{k1} = Diag(\overline{\sigma}_{k1i}^2) \quad \text{and} \quad \mathbf{V}_{k2} = Diag(\overline{\sigma}_{k2i}^2)$$

where $\overline{\sigma}_k^2$ denote a local estimate of the curvatures' variances.

Based on this, the unknown parameters $\mathbf{u}$, i. e. the coordinates, and the variances can be estimated using iterative estimation. Details are given in [16].

3 Results

In this section we want to show the results of the parameterfree information-preserving filter and compare these results with the results of other restoration techniques. For this purpose we use synthetic test data sets. The advantage of synthetic data is that the values of the true signal $\mathbf{z}_0$ are known and can be used as reference. A reference is of importance because we do not only want to compare the results qualitatively by visual inspection, but also give a quantitative comparison.

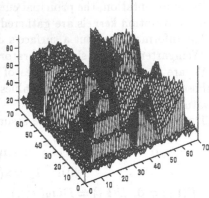

Fig. 1. Test image

Fig. 2. Test image: $\sigma = 2$ [gr], range: 20-90 [gr]

In order to derive such quantitative measures, the area of the surface $\mathcal{S}$ is devided into two components $\mathcal{R}$ and $\mathcal{B}$, where $\mathcal{B} = \{\mathcal{B}_i\}$ is the set of boundary regions, i. e. regions of discontinuities, and $\mathcal{R} = \{\mathcal{R}_i\}$ is the set of mutually exclusive segments of continous regions. Based on this division, two quantities can be computed.

The first quantity is the *property of smoothing*

$$PS = \frac{\hat{\sigma}_n(\hat{\mathbf{z}})}{\sigma_n(\mathbf{z})} \quad \text{with} \quad \hat{\sigma}_n = 1.4826 * med_{i \in \mathcal{R}}(|\hat{z}_i - z_{0i}|) \tag{5}$$

$\hat{\sigma}_n$ is the robust estimate of the noise standard deviation in homogeneous regions $\mathcal{R} = \{\mathcal{R}_j\}$ (cf. [11]) based on the restored surface. $\sigma_n(\mathbf{z})$, which in case of synthetic data is known, is the standard deviation of the observed signal $\mathbf{z}$. If all noise is removed, i. e. $\hat{\sigma}_n(\hat{\mathbf{z}}) = 0$, PS is equal to zero.

The second quantity is the *property of preserving discontinuities*

$$PP = \frac{\sigma_{\Delta s}}{\sigma_s(\mathbf{z})} \quad \text{with} \quad \sigma_{\Delta s} = \frac{\sum_{i \in \mathcal{B}} |\hat{S}_i - S_i|}{|\mathcal{B}|} \quad \text{and} \quad S_i = (\sqrt{g_r^2 + g_c^2})_i \tag{6}$$

where $\hat{S}_i$ and S_i, the local edge strength, are computed based on the restored image and the noiseless test image respectively using the Sobel-operator and $|\mathcal{B}|$ is the number of points in $\mathcal{B}$. This quantity is equal to zero, if the information is maintained.

The quantity PP is related to the Sobel's standard deviation σ_s of the observed signal and is computed based only using pixels within the boundary regions $\mathcal{B}$. Therefore the two quantities for the quantitative evaluation are independent of each other.

The test data set (Fig. 1) is similar to the image [1] used. For further examination white Gaussian noise with standard deviation $\sigma = 2$ [gr] has been added to the original data set (Fig. 2).

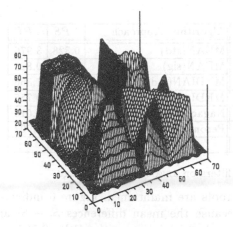

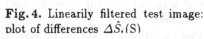

Fig. 3. Linearily filtered test image: 3D-plot

Fig. 4. Linearily filtered test image: plot of differences $\Delta\hat{S}_i(S)$

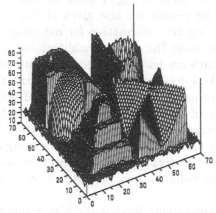

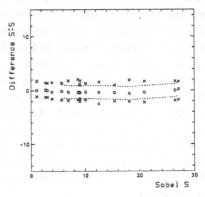

Fig. 5. Restored test image: 3D-plot

Fig. 6. Restored test image: plot of differences $\Delta\hat{S}_i(S)$

Qualitative effects of the restoration techniques can be easily seen in the 3D-plots and the additional plots (Fig. 4, Fig. 6), where the mean differences of $\hat{S}_i - S_i$ are plotted against S. $\times$ signifies the extrema and o the mean difference. The tolerance of $3\sigma_S$ is represented by the lines, where σ_S is computed based on the estimated standard deviation $\hat{\sigma}_n(\hat{\mathbf{z}})$.

Figure 3 shows the result of restoration using a linear filter, the mean filter (MEAN(std),c. f. [17]). The changes of the signal are evident. The peak almost diminishes and the edges, corners and the tops of the roofs are smeared. The effect on the edges can also easily be seen in figure 4. The values of the quantities $\hat{S}_i$ are reduced, the differences are negative. This filter has the best smoothing properties in homogeneous regions, but also the worst information preserving properties ($PS = 0.328$; $PP = 3.976$).

Figure 5 shows the result of the information-preserving filter. The smoothing properties of this filter applied to the noisy image are almost equal in the entire

Algorithm/Approach	PS	PP	Algorithm/Approach	PS	PP
Gaussian Filter	0.367	3.040	MEAN(std)	0.328	3.976
MEAN(knn)	0.823	0.762	MEAN(sig)	0.655	0.822
MEAN(snn)	0.835	1.282	MEDIAN(std)	0.476	1.366
MEDIAN(knn)	0.869	0.841	MEDIAN(sig)	0.714	0.755
MEDIAN(snn)	0.935	1.421	Nagao/Matsuyama(1979)	0.978	1.610
GRIN	0.413	0.913	Perona/Malik(1990)	0.391	1.002
Inform.Pres.Filter(IPF)	0.589	0.660			

Fig. 7. Evaluation of various filters on an artificial test image

image. The peak and the tops of the roofs are maintained. Figure 6 indicates that the information is maintained because the mean differences $\hat{S}_i - S_i$ are close to zero. These properties are also evident in the quantities $PS = 0.589$ and $PP = 0.660$.

The results for other filters can only be given in Fig. 7 using the enchantments for the filters like [17]. Some of the results are also given in [15]. The trade-off between smoothing and preserving the information for non-adaptive techniques (Gaussian, mean and median using the entire neighbourhood of a point) is evident. Adaptive techniques which are based on selecting points from the neighbourhood using a criterion like the k-Nearest-Neighbourhood (knn), the Sigma-Neighbourhood (sig), and the Symmetric-Nearest-Neighbourhood (snn) have knobs to be tuned with. The tuning of these knobs depends either on the user or the information the user has in advance, e. g. the standard deviation for the Sigma-Neighbourhood. All techniques except the information-preserving filter have no criteria, when iterations should be stopped. For the results of these techniques the knobs have been tuned in order to gain the optimal result for each technique.

The disadvantage of the information-preserving filter is the high computational effort due to solving a linear equation system of $U \times V$ unknowns, where U and V are the number of nodes in each surface coordinate direction. Furthermore the convergence of the SOR-iteration is dependent on the degree of noise. The rigorous solution via least squares adjustment can be approximated for not too high noise efficiently yielding comparable results. (c. f. [5]).

4 Conclusion

We presented an algorithm for parameterfree information-preserving surface restoration. The basic idea of this algorithm is to extract noise and signal properties of the data, which are 2.5D or 3D surfaces, and to use these properties for filtering. The properties which are estimated within a statistical framework are the variances of the noise and the smoothness of the data. The ratio of these quantities determines the parameter λ of standard regularization techniques for each point. Therefore this knob has been eliminated and no parameters have to be tuned by the user in order to obtain optimal results with regard to the smoothness and the preservation of information. The minimization of the resulting functional is done by least squares adjustment.

The results of our algorithm for 2.5D surfaces have been quantitatively compared to those of wellknown filter techniques. The comparison outlines our approach's property of preserving information. It also has been tested on images with signal-dependent noise and aerial images with similar results.

Acknowledgements

The author would like to acknowledge the helpful discussions with Prof. Hans–Peter Helfrich and Prof. Wolfgang Förstner.

References

1. P.J. Besl, J.B. Birch, and L.T. Watson. Robust Window Operators. In *Proceedings 2nd International Conference on Computer Vision*, 591–600, 1988.
2. P.J. Besl and R.C. Jain. Invariant Surface Characteristics for 3D Object Recognition in Range Images. *CVGIP*, 33(1):33 – 80, 1986.
3. A. Blake and A. Zisserman. *Visual Reconstruction*. MIT Press, Cambridge, 1987.
4. W. Förstner. Determination of the Additive Noise Variance in Observed Autoregressive Processes Using Variance Component Estimation Technique. *Statistics & Decisions*, supl. 2:263–274, 1985.
5. W. Förstner. *Statistische Verfahren für die automatische Bildanalyse und ihre Bewertung bei der Objekterkennung und -vermessung*, Volume 370 of Series *C*. Deutsche Geodätische Kommission, München, 1991.
6. K.R. Koch. *Parameter Estimation and Hypothesis Testing in Linear Models*. Springer, 1988.
7. Y.G. Leclerc. Image Partitioning for Constructing Stable Descriptions. In *Proceedings of Image Understanding Workshop, Cambridge*, 1988.
8. M. Nagao and T. Matsuyama. Edge Preserving Smoothing. *CGIP*, 9:394 ff., 1979.
9. S.I. Olsen. Estimation of Noise in Images: An Evaluation. *CVGIP-GMIP*, 55(4):319–232, 1993.
10. P. Perona and J. Malik. Scale-Space and Edge Detection Using Ansiotropic Diffusion. *IEEE T-PAMI*, 12(7):629–639, 1990.
11. P.J. Rousseeuw and A.M. Leroy. *Robust Regression and Outlier Detection*. Wiley, New York, 1987.
12. S.S. Sinha and B.G. Schunck. A Two-Stage Algorithm for Discontinuity-Preserving Surface Reconstruction. *IEEE T-PAMI*, 14(1):36–55, 1992.
13. D. Terzopoulos. Regularization of Inverse Visual Problems Involving Discontinuities. *IEEE T-PAMI*, 8(4):413–424, 1986.
14. V. Torre and T.A. Poggio. On Edge Detection. *IEEE T-PAMI*, 8(2):147–163, 1986.
15. U. Weidner. Informationserhaltende Filterung und ihre Bewertung. In B. Radig, editor, *Mustererkennung*, 193–201. DAGM, Springer, 1991.
16. U. Weidner. Parameterfree Information-Preserving Surface Restoration. accepted paper ECCV'94, extended version, 1993.
17. W.-Y. Wu, M.-J.J. Wang, and C.-M. Liu. Performance Evaluation of some Noise Reduction Methods. *CVGIP*, 54(2):134–146, 1992.

Illumination

Spatially-Varying Illumination : A Computational Model of Converging and Diverging Sources

M. S. Langer and S. W. Zucker

Research Center for Intelligent Machines
McGill University
3480 University St, Montreal, H3A 2A7, Canada.
email: langer@cim.mcgill.ca, zucker@cim.mcgill.ca

Abstract. There are three reasons for illumination to vary within a scene. First, a light source may be visible from some surfaces but not from others. Second, because of linear perspective, the shape and size of a finite source may be different when viewed from different points in a scene. Third, the brightness of a source may be non-uniform. These variations are captured by a new computational model of spatially varying illumination. Two types of source are described: a distant hemispheric source such as the sky in which light converges onto a scene, and a proximal source such as a lamp in which light diverges into a scene. Either type of source may have a non-uniform brightness function. We show how to render surfaces using this model and how to compute shape from shading under it.

1. Introduction

There are three reasons why illumination may vary within a scene. The first is that the source may be visible from some surfaces but not from others. The second is that, because of linear perspective, the shape and size of the source may be different when viewed from different points in the scene. The third is that the brightness of the source may be non-uniform.

In order to draw inferences about a scene from such illumination variations, we develop a model of how light flows through a scene. That model is computational in that it specifies data structures for representing general types of illumination variation, as well as algorithms for manipulating these data structures. Specifically we model two generic illumination scenarios: an outdoor scene illuminated by the sky, and a scene illumination by a proximal diverging source such as a lamp or window. The model generalizes our earlier papers [1, 2] in which we assumed that the light source was a uniformly bright sky.

2. Visibility Fields

We begin with an example that illustrates the fundamental issues. Consider an empty room with dark colored walls, illuminated by light from the sky, which passes through a

* This research was supported by grants from NSERC and FCAR.

Spatially Varying Illumination : A Computational Model of Converging and Diverging Sources

M. S. Langer and S.W. Zucker

Research Center for Intelligent Machines
McGill University
3480 University St. Montreal, H3A2A7, Canada
email: langer@cim.mcgill.ca, zucker@cim.mcgill.ca

Abstract. There are three reasons for illumination to vary within a scene. First, a light source may be visible from some surfaces but not from others. Second, because of linear perspective, the shape and size of a finite source may be different when viewed from different points in a scene. Third, the brightness of a source may be non-uniform. These variations are captured by a new computational model of spatially varying illumination. Two types of source are described: a distant hemispheric source such as the sky in which light converges onto a scene, and a proximal source such as a lamp in which light diverges into a scene. Either type of source may have a non-uniform brightness function. We show how to render surfaces using this model, and how to compute shape from shading under it.

1   Introduction

There are three reasons why illumination may vary within a scene. The first is that the source may be visible from some surfaces but not from others. The second is that, because of linear perspective, the shape and size of the source may be different when viewed from different points in the scene. The third is that the brightness of the source may be non-uniform.

In order to draw inferences about a scene from such illumination variations, we develop a model of how light flows through a scene. This model is computational in that it specifies data structures for representing general types of illumination variation, as well as algorithms for manipulating these data structures. Specifically, we model two general illumination scenarios: an outdoor scene illuminated by the sky, and a scene illuminated by a proximal diverging source such as a lamp or window. The model generalizes our earlier papers [1, 2] in which we assumed that the light source was a uniformly bright sky.

2   Visibility Fields

We begin with an example that illustrates the fundamental issues. Consider an empty room with dark colored walls (allowing us to ignore surface interreflections). The room is illuminated by light from the sky which passes through a

* This research was supported by grants from NSERC and AFOSR.

window. Observe that *the fundamental cause of the illumination variation is that the set of directions in which the light source is visible varies across free space.* This geometric variation is explicitly shown in Figure 1. Each disc in this figure represents the set of light rays passing through a point in free space within the room. The white sectors of each disc represent the rays which come directly from the window (and hence from the source), and the grey sectors represent the rays which come directly from the walls.

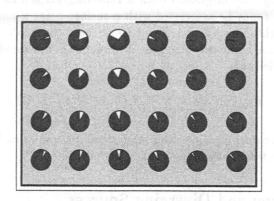

Fig. 1. An empty room illuminated by the light passing through a window.

This partition of the rays is the key tool for modelling illumination variation within a scene, and is formally defined as follows [1]. The VISIBILITY FIELD at a point $\mathbf{x}$ in free space is a set of unit length vectors, $\mathcal{V}(\mathbf{x})$, that represent the directions in which the light source is visible from $\mathbf{x}$. Observe that, as one moves away from the window in a particular direction, the solid angle of rays in which the window is visible decreases.

3   Brightness of a Light Ray

Visibility and aperture are geometric properties of free space. As such, they cannot account for photometric properties of light, in particular, that not all light rays carry the same energy density. For example, on a sunny day, certain of the light rays which pass through a window come from the sun, while others come from the blue sky.

Energy density of light is specified in terms of the brightness of a light ray, which is defined as follows [3, 5]. Consider viewing a scene through a narrow straight tube. Suppose that the near end of the tube is positioned at a point $\mathbf{x}$, and that the tube is pointing in direction $\mathbf{L}$. Let the light energy passing through the tube be d^2E. Let the solid angle subtended by the far end of the tube (when viewed from $\mathbf{x}$) be $d\Omega$. Let the cross sectional area of the tube be da. Then, the

BRIGHTNESS OF A LIGHT RAY passing through **x** from direction **L** is

$$B(\mathbf{x}, \mathbf{L}) \equiv \frac{d^2 E}{d\mathbf{a}\, d\Omega} .$$

Brightness has units lumens per square metre per steradian. The key property of the brightness is that, in the absence of scattering (eg. by fog), brightness is constant along a ray [3]. Considering each ray as a single geometric object, we may thus assign to this object a single brightness value.

For a light ray that originates from a reflecting surface rather than from a source, brightness may be associated with a surface point **x** and with the direction **L**. This brightness value is referred to as the LUMINANCE of **x** in direction **L**. In the case of a Lambertian surface, luminance is independent of direction, and may be modelled as

$$B_{out}(\mathbf{x}) = \frac{\rho}{\pi} \int_{\mathcal{V}(\mathbf{x})} B(\mathbf{x}, \mathbf{L})\, \mathbf{N}(\mathbf{x}) \cdot \mathbf{L}\, d\Omega . \tag{1}$$

This model is accurate provided that the albedo is low, that is, provided that surface interreflections may be ignored.

4 Converging and Diverging Sources

Two extreme scenarios are of special interest. The first is a light source that is much larger than a scene, so that rays from the source *converge* to the scene. The canonical example is the sky. The second is a light source that is much smaller than a scene so that rays from the source *diverge* to the scene. The canonical example is a lamp or candle.

The brightness of rays coming from a converging or a diverging source depend only on direction. This is obvious for a converging source, since the brightness of the sky does not vary as one moves within a scene. The case of the diverging source is less obvious, but may be understood in terms of an example of a room illuminated by sky light that passes through a clean window. Light rays that converge on the window diverge into the room, so that the rays entering the room inherit the brightness of rays from the sky, which depend on direction only.

Let $B_{src}(\mathbf{L})$ denote the brightness function of a converging or diverging source, and write (1) as

$$B_{out}(\mathbf{x}) = \frac{\rho}{\pi} \int_{\mathcal{V}(\mathbf{x})} B_{src}(\mathbf{L})\, \mathbf{N}(\mathbf{x}) \cdot \mathbf{L}\, d\Omega . \tag{2}$$

It is important to note that in classical photometry, a diverging source is usually approximated as a point[5] whose illumination is specified by *luminous intensity* which has units lumens per steradian. This definition, however, does not allow certain causes of illumination variation to be distinguished. For example, a source may have non-spherical shape or it may have non-uniform brightness, or both. Moreover, luminous intensity does not account for the penumbra (smooth cast shadow boundaries) produced by the finite size of the source. The advantage of the above model (2) is that it explicitly models the actual causes of illumination variation in a scene.

5 Discretization of Model

In order to perform computations, the variables of our models must be discretized. Space may be represented by an $N \times N \times N$ cubic lattice. A node in this lattice is $\mathbf{x} = (x, y, z)$. Assume that a surface seen in an image may be represented by a continuous depth map $\hat{z}(x, y)$ defined on a unit square. Given such a surface, a set of free space nodes $\mathcal{F}$ is the set of nodes lying above the surface.

Light travels from one free space node to another. Light is restricted to travel in a small number of directions, which are defined by an $M \times M$ cube, where $M \ll N$. Each node on the surface of this cube defines a direction, namely, the direction of a light ray passing through that node and through the center of the cube. In particular, we restrict our discussion to sources that are on the same side of the plane $z = 0$ as the viewer, so that the directions of light rays coming from the source may be represented by a hemicube [4], denoted $\mathcal{H}^*$.

A brightness function, $B_{src}^*(\mathbf{L})$, is defined on $\mathcal{H}^*$. Because the directions $\mathcal{H}^*$ define a non-uniform spacing of the unit sphere, to discretize the integral it is necessary to weight each of directions by a solid angle $\Delta \mathbf{L}$ that depends on $\mathbf{L} \in \mathcal{H}^*$. Finally, for each node $\mathbf{x}$, let the discrete set of directions in which the light source is visible from $\mathbf{x}$ be denoted $\mathcal{V}^*(\mathbf{x})$, so that $\mathcal{V}^*(\mathbf{x}) \subseteq \mathcal{H}^*$ Then, for either a converging or diverging source, we have the following model of surface luminance,

$$B_{out}(\mathbf{x}) = \frac{\rho}{\pi} \sum_{\mathbf{L} \in \mathcal{V}^*(\mathbf{x})} B_{src}^*(\mathbf{L}) \, \mathbf{N}(\mathbf{x}) \cdot \mathbf{L} \, \Delta \mathbf{L} . \tag{3}$$

In the next section, we present computational algorithms which are based on this model.

6 Forward and Inverse Algorithm

We present a generalization of the forward and inverse algorithms introduced in [1], where a uniform converging source was assumed. We now consider both converging and diverging sources, each having arbitrary brightness functions.

Light rays enter a scene through the boundary of free space $\mathcal{F}$. For a given scene, the set of rays coming from a source may be specified by the values of the visibility field on the boundary of free space. Both the forward and inverse algorithms depend on the computation of the visibility field over free space, $\mathcal{F}$. This computation is performed by propagating the visibility field away from the boundary of $\mathcal{F}$. The computation is by induction. The boundary condition on the visibility field is given for depth $n = 0$. Then, assuming the visibility field has been computed up to depth n, it is computed at depth $n + 1$.

FORWARD ALGORITHM: Given $z(x, y)$, compute $B^*_{out}(x, y)$.

> $n := 0$;
> repeat
>   for all (x, y),
> $\mathbf{x} := (x, y, n)$;
>   if $n \leq z(x, y)$
>   then for all $\mathbf{L} \in \mathcal{H}^*$
>   if $\mathbf{L} \in \mathcal{V}^*(\mathbf{x} + \mathbf{L})$ and $\mathbf{x} + \mathbf{L} \in \mathcal{F}$
>   then $\mathbf{L} \in \mathcal{V}^*(\mathbf{x})$
>   else $\mathbf{L} \notin \mathcal{V}^*(\mathbf{x})$;
>   if $n = z(x, y)$, then compute $B^*_{out}(x, y)$ using Eq. (3);
> $n := n + 1$;
>   until for all (x, y), $z(x, y) < n$.

The inverse problem is more challenging. As in [1, 2], we ignore the shading effects of the surface normal. This is done by replacing the factor $\mathbf{N}(\mathbf{x}) \cdot \mathbf{L}$ by its average value, 0.5, on the unit hemisphere $\mathcal{H}(\mathbf{x})$, yielding the model

$$B^*_{out}(\mathbf{x}) \equiv \frac{\rho}{2\pi} \sum_{\mathbf{L} \in \mathcal{V}^*(\mathbf{x})} B^*_{src}(\mathbf{L}) \, \Delta \mathbf{L} . \tag{4}$$

The present model is more general since it allows for directional variation in the brightness of the source.

INVERSE ALGORITHM: Given an image $I(x, y)$, compute $z(x, y)$.

> for all (x, y), $z(x, y) := 0$;
> $n := 0$;
> repeat
>   for all $(x, y) \in \mathcal{P}^*$,
> $\mathbf{x} := (x, y, n)$;
>   if $z^*(x, y) = n$
>   for all $\mathbf{L} \in \mathcal{H}^*$
>   if $\mathbf{L} \in \mathcal{V}^*(\mathbf{x} + \mathbf{L})$ and $\mathbf{x} + \mathbf{L} \in \mathcal{F}^*$
>   then $\mathbf{L} \in \mathcal{V}^*(\mathbf{x})$
>   else $\mathbf{L} \notin \mathcal{V}^*(\mathbf{x})$;
>   Compute $B^*_{out}(\mathbf{x})$ using Eq. (4);
>   if $| B^*_{out}(\mathbf{x}) - I(x, y) | > \epsilon$ then $z(\dot{x}, y) := n + 1$;
> $n := n + 1$;
>   until for all (x, y), $z(x, y) < n$.

7 Results

A slanting plane is rendered using a diverging spherical source. Three brightness functions are used: isotropic (left), weakly directed (middle), and strongly directed (right). As the brightness becomes more directed along the optical axis, the maximum of the image intensity shifts toward the center of the image.

A depth map is computed from each of the three images. The corners of the example on the right illustrate an important ambiguity in the inverse algorithm. Since a spotlight gives off a cone of light, the colums of free space at the image corners are darkest at shallow points (above the source cone), brighter as the depth increases, and darker again as the distance from the source increases. The algorithm cannot distinguish the two causes of darkness.

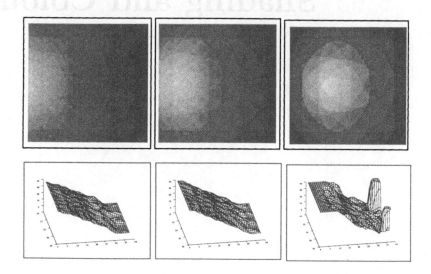

Fig. 2. The diverging source is a sphere centered at the viewer.

References

1. M. S. Langer, S.W. Zucker, "Diffuse Shading, Visibility Fields, and the Geometry of Ambient Light", *Proc. Fourth ICCV*, Berlin, Germany. May 1993.
2. M. S. Langer, S.W. Zucker, "Shape from Shading on a Cloudy Day". *J. Opt. Soc. Am.* (in press).
3. A. Gershun, "The Light Field", J.Math.Phys. 18,51-151 (1939).
4. Cohen, M.F., Greenberg, D.P. "The hemicube: A radiosity approach for complex enviroments." Computer Graphics 22(4) 155-164 (1985).
5. P. Moon, The Scientific Basis of Illuminating Engineering. (Dover Publications, 1961).

Shading and Colour

Recovery of Illuminant and Surface Colors from Images Based on the CIE Daylight

Yuichi OHTA and Yasuhiro HAYASHI

Institute of Information Sciences and Electronics
University of Tsukuba
Tsukuba, Ibaraki, 305, JAPAN

Abstract. We propose a color constancy algorithm suitable for robot vision under natural environments based on the CIE daylight hypothesis. The algorithm can recover the illuminant color and the surface color in the scene from three R, G and B values observed on two color images, typically, the current image and the past image. It utilizes the advantage of a robot which can exactly memorize images observed in the past. By exploiting the CIE daylight as a constraint, the stability and the accuracy of the color constancy algorithm based on multiple images which are proposed previously are remarkably improved. Effectiveness of the proposed method is examined theoretically by analyzing the behaviour of the algorithm under the existence of noise and also experimentally by using both real and synthesized images.

1   Introduction

Color is a useful information for a robot to recognize scenes. However, the color observed through images is often changed by the fluctuation of illumination. It is difficult to use such color as a stable feature in computer vision. On the other hand, certain visual system has a function called color constancy and we can identify objects in the scene using color as an important key under the variation of illumination. Computational theory for color constancy has been an important issue in computer vision [2], [3], [4], [5], [6], [7], [8]. By realizing a function similar to human color constancy on a robot, color can be used as a stable feature under the fluctuation of illumination in natural environments.

We think that the realization of color constancy on a robot need not to follow the features to which we human beings are constrained. A robot, in a computer, can exactly memorize huge information observed in the past. Therefore, it is reasonable to take not only the image information being observed currently but also the image information observed in the past. That is, in the color constancy, a robot can use a framework using multiple images as illustrated in figure 1. By utilizing this advantage, we can perform a color constancy algorithm which is more general and more accurate than along with color, the restriction of a single image as in the human vision.

We have proposed a color constancy algorithm using multiple images [1]. In this algorithm, when two pairs of objects are illuminated on two images observed

Recovery of Illuminant and Surface Colors from Images Based on the CIE Daylight

Yuichi OHTA and Yasuhiro HAYASHI

Institute of Information Sciences and Electronics
University of Tsukuba
Tsukuba,Ibaraki,305,JAPAN

Abstract. We propose a color constancy algorithm suitable for robot vision under natural environments based on the CIE daylight hypothesis. The algorithm can recover the illuminant color and the surface color in the scene from the R, G and B values observed on two color images, typically the current image and the past image. It utilizes the advantage of a robot which can exactly memorize images observed in the past. By employing the CIE daylight as a constraint, the stability and the accuracy of the color constancy algorithm based on multiple images, which we proposed previously, are remarkably improved. Effectiveness of the constraint is examined theoretically by analysing the behaviour of the algorithm under the existence of noise and also experimentally by using synthesized and real color images.

1   Introduction

Color is a useful information for a robot to recognize scenes. However, the color observed through images is often changed by the fluctuation of illumination. It is difficult to use such color as a stable feature in computer vision. On the other hand, human visual system has a function called color constancy and we can identify objects in the scene using color as an important key under the variation in illumination. A computational theory for color constancy has been an important target in computer vision [2] [3] [4] [5] [6] [7] [8] [9]. By realizing a function similar to human color constancy on a robot, color can be used as a stable feature under the uncontrollable illumination in natural environments.

We think that the realization of color constancy on a robot need not to follow the framework to which we human beings are constrained. A robot, or a computer, can exactly memorize image information observed in the past. Therefore, it is reasonable to use not only the image information being observed currently but also the image information observed in the past. That is, the color constancy on a robot can use a framework using multiple images as illustrated in figure 1. By utilizing this advantage, we can realize a computational algorithm which is more general and more accurate than those which follow the restriction of a single image as in the human vision.

We have proposed a color constancy algorithm using multiple images [1]. In this algorithm, when two pairs of objects are identified on two images observed under different illuminations, the colors of illuminant and the surface reflectance in the scene can be recovered from the R, G and B values observed on the two images. The algorithm does not require any specific assumption on the true color in the scene.

The problem of color constancy is ill-posed, in general, in the sense that it is very difficult to determine the solution stably. The discrepancy between the assumed ideal models and the real data sometimes guides our previous algorithm to inaccurate solutions. In order to use the algorithm in practical situations, it is essential to make the algorithm tough. Based on an error analysis, we found that the major reason for the instability is the too large freedom in the illuminant color space. When the illuminant in a scene is a daylight, it should be close to the CIE daylight illuminant. By using the CIE daylight hypothesis to reduce the freedom in the illuminant color, we have developed a more stable algorithm for recovering colors of illuminant and surface reflectance based on the R, G and B values of color images.

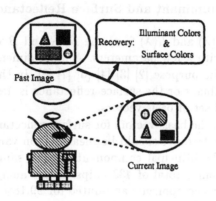

Fig. 1. A framework of color constancy for robot vision

2 Illuminant and Surface Colors from Multiple Images

2.1 A Model for Color Image Acquisition

The process to acquire the three primary components of color image can be summarized as follows. First, the light from the illuminant hits the surface of an object and it is reflected. This reflected light comes into the camera and is decomposed into three primary colors. Each of the three components is converted into an electric signal and is amplified to make the output signal values R, G and B. Thus the R, G and B values of the object are obtained by multiplying the spectral power distribution $E(\lambda)$ of reflected light from the object with the spectral sensitivity of each channel $S_R(\lambda)$, $S_G(\lambda)$ and $S_B(\lambda)$, respectively.

$$R = \int S_R(\lambda)E(\lambda)d\lambda$$

$$G = \int S_G(\lambda)E(\lambda)d\lambda$$

$$B = \int S_B(\lambda)E(\lambda)d\lambda \tag{1}$$

where λ represents the wavelength and they are integrated over the range of visible spectrum. The reflected light $E(\lambda)$ is represented as,

$$E(\lambda) = I(\lambda)R(\lambda) \tag{2}$$

where $I(\lambda)$ is the spectral power distribution of the illuminant, and $R(\lambda)$ is the surface spectral reflectance of the object. When the illuminant changes, the R, G and B values observed on the image are changed even for a same object.

2.2   Models for Illuminant and Surface Reflectance

In order to recover $I(\lambda)$ and $R(\lambda)$ from the R, G and B values in images, they should be modeled with a few parameters. A finite-dimensional linear model is often employed for the purpose [2] [3] [4] [6] [7] [8]. In the model, the spectral property of the illuminant or the surface reflectance is described by a weighted summation of a fixed set of basis vectors.

In order to obtain the basis vectors for surface reflectance, a large number of samples of spectral reflectance should be measured on various materials. Cohen [11] has computed the principal components of 150 samples of Munsell chips randomly selected from a total of 433 chips. In his analysis it turned out the mean and the first two components accounted for 99.18% of the variance of the samples. Parkkinen et al. [12] reported a similar result using 1257 samples.

As for the basis vectors for illuminant, Judd et al. [10] have examined the spectral distributions of 622 samples from typical daylights. The study showed that the mean and the first two principal components accounted for almost 100% of the variance of the samples.

We, therefore, describe $I(\lambda)$ and $R(\lambda)$ with weighted summation of three basis vectors.

$$I(\lambda) = a_1 I_1(\lambda) + a_2 I_2(\lambda) + a_3 I_3(\lambda)$$
$$R(\lambda) = b_1 R_1(\lambda) + b_2 R_2(\lambda) + b_3 R_3(\lambda) \tag{3}$$

We call the coefficients (a_1, a_2, a_3) and (b_1, b_2, b_3) in equation (3) as the characteristic parameters representing spectral properties of illuminant and surface reflectance, respectively.

2.3   Recovery of Scene Color Using Multiple Images

Equations representing the relations between the R, G and B values and the characteristic parameters of the spectral properties of illuminant and surface reflectance can be obtained by substituting equations (2) and (3) into equation (1).

$$R = \int S_R(\lambda) \sum_{i=1}^{3} a_i I_i(\lambda) \sum_{j=1}^{3} b_j R_j(\lambda) d\lambda$$

$$= \sum_{i=1}^{3} \sum_{j=1}^{3} a_i b_j \left\{ \int S_R(\lambda) I_i(\lambda) R_j(\lambda) d\lambda \right\}$$

$$G = \int S_G(\lambda) \sum_{i=1}^{3} a_i I_i(\lambda) \sum_{j=1}^{3} b_j R_j(\lambda) d\lambda$$

$$= \sum_{i=1}^{3} \sum_{j=1}^{3} a_i b_j \left\{ \int S_G(\lambda) I_i(\lambda) R_j(\lambda) d\lambda \right\}$$

$$B = \int S_B(\lambda) \sum_{i=1}^{3} a_i I_i(\lambda) \sum_{j=1}^{3} b_j R_j(\lambda) d\lambda$$

$$= \sum_{i=1}^{3} \sum_{j=1}^{3} a_i b_j \left\{ \int S_B(\lambda) I_i(\lambda) R_j(\lambda) d\lambda \right\} \tag{4}$$

We assume that the spectral sensitivities $S_R(\lambda)$, $S_G(\lambda)$ and $S_B(\lambda)$ of the camera are a priori known. Since $I_i(\lambda)$s, $R_j(\lambda)$s, $S_R(\lambda)$, $S_G(\lambda)$ and $S_B(\lambda)$ in equation (4) are known, we can compute each of the integral terms in advance. Thus equation (4) can be represented as a set of nonlinear quadratic equations of unknown characteristic parameters $a = (a_1 \ a_2 \ a_3)^T$ and $b = (b_1 \ b_2 \ b_3)^T$.

$$R = b^T S_R a$$
$$G = b^T S_G a \tag{5}$$
$$B = b^T S_B a$$

where S_R, S_G and S_B are 3×3 constant matrices, and their ijth element is the value of $\int S_R(\lambda) I_i(\lambda) R_j(\lambda) d\lambda$, etc. Now we consider these three equations as the observation equation representing the relation between the six characteristic parameters of scene color and the R, G and B values observed on an image. Let denote them in a simpler form as,

$$C = F(a, b) \tag{6}$$

where $C = (R \ G \ B)^T$, and $F()$ represents the set of three quadratic equations.

Now the color constancy problem can be treated as a problem of solving the unknown variables a and b based on equation (6). According to the relationship between the number of equations obtained from images and the number of unknown parameters, the simplest case to solve the equations is that two objects (b_1 and b_2) are identified on two images observed under two different illuminants

(a_1 and a_2) as shown in equation (7) [1]. Figure 2 illustrates the situation. Both of the number of equations and the number of unknown parameters are twelve.

$$
\begin{aligned}
C_{11} &= F(a_1, b_1) \\
C_{12} &= F(a_1, b_2) \\
C_{21} &= F(a_2, b_1) \\
C_{22} &= F(a_2, b_2)
\end{aligned}
\tag{7}
$$

where C_{pq} represents the $(R \quad G \quad B)^T$ of object q observed under illuminant p.

All terms on the right hand side of equation (7) are the form of $a_i b_j$ as shown in equation (4). This means that unless one of the twelve unknown parameters in equation (7) is fixed, all unknown parameters can not be fixed. In other words, one of the twelve equations in equation (7) is redundant. Therefore we fix a_{11} of a_1 to a constant and determine all unknown parameters using a least-square method based on equation (8).

$$
\min \left[\sum_{p=1}^{2} \sum_{q=1}^{2} \{ C_{pq} - F(a_p, b_q) \}^2 \right]
\tag{8}
$$

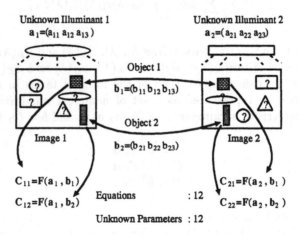

Fig. 2. Recovery of scene colors from two color images

2.4 Error Analysis

The algorithm described in the previous section works fairly well in the "ideal" situation: *i.e.*, the illuminants and the surface reflectances are exactly the summation of three basis vectors and no noise is included in the image acquisition process. In real situations, however, the color information obtained from images is not free of noise. As illustrated in figure 3, noise is included at every step of the image acquisition process. By the existence of such noise, the minimum of equation (8) becomes ambiguous and the stability of the algorithm is lost. In order to analyze the stability of the algorithm, we explicitly describe the noise factors at each step in figure 3 as follows; illuminant modeling error $\Delta I(\lambda)$, reflectance modeling error $\Delta R(\lambda)$, sensitivity measurement error $\Delta S_R(\lambda)$, $\Delta S_G(\lambda)$ and $\Delta S_B(\lambda)$, and R, G and B values observation error ΔR, ΔG and ΔB.

The non-linear simultaneous equation (7) can be converted to linear simultaneous equations with six unknowns b_1 and b_2 by fixing the characteristic parameters of illuminants a_1 and a_2.

$$Y_C = A x_b \tag{9}$$

where Y_C is a 6×2 matrix which has R_{pq}, G_{pq} and B_{pq} values observed for two objects on two images ($p = 1, 2$; $q = 1, 2$), A is a 6×3 matrix whose element is determined by the S_R, S_G, S_B, a_1 and a_2, and x_b is a 3×2 matrix composed of the unknown characteristic parameters of surface reflectances. When we describe the error explicitly, equation (9) can be written as follows.

$$Y_C + \Delta Y_C = (A + \Delta A)(x_b + \Delta x_b) \tag{10}$$

where ΔY_C represents errors in the observed data as stated, ΔA is the variation in A caused by the fluctuation of the characteristic parameters a_1 and a_2. The fluctuation in the solution is represented as

$$\frac{\|\Delta x_b\|}{\|x_b\|} \leq (\frac{\sigma_1}{\sigma_3})(\frac{1}{1 - (\frac{\sigma_1}{\sigma_3})\frac{\|\Delta A\|}{\|A\|}})(\frac{\|\Delta Y_C\|}{\|Y_C\|} + \frac{\|\Delta A\|}{\|A\|}) \tag{11}$$

where $\| \cdot \|$ represents norm, σ_1 and σ_3 are the maximum and the minimum singular values of matrix A, respectively, and σ_1/σ_3 is called the condition number of matrix A. Equation (11) shows that the fluctuation in the b_1 and b_2 caused by the ΔY_C and ΔA is magnified by the condition number of matrix A.

By fixing the characteristic parameters of surface reflectances b_1 and b_2, equation (7) can be converted into linear simultaneous equations with six unknowns a_1 and a_2.

$$Y_C = B x_a \tag{12}$$

B is a 6×3 matrix determined by the S_R, S_G, S_B, b_1 and b_2, and x_a is a 3×2 matrix composed of the unknown characteristic parameters of illuminants. Following the same steps as equation (11), we can obtain equation (13).

$$\frac{\|\Delta x_a\|}{\|x_a\|} \leq (\frac{\sigma_1'}{\sigma_3'})(\frac{1}{1 - (\frac{\sigma_1'}{\sigma_3'})\frac{\|\Delta B\|}{\|B\|}})(\frac{\|\Delta Y_C\|}{\|Y_C\|} + \frac{\|\Delta B\|}{\|B\|}) \tag{13}$$

where σ_1' and σ_3' are the maximum and the minimum singular values of matrix B, respectively, and σ_1'/σ_3' is the condition number of matrix B.

We have examined the condition numbers of matrices A and B by setting the characteristic parameters a and b to various values observable in real scenes. Table 1 shows their maximum, minimum, and mean values. In this examination, we used the spectral sensitivities actually measured on a 3CCD-TV camera for the $S_R(\lambda)$, $S_G(\lambda)$ and $S_B(\lambda)$. The basis vectors by Judd are used for $I_i(\lambda)$s. For $R_j(\lambda)$s, basis vectors derived from the actual spectral reflectance of the color chips on the Macbeth Color Checker [13], which are similar to the vectors by Cohen, are used. It will be clear from table 1 that equation (13) is far more sensitive to noise than equation (11). This means the characteristic parameters of illuminant easily become unstable under the existence of noise and it is necessary to introduce an additional constraint for the illuminant to make the algorithm more stable.

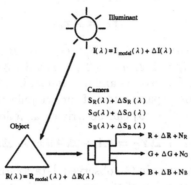

Fig. 3. Noise factors

Table 1. Condition numbers of matrix A and B

	max.	mean	min.
matrix A	2.62	1.54	1.27
matrix B	291.35	89.23	50.62

3 Recovery Based on the CIE Daylight Hypothesis

3.1 The CIE Daylight Hypothesis

In order to improve the stability and the accuracy of the color constancy algorithm by giving an additional constraint to the illuminant color, we introduce the CIE daylight hypothesis.

The CIE daylight hypothesis: "When the illuminant is a daylight, its spectral power distribution should be close to the CIE daylight at a certain color temperature."

The CIE daylight is a model of typical daylights proposed by the CIE (Commission Internationale de l'Eclairage) in 1966 [10], and its spectral distribution depends on a single parameter called color temperature. A relative power distribution $I_{day}(\lambda)$ can be modeled by

$$I_{day}(\lambda) = I_{mean}(\lambda) + M_1 I_{first}(\lambda) + M_2 I_{second}(\lambda) \tag{14}$$

where $I_{mean}(\lambda)$, $I_{first}(\lambda)$ and $I_{second}(\lambda)$ correspond to the mean, the first and the second components obtained by Judd, respectively. M_1 and M_2 are calculated from the chromaticity coordinates x and y corresponding to the position on the CIE chromaticity chart where the color of the given light would appear.

$$M_1 = \frac{-1.3515 - 1.7703x + 5.9114y}{0.0241 + 0.2562x - 0.7341y}$$

$$M_2 = \frac{0.0300 - 31.4424x + 30.0717y}{0.0241 + 0.2562x - 0.7341y} \tag{15}$$

The chromaticity coordinates in turn can be calculated from a given correlated color temperature T_C as follows.

$$x = -4.6070\frac{10^9}{T_C^3} + 2.9678\frac{10^6}{T_C^2} + 0.09911\frac{10^3}{T_C} + 0.244063 \quad \text{\small(for } 4000K \leq T_C < 7000K\text{)}$$

$$x = -2.0064\frac{10^9}{T_C^3} + 1.9018\frac{10^6}{T_C^2} + 0.24748\frac{10^3}{T_C} + 0.237040 \quad \text{\small(for } 7000K \leq T_C < 25000K\text{)}$$

$$y = -3.000x^2 + 2.870x - 0.275 \tag{16}$$

3.2 Recovery Based on The CIE Daylight Hypothesis

The basis vectors $I_1(\lambda)$, $I_2(\lambda)$ and $I_3(\lambda)$ for illuminant color in equation (3) correspond to $I_{mean}(\lambda)$, $I_{first}(\lambda)$ and $I_{second}(\lambda)$ in equation (14), respectively. When we assume $a_1 = 1$, the characteristic parameters (a_2, a_3) correspond to (M_1, M_2) in equation (14). From the equations (15) and (16), the (a_2, a_3) of CIE daylights should be on the curve illustrated in figure 4. Then the difference between an illuminant and the CIE daylight can be measured by the distance $E(a)$ on the (a_2, a_3) plane as shown in figure 4. The illuminants recovered by the color constancy algorithm should minimize both of equation (8) and the distance $E(a)$ simultaneously. Then we define equation (17) for the target of minimization.

$$\min \left[\sum_{p=1}^{2} \sum_{q=1}^{2} \{C_{pq} - F(a_p, b_q)\}^2 + \alpha \sum_{p=1}^{2} E^2(a_p) \right] \tag{17}$$

where α is a weight.

In order to find the set of parameters which minimize equation (8) and equation (17), we employed the non-linear simplex method [14]. In oder to find a set of 11 parameters which minimizes the objective function, the simplex method generates a general simplex with 12 vertices in the 11 dimensional parameter space. Comparing the function values at the 12 vertices, the vertex with the largest value is replaced with a new vertex by one of the three operations, reflection, contraction and expansion. A unit general simplex with 12 vertices, one of which is located at the origin, is set for the initial simplex and the replacement repeats until the simplex converges. The coefficients for the reflection, the contraction and the expansion are set to 1.0, 0.5 and 2.0, respectively.

4 Experiments

In order to demonstrate the validity of our new algorithm proposed in this paper, experiments using synthesized color images and real color images have been performed. The Macbeth Color Checker was used in both experiments as the color object.

4.1 Experiments with Synthesized Images

The color images used in this experiment are synthesized in the following condition. The two illuminants are the CIE daylights at the color temperatures $4800K$ and $10000K$. In order to simulate the modeling error in the illuminant, the fourth basis vector of Judd, i.e., the vector corresponding to the third component, is added to the ideal CIE daylight. The weight for the fourth vector is controlled to make the error between the synthesized illuminant and the CIE daylight to be 0.1 in the definition of equation (18). The spectral reflectances of objects are the actual measurements from the color chips on the Macbeth Color Checker. The spectral sensitivities of camera are the actual measurements of a 3CCD-TV camera. Two color images which simulate the appearance of the Macbeth Color Checker under the daylights of $4800K$ and $10000K$ are generated. Then four sets of R, G and B values, two color chips on two images, are supplied to the recovering algorithm.

Figure 5 shows a result obtained by using "orange" and "blue" color chips. Figure 5(a) shows the spectral distribution of illuminant at $4800K$ and figure 5(b) shows the spectral reflectance of the "orange" color chip. In each figure, "with" / "without" means the result obtained with / without the CIE daylight hypothesis. In order to quantitatively evaluate the performance of the results, we define the error measure of a spectral function $X(\lambda)$ compared to its true value $X_{true}(\lambda)$ as equation (18).

$$Error = \sqrt{\frac{\int_{400}^{700} \left\{X_{true}(\lambda) - X(\lambda)\right\}^2 d\lambda}{700 - 400}} \tag{18}$$

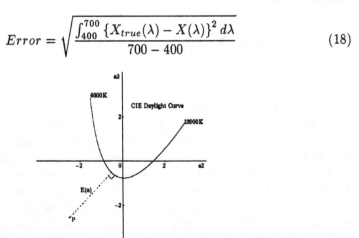

Fig. 4. The CIE daylight curve on the (a_2, a_3) plane and the distance $E(a)$

The results shown in figure 5(a) indicate 0.26 and 0.10 for "without" and "with" cases, respectively. The results shown in figure 5(b) indicate 0.13 and 0.05. In order to examine the influence of the selection of two color chips to the accuracy of the recovered scene colors, the recovery experiments were performed for all the combinations of selecting two color chips from the nineteen chips on the Macbeth Color Checker, *i.e.*, 171 cases. Figure 6 shows the error distribution for recovered colors of illuminant and surface reflectance.

4.2 Experiments with Real Images

We used a monochrome CCD camera with $\gamma = 1$ for the acquisition of R, G and B images. Three color separating filters, No.25, No.58 and No.47, are used for color separation. In order to obtain a good linearity between the input irradiance to the camera and the output R, G and B values, images observed by changing the iris size are combined into an image with a wide dynamic range. We used a lamp which has a spectral power distribution close to a daylight at $6500K$ for the illuminant. An optical filter for color conversion is used to change the color temperature from $6500K$ to $10000K$. The Macbeth Color Checker is illuminated by the lamp with and without the color conversion filter and two sets of RGB images are digitized.

It should be noted that obtaining two images with and without the color conversion filter is a convenience for the experiment and it never means that our algorithm needs more than three different sensor channels as Maloney [8]. The true spectral properties of the lamp, the color conversion filter, and the Macbeth Color Checker are blind to the recovering process, of course, and they are only used to evaluate the accuracy of the results obtained by the color constancy algorithm.

Figure 7 shows the results obtained by using "blue flower" and "moderate red" color chips. Figure 7(a) shows the results for illuminant color at $6500K$ and figure 7(b) shows the results for surface color of "blue flower". The results shown in figure 7(a) have errors of 0.50 and 0.10 defined by equation (18) for "without" and "with" cases, respectively. The results shown in figure 7(b) indicate 0.13 and 0.06. Figure 8 shows the error distribution for recovered illuminant colors and surface colors for the 171 pairs.

5 Conclusion

We proposed a new color constancy algorithm suitable for robot vision based on the CIE daylight. The algorithm uses multiple color images considering the advantage of the robot to the human. The algorithm requires no assumption on the true value of the scene color as the algorithms which use a single image following the human color constancy. By employing the CIE daylight hypothesis for a constraint on the illuminant, the stability and the accuracy of the color constancy algorithm were remarkably improved. We think that the algorithm is effective to recover the scene colors in natural environments.

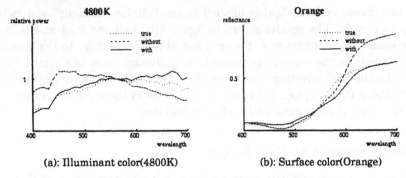

(a): Illuminant color(4800K)

(b): Surface color(Orange)

Fig. 5. Results by using synthesized images

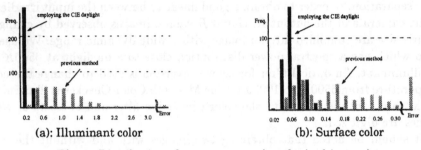

(a): Illuminant color

(b): Surface color

Fig. 6. Distribution of recovery error (synthesized images)

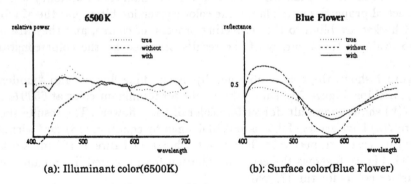

(a): Illuminant color(6500K)

(b): Surface color(Blue Flower)

Fig. 7. Results by using real images

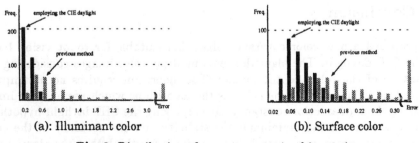

(a): Illuminant color

(b): Surface color

Fig. 8. Distribution of recovery error (real images)

Acknowledgments

We appreciate the kindness of Prof. Steven A. Shafer and Miss Carol L. Novak at Carnegie Mellon University who have offered us the spectral data of the Macbeth Color Checker.

References

1. M.Tsukada,Y.Ohta, "An Approach to Color Constancy Using Multiple Images," *IEEE 3rd International Conference on Computer Vision*, pp.385–389,(1990).
2. C.L.Novak,S.A.Shafer, "Supervised Color Constancy Using A Color Chart," *Technical Report CS-90-140,School of Computer Science, Carnegie Mellon University*, (1990).
3. R.Bajcsy,S.W.Lee,A.Leonardis, "Image Segmentation with Detection of Highlights and Inter-reflections Using Color," *Image Understanding and Machine Vision*, Vol.14,pp.16–19(1989).
4. B.Funt,J.Ho, "Color from Black and White," *IEEE 2nd International Conference on Computer Vision*, pp.2–8,(1988).
5. E.Land,J.J.McCann, "Lightness and retinex theory," *J.Opt.Soc.Am.*, 61,pp.1–11,(1971).
6. R.Gershon,A.D.Jepson,J.K.Tsotsos, "From R,G,B to Surface Reflectance: Computing Color Constancy Descriptors in Images," *Proc. of 10th Int. Joint Conf. on Artificial Intelligence*,pp.755 – 758, (1987).
7. G.Buchsbaum, "A Spatial Processor Model for Object Colour Perception," *J.Franklin.Inst.*, 310(1),pp.1–26,(1980).
8. L.T.Maloney,B.A.Wandell, "Color Constancy: a method for recovering surface spectral reflectance," *J.Opt.Soc.Am.*, Vol.3,No.1,pp.29–33,(1986).
9. D.A.Forsyth, "A Novel Algorithm for Color Constancy," *Int. J. Computer Vision*, Vol.5,No.1,pp.5–36,(1990).
10. D.B.Judd,D.L.MacAdam,G.Wyszecki, "Spectral Distribution of Typical Daylight as a Function of Correlated Color Temperature," *J.Opt.Soc.Am.*, Vol.54, No.8, pp.1031 – 1046, (1964).
11. J.Cohen, "Dependency of the spectral reflectance curves of the Munsell color chips," *Psychonomical Science*,Vol.1,pp.369–370,(1964).
12. J.P.S.Parkkinen, J.Hallikainen, T.Jaaskelainen, "Characteristic spectra of Munsell colors," *J.Opt.Soc.Am.A*,Vol.6,No.2,pp.318–322,(1989).
13. C.S.McCamy,H.Marcus,J.G.Davidson, "A Color-Rendition Chart," *Journal of Applied Photographic Engineering*, Vol.2,No.3,pp.95–99,(1976).
14. J.A.Nelder,R.Mead, "A simplex method for function minimization," *The Computer Journal*,Vol.7,pp.308–313,(1965).

3-D Stereo Using Photometric Ratios

Lawrence B. Wolff and Elli Angelopoulou

Computer Vision Laboratory
Department of Computer Science, The Johns Hopkins University
Baltimore, MD 21218

Abstract. We present a novel robust methodology for corresponding a dense set of points on an object surface from photometric values, for 3-D stereo computation of depth. We use two stereo pairs of images, each pair taken of exactly the same scene but under different illumination. By respectively dividing the left images and the right images of these pairs, a stereo pair of photometric ratio images is produced. We formally show that for diffuse reflection the photometric ratio is invariant to camera characteristics, surface albedo, and viewpoint. Therefore the same photometric ratio in both images of a stereo pair implies the same equivalence class of geometric physical constraints. We derive a shape-from-stereo methodology applicable to perspective views and not requiring precise knowledge of illumination conditions. This method is particularly applicable to smooth featureless surfaces. Experimental results of our technique on smooth objects of known ground truth shape are accurate to within 1% depth accuracy.

1 Introduction

There has been extensive work on computational stereo vision (see [12], [11], [5], [15], [1], and [13]). Most of the methods for computing depth from stereo vision involves the correspondence of image features such as intensity discontinuities or zero crossings determining image edges. A possible disadvantage of these techniques is that such data can be sparse and a number of methods have been developed to interpolate smooth surfaces to sparse depth data from stereo [5], [18]. There are considerable problems with shape determination of smooth featureless objects using feature-point based stereo vision algorithms.

Grimson [6] was the first to consider utilizing the diffuse shading information from two camera views to determine surface orientation at zero crossings. This additional information increased the accuracy of the surface interpolation. Smith [17] considered the correspondence of points in a stereo pair of images of a smooth featureless Lambertian reflecting surface utilizing an elegant mathematical formulation he termed the *Stereo Integral Equation*. There has been work by Blake, Brelstaff,

This research was supported in part by an NSF Research Initiation Award, grant IRI-9111973, DARPA contract F30602-92-C-0191 and an NSF Young Investigator Award IRI-9357757.

Zisserman and others [2], [3], [24] that has exploited the geometry of specular reflection viewed from a stereo pair of cameras to derive constraints on surface shape.

The major advantage of being able to accurately correspond photometric values between a stereo pair of images, besides being able to determine the shape of smooth featureless surfaces, is that it provides a very dense depth map. We utilize 2 illumination conditions but do not need to know them precisely. Our methodology corresponds the left and right ratio images of the same scene produced under these illumination conditions. We prove that the photometric ratios arising from diffuse reflection are invariant to almost all characteristics varying between a stereo pair of cameras as well as viewpoint and diffuse surface albedo. These varying characteristics make pixel gray values by themselves unreliable for stereo correspondence. In general, photometric ratios are invariant for reflectance functions that are separable with respect to incident light angular variables, and, viewing angular variables. Corresponding photometric ratios is equivalent to corresponding classes of well-defined physical constraints on object points, which makes this method formally robust. Furthermore, correspondence of photometric ratios can be done to subpixel accuracy using interpolation. We examine the *isoratio image curves* produced from these geometric physical constraints, which are image curves with equal photometric ratio. Due to their invariance to viewpoint and surface albedo, isoratio image curves may be useful for object recognition.

A technique that is somewhat related to our stereo methodology is "dual photometric stereo" pioneered by Ikeuchi [9]. There are however major conceptual and implementation differences. Ikeuchi does have the extra information provided by surface orientation to refine his depth map. However, his method is restricted to nearly orthographic views and known incident orientation of at least 3 distant light sources. The 3-D stereo method using multiple illumination that we are proposing does not require precise knowledge of any of the multiple illumination conditions and is applicable to full perspective views.

The experimentation that we present with ground truth objects shows that we can determine the shape of cylindrical and spherical objects, using stereo correspondence of photometric ratios, with a depth accuracy to well within 1%. Our stereo correspondence algorithm can recover the shape of more complex surfaces (like a face mask) with comparable accuracy.

2 Problem Background

To describe the problematic issues of comparing image intensities between a stereo pair of cameras we need to understand the image formation process. We describe the formation of image intensity values beginning with the familiar relation from Horn and Sjoberg[8]:

$$E = L_r (\pi/4) (D/i)^2 \cos^4 \alpha \qquad (1)$$

which relates image irradiance, E, to reflected radiance, L_r. Let D be the lens diameter, i the image distance, and α the light angle relative to the optic axis incident on the camera lens. Equation (1) assumes ideal pinhole optics. The effective diameter, D, of a lens can be controlled with an aperture iris the size of which is measured on an F-stop scale. Image irradiance is therefore very sensitive to F-stop. While a stereo pair of cameras can use identical model lenses at exactly the same F-stop setting, the effective lens diameters can still be slightly different. The focal lengths as well can be slightly different and by the classical thin lens law this will influence the image distance, i, in turn effecting the image irradiance. Even in the ideal case where focal lengths are precisely equal, the image distance, i, can be slightly different for a stereo pair of images even though the images "appear" equivalently in focus. On top of all this is the dependence of image irradiance in perspective images on pixel location relative to the optical center of the image plane. The farther a pixel is radially away from the optical center, the larger is the light incident angle, α, which strongly affects image irradiance. Image irradiances arising from the same object point appear in different parts of a stereo pair of images making them difficult to compare.

Equation (1) only takes into account the optics involved in image formation. Image irradiance is converted into pixel gray value using electronics. In general, the conversion of image irradiance, E, into pixel gray value, I, can be described by the expression

$$I = g E^{1/\gamma} + d \qquad (2)$$

where g is termed the *gain*, d is the *dark reference*, and, γ, controls the non-linearity of gray level contrast. It is typically easy to set $\gamma = 1.0$ producing a linear response, and easy to take a dark reference image with the lens cap on, then subtracting d out from captured images. However, we have observed that not only can the gain, g, be variable between identical model cameras but this can change over time especially for relatively small changes in temperature. Unless g is calibrated frequently, comparing pixel gray values for identical image irradiances between a stereo pair of cameras can be difficult.

A widely used assumption about diffuse reflection from materials is that they are Lambertian [10] meaning that light radiance, L, incident through solid angle, $d\omega$, at angle of incidence, ψ, on an object point with diffuse albedo ρ, produces reflected radiance:

$$L \cdot \rho \cdot \cos \psi \cdot d\omega$$

independent of viewing angle. The independence of diffuse reflected radiance with respect to viewing angle makes it theoretically feasible to associate radiance values with object points in a stereo pair of images.

Reflectance Models

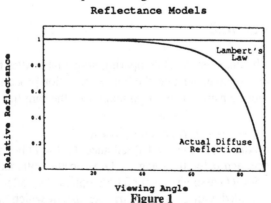

Figure 1

The physical reality of diffuse reflection makes it even more practically difficult to associate diffuse reflected radiance with object points across a stereo pair of images. A recently proposed diffuse reflectance model for smooth dielectric surfaces [19], [20], empirically verified to be more accurate than Lambert's Law, expresses the dependence of diffuse reflected radiance on both angle of incidence, ψ, and viewer angle, ϕ, as

$$L \cdot \rho \cdot [1 - F(\psi, n)] \cdot \cos\psi \cdot \left[1 - F(\sin^{-1}(\frac{\sin\phi}{n}), 1/n)\right] \cdot d\omega \tag{3}$$

where the functions, $F()$, are the Fresnel reflection coefficients [16], and, n, is the index of refraction of the dielectric surface, and, ρ, is the diffuse albedo computed from physical parameters. Figure 1 shows the significant dependence of diffuse reflection upon viewer angle.

Diffuse reflected radiance from an object point as seen from the two different viewpoints of a stereo pair of cameras will almost always not be equal. The dependence of specular reflection upon viewpoint is even more severe due to its highly directional nature and the geometry of angle of incidence equals angle of reflection.

3 Using Photometric Ratios for 3-D Stereo

We show that the ratio image produced by dividing 2 images of diffuse reflection from the same scene with respect to 2 different illumination conditions is invariant to the differences in physical characteristics of cameras discussed in the previous section, as well as viewpoint and diffuse surface albedo. Furthermore, these photometric ratios can be associated with well-defined geometric physical constraints on object points making them suitable for robust correspondence in a stereo pair of images.

3.1 Photometric Ratios as an Invariant

Combining equations (1), (2) and (3) gives us an expression which precisely relates pixel gray value, I, to diffuse reflection as a function of imaging geometry and camera parameters. For incident radiance L through a small solid angle, $d\omega$, at an angle of incidence, ψ, the gray value formed from viewing angle, ϕ (assuming we subtract out the dark reference, d) is:

$$I = g\left\{ (\pi/4)(D/i)^2 \cos^4\alpha \left(L\rho[1 - F(\psi, n)]\cos\psi\left[1 - F(\sin^{-1}(\frac{\sin\phi}{n}), 1/n)\right]d\omega\right)\right\}^{1/\gamma}$$

For a general incident radiance distribution, $L(\psi, \theta)$, (θ is azimuth about the surface normal) with respect to an object point, integrating over the incident hemisphere, the gray value will be:

$$I = g\left\{ (\frac{\pi}{4})(\frac{D}{i})^2 \cos^4\alpha \int (L(\psi, \theta)\rho[1 - F(\psi, n)]\cos\psi\left[1 - F(\sin^{-1}(\frac{\sin\phi}{n}), \frac{1}{n})\right]d\omega)\right\}^{1/\gamma}$$

$$= g\left\{ (\frac{\pi}{4})(\frac{D}{i})^2 \cos^4\alpha\left[1 - F(\sin^{-1}(\frac{\sin\phi}{n}), \frac{1}{n})\right]\rho\right\}^{1/\gamma} \left\{\int L(\psi, \theta)[1 - F(\psi, n)]\cos\psi\, d\omega\right\}^{1/\gamma} \tag{4}$$

Consider this object point first illuminated with an incident radiance distribution, $L_1(\psi, \theta)$, and then illuminated with an incident radiance distribution, $L_2(\psi, \theta)$. From equation (4) the photometric ratio of gray values is:

$$\frac{I_1}{I_2} = \frac{\{\int L_1(\psi, \theta)\,[1 - F(\psi, n)]\cos\psi\,d\omega\}^{1/\gamma}}{\{\int L_2(\psi, \theta)\,[1 - F(\psi, n)]\cos\psi\,d\omega\}^{1/\gamma}} \tag{5}$$

where the terms outside the integral signs in the numerator and the denominator cancel out. This photometric ratio expresses a well-defined geometric physical constraint determined by an illumination distribution relative to surface orientation at an object point. It is a function of only incident light geometry relative to local surface orientation, and is invariant to all camera parameters (except γ), viewing angle, ϕ, and diffuse surface albedo, ρ.

It is important to note that the reason why the viewing angle cancels out in the photometric ratio, expression (5), is because expression (3) for diffuse reflection is a separable function with respect to incident and viewing angular variables, ψ, and, ϕ. In general, it is clear that this photometric ratio is invariant to viewing for any reflectance function that is separable with respect to incident light and viewing angular variables, including azimuth dependent reflectance functions. This photometric ratio will not be such an invariant for combined specular and diffuse reflection, since specular reflection at an object point adds the term

$$L \cdot F(\psi, n) \cdot \delta\,(\psi - \phi) \cdot \delta\,(\theta_0 + 180 - \theta)$$

(incidence angle ψ, incident azimuth angle θ_0, emittance angle ϕ and emittance azimuth angle θ) to expression (3), and therefore combined specular and diffuse reflection is not separable with respect to ψ and ϕ.

3.2 Isoratio Image Curves and Physical Constraints

The ratio of equation (5) expresses a physical constraint consisting of the interrelationship between the local surface orientation at an object point and the two illumination distributions, $L_1(\psi,\theta)$, and, $L_2(\psi,\theta)$. Object points producing the same photometric ratios form equivalence classes that project onto the image plane forming what we term in this paper *isoratio image curves*. Different than isophotes which are image curves of equal gray value, an object point belongs to an isoratio image curve based on the geometric relationship of its surface normal with respect to two illuminations, independent of diffuse surface albedo, and independent of viewpoint even as diffuse reflection is viewpoint dependent. Corresponding photometric ratios along epipolar lines between a stereo pair of images is identical to corresponding points that are at the intersection of isoratio image curves and the epipolar lines. For best correspondence of photometric ratios we would like isoratio image curves to intersect epipolar lines as perpendicularly as possible. This tends to maximize the spatial variability (i.e., gradient) of photometric ratios along an epipolar line so that correspondences can be more accurately localized. See [21] for more detailed analysis.

3.3 Corresponding Photometric Ratios

Most cameras have a default setting of linear response (i.e., γ=1.0). If not, the intensity values can be linearized by inverse γ-correction computational processing.

For monotonically varying photometric ratios across an epipolar line, the numerical value I_1/I_2 in the left image can be matched accurately with the corresponding one in the right image and by using interpolation we get subpixel accuracy. We have found the photometric ratio I_1/I_2 in general to be remarkably smoothly varying across epipolar lines, particularly as compared with gray values themselves which typically fluctuate more. Below we present two algorithms for non-monotonic distributions of photometric ratios across epipolar lines. The first one is based on the preservation of left-to-right ordering. The second one is a more sophisticated hierarchical algorithm that can handle complex photometric ratio distributions produced from complex object surfaces.

4 Experimental Results

We tested the accuracy of a dense depth map determined from correspondence of photometric ratios between a stereo pair of images on two objects of known ground truth, a cylinder Figure 3 and a sphere Figure 8, and then experimented with the recovery of the depth of a far more complicated surface, a face mask Figure 12.

Figure 2	Figure 3

A pair of Sony XC-77 cameras (about 100:1 signal-to-noise ratio) with 25mm lenses were used with a stereo baseline of 3 inches. The cameras were mounted on precision controlled vertical moving platforms, and camera roll was precision controlled so that the corresponding epipolar lines were the scanlines themselves (Figure 2). The radius of the smooth plastic cylinder was precisely machined to 1 3/8 inches, and the radius of the smooth sphere is a precisely 1 3/16 inch radius billiard cue ball. The objects were placed so that their closest point was 20 inches from the stereo baseline which is far relative to the sizes of these objects themselves. At the distance that the cylinder and sphere were placed away from the baseline, the maximum depth variation across each object is about 5% of the total distance from the baseline. This means that for a depth map to have any resemblance to the shape of these objects our depth recovery from stereo correspondence must have an accuracy significantly better than 5%. Each illumination condition was produced from one of 2 point light sources incident at approximately 20° on each side of the horizontal perpendicular bisector of the baseline, and at about 12 inches away from the objects. The light sources were not precision mounted, nor were their incident orientations precisely known. To minimize the occurrence of specularities on the objects, we used cross-polarization.

Figure 4

Figures 4 and 6 show the photometric ratio images with respect to the left and right views of a cylinder (shown in Figure 3) and a sphere (shown in Figure 5) respectively. All the photometric ratio images were derived by dividing the image of the object illuminated by the left light source, by the image of the object illuminated by the right light source. Notice that more of the left side of the cylinder is visible from the left view than from the right view, as can be seen by the width of the left-most dark isoratio curve. The inverse is noticeable on the right side of the cylinder. The shape of the isoratio image curves on the various objects shows the well-ordered structure that is induced on objects by photometric ratios. Note the two tiny spots near the center of the sphere on each of the isoratio image curve images. These are due to parts of specularities that we did not completely cancel out by cross polarization.

Figure 5   **Figure 6**

Figures 7, 8 show the actual photometric ratio values going across a pair of corresponding epipolar horizontal scanlines in the left and right images, approximately midway through the cylinder, and the sphere respectively. In Figure 8 the displayed corresponding epipolar scanlines pass through where specular reflections are produced from the left light source (the small peak) and from the right light source (the small valley).

Scan Lines of Left and Right Images of Cylinder

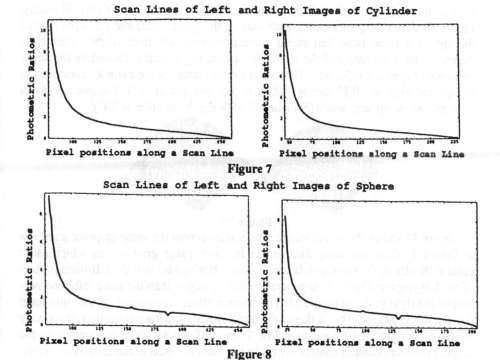

Figure 7

Scan Lines of Left and Right Images of Sphere

Figure 8

For these simpler objects we had success with the following photometric ratio matching algorithm.

Correspondence_Algorithm_1

> For each scan line
>> Repeat
>>> 1. In the **left image**, find the *leftmost* uncorresponded pixel that has some ratio value.
>>> 2. In the **right image**, find the corresponding pixel, which has to be to the *right* of the last match. To do this:
>>>> * either find the *leftmost* pixel with the same ratio value;
>>>> * or a) find the *two adjacent leftmost* pixels with values larger and smaller than that ratio value.
>>>>> b) interpolate linearly.

Figure 9

Figure 9 shows the ground truth depth map of the cylinder (left) and the depth map of that cylinder derived from Correspondence_Algorithm_1 (right). Similarly, Figure 10 shows the ground truth depth map of the sphere (left) and the depth map of the sphere derived from that stereo correspondence algorithm (right). The slight "dimple" near the center of the recovered sphere depth map is caused by the slight presence of specular reflection. The average depth error for the cylinder compared to the ground truth was 0.17 inches (0.85% depth variation at 20"). The average depth error across the sphere, was 0.09 inches (0.45% depth variation at 20")!

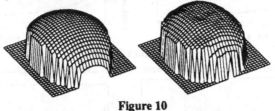

Figure 10

Figure 11 shows the actual image gray values across the same epipolar scanlines as Figure 7. There are noisy fluctuations in these image gray values, which cause great difficulty to the correspondence problem. Notice also that the left-hand portion of the left graph in Figure 11 is generally slightly higher than the same left-hand portion of the right graph in Figure 11. The reverse effect is noticeable at the right-hand portion of the graphs. This is due to the dependence of diffuse reflection on viewing angle, ϕ, as described by equation (3). These differences are compounded by the slightly different camera characteristics in the cameras used in the stereo pair resulting in large errors.

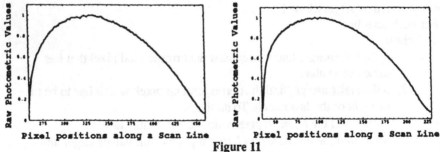

Figure 11

Figure 12 shows a much more complicated surface, a face mask. Figure 13 shows the resulting isoratio image curves for left and right views. Due to the significant complexity of the surface of the face mask some isoratio image curves appear thicker and sometimes more like "regions" rather than curves on some of the flatter portions of the mask.

Figure 14 shows photometric ratio distributions across corresponding epipolar scanlines going through the eyes and the bridge of the nose on the face mask. This is an example of one of the more difficult photometric ratio distributions to correspond. There are significantly wide flat plateaus across which there are many minor fluctuations due to noise that do not consistently appear across corresponding epipolar scanlines. It is straightforward to distinguish peaks and valleys produced by noise, from true peaks and valleys caused by real object characteristics.

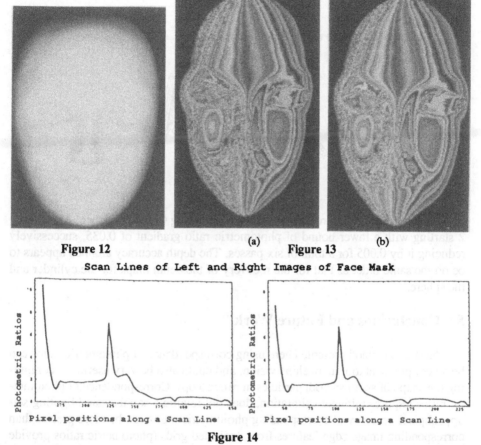

Figure 12   (a)   **Figure 13**   (b)

Scan Lines of Left and Right Images of Face Mask

Figure 14

Let the *degree of non-monotonicity* of a photometric ratio distribution across an epipolar line be the total number of occurring maxima and minima. The two properties most salient to peaks and valleys due to noise are that: (i) their degree of non-monotonicity is high over small local pixel neighborhoods, typically of degree at least 3 within a 4 pixel neighborhood; (ii) they typically have a much smaller photometric ratio gradient, ε, than true peaks and valleys. These observations motivated us to develop the following hierarchical stereo matching algorithm.

Correspondence_Algorithm_2

For each scan line

Set the gradient ε to some prescribed lower bound

Repeat for current ε

Repeat

Choose the *uncorresponded* non-noisy pixels in the **left image**, that satisfy ε. Run Correspondence_Algorithm_1 on these pixels, using the previously corresponded pixels to calculate the region where the matching pixel should lie.

Until no more pixels
Decrease ε
Until ε very small
Linearly interpolate uncorresponded pixels.

Figure 15

The depth map in Figure 15 was produced by using Correspondence_Algorithm_ 2 starting with a lower bound of photometric ratio gradient of 0.035, successively reducing it by 0.005 for a total of six passes. The depth accuracy attained appears to be on the same order as that for the recovery of the depth maps for the cylinder and the sphere.

5 Conclusions and Future Work

The stereo method presented here using correspondence of photometric ratios can be a very practical tool in machine vision, and could also be very useful for computing the shape of small smooth particles in microscopy. Correspondence of photometric ratios requires minimal calibration, does not require a sophisticated lighting set-up, subpixel accuracy of corresponding photometric ratios can be more precise than corresponding image edge features from projected grids (photometric ratios provide denser depth maps literally providing depth data at every single pixel where there is diffuse reflection), and, is relatively computationaly inexpensive.

In addition to proposing photometric ratios as a reliable way of corresponding a stereo pair of images, we introduced the notion of the isoratio image curve which (unlike isophotes) are invariant to diffuse surface albedo. Therefore isoratio curves are more directly related to the actual geometry of the surface itself and can yield more of information for object recognition. We are currently studying the use of isoratio image curves for improving the performance of object recognition in robotic environments.

References

1. N. Ayache. *Artificial Vision for Mobile Robots: Stereo Vision and Multisensory Perception.* MIT Press, 1989.
2. A. Blake. "Specular Stereo." *Proceedings of IJCAI*, pp. 973-976, 1985.
3. G.J. Brelstaff and A. Blake."Detecting specular reflections using Lambertian

constraints." *Proceedings of the IEEE Second International Conference on Computer Vision (ICCV)*, pp.297-302, Tampa, Florida, December 1988.

4. D. Clarke and J.F. Grainger. *Polarized Light and Optical Measurement*. Pergamon Press, 1971.

5. W.E.L. Grimson. *From Images to Surfaces: A Computational Study of the Human Early Visual System*. MIT Press, 1981.

6. W.E.L. Grimson. "Binocular Shading and Visual Surface Reconstruction." *Computer Vision Graphics and Image Processing*, 28 (1): 19-43, 1984.

7. B.K.P. Horn. "Understanding Image Intensities." *Artificial Intelligence*, pp. 1-31, 1977.

8. B.K.P. Horn and R.W. Sjoberg. "Calculating the Reflectance Map." *Applied Optics*, 18 (11): 1770-1779, June 1979.

9. K. Ikeuchi. "Determining a Depth Map Using a Dual Photometric Stereo." *International Journal of Robotics Research*, 6 (1): 15-31, 1987.

10. J.H. Lambert. "Photometria sive de mensura de gratibus luminis, colorum et umbrae" *Eberhard Klett*. Ausberg, Germany, 1760.

11. D.Marr. Vision. Freeman, San Francisco, 1982.

12. D. Marr and T. Poggio. "A theory of human vision." *Proceedings of the Royal Society of London*. B, 204: 301-328, 1979.

13. J.E.W. Mayhew and J.P. Frisby. *3D Model Recognition from Stereoscopic Cues*. MIT Press, 1991.

14. B.T. Phong. "Illumination for computer generated images." *Communications of the ACM*, 18(6): 311-317, June 1975.

15. S. Pollard and J. Mayhew and J. Frisby. "PMF: a stereo correspondence algorithm using the disparity gradient limit." *Perception*, 14: 449-470, 1985.

16. R. Siegal and J.R. Howell. *Thermal Radiation Heat Transfer*. McGraw-Hill, 1981.

17. G.B. Smith. "Stereo Integral Equation." *Proceedings of the AAAI*, pp. 689-694, 1986.

18. D. Terzopoulos. "The role of constraints and discontinuities in visible-surface reconstruction." *Proceedings of IJCAI*, pp. 1073-1077, 1983.

19. L.B. Wolff. "Diffuse Reflection." *Proceedings of IEEE Conference on Computer Vision and Pattern Recognition (CVPR)*, pp. 472-478, June 1992.

20. L.B. Wolff. "Diffuse and Specular Reflection." *Proceedings of the DARPA Image Understanding Workshop*, April 1993.

21. L.B. Wolff and E. Angelopoulou. "3-D Stereo Using Photometric Ratios." *Johns Hopkins University Technical Report CS-93-10*, October 1993.

22. L.B. Wolff and T.E. Boult. "Constraining Object Features Using a Polarization Reflectance Model." *IEEE Transactions on Pattern Analysis and Machine Intelligence (PAMI)*, 13 (7): 635-657, July 1991.

23. R.J. Woodham. "Reflectance map techniques for analyzing surface defects in metal castings." *Ph.D. thesis, MIT AI Lab Tech Report AI-TR-457*, June 1978.

24. A. Zisserman and P. Giblin and A. Blake. "The information available to a moving observer from specularities". *Image and Vision Computing*, 7 (1): 38-42, 1989.

Shape from Shading: Provably Convergent Algorithms and Uniqueness Results

Paul Dupuis[1] and John Oliensis[2]*

[1] Division of Applied Mathematics, Brown University, Providence, Rhode Island 02912, USA

[2] Department of Computer Science, University of Massachusetts at Amherst, Amherst, Massachusetts 01003, USA

Abstract. An explicit representation for the surface corresponding to a shaded image is presented and proven to be correct (under standard conditions). Uniqueness of the surface is an immediate consequence. Using this representation, various iterative algorithms for shape reconstruction are derived. It has been proven that all these algorithms converge monotonically to the correct surface reconstruction, and they have been shown experimentally to be fast and robust. Some of the results of this paper extend previous ones to the case of illumination from a general direction.

1 Introduction

Shape from shading has proven to be a difficult problem, even under the standard idealizing assumptions of a Lambertian surface, known light source, and no shadowing or occlusion. Recently, a new approach has been developed, based on relating shape from shading to an "equivalent" optimal control problem [7,8,4,9,13,14,1]. The advantages of this approach are both theoretical and practical. First, it makes possible an easy uniqueness proof for the surface corresponding to a shaded image (under standard conditions); thus shape from shading, contrary to previous belief, is often a well–posed problem. Second, the approach leads naturally to an algorithm for surface reconstruction that is simple, fast, provably convergent, and (under standard conditions) provably convergent to the correct surface. In contrast, traditional algorithms typically require thousands of iterations for reconstruction with no guarantee of convergence [5].

In this paper we prove the correctness of an optimal control representation for shape from shading, extending previous work to the case of illumination from a general direction (Section 2). Uniqueness of the surface is an immediate consequence.

From this representation, we derive in Section 3 two provably correct surface reconstruction algorithms (see also [8]). An advantage of our approach is that it gives a great deal of freedom in constructing algorithms, all of which can be proven to produce the same surface approximation. This is useful since one

* This research was supported in part by National Science Foundation grants DMS-9115762, IRI-9113690, and CDA-8922572.

of the presented algorithms has a simple theoretical interpretation and can be used to prove the correctness of the surface reconstruction [3], while the other is more efficient computationally. Note that although the algorithms described here require some information about the imaged surface in order to reconstruct it, they have recently been embedded in a global algorithm capable of surface reconstruction with no a priori information about the surface [7].

2 The Representation Theorem

We consider the idealized problem of shape from shading under the usual assumptions. Note that although we assume Lambertian surface reflectance and illumination from a single direction, our results can be extended easily to any "convex" reflectance function. Under these assumptions, the intensity at an image point $r \equiv (x, y)$ is given by $I(x, y) = \hat{L} \cdot \hat{n}$, where $\hat{L}$ is a unit vector in the light source direction, the optical axis is along the $-z$ direction, and $\hat{n}$ is the surface normal at the corresponding surface point. $I(\cdot)$ is defined on a bounded open subset $\mathcal{D}$ of $\Re^2$. In terms of the surface height function $z(x, y)$, which is assumed continuously differentiable (though this is not essential),

$$\hat{n} \equiv \frac{(-\nabla z, 1)}{(1 + \|\nabla z\|^2)^{1/2}}.$$

For illumination from a general direction, we represent the surface not by $z(\cdot)$ but by its height $f(x, y) \equiv \hat{L} \cdot (x, y, z(x, y))$ measured along the light direction $\hat{L}$. Without loss of generality, assume that $L_x = 0$, $L_z > 0$. In terms of $f(\cdot)$, the image irradiance equation can be rewritten after some algebra as $H(r, \nabla f(x)) = 0$, where the Hamiltonian

$$H(r, \alpha) = I(r) \left(1 + \|\alpha\|^2 - 2\alpha_y L_y\right)^{1/2} + \alpha_y L_y - 1.$$

Note that $H(r, \alpha)$ is a strictly convex function of α. The fact that the image irradiance equation can be rewritten in terms of a strictly convex H is the essential property used below. Our results can be extended to essentially any image irradiance equation that can be so written.

Singular points—those image points where the intensity achieves its maximal brightness $I(\cdot) = 1$—play a critical role in constraining the surface corresponding to a shaded image [8,11,16,2]. Only at these points is the local surface orientation determined from the intensity alone. Let S denote the set of singular points in the image. It is easy to see that $\nabla f = 0$ on S, so that S includes all local maxima and minima of $f(x, y)$. We will focus on those singular points corresponding essentially to the local minima, and use these in determining the surface from its image. (Alternatively, our results could be derived using the local maxima.)

To specify precisely the conditions under which our results hold, we introduce some nonstandard terminology. We say that a set $A \subset \Re^2$ is smoothly connected if given any two points r and r' in A there is an absolutely continuous ("smooth") path connecting the two. We will assume that the set of singular points is a finite collection of smoothly connected sets. Then since $\nabla f = 0$ on $\mathcal{S}$, $f(\cdot)$ is constant over each connected component $\mathcal{S}_C \subset \mathcal{S}$. We will refer to a connected subset $\mathcal{S}_C$ as a set of local minima if there exists an $\varepsilon > 0$ such that $d(r, \mathcal{S}_C) < \varepsilon$ implies $f(r) \geq f(r')$ for $r' \subset \mathcal{S}_C$, i.e., if the "heights" f of nearby points are larger than the value of f on $\mathcal{S}_C$. We will refer to a point as a local minimum of f only if it is contained in such a connected subset $\mathcal{S}_C$. An analogous definition is used for local maxima. Finally, a connected subset that is neither a set of local maxima or local minima will be called a set of saddle points. Let $\mathcal{M}$ be the set of all the local minima in the above sense.

The Lagrangian corresponding to $H(\cdot)$ is:

$$L(r, \beta) = \sup_\alpha \left[-\alpha \cdot \beta - H(r, \alpha) \right]$$
$$= L_z^2 - L_y \beta_y - L_z \left(I^2(r) - |\beta_x|^2 - |\beta_y + L_y|^2 \right)^{1/2} \tag{2.1}$$

if $|\beta_x|^2 + |\beta_y + L_y|^2 \leq I^2(r)$ and ∞ if $|\beta_x|^2 + |\beta_y + L_y|^2 > I^2(r)$. Define

$$\mathcal{U}(r) = \left\{ \beta : |\beta_x|^2 + |\beta_y + L_y|^2 \leq I^2(r) \right\}.$$

Thus $\mathcal{U}(r)$ is the domain on which $L(r, \cdot)$ is finite. The Lagrangian L serves as the running cost in the "equivalent" optimal control problem, which we now define. Consider an arbitrary path ϕ in the image plane starting at some r, and continuing for a time ρ. More precisely, the path is defined by $\phi(0) = r, \dot{\phi} = u(t)$, where the control $u : [0, \infty) \to \Re^2$ is any integrable function. For each such path, we define a cost which is the sum of two terms: 1) the total running cost, given by the integral of the running cost $L(\phi, u(\phi))$ over the path, and 2) a terminal cost, which depends only on the end point of the path. The control problem is to find the path giving the minimal total cost. The representation theorem states that under appropriate conditions the infimal value of the cost for starting point r is just $f(r)$.

Assume we are given an upper bound B for $\{f(r) : r \in \mathcal{D}\}$. Then define the terminal cost

$$g(r) = \begin{cases} f(r) & \text{for } r \in \mathcal{M} \\ B & \text{for } r \notin \mathcal{M} \end{cases} \tag{2.2}$$

The terminal cost imposes the large penalty B on any path terminating at a point $r \notin \mathcal{M}$. Finally, the total cost is the sum of the running and terminal costs

$$V(r) = \inf \left[\int_0^{\rho \wedge \tau} L(\phi(s), u(s)) ds + g(\phi(\rho \wedge \tau)) \right], \tag{2.3}$$

where $\rho \wedge \tau$ denotes $\min(\rho, \tau)$, $\tau = \inf\{t : \phi(t) \in \partial \mathcal{D} \cup \mathcal{M}\}$ and the infimum is over all paths ϕ and stopping times $\rho \in [0, \infty)$. Thus, V is the "minimal" cost over all finite time paths, where the path terminates either at time ρ determined by the controller, or else at the first time that the path exits $\mathcal{D}$ or enters $\mathcal{M}$. We want to show that $f(r) = V(r)$.

Preliminaries. For any H, it is easy to show that the definition (2.1) implies that the running cost $L(r, \cdot)$ is convex on $\mathcal{U}(r)$: here it is strictly convex. Moreover, a direct calculation shows that $L(\cdot, \cdot) \geq 0$, and $L(r, \beta) = 0$ only for $r \in \mathcal{S}$

and $\beta = 0$. Also, since $H(r, \cdot)$ is strictly convex, it follows by standard arguments that

$$H(r, \alpha) = \sup_{\beta \in \mathcal{U}(r)} [-\alpha \cdot \beta - L(r, \beta)], \qquad (2.4)$$

and for each $\alpha \in \Re^2$ there exists a unique vector $u(r, \alpha)$ such that

$$H(r, \alpha) = -\alpha \cdot u(r, \alpha) - L(r, u(r, \alpha)).$$

Define $\bar{u}(r)$ for $r \in \mathcal{D}$ by

$$0 = H(r, \nabla f(r)) = -\nabla f(r) \cdot \bar{u}(r) - L(r, \bar{u}(r)). \qquad (2.5)$$

From (2.1), $\bar{u}(r)$ is given by

$$\nabla_\alpha H(r, \alpha)|_{\nabla f} = -\bar{u}(r).$$

If (as we assume) $\nabla f(r)$ is continuous, then the fact that $H(r, \cdot)$ is C^1 implies $\bar{u}(r)$ is continuous on $\mathcal{D}$. An explicit calculation shows that $\bar{u}(r)$ is proportional to the projection in the (x, y) plane of the steepest descent direction on the surface [10], where "steepest descent" is defined with respect to the light direction $\hat{L}$, rather than the vertical direction $(0, 0, 1)$.

We consider subsets $\mathcal{G}$ of $\mathcal{D}$ satisfying the following assumption.

A2.1 *Assume that S consists of a finite collection of disjoint, compact, smoothly connected sets, and that $\nabla f(\cdot)$ is continuous on the closure of $\mathcal{D}$. Let $\mathcal{G} \subset \mathcal{D}$ be a compact set, and assume $\mathcal{G}$ is of the form $\mathcal{G} = \cap_{j=1}^J \mathcal{G}_j$, $J < \infty$, where each $\mathcal{G}_j$ has a continuously differentiable boundary. Let $\mathcal{M}$ be the set of local minima of $f(\cdot)$ inside $\mathcal{G}$. Then we assume that the value of $f(\cdot)$ is known at all points in $\mathcal{M}$. Let $\bar{u}$ denote the "steepest descent" direction given by (2.5) above. Define $n_j(r)$ to be the inward (with respect to $\mathcal{G}$) normal to $\partial \mathcal{G}_j$ at r. Then we also assume that $\bar{u}(r) \cdot n_j(r) > 0$ for all $r \in \partial \mathcal{G} \cap \partial \mathcal{G}_j, j = 1, ..., J$.*

It will turn out that the minimizing trajectories correspond to paths of steepest descent on the surface. The assumption on $\mathcal{G}$ above thus guarantees that any minimizing trajectory that starts in $\mathcal{G}$ stays in $\mathcal{G}$. When this assumption is violated for some point r, then $f(r)$ cannot be represented as the minimal cost $V(r)$ but may be computable in terms of a maximum cost for an analogous optimal control problem. If neither of these possibilities holds, then the surface at r is not well determined. In general, this will occur only for small image sections near the image boundary [10].

Theorem 2.1 *Assume A2.1, and that B is an upper bound for $f(\cdot)$ on $\mathcal{G}$. Define $L(\cdot, \cdot)$ by (2.1), $g(\cdot)$ by (2.2), and $V(r)$ by (2.3). Then $V(r) = f(r)$ for all $r \in \mathcal{G}$.*

Proof. We first show that $V(r) \geq f(r)$. Let $u(\cdot)$ be any admissible control and define

$$\phi(t) = r + \int_0^t u(s)ds, \quad \tau = \inf\{t : \phi(t) \in \partial D \cap \mathcal{M}\}. \tag{2.6}$$

Since L is the Legendre transform of H and since $H(r, \nabla f(r)) = 0$ for $r \in \mathcal{G}$, $0 \geq -\nabla f(r) \cdot \beta - L(r, \beta)$ for all $\beta \in \Re^2$, and in particular $-\nabla f(\phi(t)) \cdot u(t) \leq L(\phi(t), u(t))$ for $t \in [0, \rho \wedge \tau]$. This implies that

$$-f(\phi(\rho \wedge \tau)) + f(r) = -\int_0^{\rho \wedge \tau} \nabla f(\phi(t)) \cdot u(t)dt \leq \int_0^{\rho \wedge \tau} L(\phi(t), u(t))dt,$$

and thus

$$\int_0^{\rho \wedge \tau} L(\phi(t), u(t))dt + f(\phi(\rho \wedge \tau)) \geq f(r).$$

Since $g(\phi(\rho \wedge \tau)) \geq f(\phi(\rho \wedge \tau))$, we obtain $V(r) \geq f(r)$.

Next we show $V(r) \leq f(r)$. In order to do so we will verify that for each $\varepsilon > 0$ there exists a control $u(\cdot)$ such that for ϕ and τ defined by (2.6) we have

$$\int_0^\tau L(\phi(t), u(t))dt + g(\phi(\tau)) \leq f(r) + \varepsilon. \tag{2.7}$$

Let S_C be a maximal smoothly connected component of S. For any two points r, r' in S_C, there exists a path $\phi(t)$ and a time $t^* < \infty$ such that $\phi(t) \in S_C$ for $t \in [0, t^*]$, $r = \phi(0)$ and $r' = \phi(t^*)$. Write $\phi(t) = r + \int_0^t u(s)ds$ in terms of the control $u(t)$. Define a new control $u_\lambda(t) \equiv \lambda u(t\lambda)$, where $\lambda > 0$ is a constant, and let $\phi_\lambda(t) = \phi(t\lambda)$ be the corresponding path. Since $L(r, u)/\|u\| \to 0$ as $\|u\| \to 0$, for r such that $I(r) = 1$, we can choose λ such that

$$\int_0^{\lambda t^*} L(\phi_\lambda(t), u_\lambda(t))dt = \int_0^{t^*} \frac{L(\phi(t), \lambda u(t))}{\lambda}dt \leq \frac{\varepsilon}{3}.$$

Further, since $|L_y| < 1$, there exists $a > 0$ such that for any component S_C as above, and r such that $d(r, S_C) \leq a$, we have the following. Let r' be the point in S_C closest to r. Then there exists a time $t_a \in [0, \infty)$, constant control $u(\cdot) = (r' - r)/t_a$ and corresponding path $\phi(t) = r + \int_0^t u(s)ds$, such that $\phi(t_a) = y$ and $\int_0^{t_a} L(\phi(t), u(t))dt \leq \varepsilon/3$. Finally, this shows that for any S_C, and r, r' such that $d(r, S_C) \leq a$ and $d(r', S_C) \leq a$, there exists a control $\tilde{u}_{rr'}(t)$ and time $\sigma_{rr'} \in [0, \infty)$ such that for the corresponding path $\phi_{rr'}(t)$ we have $\phi_{rr'}(0) = r$, $\phi_{rr'}(\sigma_{rr'}) = r'$,

and

$$\int_0^{\sigma_{rr'}} L(\phi_{rr'}(t), \tilde{u}_{rr'}(t))dt \leq \varepsilon.$$

Since f is constant on S_C, then by choosing $a > 0$ smaller if need be we can also assume that $|f(r) - f(r')| \leq \varepsilon$.

We now construct the control that satisfies (2.7). If r is a local minimum then we simply take $\tau = 0$ and are done. There are then two remaining cases: (1) r is contained in some S_C with $S_C \cap \mathcal{M} = \emptyset$, or (2) $r \notin S$. If case (1) holds then $S_C \cap M = \emptyset$ implies the existence of a point r' such that $f(r') < f(r)$ and $d(r', S_C) \leq a$. Since A2.1 implies $S \subset \mathcal{G}^0$, we can assume that $r' \in \mathcal{G}$. In this case we will set $u(t) = \bar{u}_{rr'}(t)$ for $t \in [0, \sigma_{rr'})$.

Next consider the definition of the control for $t \geq \sigma_{rr'}$. For $c > 0$ let $b = \inf\{L(r, u) : r \in \mathcal{D}, d(r, S) > c, u \in \Re^2\}$. The continuity of $I(\cdot)$ and the fact that $I(r) < 1$ for $r \notin S$ imply $b > 0$. Consider any solution (there may be more than one) to

$$\dot{\phi}(t) = \bar{u}(\phi(t)), \ \phi(0) = r'. \tag{2.8}$$

According to (2.5), for any t such that $\phi(t) \in \mathcal{G} \backslash S$ and $d(\phi(t), S) > c$

$$\begin{aligned} \frac{d}{dt} f(\phi(t)) &= \nabla f(\phi(t)) \cdot \bar{u}(\phi(t)) \\ &= -L(\phi(t), \bar{u}(\phi(t))) \\ &\leq -b. \end{aligned} \tag{2.9}$$

A2.1 implies $\phi(t)$ cannot exit $\mathcal{G}$. Thus, since $f(r)$ is bounded on $\mathcal{G}$, (2.9) implies that $\phi(t)$ must enter the set $\{r : d(r, S) \leq c\}$ in finite time, for any c. If $\phi(t) \in S$ for some $t < \infty$ we define $\eta_{r'} = \inf\{t : \phi(t) \in S\}$ and $w = \phi(\eta_{r'})$. Otherwise, let t_i be any sequence tending to ∞ as $i \to \infty$. Since $\mathcal{G}$ is compact we can extract a subsequence (again labeled by i) such that $\phi(t_i) \to v$ for some $v \in S$. Let $\bar{i}$ be large enough that $\|\phi(t_{\bar{i}}) - v\| \leq a$. Since $f(\phi(t_i)) \downarrow f(v)$, we have $f(\phi(t_{\bar{i}})) > f(v)$. For this case we define $\eta_{r'} = t_{\bar{i}}$ and $w = \phi(\eta_{r'})$.

Integrating (2.9) gives

$$f(r') - f(w) = \int_0^{\eta_{r'}} L(\phi(t), \bar{u}(\phi(t))) dt.$$

The control $u(t)$ for $t \in [\sigma_{rr'}, \sigma_{rr'} + \eta_{r'})$ is defined to be $\bar{u}(\phi(t + \sigma_{rr'}))$.

We now consider the point w. We first examine the case in which the solution to (2.8) does not enter S in finite time. Since $\|w - v\| \leq a$, $\bar{u}_{wv}(t)$ gives a control such that the application of this control moves $\phi(\cdot)$ from w to v with accumulated running cost less than or equal to ε. We define $u(t) = \bar{u}_{wv}(t - (\eta_{r'} + \sigma_{rr'}))$ for $t \in [\sigma_{rr'} + \eta_{r'}, \sigma_{rr'} + \eta_{r'} + \sigma_{wv})$. If the solution to (2.8) reached S in finite time we define $w = v$ and $\sigma_{wv} = 0$. Let $\sigma = \sigma_{rr'} + \eta_{r'} + \sigma_{wv}$.

Let us summarize the results of this construction. Given any point $r \in S$ that is not a local minimum we have constructed a piecewise continuous control $u(\cdot)$ and $\sigma < \infty$ such that if $\phi(t) = r + \int_0^\sigma u(s) ds$, then

$$\begin{aligned} f(r) - f(\phi(\sigma)) &= f(r) - f(r') + f(r') - f(w) + f(w) - f(v) \\ &\geq \int_{\sigma_{rr'}}^{\sigma_{rr'} + \eta_{r'}} L(\phi(t), u(t)) dt \\ &\geq -2\varepsilon + \int_0^\sigma L(\phi(t), u(t)) dt. \end{aligned}$$

We have also shown that $f(r) > f(v) = f(\phi(\sigma))$, $\phi(\sigma) \in S$. Thus, either the component S_C containing $\phi(\sigma)$ satisfies $S_C \cap M \neq \emptyset$, and we are essentially done, or we are back into case (1) above, and can repeat the procedure. Let K be the number of disjoint compact connected sets that comprise S. Then the strict decrease $f(r) > f(\phi(\sigma))$ and the fact that $f(\cdot)$ is constant on each S_C imply the procedure can be repeated no more than K times before reaching some S_C containing a point from $\mathcal{M}$. If case (2) holds we can use the same procedure, save that the very first step is omitted. Thus, in general, we have exhibited a control $u(\cdot)$ such that

$$\int_0^\tau L(\phi(t), u(t))dt + g(\phi(\tau)) \le f(r) + (2K + 1)\varepsilon.$$

Since $\varepsilon > 0$ is arbitrary, the theorem is proved. ∎

3 Shape Reconstruction Algorithms

In this section, we describe how algorithms for shape reconstruction can be derived from control representations such as (2.3). It is important to note that many different algorithms can be derived, depending on how the image irradiance equation is rewritten as a Hamiltonian, and that all compute the same surface approximation from the image. Thus, for example, an algorithm can be generated from the Hamiltonian of the previous section, which we henceforth denote by $H^{(1)}$. Another possibility [8] is to write the image irradiance equation in the form $H^{(2)}(r, \nabla f(r)) = 0$, with

$$H^{(2)}(r, \alpha) \equiv \frac{1}{2} \left[I^2 \alpha_x^2 + v \alpha_y^2 + 2(1 - I^2)L_y \alpha_y - (1 - I^2) \right], \qquad (3.10)$$

where $v(r) = I^2(r) - L_y^2$. Note that when $v(r) < 0$ $H^{(2)}(r, \alpha)$ is not a convex function of α. Nevertheless, an algorithm can be derived from this form of the Hamiltonian, which, although it differs from the algorithm generated from $H^{(1)}$, reconstructs the same surface approximation.

The algorithms are derived using a discrete approximation of the continuous control representation. In this discrete control problem, the object is to minimize the cost over all discrete paths on a grid of pixels. A difficulty in doing this is that a discrete trajectory, in which at each time step the path jumps between neighboring pixels, is generally a poor approximation to a continuous trajectory. In order to better approximate a continuous trajectory on a discrete grid, an element of randomness is introduced. Thus the continuous optimal control problem is approximated by a discrete stochastic optimal control problem, and the cost of the continuous problem is approximated by the expectation of the cost for the discrete problem. Note that the algorithms themselves are deterministic, even though the discrete control problem is stochastic.

Thus, given a control u, we define the probabilities for the path to jump to neighboring pixels so that on average the discrete motion approximates the continuous motion $\dot{\phi} = u$. Let $p(r, r'|u)$ denote the transition probability for the path to move from r to a 4-nearest neighbor site r' in the current time step, given that control u is applied. We define

$$p(r, r + \text{sign}(u_x)(1,0)|u) = \frac{|u_x|}{|u_x| + |u_y|} \qquad (3.11)$$

$$p(r, r + \text{sign}(u_y)(0,1)|u) = \frac{|u_y|}{|u_x| + |u_y|}, \qquad (3.12)$$

with all other probabilities zero. We also define the size of the time step to be $\Delta t(u) \equiv 1/(|u_x| + |u_y|)$. With this definition, and assuming for example $u_x, u_y > 0$, the average motion is

$$\frac{(1,0)u_x + (0,1)u_y}{|u_x| + |u_y|} = u\Delta t(u),$$

which approximates the continuous motion. This definition actually makes sense only when $u \neq 0$. For $u = 0$, we define $p(r, r|0) = 1$, and $\Delta t(0) = 1$.

For a given sequence of controls $\{u_i\}$, let $\{\xi_i : \xi_0 = r\}$ denote the path starting at r which evolves at each time step i as determined by the control sequence $\{u_i\}$ and the transition probabilities. Then for the representation and Lagrangian (now denoted $L^{(1)}$) of the previous section, the approximating stochastic control problem is

$$V^{(1)}(r) = \inf E_x \left[\sum_{i=0}^{(N \wedge M)-1} L^{(1)}(\xi_i, u_i)\Delta t(u_i) + g(\xi_{(N \wedge M)}) \right],$$

where $N = \inf\{i : \xi_i \notin \mathcal{D} \text{ or } \xi_i \in \mathcal{M}\}$, and the minimization is over all control sequences $\{u_i\}$ and stopping times M. E_x denotes the expectation. Thus, $V^{(1)}$ is the minimum of the expectation of the cost over all finite length control sequences, where the path terminates either at discrete time M chosen by the controller, or else at the first time that the path exits $\mathcal{D}$ or enters $\mathcal{M}$.

Suppose that instead of considering paths of arbitrary length, we consider paths continuing for at most n time steps:

$$V_n^{(1)}(r) \equiv \inf E_x \left[\sum_{i=0}^{(N \wedge M \wedge n)-1} L(\xi_i, u_i)\Delta t(u_i) + g(\xi_{(N \wedge M \wedge n)}) \right], \qquad (3.13)$$

Then $V_n^{(1)}(r)$ is clearly nonincreasing in n and $V_n^{(1)}(r) \downarrow V^{(1)}(r)$ as $n \to \infty$. As discussed in [8], it follows from the principle of dynamic programming that $V_n^{(1)}(r)$ and $V_{n+1}^{(1)}(r)$ are related by

$$V_{n+1}^{(1)}(r) = \min \left[\inf_{u \in \mathbb{R}^2} \left(L^{(1)}(r, u)\Delta t(u) + \sum_{r'} p(r, r'|u)V_n^{(1)}(r') \right), g(r) \right] \qquad (3.14)$$

Clearly, we also have the initial condition $V_0^{(1)}(r) = g(r)$. This, together with the recursive equation (3.14), gives an algorithm which converges monotonically down to V.

For the second control problem, we get a similar algorithm. $V_0^{(2)}(r) = g(r)$, and

$$V_{n+1}^{(2)}(r) = \min \left[\inf_{u \in \mathbb{R}^2} \left(L^{(2)}(r,u)\Delta t(u) + \sum_{r'} p(r,r'|u)V_n^{(2)}(r') \right), g(r) \right] \text{ or}$$

$$V_{n+1}^{(2)}(r) = \min \left[\sup_{u_y, L_y < 0} \inf_{u_* \in \mathbb{R}} \left(L^{(2)}(r,u)\Delta t(u) + \sum_{r'} p(r,r'|u)V_n^{(2)}(r') \right), g(r) \right]$$

(3.15)

where the first expression applies when $v(r) \geq 0$ and the second when $v(r) < 0$. The Lagrangian $L^{(2)}$ is derived from an equation analogous to (2.1):

$$L^{(2)}(r,\beta) = \sup_\alpha \left[-\alpha \cdot \beta - H^{(2)}(r,\alpha) \right] \qquad \text{if } v(r) > 0$$
$$= \inf_{\alpha_y} \sup_{\alpha_*} \left[-\alpha \cdot \beta - H^{(2)}(r,\alpha) \right] \text{ if } v(r) < 0.$$

(The case $v(r) = 0$ is given by the appropriate limit as $v(r) \to 0$ from either direction.) The difference from the previous algorithm is due to the nonconvexity in the Hamiltonian for image regions where $v(r) < 0$. For more detail, and experimental results obtained with the second algorithm above, consult [8, 3].

The algorithms described above are of the Jacobi type, with the surface updated everwhere in parallel at each iteration. The algorithms can also be shown to converge if implemented via Gauss–Seidel, with updated surface estimates used as soon as they are available. In fact, the Gauss–Seidel algorithms converge for any sequence of pixel updates [3]; for example, it is possible to change the direction of the sweep across the image after each pass [1]. Our experiments show that this produces a significant speedup, changing the computation time from order N to order 1 with a small constant, where N is the linear dimension of the image. Specifically, we have proven the following [3]:

Proposition 3.1 *Consider either of the recursive algorithms derived in (3.14) or (3.15). Let an initial condition $V_0^{(a)}$, where $a \in \{1, 2\}$, be given and define the sequence $\{V_i^{(a)}, i \in N\}$ according to either the Jacobi iteration [e.g. (3.14)] or the Gauss-Seidel iteration, where the pixel sites are updated in an arbitrary sequence. Assume that $V_0^{(a)}(r) \geq g(r)$ for all $r \in D$. Then the following conclusions hold.*

1. *For each $r \in D$, $V_i^{(a)}(r)$ is nonincreasing in i and bounded from below. Define $V^{(a)}(r) = \lim_{i \to \infty} V^{(a)}(r)$. Then the function $V^{(a)}(\cdot)$ is a fixed point of (3.14) (or (3.15) if appropriate).*
2. *The function $V^{(a)}(\cdot)$ can be uniquely characterized as the largest fixed point of (3.14) (or (3.15) if appropriate) that satisfies $V^{(a)}(r) \leq V_0^{(a)}(r)$ for all $r \in D$.*
3. *A function $w(r)$ is a fixed point of (3.14) if and only if it is a fixed point of (3.15).*

Remark. Thus, taking $V_0^{(a)}(r) = g(r)$, where $g(r)$ is defined by (2.2), both algorithms reconstruct the same surface approximation: $V^{(1)}(r) = V^{(2)}(r)$. The correct surface approximation is obtained by taking the largest of all the fixed points of the iterations in (3.14) or (3.15).

References

1. M. Bichsel, A. P. Pentland, , "A Simple Algorithm for Shape from Shading," *Proc. IEEE Conference on Computer Vision and Pattern Recognition*, Champaign, Illinois, pp. 459-465, June 1992.
2. A. R. Bruss, "The Eikonal Equation: Some Results Applicable to Computer Vision," *Journal of Mathematical Physics*, Vol. 23, No. 5, pp. 890-896, May 1982.
3. P. Dupuis and J. Oliensis, "An Optimal Control Formulation and Related Numerical Methods for a Problem in Shape Reconstruction," to appear in *Annals of Applied Probability*.
4. P. Dupuis and J. Oliensis, "Direct Method for Reconstructing Shape from Shading," in *IEEE Computer Vision and Pattern Recognition*, Champaign, Illinois, June 1992, pp. 453-458.
5. B. K. P. Horn and M.J. Brooks (eds.) *Shape from Shading*. MIT Press: Cambridge, MA, 1989.
6. H. J. Kushner and P. Dupuis, *Numerical Methods for Stochastic Control Problems in Continuous Time*, Springer–Verlag: New York, 1992.
7. J. Oliensis and P. Dupuis, "A Global Algorithm for Shape from Shading," long paper, *Proc. of the Fourth International Conference on Computer Vision*, Berlin, Germany 1993, pp. 692–701.
8. J. Oliensis and P. Dupuis, "Direct Method for Reconstructing Shape from Shading," in *Physics–Based Vision: Principles and Practice, Shape Inference Volume*, L. Wolff, S. Shafer, G. Healey, editors, Jones and Bartlett, Boston, June 1992, pp. 17–28.
9. J. Oliensis and Paul Dupuis, "Direct method for reconstructing shape from shading," *Proc. SPIE Conf. 1570 on Geometric Methods in Computer Vision*, San Diego, California, July 1991, pp. 116-128.
10. J. Oliensis, "Shape from Shading as a Partially Well–Constrained Problem," *Computer Vision, Graphics, and Image Processing: Image Understanding*, Vol. 54, No. 2, September 1991, pp. 163-183.
11. J. Oliensis, "Uniqueness in Shape From Shading," *The International Journal of Computer Vision*, Vol. 6 no. 2, pp. 75-104, 1991.
12. R. T. Rockafellar, *Convex Analysis*, Princeton University Press: Princeton, 1970.
13. E. Rouy, A. Tourin, "A Viscosity Solutions Approach To Shape–From–Shading," *SIAM J. on Numerical Analysis* 29:867-884, 1992.
14. E. Rouy, A. Tourin, "A Viscosity Solutions Approach To Shape–From–Shading," unpublished report.
15. B. V. H. Saxberg, "An Application of Dynamical Systems Theory to Shape From Shading," in *Proc. DARPA Image Understanding Workshop*, Palo Alto, CA, pp. 1089–1104, May 1989.
16. B. V. H. Saxberg, "A Modern Differential Geometric Approach to Shape from Shading," MIT Artificial Intelligence Laboratory, TR 1117, 1989.

Seeing Beyond Lambert's Law

Michael Oren and Shree K. Nayar

Department of Computer Science, Columbia University, New York, N.Y. 10027, U.S.A

Abstract: Lambert's model for diffuse reflection is extensively used in computational vision. For several real-world objects, the Lambertian model can prove to be a very inaccurate approximation to the diffuse component. While the brightness of a Lambertian surface is independent of viewing direction, the brightness of a rough diffuse surface increases as the viewer approaches the source direction. A comprehensive model is developed that predicts reflectance from rough diffuse surfaces. Experiments have been conducted on real samples, such as, plaster, clay, and sand. The reflectance measurements obtained are in strong agreement with the reflectance predicted by the proposed model.

1 Introduction

A surface that obeys Lambert's Law appears equally bright from all viewing directions [Lambert-1760]. This model for diffuse reflection was advanced by Lambert over 200 years ago and remains one of the most widely used models in machine vision. It is used explicitly by shape recovery techniques such as shape from shading and photometric stereo. It is also invoked by vision techniques such as binocular stereo and motion detection to solve the correspondence problem. For several real-world objects, however, the Lambertian model can prove to be a poor and inadequate approximation to the diffuse component. It is shown in this paper, that surface roughness plays a critical role in the deviation from Lambertian behavior. This deviation is significant for very rough surfaces, and increases with the angle of incidence.

The topic of rough diffuse surfaces has been extensively studied in the areas of applied physics and geophysics. The following is a very brief summary of previous results on the subject. In 1924, Opik [Öpik-1924] designed an empirical model to describe the non-Lambertian behavior of the moon. In 1941, Minnaert [Minnaert-1941] modified Opik's model to obtain the following reflectance function:

$$f_r = \frac{k+1}{2\pi} (\cos \theta_i \cos \theta_r)^{(k-1)} \qquad (0 \le k \le 1)$$

where, θ_i and θ_r are the polar angles of incidence and reflection, and k is a measure of surface roughness. This function was designed to obey Helmholtz's reciprocity principle but is not based on any theoretical foundation. It assumes that the radiance of non-Lambertian diffuse surfaces is symmetrical with respect to the surface normal, an assumption that proves to be incorrect.

The above studies were attempts to design reflectance models based on measured reflectance data. In contrast, several investigators developed theoretical models for diffuse reflection from rough surfaces (see [Oren and Nayar-1992] for a more detailed survey). These efforts were motivated primarily by the reflectance characteristics of the moon. Infrared emission and visible light reflection from the moon indicate that the moon's surface radiates more energy back in the direction of the source (the sun) than in the normal direction (like Lambertian surfaces) or in the forward direction (like specular surfaces). This phenomenon is referred to as *backscattering* [1]. Though several models were developed to describe this phenomenon [Smith-1967] [Buhl *et al.*-1968] [Hering and Smith-1970], these models are limited either because they assume restrictive surface geometries, or because they are confined to reflections in the plane of incidence.

In contrast, the model presented here can be applied to isotropic as well as anisotropic rough surfaces, and can handle arbitrary source and viewer directions. Further, it takes into account complex geometrical effects such as *masking*, *shadowing*, and *interreflections* between points on the surface. We begin by modeling the surface as a collection of long symmetric V-cavities with Lambertian facets. First, a reflectance model is developed for anisotropic surfaces with one type (facet-slope) of V-cavities, and with all cavities aligned in the same direction on the surface plane. This result is then used to derive a model for the more general case of isotropic surfaces that have normal facet distributions with zero mean and arbitrary standard deviation (σ). The standard deviation parametrizes the macroscopic roughness of the surface. The Lambertian model is a special case, or instance, of the derived model.

Figure 1 shows three images of spheres rendered using the proposed reflectance model. In all three cases, the sphere is illuminated from the viewer direction. In the first case, $\sigma = 0$, and hence the sphere is Lambertian in reflectance. As the roughness increases, the sphere begins to appear flatter. In the extreme roughness case shown in Figure 1(c), the sphere appears like a flat disc with nearly constant brightness. This phenomenon has been widely observed and reported in the case of the full moon.

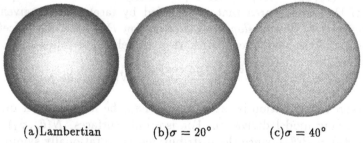

(a)Lambertian   (b)$\sigma = 20°$ (c)$\sigma = 40°$

Fig. 1. Images of spheres rendered using the proposed reflectance model.

---

[1] A different backscattering mechanism produces a sharp peak close to the source direction (see [Hapke and van Horn-1963, Oetking-1966, Tagare and deFigueiredo-1991]). This is not the mechanism discussed in this paper. Hapke *et al.* [Hapke *et al.*-1993] attribute this backscatter peak to a physical-optics phenomenon called the "opposition effect." This phenomenon is seldom encountered in machine vision since it is observed only when the sensor and source are within a few degrees from each other; a situation difficult to emulate in practice without the source or the sensor occluding the other.

Several experimental results are presented to demonstrate the accuracy of the diffuse reflectance model. These experiments were conducted on commonplace samples such as sand and plaster. In all cases, reflectance predicted by the model was found to be in strong agreement with measurements. These results illustrate that the deviation from Lambertian behavior can be substantial. We conclude with a discussion on the implications of the proposed model for machine vision. Specifically, the effect of the described reflectance characteristics on image brightness, reflectance maps, and shape recovery algorithms is examined. These results demonstrate that the findings reported here are fundamental to the problem of visual perception.

2   Surface Roughness Model

The effects of shadowing, masking, and interreflection need to be analyzed in order to obtain an accurate reflectance model. To accomplish this, we use the roughness model proposed by Torrance and Sparrow [Torrance and Sparrow-1967] that assumes the surface to be composed of long symmetric V-cavities (see Figure 2). Each cavity consists of two planar facets. The width of each facet is assumed to be small compared to its length. We assume each facet area da is small compared to the area dA of the surface patch that is imaged by a single sensor pixel. Hence, each pixel includes a very large number of facets. Further, the facet area is large compared to the wavelength λ of incident light and therefore geometrical optics can be used to derive the reflectance model. The above assumptions can be summarized as: $\lambda^2 \ll da \ll dA$

We denote the slope and orientation of each facet in the V-cavity model as (θ_a, ϕ_a), where θ_a is the polar angle and ϕ_a is the azimuth angle. Torrance and Sparrow have assumed all facets to have equal area da. They use the distribution $N(\theta_a, \phi_a)$ to represent the number of facets per unit surface area that have the normal $\hat{a} = (\theta_a, \phi_a)$. Here, we use a probability distribution to represent the fraction of the surface area that is occupied by facets with a given normal. This is referred to as the *slope-area distribution* $P(\theta_a, \phi_a)$. The facet-number distribution and the slope-area distribution are related as follows:

$$P(\theta_a, \phi_a) = \frac{dA\, N(\theta_a, \phi_a)\, da\, \cos\theta_a}{dA} = N(\theta_a, \phi_a)\, da\, \cos\theta_a \qquad (1)$$

The slope-area distribution is easier to use than the facet-number distribution in the following model derivation. For isotropic surfaces, $N(\theta_a, \phi_a) = N(\theta_a)$ and $P(\theta_a, \phi_a) = P(\theta_a)$, since the distributions are rotationally symmetric with respect to the global surface normal $\hat{n}$ (Figure 2).

3   Reflectance Model

In this section, we derive a reflectance model for rough diffuse surfaces. For lack of space, only important results are discussed. For details we refer the reader to [Oren and Nayar-1992]. During the derivation, we will draw on several well-known radiometric definitions that are given in [Nicodemus *et al.*-1977].

Consider a surface area dA that is imaged by a single sensor element in the direction $\hat{v} = (\theta_r, \phi_r)$ and illuminated by a distant point light source in the direction $\hat{s} = (\theta_i, \phi_i)$. The area dA is composed of a very large number of

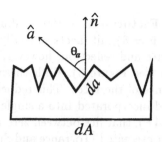

Fig. 2. Surface modeled as a collection of V-cavities.

symmetric V-cavities. Each V-cavity is composed of two facets with the same slope but facing in opposite directions. Consider the flux reflected by a facet with area da and normal $\hat{a} = (\theta_a, \phi_a)$. The projected area on the surface occupied by the facet is $da \cos\theta_a$ (see Figure 2). Thus, while computing the contribution of the facet to the radiance of the surface patch, we need to use the projected area $da \cos\theta_a$ and not the actual facet area da. This radiance contribution is what we call the *projected radiance* of the facet:

$$L_{rp}(\theta_a, \phi_a) = \frac{d\Phi_r(\theta_a, \phi_a)}{(da \cos\theta_a) \cos\theta_r \, d\omega_r} \tag{2}$$

where, $d\omega_r$ is the solid angle subtended by the sensor optics. For ease of description, we have dropped the source and viewing directions from the notations for projected radiance and flux. Now consider the slope-area distribution of facets given by $P(\theta_a, \phi_a)$. The total radiance of the surface can be obtained as the aggregate of $L_{rp}(\theta_a, \phi_a)$ over all facets on the surface:

$$L_r(\theta_r, \phi_r; \theta_i, \phi_i) = \int_{\theta_a=0}^{\frac{\pi}{2}} \int_{\phi_a=0}^{2\pi} P(\theta_a, \phi_a) \, L_{rp}(\theta_a, \phi_a) \sin\theta_a \, d\phi_a \, d\theta_a \tag{3}$$

3.1 Model for Uni-directional Single-Slope Distribution

The first surface type we consider has all facets with the same slope θ_a. Further, all V-cavities are aligned in the same direction; azimuth angles of all facets are either ϕ_a or $\phi_a + \pi$. Consider a Lambertian facet with albedo ρ, that is fully illuminated (no shadowing) and is completely visible (no masking) from the sensor direction. The radiance of the facet is proportional to its irradiance and is equal to $\frac{\rho}{\pi} E(\theta_a, \phi_a)$. The irradiance of the facet is $E(\theta_a, \phi_a) = E_0 <\hat{s}, \hat{a}>$, where, E_0 is the irradiance when the facet is illuminated head-on (i.e. $\hat{s} = \hat{n}$), and $<, >$ denotes the dot product between two vectors. Using the definition of radiance [Nicodemus *et al.*-1977], the flux reflected by the facet in the sensor direction is: $d\Phi_r = \frac{\rho}{\pi} E_0 <\hat{s}, \hat{a}> <\hat{v}, \hat{a}>$. Substituting this expression in (2), we get:

$$L_{rp}(\theta_a, \phi_a) = \frac{\rho}{\pi} E_0 \frac{<\hat{s}, \hat{a}> <\hat{v}, \hat{a}>}{<\hat{a}, \hat{n}> <\hat{v}, \hat{n}>} \tag{4}$$

The above expression clearly illustrates that the projected radiance of a tilted Lambertian facet is not equal in all viewing directions.

Geometric Attenuation Factor: If the surface is illuminated and viewed from the normal direction ($\hat{s} = \hat{v} = \hat{n}$), all facets are fully illuminated and visible. For larger angles of incidence and reflection, however, facets are shadowed and masked by adjacent facets (see Figure 3). Both these geometrical phenomena reduce the projected radiance of the facet. This reduction in brightness can be derived using geometry and incorporated into a single term, called the *geometrical attenuation factor ($\mathcal{GAF}$)*, that lies between zero and unity. Several derivations of the $\mathcal{GAF}$ have been presented [Torrance and Sparrow-1967] [Blinn-1977] [Oren and Nayar-1992]. The final result can be compactly represented as:

$$\mathcal{GAF} = Min\left[1, Max\left[0, \frac{2<\hat{s},\hat{n}><\hat{a},\hat{n}>}{<\hat{s},\hat{a}>}, \frac{2<\hat{v},\hat{n}><\hat{a},\hat{n}>}{<\hat{v},\hat{a}>}\right]\right] \quad (5)$$

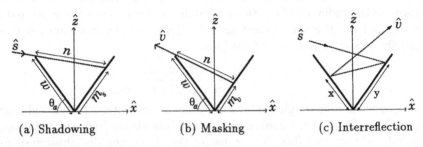

(a) Shadowing   (b) Masking   (c) Interreflection

Fig. 3. Shadowing, masking, and interreflection in a V-cavity

Projected Radiance and $\mathcal{GAF}$: The projected radiance of a Lambertian facet is obtained by multiplying the $\mathcal{GAF}$ with the projected radiance given by (4). Table 1 details the $\mathcal{GAF}$ and the corresponding projected radiance for all cases of shadowing and masking. Note that the projected radiance is denoted as L_{rp}^1; the superscript is used to indicate that the radiance is due to direct illumination by the source. In the following discussion, we will use L_{rp}^2 to denote radiance due to interreflections.

Table 1. Projected radiance of a facet for different masking/shadowing conditions.

	$\mathcal{GAF}$	$L_{rp}^1(\theta_a, \phi_a)$
No Masking or Shadowing	1	$\frac{\rho}{\pi}E_0 \frac{<\hat{s},\hat{a}><\hat{v},\hat{a}>}{<\hat{a},\hat{n}><\hat{v},\hat{n}>} =$ $\frac{\rho}{\pi}E_0 \cos\theta_i \cos\theta_a \left(1 + \tan\theta_i \tan\theta_a \cos(\phi_i - \phi_a)\right)$ $\left(1 + \tan\theta_r \tan\theta_a \cos(\phi_r - \phi_a)\right)$
Masking	$\frac{2<\hat{v},\hat{n}><\hat{a},\hat{n}>}{<\hat{v},\hat{a}>}$	$\frac{\rho}{\pi}E_0 \, 2<\hat{s},\hat{a}> =$ $\frac{\rho}{\pi}E_0 \cos\theta_i \cos\theta_a \, 2\left(1 + \tan\theta_i \tan\theta_a \cos(\phi_i - \phi_a)\right)$
Shadowing	$\frac{2<\hat{s},\hat{n}><\hat{a},\hat{n}>}{<\hat{s},\hat{a}>}$	$\frac{\rho}{\pi}E_0 \frac{2<\hat{s},\hat{a}><\hat{v},\hat{a}>}{<\hat{v},\hat{n}>} =$ $\frac{\rho}{\pi}E_0 \cos\theta_i \cos\theta_a \, 2\left(1 + \tan\theta_r \tan\theta_a \cos(\phi_r - \phi_a)\right)$

Interreflection Factor: We have the task of modeling interreflections in the presence of masking and shadowing effects. In the case of Lambertian surfaces, the energy in an incident light ray diminishes rapidly with each interreflection bounce. Therefore, we model only two-bounce interreflections and ignore subsequent bounces. Since the length l of the V-cavity is much larger than its width w, i.e. $l \gg w$, it can be viewed as a one-dimensional shape with translational symmetry. For such shapes, the two-bounce interreflection component can be determined as an integral over the one-dimensional cross-section of the shape [Siegel and Howell-1972]:

$$L_r^2(x) = \frac{\rho}{\pi} \int K'(x,y) L_r^1(y) dy \qquad (6)$$

where x and y are the shortest distances of facet points from the intersection of the two facets (see Figure 3(c)). K' is the kernel for the translational symmetry case and is derived in [Jakob-1957] and [Forsyth and Zisserman-1989] to be:

$$K'(x,y) = \frac{\pi \sin^2{(2\theta_a)}}{2} \frac{xy}{(x^2 + 2xy\cos{(2\theta_a)} + y^2)^{3/2}} \qquad (7)$$

We know that the orientation of the considered facet is $\hat{a} = (\theta_a, \phi_a)$ and the orientation of the adjacent facet is $\hat{a}' = (\theta_a, \phi_a + \pi)$. The limits of the integral in the interreflection equation are determined by the masking and shadowing of these two facets. Let m_v be the width of the facet which is visible to the viewer, and m^s be the width of the *adjacent* facet that is illuminated. From the definitions of radiance and projected radiance we get:

$$L_{rp}^2 = \frac{l <\hat{a}, \hat{v}>}{da <\hat{a}, \hat{n}> <\hat{v}, \hat{n}>} \int_{x=m_v}^{w} L_r^2(x)\, dx \qquad (8)$$

Using the following change of variables: $r = \frac{y}{w}$; $t = \frac{x}{w}$, the radiance due to two-bounce interreflections given by (6) and (8) can be written as:

$$L_{rp}^2 = (\frac{\rho}{\pi})^2 E_0 \frac{<\hat{a}', \hat{s}> <\hat{a}, \hat{v}>}{<\hat{a}, \hat{n}> <\hat{v}, \hat{n}>} \int_{t=\frac{m_v}{w}}^{1} \int_{r=\frac{m^s}{w}}^{1} K'(t,r) dr\, dt \qquad (9)$$

Using (7), the above integral is evaluated as:

$$\int_{t=\frac{m_v}{w}}^{1} \int_{r=\frac{m^s}{w}}^{1} K'(r,t) dr\, dt = \frac{\pi}{2}\left[d(1, \frac{m_v}{w}) + d(1, \frac{m^s}{w}) - d(\frac{m^s}{w}, \frac{m_v}{w}) - d(1,1) \right] (10)$$

where: $d(x,y) = \sqrt{x^2 + 2xy\cos{(2\theta_a)} + y^2}$. We refer to (10) as the *interreflection factor* ($\mathcal{IF}$). From (9), the interreflection component of the projected radiance of a facet with orientation (θ_a, ϕ_a) is:

$$L_{rp}^2(\theta_a, \phi_a) = (\frac{\rho}{\pi})^2 E_0 \cos\theta_i \cos\theta_a \qquad (11)$$

$$\left(1 - \tan\theta_i \tan\theta_a \cos{(\phi_i - \phi_a)}\right)\left(1 + \tan\theta_r \tan\theta_a \cos{(\phi_r - \phi_a)}\right) \mathcal{IF}(\hat{v}, \hat{s}, \hat{a})$$

The total projected radiance of the facet is the sum of the projected radiance due to source illumination (given in Table 1) and the above interreflection component: $L_{rp}(\theta_a, \phi_a) = L_{rp}^1(\theta_a, \phi_a) + L_{rp}^2(\theta_a, \phi_a)$ The uni-directional single-slope surface considered here has only two types of facets with normals (θ_a, ϕ_a) and $(\theta_a, \phi_a + \pi)$. Hence, the radiance of the surface for any given source and sensor directions is simply the average of the projected radiances of the two facet types.

3.2 Model for Isotropic Single-Slope Distribution

All facets on this isotropic surface have the same slope θ_a but are uniformly distributed in ϕ_a. From the previous section, we know the radiance $L_{rp}(\theta_a, \phi_a)$ of a facet with normal $\hat{a} = (\theta_a, \phi_a)$. Therefore, the radiance of the isotropic surface is determined as an integral of the projected radiance over ϕ_a:

$$L_{rp}(\theta_a) = \frac{1}{2\pi} \int_{\phi_a=0}^{2\pi} L_{rp}(\theta_a, \phi_a) d\phi_a \tag{12}$$

Given a source direction (θ_i, ϕ_i) and a sensor direction (θ_r, ϕ_r), we first need to find the ranges of facet orientation ϕ_a for which the facets are masked, shadowed, masked and shadowed, and neither masked nor shadowed[2]. This requires a careful geometrical analysis. Once this is done the above integral can be decomposed into parts corresponding to masking/shadowing ranges. Each range is evaluated using the corresponding radiance expression in Table 1. We refer the interested reader to [Oren and Nayar-1992] for details on the evaluation of direct illumination and interreflection components of (12).

3.3 Model for Gaussian Slope-Area Distribution

In the case of isotropic surfaces, the slope-area distribution can be described using a single parameter, namely, θ_a, since the facets are uniformly distributed in ϕ_a. The radiance of any isotropic surface can therefore be determined as:

$$L_r(\theta_r, \theta_i, \phi_r - \phi_i) = \int_0^{\frac{\pi}{2}} P(\theta_a) L_{rp}(\theta_a) \sin\theta_a d\theta_a \tag{13}$$

where $L_{rp}(\theta_a)$ is the projected radiance obtained in the previous section. Here, we assume the isotropic distribution to be Gaussian with mean μ and standard deviation σ, i.e. $P(\theta_a; \sigma, \mu)$. Reasonably rough surfaces can be described using a zero mean ($\mu = 0$) Gaussian distribution: $P(\theta_a) = c \exp\left(-\theta_a^2/2\sigma^2\right)$ where, the c is the normalization constant.

The above integral cannot be easily evaluated. Therefore, we pursued a functional approximation [Oren and Nayar-1992] to the integral that is accurate for arbitrary surface roughness and angles of incidence and reflection. The final approximation results are given below. Let $\alpha = Max[\theta_r, \theta_i]$ and $\beta = Min[\theta_r, \theta_i]$. The source illumination component of radiance of a surface with roughness σ is:

$$L_r^1(\theta_r, \theta_i, \phi_r - \phi_i; \sigma) = \frac{\rho}{\pi} E_0 \cos\theta_i \left[C_1(\sigma) + \right. \tag{14}$$

$$\cos(\phi_r - \phi_i) C_2(\alpha; \beta; \phi_r - \phi_i; \sigma) \tan\beta + \left(1 - |\cos(\phi_r - \phi_i)|\right) C_3(\alpha; \beta; \sigma) \tan\left(\frac{\alpha + \beta}{2}\right) \right]$$

where the coefficients are:

$$C_1 = 1 - 0.5 \frac{\sigma^2}{\sigma^2 + 0.33}$$

$$C_2 = \begin{cases} 0.45 \frac{\sigma^2}{\sigma^2 + 0.09} \sin\alpha & \text{if } \cos(\phi_r - \phi_i) \geq 0 \\ 0.45 \frac{\sigma^2}{\sigma^2 + 0.09} \left(\sin\alpha - \left(\frac{2\beta}{\pi}\right)^3\right) & \text{otherwise} \end{cases}$$

$$C_3 = 0.125 \left(\frac{\sigma^2}{\sigma^2 + 0.09}\right) \left(\frac{4\alpha\beta}{\pi^2}\right)^2$$

---

[2] Imagine a V-cavity rotated about the global surface normal for any given source and sensor direction. Various masking/shadowing scenarios can be visualized.

Using a similar approach, an approximation to the interreflection component
was also derived:

$$L_r^2(\theta_r, \theta_i, \phi_r - \phi_i; \sigma) = 0.17 \frac{\rho^2}{\pi} E_0 \cos \theta_i \frac{\sigma^2}{\sigma^2 + 0.13} \left[1 - \cos(\phi_r - \phi_i) \left(\frac{2\beta}{\pi} \right)^2 \right] (15)$$

The two components are combined to obtain the total surface radiance: $L_r(\theta_r, \theta_i,$
$\phi_r - \phi_i; \sigma) = L_r^1(\theta_r, \theta_i, \phi_r - \phi_i; \sigma) + L_r^2(\theta_r, \theta_i, \phi_r - \phi_i; \sigma)$. Finally, the *BRDF* of
the surface is obtained from its radiance and irradiance as $f_r(\theta_r, \theta_i, \phi_r - \phi_i; \sigma) =$
$L_r(\theta_r, \theta_i, \phi_r - \phi_i; \sigma) / E_0 \cos \theta_i$. It is important to note that the above model
obeys Helmholtz's reciprocity principle. *Also note that the model reduces to the
Lambertian model when $\sigma = 0$.*

Qualitative Model: A further simplification to the above model can be achieved
with a slight sacrifice in accuracy. The following model was arrived at by studying, through numerous simulations, the relative contributions of various terms in
the functional approximation given by (14). The simulations showed that coefficient C_3 makes a relatively small contribution to the total radiance. A simpler
model is thus obtained by discarding C_3 and ignoring interreflections:

$$L_r(\theta_r, \theta_i, \phi_r - \phi_i; \sigma) = \frac{\rho}{\pi} E_0 \cos \theta_i (C_1 + C_2 Max \left[0, \cos(\phi_r - \phi_i) \right] \tan \beta) (16)$$

This model can be of significant practical value in applications where very high
accuracy is not critical.

4   Experiments

We have conducted several experiments to verify the accuracy of the diffuse
reflectance model. The experimental set-up used to measure the radiance of
samples is described in [Oren and Nayar-1992]. Figures 4 and 5 shows results
obtained for samples of wall plaster (A) and sand (B). The radiance of each sample is plotted as a function of sensor direction θ_r for different angles of incidence
θ_i. These measurements are made in the plane of incidence ($\phi_r = \phi_i = 0$). For
these two samples (A and B), σ and ρ were selected empirically to obtain the
best match between measured and predicted reflectance. Here, we have used the
numerical evaluation of the model (equation 13). For both samples, radiance increases as the viewing direction θ_r approaches the source direction θ_i (backward
reflection). This is in contrast to the behavior of rough specular surfaces that reflect more in the forward direction, or Lambertian surfaces where radiance does
not vary with viewing direction. For both samples, the model predictions and
experimental measurements match remarkably well. In both cases, a small peak
is noticed near the source direction. This phenomenon, known as the opposition
effect [Hapke and van Horn-1963], was discussed earlier in the introduction and
is different from the one described by our model.

   Figure 6 shows results for a sample (foam) that has not only a diffuse component but also a significant specular component. In this case, the reflectance
model used is a linear combination of new model and the Torrance-Sparrow
model [Torrance and Sparrow-1967] that describes specular, or surface, reflection from rough surfaces: $L_r = k_d L_r^d + k_s L_r^s$ where L_r^d and L_r^s are the diffuse
and specular components, respectively, and k_d and k_s are weighting coefficients

Wall Plaster

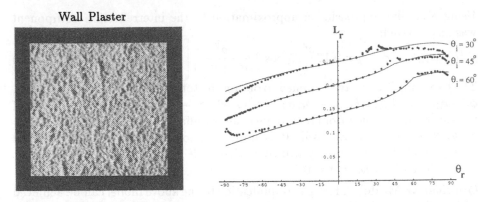

Fig. 4. Reflectance measurement (dots) and reflectance model (solid lines) ($\sigma = 30°$, $\rho = 0.90$) plots for wall plaster (sample A). Radiance is plotted as a function of sensor direction (θ_r) for different angles of incidence ($\theta_i = 30°, 45°, 60°$).

Sand

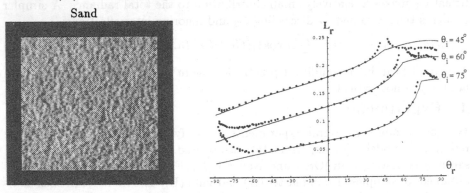

Fig. 5. Reflectance measurement and reflectance model ($\sigma = 35°$, $\rho = 0.80$) plots for sand (sample B).

Foam

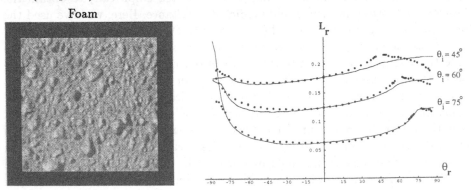

Fig. 6. Reflectance measurement and reflectance model ($\sigma = 20°$, $\rho = 0.8$, $k_s/k_d = 0.02$) plots for foam (sample C). The reflectance model used includes a specular component.

for the two components. For this experiment, we used the functional approximation (14) and the reflectance parameters σ, ρ, k_d, and k_s were estimated by fitting (using non-linear optimization) the model (14) to measured data. Other experiments based on the combined model are reported in [Oren and Nayar-1992].

5 Implications for Machine Vision

Numerous algorithms in computer vision use assumptions regarding reflectance properties of objects in the scene. Incorrect modeling of reflectance properties naturally leads to inaccurate results. We begin by examining images of rough diffuse surfaces. Figure 7(a) shows an image of the rough cylindrical clay vase taken using a CCD camera. The vase is illuminated by a single light source close to the sensor direction. Clearly, the real vase appears much flatter, with less brightness variation along its cross-section, than the Lambertian vase. Note that the proposed model does well in predicting the appearance of the vase. Here, roughness and albedo were selected empirically; $\sigma = 40°$ and $\rho = 0.70$. Figure 7(d) compares brightness values along the cross-section of the three different vase images. Note that the brightness of the real vase remains nearly constant over most of the cross-section and drops quickly to zero very close to the limbs. The proposed model does very well in predicting this behavior, while the Lambertian model produces large brightness errors.

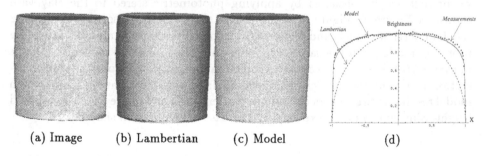

(a) Image   (b) Lambertian   (c) Model   (d)

Fig. 7. (a-c) Real image of a cylindrical clay vase compared with images rendered using the Lambertian and proposed models. Illumination is from the direction $\theta_i = 0°$. (d) Comparison between image brightness along the cross-sections of the three vases.

Reflectance maps are widely used in vision for obtaining shape information from brightness images [Horn and Brooks-1989]. For a given reflectance model and source direction, the reflectance map establishes the relationship between surface orientation, given by the gradient space parameters (p, q), and image brightness. Figure 8(a) shows the reflectance map of a Lambertian surface for illumination from the direction $(\theta_i = 10°, \phi_i = 45°)$. The same reflectance map is obtained using the proposed model with roughness $\sigma = 0$. Figure 8(b) shows the reflectance map of a rough Lambertian surface with $\sigma = 60°$. Note that the rough Lambertian surface produces a map that appears very similar to the linear reflectance map [Horn and Brooks-1989] hypothesized for the lunar surface.

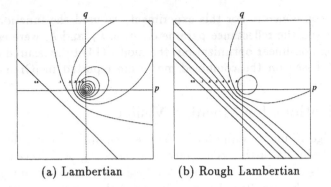

(a) Lambertian   (b) Rough Lambertian

Fig. 8. Reflectance maps for (a) Lambertian surface ($\rho = 0.9$), and (b) rough Lambertian surface ($\sigma = 60°$, $\rho = 0.9$). For both maps the angles of incidence are $\theta_i = 10°$ and $\phi_i = 45°$. Note the similarity between the second map and the well-known linear reflectance map previously suggested for lunar reflectance.

The proposed reflectance model therefore establishes a continuum from pure Lambertian to lunar-like reflectance.

The problem of recovering shape from brightness images has been intensely researched in the past two decades. Several algorithms have been proposed, the most noteworthy of these being shape from shading [Horn and Brooks-1989] and photometric stereo [Woodham-1980]. For these methods to produce meaningful shape estimates, it is imperative that accurate reflectance models be used. Here, we present results obtained by applying photometric stereo to the clay vase shown in Figure 7. Figure 9(a) shows the shape of the vase recovered using the Lambertian model, and Figure 9(b) shows the shape computed using the proposed model with the same roughness and albedo used to render the image in Figure 7(c). Figure 9(c) compares height values computed along the vase cross-section using the two models. It is evident from this plot that the Lambertian model results in large errors in computed orientation and hence also in computed height. Similar errors are expected in the case of shape from shading.

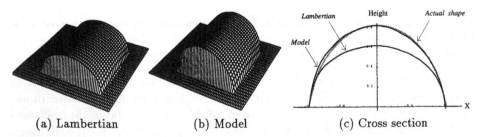

(a) Lambertian   (b) Model   (c) Cross section

Fig. 9. Shape of the vase in Figure 7(a) determined by photometric stereo using (a) the Lambertian model, and (b) the proposed model. In both cases, images were obtained using two light sources at angles $-10°$ and $10°$ with respect to the sensor direction. (c) Actual profile of the vase compared with profiles computed using the Lambertian model and the proposed model ($\sigma = 40°$, $\rho = 0.70$). The Lambertian model produces large errors in computed shape.

References

[Blinn, 1977] J. F. Blinn. Models of light reflection for computer synthesized pictures. *ACM Computer Graphics (SIGGRAPH 77)*, 19(10):542–547, 1977.

[Buhl et al., 1968] D. Buhl, W. J. Welch and D. G. Rea. Reradiation and thermal emission from illuminated craters on the lunar surface. *Journal of Geophysical Research*, 73(16):5281–5295, August 1968.

[Forsyth and Zisserman, 1989] D. Forsyth and A. Zisserman. Mutual illumination. *Proc. Conf. Computer Vision and Pattern Recognition*, pages 466–473, 1989.

[Hapke and van Horn, 1963] B. W. Hapke and Huge van Horn. Photometric studies of complex surfaces, with applications to the moon. *Journal of Geophysical Research*, 68(15):4545–4570, August 1963.

[Hapke et al., 1993] B. W. Hapke, R. M. Nelson and W. D. Smythe. The opposition effect of the moon: The contribution of coherent backscatter. *Science*, 260(23):509–511, April 1993.

[Hering and Smith, 1970] R. G. Hering and T. F. Smith. Apparent radiation properties of a rough surface. *AIAA Progress in Astronautics and Aeronautics*, 23:337–361, 1970.

[Horn and Brooks, 1989] B. K. P. Horn and M. J. Brooks, editors. *Shape from Shading*. The MIT Press, 1989.

[Jakob, 1957] M. Jakob. *Heat Transfer*. Wiley, 1957.

[Lambert, 1760] J. H. Lambert. Photometria sive de mensure de gratibus luminis, colorum umbrae. *Eberhard Klett*, 1760.

[Öpik, 1924] E. Öpik. Photometric measures of the moon and the moon the earthshine. *Publications de L'Observatorie Astronomical de L'Universite de Tartu*, 26(1):1–68, 1924.

[Minnaert, 1941] M. Minnaert. The reciprocity principle in lunar photometry. *Astrophysical Journal*, 93:403–410, 1941.

[Nicodemus et al., 1977] F. E. Nicodemus, J. C. Richmond and J. J. Hsia. *Geometrical Considerations and Nomenclature for Reflectance*. National Bureau of Standards, October 1977. Monograph No. 160.

[Oetking, 1966] P. Oetking. Photometric studies of diffusely reflecting surfaces with application to the brightness of the moon. *Journal of Geophysical Research*, 71(10):2505–2513, May 1966.

[Oren and Nayar, 1992] M. Oren and S. K. Nayar. Generalization of the lambertian model and implications for machine vision. Technical Report CUCS-057-92, Department of Computer Science, Columbia University, New York, NY, USA, 1992.

[Siegel and Howell, 1972] R. Siegel and J. R. Howell. *Thermal Radiation Heat Transfer*. Hemisphere Publishing Corporation, third edition, 1972.

[Smith, 1967] B. G. Smith. Lunar surface roughness: Shadowing and thermal emission. *Journal of Geophysical Research*, 72(16):4059–4067, August 1967.

[Tagare and deFigueiredo, 1991] H. D. Tagare and R. J. P. deFigueiredo. A theory of photometric stereo for a class of diffuse non-Lambertian surfaces. *IEEE Transactions on Pattern Analysis and Machine Intelligence*, 13(2):133–152, February 1991.

[Torrance and Sparrow, 1967] K. Torrance and E. Sparrow. Theory for off-specular reflection from rough surfaces. *Journal of the Optical Society of America*, 57:1105–1114, September 1967.

[Woodham, 1980] R. J. Woodham. Photometric method for determining surface orientation from multiple images. *Optical Engineering*, 19(1):139–144, January-February 1980.

Using 3–Dimensional Meshes To Combine Image-Based and Geometry-Based Constraints

P. Fua and Y.G. Leclerc

SRI International
333 Ravenswood Avenue, Menlo Park, CA 94025, USA
(fua@ai.sri.com   leclerc@ai.sri.com)

Abstract. To recover complicated surfaces, single information sources often prove insufficient. In this paper, we present a unified framework for 3–D shape reconstruction that allows us to combine image-based constraints, such as those deriving from stereo and shape-from-shading, with geometry-based ones, provided here in the form of 3–D points, 3–D features or 2–D silhouettes.

Our approach to shape recovery is to deform a generic object-centered 3–D representation of the surface so as to minimize an objective function. This objective function is a weighted sum of the contributions of the various information sources. We describe these various terms individually, our weighting scheme and our optimization method. Finally, we present results on a number of difficult images of real scenes for which a single source of information would have proved insufficient.

1   Introduction

The problem of recovering surface shape from image cues, the so-called "shape from X" problem, has received tremendous attention in the computer vision community. But no single source of information "X," be it stereo, shading, texture, geometric constraints or any other, has proved to be sufficient across a reasonable sampling of images. To get good reconstructions, it is necessary to use as many different kinds of cues with as many views of the surface as possible. In this paper, we present and demonstrate a working framework for surface reconstruction that combines image cues, such as stereo and shape-from-shading, with geometric constraints, such as those provided by laser range finders, area- and edge-based stereo algorithms, linear features and silhouettes.

Our framework can incorporate cues from many images, including images taken from widely differing viewpoints. It accomodates such viewpoint-dependent effects as self-occlusion and self-shadowing. It accomplishes this by using a full 3–D object-centered representation of the estimated surface. This representation is used to generate synthetic views of the estimated surface from the viewpoint of each input image. Using standard computer graphics algorithms, those parts of the surface that are hidden from a given viewpoint can be identified and eliminated from the reconstruction process. The remaining parts are then in correspondence with the input images. The corresponding cues are applied in an iterative manner using an optimization algorithm.

Lecture Notes in Computer Science, Vol. 801
Jan-Olof Eklundh (Ed.)

In many recent publications about surface reconstruction, such as [Delingette et al., 1991, Terzopoulos and Vasilescu, 1991, Szeliski and Tonnesen, 1992], the authors fit a surface to previously computed 3–D data, such as the output laser range finders or correlation-based stereo algorithms. In other words, the derivation of the 3–D data from the images is completely divorced from the surface reconstruction. In contrast, our framework allows us to directly use such image cues as stereo, shading, and silhouette edges in the reconstruction process while simultaneously incorporating previously computed 3–D data. In a previous publication [Fua and Leclerc, 1993] we describe how stereo and shading are used within the framework described below, and the relationship of this approach to previous work. Here, we focus on the incoporation of additional image cues, silhouette edges and previously computed 3–D data.

Combining these different sources of information is not a new idea in itself. For example, Blake et al. [1985] discuss the complementary nature of stereo and shape from shading. Both Cryer et al. [1992] and Heipke et al. [1992] have proposed algorithms to combine shape-from-shading and stereo while Liedtke et al. [1991] use silhouettes to derive an initial estimate of the surface and improve the result using multi-image stereo. However, none of the algorithms we know of uses an object-centered representation and an optimization procedure that are general enough to incorporate all of the cues that we present here. This generality should also make possible the use of a very wide range of other sources of information, such as shadows, in addition to those actually discussed here.

We view the contribution of this paper as providing both the framework that allows us to combine diverse sources of information in a unified and computationally effective manner, and the specific details of how these diverse sources of information are derived from the images.

In the next section, we describe our framework and the new information sources introduced here. We then demonstrate that the framework successfully performs its function on real images and allows us to achieve results better than those we could derive from any one, or even two, sources of information.

2 Framework

Our approach to recovering surface shape and reflectance properties from multiple images is to deform a 3–D representation of the surface so as to minimize an objective function. The free variables of this objective function are the coordinates of the vertices of the triangulation representing the surface, and the process is started with an initial surface estimate. Here we assume that images are monochrome, and that their camera models are known *a priori*.

We represent a surface S by a hexagonally connected set of vertices called a *mesh*. Such a mesh is shown in Figure 1(a). The position of a vertex v_j is specified by its Cartesian coordinates (x_j, y_j, z_j).

For each input image, we generate a "Facet-ID" image by encoding the index i of each facet f_i as a unique color, and projecting the surface into the image plane, using a standard hidden-surface algorithm. As discussed in Sections 2.3

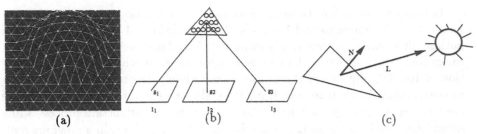

Fig. 1. Mesh representation and computation of the image terms of the objective function: (a) Wireframe representation of the a mesh. (b) Facets are sampled at regular intervals, the circles represent the sample points. The stereo component of the objective function is computed by summing the variance of the grey level of the projections of these sample points, the g_is. (c) Each facet's albedo is estimated using its normal N, the light source direction L and, the average gray level of the projection of the facet into the images. The shading component of the objective function is the sum of the squared differences in estimated albedo across neighboring facets.

and 2.4, we use it to determine which surface points are occluded in a given view and on which facets geometric constraints should be brought to bear.

2.1 Objective Function and Optimization Procedure

The objective function $\mathcal{E}(\mathcal{S})$ that we use to recover the surface is a sum of terms that take into account the image-based constraints—stereo and shape from shading—and the geometry-based constraints—features and silhouettes—that are brought to bear on the surface. To minimize $\mathcal{E}(\mathcal{S})$, we use an optimization method that is inspired by the heuristic technique known as a continuation method [Terzopoulos, 1986, Leclerc, 1989] in which we add a regularization term to the objective function and progressively reduce its influence. We define the total energy of the mesh, $\mathcal{E}_T(\mathcal{S})$, as

$$\mathcal{E}_T(\mathcal{S}) = \lambda_D \mathcal{E}_D(\mathcal{S}) + \mathcal{E}(\mathcal{S}) \text{ with } \mathcal{E}(\mathcal{S}) = \sum_i \lambda_i \mathcal{E}_i(\mathcal{S}) . \tag{1}$$

The $\mathcal{E}_i(\mathcal{S})$ represent the image and geometry-based constraints discussed below, and the λ_i their relative weights. $\mathcal{E}_D(\mathcal{S})$, the regularization term, serves a dual purpose. First, we define it as a quadratic function of the vertex coordinates, so that it "convexifies" the energy landscape when λ_D is large and improves the convergence properties of the optimization procedure. Second, in the presence of noise, some amount of smoothing is required to prevent the mesh from overfitting the data, and wrinkling the surface excessively [Fua and Leclerc, 1993].

In our implementation, we take $\mathcal{E}_D$ to be a measure of the curvature or local deviation from a plane at every vertex. Using finite differences, $\mathcal{E}_D$ can be expressed as a quadratic form [Fua and Leclerc, 1993]

$$\mathcal{E}_D(\mathcal{S}) = 1/2(X^T K X + Y^T K Y + Z^T K Z) , \tag{2}$$

where X, Y, and Z are the vectors of the x, y and z coordinates of the vertices, and K is a sparse and banded matrix.

Because $\mathcal{E}_D$ is quadratic and decouples the three spatial coordinates, our energy term is amenable to a "snake-like" optimization technique [Kass *et al.*, 1988]. We treat S as a physical surface embedded in a viscous medium and evolving under the influence of the potential $\mathcal{E}_T$. We solve the minimization problem by solving the dynamics equation of this system. We can either optimize the three spatial components, X, Y and Z simultaneously or separately.

To speed the computation and prevent the mesh from becoming stuck in undesirable local minima, we typically use several levels of mesh size—three in the examples of Section 3—to perform the computation. We start with a relatively coarse mesh that we optimize. We then refine it by splitting every facet into four smaller ones and reoptimizing. Finally, we repeat the split and optimization processes one more time.

2.2 Combining the Components

The total energy of Equation 1 is a sum of terms whose magnitudes are image- or geometry-dependent and, as a result, not necessarily commensurate. One therefore needs to scale them appropriately, that is to define the λ weights so as to make the magnitude of their contributions commensurate and independent of the specific radiometry or geometry of the scene under consideration. Since the dynamics of the optimization are controlled by the gradient of the objective function, an effective way to normalize the contributions is to introduce a set of weights λ'_i such that $\lambda'_D = 1 - \sum_{1 \le i \le n} \lambda'_i > 0$. The λs are taken to be

$$\lambda_i = \frac{\lambda'_i}{\| \vec{\nabla} \mathcal{E}_i(\mathcal{S}^0) \|} \,, \quad \lambda_D = \frac{\lambda'_D}{\| \vec{\nabla} \mathcal{E}_D(\mathcal{S}^0) \|} \,, \tag{3}$$

where $\mathcal{S}^0$ is the surface estimate at the start of each optimization step. In practice we have found that, because the normalization makes the influence of the various terms comparable irrespective of actual radiometry or dimensions, the user-specified λ'_i weights are context-specific but not image-specific. In other words, we use one set of parameters for images of faces when combining stereo, shape-from-shading, and silhouettes, and another when dealing with aerial images of terrain using stereo and 3-D point constraints, but we do not have to change them for different faces or different landscapes. The continuation method of Section 2.1 is implemented by first taking λ'_D to be 0.5 and then reducing it while keeping the relative values of the λ'_is constant.

2.3 Geometric Constraints

We have explored the constraints generated by 3–D points, 3–D linear features, and 2–D silhouettes.

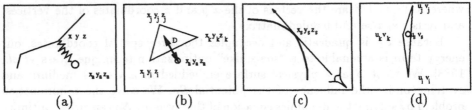

Fig. 2. 3–D and 2–D point constraints: (a) Point attractor modeled as a spring attached to a vertex. (b) Point attractor modeled as a spring attached to the closest surface point. (c) Occlusion contours are the locus of the projections of the (x_s, y_s, z_s) surface points for which a camera ray is tangential to the surface. (d) In practice, the (u_s, v_s) projection of such a point must be colinear with the projections of the vertices of the facet that produces the observed silhouette edge.

3–D Points They are treated as attractors and 3–D linear features are taken to be collections of such points. The easiest way to handle attractors is to model each one as a spring by adding the following term to the objective function

$$e_a = 1/2((x_a - x_i)^2 + (y_a - y_i)^2 + (z_a - z_i)^2) \qquad (4)$$

where x_i, y_i, and z_i are the coordinates of the mesh vertex closest to the attractor (x_a, y_a, z_a). This, however, is inadequate if one wishes to use facets that are large enough so that attracting the vertices, as opposed to the surface point closest to the attractor, would cause unwarranted deformations of the mesh. This is especially important when using a sparse set of attractors. In this case, the energy term of Equation 4 must be replaced by one that attracts the surface without warping it. In our implementation, this is achieved by redefining e_a as

$$e_a = 1/2d_a^2 \qquad (5)$$

where d_a is the orthogonal distance of the attractor to the closest facet. It is easy to show that d_a^2 can be expressed as the ratio of two second order polynomial in terms of the vertex coordinates. These two sorts of attractors are depicted in Figure 2 (a,b). The search for the "closest facet" is made efficient and fast by assuming that the attractors can be identified by their projection in an image. We project the mesh into that image, generate the corresponding Facet-ID image—which must be done in any case for other computations—and look up the facet number of the point's projection. This applies, for example, to range maps, edge- or correlation-based stereo data, and hand-entered features that can be overlaid on various images. We typically recompute the facet attachments at every iteration of the optimization procedure so as to allow facets to slide as necessary. Since the points can potentially come from any number of images, this method can be used to fuse 3–D data from different sources.

Silhouettes Contrary to 3–D edges, silhouette edges are typically 2–D features since they depend on the viewpoint and cannot be matched across images. However, as shown in Figure 2(c), they constrain the surface tangent. Each point of the silhouette edge defines a line that goes through the optical center of the camera and is tangent to the surface at its point of contact with the surface. The points of a silhouette edge therefore define a ruled surface that is tangent to the surface. In terms of our facetized representation, this can be expressed as follows. Given a silhouette point (u_s, v_s) in an image, there must be a facet with vertices $(x_i, y_i, z_i)_{1 \leq i \leq 3}$ whose image projections $(u_i, v_i)_{1 \leq i \leq 3}$, as well as (u_s, v_s), all lie on a single line as depicted by Figure 2(d). This is enforced by adding, for each silhouette point, a term of the form

$$e_s = 1/2 \sum_{1 \leq i \leq 3, i < j \leq 3} \begin{vmatrix} u_i & u_j & u_s \\ v_i & v_j & v_s \\ 1 & 1 & 1 \end{vmatrix}^2 , \tag{6}$$

where the (u_i, v_i)s are the projections of the (x_i, y_i, z_i) using the camera model. This term constrains the determinants to be small and, therefore, the projections of the vertices and the silhouette point to be collinear.

As with the 3–D attractors, the main problem is to find the "silhouette facet" to which the constraint applies. Since the silhouette point (u_s, v_s) can lie outside the projection of the current estimate of the surface, we search the Facet-ID image in a direction normal to the silhouette edge for a facet that minimizes e_s and that is therefore the most likely to produce the silhouette edge. This, in conjunction with our coarse-to-fine optimization scheme, has proved a robust way of determining which facets correspond to silhouette points.

2.4 Image Constraints

In this work, we use two complementary image-based constraints: stereo and shape-from-shading.

The stereo component of the objective function is derived by comparing the gray-levels of the points in all of the images for which the projection of a given point on the surface is visible, as determined using the Facet-ID image. As shown in Figure 1(b), this comparison is done for a uniform sampling of the surface. This method allows us to deal with arbitrarily slanted regions and to discount occluded areas of the surface.

The shading component of the objective function is computed using a method that does not invoke the traditional constant albedo assumption. Instead, it attempts to minimize the variation in albedo across the surface, and can therefore deal with surfaces whose albedo varies slowly. This term is depicted by Figure 1(c).

Stereo information is very robust in textured regions but potentially unreliable elsewhere. We therefore use it mainly in textured areas by weighting the stereo component most strongly for facets of the triangulation that project into

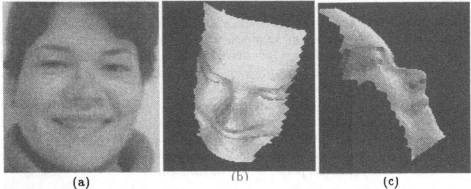

(a)   (b)   (c)

Fig. 3. Combining stereo and shape-from-shading: (a) First image of a triplet (courtesy of INRIA). (b,c) Shaded views of the reconstructed surface.

textured image areas. Conversely, the shading information is more reliable where there is little texture and is weighted accordingly.

These two terms are central to our approach: they are the ones that allow the combination of geometric information with image information. However, since their behavior and implementation have already been extensively discussed elsewhere, we do not describe them any further here and refer the interested reader to our previous publication [Fua and Leclerc, 1993]. In Figure 3, we show the reconstruction of a face using only stereo and shape-from-shading.

3 Applications

Our framework lets us combine geometric constraints with image-based constraints either to derive surface reconstructions or to refine previously computed surfaces. We now demonstrate its capabilities using difficult imagery.

Our system deals with the various sources of 3–D information, whether dense, such as range maps or correlation-based stereo disparity maps, or linear, such as edge-features, in the same fashion. They are sampled at regular intervals to generate collections of 3–D attractors or 2–D silhouette points.

Dense 3–D Data In Figure 4, we show an image of a face and a corresponding range map computed using structured light. Although fairly accurate, this particular method introduces artifacts in the range image. As a result, fitting a surface to this data by treating the range points as attractors yields the excessively wrinkly result shown in Figure 4(c). Simply smoothing would lose important details such as the mouth or the fine structures on the side of the nose. Our approach provides us with a better way of dealing with this problem: we can fuse the range information with the shading information of the intensity image of Figure 4(a) by taking the objective function to be a weighted sum of the term that attracts the surface towards the range data and of the the shading term. The result, shown in Figure 4(d,e,f), is much smoother, but the mouth is well

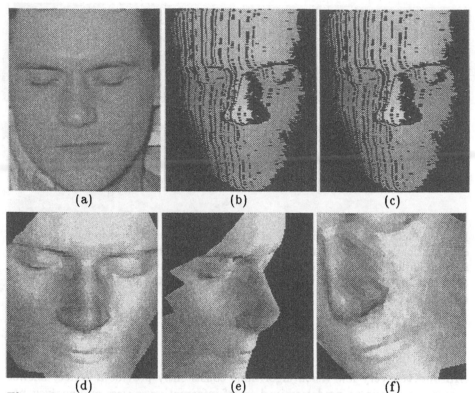

(a)   (b)   (c)

(d)   (e)   (f)

Fig. 4. Combining range data with shape–from–shading information: (a) Image of a face (Courtesy of ETH Zürich). (b) Corresponding range image computed using structured light. (c) Shaded views of the surface reconstructed by using the range-data points as attractors. (d)(e)(f) Shaded views of the reconstruction refined using shading.

preserved and the side of the nose better defined. Note, however, that in the side view the bottom of the nose is not flat enough. This is not surprising since the shading information is of no use there. We address this problem below.

Sparse 3–D Data We now turn to sparse 3–D data. In Figure 5, we show a stereo pair of a rock outcrop forming an almost vertical cliff. Correlation-based algorithms typically fail in the cliff area. To demonstrate the data-fusion capabilities of our approach, we have used the 3D–snakes embedded in the SRI Cartographic Modeling Environment to supply 3–D edges whose projections are shown in Figure 5(c,d).

We first attract an initially flat surface to both the output of a simple correlation-based algorithm—it yields information only in the flat parts of the scene—and the 3–D outlines and produce the roughly correct but excessively smooth estimate of Figure 5 (e). By adding either the stereo term alone to $\mathcal{E}_T$, Figure 5 (f), or both the stereo and shading terms, Figure 5 (g,h), we can generate a much more realistic model of the surface.

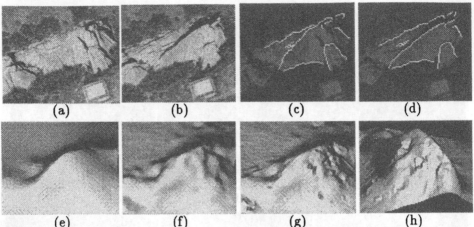

(a) (b) (c) (d)

(e) (f) (g) (h)

Fig. 5. Semiautomated cartography of a rugged site: (a,b) A hard-to-fuse stereo pair of a rock outcrop with an almost vertical cliff. (c,d) The projections of a few 3–D features outlined using 3–D snakes. (e) Reconstructed surface using the 3–D features as attractors. (f) Refinement using stereo. (g,h) Refinement using both stereo and shape from shading.

Silhouettes Very few vision algorithms consistently provide a perfect answer across scenes using a predetermined set of information sources and analysis parameters. It is often important to be able to easily refine a previously derived result, and silhouettes are very effective for this purpose. For example, the reconstruction of the bottom of the nose in Figure 4(e) is not quite right, as can be seen in Figure 6(b). To correct this, we use the silhouettes of Figure 6(a,b) that have been outlined using 2–D snakes. We take the total energy $\mathcal{E}_T$ to be a weighted sum of the silhouette attraction terms of Equation 5 and of the shading term of Section 2.4. We use these terms to deform the nose region and generate the improved result of Figure 6(c).

The face reconstruction of Figure 3 presents us with a slightly different problem. We have used a correlation-based stereo algorithm to provide us with an initial estimate. This algorithm gave us no information on the sharply slanted parts of the face, which are therefore missing from the reconstruction. The silhouettes of the face, however, are clearly visible and easy to outline, as shown in Figure 6(d). To take advantage of these, we start with a larger and coarser mesh that evolves under the influence of the silhouettes and the vertices of the original reconstruction that are treated as attractors. When the mesh has been refined and optimized, we complete the optimization procedure by turning on the full objective function including stereo and shape-from-shading. The results are shown in Figure 6(e,f).

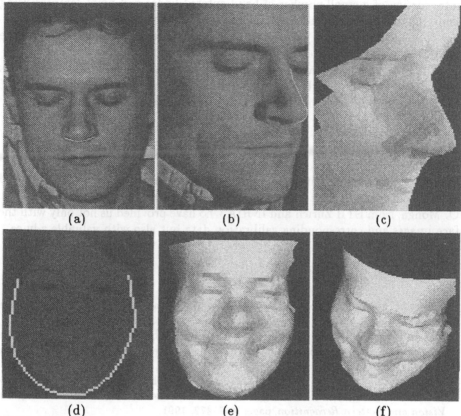

(a) (b) (c)

(d) (e) (f)

Fig. 6. Using silhouettes to improve a reconstruction: (a) The face of Figure with a silhouette at the bottom of the nose outlined. (b) A side view of the same face with a second nose silhouette. (c) Shaded views of the refined reconstruction using both shading and the two silhouettes. (d) Face silhouette outlined in the first image of the triplet of Figure . (e,f) Shaded views of the reconstructed surface after optimization using stereo, shading, and the constraints provided by the silhouettes.

4 Summary and Conclusion

We have presented a surface reconstruction method that uses an object-centered representation to recover 3–D surfaces. Our method uses both monocular shading cues and stereoscopic cues from any number of images while correctly handling self-occlusions. It can also take advantage of the geometric constraints derived from measured 3–D points and 2–D silhouettes. These complementary sources of information are combined in a unified manner so that new ones can be added easily as they become available.

Using a variety of real imagery, we have demonstrated that the resulting method is quite powerful and flexible, allowing for both completely automatic reconstruction in straightforward circumstances, and for user-assisted reconstruction in more complex ones. User assistance is provided primarily through the introduction of a small number of hand-entered linear and point features using semi-automated "snake" technology. The method is controlled by a small number of image-independent parameters that specify the relative importance of the various information sources.

The method has valuable capabilities for applications such as 3-D graphics model generation and high-resolution cartography in which a human can select the sources of information to be used and their relative importance.

Acknowledgments

Support for this research was provided by various contracts from the Advanced Research Projects Agency. We wish to thank O. Kübler, M. Trobina, H. Matthieu, O. Monga, from ETH Zurich and INRIA who have provided us not only with the face images and corresponding calibration data but also with valuable advice.

References

[Blake et al., 1985] A. Blake, A. Zisserman, and G. Knowles. Surface descriptions from stereo and shading. *Image Vision Computation*, 3(4):183–191, 1985.

[Cryer et al., 1992] J. E. Cryer, Ping-Sing Tsai, and Mubarak Shah. Combining shape from shading and stereo using human vision model. Technical Report CS-TR-92-25, U. Central Florida, 1992.

[Delingette et al., 1991] H. Delingette, M. Hebert, and K. Ikeuchi. Shape representation and image segmentation using deformable surfaces. In *Conference on Computer Vision and Pattern Recognition*, pages 467–472, 1991.

[Fua and Leclerc, 1993] P. Fua and Y.G. Leclerc. Object-centered surface reconstruction: Combining multi-image stereo and shading. In *ARPA Image Understanding Workshop*, Washington, D.C., April 1993.

[Heipke, 1992] C. Heipke. Integration of digital image matching and multi image shape from shading. In *International Society for Photogrammetry and Remote Sensing*, pages 832–841, Washington D.C., 1992.

[Kass et al., 1988] M. Kass, A. Witkin, and D. Terzopoulos. Snakes: Active contour models. *International Journal of Computer Vision*, 1(4):321–331, 1988.

[Leclerc, 1989] Y.G. Leclerc. Constructing simple stable descriptions for image partitioning. *International Journal of Computer Vision*, 3(1):73–102, 1989.

[Liedtke et al., 1991] C. E. Liedtke, H. Busch, and R. Koch. Shape adaptation for modelling of 3D objects in natural scenes. In *Conference on Computer Vision and Pattern Recognition*, pages 704–705, 1991.

[Szeliski and Tonnesen, 1992] R. Szeliski and D. Tonnesen. Surface modeling with oriented particle systems. In *Computer Graphics (SIGGRAPH'92)*, pages 185–194, July 1992.

[Terzopoulos and Vasilescu, 1991] D. Terzopoulos and M. Vasilescu. Sampling and reconstruction with adaptive meshes. In *Conference on Computer Vision and Pattern Recognition*, pages 70–75, 1991.

[Terzopoulos, 1986] D. Terzopoulos. Regularization of inverse visual problems involving discontinuities. *IEEE Transactions on Pattern Analysis and Machine Intelligence*, 8:413–424, 1986.

Motion Segmentation

Determination of Optical Flow and its Discontinuities using Non-Linear Diffusion

M. Proesmans, L. Van Gool, E. Pauwels, A. Oosterlinck

ESAT-MI2, Katholieke Universiteit Leuven,
K. Mercierlaan 94, B-3001 Leuven, Belgium

Abstract. A new method for optical flow computation by means of a coupled set of non-linear diffusion equations is presented. This approach integrates the classical differential approach with the correlation type of motion detectors. A measure of inconsistency within the optical flow field which indicates optical flow boundaries. This information is fed back to the optical flow equations in a non-linear way and allows the flow field to be reconstructed while preserving the discontinuities. The whole scheme is also applicable to stereo-matching. The model is applied to a set of synthetic and real image sequences to illustrate the behaviour of the coupled diffusion equations.

1. Introduction

Most methods for computing motion fields rely on spatial and temporal gradients. The image intensity traces the optical flow problem is ill-posed, additional constraint must be required. The simplest is the quadratic smoothness constraint [5]. Other constraints have been introduced using higher order spatial and temporal derivatives [6]. Some methods use overconstrained systems of equations [3, 14], rather than the functional to emphasize. Other methods try to look for specific features - such as corners [ ]. It is a priori not to capture smoothness of the flow field across the discontinuities. Part of the problem lies in the required size of the operator mask to estimate the spatio-temporal derivatives of the greyvalue distribution. Large masks may be called for in order to eliminate the effect of noise and to handle relatively large inter-frame distances. The method presented this issue offers an alternative solution which roughly consists of three parts.

– Basically the method starts from the differential approach of the optical flow problem.
– Unlike other differential methods, our approach is provided with a mechanism very similar to the matching process of correlation based approaches [1]. This mechanism allows for a clear implementation and inconsistencies within the resulting scheme turn out to be explicit near by flow discontinuities.
– Finally, the discontinuity information is fed back to the optical flow scheme in a non-linear way in order to reconstruct the optical flow field while preserving its discontinuities.

Determination of Optical Flow and its Discontinuities using Non-Linear Diffusion

M. Proesmans[1], L. Van Gool[1], E. Pauwels[1], A. Oosterlinck[1]

ESAT-MI2, Katholieke Universiteit Leuven,
K. Mercierlaan 94, B-3001 Leuven, Belgium

Abstract. A new method for optical flow computation by means of a coupled set of non-linear diffusion equations is presented. This approach integrates the classical differential approach with the correlation type of motion detectors. A measure of inconsistency within the optical flow field which indicates optical flow boundaries. This information is fed back to the optical flow equations in a non-linear way and allows the flow field to be reconstructed while preserving the discontinuities. The whole scheme is also applicable to stereo matching. The model is applied to a set of synthetic and real image sequences to illustrate the behaviour of the coupled diffusion equations.

1 Introduction

Most methods for computing motion fields rely on spatial and temporal gradients of the image intensity. Since the optical flow problem is ill-posed, additional constraints are required. The simplest is the quadratic smoothness constraint [5]. Other constraints have been introduced using higher order spatial and temporal derivatives [6]. Some methods use overconstrained systems of equations [3, 14], rather than functional descriptions. Other methods try to look for specific features - such as corners [7]. It is a problem not to enforce smoothness of the flow field across flow discontinuities. Part of the problem lies in the required size of the operator masks to estimate the spatio-temporal derivatives of the grayvalue distribution. Large masks may be called for in order to eliminate the effect of noise, and to handle relatively large interframe distances. The method presented in this paper offers an alternative solution which roughly consists of three parts.

- Basically, the method starts from the differential approach of the optical flow problem.
- Unlike other differential methods, our approach is provided with a mechanism very similar to the matching process of correlation based approaches [11]. This mechanism allows for a dual implementation and inconsistencies within the resulting scheme turn out to be concentrated nearby flow discontinuities.
- Finally, the discontinuity information is fed back to the original optical flow scheme in a non-linear way in order to reconstruct the optic flow field while preserving its discontinuities.

Lecture Notes in Computer Science, Vol. 801
Jan-Olof Eklundh (Ed.)

2   Optical Flow

The classical differential techniques used for computation of optical flow are based on the image flow constraint equation.

$$I_x.u + I_y.v + I_t = 0 \ .$$

This equation relates spatio-temporal intensity changes to the velocity (u, v). It states that the image irradiance remains constant during the motion process. This single equation cannot fix the two motion components. Therefore most techniques use some kind of smoothness constraint such as introduced by Horn & Schunck [5] which led to the following minimizing functional

$$E = \int \int (\lambda(I_x.u + I_y.v + I_t) + (u_x^2 + u_y^2 + v_x^2 + v_y^2))dxdy \ .$$

Its main advantage is its simplicity, since minimizing the functional leads to a set of linear equations. In fact the corresponding evolution equations are

$$\frac{\partial u}{\partial t} = \nabla^2 u - \lambda I_x(I_x.u + I_y.v + I_t)$$
$$\frac{\partial v}{\partial t} = \nabla^2 v - \lambda I_y(I_x.u + I_y.v + I_t) \ .$$
$$(1)$$

The smoothness constraint thus allows to estimate both velocity components, yet also forces the estimated vector field to vary smoothly across boundaries. A number of methods have been introduced [1, 6, 4, 10] to allow the optical flow field to be discontinuous, by appropriately exploiting the gradient information of the flow field. Nevertheless, the original Horn & Schunck scheme did not loose its popularity since its performance is quite satisfactory [2, 15] and this all the more in view of its simplicity. In the next sections, an alternative way of detecting discontinuities in the flow field will be derived.

3   The Dual Optical Flow Scheme

Since the optical flow equation relates spatio-temporal derivatives in a point, it can only hold locally. If accurate results are required for larger velocities, the gradient information has to be estimated with larger operator masks, resulting in a further degradation of discontinuities in the flow field. The method to be expounded, on the other hand, is bi-local.

Consider a point (x, y) in a frame at time t, for which we have some velocity estimates $(\tilde{u}, \tilde{v})$, and a point $(x - \tilde{u}dt, y - \tilde{v}dt)$ in a previous frame at time $t - dt$. For the 1D case, assuming an estimate $\tilde{u} = \frac{dx}{dt}$, we could rewrite the optical flow constraint as follows

$$\frac{dI}{dt} = I_x.u + I_t = 0$$

$$I_x.u + \frac{I(x, t) - I(x, t - dt)}{dt} = 0$$

$$I_x . u + \frac{I(x,t) - I(x - \tilde{u}dt, t - dt)}{dt} + \frac{I(x - \tilde{u}dt, t - dt) - I(x, t - dt)}{dt} = 0$$

and using the approximations

$$I(x - \tilde{u}dt, t - dt) = I(x,t) - \tilde{u}I_x dt - I_t dt$$
$$I(x, t - dt) = I(x,t) - I_t dt$$

$$I_x(u - \tilde{u}) + \frac{I(x,t) - I(x - \tilde{u}dt, t - dt)}{dt} = 0 . \tag{2}$$

This *residual optical flow* equation yields – if we were able to estimate the intensity variations at a shifted location $x - \tilde{u}dt$ at time $t - dt$ – the residual velocity $u - \tilde{u}$. Figure 1 depicts more clearly the relationship between the different components in equation 2. Note that if $\tilde{u}$ were the real velocity u, the constraint would reduce to $I(x,t) - I(x - dx, t - dt) = 0$ which agrees with the constant irradiance assumption.

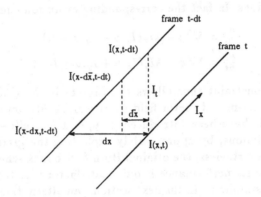

Fig. 1. interpretation of 1D optic flow equation

In two dimensions, the constraint equation yields

$$I_x u + I_y v + \mathbf{I}_t(\tilde{u}, \tilde{v}) = 0 \ , \quad \mathbf{I}_t(\tilde{u}, \tilde{v}) = -I_x \tilde{u} - I_y \tilde{v} + \frac{I(x,y,t) - I(x - \tilde{u}dt, y - \tilde{v}dt, t - dt)}{dt} .$$
$$\tag{3}$$

If we introduce this constraint into the original evolution equations (1), we would end up with the following scheme

$$\frac{\partial u}{\partial t} = \nabla^2 u - \lambda I_x(I_x u + I_y v + \mathbf{I}_t(\tilde{u}, \tilde{v}))$$
$$\frac{\partial v}{\partial t} = \nabla^2 v - \lambda I_y(I_x u + I_y v + \mathbf{I}_t(\tilde{u}, \tilde{v})) . \tag{4}$$

In the most general case $(\tilde{u}, \tilde{v})$ can be any estimate of the velocity components, From a practical point of view, they are chosen to be the estimates of the previous iteration. The resulting scheme is quite similar to correlation-based approaches, since a matching point is assigned to each point in the reference frame, based on equality of intensity.

Up to now the estimates $(\tilde{u}, \tilde{v})$ have been used to allocate a position in a previous frame. Similarly, one can start from the previous frame and search the corresponding point $(x + \tilde{u}dt, y + \tilde{v}dt)$ in the next frame. At first glance both schemes – forward and backward – seem to be equivalent, but they are not! In fact, nearby optical flow boundaries and occluding regions large inconsistencies between the two schemes are found. This characteristic can be used to create a motion edge indicator.

4 Discontinuities and Non-Linear Diffusion

4.1 Detection of discontinuities in the flow field

For the main part of the flow field, the dual scheme is consistent, i.e. they yield the same result. For two frames a and b, this means that

$$\mathbf{v}_a(x, y) = -\mathbf{v}_b(x - u_a\Delta t, y - v_a\Delta t) \text{ and } \mathbf{v}_b(x, y) = -\mathbf{v}_a(x - u_b\Delta t, y - v_b\Delta t)$$

with $\mathbf{v}_a = (u_a, v_a)$ and $\mathbf{v}_b = (u_b, v_b)$. Note that the velocity estimates in both schemes will be opposite to each other, since the roles of the frames are reversed. In the neighbourhood of discontinuities, the dual scheme is very likely to be inconsistent. Indeed, for a number of points in frame a, one can not find matching points in frame b, and vice versa, when they are occluded by the moving object. Using the difference vectors

$$\mathbf{C}_a = \mathbf{v}_a(x, y) + \mathbf{v}_b(x - u_a\Delta t, y - v_a\Delta t) \text{ and } \mathbf{C}_b = \mathbf{v}_b(x, y) + \mathbf{v}_a(x - u_b\Delta t, y - v_b\Delta t)$$

one can define inconsistency measures c_a and c_b which can be fed back to the dual optical flow scheme. In order to make them less sensitive to noise and independent of the velocity magnitude, an additional diffusion process is used:

$$\frac{\partial c}{\partial t} = \rho\nabla^2 c - \frac{c}{\rho} + 2\alpha(1 - c)\|\mathbf{C}\|$$

following Shah's [12] procedure for generating edge maps from intensity gradients. In this expression c indicates the likelihood of there being an edge at some position in the flow field. Hence, c is assumed to be smooth and close to 1 in the vicinity of a flow boundary, and close to zero away from such discontinuities.

4.2 Measures to prevent blurring of flow discontinuities

The smoothing process in the equations 4, which risk to blur the discontinuities in the optical flow field, can be controlled by introducing non-linear diffusion terms. Perona & Malik [9] proposed a method to locally sharpen edges in gray-value images, in order to preserve contrast. This can be achieved by making the diffusion coefficient γ dependent on the gray-level f

$$\frac{\partial f}{\partial t} = div(\gamma(f)\nabla f) .$$

Choosing $\gamma = 0$ at the boundaries and $\gamma = 1$ elsewhere, encourages smoothing within the regions but attenuates smoothing across the boundaries. Since the boundaries are not known yet, one chooses γ locally as a function of the gradient: $\gamma(f) = \gamma(\| \nabla f \|)$. Possible functions are

$$\gamma(f) = e^{-(\|\nabla f\|/K)^2} \quad \text{and} \quad \gamma(f) = \frac{1}{1 + (\|\nabla f\|/K)^2} \ .$$

Introducing a similar edge sharpening process into the optical flow equations will prevent smoothing across inconsistent regions. However, there are some serious shortcomings. The effect of the non-linearity is that smoothing is prohibited at each point containing inconsistent values. During the iteration process, velocity components can be inconsistent temporarily, especially if local gradient information is not consistent with the direction of the optical flow. If so, these components are restrained from converging to their correct values since any communication with neighbouring velocities is restricted. What we really need is a process which prevents consistent regions to suffer interference from inconsistent ones. This can be formulated mathematically by a diffusion coefficient γ which is weighted over a region of interest Ω, e.g.

$$\frac{\partial u}{\partial t} = div(\gamma(c)\nabla u)\ldots \ , \ \gamma(c) = \frac{\xi}{1 + (\frac{c}{K})^2} \ \text{with} \ \xi \ \text{such that} \ \int_\Omega \gamma(c) = 1 \ .$$

5   Integration

If we integrate all of the above ideas, we have a system of 6 coupled diffusion maps, four of which describe optical flow constraints, while the other two measure the consistency of the dual scheme. A bloack scheme of this algorithm is visualized in figure 2. These maps undergo a coupled development towards an equilibrium state.

$$
\begin{aligned}
\frac{\partial u_1}{\partial t} &= div(\gamma(u_1)\nabla u_1) - \lambda I_x(I_x u_1 + I_y v_1 + \mathbf{I}_t(\tilde{u_1}, \tilde{v_1})) \ , \\
\frac{\partial v_1}{\partial t} &= div(\gamma(v_1)\nabla v_1) - \lambda I_y(I_x u_1 + I_y v_1 + \mathbf{I}_t(\tilde{u_1}, \tilde{v_1})) \ , \\
\frac{\partial u_2}{\partial t} &= div(\gamma(u_2)\nabla u_2) - \lambda I_x(I_x u_2 + I_y v_2 + \mathbf{I}_t(\tilde{u_2}, \tilde{v_2})) \ , \\
\frac{\partial v_2}{\partial t} &= div(\gamma(v_2)\nabla v_2) - \lambda I_y(I_x u_2 + I_y v_2 + \mathbf{I}_t(\tilde{u_2}, \tilde{v_2})) \ , \\
\frac{\partial c_1}{\partial t} &= \rho\nabla^2 c_1 - \frac{c_1}{\rho} + 2\alpha(1 - c_1)\|\mathbf{C}_1(u_1, v_1, u_2, v_2)\| \ , \\
\frac{\partial c_2}{\partial t} &= \rho\nabla^2 c_2 - \frac{c_2}{\rho} + 2\alpha(1 - c_2)\|\mathbf{C}_2(u_1, v_1, u_2, v_2)\| \ .
\end{aligned}
\tag{5}
$$

The iteration process proceeds by updating the above equations, and at the same time, recomputing the spatio-temporal information. The latter has been carried out by simple truncation of the shifted coordinates or by bilinear interpolation. In case of truncated coordinates, however, one can expect to observe oscillatory behaviour of the iterative scheme especially nearby flow discontinuities. The bilinear interpolation approach on the other hand converges much more smoothly, be it at a higher computational cost.

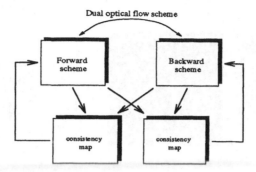

Fig. 2. Dual optical flow scheme with feed back loops

6 Stereo Matching

Stereo matching can be considered to be a special case of this optical flow scheme. In preliminary experiments, excluding vergence and occulo-torsion, the simplifying assumption was made that the disparities can be found as purely horizontal shifts (i.e. disparity $d = u$) and the v-maps were suppressed. This results in a system of 4 coupled diffusion equations which is reminiscent of a stereo approach proposed by Shah [13] who considers gradients instead of inconsistency measures.

7 Experimental Results

We applied the algorithm to a set of non-trivial synthetic image sequences which consist of a textured object moving on an identically textured background. The object can only be discriminated from the background by the motion cue. Figure 3 shows a circle translating diagonally at 3, 5 pixels/frame. The operator mask is 3×3, which is small compared to a real velocity of about 3.5 pixels/frame. The classical Horn & Schunck approach, although able to extract the optic flow field, shows clear distorsions in the flow field for these small mask sizes. The dual approach (figure 4) succeeds in finding the correct displacement field. Each of the inconsistency images contains part of the information concerning flow boundaries or occluding regions. The latter can be observed as a thickening of the boundary contours. The left image shows the region which is about to become visible, while the right image contains the region which is going to be occluded. It is interesting to note that these data can be rearranged into a boundary image δ and an occluded region image ω.

$$\delta = min(c_1, c_2) \quad \text{and} \quad \omega = max(c_1 - \delta, c_2 - \delta) \ .$$

These operations are equivalent to the AND and EXOR operation on binary signals.

Figure 5a shows a circle rotating at 5 degrees/frame. Obviously, there aren't any occluding regions, and for each point a match can be found. As shown in figure

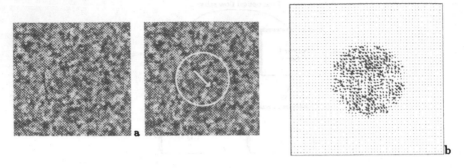

Fig. 3. a: Translating circle. b: Horn & Schunck using 3×3 masks ($\lambda = 0.001$).

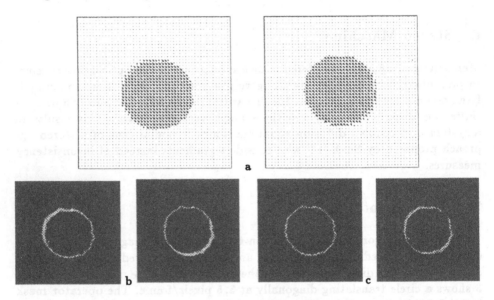

Fig. 4. a: Optic flow fields of the dual scheme ($\lambda = 0.001, K = 0.2, \rho = 0.5, \alpha = 10.0$).
b: Inconsistencies c_1 and c_2. c: Boundary δ and occluded regions ω.

6c w is practically non-existent, whereas non-zero values can be accounted for by discretization errors and noise. The 3D plot of figure 5b shows that the velocity magnitude increases linearly from the center to the object boundaries.

Figure 7 shows experiments on a real sequence, a fish moving to the left. The optical flow field is quite reasonable. As for the optical flow boundaries, local thickening can be observed in the inconsistency images, indicating the existence of occluding regions. It must be noted that at some points the inconsistency images are blurred or interrupted. This is due to a lack of contrast with and in the background.

Figure 9 shows a stereo image pair of a shell on a textured background and the resulting disparities. The dips at the center of the shell (figure 10) are due to specular reflections of overhead neon tubes. Such reflections cause problems

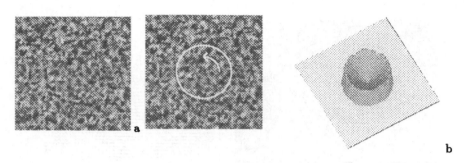

Fig. 5. a: Rotating circle. b: 3-dimensional plot of velocity magnitude.

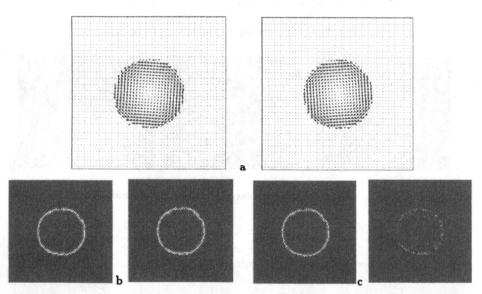

Fig. 6. a: Optic flow fields of the dual scheme ($\lambda = 0.001, K = 0.2, \rho = 0.5, \alpha = 10.0$).
b: Inconsistencies c_1 and c_2. c: Boundary δ and occluded regions ω

to stereo. Otherwise, the disparity fields are remarkably smooth, yet sharply delineated. Together with the boundary image (δ) one can reconstruct a depth image while preserving the discontinuity (figure 9b).

8 Conclusions and Future Research

A method was proposed that can be considered a merger of correlation and differential techniques. Although the inclusion of correlation aspects does not really unify the analysis of short-range and long-range motion, a wider range of velocities can be handled without the introduction of larger filters. Therefore the optical flow field can be determined more accurately. A dual scheme has been worked out that provides measures of inconsistency which together indicate the

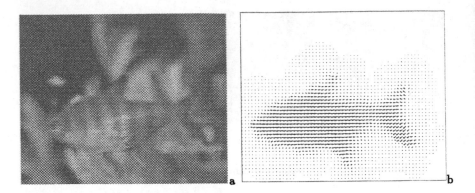

Fig. 7. a: Fish moving to the left. b: Flow field

Fig. 8. a: Inconsistencies. b: Segmented image

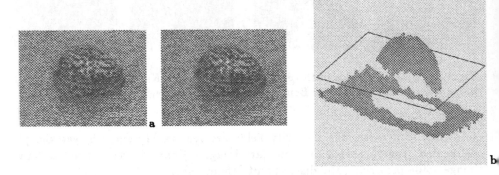

Fig. 9. a: Stereo view of shell on textured background. b: 3D reconstruction.

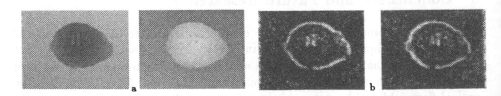

Fig. 10. a: Disparities of left and right scheme. b: Inconsistencies

presence of flow boundaries and occluding regions. Another important aspect
of the method is the introduction of non-linearity. It allows to reconstruct the
optical flow field preserving its discontinuities.

Ongoing research is aimed at integrating information coming from dual schemes
working on different spatial scales. In a further stage the introduction of additional spatio-temporal filters can provide more information about the resulting
flow field [14]. Another aspect we intend to address is the problem of changing
brightness patterns in time, for which more flexibel motion constraint equations
have to be introduced [8].

References

1. Aisbett J.: Optical flow with an intensity-weighted smoothing. IEEE Transactions
   on PAMI. **11.5** (1989) 512–522
2. Barron J.L., Fleet D.J., Beauchemin S.S., and Burkitt T.A.: Performance of optical
   flow techniques. IEEE Proceedings of CVPR, Illinois. (1992) 236–242
3. Campani M. and Verri A.: Computing Optical Flow from an Overconstrained Sytem
   of Linear Algebraic Equations. Proc. Third Int. Conf. on Comp. Vision. Osaka,
   Japan. (1990) 22–26,
4. Cohen I.: Nonlinear Variational Method for Optical flow computation. Proc. of the
   8th Scandinavian Conf. on Image Analysis. **1** (1993) 523–530
5. Horn B.K.P. and Schunck G.: Determining optical flow. Artificial Intelligence. **17**
   (1981) 185–203
6. Nagel H.H. and Enkelmann W.: An investigation of smoothness constraints for the
   estimation of displacement vector fields from image sequence. IEEE Transactions
   on PAMI. **8.5** (1986) 565–593
7. Nagel H.H.: Displacement Vectors Derived from Second-Order Intensity Variations
   in Image Sequences. Comp. Vision, Graphics, and Image Proc. **21** (1983) 85–117
8. Negahdaripour S. and Yu C.: A generalized Brightness Change Model for Computing
   Optical Flow. 4th Int. Conf. on Comp. Vision. (1993) 2–11
9. Perona P. and J. Malik J.: Scale-Space and Edge Detection Using Anisotropic Diffusion. IEEE Transactions on PAMI. **12.7** (1990)
10. Pauwels E.J., Proesmans M., Van Gool L.J., T. Moons and Oosterlinck A.: Im-
    age Enhancement using coupled anisotropic diffusion equations. Proc. on the 11th
    European Conf. on circuit theory and design, **2** (1993) 1459–1464
11. Reichardt W.E. and Poggio T.: Figure-ground discrimination by relative movement
    in the visual system of the fly. Part I: Experimental results. Biological Cybernetics.
    35 (1980) 81–100
12. Shah J.: Segmentation by non-linear diffusion. Proc. IEEE CVPR Hawai (1991)
13. Shah J.: (1993) A Nonlinear Diffusion Model for Discontinuous Disparity and Half-
    Occlusion in Stereo. Proc. IEEE CVPR NY (1993)
14. Weber J. and J. Malik J.: Robust Computation of Optical Flow in a Multi-Scale
    Differential Framework. 4th Int. Conf. on Comp. Vision. (1993) 12–20
15. Willick D. and Yang Y.: Experimental Evaluation of Motion Constraint Equations.
    CVGIP: Image Understanding. **54.2** (1991) 206–214

Motion Boundary Detection in Image Sequences by Local Stochastic Tests

H.-H. Nagel[1,2], G. Socher[2], H. Kollnig[2], and M. Otte[2]

[1] Fraunhofer-Institut für Informations- und Datenverarbeitung IITB
Fraunhoferstr. 1, D-76131 Karlsruhe
Telephone +49 (721) 6091-210 (Fax -413)
[2] Institut für Algorithmen und Kognitive Systeme
Fakultät für Informatik der Universität Karlsruhe

Abstract. While estimating both components of optical flow based on the postulated validity of the Optical Flow Constraint Equation (OFCE), it has been tacitly assumed so far that the partial derivatives of the gray value distribution - which are required for this approach at the pixel positions involved - are independent from each other. [Nagel 94] has shown in a theoretical investigation how dropping this assumption affects the estimation procedure. The advantage of such a more rigorous approach consists in the possibility to replace heuristic tests for the local detection of discontinuities in optical flow fields by well known stochastic tests. First results from various experiments with this new approach are presented and discussed.

1 Introduction

Most attempts to estimate optical flow so far took only partial account of the stochastic nature of the observed digitized image sequences. As a consequence, heuristic procedures to cope with signal variations as well as 'intuitive' choices of threshold parameters have been used to select results upon which further inferences had to be based. A careful discussion about the assumptions underlying various approaches towards the estimation of optical flow can be found, too, in [Fleet 92] and in [Nagel 92]. [Barron et al. 92] offer an in-depth comparison between various approaches. In the following, therefore, we concentrate on recent approaches towards the segmentation of estimated optical flow fields.

In cases of relative motion between camera and scene background, one can attempt to segment the field of view based on significant discontinuities in the optical flow field. [Spoerri & Ullman 87] discuss local computations to detect motion boundaries. [Bouthemy & Francois 93] and [Irani et al. 92] have exploited the evaluation of more than two or three consecutive frames from an image sequence in order to acquire clues to regions corresponding to the images of moving objects. [Thompson & Pong 90] compare - in qualitative terms - various approaches towards the segmentation of images of moving objects from the image of moving background. A valuable update on detecting images of moving objects can be found in [Letang et al. 93]. More recent approaches have been reported by [Wang & Adelson 93], [Gu et al. 93], [Torr & Murray 92], and [Kollnig et al.

94]. None of these approaches investigates the influence of uncertainties in the raw digitized gray values on the final segmentation results in a stringent manner.

[Negahdaripour & Lee 92] tessellate frames from an image sequence and estimate optical flow as well as its first spatial derivatives within each image region by a fit to the Optical Flow Constraint Equation (OFCE), see [Horn 86]. They do not, however, take into account that the estimates for the spatio-temporal gray value gradient at neighboring pixel positions are not independent from each other.

In most cases, the assumption is not even made explicit that the partial derivatives $\partial g(x, y, t)/\partial x$, $\partial g(x, y, t)/\partial y$, and $\partial g(x, y, t)/\partial t$ of the gray value distribution $g(x, y, t)$ at neighboring pixel positions are treated as independent estimates. Each such estimate is tacitly associated with an error taken to be an independently identically distributed (i.i.d.) sample from a Gaussian and then used in a Least Squared Error approach - see, for example, [Burt et al. 91], [Campani & Verri 92], [Torr & Murray 92], and [Otte & Nagel 94]. [Gu et al. 93], however, at least mention this assumption explicitly in their study to segment images of moving objects from those of moving background, see also [Etoh & Shirai 93]. Similarly, [Weber & Malik 93] emphasize the fact that all partial derivatives of the gray value distribution used for estimating optical flow are in principle corrupted by noise, not only the temporal derivative. They treat, however, each estimated spatio-temporal partial derivative of the gray value distribution as being an independent measurement.

Some authors explicitly posit that the deviation from an exact validity of the OFCE at each pixel position is i.i.d. Gaussian, for example [Bouthemy & Francois 93]. An analogous remark is made by [Simoncelli et al. 91]. Similarly, [Chou & Chen 93] point out that noise could be taken into account by associating their version of the OFCE with a suitably chosen noise term. [Bouthemy & Santillana Rivero 87] postulated that the difference between a constant optical flow for a region and a local estimate, projected onto the local gradient direction, is i.i.d. Gaussian. [De Micheli et al. 93] pointed out that in case the Hessian is well conditioned, the technique to estimate optical flow from second order spatial derivatives of the gray value distribution 'can be computed almost independently at any pixel position' - if one neglects the correlation between adjacent estimates introduced by a smoothing step in their approach.

In his study of uncertainty in Low-Level Vision, [Szeliski 89], [Szeliski 90] does not treat the influence of uncertainties of the individual gray values on the uncertainty of the resulting optical flow estimates. His approach clearly shows that i.i.d. Gaussian noise is assumed for each estimate of the gradient at a location x, but the interrelationship between the various gray values contributing to gradient estimates at adjacent pixel positions is not treated in detail.

Based on well established approaches of estimation theory, [Nagel 94] describes an estimation of optical flow vector fields which takes the dependencies between estimates of partial derivatives of gray values into account.

2   Notation

A vector in the spatio-temporal domain of image plane location (x, y) at time t

is denoted by a bold face character, i.e. $\boldsymbol{x} = (x, y, t)^T = (x_1, x_2, x_3)^T$ where the latter notation is used if a coordinate should be referenced by a running index.

It is assumed that the irradiance distribution $g(x, y, t)$ impinging at the image plane location (x, y) at time t is transduced into a gray value $g_{observed}(x, y, t)$. The continuum $\boldsymbol{x} = (x, y, t)^T$ is sampled at grid position $\boldsymbol{x}_{k_{sample}} = (x_{k_{sample}}, y_{k_{sample}}, t_{k_{sample}})^T$ with $n_{sample} = n_{x_{sample}} \times n_{y_{sample}} \times n_{t_{sample}}$ and $k_{sample} \in \{1, ..., n_{sample}\}$. Let $g(\boldsymbol{x}_{k_{sample}})$ denote the undistorted irradiance value at the raster position $\boldsymbol{x}_{k_{sample}}$. The sensing process is assumed to distort the incoming signal by noise $\delta g(\boldsymbol{x}_{k_{sample}})$ which is taken to be independently identically distributed with zero mean and variance σ_g^2, thus

$$g_{observed}(\boldsymbol{x}_{k_{sample}}) = g(\boldsymbol{x}_{k_{sample}}) + \delta g(\boldsymbol{x}_{k_{sample}}) \qquad . \qquad (1)$$

The pixel position at the center of the sampling area is indicated by the position vector $\boldsymbol{x}_{0_{test}} = (x_{0_{test}}, y_{0_{test}}, t_{0_{test}})^T$ with $t_{0_{test}} = t_0$. We select a subset from the digitized image around location $\boldsymbol{x}_{0_{test}}$ in order to estimate the optical flow vector. This subset is denoted as the test area around $\boldsymbol{x}_{0_{test}}$ and comprises - for example - a cube of pixels around the central pixel $\boldsymbol{x}_{0_{test}}$ in the image plane at time t_0. The other pixel positions are serialized in raster scan order starting at the northwest position of $\boldsymbol{x}_{0_{test}}$ - but in the preceding frame - with $j_{test} = 1, ..., n_{test} - 1$, skipping $\boldsymbol{x}_{0_{test}}$ since this center pixel of the test area is taken to be the first in this serialization.

It is postulated that the structure of the impinging irradiance distribution is such that the Optical Flow Constraint Equation (OFCE) [Horn 86] is satisfied at location $\boldsymbol{x}_{test}$. Although other constraint equations - see, e.g., [Negahdaripour & Yu 93] - could be introduced, the emphasis of this study can be demonstrated based on the well-known OFCE. We thus have

$$u_1(\boldsymbol{x}_{test}) \left.\frac{\partial g(\boldsymbol{x})}{\partial x}\right|_{\boldsymbol{x} = \boldsymbol{x}_{test}} + u_2(\boldsymbol{x}_{test}) \left.\frac{\partial g(\boldsymbol{x})}{\partial y}\right|_{\boldsymbol{x} = \boldsymbol{x}_{test}} + \left.\frac{\partial g(\boldsymbol{x})}{\partial t}\right|_{\boldsymbol{x} = \boldsymbol{x}_{test}} = 0 \ . \ (2)$$

Moreover, it is assumed that the optical flow vector $\mathbf{u}(\boldsymbol{x})$ varies only linearly within the test area, i.e.

$$\begin{pmatrix} u_1(\boldsymbol{x}_{test}) \\ u_2(\boldsymbol{x}_{test}) \end{pmatrix} = \begin{pmatrix} u_1(\boldsymbol{x}_{0_{test}}) \\ u_2(\boldsymbol{x}_{0_{test}}) \end{pmatrix}$$

$$+ \begin{pmatrix} \left.\frac{\partial u_1(\boldsymbol{x})}{\partial x}\right|_{\boldsymbol{x} = \boldsymbol{x}_{0_{test}}} & \left.\frac{\partial u_1(\boldsymbol{x})}{\partial y}\right|_{\boldsymbol{x} = \boldsymbol{x}_{0_{test}}} & \left.\frac{\partial u_1(\boldsymbol{x})}{\partial t}\right|_{\boldsymbol{x} = \boldsymbol{x}_{0_{test}}} \\ \left.\frac{\partial u_2(\boldsymbol{x})}{\partial x}\right|_{\boldsymbol{x} = \boldsymbol{x}_{0_{test}}} & \left.\frac{\partial u_2(\boldsymbol{x})}{\partial y}\right|_{\boldsymbol{x} = \boldsymbol{x}_{0_{test}}} & \left.\frac{\partial u_2(\boldsymbol{x})}{\partial t}\right|_{\boldsymbol{x} = \boldsymbol{x}_{0_{test}}} \end{pmatrix} \cdot (\boldsymbol{x}_{test} - \boldsymbol{x}_{0_{test}})$$

or − with the abbreviated notation $(u_1(\boldsymbol{x}_{0_{test}}), u_2(\boldsymbol{x}_{0_{test}}))^T = (u_1, u_2)^T$ −

$$\begin{pmatrix} u_1(\boldsymbol{x}_{test}) \\ u_2(\boldsymbol{x}_{test}) \end{pmatrix} = \begin{pmatrix} u_1 \\ u_2 \end{pmatrix} + \begin{pmatrix} u_{1x} & u_{1y} & u_{1t} \\ u_{2x} & u_{2y} & u_{2t} \end{pmatrix} \cdot (\boldsymbol{x}_{test} - \boldsymbol{x}_{0_{test}}) \qquad . \qquad (3)$$

The partial derivatives of $g(x)$ with respect to x, y, and t are computed by discrete convolution of $g(x_{k_{sample}})$ with discretized versions of the corresponding partial derivatives of a trivariate spatiotemporal Gaussian distribution

$$w(x) = \frac{1}{(2\pi)^{\frac{3}{2}}\sqrt{|\Sigma_w|}} \exp^{-\frac{1}{2}x^T \Sigma_w^{-1} x} \quad , \tag{4}$$

$$\left. \frac{\partial g(x)}{\partial x_i} \right|_{x = x_{test}} = \iiint d\xi \cdot \frac{\partial w(\xi)}{\partial \xi_i} g(x_{test} - \xi) = \iiint d\xi \cdot \left. \frac{\partial w(x - \xi)}{\partial x_i} \right|_{x = x_{test}} g(\xi) \ . \tag{5}$$

The samples of $\left. \frac{\partial w(x-\xi)}{\partial x_i} \right|_{x = x_{test}}$ are arranged into column vectors

$$\mathbf{w}_i(x_{test}) = \left(\left. \frac{\partial w(x - x_{k_{sample}})}{\partial x_i} \right|_{x = x_{test}} \right) = \left(w_{i k_{sample}}(x_{test}) \right) \tag{6}$$

where $i = 1, 2, 3$ corresponds to x, y, t, respectively, and $k_{sample} = 1, ..., n_{sample}$. The convolution can then be written as the scalar product

$$\left. \frac{\partial g(x)}{\partial x_i} \right|_{x = x_{test}} = \mathbf{w}_i(x_{test})^T \mathbf{g} = \sum_{k_{sample}=1}^{n_{sample}} w_{i k_{sample}}(x_{test}) \cdot g_{k_{sample}}, \ i = 1, 2, 3 \ . \tag{7}$$

Since we shall have to study the optical flow vector $(u_1(x_{test}), u_2(x_{test}))^T$ as some function of all n_{test} pixel positions x_{test} in the test area, it will be convenient to index these positions and to write

$$\mathbf{w}_i(x_{j_{test}}) = \mathbf{w}_{i j_{test}} = \left(w_{i k_{sample}}(x_{j_{test}}) \right) = \left(w_{i j_{test} k_{sample}} \right)$$

$$i = 1, 2, 3; \ j_{test} = 0, 1, ..., n_{test} - 1; \ k_{sample} = 1, 2, ..., n_{sample}. \tag{8}$$

3 Estimation Problem and Solution Approach

We may now write the OFCEs as a set of n_{test} equations

$$u_{1 j_{test}}(\mathbf{w}_{1 j_{test}}^T \mathbf{g}) + u_{2 j_{test}}(\mathbf{w}_{2 j_{test}}^T \mathbf{g}) + (\mathbf{w}_{3 j_{test}}^T \mathbf{g}) = 0 \qquad \text{or}$$

$$(u_{1 j_{test}} \mathbf{w}_{1 j_{test}} + u_{2 j_{test}} \mathbf{w}_{2 j_{test}} + \mathbf{w}_{3 j_{test}})^T \mathbf{g} = 0, \ j_{test} = 0, ..., n_{test} - 1. \tag{9}$$

This formulation exhibits the linear dependence of the n_{test} OFCEs on the set of all samples from the irradiance field within the sampling area. It will be advantageous to consider this set of n_{test} OFCEs as a column vector with n_{test} components, where each component depends on the gray values $\mathbf{g}$ and on the set of $n_{parameter} = 8$ parameters written as components of

$$\mathbf{u} = (u_1, u_{1x}, u_{1y}, u_{1t}, u_2, u_{2x}, u_{2y}, u_{2t})^T \qquad . \tag{10}$$

We then have for each component $c_{j_{test}}(\mathbf{g}, \mathbf{u})$ of this column vector

$$c_{j_{test}}(\mathbf{g}, \mathbf{u}) = \left\{ \left[u_1 + \begin{pmatrix} u_{1x} \\ u_{1y} \\ u_{1t} \end{pmatrix}^T (\boldsymbol{x}_{j_{test}} - \boldsymbol{x}_{0_{test}}) \right] \mathbf{w}_{1j_{test}} + \right. \tag{11}$$

$$\left. \left[u_2 + \begin{pmatrix} u_{2x} \\ u_{2y} \\ u_{2t} \end{pmatrix}^T (\boldsymbol{x}_{j_{test}} - \boldsymbol{x}_{0_{test}}) \right] \mathbf{w}_{2j_{test}} + \mathbf{w}_{3j_{test}} \right\}^T \mathbf{g} = 0,$$

$$j_{test} = 0, 1, 2, ..., n_{test} - 1 \ .$$

Since by assumption - see equ. (1) - we can write $\mathbf{g}_{observed} = \mathbf{g} + \delta\mathbf{g}$ where the error vector $\delta\mathbf{g}$ is assumed to be distributed according to

$$p(\delta\mathbf{g}) = \frac{1}{(2\pi\sigma_g^2)^{n_{sample}/2}} \exp^{-\frac{1}{2}\delta\mathbf{g}^T \Sigma_g^{-1}\delta\mathbf{g}} \tag{12}$$

with - $I_{n\times n}$ denoting the $n \times n$ unity matrix -

$$\Sigma_g = \sigma_g^2 \cdot I_{n_{sample}\times n_{sample}}. \tag{13}$$

We are now in a position to precisely formulate the estimation problem: given the assumptions introduced above, determine the estimate $\hat{\mathbf{u}}$ for the parameter vector $\mathbf{u}$ which maximizes the joint probability to observe $\delta\mathbf{g}$, subject to the constraints $c_{j_{test}}(\mathbf{g}, \mathbf{u}) = 0$ for $j_{test} = 0, 1, ...n_{test-1}$. This is equivalent to minimizing

$$\delta\mathbf{g}^T \Sigma_g^{-1}\delta\mathbf{g} + 2\boldsymbol{\lambda}^T \left(c_{j_{test}}(\mathbf{g}, \mathbf{u}) \right) \implies \text{minimum} \tag{14}$$

by suitable choices of $\boldsymbol{\lambda} = (\lambda_0, \lambda_1, ..., \lambda_{n_{test}-1})^T$ and of the components of $\mathbf{u}$. This is a non-linear constraint problem which is solved by an iterative approach - see [Nagel 94]. As usual, it is assumed that all higher than first order terms in the constraint equations can be neglected, i.e.

$$c_{j_{test}}(\mathbf{g}, \mathbf{u}) = c_{j_{test}} \left(\mathbf{g}_{(k)} + \Delta_{(k)}\mathbf{g} , \mathbf{u}_{(k)} + \Delta_{(k)}\mathbf{u} \right) \tag{15}$$

$$= c_{j_{test}}(\mathbf{g}_{(k)}, \mathbf{u}_{(k)}) + \left(\left. \frac{\partial c_{j_{test}}}{\partial \mathbf{g}} \right|_{\mathbf{g}_{(k)}, \mathbf{u}_{(k)}} \cdot \Delta_{(k)}\mathbf{g} \right)$$

$$+ \left(\left. \frac{\partial c_{j_{test}}}{\partial \mathbf{u}} \right|_{\mathbf{g}_{(k)}, \mathbf{u}_{(k)}} \cdot \Delta_{(k)}\mathbf{u} \right) = 0$$

where (k) denotes an iteration index, $k = 0, 1, ...$, and $\Delta_{(k)}\mathbf{g}$ as well as $\Delta_{(k)}\mathbf{u}$ are assumed to be small corrections so that higher than first powers of the components of $\Delta_{(k)}\mathbf{g}$ and $\Delta_{(k)}\mathbf{u}$ can be neglected.

It is further assumed that a start estimate $\hat{\mathbf{u}}_{(0)}$ for $\mathbf{u}$ is available and that the observed gray values $\mathbf{g}_{observed}$ may serve as start values for the undistorted gray values $\mathbf{g}$ to be determined during the iterative estimation procedure, i.e. $\mathbf{g}_{(0)} = \mathbf{g}_{observed}$. In order to simplify the notation, the iteration index (k) will be suppressed in subsequent expressions unless it is explicitly manipulated. The following abbreviations are introduced :

$$\mathbf{c} = \left(c_{j_{test}}(\mathbf{g}_{(k)}, \mathbf{u}_{(k)}) \right) , \text{ a } n_{test} \times 1 \qquad \text{vector}, \qquad (16a)$$

$$C_g = \left(\frac{\partial c_{j_{test}}}{\partial \mathbf{g}} \bigg|_{\mathbf{g}_{(k)}, \mathbf{u}_{(k)}} \right) , \text{ a } n_{test} \times n_{sample} \quad \text{matrix}, \qquad (16b)$$

$$C_u = \left(\frac{\partial c_{j_{test}}}{\partial \mathbf{u}} \bigg|_{\mathbf{g}_{(k)}, \mathbf{u}_{(k)}} \right) , \text{ a } n_{test} \times n_{parameter} \text{ matrix} . \qquad (16c)$$

The minimization problem can now be rewritten as:

$$\Delta \mathbf{g}^T \Sigma_g^{-1} \Delta \mathbf{g} + 2\lambda^T (\mathbf{c} + C_g \Delta \mathbf{g} + C_u \Delta \mathbf{u}) \implies \text{minimum} . \qquad (17)$$

If we define

$$\Sigma_u = \left(C_u^T \left(C_g \Sigma_g C_g^T \right)^{-1} C_u \right)^{-1} , \qquad (18)$$

the solution to this constrained minimization problem is given in [Nagel 94] :

$$\Delta \hat{\mathbf{g}} = -\Sigma_g C_g^T \left(C_g \Sigma_g C_g^T \right)^{-1} \left[I - C_u \Sigma_u C_u^T \left(C_g \Sigma_g C_g^T \right)^{-1} \right] \mathbf{c} , \qquad (19)$$

$$\Delta \hat{\mathbf{u}} = -\Sigma_u C_u^T \left(C_g \Sigma_g C_g^T \right)^{-1} \mathbf{c} , \qquad (20)$$

$$\hat{\lambda} = \left(C_g \Sigma_g C_g^T \right)^{-1} \left[I - C_u \Sigma_u C_u^T \left(C_g \Sigma_g C_g^T \right)^{-1} \right] \mathbf{c} . \qquad (21)$$

We thus have

$$\hat{\mathbf{g}}_{(k+1)} = \hat{\mathbf{g}}_{(k)} + \Delta \hat{\mathbf{g}}_{(k)} \qquad \text{for } k = 0, 1, \dots \qquad (22)$$

with $\mathbf{g}_{(0)} = \mathbf{g}_{observed}$, $\Delta \hat{\mathbf{g}}_{(0)} = 0$,

$$\hat{\mathbf{u}}_{(k+1)} = \hat{\mathbf{u}}_{(k)} + \Delta \hat{\mathbf{u}}_{(k)} \qquad \text{for } k = 0, 1, \dots \qquad (23)$$

with $\Delta \hat{\mathbf{u}}_{(0)} = 0$, and $\hat{\mathbf{u}}_{(0)} = -(G^T G)^{-1} G^T \mathbf{g}_t$. The matrix G is built from partial spatial derivatives of the grayvalues - see [Nagel 94]. The iteration will be stopped if

$$\|\Delta \hat{\mathbf{u}}_{(k+1)} - \Delta \hat{\mathbf{u}}_{(k)}\| < \text{ iteration threshold} . \qquad (24)$$

As is well known, $\Delta \hat{\mathbf{g}}^T \Sigma_g^{-1} \Delta \hat{\mathbf{g}}$ follows a χ^2-distribution with $(n_{test} - n_{parameter})$ degrees of freedom.

If we possess an estimate of σ_g^2, for example from measurements, we can compute

$$\Delta\hat{g}^T \Sigma_g^{-1} \Delta\hat{g} = \sigma_g^{-2} \Delta\hat{g}^T \Delta\hat{g} \tag{25}$$

and test whether this result is compatible with the assumptions: if

$$\sigma_g^{-2} \Delta\hat{g}^T \Delta\hat{g} > \chi^2(n_{test} - n_{parameter}; 1 - \alpha) , \tag{26}$$

then the estimate $\hat{u}$ is rejected, the estimated error being incompatible at a confidence level of $1 - \alpha$ with the assumptions made.

As can be seen from equ. 20, the inverse of Σ_u - i.e. $C_u^T (C_g \Sigma_g C_g^T)^{-1} C_u$ - has to have sufficiently large eigenvalues in order to ensure that it can be inverted without numerical problems. We thus may require that the smallest eigenvalue of Σ_u^{-1} does exceed a threshold.

We are now able to detect algorithmically not only instability due to insufficient gray value variations. In addition, we may use equ. (26) in order to perform a test on inappropriately large variations of the gray value distribution which will result in an excessively high value for $\sigma_g^{-2} \Delta\hat{g}^T \Delta\hat{g}$ and thus can be detected with a given confidence $1 - \alpha$.

As a result of this analysis, we thus have tests for both situations, inappropriately small as well as inappropriately large variations of the gray value distribution within the test area ! These tests can, of course, be easily extended for larger and less regular areas than discussed so far.

4   Results

Quantitative experiments with the approach outlined in the preceding section have been performed with image frames from a sequence recorded by a camera on the moving arm of a calibrated robot - see Figure 1 [Otte & Nagel 94].

Since the χ^2-distribution requires the knowledge of the variance of the original measurements, a subseries of 29 image frames has been recorded at a fixed position of the robot hand with the illumination kept stationary, yielding 3.6 as the average gray value variance. Optical flow vectors estimated according to the

Fig. 1. Three frames from a sequence of non-interlaced images. The video camera translates into the scene. In addition, the white marble parallelepiped is moving to the left with respect to the rest of the scene.

approach of [Nagel 94] outlined in the preceding section in an image area where we do not expect discontinuities of the optical flow field do not differ significantly from those obtained according to a version of the approach of [Campani & Verri 92] extended by the inclusion of temporal derivatives of the optical flow. Differences are significant only at those locations where the estimation has been suppressed in the approach of [Nagel 94] due to insufficient structure in the local gray value variation.

It turned out, however, that in image areas with sufficient structure to determine all unknown components of the vector $\mathbf{u}$, the estimated gray value variances are greater than expected. These image areas are selected by requiring that the smallest singular value exceeds 0.3 as a threshold. If we plot the histogram of $\Delta \hat{\mathbf{g}}^T \Delta \hat{\mathbf{g}} / (4.2)^2$ instead of $\sigma_g^{-2} \Delta \hat{\mathbf{g}}^T \Delta \hat{\mathbf{g}}$ with $\sigma_g^2 = (1.902)^2$, we observe acceptable compatibility with a χ^2-distribution for 3 degrees of freedom. The standard deviation of the gray values had to be increased, however, by a factor of roughly 2.3 compared to the measured standard deviation in order to shift the maximum of the histogram to the expected position. This observation could be taken as a hint that the OFCE imposes constraints onto the recorded spatiotemporal data which are not quite compatible with the true variations. It should not come as a surprise that these constraints make themselves felt more strongly in image areas with sufficient spatiotemporal variation to facilitate the estimation of all components of the unknown vector $\mathbf{u}$ than in image areas with only small variations.

Significant differences in the histogram of $\sigma_g^{-2} \Delta \hat{\mathbf{g}}^T \Delta \hat{\mathbf{g}}$ can be observed if we compare one obtained from image areas where we do not expect discontinuities of the optical flow and a histogram computed for an image area in which discontinuities of the optical flow field occur. The tail of $\sigma_g^{-2} \Delta \hat{\mathbf{g}}^T \Delta \hat{\mathbf{g}}$ extends to much larger values in the latter case. A threshold applied to such χ^2-values appears as a suitable local means to discriminate discontinuities in the optical flow field from image areas with a smooth variation of the optical flow field. This hypothesis is well supported by the results shown in Figure 2. Image locations with large values of $\sigma_g^{-2} \Delta \hat{\mathbf{g}}^T \Delta \hat{\mathbf{g}}$ clearly cluster along the expected lines of discontinuity - in this case caused by both depth discontinuities and, in addition, by the movement of the white marble block relative to the scene background which itself moves relative to the camera due to the camera motion on the robot arm.

Figure 3 illustrates how moving object contours can be extracted in real world image sequences without depending on a-priori knowledge about a stationary camera. Significant contour segments of the moving bus can be detected solely by the requirement that χ^2 exceeds a threshold, in this case of 48. For a gray value standard deviation of $\sigma_g = 1.902$, the χ^2-threshold at the 99% confidence level is 11.37. The estimate $\sigma_g = 1.902$ for the standard deviation of the observed gray values has been obtained by recording with a CCD-camera whereas the image sequence 'Ettlinger-Tor-Platz' has been recorded with an older tube TV-camera. We thus expect that analogous noise measurements for this latter camera would yield larger values than those obtained with the CCD-camera under controlled laboratory conditions. This would allow to lower the threshold for χ^2 in the 'Ettlinger-Tor-Platz' image sequence from 48 to some more reasonable value without serious deterioration of the detection ability.

5 Conclusion

Experimental evidence has been presented for the hypothesis that taking the stochastic aspects of gray value variation into account for the estimation of an optical flow field facilitates the segmentation of such a field based solely on a χ^2-test - even if the background should change due to camera motion. The pixel positions at which such a test will fail - and thus generate a cue towards the presence of a discontinuity in the estimated optical flow field - cluster around discontinuities. The width of such clusters depends on the size of the masks which are used to estimate the spatiotemporal derivatives of the gray value distribution. In the cases presented here, these masks had a width of seven pixels. It can be seen in the last Figure that the χ^2-test tends to emphasize the contour lines of the bus. Obviously, further experiments are required in order to consolidate the preliminary conclusions presented in this contribution.

6 Acknowledgements

Partial support of these investigations by the ESPRIT Basic Research Action project INSIGHT II as well as by the Deutsche Forschungsgemeinschaft (DFG) in the framework of the Sonderforschungsbereich 'Künstliche Intelligenz - Wissensbasierte Systeme' are gratefully acknowledged.

References

[Barron et al. 92] Barron, J.L., Fleet, D.J., Beauchemin, S.S., and Burkitt, T.A.: Performance of Optical Flow Techniques. In *Proc. IEEE Conference on Computer Vision and Pattern Recognition CVPR '92*, 15-18 June 1992, Champaign, IL, pp. 236-242. See, too, Int. Journal of Computer Vision 12:1 (1994) 43-77.

[Bouthemy & Santillana Rivero 87] Bouthemy, P., and Santillana Rivero, J.: A Hierarchical Likelihood Approach for Region Segmentation According to Motion-Based Criteria. In *Proc. First Intern. Conference on Computer Vision ICCV '87*, London, UK, 8-11 June 1987, pp. 463-467.

[Bouthemy & Francois 93] Bouthemy, P., and Francois, E.: Motion Segmentation and Qualitative Scene Analysis from an Image Sequence. Int. Journal of Computer Vision 10:2 (1993) 157-182

[Burt et al. 91] Burt, P.J., Hingorani, R., and Kolczynski, R.: Mechanisms for Isolation Component Patterns in the Sequential Analysis of Multiple Motion. In *Proc. IEEE Workshop on Visual Motion*, Princeton, NJ, 7-9 October 1991, pp. 187-193.

[Campani & Verri 92] Campani, M., and Verri, A.: Motion Analysis from First Order Properties of Optical Flow. CVGIP: Image Understanding 56:1 (1992) 90-107.

[Chou & Chen 93] Chou, W.-S., and Chen, Y.-C.: Estimation of the Velocity Field of Two-Dimensional Deformable Motion. Pattern Recognition 26:2 (1993) 351-364.

[De Micheli et al. 93] De Micheli, E., Torre, V., and Uras, S.: The Accuracy of the Computation of Optical Flow and of the Recovery of Motion Parameters. IEEE Transactions on Pattern Analysis and Machine Intelligence PAMI-15:5 (1993) 434-447.

[Etoh & Shirai 93] Etoh, M., and Shirai, Y.: Segmentation and 2D Motion Estimation by Region Fragments. In *Proc. Fourth Intern. Conference on Computer Vision ICCV '93*, 11-14 May 1993, Berlin, Germany, pp. 192-199.

[Fleet 92] Fleet, D.J.: Measurement of Image Velocity. Kluwer Academic Publishers: Boston, MA; London, UK; Dordrecht, NL, 1992

[Gu et al. 93] H. Gu, M. Asada, and Y. Shirai: The Optimal Partition of Moving Edge Segments. In *Proc. IEEE Conference on Computer Vision and Pattern Recognition CVPR '93*, 15-17 June 1993, New York City, NY, pp. 367-372.

[Horn 86] Horn, B.K.P.: Robot Vision. The MIT Press: Cambridge, MA, 1986

[Irani et al. 92] Irani, M., Rousso, B., and Peleg, S.: Detecting and Tracking Multiple Moving Objects Using Temporal Integration. In *Proc. Second European Conference on Computer Vision ECCV '92*, Santa Margherita Ligure, Italy, 18-23 May 1992, Lecture Notes in Computer Science 588, G. Sandini (ed.), Springer-Verlag: Berlin Heidelberg New York and others, pp. 282-287.

[Kollnig et al. 94] H. Kollnig, H.-H. Nagel, and M. Otte: Association of Motion Verbs with Vehicle Movements Extracted from Dense Optical Flow Fields. Proc. ECCV '94, Stockholm / Sweden, 2-6 May 1994.

[Letang et al. 93] Letang, J.M., Rebuffel, V., and Bouthemy, P.: Motion Detection Robust to Perturbations: a Statistical Regularization and Temporal Integration Framework. In *Proc. Fourth Intern. Conference on Computer Vision ICCV '93*, 11-14 May 1993, Berlin, Germany, pp. 21-30.

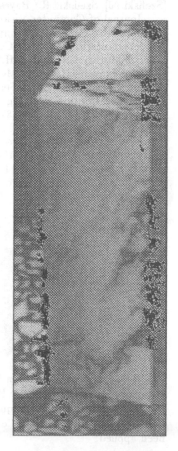

Fig. 2. A black dot is superimposed on the original image at all locations where $\sigma_g^{-2} \Delta\hat{g}^{\,T} \Delta\hat{g}$ exceeds a threshold of 100 for $\sigma_g^2 = 3.6$. This demonstrates the possibility to detect discontinuities in optical flow fields by local methods, here the boundaries of the marbled epiped which moves with respect to the rest of the field of view recorded by a camera moving itself. Obviously, the local gray value variation must be significant enough to facilitate estimation of an optical flow vector by a local approach.

315

[Nagel 92] Nagel, H.-H.: Direct Estimation of Optical Flow and of Its Derivatives. In *Artificial and Biological Vision Systems*, G. Orban and H.-H. Nagel (eds.). Springer-Verlag: Berlin Heidelberg New York and others, 1992, pp. 193-224.

[Nagel 94] Nagel, H.-H.: Optical Flow Estimation and the Interaction Between Measurement Errors at Adjacent Pixel Positions. Int. Journal of Computer Vision, to appear 1994.

[Negahdaripour & Lee 92] Negahdaripour, S., and Lee, S.: Motion Recovery from Image Sequences Using Only First Order Optical Flow Information. Int. Journal of Computer Vision 9:3 (1992) 163-184.

[Negahdaripour & Yu 93] Negahdaripour, S., and Yu, C.-H.: A Generalized Brightness Change Model for Computing Optical Flow. In *Proc. Fourth Intern. Conference on Computer Vision ICCV '93*, 11-14 May 1993, Berlin, Germany, pp. 2-11.

[Otte & Nagel 94] M. Otte and H.-H. Nagel: Optical Flow Estimation: Advances and Comparisons. Proc. ECCV '94, Stockholm / Sweden, 2-6 May 1994.

[Simoncelli et al. 91] Simoncelli, E.P., Adelson, E.H., and Heeger, D.J.: Probability Distributions of Optical Flow. In *Proc. IEEE Conference on Computer Vision and Pattern Recognition*, Lahaina, Maui, Hawaii, 3-6 June 1991, pp. 310-315.

[Spoerri & Ullman 87] Spoerri, A., and Ullman, S.: The Early Detection of Motion Boundaries. In *Proc. First Intern. Conference on Computer Vision ICCV '87*, London, UK, 8-11 June 1987, pp. 209-218.

[Szeliski 89] Szeliski, R.: Bayesian Modeling of Uncertainty in Low-level Vision. Kluwer Academic Publishers: Boston, MA; Dordrecht, NL; London, UK, 1989

[Szeliski 90] Szeliski, R.: Bayesian Modeling of Uncertainty in Low-Level Vision. Int. Journal of Computer Vision 5:3 (1990) 271-301.

[Thompson & Pong 90] Thompson, W.B., and Pong, T.-C.: Detecting Moving Objects. Intern. Journal of Computer Vision 4:1 (1990) 39-57.

[Torr & Murray 92] Torr, P.H.S., and Murray, D.W.: Statistical Detection of Independent Movement from a Moving Camera. In *Proc. British Machine Vision Conference*, Leeds, UK, 22-24 Sept. 1992, D. Hogg and R. Boyle (eds.), Springer-Verlag: London Berlin Heidelberg and others, pp. 79-88. See, too, Image and Vision Computing 11:4 (1993) 180-187.

[Wang & Adelson 93] Wang, J.Y.A., and Adelson, E.H.: Layered Representation for Motion Analysis. In *Proc. IEEE Conference on Computer Vision and Pattern Recognition CVPR '93*, 15-17 June 1993, New York City, NY, pp. 361-366.

[Weber & Malik 93] Weber, J., and Malik, J.: Robust Computation of Optical Flow in a Multiscale Differential Framework. In *Proc. Fourth Intern. Conference on Computer Vision ICCV '93*, 11-14 May 1993, Berlin, Germany, pp. 12-20.

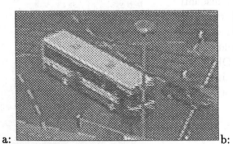 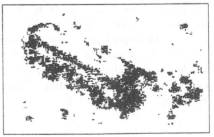

a: b:

Fig. 3. (a) Enlarged subregion from a sequence recorded at an intersection in downtown Karlsruhe, the 'Ettlinger-Tor-Platz'. (b) Moving contour segments are separated from the background solely by requiring that χ^2 exceeds a threshold of 48; no additional thresholds for the magnitude of the optical flow or for the smallest singular value have been applied.

Segmentation of moving objects by robust motion parameter estimation over multiple frames *

S. Ayer, P. Schroeter and J. Bigün

Swiss Federal Institute of Technology, Signal Processing Laboratory
CH-1015 Lausanne, Switzerland

Abstract. A method for detecting and segmenting accurately moving objects in monocular image sequences is proposed. It consists of two modules, namely a motion estimation and a motion segmentation module. The motion estimation problem is formulated as a time varying motion parameter estimation over multiple frames. Robust regression techniques are used to estimate these parameters. The motion parameters for the different moving objects are obtained by successive estimations on regions for which the previously estimated motion parameters are not valid. The segmentation module combines all motion parameters and the gray level information in order to obtain the motion boundaries and to improve them by using time integration. Experimental results on real image sequences with static or moving camera in the presence of multiple moving objects are reported.

1 Introduction

Detecting and segmenting moving objects in image sequences have been given a large attention in the research community. Most of the early research has been concentrated on the estimation of optical flow computed between image pairs. Such a flow field assigns to each pixel of one image a translational vector containing local motion information. The classical pixelwise classification based on the optical flow can be employed to detect multiple motions (see for example [1] and [11]). However, these methods are very sensitive to the quality of the optical flow, and as small spatial and temporal regions do not always carry sufficient motion information, the optical flow computation can be very inaccurate. Another approach is the use of parametric motion estimators, which describe the motion over a larger spatial region in terms of a parametric model. In this case, a model is used in order to constrain the flow field computation, so that the flow field does not vary in an uncontrolled fashion. However, when the region of analysis contains multiple moving objects, one is compelled to use an estimation method that can recover simultaneously the model parameters and the motion discontinuities. To achieve this goal, several ideas have been proposed, among

---

* This work has been supported by Thomson-CSF, Rennes,France

which we can discriminate those based on line process (discontinuities detection) [5] and outlier detection [9, 7].

In this paper, we propose a new method for time-varying motion analysis and segmentation which uses both a large spatial region and a large temporal support. The motion estimation problem is formulated as one of time-varying parameter estimation over multiple frames. A robust regression technique [12] is used to estimate the motion parameters. As these techniques are resistant to a given percentage of outliers in the data, they allow us to overcome the problem of multiple moving objects inside the region of analysis. Such techniques have recently been used in computer vision [10], e.g. motion parameter estimation and segmentation in a pair of images [3, 6, 7], detection of moving objects [16].

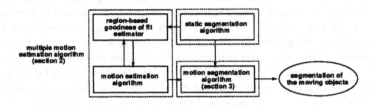

Fig. 1. Block diagram of the system

The different blocks of the method are shown in Fig. 1. Note that, in this paper, we assume that the number of moving objects does not change in the image sequence. The motion estimation algorithm is first applied to an entire region of the image (here the whole image). By means of a segmentation algorithm [13], we then obtain subregions with similar gray level and determine in which of these regions the estimated parameters are not valid. Further motion estimations are applied to these regions. Thus, by successive application of the robust motion estimation algorithm, the number of regions for which the previously estimated motion parameters could not explain the motion well is reduced to zero. Then, the motion segmentation algorithm combines the motion parameters coming from the multiple estimations and the gray level information in order to obtain the motion boundaries and to improve them by using time integration. The pixels within a statically segmented subregion are constrained to follow the same motion allowing us to classify correctly pixels with low gradient information.

Experimental results indicate that the proposed scheme is robust to the presence of different moving objects and is also general enough to deal with scenes with moving or static cameras, with objects close to or far from the camera, and in a stationary or non-stationary environment.

The time-varying robust motion estimation algorithm is presented in the next section. Section 3 describes how moving objects are segmented by using multiple frames. Finally, experimental results are reported in Sect. 4 and concluding remarks are given in Sect. 5.

2 Model-Based Time-Varying Motion Estimation

The motion estimation problem is here formulated as one of time-varying parameter estimation. In Fig. 2, we give an overview of the different basic operations which are involved in the implementation of the algorithm.

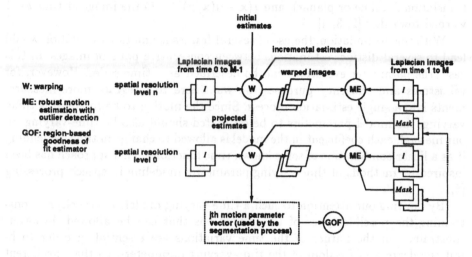

Fig. 2. General framework of the robust motion estimator

In our method, the estimation is performed in a hierarchical and iterative way. In our implementation, we use the Laplacian image pyramid as input to the algorithm. The estimation process begins at the coarsest resolution level, using zero initial estimates. An estimation step consists of two operations: the image sequence warping (using bicubic interpolation) and the estimation of the motion parameter increments. As it will be explained in Sect. 2.1 and 2.2, the incremental motion parameters are estimated by using using a robust linear regression procedure and an outlier detection technique.

Using the final time-varying motion parameter estimates (obtained at resolution level 0), a region-based goodness of fit is computed for each frame. The goal of this operation is to classify regions into two classes: the regions where the estimated parameters are valid and those where they are not. This point will be explained in more details in Sect. 2.3.

The result of the multiple motion estimation algorithm is a set of time-varying parameter vectors $p_j(t)$. As explained in Sect. 3, these vectors are used together with gray level information in order to obtain an accurate segmentation of the moving objects.

2.1 From parametric to time-varying parametric estimation

If we consider only two frames in the sequence and assume intensity constancy (i.e. the brightness of a small surface patch is not changed by motion), the problem of motion model fitting can be posed as the minimization over the region of analysis of a function of

$$I(\mathbf{x}, t) - I(\mathbf{x} - \mathbf{u}(\mathbf{x}, \mathbf{p}), t - 1), \tag{1}$$

where $\mathbf{p}$ denotes the model parameters, $\mathbf{u}(\mathbf{x}, \mathbf{p})$ the flow field in that region (e.g. translational, affine or planar), and $I(\mathbf{x} - \mathbf{u}(\mathbf{x}, \mathbf{p}), t - 1)$ the image at time $t - 1$ warped towards t [2, 3, 4].

With this formulation, the use of several frames for motion estimation would lead to several distinct estimations between consecutive pairs of images. In this case, the parameter evolutions can be described as a time series. However, for robustness and efficiency purposes, we want here to integrate more measurements into a single estimation process. Since the motion to be modeled is time-varying, the model parameters to be estimated should also be time-varying. In our method, each coefficient in the model is allowed to change in time by defining it as a linear combination of some known time functions. This approach has been inspired by methods of time-varying parametric modeling in speech processing [8].

By limiting our attention to such a time-varying model, we are clearly constraining the possible types of time variations that can be allowed. However, constraints on the nature of the time variations are essential in order to limit the degrees of freedom of the time-varying parameters, so that incoherent and noisy estimations can be avoided. A judicious choice of the basis functions can provide a good approximation of a wide variety of motion parameter time variations with only a few coefficients. In our experiments, we used the trigonometric (Fourier) functions, as well as the Legendre and Hermite polynomials. A very important point is also that this method can make use of the spatial multiresolution for determining the degree of freedom of the time-varying motion parameter estimation.

With a model of this form, the coefficients in the linear combination are to be estimated from the image sequence and the problem of motion estimation is posed as the minimization of a function of

$$I(\mathbf{x}, t_a) - I(\mathbf{x} - \mathbf{u}(\mathbf{x}, \mathbf{p}(t_a)), t_{a-1}), \qquad j = 1, \ldots, M \tag{2}$$

over the region of analysis and over $M + 1$ frames. In this formulation, $\mathbf{p}(t_a)$ denotes the motion parameter vector at time t_a, whose components are modeled as linear combinations of some known functions of time $f_k(t)$:

$$p_i(t) = \sum_{k=0}^{F-1} a_{i+Pk} \, f_k(t), \qquad i = 0, \ldots, P - 1 \tag{3}$$

where P is the number of motion parameters (e.g. translational model ($P = 2$), affine model ($P = 6$)) and F the number of time functions.

The problem of estimating the parameter vector $\mathbf{a}$ from equation (2) is non-linear, and this system of non-linear algebraic equations has no closed form solution. Consequently, one is compelled to solve the system of equations numerically in order to find an estimate of the parameter vector **a**. Suppose that an initial estimate **â** is available (in our case, it will be the parameter vector **0** at the coarsest resolution level and the projected estimates at the other levels). The problem may be linearized using **â** and the first order Taylor expansion of equation (2) leads to

$$\Delta I(\mathbf{u}(\mathbf{x},\mathbf{p}))|_{\mathbf{a}=\hat{\mathbf{a}}} = [(\nabla I(\mathbf{x}-\mathbf{u}(\mathbf{x},\mathbf{p}),t_{a-1}))^T \frac{\delta\mathbf{u}}{\delta\mathbf{p}}\frac{\delta\mathbf{p}}{\delta\mathbf{a}}]|_{\mathbf{a}=\hat{\mathbf{a}}} (\mathbf{a}-\hat{\mathbf{a}}) \quad (4)$$

where

$$\Delta I(\mathbf{u}(\mathbf{x},\mathbf{p})) = I(\mathbf{x},t_a) - I(\mathbf{x}-\mathbf{u}(\mathbf{x},\mathbf{p}(t_a)),t_{a-1}).$$

In equation (4), $\nabla\mathbf{I}(\mathbf{x}-\mathbf{u}(\mathbf{x},\mathbf{p}),t-1)$ denotes the spatial gradient vector $[\frac{\delta I}{\delta x},\frac{\delta I}{\delta y}]^T$ of the warped image, $\frac{\delta\mathbf{u}}{\delta\mathbf{p}}$ the $2 \times P$ Jacobian matrix of the vector field **u**, and $\frac{\delta\mathbf{p}}{\delta\mathbf{a}}$ the $P \times PF$ Jacobian matrix of the motion parameter vector **p**.

Equation (4) shows that, after linearization of the model, the problem of time-varying model-based motion estimation can be reformulated to one of parameter estimation. Standard or robust linear regression methods may be used to estimate the parameters $\delta\mathbf{a}$ (see Sect. 2.2).

2.2 Robust linear regression estimators

The LS estimator is known to be optimal for Gaussian noise distribution. However, more recently attention has been given to the fact that LS analysis is very sensitive to minor deviations from the Gaussian noise model and to the presence of outliers in the data. In order to reduce the impact of these negative influences, robust methods that are much less affected by outliers have been developed (e.g. LMedS and LTS [12]). In computer vision the problem of regression analysis is an important statistical tool and recently the interest for robust estimators has increased [10].

In this paper, we discuss the application of two robust estimators to the problem of time-varying motion estimation, namely the *least median of squares* (LMedS) and the *least-trimmed squares* (LTS) given by

$$\min_{\hat{\Theta}} \mathrm{median}(r_i^2) \qquad \text{and} \qquad \min_{\hat{\Theta}} \sum_{i=1}^{h} (r^2)_{i:n} \quad (5)$$

where $(r^2)_{1:n} \leq \dots \leq (r^2)_{n:n}$ are the ordered squared residuals.

In the case of motion estimation, the sensitivity of LS estimators to the presence of outliers may be exhibited by the following example. In Fig. 3, we show a 3-D plot of the translational model objective function for the TAXI sequence (see Fig. 5). In these plots, dx (not shown) and dy axes represent the two translational motion parameters (dx, dy) and the z axis represents the objective function to be minimized by the motion estimation algorithm. In this case, the minimum objective function value should be at $(dx, dy) = 0$ (zero background

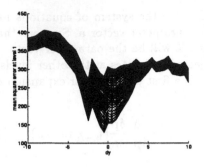
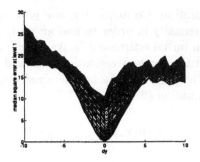

Fig. 3. Objective function plots for the TAXI sequence (translational model): (left) mean square error (right) median square error

motion). These plots exhibit the resistance of the LS and LMedS estimators to outliers, which are caused by the multiple motions present in the image sequence. The biases introduced in the LS estimates make their use difficult for outlier detection and for segmentation purposes.

2.3 Region-based goodness of fit measures

In order to detect the different moving objects present in the scene, we need to find the regions where the estimated parameters are not valid, onto which further motion estimations should be applied. For this purpose, we compute a goodness of fit measure in each region obtained from the static segmentation [13]. Note that the first computed motion is obtained generally by applying the motion estimation algorithm on the whole image.

As the robust linear regression estimators are combined with a least-squares procedure, the value minimized by the motion estimation algorithm may be expressed as

$$\gamma = (\Delta I(\mathbf{u}(\mathbf{x}, \mathbf{p})))^T \, \Delta I(\mathbf{u}(\mathbf{x}, \mathbf{p})) \tag{6}$$

which is the sum of the residuals. With the Gaussian noise assumption, this sum is the sum of the squares of MN independent scalar random variables with zero mean and unity variance (assuming that the errors are normalized), that is γ has a chi-square distribution with $n - PF$ degrees of freedom. Here, MN is the number of points in the image sequence and PF is the dimension of the parameter vector a.

Based on this, γ is a measure of the goodness of fit. This measure is computed over each statically segmented region of each original frame of the sequence and the parameters are considered as not valid if

$$\gamma > c \tag{7}$$

where the threshold c is obtained such that the probability of a $n - PF$ degree of freedom chi-square random variable exceeding it is α (here 5 %).

Once the regions have been classified as valid or not valid, connected regions are merged. In Fig. 5 (row 1, left), we show the results of this computation obtained for the TAXI sequence after the first robust motion estimation, which returns estimated parameters very close to zero. In this figure, the black regions stands for not valid regions. In order to remove tiny regions, a median filtering is applied (Fig. 5 (row 1, right)).

At this stage we need to find masks for further motion estimation. For this purpose, correspondences have to been found between the different valid regions. Due to the assumption of unchanged object configuration and to the fact that the motion estimation behaves very consistently over time, this is not a very complicated correspondence problem. Methods such that presented in [14] can be used for this purpose. The final result of the region-based goodness of fit estimator is a set of mask sequences that can be used for further motion estimations.

3 Segmentation of multiple moving objects

This section describes a method that combines motion and luminance for an accurate segmentation of multiple moving objects. An attempt in this direction was proposed in [15]. A different approach (based only on motion) consists in computing the prediction error pixelwise or in a small neighborhood and then segmenting the resulting error image [3, 9]. In our experiments, this approach worked well with sequences containing textured moving objects but failed for objects where the gradient information is low. Here, we propose to overcome this problem by constraining the pixels within a spatially segmented subregion to follow the same motion.

First, we apply a static segmentation algorithm [13] on the last frame of an image sequence in order to obtain the subregions with similar gray-level. This static segmentation is embedded in a multiresolution framework using quadtrees [17]. Multiple resolutions are very useful because at lower resolutions the noise is reduced, allowing the class-centers to be better defined, whereas higher resolutions are needed to obtain accurate borders. Here the boundary refinement step will be applied only once the motion labeling is done.

The estimates of the different motions are used to classify each subregion, thus merging the subregions with the same motion. This can be done by computing the prediction errors corresponding to the different detected motions for all the subregions, and to assign them a motion label corresponding to the minimum error. We also propose to use more frames to increase the certainty that a subregion is correctly classified. If a subregion is detected as having the same motion in successive frames then its classification certainty increases.

Figure 4 shows the block diagram of the motion segmentation algorithm. Suppose that we have a set of $M+1$ successive frames at times $t_a, a = 0, \ldots, M$. Time-varying motion parameter vectors, $\mathbf{p}_j(t_a)$ are first estimated by the multiple motion estimation algorithm (Sect. 2). The image sequence is then warped towards the last frame with the composition of all motions $C(\mathbf{p}_j(t_a), a =$

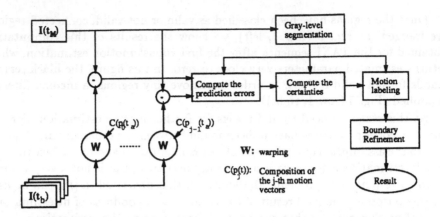

Fig. 4. Block diagram of the motion segmentation algorithm

$M - 1, \ldots, b)$, for $b = M - 1, \ldots, 0$. For example, assume that we have only translational parameters and 3 frames ($M = 2$):

$$b = 1 : C(\mathbf{p}_j(t_a), a = 1, \ldots, 1) = \mathbf{p}_j(t_1)$$
$$b = 0 : C(\mathbf{p}_j(t_a), a = 1, \ldots, 0) = \mathbf{p}_j(t_1) + \mathbf{p}_j(t_0) \qquad (8)$$

This results in $M \times N_m$ warped images where N_m is the number of detected motions.

Starting from $b = M - 1$ (until $b = 0$), the prediction errors are computed, at the coarsest level of the pyramid, by using the following robust objective function

$$e_{ij}(t_b) = \sum_{k=1}^{N_i/2} (r_{ij}^2)_{k:N_i}, \qquad j = 0, \ldots, N_m - 1, \qquad i = 0, \ldots, N_s - 1 \qquad (9)$$

where

$$r_{ij} = I(\mathbf{x}_{ik}, t_M) - I(\mathbf{x}_{ik} - \mathbf{u}(\mathbf{x}_{ik}, C(\mathbf{p}_j(t_a), a = M - 1, \ldots, b)), t_b) \qquad (10)$$

and $(r_{ij}^2)_{1:N_i} \leq \ldots \leq (r_{ij}^2)_{N_i:N_i}$. Here, I represents the original frames, N_i is the size of region S_i, $\mathbf{x}_{ik} \in S_i$, N_s the number of subregions and $\mathbf{u}(\mathbf{x}_{ik}, C(\mathbf{p}_j(t_a), a = M - 1, \ldots, b))$ is the flow field obtained with the composition of the parameter vectors. A robust objective function (like in equation (5)) is used because a small fraction of pixels of a subregion with high residuals can have a strong influence on the motion labeling and can even cause a false classification of a subregion.

The motion labeling is computed by means of a measure of classification certainty that evolves with the number of frames. For each subregion i and for each motion j, the certainty $c_{ij}(t_b)$ is obtained by computing the normalized difference between products of prediction errors:

$$c_{ij}(t_b) = \frac{Pd_2 - Pd_1}{Pd_2 + Pd_1} \qquad 0 \le j' \ne j < N_m$$

$$Pd_1 = \prod_{a=b}^{M-1} e_{ij}(t_a) \qquad\qquad Pd_2 = \prod_{a=b}^{M-1} e_{ij'}(t_a) \tag{11}$$

where $e_{ij'}(t_a)$ is the closest prediction error at time t_a (corresponding to motion j') smaller than $e_{ij}(t_a)$ if it exists, or the closest prediction error greater than $e_{ij}(t_a)$ otherwise. Note that $c_{ij}(t_b)$ may take negative values when $Pd_2 \le Pd_1$. If the motion label j corresponding to the minimum error of prediction remains the same (i.e. $e_{ij'}(t_a) > e_{ij}(t_a)$ for all t_a) then the certainty $c_{ij}(t_b)$ will tend to increase. However, if the motion labels change with time or if more than one motion is present within a subregion (i.e. $e_{ij'}(t_a) \approx e_{ij}(t_a)$), $c_{ij}(t_b)$ will be close to or smaller than zero.

After all frames have been considered (i.e. $b = 0$), the subregions can be classified according to the maximum certainty, resulting in a motion label image $L(\mathbf{x}_{ik})$ at the coarsest level of the quadtree:

$$L(\mathbf{x}_{ik}) = \arg\max_j c_{ij}(t_b = 0) \qquad 0 \le i < N_s, \quad 0 \le j < N_m, \quad 1 \le k \le N_i \tag{12}$$

The tiny subregions of $L(\mathbf{x}_{ik})$ can then be reassigned to their neighborhood. Here, we assume that a small subregion enclosed in a larger subregion must have the same motion than the larger one. Finally, the boundary refinement [13] is applied only on the boundaries corresponding to motion boundaries of $L(\mathbf{x}_{ik})$.

4 Results

The method described in the previous sections has been applied to different sequences. The first one, called the BBC sequence, shows a car moving to the left and tracked by the camera inducing a motion of the background to the right. The difficulties of this sequence are due to the fact that the car is close to the camera and that the car motion is not parallel to the image plane. For simplicity, we used here a translational model but the affine model yields, in this case, similar results. Figure 5 (row 3, right) shows the last frame of the sequence ($M = 4$) and its static segmentation (row 3, left) computed with $c = 4$ classes at the second level of the quadtree, yielding 251 subregions. In order to prevent subregions having different motions from being merged, different values of c ($c = 4, 5$ or 6 typically) can be used in the clustering algorithm, causing only slight changes in the final segmentation result.

Figure 5 (row 2) shows the evolution of the motion labeling. Black labels correspond to subregions that are classified with certainty under a threshold of 0.9. We can observe that the number of such subregions is reduced as the number of frames increases. Only tiny subregions remain unclassified after the last iteration partly because of unrecovered areas caused by the warping operation. Figure 5 (row 3) shows the final motion labeling after the reassignment of the tiny unclassified (or misclassified) subregions and boundary refinement. Accurate boundaries can be observed and it can be seen that small details like most parts of the antenna are preserved. As the shade underneath the car is moving with the same motion as the car, the segmentation at this place is correct. However, the back window of the car is misclassified because it is merged to the background by the static segmentation algorithm.

The same procedure (with the same parameters) was applied to the TAXI sequence that contains three moving cars on a static background. The final segmentation results and the superimposed boundaries can be seen in Fig. 5 (row 4). First, it can be noticed that the three cars are correctly classified and that the white taxi boundaries are accurate. On the left car, the gray level of part of the roof was merged to the background by the static segmentation. On the right, the car is passing behind a tree disturbing the motion segmentation. Results for a sequence (SAL) where only the camera is moving and where different motions are induced due to depth discontinuities is also shown in Fig. 5 (row 4).

5 Conclusion

In this paper, we presented a method that combines motion and gray level information in a set of successive frames in order to detect and segment multiple moving objects. We showed that robust regression methods allow us to estimate accurate motion parameters where the standard least squares estimation scheme fails. Unlike two-frames based motion estimation, our scheme estimates time varying motion parameters over a set of successive frames by defining them as linear combinations of a set of known time functions. This approach constrains temporally the motion parameters in order to avoid incoherent and noisy estimations. Here, we assume that the number of different moving objects does not change in the considered sequence. A strategy to detect the appearance or disappearance of moving objects still needs to be investigated. More attention should also be devoted to the automatic choice of the motion model to be used and of the degree of freedom of the time-varying parameter estimation.

The second part of the algorithm finds accurate boundaries between the moving objects by combining all the detected motions over the successive frames and the gray level information. Subregions with similar gray levels are given a motion label according to the a motion certainty that increases with the number of frames. Here, we first find the different subregions of a frame by means of a clustering algorithm which constrains the pixels of a subregion to move with the same motion. This approach allows to assign a motion label to pixels where the motion information alone is not sufficient for a correct motion labeling. However, problems might arise if a statically segmented subregion contains two or more different motions. In this case, some pixels of such a subregion will be misclassified. With robust objective functions we already reduced the risk of subregion misclassification. We are currently investigating a method that re-segments (into more classes) subregions with low motion certainty. This operation should further reduce the number of misclassified pixels.

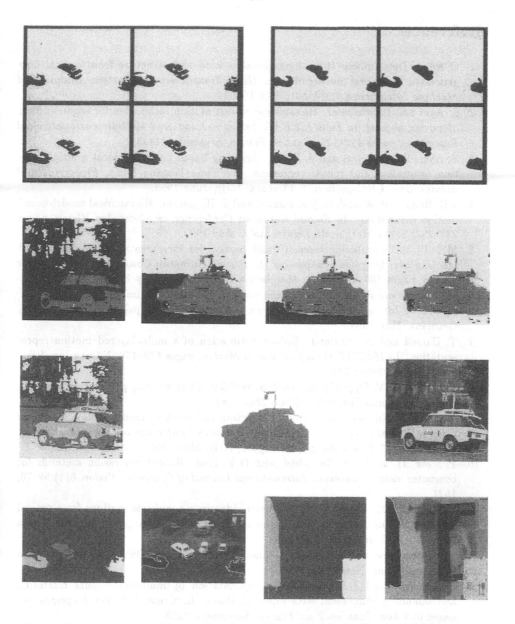

Fig. 5. (Row 1 from top) Region-based goodness of fit masks for the TAXI sequence after the first motion estimation (increasing time from left to right and from top to bottom) (Row 2) Evolution of the motion labeling by using 2, 3, 4 and 5 frames. Black labels correspond to subregions that are classified with certainty under a threshold of 0.9. (Row 3) (left) Static segmentation of the last frame (middle) Segmentation result using 5 frames after the reassignment of tiny subregions. (right) Boundaries superimposed on the fifth frame. (Row 4) (left) Segmentation result on the TAXI sequence (right) Segmentation result on the SAL sequence.

References

1. G Adiv. Determining three-dimensional motion and structure from optical flow generated by several moving objects. *IEEE Transactions on Pattern Analysis and Machine Intelligence*, 7:384–401, July 1985.
2. S. Ayer and P. Schroeter. Hierarchical robust motion estimation for segmentation of moving objects. In *Eigth IEEE Workshop on Image and Multidimensional Signal Processing*, pages 122–123, Cannes, France, September 1993.
3. S. Ayer, P. Schroeter, and J. Bigün. Tracking based on hierarchical multiple motion estimation and robust regression. In *Time-Varying Image Processing and Moving Object Recognition, 3*, Florence, Italy, June 1993.
4. J.R. Bergen, P. Anandan, K.J. Hanna, and J. Hingorani. Hierarchical model-based motion estimation. In *Second European Conference on Computer Vision*, pages 237–252, Santa Margherita Ligure, Italy, May 1992.
5. M.J. Black. Combining intensity and motion for incremental segmentation and tracking over long image sequences. In *Second European Conference on Computer Vision*, pages 485–493, Santa Margherita Ligure, Italy, May 1992.
6. M.J. Black and P. Anandan. A framework for the robust estimation of optical flow. In *Fourth International Conference on Computer Vision*, pages 231–236, Berlin, Germany, May 1993.
7. T. Darrell and A. Pentland. Robust estimation of a multi-layered motion representation. In *IEEE Workshop on Visual Motion*, pages 173–178, Nassau Inn, Princeton, NJ, October 1991.
8. M.G. Hall, A.V. Oppenheim, and A.S. Willsky. Time-varying parametric modeling of speech. *Signal Processing*, 5:267–285, 1983.
9. M. Irani, B. Rousso, and S. Peleg. Detecting and tracking multiple moving objects using temporal integration. In *Second European Conference on Computer Vision*, pages 282–287, Santa Margherita Ligure, Italy, May 1992.
10. P. Meer, D. Mintz, A. Rosenfeld, and D.Y. Kim. Robust regression methods for computer vision : A review. *International Journal of Computer Vision*, 6(1):59–70, 1991.
11. A. Rognone, M. Campani, and A. Verri. Identifying multiple motions from optical flow. In *Second European Conference on Computer Vision*, pages 258–266, Santa Margherita Ligure, Italy, May 1992.
12. P.J. Rousseeuw and A.M. Leroy. *Robust Regression and Outlier Detection*. John Wiley and Sons, New York, 1987.
13. P. Schroeter and J. Bigün. Image segmentation by multidimensional clustering and boundary refinement with oriented filters. In *Gretsi Fourteenth symposium*, pages 663–666, Juan les Pins, France, Septembre 1993.
14. S.K. Sethi and R. Jain. Finding trajectories of feature points in a monocular image sequence. *IEEE Transactions on Pattern Analysis and Machine Intelligence*, 9:56–73, January 1987.
15. W.B Thompson. Combining motion and contrast for segmentation. *IEEE Transactions on Pattern Analysis and Machine Intelligence*, 2:543–549, 1980.
16. W.B. Thompson, P. Lechleider, and E.R. Stuck. Detecting moving objects using the rigidity constraint. *IEEE Transactions on Pattern Analysis and Machine Intelligence*, 15:162–166, February 1993.
17. R. Wilson and M. Spann. *Image Segmentation and Uncertainty*. Research Studies Press Ltd., Letchworth, England, 1988.

Stochastic Motion Clustering

P H S Torr and D W Murray

Department of Engineering Science, University of Oxford
Parks Road, Oxford, OX1 3PJ, UK
Email: phst|dwm@robots.oxford.ac.uk

Abstract. This paper presents a new method for motion segmentation, the clustering together of features that belong to independently moving objects. The method exploits the fact that two views of a rigidly connected $3D$ point set are linked by the 3×3 Fundamental Matrix which contains all the information on the motion of a given set of point correspondences. The segmentation problem is transformed into one of finding a set of Fundamental Matrices which optimally describe the observed temporal correspondences, where the optimization is couched as a maximization of the *a posteriori* probability of an interpretation given the data. To reduce the search space, feasible clusters are hypothesized using robust statistical techniques, and a multiple hypothesis test performed to determine which particular combination of the many feasible clusters is most likely to represent the actual feature motions observed. This test is shown to be to computable in terms of a 0-1 integer programming method, alleviating the combinatorial computing difficulties inherent in such problems.

1 Introduction

Motion is a powerful cue for image and scene segmentation in the human visual system as evidenced by the ease with which we see otherwise perfectly camouflaged creatures as soon as they move, and by the strong cohesion perceived when even disparate parts of the image move in a way that could be interpreted in terms of a rigid motion in the scene.

Motion segmentation is often an essential part of the application of visual sensing to robotics. It turns out to be a most demanding problem, receiving considerable attention over the years [19, 18, 1, 14, 13, 10, 8, 5, 16]. As in [13, 8], we here pursue an optimal approach to the detection of independent motion, but one which works with unknown camera calibration and unknown camera motion. The case for algorithms that do not require calibration has been strongly made in [4]. Camera calibration is often impractical, especially when parameters are changed during the course of processing, and can introduce correlated errors into the system. As motion segmentation is a precursor to structure and motion recovery it appears unwise to predicate segmentation on knowledge of the camera motion. Instead, our approach can incorporate partial or full calibration and motion information if available, but it does not require them.

We adopt a scene-based rather than imaged-based segmentation, as suggested in [13], but, instead of adopting a specific scene model, utilise the fact that two views of a static $3D$ point set are linked by the 3×3 *Fundamental Matrix* [$\mathbf{F}$] relating the uncalibrated image coordinates of the points seen from the two camera positions [7, 4, 3]. The Fundamental Matrix encapsulates the epipolar geometry and contains all the information on the camera's intrinsic and extrinsic parameters from a given set of point correspondences.

The method in overview is:

1. Generate hypothetical clusters by randomly sampling a subset of matches and using them to calculate a solution. Include in the cluster all matches consistent with that solution.
2. Prune solutions that have too few elements or are the same as existing ones.
3. Perform a multiple hypothesis test to determine which particular combination of the many feasible clusters is most likely to represent the actual motions.

2   Optimal Clustering

Consider a set of observed motion data, consisting of temporal matches of image features between two frames. The segmentation problem is to group the data into several clusters arising from independently moving objects, together with a cluster of unexplained data, in a way that maximizes the probability of the underlying interpretation Θ given the motion data D.

The most likely interpretation is obtained by maximizing the joint likelihood function of the measurements over all possible interpretations:

$$\max_{\Theta} \Pr[\Theta|D] \ . \tag{1}$$

Using Bayes' Theorem this may be rewritten as finding

$$\max_{\Theta} \left(\frac{\Pr[D|\Theta]\Pr[\Theta]}{\Pr[D]} \right) \tag{2}$$

and, as the prior $\Pr[D]$ does not depend on Θ, this is further simplified to finding

$$\max_{\Theta} \left(\Pr[D|\Theta]\Pr[\Theta] \right) \ . \tag{3}$$

In the motion segmentation problem this optimization is far from straightforward. However we shall demonstrate a method, initially proposed for multi-target tracking problems [12, 2], which converts the optimization into a 0-1 integer programming problem. First though, we will develop a probabilistic model for $\Pr[D|\Theta]$ and $\Pr[\Theta]$.

3   Probabilistic Models

We define a segmentation or interpretation Θ as a set of s clusters such that (i) each measurement belongs to a cluster, $D(\kappa_1) \cup D(\kappa_2) \cdots \cup D(\kappa_s) = D$; and (ii) each measurement belongs to only one cluster, $D(\kappa_i) \cap D(\kappa_j) = 0$; where $D(\kappa_j)$ is the set of matches in cluster κ_j. The last cluster, κ_s, is a cluster containing all unexplained (possibly mis-matched) data. It should be noted that the number of clusters may vary from hypothesized segmentation to segmentation. It is also assumed that the data in each cluster is independent from other clusters, so that $\Pr[D|\Theta] = \prod_{j=1}^{s} \Pr[D(\kappa_j)|\Theta]$.

3.1 Cluster model

One way in which motion clustering algorithms can fail is when the motion models they employ are too restrictive. For example, clustering based on similarity of image velocities alone [17] will fail when a static scene is viewed by a camera undergoing cyclotorsion. Again, schemes based on linear variation of the motion flow field [1, 20] will produce spurious segmentations at depth discontinuities when the camera is translating. The need for a more general model is apparent.

A completely general model of rigid motion, even given an uncalibrated camera, is provided through the Fundamental Matrix. Suppose that a set of points is correctly clustered, and arise from an object which has undergone a rotation and non-zero translation. After the motion, the set of homogeneous image points $\{\mathbf{x}_i\}, i = 1, \ldots N$, is transformed to the set $\{\mathbf{x}'_i\}$ related by

$$\mathbf{x}'^T_i [\mathbf{F}] \mathbf{x}_i = 0 \tag{4}$$

where $[\mathbf{F}]$ is the 3×3 Fundamental Matrix [7, 4]. Thus there is a constraint linking rigid motion in the world to inhomogeneous image coordinates in image one (x, y) and image two (x', y'), viz:

$$f_1 x'_i x_i + f_2 x'_i y_i + f_3 x'_i + f_4 y'_i x_i + f_5 y'_i y_i + f_6 y'_i + f_7 x_i + f_8 y_i + f_9 = 0 \ . \tag{5}$$

When there is degeneracy in the data such a unique solution for $[\mathbf{F}]$ cannot be obtained, it is desirable to adopt a simpler motion model. For small independently moving objects, there may be an insufficient range of x and y to determine the quadratic constraint, and we use a linear constraint. If all the points in three space lie within a small field of view and have a small depth variation the quadratic terms in Equation (5) become insignificant and we are left with the Fundamental Matrix reduced to its affine form [21, 16]

$$[\mathbf{F}]_A = \begin{bmatrix} 0 & 0 & f_3 \\ 0 & 0 & f_6 \\ f_7 & f_8 & f_9 \end{bmatrix} \tag{6}$$

and all the points obey the constraint

$$f_3 x'_i + f_6 y'_i + f_7 x_i + f_8 y_i + f_9 = 0 \ . \tag{7}$$

Whichever constraint is used (see later), the computed Fundamental Matrix for a whole cluster provides an epipolar line for each feature in that cluster, and the quality of the proximity of the match to the epipolar yields a measure of whether the cluster is a good one.

Given a cluster, we wish to evaluate the likelihood of its existence, $\Pr[D(\kappa_j)|\kappa_j]$, where $D(\kappa_j)$ are the n_j data items comprising cluster κ_j. Let us assume that the distance from a match to its epipolar line is normally distributed with zero mean and variance σ^2, a value which we can estimate from an analysis of the characteristics of the feature matcher. The sum of squares of these distances is a χ^2 variable with degrees of freedom $N_j = n_j - 7$ (or $n_j - 4$ in the case of the affine camera). If we let V_j be the sum of squares divided by the variance then the probability density function of the cluster is

$$Pr[D(\kappa_j)|\kappa_j] = \frac{1}{2^{d_j}\Gamma(d_j)}V_j^{d_j-1}e^{-\frac{V_j}{2}}, \qquad (8)$$

where $d_j = \frac{N_j}{2}$ and $\Gamma()$ is the Gamma function [11]. The matches not originating from any cluster (mis-matches or false matches) are modelled as independent identically distributed events with a uniform probability density function $\frac{1}{v}$ and so

$$Pr[D(\kappa_s)|\kappa_s] = \left(\frac{1}{v}\right)^{n_s} \qquad (9)$$

where n_s is the number of mis-matches.

In [13] a prior $Pr[\Theta]$ was used which favoured spatial clustering. In this work however potential clusters are hypothesized by a cluster generation stage, and so we choose $Pr[\Theta]$ as a uniform distribution. Thus the total likelihood function for a given partition is:

$$Pr[D|\Theta] = \Pi_{j=1}^{s-1}\left[\frac{1}{2^{d_j}\Gamma(d_j)}V_j^{d_j-1}e^{-\frac{V_j}{2}}\right]\left(\frac{1}{v}\right)^{n_s}. \qquad (10)$$

The optimum segmentation is that which maximizes the likelihood function given in Equation (10). One approach might be to form every segmentation Θ of data into clusters and mis-matches and so arrive at the maximum likelihood data association, but of course this brute force approach is computationally feasible only in trivial cases. The key to reducing the computational complexity is inferring the existence of clusters. Thus, using theory developed for data association in tracking [12, 2], we have devised a clustering algorithm consisting of two parts: feasible cluster construction, followed by a Bayesian decision process that selects the optimal combination of clusters. We describe these in the next sections.

4   Cluster Hypothesis Generation

Given that a large proportion of our data may belong to different populations the approach is the opposite to conventional smoothing techniques. Rather than using as much data as is possible to obtain an initial solution and then attempting to identify the cluster, we randomly sample as small a subset of the data as is feasible to estimate the parameters to generate hypotheses.

To estimate the Fundamental Matrix we select seven points and form the data matrix:

$$[\mathbf{D}] = \begin{bmatrix} x'_1x_1 & x'_1y_1 & x'_1 & y'_1x_1 & y'_1y_1 & y'_1 & x_1 & y_1 & 1 \\ \vdots & \vdots & \vdots & \vdots & \vdots & \vdots & \vdots & \vdots & \vdots \\ x'_7x_7 & x'_7y_7 & x'_7 & y'_7x_7 & y'_7y_7 & y'_7 & x_7 & y_7 & 1 \end{bmatrix}. \qquad (11)$$

The selection process exploits spatial cohesion by randomly selecting one feature and its match, then selecting the six nearest feature matches within the image [1].

Examining the null space of this matrix, we find a one parameter family of solutions for $[\mathbf{F}]$: $\alpha[\mathbf{F}]_1 + (1 - \alpha)[\mathbf{F}]_2$. Introducing the constraint $|[\mathbf{F}]| = 0$ [4] allows us to obtain a cubic in α from which we obtain 1 or 3 solutions—all of which are examined to see which gives the best result.

The cluster of seven points is now grown by testing whether or not other feature pairs are consistent with the derived Fundamental Matrix. A t-test is made on the distance of the feature in each image to the epipolar line for that feature defined by the Fundamental Matrix. Effectively we are using a non-linear estimator to determine the Fundamental Matrix by minimizing the Euclidean distances of features to epipolar lines. Minimizing this distance has been shown to be superior to minimizing the residuals[9]. By introducing the t-test our method gains robustness to outliers.

Degeneracy in the data can be detected by testing if the null space of the matrix in Equation (11) is greater than 2. If this is the case, 4 of the 7 points are randomly selected and an affine matrix and epipolar lines computed instead [16].

We now calculate how many samples are required. Ideally, we would consider every possible sample, but this is computationally infeasible. Instead we choose m, the number of samples which gives a probability in excess of 95% that we have included a good sample within our selection. (Here a good sample means a set of low noise, consistent data.) The expression for this probability, Υ, is [15]:

$$\Upsilon = 1 - (1 - (1 - \epsilon)^p)^m , \tag{12}$$

where ϵ is the probability that each match is inconsistent with the rest, p the dimension of the parameter, m the number of samples needed. Figure 1 gives some sample values of the number m of samples required to ensure $\Upsilon \geq 0.95$ for given p and ϵ. The utilization of spatial cohesion for cluster generation significantly reduces ϵ, so we select $m = 500$.

Dimension	ϵ						
p	0.1	0.2	0.3	0.4	0.5	0.6	0.7
4	3	6	11	22	47	116	369
7	5	13	35	106	382	1827	13696

Fig. 1. *The number m of samples required to ensure $\Upsilon \geq 0.95$ for given p and ϵ, where Υ is the probability that all the data points we have selected in one of our samples are consistent.*

4.1 Pruning

After the initial cluster generation, clusters deemed too small are pruned. To determine what is a significant size for the cluster we calculate the probability

---

[1] An extension to the method would be to sample from the set of all candidate matches proposed by the feature matcher, only accepting matches as verified if they are included in a valid cluster. This would allow the segmentation to guide the matching process.

that cluster might have occurred randomly. Given a trial cluster associated with Fundamental Matrix [**F**], we accept a point as belonging to that cluster if it lies within a certain distance b of its epipolar line determined by the t-test threshold t_α. If the image size is $l \times l$ pixels then the maximum area that is swept out in the image within b of an epipolar line is below $2\sqrt{2}bl$. This gives the probability of given point lying on an epipolar line by chance as $\xi = 2\sqrt{2}b/l$.

Now the probability of obtaining a cluster of size k follows a Binomial distribution:

$$\Pr(k) = \binom{n}{k} \xi^k (1-\xi)^{n-k} \ , \tag{13}$$

which, if $\mu = n\xi < 5$ and $n > 20$, can be well-approximated by a Poisson distribution:

$$\Pr(k) = \frac{e^{-\mu}\mu^k}{k!} \ . \tag{14}$$

Summing these probabilities for $k = 0, 1, \ldots, h$ gives us the probability $\Pr(0 \le k \le h)$ of a cluster existing smaller or equal in size to h. In our work we prune all clusters κ_j with size $n_j \le h$ such that $\Pr(0 \le k \le h) \le 0.05$.

4.2 Merging clusters

Because of the way the hypotheses are generated, there may be some clusters that possess a major overlap. If the distances to epipolar lines are viewed as identically distributed Gaussian variables with zero mean, then the sum of the squares of these distances divided by their variance is a χ^2 variable and one can apply a χ^2 test to see whether or not two clusters should be merged.

However, if this was done for every pair of solutions there would be a significant rise in computation. To avoid this, a threshold β is set on a measure of the distance between any two solutions $\mathbf{f}_a$ and $\mathbf{f}_b$, and the merge χ^2 test only performed if

$$\mathbf{f}_a^T \mathbf{f}_b < \beta \ . \tag{15}$$

The vector $\mathbf{f} = (f_1, \ldots, f_9)^T$ is made from the elements of the Fundamental Matrix [**F**].

5 Selecting a segmentation

In this section we shall show, given a feasible cluster set, that the optimization process to achieve segmentation can be cast as a 0-1 integer programming problem, one for which efficient computer algorithms exist.

Suppose that we have l postulated clusters. We represent a segmentation Θ as a binary vector Θ with a number of elements equal to the number of hypothesized clusters, i.e.

$$\Theta = (\theta_1, \theta_2 \cdots \theta_l)^T \ , \tag{16}$$

where the jth cluster is included in the partition if $\theta_j = 1$ and not otherwise. For example, suppose we generated 5 potential clusters, then a segmentation corresponding to $\{\kappa_1, \kappa_3, \kappa_5\}$ would be represented by $\Theta = (1, 0, 1, 0, 1)^T$.

Let the negative log-likelihood function of cluster κ_j be:

$$c_j = -\ln(\Pr[D(\kappa_j)|\kappa_j]) \tag{17}$$

where $D(\kappa_j)$ are the n_j data items in cluster κ_j. If we define c with jth element c_j, the negative log-likelihood function of all the measurements for the segmentation Θ under consideration is

$$\mathbf{c}^T \Theta + c_s \ , \tag{18}$$

where c_s is the negative log-likelihood of the cluster of mis-matches

$$c_s = -n_s \ln v^{-1} \ . \tag{19}$$

It would be convenient for the purposes of the integer programming algorithm to make Equation (18) purely the inner product of Θ and a vector. Now c_s may be written as

$$c_s = -n_s \ln v^{-1} = -(n - \sum_j \theta_j n_j) \ln v^{-1} \tag{20}$$

where $n = \sum_j n_j$ is the total number of matches. Let us also define

$$\tilde{c}_j = c_j + n_j \ln v^{-1} \ . \tag{21}$$

Then, if we create vector $\tilde{\mathbf{c}}$ with jth element $\tilde{c}_j$, we have:

$$\mathbf{c}^T \Theta + c_s = \tilde{\mathbf{c}}^T \Theta \ . \tag{22}$$

In order to enforce the constraint that each match may only be in one cluster let us define the matrix $[\mathbf{A}]$ such that $A_{ij} = 1$ if the jth postulated cluster contains the ith datum and 0 otherwise. Then the optimization problem can be expressed as finding:

$$\begin{array}{c} \text{minimize } [\tilde{\mathbf{c}}^T \Theta] \\ \text{subject to } [\mathbf{A}]\Theta \leq 1 \end{array} \tag{23}$$

To solve this we have used the branch and bound method from NAG Library [6]. Note any cluster with $\tilde{c}_j > 0$ can be pruned as it will never form part of the feasible set.

6 Results

The first set of experiments has been performed on computer generated data. Points were generated at random 3D positions and imaged by a moving synthetic camera with a field of view of 75° (corresponding to an image size of 500 × 500 units and focal length 325 units). Between views the camera was translated a random amount between 0 and 100 units in a random direction and rotated about a randomly chosen axis between 0 and 2 degrees. After imaging, points were perturbed by Gaussian noise with zero mean and standard deviation of unity. Features belonging to another moving object were then introduced. The object had various sizes, giving rise to 10 to 50% of the total number of features, the latter being typically 250.

For each size of object, the random experiments were repeated 100 times and graphs showing the percentage of correctly classified motion matches on both the large and small object, as a function of the small objects relative size. The results are shown in Figure 2, which is a graph of the percentage of each object correctly identified against the size of the smaller object as a percentage of the total number of features. It can be seen that the algorithm performs best if there is a larger object and a smaller object, but still gives good results when the two objects are of equal size.

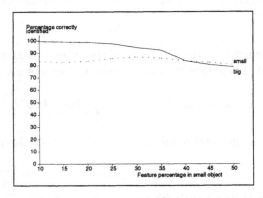

Fig. 2. *Showing the percentage of the objects correctly identified.*

Figure 3 shows typical results from experiments with real imagery. The top-left image shows motions matches obtained from two heads nodding and wagging in front of a stationary background. Two of the segmented clusters are shown at the top right and bottom-left, and the unsegmented matches shown at the bottom-right. A third cluster containing just stationary background points was also detected but is not shown here. It can seen that the largest cluster of features is on the right hand face and this also grabs some features on the left which happen to be consistent with the motion of both faces. We suggest that this sort of ambiguity can only be resolved over time, by using a sequence of images.

A considerable problem with stochastic segmentation algorithms has been their lack of speed. By introducing the hypothesis and test paradigm, the computation time of the present algorithm has been reduced substantially. In the example on real data, the segmentation algorithm took only 10% of time taken to compute and match corner features.

7 Conclusion

In this paper we have shown how robust methods may be used to solve the problem of motion segmentation. Our methods are based on scene constraints rather than image based approximations. We have set out a rigorous maximum likelihood analysis of the problem and eschewed heuristics. Combinatorial difficulties that might otherwise prevent the use of a Bayesian analysis have been alleviated

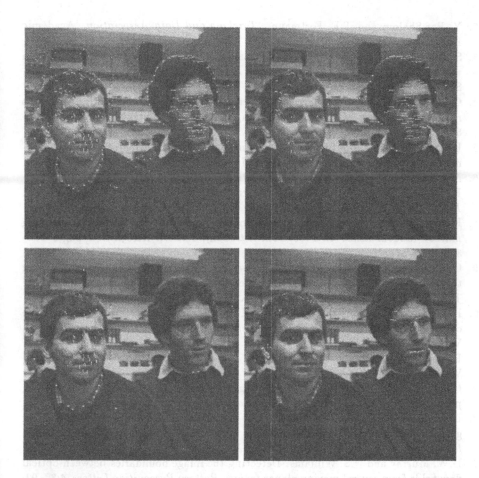

Fig. 3. *Showing an image taken from a smoothed sequence of a two heads rotating. The top left image shows the detected feature matches for two images in the sequence. All the points that are tested to see whether or not they are stationary. The top right shows the largest moving cluster detected, the bottom left the next largest cluster and the bottom right the mis-matches.*

through the use of 0-1 integer programming techniques, thus ensuring that the segmentation algorithm does not provide a significant computational overhead to the feature detection and matching algorithm. Indeed it has been shown that the segmentation algorithm may be used to aid the feature matching process.

References

1. G. Adiv. Inherent ambiguities in recovering 3-d motion and structure from a noisy flow field. In *Proceedings, CVPR '85 (IEEE Computer Society Conference on Computer Vision and Pattern Recognition, San Francisco, CA, June 10–13, 1985)*, IEEE Publ. 85CH2145-1., pages 70–77. IEEE, IEEE, 1985.

2. Y. Bar-Shalom and T.E. Fortmann. *Tracking and Data Association*. Academic Press, 1988.

3. S. Demey, A. Zisserman, and P. A. Beardsley. Affine and projective structure from motion. In D. Hogg, editor, *Proc. British Machine Vision Conference*, pages 49–58. Springer-Verlag, Sept 1992. Leeds.

4. O.D. Faugeras. What can be seen in three dimensions with an uncalibrated stereo rig? In *Proceedings of 3rd European Conference on Computer Vision*, pages 563–578, 1992.

5. E. François and P. Bouthemy. Multiframe based identification of mobile components of a scene with a moving camera. In *Proc. CVPR.*, 1991.

6. Numerical Algorithms Group. *NAG Fortran Library vol 7*. NAG, 1988.

7. R. Hartley. Estimation of relative camera positions for uncalibrated cameras. In *Proc. ECCV-92*, pages 579–87, 1992.

8. F. Heitz and P. Bouthemy. Multimodal motion estimation and segmentation using markov random fields. In *Proc. 10th Int. Conf. Pattern Recognition*, pages 378–383, 1991.

9. Q. T. Luong, R. Deriche, O. D. Faugeras, and T. Papadopoulo. On determining the fundamental matrix: analysis of different methods and experimental results. Technical Report 1894, INRIA (Sophia Antipolis), 1993.

10. P. F. McLauchlan, I. Reid, and D. W. Murray. Coarse image motion for saccade control. In D. Hogg, editor, *Proc. British Machine Vision Conference*. Springer-Verlag, Sept 1992. Leeds.

11. P. L. Meyer. *Introductory Probability and Statistical Applications*. Addison-Wesley, 1970.

12. C. L. Morefield. Applications of 0-1 integer programming to multitarget tracking problems. *IEEE Transactions on Automatic Control*, 22:302–312, 1977.

13. D.W. Murray and B.F. Buxton. Scene segmentation from visual motion using global optimization. *IEEE Transactions on Pattern Analysis and Machine Intelligence*, 8:220–228, 1987.

14. D.W. Murray and N.S. Williams. Detecting the image boundaries between optical flow fields from several moving planar facets. *Pattern Recognition Letters*, 4:87–92, 1986.

15. P. J. Rousseeuw. *Robust Regression and Outlier Detection*. Wiley, New York, 1987.

16. L.S. Shapiro. *Affine Analysis of Image Sequences*. PhD thesis, Oxford University, 1993.

17. S. M. Smith and J. M. Brady. A scene segmenter; visual tracking of moving vehicles. In *Intelligent Autonomous Vehicles*, pages 119–126, 1993.

18. W.B. Thompson and T.C. Pong. Detecting moving objects. *International Journal of Computer Vision*, 4(1):39–58, 1990.

19. S. Ullman. Relaxed and constrained optimisation by local processes. *Computer Graphics and Image Processing*, 10:115–125, 1979.

20. A.M. Waxman and J.H. Duncan. Binocular image flows: Steps toward stereo-motion fusion. *IEEE Transactions on Pattern Analysis and Machine Intelligence*, 8:715–729, 1986.

21. A. Zisserman. Notes on geometric invariance in vision. BMVC Tutorial, 1992.

Association of Motion Verbs with Vehicle Movements Extracted from Dense Optical Flow Fields

H. Kollnig[1], H.-H. Nagel[1,2], and M. Otte[1]

[1] Institut für Algorithmen und Kognitive Systeme, Fakultät für Informatik der Universität Karlsruhe (TH), Postfach 6980, D-76128 Karlsruhe, Germany
[2] Fraunhofer-Institut für Informations- und Datenverarbeitung (IITB), Fraunhoferstr. 1, D-76131 Karlsruhe, Germany

Abstract. This contribution addresses the problem of detection and tracking of moving vehicles in image sequences from traffic scenes recorded by a stationary camera. By replacing the low level vision system component for the estimation of displacement vectors by an optical flow estimation module we are able to detect all moving vehicles in our test image sequence. By replacing the edge detector and by doubling the sampling rate we improve the model-based object tracking system significantly compared to an earlier system. The trajectories of vehicles are characterized by motion verbs and verb phrases. Results from various experiments with real world traffic scenes are presented.

1 Introduction

The quality of trajectories which are now available as an output of the system reported by [Koller et al. 93] gives us the opportunity to associate motion verbs with trajectory segments which are extracted from image sequences. Therefore, object movements are described not only geometrically but also conceptually.

So far, only few approaches towards the extraction of conceptual descriptions from image signals exist. A survey of literature can be found in [Nagel 88]. The NAOS system, for instance, creates a retrospective natural language description of object movements in a traffic scene [Neumann & Novak 86], but it has so far only been tested with synthetic image data. [Mohnhaupt & Neumann 90] use natural language utterances for a top-down control in traffic scene analysis. The SOCCER system simultaneously generates running reports for short sections from soccer games [André et al. 88], which serve as a basis for recognition of intentions and interactions of multiple agents [Retz-Schmidt 91]. [Nagel 91] proposes transition diagrams to represent admissible sequences of actions used in a system for visual road vehicle guidance and shows how more complex actions can be hierarchically formalized by means of approaches used in formal language theory and how sequences of actions can be visualized. Transition diagrams are also presented by [Herzog 92] as a means for an incremental generation of motion descriptions. He shows how motion descriptions can be constructed automatically from interval-based event representations using temporal constraint propagation techniques.

Recently, [Birnbaum et al. 93] report on the BUSTER system which explains why stacked block structures are not moving. However, their system is restricted to simple static scenes and 2-D image analysis. In order to develop a traffic surveillance system by means of image sequence analysis, [Toal & Buxton 92] used spatio-temporal reasoning to analyze occlusion behavior. In their approach, temporarily occluded vehicles are correctly relabeled after re-emerging rather than being treated as completely independent vehicles.

Lecture Notes in Computer Science, Vol. 801
Jan-Olof Eklundh (Ed.)

Our system with 67 motion verbs links directly to the evaluation of real world image sequences and extracts conceptual descriptions for vehicle movements in a greater variety. In contrast to the cited papers [Neumann & Novak 86; Mohnhaupt & Neumann 90; André *et al.* 88; Herzog 92; Retz-Schmidt 91] we do not use synthetic data to extract conceptual descriptions. The problems which arise by the analysis of real and noisy data are not yet covered in literature. It is one of our main intentions to extract the conceptual descriptions from trajectory data obtained by object tracking in real image sequences.

The system reported by [Koller *et al.* 93] works as follows: Starting from a token-based estimation of a displacement vector field, hypotheses for object image candidates are created. By means of an off-line calibration, these vehicle hypotheses can be backprojected into the 3-D world which results in pose estimates to initialize a Kalman-Filter. By projecting an hypothesized 3-D polyhedral vehicle model into the image plane, 2-D model edge segments are obtained which are matched to straight-line edge segments, so called data segments, extracted from the image. This feeds into a state MAP-update step. Kalman-Filter prediction is performed by using a motion model.

Compared with the system built by [Koller *et al.* 93] we substituted both low-level image analysis modules. First, the blob feature based component for the estimation of displacement vectors (see [Koller *et al.* 91]) was replaced by an optical flow estimation module (see [Otte & Nagel 94]). The optical flow field is denser so that a redesigned clustering algorithm enables us now to obtain significantly better initial pose estimates for object candidates. This facilitates to tighten the thresholds and Kalman-Filter parameters which in turn stabilizes the tracking process. Second, the straight line segment detection process used by [Koller *et al.* 93] has been supplanted by the edge detector reported by [Otte & Nagel 92a + 92b], which provides more data segments based on image structures which improves the matching process. This in turn contributes to an enhanced a-posteriori state estimation in the Kalman-Filter update step. Moreover, by interpolating the interlaced half-frames we doubled the sampling rate from 25 Hz to 50 Hz. As a consequence of all these improvements, all vehicles in our test image sequence can be tracked with the same Kalman-Filter parameter set.

In order to associate motion verbs and verb phrases with the notably better trajectory segments, a complete rework of previously published methods [Koller *et al.* 91; Heinze *et al.* 91] was necessary. The set of German verbs was translated into English wherever translation was possible. Fuzzy sets instead of the former threshold decision approach are used to associate trajectory attributes and verbs in order to cope with the inherent vagueness of natural language descriptions. As a consequence, the automata for incremental occurrence recognition had to be redesigned. Moreover, the conceptual descriptions are visualized in the image which enables us to more thoroughly inspect the system output.

This paper is organized as follows: A brief overview regarding related work on object recognition is presented in Section 2. The improvements of our detection and tracking system are described in Sections 3 and 4. The subsequent Sections 5 – 7 deal with the extraction of conceptual descriptions from image signals. The results of our experiments are illustrated in Section 8.

2 Object segmentation and pose estimation approaches

A review of relevant literature can be found in [Koller *et al.* 93]. Here we confine ourselves to recent publications. [Zhang *et al.* 93] propose a view-independent relational model (VIRM) for 3-D object recognition. The VIRM of an object is represented as a hypergraph with attached weights to represent the covisibility of model features and with associated procedural constraints to represent view independent relationships between model features, e. g. parallelism or relative size. Given a CAD-wireframe model, their system constructs off-line a view-independent relational model, which can be applied for pose estimation without the need for information about the position and orientation of the camera (due to the VIRM).

[Tan et al. 92] propose a non-statistical linear algorithm for object pose estimation. They have no motion model and no prediction. The correspondences between data and model segments are established interactively. In [Tan et al. 93] the matching is performed automatically by histogram voting based on a generalized Hough transform. This pose estimation approach is used to extend their traffic vision system to multiple cameras and to track articulated objects, such as a lorry and a trailer. First results are reported by [Worrall et al. 93].

In contrast to interpretation-tree matching approaches, where the resulting computational costs can be reduced, for instance, by using a best-first search [Lowe 92], [Du et al. 93] establish the 3-D grouping of line segments by monotonically improving compliance with a viewpoint consistency constraint. By means of an experimental study they illustrate that their approach is more robust than Lowe's in the presence of errors of data segments.

[Liu & Huang 93] propose a vehicle centered motion model by representing a 3-D motion as a rotation around an axis through the vehicle center followed by a translation. By adding several constraints on the rotation and translation, they obtain different motion types. However, their 3-D motion estimation approach has so far only been tested on five image frames containing one vehicle.

In comparison with the above described approaches, our scenes are more complex. By exploiting the information from optical flow, we obtain a good initial guess and therefore avoid trying all possible angles for the positions of the model. Although our trajectory data are not computed in real-time, they are more densely sampled – 50 Hz – compared with 0.48 Hz [Tan et al. 92] and 5 Hz [Tan et al. 93; Worrall et al. 93]. Moreover, we do not restrict ourselves to a single aspect of image sequence analysis but present a system that covers all analysis steps from the gray value data up to conceptual descriptions.

3 Exploiting the information of a segmented optical flow field to initialize a model-based tracking system

The displacement vectors in the approach reported by [Koller et al. 91] were obtained by matching blobs generated by the monotonicity operator [Kories & Zimmermann 86] in two consecutive frames. In lots of experiments in which we exercised the system described by [Koller et al. 93], it turned out that the blob-based motion segmentation step used in their approach did not provide a very exact initial guess for each object nor detected it every object.

Reporting problems by using a similar displacement vector estimation module, [Gong & Buxton 93] improve the segmentation and 2-D tracking of moving objects by incorporating more contextual knowledge about the scene even at the earliest stages of visual processing. In contrast, we are able to simplify the cluster analysis by improving the low-level image analysis module.

We replaced this module by a more time consuming optical flow vector estimation module related to the approach of [Campani & Verri 92], which has been extended to include partial derivatives with respect to time by [Otte & Nagel

94]. This optical flow field estimation enables us to compute better initial pose estimates and thus more appropriate object hypotheses.

The optical flow field restricted to vectors exceeding a minimum magnitude, which, moreover, survived a singular value threshold, is juxtaposed to the displacement vector field used by [Koller *et al.* 91; Koller *et al.* 93] in Figure 1. Details of the clustering analysis originally developed by [Sung 88] and subsequently improved significantly by [Koller 92] can be found in Appendix A. The resulting optical flow field is significantly denser than the displacement vector field and overlaps each moving vehicle to such an extent that the subsequent cluster analysis step is significantly simplified: neighboring vectors with approximately the same magnitude and orientation are grouped into object image can-

Fig. 1. Improvements in the initialization step: The first row shows the results of the displacement vector field estimation module used by [Koller *et al.* 91; Koller *et al.* 93] and the clustered vectors; each cluster is marked by a circumscribed rectangle. A section from the lower right part of the upper left quadrant in the first row is given on the right hand side of the first row. The displacement vectors are the results of tracking blob features along four consecutive frames. The second row shows the output of the clustering step applied to an optical flow vector field related to the approach of [Campani & Verri 92], extended and implemented by [Otte & Nagel 94]. The smaller optical flow vectors show the gray value displacements in one half-frame.

didates. Moreover, the detection rate increases significantly, too. In contrast to the approach of [Koller *et al.* 93], the information from the optical flow estimation is not just exploited to obtain initial values for position and orientation of a vehicle, but also to estimate the magnitude of the velocity v for each object. Therefore, our initialization is more homogeneous than that of [Koller *et al.* 93] whose displacement vector field could only be used to separate moving regions from the static image background. Their bootstrap phase was performed using the first two or three frames in order to estimate initial magnitudes of the translational and angular velocities v and ω, respectively. Since our initial estimates are more reliable, we have been able to tighten the tolerances which in turn resulted in a more efficient exclusion of outliers.

4 Computing data segments

[Koller *et al.* 93] extracted line segments fitted to thresholded edge elements which in turn are detected as local maxima of the gray-value gradient magnitude in gradient direction. In low contrast image regions, thresholding the gradient magnitude may suppress not only noise, but also edge elements which are part of a significant image structure and may thus result in the fragmentation or total loss of edge segments. In contrast to the traditional pixel oriented gradient magnitude thresholding, [Otte & Nagel 92a + 92b] proposed to chain edge elements to edge element chains and vertices without any thresholding. The evaluation of chain properties such as average gradient magnitude, length of chains and second moments of gradient direction change rates allows to either reject edge element chains as noisy or to accept them as a structure underlying the original image. Edge element chains include much more global information as compared to the information about a single edge element. The extraction of line segments, therefore, can be improved. For this reason, we replaced the line extraction process by the novel approach of [Otte & Nagel 92b].

Furthermore, instead of selecting uncertainties of data segments interactively (as e.g. [Tan *et al.* 93; Deriche & Faugeras 90]), we estimate them from the image data and, therefore, we are able to reduce the set of free parameters. Using the midpoint representation of line segments as described in [Deriche & Faugeras 90], we calculate the smaller eigenvalue in an eigenvector line fitting process to a set of edge elements to estimate the uncertainties perpendicular to a line segment.

5 Trajectory attributes based on fuzzy sets

In the following, fuzzy sets are used to abstract from quantitative details in geometrical descriptions obtained by automatic image sequence analysis.

For every object its world coordinates $(x(t_k), y(t_k))$, its speed $v(t_k)$, orientation $\theta(t_k)$ and its angular velocity $\omega(t_k)$ are extracted from an image sequence, sampled with 50 Hz. These trajectory data are characterized by attributes modeled by fuzzy sets. For example, the attribute *A_Speed* that characterizes the speed of the agent is modeled by the fuzzy membership functions shown in Figure 2, where the speed limit of 50 km/h on German downtown roads is taken into account. Other attributes are described in [Nagel & Kollnig 94]. The changing, increasing, decreasing, staying equal, or becoming unequal of the attribute values, below defined as monotonicity conditions, are depicted by fuzzy membership functions, too.

6 Discourse world and definition of occurrences

Human beings describe important occurrences by verbs. However, the exact meaning of a verb often depends on the subjective impression of the speaker.

Table 1. Definitions of agent reference occurrences. A dash '—' denotes the irrelevance of the attribute in the occurrence definition.

occurrences	agent reference attributes A_Speed		
	Pre_C	Mon_C	Post_C
be standing	zero	—	zero
drive off	zero	increasing	≥small
accelerate	≥small	increasing	≥small
drive slowly	small	—	small
drive at regular speed	normal	—	normal
run fast	fast	—	fast
run very fast	very fast	—	very fast
drive at constant speed	≥small	staying equal	≥small
brake	≥small	decreasing	≥small
stop	≥small	decreasing	zero

To avoid ambiguity we describe occurrences detected in an image sequence not just by motion verbs but also by verb phrases. Scanning a German dictionary with 150,000 entries yielded about 9,200 verb entries. Using a set of criteria – for instance, our occurrences should be elementary, i.e. not composed of other occurrences – all those verbs are selected from this set of 9,200 verbs which describe vehicle motions for downtown roads and road intersections. After the removal of synonyms, our system retains 67 verbs, listed in Appendix B.

Each occurrence is defined by three predicates, a *precondition (Pre_C)* that determines the attribute constellation necessary for the beginning of the occurrence, a *monotonicity condition (Mon_C)* that indicates the direction and amount of change during the validity of the occurrence, and a *postcondition (Post_C)*, defining the end of the occurrence. We divided the occurrences with respect to their reference into four classes:

- **Agent Reference**: the occurrence refers only to the agent (i.e. 'to brake'),
- **Location Reference**: in addition to the agent, the occurrence refers to a location (i.e. 'to arrive at a location '),
- **Road Reference**: in addition to the agent, the occurrence refers to the road or lane (i.e. 'to leave a driving lane'),
- **Object Reference**: in addition to the agent, the occurrence refers to another object (i.e. 'to follow a car').

By combining several attributes, we obtain an occurrence definition scheme. For example, the agent reference occurrences are tabulated in Tab. 1.

7   Automata for incremental occurrence recognition

To be able to extend our system to react to evaluated image sequence data in real-time, we prefer an incremental scene analysis instead of an retrospective or a-posteriori analysis where the motion descriptions are extracted on completed trajectories. Therefore, at each half-frametime during the evaluation of an image sequence, the attribute values are determined. For each occurrence, the values of Pre_C, Mon_C, and $Post\_C$ are determined. Multiple entries are combined

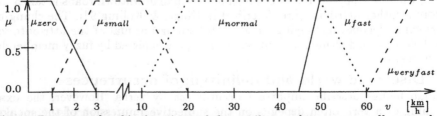

Fig. 2. Fuzzy membership functions of the attribute values *zero, small, normal, fast* and *very fast* for *A_Speed* as a function of the estimated vehicle speed.

by choosing the minimum of the attribute values, irrelevant entries are set to 1. The automata for incremental occurrence recognition are divided into four classes according to the aspect of the occurrences: details about the extraction of description of mutative, perpetuative, resultative, and inchoative occurrences can be found in [Kollnig & Nagel 93]. Each one of our occurrence descriptions contains a start frame number, an end frame number, and a degree λ of estimated validity ($0 < \lambda \leq 1$).

8 Experiments and results

As an experiment we used an image sequence of about 50 frames of a multi-lane street intersection in Karlsruhe. The size of the images of the moving vehicles varies from 25×30 to 30×35 (apart from the bus: 110×110) pixels in a frame. The smallest car images are even smaller than the 20×40 pixels in [Koller *et al.* 93].

The state vector x_k at time t_k used by our Kalman-Filter tracking module (for details see [Koller *et al.* 93]) is a five-dimensional vector consisting of the position (p_{x_k}, p_{y_k}) and orientation ϕ_k of the model as well the magnitudes v_k and ω_k of the translational and angular velocities. Due to our more precise initialization, we were able to decrease — compared with [Koller *et al.* 93] — the entries in the start covariance matrix by a factor 100. We used the initial values $\sigma_{p_{x_0}} = \sigma_{p_{y_0}} = 0.05$ m, $\sigma_{\phi_0} = 0.01$ rad, $\sigma_{v_0} = 0.032$ m/frame, $\sigma_{\omega_0} = 0.032$ rad/frame (apart from the 3 times larger bus: $\sigma_{p_{x_0}} = \sigma_{p_{y_0}} = 0.16$ m, $\sigma_{\phi_0} = 0.032$ rad). We use a process noise of $\sigma_v = 10^{-3}$ (m/frame) and $\sigma_\omega = 10^{-4}$ (rad/frame). The threshold d_r for the computed Mahalanobis distance used for establishing correspondences between model and data segments could be doubled — compared with [Koller *et al.* 93] — due to the more robust initialization and better data segments. The values of our estimated errors perpendicular to the data segments are often only one half of the value which was interactively chosen by [Koller *et al.* 93]. We set $d_r = 10$. To track the bus – despite the fact that it is partially occluded by a street-lamp post – we were forced to use $d_r = 12$. Hereby, we compensate for the fact that wheels and doors of the bus are not yet modeled and, therefore, only comparatively long line segments are expected according to our very simple box model of the bus.

The computed trajectories for each moving car are given in Fig. 3. There still remain some problems. Obj. #1 can be correctly tracked only 40 half-frames due to its partial occlusion by a road sign. Obj. #3 cannot be tracked because it emerges from a tunnel underneath the intersection on a not yet calibrated lane. Obj. #11 cannot be tracked because its image is not correctly covered by the initially detected moving region due to the street-lamp post; obj. #12 has almost left the field of view before the tracking could stabilize. Fig. 4 shows an enlarged section of the image shown in Fig. 3. The results of the conceptual description extraction module for this image area are given in Fig. 5. To be able to verify the system output, the agent trajectory is colored depending on the extracted occurrences. The degree of estimated validity for each occurrence associated with a trajectory segment is visualized by the thickness of the trajectory. If more than one description is valid at one half-frametime, the translated trajectories are projected with different colors. Fig. 6 shows the visualization of the contents of Fig. 5.

9 Acknowledgments

We gratefully acknowledge stimulating discussions with Konstantinos Daniilidis, Dieter Koller, and Karl Schäfer. Our thanks go to Markus Maier, Harald Damm, and Martin Tonko for their support in this research.

A Clustering analysis of optical flow vectors

[Koller *et al.* 93] used the following cluster analysis, originally developed by [Sung 88]: First of all, each optical flow vector is considered as a cluster seed. Around such a seed, all vectors are clustered for which the conjunction of the following three predicates is satisfied.

- Two vectors satisfy the **neighboring** predicate, if the Euclidean distance of their footpoints does not exceed a threshold t_n.
- Two vectors satisfy the **parallel** predicate, if the absolute difference of their orientations does not exceed a threshold t_p.
- Two vectors satisfy the **same_length** predicate, if their relative length difference with respect to the first vector does not exceed a threshold t_l.

Second, we create maximal disjoint clusters by merging recursively all clusters with a non-empty intersection. Third, the footpoints of all vectors in each cluster are enclosed by a rectangle. Again, it is tested if one rectangle contains a vector of another rectangle. In this case, these clusters are merged and the enclosing rectangle for the merged clusters is determined. In our experiments we used $t_n = 1, t_p = 15°, t_l = 15\%$. Due to the now available dense optical flow fields, the threshold t_n could be set to one, compared to $t_n = 15$ in [Koller *et al.* 93] (see first row in Fig. 1).

B List of occurrences in the discourse world

Agent Reference: be standing, drive off, accelerate, drive slowly, drive at regular speed, run fast, run very fast, drive at constant speed, brake, stop, run straight ahead, turn right, turn left, revolve around a vertical axis, slide, skid, reverse, run forward (18 occurrences).

Location Reference: drive to location, pass location, arrive at location, depart from location, run over location, stop at location, park at location, leave location, leave location behind (9 occurrences).

Road Reference: leave driving lane, enter lane, turn, change section, drive on lane, cross a lane (6 occurrences).

Object Reference: catch up with obj, fall behind, follow, follow closely, run into obj, pull out from behind obj, get out of the way of obj, cut in in front of obj, slip in front of obj, pull up to, flank, move past, let run into, pass, drive in front of, lose a lead on, draw ahead of obj, approach oncoming obj, make way for oncoming obj, leave an obj driving off in opposite direction, approach crossing obj, close up to obj, merge in front of obj, leave crossing obj, move towards stationary obj, stop behind stationary obj, be standing near stationary obj, start in front of stationary obj, pull out behind stationary obj, drive around stationary obj, pass stationary obj, merge in front of stationary obj, move away from stationary obj, collide with obj (34 occurrences).

References

[André *et al.* 88] E. André, G. Herzog, T. Rist, On the Simultaneous Interpretation of Real World Image Sequences and their Natural Language Descriptions: The System Soccer, in Y. Kodratoff (ed.), *Proc. 8th Europ. Conf. on Artificial Intelligence*, München, Aug. 1-5, 1988, pp. 449-454.

[Birnbaum *et al.* 93] L. Birnbaum, M. Brand, P. Cooper, Looking for Trouble: Using Causal Semantics to Direct Focus of Attention, in *Proc. Int. Conf. on Computer Vision (ICCV '93)*, Berlin, Germany, May 11-14, 1993, pp. 49-56.

[Campani & Verri 92] M. Campani, A. Verri, Motion Analysis from First-Order Properties of Optical Flow, *Computer Vision, Graphics, and Image Processing* **56** (1992) 90-107.

[Deriche & Faugeras 90] R. Deriche, O. Faugeras, Tracking line segments, *Image and Vision Computing* **8**:4 (1990) 261-270.

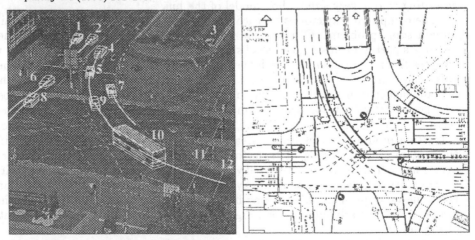

Fig. 3. The estimated trajectories of each moving vehicle of our test image sequence and a projection of the estimated trajectories into the street plane, superimposed to a digitized image of an official map for this intersection. The vehicles are referred to by numbers indicated in the left frame.

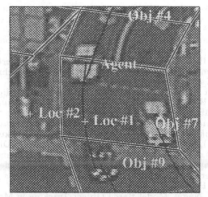

Fig. 4. Enlarged section of the image shown in Fig. 3. Obj. # 5 was selected as agent and two locations are marked as '+ Loc #1' and '+ Loc #2'. An interactively created road model is superimposed, representing road sections as polygons.

Fig. 6. The trajectory of agent #5 shown in Fig. 4 is colored by location occurrences involving location #1 shown in Fig. 5.

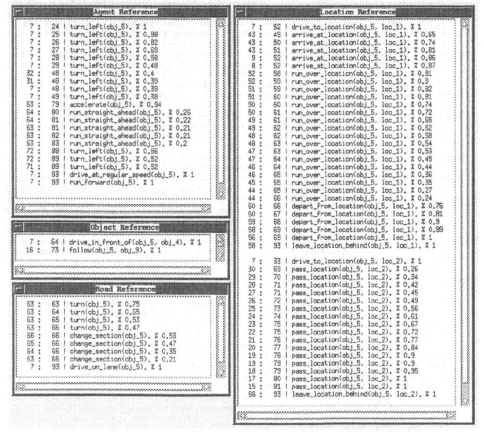

Fig. 5. The output of the computed occurrence descriptions after selecting object #5 as agent. The descriptions contain a time interval (before the exclamation mark), the involved objects and locations (in round brackets as arguments) and the fuzzy membership degree (following the percent symbol).

347

[Du et al. 93] L. Du, G. D. Sullivan, K. D. Baker, Quantitative Analysis of the Viewpoint Consistency Constraint in Model-Based Vision, in *Proc. Int. Conf. on Computer Vision (ICCV '93)*, Berlin, Germany, May 11-14, 1993, pp. 632–639.

[Gong & Buxton 93] S. Gong, H. Buxton, From Contextual Knowledge to Computational Constraints, in *Proc. Brit. Machine Vision Conf.*, Guildford, UK, Sept. 21-23, 1993, pp. 229–238.

[Heinze et al. 91] N. Heinze, W. Krüger, H.-H. Nagel, Berechnung von Bewegungsverben zur Beschreibung von aus Bildfolgen gewonnenen Fahrzeugtrajektorien in Straßenverkehrsszenen (in German), *Informatik - Forschung und Entwicklung* 6 (1991) 51–61.

[Herzog 92] G. Herzog, Utilizing Interval-Based Event Representations for Incremental High-Level Scene Analysis, in *Proc. Fourth European Workshop on Semantics of Time, Space and Movement and Spatio-Temporal Reasoning*, Château de Bonas, France, Sept. 4-8, 1992, pp. 425–435.

[Koller 92] D. Koller, *Detektion, Verfolgung und Klassifikation bewegter Objekte in monokularen Bildfolgen am Beispiel von Straßenverkehrsszenen* (in German), Dissertation, Fakultät für Informatik der Universität Karlsruhe (TH), Karlsruhe, Juni 1992, available as vol. DISKI 13, *Dissertationen zur Künstlichen Intelligenz*, infix-Verlag, Sankt Augustin, Deutschland, 1992.

[Koller et al. 91] D. Koller, N. Heinze, H.-H. Nagel, Algorithmic Characterization of Vehicle Trajectories from Image Sequences by Motion Verbs, in *IEEE Conf. Computer Vision and Pattern Recognition (CVPR '91)*, Lahaina, Maui, Hawaii/HI, June 3-6, 1991, pp. 90–95.

[Koller et al. 93] D. Koller, K. Daniilidis, H.-H. Nagel, Model-Based Object Tracking in Monocular Image Sequences of Road Traffic Scenes, *Intern. Journal of Comp. Vision* 10:3 (1993) 257–281.

[Kollnig & Nagel 93] H. Kollnig, H.-H. Nagel, Ermittlung von begrifflichen Beschreibungen von Geschehen in Straßenverkehrsszenen mit Hilfe unscharfer Mengen (in German), *Informatik - Forschung und Entwicklung* 8 (1993) 186–196.

[Kories & Zimmermann 86] R. Kories, G. Zimmermann, A Versatile Method for the Estimation of Displacement Vector Fields from Image Sequences, in *Proc. of IEEE Workshop on Motion: Representation and Analysis*, Kiawah Island Resort, Charleston/SC, May 7-9, 1986, pp. 101-106.

[Liu & Huang 93] Y. Liu, T.S. Huang, Vehicle-Type Motion Estimation from Multi-frame Images, *IEEE Trans. on Pattern Analysis and Machine Intelligence* **PAMI-15**:8 (1993) 802–808.

[Lowe 92] D. G. Lowe, Robust Model-Based Motion Tracking Through the Integration of Search and Estimation, *International Journal of Computer Vision* 8:2 (1992) 113–122.

[Mohnhaupt & Neumann 90] M. Mohnhaupt, B. Neumann, On the Use of Motion Concepts for Top-Down Control in Traffic Scenes, in O. Faugeras (ed.), *Proc. Second European Conference on Computer Vision (ECCV '90)*, Antibes, France, Apr. 23-26, 1990, Lecture Notes in Computer Science **427**, Springer-Verlag, Berlin, Heidelberg, New York/NY and others, 1990, pp. 598–600.

[Nagel 88] H.-H. Nagel, From Image Sequences towards Conceptual Descriptions, *Image and Vision Computing* 6:2 (1988) 59–74.

[Nagel 91] H.-H. Nagel, La représentation de situations et leur reconnaissance à partir de séquences d'images — The Representation of Situations and their Recognition from Image Sequences, in 8ᵉ *Congrès Reconnaissance des Formes et Intelligence Artificielle*, Lyon–Villeurbanne, 25–29 Novembre 1991, AFCET, 1991, pp. 1221–1229.

[Nagel & Kollnig 94] H.-H. Nagel, H. Kollnig, Description of the Motion of Road Vehicle Agglomerations in Image Sequences by Natural Language Verbs (1994). In preparation.

[Neumann & Novak 86] B. Neumann, H.-J. Novak, Naos: Ein System zur natürlichsprachlichen Beschreibung zeitveränderlicher Szenen, *Informatik - Forschung und Entwicklung* 1 (1986) 83-92.

[Otte & Nagel 92a] M. Otte, H.-H. Nagel, Extraction of Line Drawings from Gray Value Images by Non-Local Analysis of Edge Element Structures, in G. Sandini (ed.), *Proc. Second European Conference on Computer Vision (ECCV '92)*, S. Margherita Ligure, Italy, May 18-23, 1992, Lecture Notes in Computer Science **588**, Springer-Verlag, Berlin and others, 1992, pp. 687–695.

[Otte & Nagel 92b] M. Otte, H.-H. Nagel, *Verbesserte Extraktion von Strukturen aus Kantenelementbildern durch Auswertung von Kantenelementketten* (in German), Interner Bericht, Institut für Algorithmen und Kognitive Systeme, Fakultät für Informatik der Universität Karlsruhe (TH), Karlsruhe, Deutschland, Oktober 1992.

[Otte & Nagel 94] M. Otte, H.-H. Nagel, Optical Flow Estimation: Advances and Comparisons, in: *Proc. Third Europ. Conf. on Computer Vision ECCV '94*, Stockholm, Sweden, May 2-6, 1994.

[Retz-Schmidt 91] G. Retz-Schmidt, Recognizing Intentions, Interactions and Causes of Plan Failures, *User Modeling and User-Adapted Interaction* 1:2 (1991) 173–202.

[Sung 88] C.-K. Sung, Extraktion von typischen und komplexen Vorgängen aus einer Bildfolge einer Verkehrsszene (in German), in H. Bunke, O. Kübler, P. Stucki (Hrsg.), *Mustererkennung 1988*, Zürich, Informatik-Fachberichte **180**, Springer-Verlag, Berlin u.a., 1988, pp. 90–96.

[Tan et al. 92] T. N. Tan, G. D. Sullivan, K. D. Baker, Linear Algorithms for Object Pose Estimation, in *Proc. British Machine Vision Conference*, Leeds, UK, Sept. 22-24, 1992, pp. 600–609.

[Tan et al. 93] T. N. Tan, G. D. Sullivan, K. D. Baker, Recognising Objects on the Ground Plane, in *Proc. British Machine Vision Conference*, Guildford, UK, Sept. 21-23, 1993, pp. 85–94.

[Toal & Buxton 92] A. F. Toal, H. Buxton, Spatio-temporal Reasoning within a Traffic Surveillance System, in G. Sandini (ed.), *Proc. Second European Conference on Computer Vision (ECCV '92)*, S. Margherita Ligure, Italy, May 18-23, 1992, Lecture Notes in Computer Science **588**, Springer-Verlag, Berlin, Heidelberg, New York/NY and others, 1992, pp. 884–892.

[Worrall et al. 93] A. D. Worrall, G. D. Sullivan, K. D. Baker, Advances in Model-Based Traffic Vision, in *Proc. Brit. Machine Vision Conf.*, Guildford, UK, Sept. 21-23, 1993, pp. 559–568.

[Zhang et al. 93] S. Zhang, G. D. Sullivan, K. D. Baker, The Automatic Construction of a View-Independent Relational Model for 3-D Object Recognition, *IEEE Transactions on Pattern Analysis and Machine Intelligence* **PAMI-15**:6 (1993) 531–544.

Feature-Extraction

Comparisons of Probabilistic and Non-probabilistic Hough Transforms

Heikki Kälviäinen, Petri Hirvonen, L. Xu, and Erkki Oja

Lappeenranta University of Technology, Department of Information Technology,
P.O. Box 20, FIN-53851 Lappeenranta, Finland (kalviai@lut.fi)
Chinese University of Hong Kong, Department of Computer Science, Shatin, Hong Kong
Helsinki University of Technology, Laboratory of Information and Computer Science, Rakentajanaukio 2 C, FIN-02150, Espoo, Finland

Abstract. A new and efficient version of the Hough Transform for curve detection, the Random and Hough Transform (RHT), has been recently suggested. The RHT selects n pixels from an edge image by random sampling to solve n parameters of a curve and then accumulates only one cell in a parameter space. In this paper, the RHT is related to other recent developments of the Hough Transform by experimental tests. In line detection, Hough Transform methods are divided into two categories: probabilistic and non-probabilistic methods. Four-level extensions of the RHT are proposed to improve the RHT for complex and noisy images. These apply the RHT process to a limited neighborhood of edge pixels. Tests with synthetic and real-world images demonstrate the high speed and low memory usage of the new extensions, as compared both to the basic RHT and other versions of the Hough Transform.

1 Introduction

The Hough Transform (HT) is a common method to extract global curve segments from an image [6]. The main drawbacks of the HT are its computational complexity and large storage requirements. In recent years, the development to alleviate these problems has been typically in two areas. One kind of approach is the set of methods in the paper called recent-based on probabilistic Hough Transforms reported, e.g., in [7, 12, 10, 5, 11, 2, 14, 4, 3]. All of them use random sampling of the edge points of an input image. Furthermore, some of these use many-to-one or converging mapping from the image space into the parameter space, and replace an accumulator array by a list structure. New deterministic or non-probabilistic approaches have also been suggested, e.g. [13, 1, 10].

For more probabilistic and non-probabilistic methods see e.g. Leavers's own prehensive review [9]. In this paper, being proponents of the Randomized Hough Transform of

For this reason, the term randomized ought to be preferred. The term randomize is more differentiating also indicates that it is not the accumulator space that is randomized. However, for reasons of conformity with current practice, we choose to use the terms probabilistic and non-probabilistic here.

Comparisons of Probabilistic and Non-probabilistic Hough Transforms

Heikki Kälviäinen[1], Petri Hirvonen[1], Lei Xu[2], and Erkki Oja[3]

[1] Lappeenranta University of Technology, Department of Information Technology,
P.O. Box 20, FIN-53851 Lappeenranta, Finland, E-mail: Heikki.Kalviainen@lut.fi
[2] Chinese University of Hong Kong, Department of Computer Science, Shatin, Hong Kong
[3] Helsinki University of Technology, Laboratory of Information and Computer Science, Rakentajanaukio 2 C, FIN-02150, Espoo, Finland

Abstract. A new and efficient version of the Hough Transform for curve detection, the Randomized Hough Transform (RHT), has been recently suggested. The RHT selects n pixels from an edge image by random sampling to solve n parameters of a curve and then accumulates only one cell in a parameter space. In this paper, the RHT is related to other recent developments of the Hough Transform by experimental tests in line detection. Hough Transform methods are divided into two categories: probabilistic and non-probablistic methods. Four novel extensions of the RHT are proposed to improve the RHT for complex and noisy images. These apply the RHT process to a limited neighborhood of edge pixels. Tests with synthetic and real-world images demonstrate the high speed and low memory usage of the new extensions, as compared both to the basic RHT and other versions of the Hough Transform.

1 Introduction

The Hough Transform (HT) is a common method to extract global curve segments from an image [9]. The main drawbacks of the HT are its computational complexity and large storage requirements. In recent years, the development to alleviate these problems has been rapid in the area. A new kind of approach is the set of methods, in this paper called *randomized* or *probabilistic Hough Transforms*, reported, e.g. in [7, 15, 16, 5, 17, 2, 14, 8, 19]. All of them use random sampling of the edge points of an input image[4]. Moreover, some of them use many-to-one or converging mapping from the image space into the parameter space, and replace an accumulator array by a list structure. New *deterministic* or *non-probabilistic* approaches have also been suggested, e.g [13, 1, 10].

For more probabilistic and non-probabilistic methods see, e.g. Leaver's comprehensive review [9]. In this paper, comparisons of several Hough Transform al-

---

[4] For this reason, the term *randomized* ought to be preferred. The term *probabilistic* is more diffuse, covering also methods that e.g model the accumulator space by statistical models. However, for reasons of conformity with current practice, we choose to use the terms *probabilistic* and *non-probabilistic* here.

gorithms are presented through experimental tests. Earlier comparisons of some of the HT methods have been presented in [12, 18, 4].

Xu et al. introduced the Randomized Hough Transform (RHT) [15, 16], proposing for the first time the novel combination of random sampling, many-to-one mapping, and the use of a list structure. The RHT overcomes many problems associated with the Standard Hough Transform (SHT) [15, 16]. However, the basic RHT may have problems with complex and noisy images. In Section 2, four novel extensions of the RHT, called the Dynamic RHT (DRHT), the Random Window RHT (RWRHT), the Window RHT (WRHT), and a special version of the WRHT, called the Connective RHT (CRHT), are suggested to alleviate these problems. The extensions apply the RHT to a local neighborhood of a randomly selected binary edge point. The methods are tested with both synthetic and real-world pictures in Section 3 and compared to the SHT, the basic RHT, and several other Hough transform algorithms with good results. The properties of the tested methods are discussed in Section 4, and some conclusions are given in Section 5.

2 Extensions of the Randomized Hough Transform

2.1 The Basic RHT Algorithm

The RHT method is based on the fact that a single parameter point can be determined uniquely with a pair, triple, or generally n-tuple of points from the original picture, depending on the complexity of the curves to be detected. For example, in the case of line detection each parameter space point can be expressed with two points from the original binary edge picture. Such point pairs (d_i, d_j) are selected randomly[5], the parameter point (a, b) is solved from the curve equation, and the cell $A(a, b)$ is accumulated in the accumulator space[6]. The RHT is run long enough to detect a global maximum in the accumulator space, i.e. the cell must reach a threshold t to be considered the maximum. The parameter space point (a, b) of the global maximum describes the parameters of the detected curve, which can then be removed from the image to start the algorithm again with the remaining pixels. The algorithm is as follows:

Algorithm 1 : *The kernel of the RHT to line detection*

1. Create the set D of all edge points in a binary edge picture.
2. Select a point pair (d_i, d_j) randomly from the set D.
3. If the points do not satisfy the predefined distance limits, go to Step 2; Otherwise continue to Step 4.
4. Solve the parameter space point (a, b) using the curve equation with the points (d_i, d_j).
5. Accumulate the cell $A(a, b)$ in the accumulator space.

---

[5] This random selecting is called *random sampling*.
[6] This many-to-one mapping is also called *converging mapping*.

6. If the $A(a, b)$ is equal to the threshold t, the parameters a and b describe the parameters of the detected curve; Otherwise continue to Step 2.

To define the distance limits in Step 3 means that the points d_i and d_j must not be too near each other or too far from each other, i.e. $dist_{min} \leq dist(d_i, d_j) \leq dist_{max}$ where $dist(d_i, d_j)$ is the distance between the points d_i and d_j. In this paper, this limitation is called *the point distance criterion*. If the edge picture is complex, the use of distance limits is necessary. Here, the RHT algorithms are shortly denoted as RHT_D and RHT_ND referring to the ones with and without the point distance criterion.

The accumulator space can have the form of a dynamic structure like a tree, because now only one cell will be updated at a time. More details of the dynamic structure and some other possibilities were given in [16]. In [15] the advantages of the RHT were stated: high parameter resolution, infinite scope of the parameter space, small storage requirements, and high speed.

2.2 Novel extensions of the RHT

The extensions, like the basic RHT, use random sampling and many-to-one mapping. However, by limiting sampling to a restricted neighborhood of edge pixels, the new methods avoid the fast growth of random selections as the number of curve segments in the image increases.

The Dynamic RHT method (DRHT) is an iterative process of two RHTs. First, the original RHT is run until the accumulator threshold is reached by some accumulator cell. For the second iteration of the algorithm, the set of feature points is determined by collecting the points that are near to the line found in the first iteration. Next, the new set of points is accumulated in the zeroed accumulator and when the accumulator threshold has been exceeded again, the line is found. From that stage the algorithm follows the original RHT. For the second RHT iteration, the accumulator resolution and the accumulator threshold are usually selected to be higher than those of the first iteration.

In the Random Window RHT (RWRHT) [6] a window location is first randomly selected from the binary edge picture. The RHT procedure is performed in the $m \times m$ window, whose size m is also randomized. Random sampling is repeated R times where R could be a function of the window size m. Window sampling is repeated until a predefined threshold t is reached. Lines are detected one by one until a desired number of lines l_{max} have been found or some heuristic criterion stops the computing. When a line has been found and verified to be a true line its pixels are removed from the binary image. The algorithm for line detection is as follows:

Algorithm 2 : *The Random Window RHT Algorithm*

1. Create the set D of all edge points in a binary edge picture.
2. Select one point d_i randomly from the set D.
3. Randomize a window size m where $m_{min} \leq m \leq m_{max}$.

4. Create a pixel data set W of the $m \times m$ neighborhood of the point d_i.
5. Repeat the RHT procedure in the set W at maximum R times.
6. If the $A(a, b)$ is equal to the threshold t, the parameters a and b describe the parameters of the detected curve; Otherwise continue to Step 2.

The Window RHT (WRHT) [6] is a simpler version that selects one edge point randomly, fits a curve to a fixed size neighborhood of the edge point, and defines the curve parameters. The curve fitting can be done for example by the least squares method. Only the parameters satisfying a certain goodness of the fitting are accepted to update the accumulator space. The WRHT process is continued until the maximum score in the accumulator is equal to the threshold t. This approach determines line segments curve by curve, too. In detail, the WRHT algorithm for line detection is as follows:

Algorithm 3 : *The Window RHT Algorithm*

1. Create the set D of all edge points in a binary edge picture.
2. Select a point d_i randomly from the set D.
3. If enough points are found in an $m \times m$ neighborhood of the point d_i, fit a curve to the points and calculate the line parameters (a, b); Otherwise go to Step 2.
4. If the fitting error is within a tolerance, accumulate the cell $A(a, b)$ in the accumulator space; Otherwise go to Step 2.
5. If the $A(a, b)$ is equal to the threshold t, the parameters a and b describe the parameters of the detected curve; Otherwise continue to Step 2.

Both the RWRHT and WRHT renew the random sampling mechanisms of the RHT but leave the accumulation technique the same as earlier. Some new accumulation approaches are proposed in [16]: the curve parameters can be stored in quantized values or a mixture structure of two hash tables and one linear list can be used. These two approaches can be combined to the RWRHT and the WRHT, too.

The most critical constraint of the algorithm for correct and reliable operation is the window size. It must be large enough so that desired detection accuracy can be achieved. However, the size is limited by the average separation distance of adjacent curves and by noise points increasing fitting error in large windows.

An extension to the WRHT, called the Connective RHT (CRHT), was recently developed in [6] by Kälviäinen and Hirvonen to handle these problematic situations. The extension introduces a connective component search of the windowed points. Now, for the fitting process only those points of the window are used that are connected to the center point of the window with an 8-path. Furthermore, the connective component search can be performed as sectored. In this context, the sectoring means limiting the search direction to the original one and its two most similar directions. Only in the special case of images in which the edges are not 8-connected, i.e. there are gaps between edge pixels, the connective component search does not improve performance.

3 Test Results

The methods were tested on both complex synthetic and complex real-world images[7]. Although a serious attempt was made to select the test parameters for each method as optimally as possible, the test results may vary according to both the selected parameters and the test pictures.

3.1 Methods Selected for Tests

The algorithms chosen for the tests are as follows: (a) non-probabilistic HTs: Standard Hough Transform (SHT) [3, 13], Combinatorial Hough Transform (CHT) [1], and Curve Fitting Hough Transform (CFHT) [10]; (b) probabilistic HTs: Randomized Hough Transform without the point distance criterion (RHT_ND) and with the point distance criterion (RHT_D), Dynamic RHT (DRHT), Window RHT (WRHT), Connective RHT (CRHT), Random Window RHT (RWRHT), Probabilistic Hough Transform by Kiryati et al. (ProbHT) [5], and Dynamic Combinatorial Hough Transform (DCHT) [7].

Methods allowing comparisons with the RHT are chosen. The SHT using Risse's cluster detection [13] has been selected as a reference method. In the CHT, two pixels of the image are used to calculate the line parameters. For limiting the number of pixel pair combinations, the image is segmented (typically in 64 parts) and the voting process is performed segment by segment. The CFHT duplicates several characteristics of the RHT and its variants like many-to-one mapping, curve fitting, and the use of a list structure.

The DCHT also belongs to probabilistic HT algorithms if a seed point is selected randomly among feature points. In the DCHT, many-to-one mapping is used. The ProbHT produces a small, randomly selected subset of the edge points in the image. This limited poll is used as an input for the HT. Although the ProbHT uses one-to-many mapping in contrast to the many-to-one mapping of the RHT, the idea of utilizing random sampling is similar.

3.2 Tests with a Complex Synthetic Image

The first test picture consists of 50 randomly generated synthetic lines (Fig. 1.a). Two tests were run: one to detect 50 realistic candidate lines and one to detect as many of those as possible. A realistic candidate line satisfies line criteria, i.e. the minimum number of pixels, the maximum gap between pixels etc. For all the synthetic images, the real parameters of the lines were always known and it was checked after each test if the detected line parameters were among them. The maximum differences between detected and real line parameters allowed were ± 5 pixels in ρ and ± 0.025 radians ($\approx 1.43°$) in θ. Realistic candidate lines satisfying this criterion are called real lines. Results of the test are summarized in Table 1 and the output images corresponding to Table 1.a are shown in Fig. 1.

---

[7] Test runs were performed on a standard SUN SPARCstation IPX.

Method	(a)				(b)			
	Lines	Time	Av Size	Max Size	Lines	Time	Av Size	Max Size
SHT	48	94.60	65536	65536	48	94.93	65536	65536
CHT	37	53.67	65536	65536	47	54.50	65536	65536
CFHT	28	3.06	40	80	28	3.06	40	80
ProbHT	47.0	79.52	65536	65536	47.0	79.63	65536	65536
RHT_ND	17.2	138.08	903	3164	37.6	290.10	677	3013
RHT_D	25.5	17.03	131	473	44.6	19.06	134	669
DRHT	27.8	19.09	179	794	46.3	29.13	151	730
WRHT	36.9	1.47	0	0	43.8	2.06	0	0
CRHT	43.3	1.80	0	0	46.4	2.07	0	0
RWRHT	26.9	2.64	63	261	46.0	4.55	52	242
DCHT	43.9	4.28	256	256	48.5	8.12	256	256

Table 1. Test results of the line detection from a 50-line image: (a) Detecting 50 lines; (b) Detecting as many lines as possible. The first column, Lines, lists the number of real lines detected and the second column, Time, lists CPU times in seconds[7]. The third and fourth columns, Av Size and Max Size, denote the average and maximum amount of active accumulator cells during the test run. Of course, those methods that apply a static accumulator have equal values in both the two last columns.

The most accurate, but slow methods were the SHT, the CHT and the ProbHT while the WRHT and the CRHT were the fastest. When only 50 candidate lines are detected, the SHT, the ProbHT, the CRHT and the DCHT give good results as displayed in Table 1.a and Fig. 1. However, in the case of detecting as many lines as possible (Table 1.b) the CHT, the DRHT, and the RWRHT also obtained reasonable results.

3.3 Tests with a Complex Real-World Image

The second test picture and its binary edde picture are presented in Fig. 2.a and 2.b. Results are summarized in Table 2 and Fig. 2. All methods, except the CFHT, gave quite satisfactory output images. The RHT_ND, SHT, and ProbHT were the slowest approaches, the extensions of the RHT the fastest ones. The RHT-like variants typically detected lines in more segments than the SHT.

4 Discussion and Comparisons

From analyzing the previous tests, some conclusions can be made on the relative performances of the methods.

4.1 Non-probabilistic Methods

The SHT is the most accurate method but computation speed is very low. Moreover, it needs a large predefined fixed size storage in accumulation. The CHT is

Method	SHT	CHT	CFHT	ProbHT	RHT_ND	RHT_D
Lines	61	102	83	54.0	115.0	115.0
Time	99.83	58.00	4.85	74.93	130.14	14.81

Method	DRHT	WRHT	CRHT	RWRHT	DCHT
Lines	113.0	114.8	119.7	115.4	95.2
Time	8.12	3.02	3.56	4.02	28.19

Table 2. Test results of the line detection from a complex real-world image.

faster than the SHT. A possible disadvantage of the algorithm seems to be that it may miss some lines due to small segment size. If the segment size is larger, the computation becomes slower. Also, the performance of the method depends more on the distribution of the image points than with the other methods. Generally, the computation time of the CHT is too high compared to the fastest methods.

The fastest of the non-probabilistic Hough transforms is the CFHT. The CFHT borrows the idea of the converging mapping from the RHT and combines this part of the RHT framework to curve fitting, achieving a high computational speed via a many-to-one mapping. With pictures like in Section 3 the CFHT fails to find several obvious lines. Therefore, the CFHT seems to be one of the most inaccurate methods. Some of the difficulties of the CFHT were already discussed in [11] and some improvements were suggested. We want to emphasize that results may vary with selected parameters.

4.2 Probabilistic Methods

The ProbHT uses only a subset of image points in Hough transform calculation. According to test simulations this subset has to be rather large to obtain an accuracy similar to the SHT. However, computing is always faster. New improved strategies to apply the ProbHT are suggested in [17].

The DCHT is a simple and fast algorithm which gives reasonably good detection results. Also, it needs only a small amount of memory for the accumulator. However, the new extended RHT methods, the CRHT etc., having similar detection accuracy seem to be faster than the DCHT, especially with complex real-world images.

If an image is simple enough, containing e.g. 10 lines, the RHT_ND needs clearly less computation and memory than the SHT. If the image consists of many lines or it is noisy, the computation time of the RHT_ND will increase rapidly because of waste accumulations. Furthermore, detection rate may decrease. Thus, the use of the point distance criterion (RHT_D) is necessary. Using the point distance criterion the RHT_D successfully avoids waste accumulations. The DRHT gives a bit better detection accuracy than the RHT_D, but sometimes at the cost of computation time and storage needed.

The RWRHT and the WRHT use more local information than the basic RHT. The RWRHT is highly adaptive since its window size is changing and the number of RHT processes is also varying. The test results of Section 3 show that it is very fast and rather accurate. The local window can extract local lines more powerfully than line extraction from the whole image. This method lacks the problems of the CFHT but also uses effectively local information. The choice of the random window size still needs more analysis.

The WRHT and CRHT also have low computation time and satisfactory accuracy. Both the WRHT and the CRHT can be used with accumulator threshold equal to one, i.e. no accumulator is needed. In fact, raising the threshold does not lead to significantly better results.

The RWRHT, WRHT, and CRHT seem to exceed the power of the RHT_D and thus are very promising approaches to further analysis. Especially, the CRHT was in all tests one of the fastest and most accurate methods.

5   Conclusion

We presented new versions of the Randomized Hough Transform to detect curve segments. The new extensions, called the Dynamic RHT, the Random Window RHT, the Window RHT, and the Connective RHT, were tested with synthetic and real-world pictures and compared to several Hough transforms. The RWRHT, the WRHT, and the CRHT gave promising results.

Acknowledgement: The authors thank Mr. P. Kultanen for his contributions to the development of the Dynamic RHT.

References

1. Ben-Tzvi, D., Sandler, M.B., "A Combinatorial Hough Transform," *Pattern Recognition Letters*, vol. 11, no. 3, 1990, pp. 167-174.
2. Bergen, J.R., Shvaytser, H., "A Probabilistic Algorithm for Computing Hough Transforms," *J. of Algorithms*, vol. 12., no. 4, 1991, pp. 639-656.
3. Duda, R.O., Hart, P.E., "Use of the Hough Transform To Detect Lines and Curves in Pictures," *Communications of the ACM*, vol. 15, no. 1, 1972, pp. 11-15.
4. Hare, A.R., Sandler, M.B., "General Test Framework for Straight-Line Detection by Hough Transforms," *Proc. of IEEE Int. Symp. on Circuits and Systems IS-CAS'93*, May 3-6, Chicago, USA, 1993, pp. 239-242.
5. Kiryati, N., Eldar, Y., Bruckstein, A.M., "A Probabilistic Hough Transform," *Pattern Recognition*, vol. 24, no, 4., 1991, pp. 303-316.
6. Kälviäinen, H., Hirvonen, P., Xu, L., Oja, E., "Probabilistic and Non-probabilistic Hough Transforms: Overview and Comparisons," Res. Rep. No. 45, Dept. of Inform. Techn., Lappeenranta Univ. of Techn., Lappeenranta, Finland, 1993. To appear in *Image and Vision Computing*.
7. Leavers, V.F., Ben-Tzvi, D., Sandler, M.B., "A Dynamic Combinatorial Hough Transform for Straight Lines and Circles," *Proc. of 5th Alvey Vision Conf.*, Reading, UK, September 25-28, 1989, pp. 163-168.

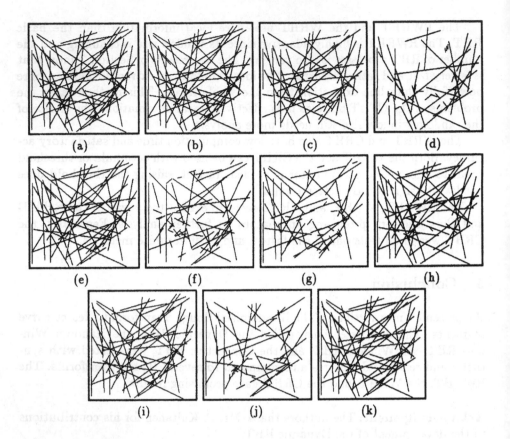

Fig. 1. Resulting images of line detection from a 50-line image by: (a) An original synthetic binary image of 50 lines; (b) SHT; (c) CHT; (d) CFHT; (e) ProbHT; (f) RHT_D; (g) DRHT; (h) WRHT; (i) CRHT; (j) RWRHT; (k) DCHT.

8. Leavers, V.F., "The Dynamic Generalized Hough Transform: Its Relationship to the Probabilistic Hough Transforms and an Application to the Concurrent Detection of Circles and Ellipses," *CVGIP: Image Understanding*, vol. 56, no. 3, 1992, pp. 381-398.

9. V.F. Leavers, "Which Hough Transform?," *CVGIP: Image Understanding*, vol. 58, no. 2, pp. 250-264, 1993.

10. Liang, P., "A New Transform for Curve Detection," *Proc. of Third Int. Conf. on Computer Vision*, Osaka, Japan, December 1990, pp. 748-751.

11. Liang, P., "A New and Efficient Transform for Curve Detection," *J. of Robotic Systems*, vol. 8, no. 6, 1991, pp. 841-847.

12. Princen, J., Yuen, H.K., Illingworth, J., Kittler, J., "A Comparison of Hough Transform Methods," *The Third Int. Conf. on Image Analysis and Its Applications*, Conf. Pub. 307, Warwick, UK, July 1989, pp. 73-77.

13. Risse, T., "Hough Transformation for Line Recognition: Complexity of Evidence Accumulation and Cluster Detection," *CVGIP*, vol. 46, 1989, pp. 327-345.

360

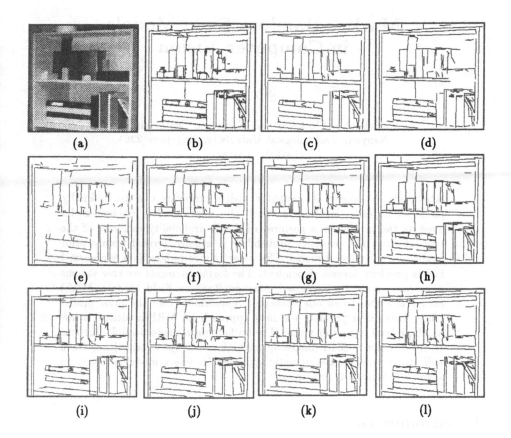

Fig. 2. Resulting images of line detection from a complex real-world image by: (a) An original gray-level image; (b) The binary edge image; (c) SHT; (d) CHT; (e) CFHT; (f) RHT_ND; (g) RHT_D; (h) DRHT; (i) WRHT; (j) CRHT; (k) RWRHT; (l) DCHT.

14. Roth, G., Levine, M.D., "Extracting Geometric Primitives," Report TR-CIM-92-13, Computer Vision and Robotics Laboratory, McGill Research Centre for Intelligent Machines, McGill Univ., Montréal, Québec, Canada, October 1992.
15. Xu, L., Oja. E., Kultanen P., "A New Curve Detection Method: Randomized Hough Transform (RHT)," *Pattern Recognition Letters*, vol. 11, no. 5, 1990, pp. 331-338.
16. Xu, L., Oja, E., "Randomized Hough Transform (RHT): Basic Mechanisms, Algorithms, and Computational Complexities," *CVGIP: Image Understanding*, vol. 57, no. 2, 1993, pp. 131-154.
17. Ylä-Jääski, A., Kiryati N, "Automatic Termination Rules for Probabilistic Hough Algorithms", *Proc. of 8th Scand. Conf. on Image Analysis*, Tromsø, Norway, May, 1993, pp. 121-128.
18. Yuen, H.K., Princen, J., Illingworth, J., Kittler, J., "Comparative Study of Hough Transform Methods for Circle Finding," *Image and Vision Computing*, vol. 8, no.1, 1990, pp. 71-77.
19. Yuen, K.S.Y., Lam, L.T.S., Leung, D.N.K., "Connective Hough Transform," *Image and Vision Computing*, vol. 11, no. 5, 1993, pp. 295-301.

Markov Random Field Models
in Computer Vision

S. Z. Li

School of Electrical and Electronic Engineering
Nanyang Technological University, Singapore 2263
szli@ntu.ac.sg

Abstract. A variety of computer vision problems can be optimally posed as Bayesian labeling in which the solution of a problem is defined as the maximum *a posteriori* (MAP) probability estimate of the true labeling. The posterior probability is usually derived from a prior model and a likelihood model. The latter relates to how data is observed and is problem domain dependent. The former depends on how various prior constraints are expressed. Markov Random Field Models (MRF) theory is a tool to encode contextual constraints into the prior probability. This paper presents a unified approach for MRF modeling in low and high level computer vision. The unification is made possible due to a recent advance in MRF modeling for high level object recognition. Such unification provides a systematic approach for vision modeling based on sound mathematical principles.

1 Introduction

Since its beginning in early 1960's, computer vision research has been evolving from heuristic design of algorithms to systematic investigation of approaches for solving vision problems. In their search for solutions, researchers have realized the importance of contextual information in image understanding. In this process, a variety of vision models using context have been proposed. Among these are Markov Random Field (MRF) theory based models (of which analytic regularization theory based models are special cases).

MRF modeling is appealing for the following reasons (Preface of [4]): (1) One can systematically develop algorithms based on sound principles rather than on some *ad hoc* heuristics for a variety of problems; (2) It makes it easier to derive quantitative performance measures for characterizing how well the image analysis algorithms work; (3) MRF models can be used to incorporate various prior contextual information or constraints in a quantitative way; and (4) The MRF-based algorithms tend to be local, and tend themselves to parallel hardware implementation in a natural way.

Complete stochastic vision models based on MRF are formulated within the Bayesian framework. The optimal solution of a problem is defined as the maximum *a posteriori* (MAP) probability estimate of the truth, the best that one can get from random observations. Most of vision problems can be posed as one of labeling using constraints due to prior knowledge and observations. In this case, the optimal solution is defined as the MAP labeling and is computed by minimizing a posterior energy. The posterior probability is derived, using the Bayesian rule, from a prior model and a likelihood model. The latter relates to how data is observed and is problem domain dependent. The former depends on how various prior constraints are expressed. Results from MRF theory provide us tools to encode contextual constraints into the prior probability. This is the main reason for MRF vision modeling.

MRF based approaches have been successful in modeling low level vision problems such as image restoration, segmentation, surface reconstruction, texture analysis, optical flow, shape from X, visual integration and edge detection (There are a long list of references. Readers may refer to collections of papers in [15, 4] and references therein). Relationships between low level MRF models are discussed in [16, 7] and those between MRF models and regularization models in [16]. The unifying theme of Bayesian modeling for low level problems appear for example, in [7, 2, 18]. A prototypical Bayesian formulation using MRF is that of Geman and Geman [8] for image restoration.

Investigation of MRF modeling in high level vision such as object matching and recognition, which is more challenging (Introduction of [15]), begins only recently. In an initial development of an MRF model for image interpretation [17], the optimal solution is defined as the MAP labeling. Unfortunately, the posterior probability therein is derived using heuristic rules instead of the laws of probability, which dissolves the original promises of MRF vision modeling. A coupled MRF network for simultaneous object recognition and segmentation is described in [5].

In a recent work [11], an MRF model for high level object matching and recognition is formulated based on sound mathematical principles. Mathematically, like the typical low level MRF model of Geman and Geman [8], the model utilizes MRF theory to characterize prior contextual constraints. This, plus an observation model for the joint likelihood, enables the derivation of the posterior probability. The model [11] is more general than the low level model [8] in that it makes use of contextual observations and allows non-homogeneous sites and non-isotropic neighborhood systems.

This makes it possible to formulate a larger number of low and high level problems in the single Bayesian framework in a systematic way. This is of significance in both theory and practice. It provides a rational approach on a sound basis. It implies some intrinsic properties or common mechanisms in seemingly different vision problems. It also suggests that these problems could be solved using a similar architecture.

This paper presents such a unified MRF modeling approach [10]. The systematic way to the MRF modeling is summarized as five steps:

1. Pose the vision problem as one of labeling in which a label configuration represents a solution (Sec.2).
2. Further pose it as a Bayesian labeling problem in which the optimal solution is defined as the MAP label configurations (Sec.3),
3. Use Gibbs distribution to characterize the prior distribution of label configurations (Sec.3.2),

4. Figure out the likelihood density of data based on an assumed observation model (domain dependent and exemplified in Sec.4) and

5. Use the Bayesian rule to derive the posterior distribution of label configurations, to measure the cost of a solution (Sec.3.3 and Sec.4).

(How to search for the MAP configuration is not discussed in this paper.) Two MRF models are described as cases in low and high level vision, respectively. The first is the prototypical Geman and Geman's low level model (Sec.4.1) and the second is the recent high level object recognition model [11] (Sec.4.2). The latter is described using the Geman-Geman's model as the reference point. The presentation is done in such as way that parallel concepts are seen clearly.

2 Vision Problems as Labeling

2.1 The Labeling Problem

A *labeling problem* is specified in terms of a set of sites and a set of labels. Let $\mathbf{d}$ be a set of m discrete *sites*.

$$\mathbf{d} = \{1, \ldots, m\} \tag{1}$$

The ordering of the sites is not important; their relationship is determined by a *neighborhood system* (the definition of neighborhood systems is central in MRF theory and will be introduced later). Let $\mathbf{D}$ be a set of *labels*. Labeling is to assign a label from $\mathbf{D}$ to each of the sites in $\mathbf{d}$.

A set of sites can be categorized in terms of their "homogeneity" and a set of labels in terms of their "continuity". Sites on a lattice such as those corresponding to array of image pixels are considered as being spatially homogeneous whereas those corresponding to features extracted from images such as critical points, line segments or surface patches are considered as being inhomogeneous. Usually, homogeneous sites lead to an isotropic neighborhood system and inhomogeneous sites to an anisotropic neighborhood system.

A label can be continuous such as a continuous intensity or range value. The value can usually be confined to a real interval

$$f_i \in \mathbf{D} = [x_l, x_h] \tag{2}$$

In this case, there are an infinite number of labels. In the other case, a label may be discrete

$$f_i \in \mathbf{D} = \{1, \cdots, M\} \tag{3}$$

For example, a label may index to one of model object lines or regions.

Let $F = \{F_1, \ldots, F_m\}$ be a family of random variables defined on $\mathbf{d}$, in which each random variable F_i assumes a value in $\mathbf{D}$. A joint event $\{F_1 = f_1, \ldots, F_m = f_m\}$, abbreviated $F = f$, is a realization of F where $f = \{f_1, \ldots, f_m\}$ is called a *configuration* of F. A configuration may represent an image, an edge map, or a matching (mapping) from image features to object features. The set of all configurations is

$$\mathbf{S} = \mathbf{D}^m = \underbrace{\mathbf{D} \times \mathbf{D} \cdots \times \mathbf{D}}_{m \text{ times}} \tag{4}$$

The space of admissible solutions may be identical to **S** or if additional constraints are imposed, a subset of it. A configuration f can be interpreted in one of the two ways: It is a mapping $f : \mathbf{d} \longrightarrow \mathbf{D}$; or it is a labeling $\{f_1, \ldots, f_m\}$ of the sites.

2.2 Labeling Problems in Vision

In terms of the homogeneity and the continuity, we may classify a vision labeling problem into one of the following four categories:

LP1: Homogeneous sites with continuous labels.
LP2: Homogeneous sites with discrete labels.
LP3: Inhomogeneous sites with discrete labels.
LP4: Inhomogeneous sites with continuous labels.

The former two categories characterize low level processing performed on observed images and the latter high level processing on extracted token features. The following describes some vision problems in terms of the categories.

Restoration of grey scale images, or image smoothing, is an LP1. The set **d** of sites corresponds to image pixels and the set **D** of labels is a real interval. The restoration is to estimate the true image signal from a degraded or noise-corrupted image.

Restoration of binary or multi-level images is an LP2. Similar to the continuous restoration, the aim is also to estimate the true image signal. The difference is that each pixel in the resulting image here assumes a discrete value and thus **D** in this case is a set of discrete labels.

Image segmentation is an LP2. It partitions an observation image into mutually exclusive regions, each of which has some uniform and homogeneous properties whose values are significantly different from those of neighboring regions. The property can be for example grey tone, color or texture. Pixels within each region is assigned a unique label.

The prior assumption in these problems is that the signal is smooth or piecewise smooth. This is complimentary to the assumption about edges at which abrupt changes occur.

Edge detection is also an LP2. Each pixel (more precisely, between each pair of neighboring pixels) is assigned a label in {edge, non-edge} if along an arc passing through the pixel there are abrupt changes in some properties in the direction tangent to the arc. The property can be the pixel value or directional derivatives of pixel value function. Continuous restoration with discontinuities [8, 16, 3] is a combination of LP1 and LP2.

Perceptual grouping [14] is an LP3. The sites usually correspond to initially segmented features (points, lines and regions) which are inhomogeneously arranged. The fragmentary features are to be organized into perceptually meaningful groups. Between each pair of the features can be assigned a label in {connected,disconnected}, indicating whether the two features should be joined.

Feature-based object matching and recognition is an LP3. Each site indexes an image feature such as a point, a line segment or a region. Labels are discrete in nature and each of them indexes a model feature. The resulting configuration is a mapping from the image features to those of a model object. Stereo matching is a similar LP3.

Pose estimation from a set of point correspondences might be formulated as an LP4. Each label may assume the value of a real matrix, representing an admissible (orthogonal, affine or perspective) transformation. A prior (unary) constraint is that the label of transformation itself must be orthogonal, affine or perspective. A mutual constraint is that the labels $f_1, \cdots, f_m$ should be close to each other to form a consistent transformation. When outliers are present, a line process field [8, 16, 3] may be introduced to separate transformation labels which form a consistent cluster from those due outliers.

3 Bayesian Labeling based on MRF

3.1 Bayesian Labeling

Bayesian statistics is of fundamental importance in estimation and decision making. Let $\mathbf{D}$ be a set of truth candidates and $\mathbf{r}$ the observation. Suppose that we know both the *a priori* probabilities $P(f)$ of configurations f and the likelihood densities $p(\mathbf{r} \mid f)$ of the observation $\mathbf{r}$. The best estimate one can get from these is that maximizes the *a posteriori* probability (MAP). The posterior probability can be computed by using the Bayesian rule

$$P(f \mid \mathbf{r}) = p(\mathbf{r} \mid f)P(f)/p(\mathbf{r}) \tag{5}$$

where $p(\mathbf{r})$, the density function of $\mathbf{r}$, does not affect the MAP solution. The *Bayesian labeling problem* is that given the observation $\mathbf{r}$, find the MAP configuration of labeling $f^* = \arg\max_{f \in \mathbf{S}} P(F = f \mid \mathbf{r})$.

To find the MAP solution, we need to derive the prior probabilities and the likelihood functions. The likelihood function $p(\mathbf{r} \mid F = f)$ depends on the noise statistics and the underlying transformation from the truth to the observation. It will be discussed in conjunction with specific problems. Knowing the *a priori* joint probability $P(F = f)$ is difficult, in general. Fortunately, there exists a theorem which helps us specify the *a priori* probabilities of MRFs. This is the main reason for MRF modeling.

3.2 MRF Prior and Gibbs Distribution

MRF is a branch of probability theory which provides a tool for analyzing spatial or contextual dependencies of physical phenomena. Define a neighborhood system for $\mathbf{d}$

$$\mathcal{N} = \{\mathcal{N}_i \mid \forall i \in \mathbf{d}\} \tag{6}$$

where $\mathcal{N}_i$ is the collection of sites neighboring to i for which (1) $i \notin \mathcal{N}_i$ and (2) $i \in \mathcal{N}_j \iff j \in \mathcal{N}_i$. The pair $(\mathbf{d}, \mathcal{N})$ is a graph in the usual sense. A *clique c* for $(\mathbf{d}, \mathcal{N})$ is a subset of $\mathbf{d}$ such that c consists of a single site $c = \{i\}$, or a pair of neighboring sites $c = \{i, j\}$, or a triple of neighboring sites $c = \{i, j, k\}$, and so on. We denote the collection of single-site cliques, that of two-site cliques, $\cdots$, by $C_1, C_2, \cdots$, respectively. The collection of all cliques for $(\mathbf{d}, \mathcal{N})$ is $C = C_1 \cup C_2 \cup \cdots$.

A family F of random variables is said to be an MRF on $\mathbf{d}$ with respect to $\mathcal{N}$ if and only if the following two conditions are satisfied: (1) $P(F = f) > 0, \forall f \in \mathbf{S}$ (positivity), and (2) $P(F_i = f_i \mid F_j = f_j, j \in \mathbf{d}, j \neq i) = P(F_i = f_i \mid F_j = f_j, j \in \mathcal{N}_i)$ (Markovianity). Condition (1) above is for F to be a random field. Condition (2) is called the local characteristics. It says that the probability of a local event at i conditioned on all the remaining events is equivalent to that conditioned on the events at the neighbors of i. It can be shown that the joint probability $P(F = f)$ of any random field is uniquely determined by these local conditional probabilities [1]. However, it is usually difficult to specify the set of the conditional probabilities. Nonetheless, the Hammersley-Clifford theorem [1] of Markov-Gibbs equivalence provides a solution.

According to the Hammersley-Clifford theorem [1], F is an MRF on $\mathbf{d}$ with respect to $\mathcal{N}$ if and only if the probability distribution $P(F = f)$ of the configurations is a Gibbs distribution with respect to $\mathcal{N}$. A Gibbs distribution of the configurations f with respect to $\mathcal{N}$ is of the following form

$$P(f) = Z^{-1} \times e^{-\frac{1}{T}U(f)} \tag{7}$$

In the above, Z is a normalizing constant, T is a global control parameter called the temperature and $U(f)$ is the *prior energy*. The prior energy has the form

$$U(f) = \sum_{c \in C} V_c(f) = \sum_{\{i\} \in C_1} V_1(f_i) + \sum_{\{i,j\} \in C_2} V_2(f_i, f_j) + \cdots \tag{8}$$

where "$\cdots$" denotes possible higher order terms. The practical value of the theorem is that it provides a simple way of specifying the joint prior probability $P(F = f)$ of the configurations by specifying the prior potentials $V_c(f)$ for all $c \in C$. One is allowed to choose appropriate potentials for desired system behavior. The potential functions contain the *a priori* knowledge of interactions between labels assigned to neighboring sites and reflect how individual matches affect one another — *a priori*.

3.3 Posterior MRF Energy

Let the likelihood function be expressed in the exponential form

$$p(\mathbf{r} \mid F = f) = Z_r^{-1} \times e^{-U(\mathbf{r} \mid f)} \tag{9}$$

where $U(\mathbf{r} \mid f)$ is called the *likelihood energy*. Then the posterior probability is a Gibbs distribution

$$P(F = f \mid \mathbf{r}) = Z_E^{-1} \times e^{-E(f)} \tag{10}$$

with *posterior energy*

$$E(f) = U(f \mid \mathbf{r}) = U(f)/T + U(\mathbf{r} \mid f) \tag{11}$$

Hence, given a fixed **r**, F is also an MRF on **d** with respect to $\mathcal{N}$. The MAP solution is equivalently found by

$$f^* = \arg\min_{f \in \mathbf{S}} U(f \mid \mathbf{r}) \tag{12}$$

To summarize, the MRF modeling process consists of the following steps: Defining a neighborhood system $\mathcal{N}$, defining cliques $\mathcal{C}$, defining the prior clique potentials, deriving the likelihood energy, and deriving the posterior energy.

4   Two Cases of MRF Vision Modeling

In this section, the prototypical low level MRF model of Geman and Geman [8] for image restoration is described first and is taken as the reference point. It is prototypical because it can model problems falling in categories LP1 and LP2. It forms the basis for other low level problems such as edge detection, motion, stereo and texture [16, 7, 15, 4]. The high level MRF model for object matching [11] is described next as a prototype for LP3.

4.1   Image Restoration at Low Level

Low level processing is performed on images. The set of sites $\mathbf{d} = \{1, \ldots, m\}$ index image pixels in a 2D plane and the observation **r** represents the array of pixel values. The set **D** contains discrete label to be assigned to the pixels. The configuration $f = \{f_i \in \mathbf{D} \mid i \in \mathbf{d}\}$, or the state of labeling, is a realization of a Markov random intensity field.

Let the neighbors of pixel i consist of the four nearest pixels

$$\mathcal{N}_i = \{j \mid dist(\text{pixel}_i, \text{pixel}_j) \leq 1\} \tag{13}$$

where $dist(A, B)$ is the distance between A and B. For simplicity, here consider only two-site cliques

$$\mathcal{C} = \mathcal{C}_2 = \{\{i, j\} \mid j \in \mathcal{N}_i, \forall i \in \mathbf{d}\} \tag{14}$$

Examples of more complex cliques can be found in Fig.5 of [8].

Now define the prior clique potentials in Eq.(8). When only two-site cliques are considered, only second order prior potentials are nonzero. The second order potential is defined by

$$V_2(f_i, f_j) = v_{20}\, g(f_i - f_j) \tag{15}$$

where v_{20} is a real scalar and $g(\eta)$ is a function measuring the cost due to the smoothness violation caused by $f_i - f_j$. For continuous restoration with discontinuities [8, 3], $g(\eta) = \min(\eta^2, \alpha)$. For piecewise constant reconstruction with discontinuities [8, 9], $g(\eta) = [1 - \delta(f_i - f_j)]$ where $\delta(\eta)$ is the Dirichlet function. A general definition of g for discontinuity-adaptive restoration is given in [13].

Geman and Geman [8] describe a general degraded image model based on which the likelihood function is obtained. In an important special case, each observed pixel value is assumed to be $r_i = f_i + n$ where $n \sim N(0, \sigma)$ is independent Gaussian noise. In this case, the likelihood energy is

$$U(\mathbf{r} \mid f) = \sum_{i \in \mathbf{d}} (r_i - f_i)^2 / \sigma \qquad (16)$$

The posterior energy $E(f) = U(f \mid \mathbf{r})$ can be computed from $U(f)$ and $U(\mathbf{r} \mid f)$ using (11)

$$U(f \mid \mathbf{r}) = \sum_{i \in \mathbf{d}} \sum_{j \in \mathcal{N}_i} v_{20}\, g(f_i - f_j)/T + \sum_{i \in \mathbf{d}} (r_i - f_i)^2 / \sigma \qquad (17)$$

The above with $g(\eta) = \min(\eta^2, \alpha)$ is the notion of the weak string model [3] and that with $g(\eta) = [1 - \delta(f_i - f_j)]$ is the minimal length coding model [9].

4.2 Object Matching at High Level

High level processing is performed on token features extracted from images. A typical problem is (partial) matching from image features to those of a modeled object. Unlike the previous case, the observation $\mathbf{r}$ in this case include not only components describing each feature itself but also those describing contextual relations between them. Moreover, the neighborhood relationship between features is not isotropic as is in the image case.

Both an object and a scene are represented by a set of features, (unary) properties of the features and (bilateral or higher order) contextual relations between them. The features, properties and relations can be denoted compactly as a *relational structure* (RS). An RS describes a scene or a (part of) model object.

The scene RS is denoted by $\mathbf{g} = (\mathbf{d}, \mathbf{r})$ where $\mathbf{d} = \{1, \ldots, m\}$ indexes a set of m features and $\mathbf{r} = \{r_1, r_2, \ldots, r_H\}$ denotes the set of observation data of order 1 through order H (When $H = 2$, the RS is reduced to a *relational graph* (RG)). For order $n = 2$, $r_2(i, j) = [r_{2,1}(i, j), \ldots, r_{2,K_2}(i, j)]^T$ consists of K_2 binary (bilateral) relations between features i and j.

A model RS is similarly denoted as $\mathbf{G} = (\mathbf{D}, \mathbf{R})$ where $\mathbf{D} = \{1, \ldots, M\}$ and $\mathbf{R} = \{R_1, R_2, \ldots, R_H\}$. For particular n and k ($1 \leq k \leq K_n; 1 \leq n \leq h$), $R_{n,k}$ represent the same type of constraint as $r_{n,k}$. Introduce a virtual NULL model $\mathbf{D}_0 = \{0\}$ to represents everything not modeled by $\mathbf{G}$. Then in matching the scene to the model object plus the NULL , the set of all labels is

$$\mathbf{D}^+ = \mathbf{D}_0 \cup \mathbf{D} = \{0, 1, \ldots, M\} \qquad (18)$$

$\mathbf{S} = (\mathbf{D}^+)^m$ is the admissible space of label configurations.

In RS matching, the set $\mathcal{N}_i$ of neighbors of $i \in \mathbf{d}$ can comprises all related sites. But when the scene is very large, $\mathcal{N}_i$ needs to include only those which are within a spatial distance α from i.

$$\mathcal{N}_i = \{j \neq i \mid dist(\text{feature}_j, \text{feature}_i) < \alpha, j \in \mathbf{d}\} \qquad (19)$$

The size α may reasonably be related to the size of the considered model object.

Now define the prior clique potentials in Eq.(8). The single-site potential is defined as

$$V_1(f_i) = \begin{cases} v_{10} & \text{if } f_i = 0 \\ 0 & \text{otherwise} \end{cases} \tag{20}$$

where v_{10} is a constant. This definition says that if f_i is the NULL label, it incurs a penalty v_{10}; or otherwise no penalty. The two-sites potential is defined as

$$V_2(f_i, f_j) = \begin{cases} v_{20} & \text{if } f_i = 0 \text{ or } f_j = 0 \\ 0 & \text{otherwise} \end{cases} \tag{21}$$

where v_{20} is a constant. This says that if either f_i or f_j is the NULL , it incurs a penalty v_{20}; or otherwise no penalty.

The joint likelihood function $p(\mathbf{r} \mid F = f)$ has the following properties: (1) It is conditioned on pure non-NULL matches $f_i \neq 0$; (2) It is regardless of the neighborhood system $\mathcal{N}$; and (3) It depends on how the model object is observed in the scene, which depends on the underlying transformations and noise. Assume that $\mathbf{R}$ and $\mathbf{r}$ consist of types of relations which are invariant under the group of underlying transformations and that the observation model is $\mathbf{r} = \mathbf{R} + \mathbf{n}$ where $\mathbf{n}$ is independent Gaussian noise. Then the likelihood energy is

$$U(\mathbf{r} \mid F = f) = \sum_{i \in \mathbf{d}, f_i \neq 0} V_1(\mathbf{r} \mid f_i) + \sum_{i \in \mathbf{d}, f_i \neq 0} \sum_{j \in \mathbf{d}, f_j \neq 0} V_2(\mathbf{r} \mid f_i, f_j) \tag{22}$$

Because the noise is independent, we have $U(\mathbf{r} \mid f_i) = U(r_1(i) \mid f_i)$ and $U(\mathbf{r} \mid f_i, f_j) = U(r_2(i, j) \mid f_i, f_j)$. The likelihood potentials are

$$V_1(r_1(i) \mid f_i) = \sum_{k=1}^{K_1} [r_{1,k}(i) - R_{1,k}(f_i)]^2 / 2\sigma_{1,k}^2 \tag{23}$$

and

$$V_2(r_2(i, j) \mid f_i, f_j) = \sum_{k=1}^{K_2} [r_{2,k}(i, j) - R_{2,k}(f_i, f_j)]^2 / 2\sigma_{2,k}^2 \tag{24}$$

where $\sigma_{n,k}^2$ ($k = 1, \ldots, K_n$ and $n = 1, 2$) are the standard deviations of the noise components. The vectors $R_1(f_i)$ and $R_2(f_i, f_j)$ is the "mean vector" for the random vectors $r_1(i)$ and $r_2(i, j)$, respectively. When the noise is correlated, there are correlating terms in the likelihood potentials. The assumption of independent Gaussian may not be accurate but offers a good approximation when the accurate likelihood is not available.

The posterior energy $E(f)$ can be computed from $U(f)$ and $U(r \mid f)$ using (11)

$$U(f \mid \mathbf{d}) = \sum_{i \in \mathbf{d}} V_{10}(f_i)/T + \sum_{i \in \mathbf{d}} \sum_{j \in \mathcal{N}_i} V_{20}(f_i, f_j)/T +$$

$$\sum_{i \in \mathbf{d}} V_1(r_1(i) \mid f_i) + \sum_{i \in \mathbf{d}} \sum_{j \in \mathbf{d}} V_2(r_2(i, j) \mid f_i, f_j) \tag{25}$$

The MAP configuration f^* of (12) is the optimal labeling of the scene in terms of the model object. Matching to multiple model objects can be resolved after matching to each of the objects [11].

5 Conclusion

A variety of low and high level vision problems can formulated as Bayesian labeling using a unified MRF modeling approach. A labeling of an image, of an edge map or of a scene is considered as a configuration of an MRF. The solution to a problem is defined as the MAP label configuration which minimizes the posterior energy. The MRF modeling provides a systematic approach for vision modeling based on the rationale principles.

Related to the MRF modeling is estimation of involved parameters. In LP1 and LP2 at low level, the estimation can be done, for example, using the coding method [1] and least square error method [6]. A learning-from-example method for MRF parameter estimation in object recognition (LP3) is proposed in [12].

References

1. J. Besag. "Spatial interaction and the statistic analysis of lattice systems". *J. Royal. Statist. Soc. B*, 36:192–293, 1974.
2. J. Besag. "Towards Bayesian image analysis". *Journal of Applied Statistics*, 16(3):395–406, 1989.
3. A. Blake and A. Zisserman. *Visual Reconstruction*. MIT Press, Cambridge, MA, 1987.
4. R. Chellappa and A. Jain, editors. *Markov Random Fields: Theory and Applications*. Academic Press, 1993.
5. P. R. Cooper. "Parallel structure recognition with uncertainty: coupled segmentation and matching". In *Proceedings of IEEE International Conference on Computer Vision*, pages 287–290, 1990.
6. H. Derin and H. Elliott. "Modeling and segmentation of noisy and textured images using Gibbs random fields". *IEEE Transactions on Pattern Analysis and Machine Intelligence*, PAMI-9(1):39–55, January 1987.
7. R. C. Dubes and A. K. Jain. "Random field models in image analysis". *Journal of Applied Statistics*, 16(2):131–164, 1989.
8. G. Geman and D. Geman. "Stochastic relaxation, gibbs distribution and bayesian restoration of images". *IEEE Transactions on Pattern Analysis and Machine Intelligence*, PAMI-6(6):721–741, November 1984.
9. Y. G. Leclerc. "Constructing simple stable descriptions for image partitioning". *International Journal of Computer Vision*, 3:73–102, 1989.
10. S. Z. Li. " Towards 3D vision from range images: An optimization framework and parallel networks". *CVGIP: Image Understanding*, 55(3):231–260, May 1992.
11. S. Z. Li. "A Markov random field model of object matching". *submitted*, 1993.
12. S. Z. Li. "Optimal selection of MRF parameters in object recognition". *in preparation*, 1993.
13. S. Z. Li. "On discontinuity adaptive regularization". *IEEE Transactions on Pattern Analysis and Machine Intelligence*, accepted.
14. D. G. Lowe. *Perceptual Organization and Visual Recognition*. Kluwer, 1985.
15. K. V. Mardia. *Technical Editor*. Special Issue on Statistic Image Analysis. *Journal of Applied Statistics*, 16(2), 1989.
16. J. Marroquin, S. Mitter, and T. Poggio. "Probabilistic solution of ill-posed problems in computational vision". *Journal of the American Statistical Association*, 82(397):76–89, March 1987.
17. J. W. Modestino and J. Zhang. "A Markov random field model-based approach to image interpretation". In *Proceedings of the IEEE Computer Society Conference on Computer Vision and Pattern Recognition*, pages 458–465, 1989. Also *IEEE Transactions on Pattern Analysis and Machine Intelligence*, Vol.14, No.6, pp.606–615, June 1992.
18. R. Szeliski. "Bayesian modeling of uncertainty in low-level vision. *International Journal of Computer Vision*, pages 271–301, 1990.

The Role of Key-Points in Finding Contours *

O. Henricsson and F. Heitger

Communication Technology Laboratory,
Swiss Federal Institute of Technology ETH
CH-8092 Zürich, Switzerland

Abstract. This paper describes a method for aggregating local edge evidences into coherent pieces of contour. An independent representation of corner and junction features provides suitable stop-conditions for the aggregation process and allows to divide contours into meaningful sub-strings, right from the beginning. The active role of corner and junction points makes the contours converge onto them and greatly reduces the problems associated with purely edge-based methods. A second stage is concerned with completing established contours across regions that are less well-defined by contrast. The algorithm suggested uses the attributes of established structures (e.g. direction of termination) as well as local orientation and edge evidences to constrain possible completions in a rigorous way.

Keywords: edge detection, key-point detection, edge linking, contour completion

1 Introduction

Intensity discontinuities are considered one of the primary image features that allow to segment a scene into meaningful parts. Based on the assumption that object boundaries are generally smooth and mostly contrast defined, much effort has been devoted to design suitable edge detectors (e.g. [3]) that reliably indicate these 1-D intensity discontinuities. The deficiencies of edge-maps, such as fragmentation, gaps at junctions, as well as clutter and faulty connections are well known. Also, object boundaries are not guaranteed to be contrast defined. To obtain more complete and unambiguous boundary definitions, additional processing is needed that accounts for more global relationships among image features.

Perceptual grouping methods have demonstrated a promising potential in this respect. Most approaches use geometrical criteria (e.g. distance, co-curvilinearity, symmetry) to group local edge evidences into larger entities, thus also separating salient structures from clutter [11, 19, 14, 6]. The use of binary edge-maps as input, however, neglects information that could assert the validity of connections on grounds other than geometry.

2-D image features, such as junctions, corners and line-ends represent an-

---

* The research described in this paper has been supported by the Swiss National Science Foundation, Grant no. 20-36431.92

other important class of image information that can serve the definition of object boundaries. With respect to this task the role of these features is a dual one: First, they reflect prominent events in the course of a boundary that allow to divide it into "natural" parts and to extract meaningful shape decompositions [2, 13]. A corner or a junction together with the directions of their constituent components often characterizes an object more succinctly than edge fragments. Fig. 1 illustrates this aspect. Second, 2-D features occur abundantly in situations of occlusion and within this context they can serve to indicate object contours even if the contrast is vanishing or null. A model of visual cortical contour processing that infers such contours as well as figure ground direction from termination evidences has been presented earlier [9]. Because the 2-D features are so significant, we use the term *key-points*.

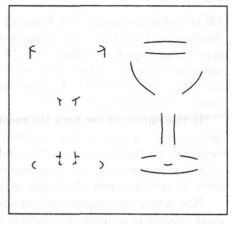

Fig. 1.: The information at corners and junctions (left) is often more important for object definition than edge fragments (right).

In this paper we want to discuss the role that an independent representation of such key-points can take in aggregating local edge evidences to larger, coherent pieces of contour (called *contour-strings* in the sequel). The goal is to represent the contrast defined image features as a collection of meaningful parts, subdivided at locations of high key-point evidence. Of course, this idea is not new, but previous implementations used post-processing of binary edge-maps to achieve segmentation (e.g. [13]), rather than utilizing independent representations of 2-D features. We will show that the complementary nature of edges and key-points can provide a better and more stable definition of image structures.

In a first instance key-points serve as stop-conditions for the aggregation process which is started at points that can most reliably be classified as "edge" points. In a second stage, the key-points that are connected to contour-strings serve as "bridge-heads" for closing gaps across regions of low or vanishing contrast. Connections are only accepted if they satisfy a variety of geometrical constraints, but also provide evidence for residual contrast definition.

For the moment, we deliberately exclude completions of the "illusory contour" type as described in [9]. The boundaries obtained with the present approach are therefore still incomplete. However, this complies with the general philosophy of the present approach: Contour-strings are established in a strictly hierarchical fashion, starting with the most reliable ones and using the information of already established structures to expand into more uncertain regions. Decisions are adapted to the level of uncertainty, with weaker evidences requiring more constraints to satisfy than stronger ones.

2 Filtering and Key-point Detection

2.1 Filters

We convolve the image with filters of even and odd symmetry (6 orientations, channels) and combine their output to response modulus (square-root of oriented energy), an approach similar to [5, 16, 15, 1, 17]. The filters have the following properties (see [8, 18] for a detailed description): They form a quadrature pair, are polar separable in the Fourier domain, and the response modulus yields a unified response to edges and lines.

In this paper we use both the modulus representations and their 2nd derivatives perpendicular to channel direction. The second derivative enhances the negative curvature occurring at modulus peaks and has further shown smaller gaps at junctions with non-maximum suppression. We denote the modulus maps with $\mathcal{M}$ and the second derivative maps $\mathcal{M}^{(2)}$.

Non-maximum suppression is applied on clipped 2nd derivative channels, i.e. local maxima in a direction perpendicular to the dominant channel orientation. This binary map (denoted $\mathcal{N}$) is used as a seed structure for the contour aggregation.

2.2 Key-points

Key-points are defined as strong 2D intensity variations, i.e. the signal not only varies in one direction, but also in other directions. We implemented a detection scheme based upon a model of visual cortical end-stopped cells.

In principle, the 1st and 2nd derivatives in the direction of modulus channels are used, the 1st derivatives being sensitive to the termination of oriented structures (line-ends, corners, junctions) and the 2nd derivatives to blobs and strong curvature. 1st and 2nd derivatives are combined to localize the key-points. A compensation map is used to eliminate spurious responses to 1D structures (straight edges, lines). The key-point detection scheme is described in detail in [8, 18]. We denote the set of detected key-points $\mathcal{K}$ and the 3×3 surround by $\mathcal{K}_s$. Reliable detection as well as accurate localization of key-points is a prerequisite for the contour aggregation as described below.

2.3 Local Orientation and Edge Quality

The response modulus in the six channels is used to determine the local orientation of the underlying structure. We use the real and imaginary coefficients of the first Fourier harmonic to approximate the local orientation, (similar to the approaches of [4, 10]).

$$\theta_{loc} = \frac{1}{2} tan^{-1} \left(\frac{\mathcal{Im}}{\mathcal{Re}} \right), \quad where \quad \theta_{loc} \in [-\frac{\pi}{2}, \frac{\pi}{2}]$$

Because we use filters that are polar separable in the Fourier domain, the response magnitudes in the different orientation channels are entirely determined by the orientation of an edge/line and the orientation tuning of the filters, defined as $\Omega(\psi) = cos^n(\psi)$.

The residual between the actual response distribution and the edge/line prediction is then used as a measure for edge quality (cf. [18] for details).

$$Residual = \sum_{k=0}^{nori-1} \left(\frac{\mathcal{M}_k}{\mathcal{M}_{max}} - \frac{\Omega(|\theta_{loc} - \theta_k|)}{\Omega(min_{j=0,...,nori-1}|\theta_{loc} - \theta_j|)} \right)^2$$

$$Q(\theta_{loc}) = \frac{1}{1 + Residual} \quad , [0 \le Q(\theta_{loc}) \le 1] \tag{1}$$

Edge quality will be used for selecting appropriate start points for contour aggregation as will be explained below.

3 Contour Aggregation

The contour aggregation algorithm can be described as a process linking initial edge-markings into coherent contour-strings. The selection of the appropriate track is based upon (1) connectivity, (2) modulus strength, and (3) key-point markings.

3.1 Selecting Start-points

Adequate start points are positions with high edge quality and low influence from surrounding key-points. Such points have per definition (1) a well defined local orientation, as needed for the start condition.

The normalized difference of modulus and key-point value is used to define the key-point influence. The product of edge quality and key-point influence yields a suitable start measure,

$$S(x,y) = \begin{cases} Q(x,y)^2 \cdot \left(\frac{\mathcal{M}_{max}(x,y) - \mathcal{K}(x,y)}{\mathcal{M}_{max}(x,y) + \mathcal{K}(x,y)} \right) & , (x,y) \in \mathcal{N} \\ 0 & , otherwise \end{cases}$$

where $\mathcal{M}_{max}(x,y)$ is the response modulus in the dominant orientation channel, and $\mathcal{K}(x,y)$ the key-point map value. Notice that only points marked by non-maximum suppression $(\mathcal{N})$ are used as start points.

The start points are transferred to a sorted list, the first entry being the point with the highest start value. The contour aggregation algorithm successively picks the currently best start point from the sorted list. After a contour segment has been established, all start points along the segment are eliminated to prevent multiple chaining of the same contour-string.

3.2 Chaining Algorithm

Contour aggregation (pixel chaining) is done by locally evaluating a small set of valid paths within directional masks as depicted in Fig. 2. The evaluation is a two stage process, (1) a priority is assigned to each path, and (2) a path value depending on the priority is assigned, as shown in Table 1. The current position P_0 and the chaining history defines the chaining direction, $\alpha \in [-\pi, \pi]$. At the start point, the chaining direction is initialized as one of the two opposing directions defined by the local orientation map. Each α is associated with a two-level directional mask j, defined in eight possible directions $(\beta(j) = j\frac{\pi}{4})$. Within each mask there are nine distinct paths extending from P_0 through a pixel P_1 in level one to a neighboring pixel P_2 in level two. Each path $i = 0, 1, \ldots, 8$ within the mask j is thus defined by the triplet $[P_0, P_1(i), P_2(i)]$ and evaluated according to the table below. The function f penalizes paths deviating from the current chaining direction α. In a first selection the path(s) with the highest priority is(are) selected. If there is more than one path, the value of $E(i)$ determines the selection. The selected path i' defines the next pixel $P_1(i')$ and an updated chaining direction α'. The chaining continues until one of the following stop conditions is encountered.

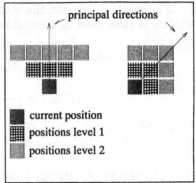

Fig. 2.: Two-level directional masks. The other six masks are only rotated versions of the two.

- $P_0 \in K$, the current position is a key-point. At priority level 3 the chaining algorithm captures the key-point position in a deterministic fashion and the stop condition is set.
- priority 0, termination without key-point marking.
- collision with another, already established, contour-string.

When the chaining algorithm encounters a stop condition it generates a stop marker of the corresponding type.

Priority	Condition	Evaluation/Action
3	$P_0 \in K_s$	Key-Point capture, no path evaluation.
2	$(P_1(i) \in \{\mathcal{N}, \mathcal{K}_s\}) \cap$ $(P_2(i) \in \{\mathcal{N}, \mathcal{K}, \mathcal{K}_s\})$	Normal chaining, evaluating $E(i) = \left(\mathcal{M}_{max}^{(2)}(P_1(i)) + \mathcal{M}_{max}^{(2)}(P_2(i)) \right) \cdot f(\beta(j), \gamma(i))$ $\gamma(i)$ is the direction of the path i and $f(\beta(j), \gamma(i)) = cos(\beta(j) - \gamma(i))$.
1	$(P_1(i) \in \mathcal{N}) \cap$ $(P_2(i) \ni \{\mathcal{N}, \mathcal{K}, \mathcal{K}_s\})$	terminating in the next step, evaluating $E(i) = \mathcal{M}_{max}^{(2)}(P_1(i))$
0	$P_1(i) \ni \{\mathcal{N}, \mathcal{K}, \mathcal{K}_s\}$	path terminated

Table. 1. Chaining algorithm.

The chaining algorithm generates contour-strings and stop markers in a connected fashion, inferring a graph-like data structure. Each contour-string is delimited at both ends with a key-point. The order of a key-point is defined as the number of contours strings connected to it. Apart from cross references, semi-global attributes are assigned to contour-strings and key-points (Table 2).

3.3 Post-processing of Established Contour-strings

The established contour-strings can still have strong orientation discontinuities. We therefore divide each contour-string with orientation discontinuities into substrings by using the algorithm suggested by Medioni [13]. The points marked by

feature type	attribute
contour-string	- length, - integrated modulus response (contrast) - type and polarity of contrast, - termination directions (linear and quadratic fits)
key-point	- order = number of connected contours, - termination direction of connected contour, - key-point value (contrast dependent) - key-point type

Table. 2. Attributes of contours and key-points.

the algorithm are further tested by linear fits on the contour-strings to either side of the marked point. If the angular difference of the two opposing directions is large enough ($> \frac{\pi}{4}$), the point is accepted as an additional key-point.

Contour-strings that are connected to a key-point of order ≥ 2 and that have a low integrated modulus value when compared to the remaining contour-strings are pruned. An additional requirement is that the contour-string is not connected to any other structure. Thus, unnecessary high orders of key-points due to these spurious contour-strings are precluded. Furthermore, short and isolated contour-strings are pruned as well if their integrated modulus is below a given threshold (we use 1% of the global average). All pruned structures are transferred to a stack and can be used for later processing. The pruning of spurious contour-strings is important with respect to gap-closing and a robust vertex classification.

4 Bridging Gaps Supported by Contrast Evidences

Recapitulating the process history of the present contour representation, we started with the initial edge map and applied the chaining algorithm as an aggregation process yielding a graph-like representation of the contours. The key-points were used as natural stop-markers during the chaining process. A pruning stage was applied to retain only significant structures.

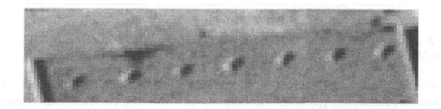

Fig. 3. Cut-out from the aerial image in Fig. 7, showing poor contrast definition.

We can now use the information gained with the contour aggregation process to find other contour strings that are less well defined by contrast, (a typical example is shown in Fig. 3). In other words, already established structures are used to constrain possible extensions across areas of low or vanishing contrast. We have tacitly assumed that all important image structures are in some sense connected to key-points, thus possible contrast defined connections are only allowed between pairs of key-points. However, bridging contrast defined gaps between pairs of key-points extends also to connections that do not comply with co-curvilinearity constraints. Our approach to close contrast defined gaps consists of four stages.

Pre-selection: all connections are checked and those which (1) exceed a predefined distance, (2) are already established or (3) intersect with already established contour string, are eliminated. The pre-selection stage is fast and greatly reduces the number of connections that are further analyzed. This stage is done without analyzing the connection for contrast evidences.

Classification: each remaining connection is classified as either two-, one-, none-sided, depending on distance and angular criteria (see below).

Evaluation: collecting contrast evidences along the connection line. Connections not passing predefined criteria are eliminated.

Selection: the remaining connections compete in a local winners-take-all procedure, leaving only the most significant connections.

4.1 Classification According to Geometrical Criteria

The connections surviving the pre-selection stage are classified as either two-, one- or none-sided depending on angular criteria, as shown in Fig. 4. The classification is done by analyzing the termination directions of the contour strings in relation to a given connection. Analyzing key-point A we have n attached con-

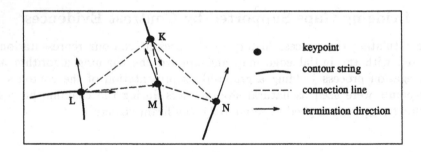

Fig. 4. Examples of connection classification (with parameters below), two-sided KM (or MK), one-sided LM, and none-sided ML, LK, KL, KN, NK, NM, MN.

tour strings $a_1, \ldots, a_n$ with their respective termination angles $\alpha_1, \ldots, \alpha_n$. Each connection from key-point A to B defines a direction, $\beta_{A \to B}$. The connection AB $(A \to B)$ is one-sided if,

$$\min_i \left(|\beta_{A \to B} - \alpha_i| \right) \leq \left(\frac{\pi}{2} - c \right) \cdot e^{-\frac{d^2}{2\sigma^2}} + c \tag{2}$$

where d is the Euklidian distance between A and B. The parameters σ and c control distance and angular criteria. (we used $\sigma = 5.0$ and $c = 15°$). If the connection BA $(B \to A)$ also satisfies (2) we have a two-sided connection. If neither

AB nor BA satisfy (2) the connection is classified as none-sided. This classification is thought to also reflect the level of uncertainty of a given connection, the most certain being the two-sided and the least certain the none-sided.

4.2 Evaluating the Connections for Contrast Evidences

The remaining connections are then tested for contrast evidences. We use two maps for this purpose; (1) the modulus channel that best matches the orientation connection between the key-points and (2) the local orientation map.

If there exists a smooth contrast defined structure between the key-points, we assume that (1) it is best defined by the modulus channel matching the connection orientation and (2) that the average deviation between the connection orientation and the local orientation along the connection line will be small.

Local maxima are searched for along scan-lines orthogonal to the orientation of the connection. As a potential structure between the key-points is expected to have low or vanishing contrast, we also expect the local maxima markings to have a high positional uncertainty (due to noise). Furthermore, the connection is constrained to go through the two key-points but must not necessarily be straight. This suggests the use of a lenticular-shaped region to search for local maxima as depicted in Fig. 5.

Local maxima found along each orthogonal scan line are marked as illustrated in Fig. 5. Not only the number of maxima markings, compared to the number of scan lines (ratio), is important but also their spatial distribution (scatter). Maxima markings are approximated with a second degree polynomial, constraining the fit-curve to go through the key-points. The mean squared error between the maxima markings and the fitted polynomial serves as a measure for scatter. Note however, that this measure does not discriminate between scatter due to noise and inter-

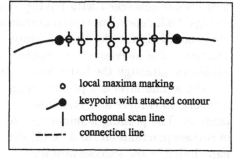

Fig. 5.: Evaluation of a connection.

ferences stemming from neighboring structures. A connection is only accepted when both, the local maxima analysis (ratio, scatter) and the orientation analysis (average deviation of local orientation) individually pass given thresholds.

4.3 Selection Through Competition

The connections remaining at this stage are few and must all have a residual contrast definition. We further reduce the number of connections by local competion, allowing only one connection *from* a given key-point to another. Notice, however, that this winner-takes-all approach still allows a given key-point to *receive* connections from other key-points. We let the competition take place only within the classes two-, one- and none-sided and the selection among the them is strictly hierachical, with the two-sided connection having the highest priority. The competition is based upon geometrical criteria and the evidence for residual contrast definition. A measure reflecting contrast definition is calculated by additively combining the ratio of maxima markings, the scatter and the average deviation of local orientation (see above). The geometrical criterion penalizes deviations from collinearity and applies only to one- and two-sided connections. As a measure we use the cosine of the enclosed angle(s) between the connection line and the termination direction(s) of the contour strings.

5 Results

In this section we show the results that can be obtained with our approach, using two rather complex images, an aerial and a telephone image. In addition we also show feature maps such as the 2nd derivative of response modulus taken in the dominant orientation and key-point map. (Fig. 6, 7, and 8). Image dimensions are 256×256 with 8-bit grey-level resolution. Tests were carried out on SUN Sparc 2 and 10 stations using ANSI-C programming language.

The gap closing algorithm successively reduces the number of connections. We have confirmed this by counting the number of connections in each stage. For the aerial image there were initially 223729 (473^2) connections and remaining after pre-selection 3450, evaluation 995, and selection 89.

6 Conclusions

We have presented a contour aggregation scheme on three distinct levels. The first level is concerned with linking local edge evidences into coherent contour-strings. An independent representation of key-points is used to define appropriate stop-conditions for the linking process. Knowing the location of corners and junctions also alleviates the problem of reconstructing them from edge map evidences, although the latter approach has proven quite successful [12].

The second level is a pruning stage, intended to eliminate spurious contours attached to corners and junctions as well as isolated contour fragments of low contrast. The pruning is important for (1) obtaining more stable classifications of corners junctions etc. and for (2) eliminating spurious contours that may block gap closing in the successive stage.

The third level deals with bridging gaps that are caused by poor contrast definition. The suggested algorithm not only incorporates geometrical information of already established structures, but also residual low-level contrast evidences for making a final decision. We have shown that this strategy effectively selects completions between pairs of key-points that are weakly defined by contrast. Currently we can only deal with fairly straight completions, but we intend to expand the scheme also for curved segments. A distinctive feature of the present approach is that a given completion must not necessarily comply with geometric (e.g. collinearity) constraints, as long as there is sufficient contrast definition. Some examples for this have been shown in Fig. 7.

In general, we believe that before invoking any type of perceptual grouping it is necessary to first find stable representations of the contrast defined features and their connectivity. Having this basis, it seems much easier to infer structures that are not defined by contrast and to discriminate between different completion types (e.g. foreground or background structures).

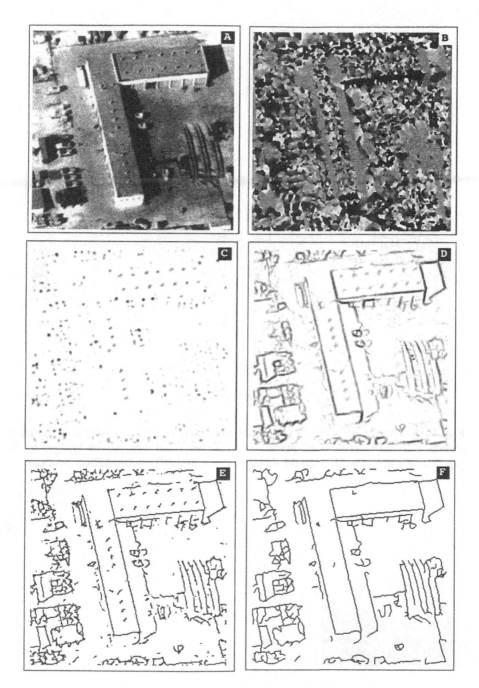

Fig. 6. (A) original aerial image, (B) local orientation coded with grey-values ranging from black 0° via grey 90° to white 180°, (C) key-point map, (D) clipped negative second derivative of modulus, (E) initial edge-map, and (F) the resulting contour representation after the gap closing procedures.

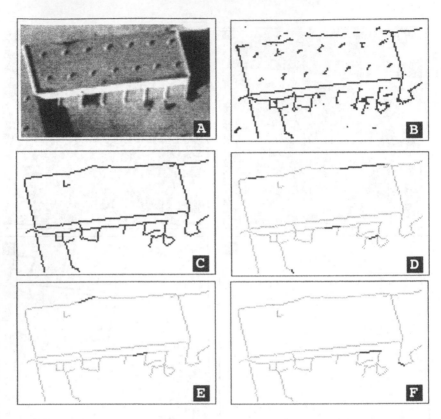

Fig. 7. (A) cut-out from Fig. 6, (B) initial edge-map, (C) the resulting contour representation after the gap closing procedures, (D) two-sided connections bridged by the gap closing algorithm, (E) one-sided connections, and (F) none-sided connections.

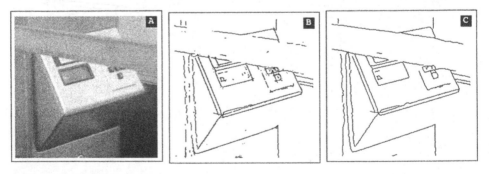

Fig. 8. (A) original telephone image, (B) initial edge-map, and (C) resulting contour representation after the gap-closing procedures

References

1. E. H. Adelson and J. R. Bergen. Spatiotemporal energy models for the perception of motion. *J. Opt. Soc. Am. A*, 2(2):pp. 284–299, 1985.
2. H. Asada and M. Brady. The Curvature Primal Sketch. *IEEE Trans. Pattern Anal. Machine Intell.*, PAMI-8(1):pp. 2–14, 1986.
3. J. F. Canny. A Computational Approach to Edge Detection. *IEEE Trans. Pattern Anal. Machine Intell.*, PAMI-8(6):pp. 679–698, 1986.
4. W. T. Freeman. *Steerable filters and local analysis of image structure.* PhD thesis, MIT, Media Laboratory, Cambridge MA, 1992.
5. G. H. Granlund. In Search of a General Picture Processing Operator. *Computer Graphics and Image Processing*, 8:pp. 155–173, 1978.
6. G. Guy and G. Medioni. Perceptual Grouping Using Global Saliency-Enhancing Operators. In *ICPR'92*, pages 99–103, 1992.
7. F. Heitger, G. Gerig, L. Rosenthaler, and O. Kübler. Extraction of boundary keypoints and completion of simple figures. In *SCIA'89*, pages 1090–1097, 1989.
8. F. Heitger, L. Rosenthaler, R. von der Heydt, E. Peterhans, and O. Kübler. Simulation of neural contour mechanisms: From simple to end-stopped cells. *Vision Research*, 32:pp. 963–981, 1992.
9. F. Heitger and R. von der Heydt. A Computational Model of Neural Contour Processing: Figure–Ground Segregation and Illusory Contours. In *ICCV'93*, pages 32–40, Berlin, Germany, 1993.
10. H. Knutsson and G. Granlund. Texture analysis using two-dimensional quadrature filters. In *IEEE Computer Society Workshop on Computer Architecture for Pattern Analysis and Image Database Management*, pages 206–213, 1983.
11. D. G. Lowe. *Perceptual organization and visual recognition.* Kluwer Academic Publishers, Boston, MA, 1985.
12. J. Matas and J. Kittler. Junction detection using probabilistic relaxation. *Image and Vision Computing*, 11(4):pp. 197–202, 1993.
13. G. Medioni and Y. Yasumoto. Corner Detection and Curve Representation Using Cubic B-Splines. *Comput. Vision, Graphics and Image Process.*, 39:pp. 267–278, 1987.
14. R. Mohan and R. Nevatia. Perceptual Organization for Scene Segmentation and Dsecription. *IEEE Trans. Pattern Anal. Machine Intell.*, PAMI-14(6):pp. 616–635, 1992.
15. M. C. Morrone and D. C. Burr. Feature detection in human vision: a phase-dependent energy model. *Proc. R. Soc. Lond.*, B 235:pp. 221–245, 1988.
16. M. C. Morrone and R. A. Owens. Feature detection from local energy. *Pattern Recognition Letters*, 6:pp. 303–313, 1987.
17. P. Perona and J. Malik. Detecting and localizing edges composed of steps, peaks and roofs. Technical Report UCB/CSD 90/590, Computer Science Division, University of California at Berkley, 1990.
18. L. Rosenthaler, F. Heitger, O. Kübler, and R. von der Heydt. Detection of General Edges and Keypoints. In G. Sandini, editor, *Lecture Notes in Computer Science*, pages 78–86. Springer Verlag, Berlin, 1992.
19. A. Sha'ashua and S. Ullman. Structural Saliency: The Detection of Globally Salient Structures Using a Locally Connected Network. In *ICCV'88*, pages 321–327, 1988.

A Framework for Low Level Feature Extraction

Wolfgang Förstner

Institut für Photogrammetrie, Universität Bonn, Nußallee 15, D-53115 Bonn
e-mail: wf@ipb.uni-bonn.de

Abstract. The paper presents a framework for extracting low level features. Its main goal is to explicitly exploit the information content of the image as far as possible. This leads to new techniques for deriving image parameters, to either the elimination or the elucidation of "buttons", like thresholds, and to interpretable quality measures for the results, which may be used in subsequent steps. Feature extraction is based on local statistics of the image function. Methods are available for blind estimation of a signal dependent noise variance, for feature preserving restoration, for feature detection and classification, and for the location of general edges and points. Their favorable scale space properties are discussed.

Keywords: low level features, keypoints, edge detection, segments, local image statistics, noise estimation, restoration, adaptive thresholds, scale space, quality evaluation.

1 Introduction

Feature extraction is the first crucial step of all image analysis procedures which aim at symbolic processing of the image content. Basic features of nearly all symbolic, i. e. non-iconic image descriptions, are points, edges and regions. The research in feature extraction is rich and dozens of procedures have been proposed for the extraction of these feature types. However, no coherent theory seems to be available suited to extract features of all types simultaneously. The lack of a theoretical basis for feature extraction was the stimulus to search for the framework documented in this paper. It had to fulfill the following requirements:

1. Since feature extraction is meant to support image interpretation, modelling needs to start in object space, from which via the sensing model an image model can be derived. This excludes all models starting at the grid structure of the digital image.
2. Feature extraction has to treat the basic features simultaneously in order to avoid the necessity of developing conflict resolution strategies.
3. For self-diagnosis, only models including stochastic components for describing the image content are suitable. This, at the same time, allows to reduce the number of "buttons" controlling the result and to retain those with a clear interpretation.
4. The features should show "nice behaviour" over scale space (cf. [24]) and should have small bias supporting coarse-to-fine strategies. Therefore, only nonlinear filters seem to be suited for feature extraction (cf. [1]).

Lecture Notes in Computer Science, Vol. 801
Jan-Olof Eklundh (Ed.)

The proposed framework intentionally restricts to low level features. No attempt is made to include specific scene knowledge. The following four steps for low-level feature extraction are discussed: 1.) estimation of noise characteristics, 2.) information preserving restoration 3.) feature detection and 4.) feature location. Unification of the steps is obtained by analysing the local autocovariance function or - equivalently - the local power spectrum. This technique has received a great deal of attention for more than 15 years, due to its versability in representing local image properties both using geometric and statistical tools (cf. [10], [17], [16], [2], [14], [23], [18]).

The novelty of the proposed approach lies in the *integration* and - as a by product - in the *simplification* of existing techniques for feature extraction and the provision of statistically founded *evaluation measures* for making the quality of the individual steps transparent and *objective*.

2 Image Model

Describing image analysis, with feature extraction being a part of it, requires the setting up of models of the scene to be recovered, of the sensing process used for observation, of the image as information memory, and of the tools used for inverting the imaging process, yielding an estimated or inferred description of the scene (cf. [12], [20]). The image model is derived in three steps.

The Ideal Continuous Image: We first assume the camera to be modelled as a pinhole camera, the lighting to be diffuse and the light sensitive image area to be of unlimited resolution.

The image area $\mathcal{I}$ therefore consists of the ideal or true *homogeneous segments* $\tilde{S}_i$, where the intensity function $\tilde{f}(x, y)$ or some locally computable function of $\tilde{f}$ is assumed to be *piecewise smooth*. The segments are assumed to show *piecewise smooth boundary lines* $\tilde{\mathcal{L}}_j$. Points $\tilde{\mathcal{P}}_k$ are either boundary points of high curvature or junctions (cf. Fig. 1a). A classification of all image points (x, y) is thus possible:

$$\mathcal{I} = \tilde{\mathcal{S}} + \tilde{\mathcal{L}} + \tilde{\mathcal{P}} = \bigcup_{i=1}^{\tilde{n}_s} \tilde{\mathcal{S}}_i + \bigcup_{j=1}^{\tilde{n}_l} \tilde{\mathcal{L}}_j + \bigcup_{k=1}^{\tilde{n}_p} \tilde{\mathcal{P}}_k \qquad (1)$$

The Real Continuous Image: Assuming a real objective, more general lighting condition and a light sensitive image area of limited resolution, in general leads to, though continuous, blurred images; the blur generally being non-homogenous and anisotropic. Due to the blurring defining a possibly local and anisotropic scale $\Sigma_1(x, y)$ we obtain *segment-regions* $\mathcal{S}_i$, often referred to as *blobs*, *line-regions* $\mathcal{L}_j$ and *point-regions* $\mathcal{P}_k$ with a partitioning similar to eq. (1) (cf. Fig. 1b). As far as they are observable, the true points $\tilde{\mathcal{P}}_k$ and lines $\tilde{\mathcal{L}}_j$ are assumed to lie in the point- and line-regions.

The Observed Image: The observed image is a sampled and noisy version of the real image, now referring to a row-columm grid (r, c): $g(r, c) = f(r, c) + n(r, c)$. The noise is at least caused by the Poisson-process of the photon flux,

Fig. 1. shows the structure of the ideal image (a), with points, lines (edges), and segments as basic features and of the real image (b) containing point-, line- and segment-type regions. (c) shows the classification tree for image features.

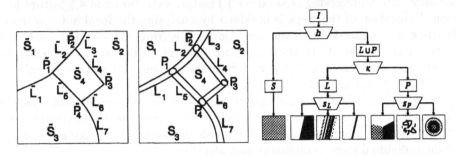

by the electronic noise of the camera and - in case g is rounded to integers - by the rounding errors. For modelling purposes an approximation of $n(r,c)$ by a Gaussian distribution seems to be sufficient. The variance in general depends on the signal and in case of no over exposition can be assumed to be linearly dependent on f, thus $\sigma_n^2(r,c) = a + bf(r,c)$.

The task of feature extraction is to recover the position of the points and lines and the mutual relations between all features in order to obtain a relational description in the sense of a feature adjacency graph (cf. [9]) used for further processing steps.

3   Feature Extraction

3.1   Local Image Characteristics

We use measures for locally characterizing the image: the average squared gradient and the regularity of the intensity function with respect to junctions and circular symmetric features (cf. [8]).

The Average Squared Gradient: With the gradient $\nabla g = (g_x, g_y)^T$ we obtain the squared gradient $\boldsymbol{\Gamma} g$ as dyadic product

$$\boldsymbol{\Gamma} g = \nabla g \nabla g^T = \begin{pmatrix} g_x^2 & g_x g_y \\ g_y g_x & g_y^2 \end{pmatrix}. \tag{2}$$

The rotationally symmetric Gaussian function with centre **o** and standard deviation σ is denoted by $G_\sigma(x,y) = G_\sigma(x) * G_\sigma(y)$. This yields the *average squared gradient* image

$$\overline{\boldsymbol{\Gamma}_\sigma g}(x,y) = G_\sigma * \boldsymbol{\Gamma} g = \int \int \boldsymbol{\Gamma} g(u,v) G_\sigma(x-u, y-v) dx dy. \tag{3}$$

The three essential elements of $\overline{\boldsymbol{\Gamma}_\sigma g}$ can be derived by three convolutions.

Thus we have to distinguish *two* scales:

- the *natural scale* σ_1, which is used to describe the blurring process (cf. above) or to generate the classical, 'natural' pyramids $G_{\sigma_1} * g$.
- the *artificial scale* $\sigma \doteq \sigma_2$, which is used to integrate the nonlinear function $\boldsymbol{\Gamma}g$ of g [15] [19] leading to the notion of an 'artificial' image pyramid $G_{\sigma_2} * \boldsymbol{\Gamma}g$.

Remark: The power spectrum $P_g(\boldsymbol{u})$ can be characterized by the effective bandwidth $\boldsymbol{B}_g \doteq \int \boldsymbol{u}\boldsymbol{u}^T P_g(\boldsymbol{u})d\boldsymbol{u} / \int P_g(\boldsymbol{u})d\boldsymbol{u}$ which, due to the moment theorem [22] is closely related to the average squared gradient by $\boldsymbol{B}_g = \overline{\boldsymbol{\Gamma}g}/(4\pi^2\sigma_g^2)$ with the constant variance σ_g^2. We will use this relation for *estimating the natural local scale.* •

Obviously the average squared gradient grasps essential parts of the *statistics* of the image function and - assuming local stationarity - may be estimated easily from (2) and (3). Diagonalization $\overline{\boldsymbol{\Gamma}g} = \boldsymbol{T}\boldsymbol{\Lambda}_g\boldsymbol{T}^T = \lambda_1(g)\boldsymbol{t}_1\boldsymbol{t}_1^T + \lambda_2(g)\boldsymbol{t}_2\boldsymbol{t}_2^T$ leads to an intuitive description of $\overline{\boldsymbol{\Gamma}g}$ with three parameters, each having very specific interpretations going beyond the ones discussed in [8], [5], and [13] and being the basis for the proposed framework:

1. The trace $h \doteq tr\overline{\boldsymbol{\Gamma}g} = \lambda_1(g) + \lambda_2(g) = \overline{\| \nabla g \|^2} \doteq \sigma_{g'}^2 = \sigma_{g_x}^2 + \sigma_{g_y}^2$ yields the total energy of the image function at (x,y), the edge busyness. We will use $tr\overline{\boldsymbol{\Gamma}_\sigma g}$ for *measuring the homogeneity* of segment-type features. It is approximately χ_m^2-distributed, where m is the number of pixels involved in the integration, allowing to fix a threshold solely based on some prespecified significance level and the noise variance. Assuming the image model $g = f + n$ with white noise, $\sigma_{g'}^2$ may be split into a signal and a noise component $\sigma_{g'}^2 = \sigma_{f'}^2 + \sigma_{n'}^2$. This will be the basis for *estimating the noise variance* and for *determining regularization factors* during restoration.

2. The ratio $v = \lambda_2/\lambda_1$ of the eigenvalues yields the degree of orientation or of an isotropy. If $\lambda_2 = 0$, we have anisotropic texture or straight general edges with arbitrary cross-sections. Using the local approximation $z = au + bv^2$ of a curved edge, one can easily show that the square κ^2 of the curvature of the isophote is given [7]: $\kappa^2 = v/\sigma^2$, ($\mid 2b \mid < \mid a \mid$). We will therefore use κ^2 for measuring the *smoothness of line-type features*.

3. The largest eigenvalue is an estimate for the *local gradient* of the texture or the edge. Due to the squaring, the phase information is lost [16]. The variance of this orientation is proportional to $\lambda_2/(\lambda_1 - \lambda_2)$, yielding an additional interpretation and showing that the variance of orientation is large for $\lambda_1 \approx \lambda_2$.

Regularity Measures: Junctions and circular symmetric features can be distinguished by analysing the local gradient field.

We use the weighted sums of the squared distances $d(\boldsymbol{p}, \boldsymbol{q})$ and $d^\perp(\boldsymbol{p}, \boldsymbol{q})$ of the reference point $\boldsymbol{p}$ to the line passing through $\boldsymbol{q}$ in the direction parallel and orthogonal to $\nabla g(\boldsymbol{q})$ resp. (cf. Fig. 2 a, b), where the weights are the squared gradient magnitude and the window is given by the Gaussian $G_\sigma(\boldsymbol{p})$.

The regularity measure for junctions is given by

$$S(\boldsymbol{p}, \sigma) = \int \int d^2(\boldsymbol{p}, \boldsymbol{q}) \parallel \nabla g(\boldsymbol{q}) \parallel^2 G_\sigma(\boldsymbol{p} - \boldsymbol{q})d\boldsymbol{q} = tr\{\boldsymbol{\Gamma}^p(\boldsymbol{p}) * [\boldsymbol{p}\boldsymbol{p}^T G_\sigma(\boldsymbol{p})]\} \quad (4)$$

Fig. 2. relation between **p** and a feature at **q**, the degree of fit of $g(x, y)$ at **p** wrt. a junction (a), circular symmetric feature (b).

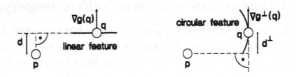

for corners or junctions. $S^\perp(\boldsymbol{p}, \sigma)$ is obtained by replacing d by $d^\perp$.

Both types are unified by BIGÜN [2] showing them to be special spiral type features. Whereas BIGÜN uses the regularity measures for classifying pixels, we will also use them for locating features. S and $S^\perp$ correspond to the keypoint map $\hat{K}$ in [23]). They, however, are simpler and – what is essential – again allow statistical testing, as they are independent and approximately χ_m^2-distributed, with m being the number of pixels involved (cf. [5]).

An Important Link: The measures $\overline{\Gamma g}$, S and $S^\perp$ have been independently motivated. However, they are not only loosely coupled by having the three elements $g_x^2, g_x g_y$ and g_y^2 of the squared gradient Γg in common. Much more, they are linked by a very important relation, namely by the covariance matrix $C_{\hat{p}\hat{p}}$ of the estimated feature location $\hat{p}$ (cf. [8]).

Assuming a *fixed* position $\boldsymbol{p}_0$ of the window minimizing $S_{p_0}(\boldsymbol{p}, \sigma) = \int\int (\boldsymbol{p} - \boldsymbol{q})^T \nabla g(\boldsymbol{q}) \nabla g^T(\boldsymbol{q})(\boldsymbol{p} - \boldsymbol{q}) G_\sigma(\boldsymbol{p}_0 - \boldsymbol{q}) d\boldsymbol{q}$ with respect to $\boldsymbol{p}$ we obtain the estimate $\hat{\boldsymbol{p}}(\sigma) = \left(\int\int \Gamma g(\boldsymbol{p}) G_\sigma(\boldsymbol{p}_0 - \boldsymbol{p}) d\boldsymbol{p}\right)^{-1} \int\int \Gamma g(\boldsymbol{p}) G_\sigma(\boldsymbol{p}_0 - \boldsymbol{p}) \boldsymbol{p} d\boldsymbol{p}$. With (3) this can be written as $\hat{\boldsymbol{p}}(\sigma) = (\overline{\Gamma_\sigma g})^{-1} \overline{\Gamma_\sigma g} \cdot \boldsymbol{p}$. With the estimated variance factor $\hat{\sigma}_0^2 = S(\hat{p}, \sigma)/(m-2)$, assuming m pixels being used, the covariance matrix of the estimated position is given by

$$C_{\hat{p}\hat{p}}(\sigma) = \frac{S(\hat{p}, \sigma)}{m-2} \cdot (\overline{\Gamma_\sigma g})^{-1} . \tag{5}$$

The regularity measure $S(\hat{p}, \sigma) = S(\boldsymbol{p}, \sigma) - \hat{\beta}^T(\sigma) \overline{\Gamma_\sigma g} \, \hat{\beta}(\sigma)$ at $\hat{p}$ is reduced by the bias $\hat{\beta}(\sigma) = \hat{\boldsymbol{p}}(\sigma) - \boldsymbol{p}$ weighted with $\overline{\Gamma_\sigma g}$. Thus the average squared gradient $\overline{\Gamma_\sigma g}$ and the regularity measure S are needed for determining the covariance of the location of a junction point. A similar reasoning holds for circular symmetric features, e. g. isolated points, replacing S by $S^\perp$ and $\Gamma = \nabla g \nabla^T g$ by $\Gamma^\perp = \nabla^\perp g \nabla^{\perp T} g$. The weight of $\hat{p}$, being proportional to the inverse of (5), equals $\overline{\Gamma_\sigma g}$, motivating the weight $tr\Gamma g = \|\nabla g\|^2$ in (4).

We are now prepared to discuss the four steps of feature extraction.

3.2   Step 1: Estimation of Noise Characteristics

The noise characteristics are decisive for thresholding. Thresholding always is performing a hypothesis test of some kind. Therefore, thresholds should depend on the distribution of the test statistic and the significance level. Whereas the distribution of the test statistic can be derived from the noise characteristics, the significance level may be fixed for all tests and/or be related to some cost function making the choice of thresholds a transparent operation.

We have developed a blind estimation scheme for the case of a linear increase of the noise variance with the signal $\sigma_n^2 = a + bf$ (cf. [3]), as real images show a significant linear portion in the noise variance. It is based on the ability to separate signal and noise in the distribution of $g_x^2 + g_y^2$ (cf. also [25]). The procedure also gives quality measures for these estimates, revealing them to be quite accurate, (in general $< 10\%$) which is consistent with the simulation results in [21] and fully sufficient.

3.3 Step 2: Information Preserving Restoration

Restoration in general aims at recovering the original signal $\tilde{f}$ from g, undoing the effects of blur and noise. This requires the estimation of the noise characteristics (cf. step 1), of the possibly local scale and of the image smoothness. We first discuss how to automatically estimate the image smoothness, assuming the local scale to be known, estimated (cf. below) or negligible.

We want to apply an adaptive Wiener filter which exploits the local statistics of the image function referring to the image model. The homogeneity of the image function g is measured by the local variance of the gradient. As the gradient varies in direction, we use the diagonalization of $\overline{\Gamma g}$ which can be written as $\overline{\Gamma g} = \overline{\Gamma f} + \sigma_n^2 I = (\sigma_{f_1}^2 + \sigma_{n_1}^2) t_1 t_1^T + (\sigma_{f_2}^2 + \sigma_{n_2}^2) t_2 t_2^T$. The eigenvalues of $\overline{\Gamma g}$ can be split into the variances $\sigma_{f_1}^2$ and $\sigma_{f_2}^2$ of the slopes in the principle directions 1 and 2 and the corresponding (equal) variances $\sigma_{n_1}^2$ and $\sigma_{n_2}^2$ of the first derivative of the noise, resp. allowing to estimate $\sigma_{f_i}^2, i = 1, 2$ from $\overline{\Gamma g}$, in case σ_n^2 is known. We can now restore the image by optimizing the energy function which explicitly reflects the image model, especially $E(\nabla \hat{f}) = 0$:

$$E = \sum_{r,c} \left(\frac{g(r,c) - \hat{f}(r,c)}{\sigma_n(r,c)} \right)^2 + \sum_{r,c} \left[\left(\frac{\hat{f}_1(r,c)}{\sigma_{f_1}(r,c)} \right)^2 + \left(\frac{\hat{f}_2(r,c)}{\sigma_{f_2}(r,c)} \right)^2 \right] \quad (6)$$

$\hat{f}_i(r,c), i = 1, 2$ are the derivatives of the restored image in the local principle directions 1 and 2. As *all* standard deviations can be estimated from the data *no tuning of parameters is necessary*. The procedure can be extended to second derivatives, thus a more general image model [26], and to more general surfaces [27].

The *selection* of a proper possibly tensor valued *scale* Σ_1 can also be based on the local image statistics [6] [19]. Approximating the local power spectrum by a Gaussian, one can show $\Sigma_1 = \sigma_g^2 \overline{\Gamma g}^{-1}$ (cf. the remark above). Using a small integration scale for $\overline{\Gamma g}$ and a large integration scale for σ_g^2, reduces bias and gathers the image contrast resp.

3.4   Step 3: Feature Detection

The classification of all image pixels into the three classes can be interpreted as feature detection in the sense that only the existence and approximate location of the features is of primary concern. The segmentation of the image area (cf. Fig. 1c) leads to a *ternary image* whose connected components give initial limitation of the search space and – in case of point- and line-regions – steer the location procedure. Moreover, a classification of the point- and line-regions can be performed.

Given the discrete version L of the average squared gradient $\overline{\Gamma_\sigma g}$ and the regularity functions S and $S^\perp$. Since the covariance of an estimated point is $D(\hat{p}) \propto S \cdot L^{-1}$ or $D(\hat{p}) \propto S^\perp \cdot L^{\perp-1}$ the 2×2-matrix L and $L^\perp$ also have to be checked for size and form using the eigenvalues λ_i common to L and $L^\perp$.

Detecting Regions: The procedure starts with the classification of pixels into homogeneous and nonhomogeneous ones by investigating $L \doteq trL = L_{11} + L_{22} = \lambda_1 + \lambda_2$. If $L < T_h$, the pixel will be considered as homogeneous.

Approximating the χ^2_m-distribution of h by a normal distribution which holds for windows larger than 5×5 the local threshold T_h is given by $T_h(x) = const. \cdot \sigma^2_n(x)(1 + z_{1-\alpha}/\sqrt{m})$ where $\sigma^2_n(x)$ is the local noise variance, *const.* a factor depending on the convolution kernels for determining L, e. g. 3/8 when using the Sobel-operator, m the number of pixels involved during integrations with G_σ and $z_{1-\alpha}$ the α-quantile of the normal distribution. The threshold only holds for unfiltered images. Otherwise the reduction in noise variance has to be taken into account, which for a Gaussian with σ_1 leads to a reduction factor of $1/(4\pi\sigma^2_1)$.

Classifying Point and Edge Regions: The second step is to investigate the form of L or $L^\perp$. It is described by the ratio $v = \lambda_2/\lambda_1$. If $v = 1$, thus $\lambda_2 = \lambda_1$ then the form of $x^T L x$ is circular indicating isotropy of the gradient caused by a corner, an isolated point or by isotropic texture. It easily can be derived from the form factor $q = 4detL/tr^2L = 4\lambda_1\lambda_2/(\lambda_1 + \lambda_2)^2$ via $v = \lambda_2/\lambda_1 = (1 - \sqrt{1-q})/(1 + \sqrt{1-q})$. As it is related to the curvature κ^2 of the isophote by $\kappa^2 = v/\sigma^2$ (cf. above), it is useful to distinguish points and smooth edges. The threshold T_κ should reflect the minimum curvature κ_{min} required for an image curve to contain a corner. T_κ can be made independent on the used scale σ. If $\|\kappa\| > T_\kappa = \kappa_{min}$, the pixel will be considered to be a candidate for a point pixel, otherwise for an edge pixel.

3.5   Step 4: Feature Location

The precise location of the point- and line-type features requires generic models which in principle allow to estimate the real-valued position of points and edges of the ideal image using the appropriate local scale of the feature. We use the two models for points, namely junctions and circular symmetric features, optimizing, i. e. minimizing, the regularity measures S (4) and $S^\perp$ from section 3.1.2. We may also use S for the location of edges, as they can be seen to be special junctions with two edges of the same orientation meeting.

Fig. 3. shows the ternary images (b, d; labels from left to right) indicating point and edge regions for a line entering an area (a). The local minima of S (bright) within the point, edge and segment regions are given in (c) and (e). Observe the unbiasedness of the optima. The integration scale is $\sigma = 4$ in (b, c). The centre of the *line* not the two edges is indicated in (c). In (d) and (e) with $\sigma = 0.7$ the two edges are detected, which are 3 pixels apart

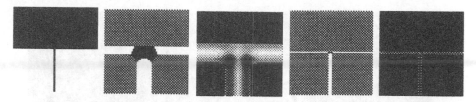

Fig. 4. shows the test image from Rosenthaler et al. with the ternary image. All junctions and corners have been detected. The integration scale is $\sigma = 2$.

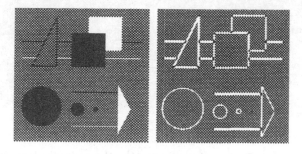

Locating Point-Type Features: There are two ways to estimate the location of point features:

- One-Step Procedure: First pixels are classified as junctions or circular features (cf. below). Pixels where S or $S^\perp$ shows a local minimum in a 8-neighborhood are considered to be point-type pixels. This yields approximate integer positions (r_0, c_0). A subpixel position (r, c) may be obtained by a parabolic fit to S or $S^\perp$, resp.
- Two-Step Procedure [8]: We first search for a relative maximum of the weight $1/tr(\boldsymbol{L}^{-1})$ in a 8-neighbourhood. *Independent on the classification* this yields the optimal window position, i. e. where the highest accuracy for the location is to be expected. After classification the subpixel position then is estimated yielding $S(\hat{\boldsymbol{p}}, \sigma)$. For circular features similar relations hold, yielding $\hat{\boldsymbol{p}}^\perp$ and $S^\perp(\hat{\boldsymbol{p}}^\perp, \sigma)$.

Classifying Junctions and Circular Symmetric Features: The classification of points (cf. Fig. 1c) can be based on the ratio $s_P = S/S^\perp \sim F_{m,m}$ [5], which again is Fisher distributed in case of white noise and orthogonal kernels for determining the derivatives $g_r(r, c)$ and $g_c(r, c)$. Two one-sided tests may be

Fig. 5. shows the recovery of the image structure with the proposed procedure (labels from left to right). The pixels of the original image (a) are classified into point, line, and segment regions (b), corresponding to the structure of the image model. The extracted and located points and edges are shown in (c) and (d) Including the blobs in (e), we obtain a partial reconstruction of the true image. The mutual relation between all feature types can be derived from the exoskeleton (f).

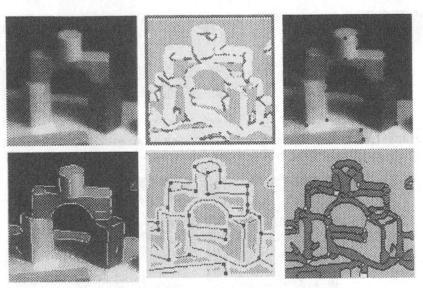

applied: 1. If $s_P < F_{m,m,\alpha}$ then $S \ll S^\perp$; the point is hypothesized to be a junction. 2. If $s_P > F_{m,n,1-\alpha}$ then $S \gg S^\perp$; the point is hypothesized to be an isolated point or, more generally, a circular symmetric feature. Otherwise no decision is made. It is meaningful to hypothesize a junction in this case. The neighborhood of p may still show regularities, e. g. being a spiral type feature [2], or may be pure texture.

Locating Edges: Similarily the location of edges may be performed in two ways:

- One-Step Procedure: Pixels where S shows a local minimum in the direction of the maximal gradient are considered as edge pixel. The direction of the gradient may be taken from the largest eigenvector of L. The procedure is then similar to the one of CANNY [4].
- Two-Step Procedure: Again we first maximize $1/tr(L^{-1})$ in the direction of the maximal gradient. This may be performed to subpixel accuracy already yielding acceptable results (cf. Fig. 5d). The integer position can then be used as the centre of a window within the optimal edge position is estimated finally.

Classifying Edge- and Line-type Features: The test whether a linear feature is a line or an edge (cf. Fig. 1c) can be based on a test comparing the significance of the vectors $(\bar{g}_x, \bar{g}_y)$ and $(\bar{g}_{xx}, \bar{g}_{xy}, \bar{g}_{yy})$ of the smoothed first and second derivatives with $\bar{z} = G_\sigma * z$. The test statistic

$$s_L = \frac{\left[(\bar{g}_x/\sigma_{\bar{g}_x})^2 + (\bar{g}_y/\sigma_{\bar{g}_y})^2\right]/2}{\left[(\bar{g}_{xx}/\sigma_{\bar{g}_{xx}})^2 + (\bar{g}_{xy}/\sigma_{\bar{g}_{xy}})^2 + (\bar{g}_{yy}/\sigma_{\bar{g}_{yy}})^2\right]/3} \sim F_{2,3} \qquad (7)$$

is used for a two-sided test: if $s_L < F_{2,3,\alpha}$ the feature is supposed to be a line, if $s_L > F_{2,3,1-\alpha}$ the feature is supposed to be an edge, otherwise it is assumed to be oriented texture. The kernels for the derivatives are supposed to be mutually orthogonal. The standard deviations are to be derived by error propagation.

In both cases, the two-step-procedure gives satisfying results, as the locally optimal window for estimation is used. The one step procedure, however, is theoretically more transparent allowing to analyze the scale behaviour more easily.

The principle and an example for the techniques are shown in figures 3 to 5.

3.6   Scale Space Properties

The favorable scale space properties of this approach have been found be HEIKKI-LÄ [15]. Compared to zero crossings of $\nabla^2 G_{\sigma_1} g$ no bias occurs at corners. In addition less spurious effects occur when σ becomes large.

Fig. 6.

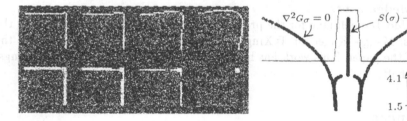

(a) shows effect of the scale for zero crossings of $\nabla^2 G_\sigma g$ at a corner compared with the minima of the regularity measure S. Points are indicated thick: No bias occurs (taken from HEIKKILÄ 1989). (b) shows the scale behaviour of the zero crossings of $\nabla^2 G_\sigma g$ and of the regularity measure S for a 1D-bar edge. The scale dependent bias (cf. BERZINS 1984) of the zero crossings is clearly visible. The bias of the feature location with S is below 10 % of the width of the bar edge, here with a width of $2a = 6$.

The interference of multiple edges can be studied analytically. We only give the result of a cross-section through a line, i. e. a bar-edge of width 2a. Assuming the squared gradient $g_x^2(x) = \delta(x+a) + \delta(x-a)$ convolution with $x^2 G_\sigma(x)$, the one dimensional version of 4, yields $S(x, \sigma) = (x+a)^2 G_\sigma(x+a) + (x-a)^2 G_\sigma(x-a)$.

At larger scales the procedure selects dark or light lines instead of edges (cf. Fig. 3). The bifurcation takes place at that scale where the second derivative $S(x, \sigma)$ vanishes at $x = 0$. This is at $\sigma = 2a/(5 - \sqrt{15}) \approx 1.5a$ (cf. Fig. 6). The maximum bias is approximately at scale $\sigma = 1.2a$ and has a size of approximately 10% of the width of the bar. At scales below $\sigma = a/2$ the bias is negligible.

4 Summary

We have sketched a framework for an integrated approach to low-level feature extraction. It covers all steps from the raw digital image to an initial symbolic image description. The main scope was to provide statistically sound measures for steering the individual steps and for evaluating the results. All analysis steps are explicitly motivated by the chosen image model. The feature extraction allows an efficient implementation and shows favorable scale space properties.

The techniques reveal fruitful links to existing ones suggesting to exploit these relations for further extension of the concept. This especially holds for transferring the techniques to range images or truely 3D/volumetric images, which can be achieved by using the 3D-version of the smoothness measures [11]. The extension to multispectral/multichannel is straight forward by weighting the channel information according to the individual noise characteristics [3]. The extension towards texture analysis may use the quadratic filter approaches [18] to an advantage. As the goal was not to explicitly include high-level or scene knowledge, the integration with interpretation modules having top-down queries to the low-level processing needs to be investigated.

Acknowledgements:
I thank Udo Tempelmann for the programming, Claudia Fuchs for providing the examples, Maggie Kugel for TEXing the manuscript and Uwe Weidner for the layout of the paper. This work has been supported by the Deutsche Forschungsgemeinschaft.

References

1. V. Berzins. Accuracy of Laplacian Edge Detectors. *CVGIP*, 27:185–210, 1984.
2. J. Bigün. A Structure Feature for Some Image Processing Applications Based on Spiral Functions. *CVGIP*, 51:166–194, 1990.
3. R. Brügelmann and W. Förstner. Noise Estimation for Color Edge Extraction. In W. Förstner and S. Winter, editors, *Robust Computer Vision*, 90–107. Wichmann, Karlsruhe, 1992.
4. J. Canny. A Computational Approach to Edge Detection. *IEEE T-PAMI*, 8(6):679–698, 1986.
5. W. Förstner. *Statistische Verfahren für die automatische Bildanalyse und ihre Bewertung bei der Objekterkennung und -vermessung*, Volume 370 of Series *C*. Deutsche Geodätische Kommission, München, 1991.
6. W. Förstner. Determination of Local Scale in an Image. Technical report, Institut für Photogrammetrie, Bonn, 1993.

7. W. Förstner. Feature Extraction in Digital Photogrammetry. *Photogrammetric Record*, 14(82):595–611, 1993.
8. W. Förstner and E. Gülch. A Fast Operator for Detection and Precise Location of Distinct Points, Corners and Circular Features. In *Proceedings of the Intercommission Conference on Fast Processing of Photogrammetric Data, Interlaken*, 281–305, 1987.
9. C. Fuchs, T. Löcherbach, H.-P. Pan, and W. Förstner. Land Use Mapping from Remotely Sensed Images. In *Colloquim on Advances in Urban Spatial Information and Analysis, Wuhan*, 1993.
10. G. H. Granlund. In Search for a General Picture Processing Operator. *CVIP*, 8:155–178, 1978.
11. G. H. Granlund. Image Sequence Analysis. In S. J. Pöppl and H. Handels, editors, *Mustererkennung*, 1–18. DAGM, 1993.
12. U. Grenander. Advances in Pattern Theory. *The Annals of Statistic*, 17:1–30, 1989.
13. R. M. Haralick and L. G. Shapiro. *Robot and Computer Vision*. Addison-Wesley, 1992.
14. D. Heeger. Optical Flow from Spatiotemporal Filters. In *Proceedings of 1st ICCV*, 181–190, 1987.
15. J. Heikkilä. Multiscale Representation with Förstner Operator. *The Photogrammetric Journal of Finland*, 11(2):40–59, 1989.
16. M. Kass and A. Witkin. Analyzing Oriented Patterns. *CVGIP*, 37:362–385, 1987.
17. H. Knutson and G. H. Granlund. Texture Analysis Using Two-Dimensional Quadrature Filters. In *Workshop Computer Architecture for Pattern Analysis and Image Data Base Management, Pasadena*, 1983.
18. T. S. Lee, D. Mumford, and A. Yuille. Texture Segmentation by Minimizing Vector-Valued Energy Functionals: The Coupled Membrane Model. In *Computer Vision - ECCV '92, Proceedings*, 165–173. Springer, 1992.
19. T. Lindeberg and J. Gårding. Direct Computation of Shape Cues by Multi-Scale Retinoptic Processing. Technical Report 117, Computational Vision and Active Perception Laboratory, Stockholm University, 1993.
20. D. E. McClure. Image Models in Pattern Theory. In A. Rosenfeld, editor, *Image Modelling*, 259–275. Academic Press Inc. , Orlando Florida, 1980/81.
21. P. Meer, J. Jolion, and A. Rosenfeld. A Fast Parallel Algorithm for Blind Estimation of Noise Variance. *IEEE T-PAMI*, 12(2):216–223, 1990.
22. A. Papoulis. *Probability, Random Variables, and Stochastic Processes*. Electrical Engineering. McGraw-Hill, 2 edition, 1984.
23. L. Rosenthaler, F. Heitger, O. Kübler, and R. von der Heydt. Detection of General Edges and Keypoints. In *Computer Vision - ECCV '92, Proceedings*, 78–86. Springer, 1992.
24. V. Torre and T. A. Poggio. On Edge Detection. *IEEE T-PAMI*, 8(2):147–163, 1986.
25. H. Vorhees and T. Poggio. Detecting Blobs as Textons in Natural Images. In *Image Understanding Workshop, LA, Proceedings*, 1987.
26. U. Weidner. Informationserhaltende Filterung und ihre Bewertung. In B. Radig, editor, *Mustererkennung, Proceedings*, 193–201. DAGM, Springer, 1991.
27. U. Weidner. Parameterfree Information-Preserving Surface Restoration. In *Computer Vision - ECCV '94, Proceedings*, 1994.

Registration and Reconstruction

Rigid and Affine Registration
of Smooth Surfaces
using Differential Properties

Jacques Feldmar and Nicholas Ayache

INRIA SOPHIA, Projet EPIDAURE
2004 Route des Lucioles, B.P. 93
06902 Sophia Antipolis Cedex, France
Jacques.Feldmar@sophia.inria.fr

Abstract. Recently, several researchers ([BM92], [Zha92], [CM92], [ML92], [GLP91]) have proposed very interesting methods based on an iterative algorithm to rigidly register surfaces represented by a set of 3d points, when a coarse estimate of the displacement is available. In this paper, we propose to introduce differential informations on points to extend this algorithm. First, we show how to efficiently use curvatures to superpose principal frames at potential corresponding points in order to find a much better rough estimate of the displacement. Then, we explain how to extend this algorithm to look for an affine transformation between two surfaces. We introduce differential informations in point coordinates: this allows us to register locally similar surfaces. We show how this differential information is transformed by an affine transformation. Finally, we introduce curvatures in the best affine transformation criterion. All this extensions are illustrated with experiments on various real biomedical surfaces: teeth, faces, skulls and brain.

1 Introduction

In this paper, we are interested in surface registration. When two surfaces represents the same object, it is often useful to superpose them. For instance, this is the case for the medical diagnosis: to compare images acquired at different times or coming from different modalities. See the article of Lisa Gottesfeld Brown [Bro92] for a review of the existing techniques. Our work is an extension of an iterative algorithm used in [BM92], [Zha92], [ML92], [CM92] and [GLSB92]. This algorithm is described in section 2.1 and is named "the iterative algorithm" in this article. Of course, classical techniques to register non-smooth objects have influenced us. The book of Grimson ([Gri90]) is a very good review of them. The geometric hashing method proposed in [LSW88] to match cross lines and the method based on mechanics of [MHS92] have also influenced us.

When the two surfaces do not come from the same object, but from objects of the same class (for example two faces), it is very useful to find the match. An example of application is to match a brain with an atlas in order to find abnormalities or to segment the brain into anatomical regions. See again [Bro92]

Rigid and Affine Registration of Smooth Surfaces using Differential Properties

Jacques Feldmar and Nicholas Ayache

INRIA SOPHIA, Projet EPIDAURE
2004 route des Lucioles, B.P. 93
06902 Sophia Antipolis Cedex, France.
Email : Jacques.Feldmar@sophia.inria.fr

Abstract. Recently, several researchers ([BM92], [Zha93], [CM92], [ML92], [CLSB92]) have proposed very interesting methods based on an iterative algorithm to rigidly register surfaces represented by a set of 3d points, when an estimate of the displacement is available. In this paper, we propose to introduce differential informations on points to extend this algorithm. First, we show how to efficiently use curvatures to superpose principal frame at possible corresponding points in order to find the needed rough estimate of the displacement. Then, we explain how to extend this algorithm to look for an affine transformation between two surfaces. We introduce differential informations in points coordinates : this allows us to match locally similar points. We show how this differential information is transformed by an affine transformation. Finally, we introduce curvatures in the best affine transformation criterion and we minimize it using extended Kalman filters. All this extensions are illustrated with experiments on various real biomedical surfaces : teeth, faces, skulls and brains.

1 Introduction

In this paper, we are interested in surface matching. When two surfaces represent the same object, it is often useful to superpose them. For instance, this is important for the medical diagnosis to compare images acquired at different times or coming from different modalities. See the article of Lisa Gottesfeld Brown [Bro92] for a review of the existing techniques. Our work is an extension of an iterative algorithm used in [BM92], [Zha93], [ML92], [CM92] and [CLSB92]. This algorithm is described in section 2.1 and is called "the iterative algorithm" in this article. Of course, classical techniques to register non-smooth objects have influenced us. The book of Grimson ([Gri90]) is a very good review of these. The geometric hashing method proposed in [GA92] to match crest lines and the method based on mechanic of [MR92] have also influenced us.

When the two surfaces do not come from the same object, but from objects of the same class (for example two faces) it is very useful too to find the match. An example of application is to match a brain with an atlas in order to find abnormalities or to segment the brain into anatomical regions. See again [Bro92] for a review. We just quote [CAS92] because their use of curvature to track points on deformable objects has influenced us.

We propose to introduce differential information to extend the iterative algorithm. In section 2, we first present this algorithm (2.1). Then we present our method to efficiently find the requisite initial estimate (2.2). In section 3, we explain how we have extended the iterative algorithm in order to find a good affine transformation. We first introduce differential informations in point coordinates (3.2). Then we modify the definition of the best affine transformation (3.3). Finally, we present results on real data (3.4).

2 Computing the rigid displacement

2.1 The iterative algorithm

We now briefly describe the iterative algorithm. (refer to the original papers for details). The goal is to find the rigid displacement $(\mathbf{R}, \mathbf{t})^1$ to superpose two surfaces, S_1 on S_2, given a rough estimate $(\mathbf{R}_0, \mathbf{t}_0)$ of this rigid displacement. Each surface is described by a set of 3d-points. The algorithm consists of two iterated steps, each iteration i computing a new estimation $(\mathbf{R}_i, \mathbf{t}_i)$ of the rigid displacement.

(1) The first step builds a set $Match_i$ of pairs of points. The construction is very simple : for each point M on S_1, a pair (M, N) is added to $Match_i$, where N is the closest point on S_2 to the point $\mathbf{R}_{i-1}M + \mathbf{t}_{i-1}$. To compute the closest point, different methods are proposed but one can use for example the distance map method [Dan80].

(2) The second step is just the least square evaluation of the best rigid displacement $(\mathbf{R}_i, \mathbf{t}_i)$ to superpose the pairs of $Match_i$ (see for example [FH86] for the quaternion method).

The termination criterion depends on the authors : the algorithm stops either when a) the distance between the two surfaces is below a fixed threshold, b) the variation of the distance between the two surfaces at two successive iterations is below a fixed threshold or c) a maximum number of iterations is reached.

This algorithm is very efficient and finds the right solution when the initial estimate $(\mathbf{R}_0, \mathbf{t}_0)$ of the rigid displacement is "not too bad" and when each point on S_1 has a correspondent on S_2. But, in practice, this is often not the case and we have to find the prior estimate $(\mathbf{R}_0, \mathbf{t}_0)$ and to deal with occlusion.

2.2 Finding the initial rigid displacement

We use differential informations to get it. The surfaces we have to superpose come from techniques described in [TG92], [Gué93]. So, for each point M on the surface, we know the principal curvatures and the principal frame.

---

[1] A rigid displacement $(\mathbf{R}, \mathbf{t})$ maps each point M to $\mathbf{R}M + \mathbf{t}$ where $\mathbf{R}$ is a 3x3 rotation matrix and $\mathbf{t}$ a translation vector.

In the ideal case, because principal curvatures are invariant under rigid displacement, given a point M on S_1 with principal curvatures (k_1, k_2), a point N on S_2 must have the same curvatures to be a possible correspondent. Moreover, if the pair (M, N) is a good match, then the rigid displacement which superposes S_1 on S_2 is also the one which superposes the principal frames attached to M and N respectively on S_1 and S_2. Hence, in the ideal case, the following algorithm would be very efficient : (1) choose a point M on S_1, (2) compute the set $SameCurvature(M)$ of points on S_2 which have the same curvatures as M, (3) for each point N in $SameCurvature(M)$, compute the rigid displacement corresponding to the superposition of the two principal frames and stop when this rigid displacement exactly superposes S_1 on S_2.

But in practice, the two surfaces cannot be exactly superposed, and there is the principal frame orientation problem. To deal with imprecision on curvatures, we register the points of S_2 in a hash table or in a kd-tree (see [PS85]) indexed by the two principal curvatures. This way, given a point M on S_1, with curvatures (k_1, k_2), we can quickly find the set of points $CloseCurvature(M)$ on S_2 whose curvatures are close to (k_1, k_2). Then, we apply the following algorithm :

1. we randomly choose a point M on the surface S_1
2. we compute the set $CloseCurvature(M)$
3. for each point N in $CloseCurvature(M)$, we compute the rigid displacements corresponding to the superposition of the two principal frames. If $R_1 = (M, \mathbf{e}_{11}, \mathbf{e}_{21}, \mathbf{n}_1)$ is the principal frame at point M and $R_2 = (N, \mathbf{e}_{12}, \mathbf{e}_{22}, \mathbf{n}_2)$ the principal frame at point N, we compute two rigid displacements d and d'. d corresponds to the superposition of R_1 on R_2. d' corresponds to the superposition of R_1 on R_2', where $R_2' = (N, -\mathbf{e}_{12}, -\mathbf{e}_{22}, \mathbf{n}_2)$. We have to compute these two rigid displacements because R_2 and R_2' are both direct, and there is no way to choose between them[2].
4. we now estimate the ratio of the number of points on the transformed surface $\mathbf{R}S_1 + \mathbf{t}$ which have their closest point on S_2 below a given distance, on the number of points of the surface S_1 to check if either d or d' reaches our termination criterion. First, we randomly choose a subset S_1' of points on S_1. Then, for each point P in S_1', we compute the closest point Q to $\mathbf{R}P + \mathbf{t}$ on S_2 and if $\|\mathbf{R}P + \mathbf{t} - Q\|$ is below a given threshold δ, then we add the pair (P, Q) in a set $Pair\_ok$. Finally, if the ratio $|Pair\_ok|/|S_1'|$ is bigger than $Threshold$ $(0 < Threshold < 1)$, we decide that $(\mathbf{R}, \mathbf{t})$ is a good estimate of the rigid displacement which superposes S_1 on S_2 and we stop the algorithm. If neither d nor d' reaches the termination criterion, then we return to point 1.

The parameter δ is the estimation of the maximal distance between one point on the surface S_1 and its closest point on S_2 after the best rigid registration (depends on the noise). $Threshold$ is the estimation of the ratio of the number of points on S_1 which have a correspondent on S_2, on the number of points

---

[2] Note that we are able to orient the normals because, in practice, we know the interior and the exterior of the objects.

on S_1 (depends on the occlusion). In practice, for our problems, it is not difficult to choose them and a good solution is found after a very small number of iterations (two or three). Typical surfaces we work with have around 10000 points. $CloseCurvature(M)$ is the set of points N on S_2 whose the principal curvatures (k'_1, k'_2) are such that $((k'_1 - k_1)^2 + (k'_2 - k_2)^2)^{1/2} < Dim/20$ where $Dim = \max(Dim\_k_1, Dim\_k_2)$ (Dim_k_1 (respectively Dim_k_2) is the difference between the maximum and the minimum value of k_1 (respectively k_2) in S_2). For S'_1, we randomly choose 5% of points of S_1. For example, the figure 1 (left) shows the initial estimate found for teeth data. We have chosen $Threshold = 0.8$ and $\delta = D/30$ where D is the largest surface diameter. The rigid displacement is found after two iterations in less than twenty seconds on a DEC 5000 workstation.

 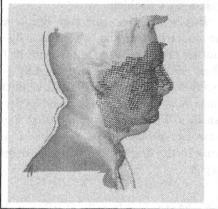

Fig. 1. Left : the rough estimate of the rigid displacement for teeth data acquired by Sopha-Bioconcept using a laser technique. One surface is dark, the other one is bright. **Right** : The best rigid displacement found between two faces of two different people. They have been acquired using a Cyberware machine. One surface is transparent, the other one is represented by lines. When the lines are dark, they are in front of the transparent surface, when they are not, they are behind.

This algorithm to find initial estimates associated with the iterative algorithm yields to an efficient framework to find very accurate rigid displacements. When the two surfaces are not complete because of occlusion, we just make use of covariance matrices and generalized Mahalanobis distances to decide if a point on S_1 has a correspondent on S_2 or not, as described in [Aya91]. For example, for teeth data of figure 1, the final displacement is such that 75% of points on the transformed surface have their closest point on the other surface at a distance lower than 0.75% of the largest surface diameter. This approximatively corresponds to the occlusion.

3   Non rigid matching of two different surfaces

When the two surfaces do not come from the same object, but from objects of the same kind, the framework described in section 2 is robust enough to find the best rigid displacement to register them. For example, figure 1 (right) shows it for two faces of two different people. In order to improve the superposition, a natural extension from rigid transformations to non rigid ones is the search for an unconstrained affine transformation $(\mathbf{A}, \mathbf{b})$[3].

3.1   Finding an affine transformation

We could use the rigid displacement found as described in the previous section as an initial estimate $(\mathbf{A}_0, \mathbf{b}_0)$ and just modify the second step of the iterative algorithm. It would just be the least square evaluation of the best affine transformation $(\mathbf{A}_i, \mathbf{b}_i)$ to superpose the pairs of $Match_i$. This evaluation is a classical least square problem.

But in practice, this very simple algorithm does not find a good solution : the similarities on the two surfaces do not tend to be brought nearer. Moreover, another major problem occurs with it. It often does not tend to a stable solution : when the transformed surface $\mathbf{A}S_1 + \mathbf{b}$ becomes very small or very flat, the criterion is minimized and nothing in the algorithm tends to avoid it. Especially, when $\mathbf{A}$ is the null matrix and $\mathbf{b}$ corresponds to a point on S_2, the criterion vanishes. This is for example what happens with the faces of figure 1. To avoid these two problems, we describe in sections 3.2 and 3.3 the modifications we bring to the original iterative algorithm (section 2.1), respectively to step 1 and step 2.

3.2   Matching locally similar points

Because points belong to surfaces, we would like that points with local similarity of shape tend to be matched in step 1 of the iterative algorithm. Because a point on a surface is very locally described by the principal curvatures and the principal frame, adding coordinates corresponding to this differential informations to the three spatial coordinates, we obtain the desired effect. In our formulation, surface points are no longer 3d points : they are 8d points. Coordinates of a point M on the surface S are $(x, y, z, n_x, n_y, n_z, k_1, k_2)$ where (n_x, n_y, n_z) is the normal on S at M, and k_1, k_2 are the principal curvatures. Between two points $M(x, y, z, n_x, n_y, n_z, k_1, k_2)$ and $N(x', y', z', n'_x, n'_y, n'_z, k'_1, k'_2)$ we now define the distance :

$$d(M, N) = (\alpha_1(x - x')^2 + \alpha_2(y - y')^2 + \alpha_3(z - z')^2 + \alpha_4(n_x - n'_x)^2 +$$
$$\alpha_5(n_y - n'_y)^2 + \alpha_6(n_z - n'_z)^2 + \alpha_7(k_1 - k'_1)^2 + \alpha_8(k_2 - k'_2)^2)^{1/2}$$

where α_i is the inverse of the difference between the maximal and minimal value of the ith coordinate of points in S_2. Using this new definition of the distance, the

---

[3] An affine transformation $(\mathbf{A}, \mathbf{b})$ maps each point M to $\mathbf{A}M + \mathbf{b}$ where $\mathbf{A}$ is a 3x3 matrix and $\mathbf{b}$ a translation vector.

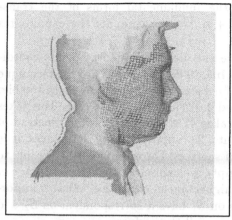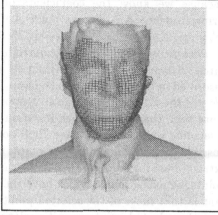

Fig. 2. The final affine transformation between the two faces. This has to be compared with the rigid displacement of figure 1 (right). One can see that the nose, the mouth and the chin are now much closer.

closest point to P on S_2 is a compromise between the 3d distance, the difference of normal orientation[4] and the difference of curvatures.

But this new definition of points coordinates introduces an interesting problem. At step 1 of the iterative algorithm, we have to compute $ClosestPoint(\mathbf{A}_iM + \mathbf{b}_i)$ where M is a point on S_1. Hence, we have to compute the new coordinates $(x', y', z', n'_x, n'_y, n'_z, k'_1, k'_2)$ of $\mathbf{A}_iM + \mathbf{b}_i$, where $(x', y', z')^t = \mathbf{A}_i(x, y, z)^t + \mathbf{b}_i$, (n'_x, n'_y, n'_z) is the normal on the transformed surface $\mathbf{A}_iS_1 + \mathbf{b}_i$ at point (x', y', z'), and k'_1 and k'_2 are the principal curvatures. In fact, because we need this result in section 3.3 we show in [FA94b] that :

proposition 1 :

When a surface S is transformed into a surface $\mathbf{A}S + \mathbf{b}$ by an affine transformation $(\mathbf{A}, \mathbf{b})$, the principal frame and the curvatures at point $\mathbf{A}M + \mathbf{b}$ on $\mathbf{A}S + \mathbf{b}$ depend only on the principal frame and the curvatures at point M on S.

More precisely, there exists a parameterization of $\mathbf{A}S_1 + \mathbf{b}$ such that, denoting E', F', G' the coefficients of the first fundamental form at point $\mathbf{A}M + \mathbf{b}$ on $\mathbf{A}S_1 + \mathbf{b}$, e', f', g' the coefficients of the second fundamental form and $(M, \mathbf{e}_1, \mathbf{e}_2, \mathbf{n})$ the principal frame at point M on S_1, we have :

$$\begin{cases} E' = \mathbf{Ae}_1.\mathbf{Ae}_1, & F' = \mathbf{Ae}_1.\mathbf{Ae}_2, & G' = \mathbf{Ae}_2.\mathbf{Ae}_2 \\ e' = \dfrac{det(\mathbf{A})k_1}{\|\mathbf{Ae}_1 \wedge \mathbf{Ae}_2\|}, & f' = 0, & g' = \dfrac{det(\mathbf{A})k_2}{\|\mathbf{Ae}_1 \wedge \mathbf{Ae}_2\|} \end{cases} \quad (1)$$

---

[4] Of course, only two parameters are necessary to describe the orientation of the normal (for example the two Euler angles). But we use (n_x, n_y, n_z) because, this way, the Euclidean distance really reflects the difference of orientation between the normals (that is not the case with the Euler angles) and we can use the kd-trees to find the closest point as explained later.

Because we know the coefficients of the fundamental forms of the transformed surface $\mathbf{A}S_1 + \mathbf{b}$ at point $\mathbf{A}M + \mathbf{b}$, we can compute the coordinates $(x', y', z', n'_x, n'_y, n'_z, k'_1, k'_2)$ (see [dC76]).

Just a problem remains to introduce this new definition of points coordinates : computing $ClosestPoint(\mathbf{A}_iM + \mathbf{b}_i)$. In 8d, we cannot use the technique described in [Dan80] as in the 3d case. The distance map would be much too big. We use the kd-tree technique as proposed in [Zha93] for the 3d case. This takes more time than before. Each iteration takes 45 seconds (CPU time) instead of 9 seconds when surfaces have 7000 points. To improve the performances, it is possible to work on a subset of points of surfaces. For example, it is possible to extract crest lines points [TG92]. Or simply, we can select a given percentage of points, choosing points which have the highest mean curvature. What is important is that most of the selected points on S_1 have a correspondent on S_2 and that the selected points describe relatively well the surfaces.

3.3   Constraints on the affine transformation

We have now to focus on a major drawback in the previous search for the affine transformation which best superposes S_1 on S_2. The criterion we minimize at step 2 of the iterative algorithm can always vanish as explained in section 3.1. To avoid this problem, we propose to define a new criterion. Let $(x, y, z, k_1, k_2, \mathbf{e}_1, \mathbf{e}_2)_k$ be the 3d coordinates, principal curvatures and principal directions of points M_k on S_1. Let $(x', y', z', k'_1, k'_2)_k$ be the 3d coordinates and principal curvatures of points $\mathbf{A}M_k + \mathbf{b}$ on the transformed surface. We call $\mathbf{g}$ the function which associates $(x', y', z', k'_1, k'_2)_k$ to $((x, y, z, k_1, k_2, \mathbf{e}_1, \mathbf{e}_2)_k, \mathbf{A}, \mathbf{b})$. The existence of this function is a consequence of the proposition 1 and we use the equations (1) to compute it. The new criterion we propose to minimize at step 2 of the algorithm is :

$$\sum_{(M_k, N_k) \in Match_i} p_k \|\mathbf{g}((x, y, z, k_1, k_2, \mathbf{e}_1, \mathbf{e}_2)_k, \mathbf{A}, \mathbf{b})) - N_k\|^2 \qquad (2)$$

where the coordinates of N_k are $(x'', y'', z'', k''_1, k''_2)_k$: the 3d coordinates and the two principal curvatures. This new criterion measures both the 3d distance and the difference of curvature between S_2 and the transformed surface $\mathbf{A}S_1 + \mathbf{b}$. Moreover, the coefficients p_k allow us to increase the importance in the criterion of the match for high curvature points because they seem to have a strong anatomical meaning ([Aya93]). These coefficients can be, for example, the mean curvature or $max(|k_1|, |k_2|)$.

We use the extended Kalman filter formalism (EKF) to minimize this new criterion (2). The details are given in [FA94b]. The only difficulty is to derive $\mathbf{g}$ with respect to $\mathbf{A}, \mathbf{b}$ and (x, y, z, k_1, k_2). In practice, we made numerous experiments and even if the minimized criterion is nonlinear, the minimization works very well. Using the new definition of the closest point (section 3.2) at step 1 and this new criterion at step 2, the modified iterative algorithm find good and stable solutions. Figure 2 shows the affine transformation found for the faces of figure

1. The solution is found after ten iterations in about 7.5 minutes (CPU time) on a DEC 5000 workstation[5]. It is to compare with the rigid transformation of figure 1. The chin, the mouth, the nose and the eyebrows of the two faces are now much closer. Note that the surfaces are now so close, that each one alternatively tends to appear in front of the other. To quantitatively evaluate the error, we have computed the average distance between a point of the transformed surface $AS_1 + b$ and its closest point on S_2. Setting the largest surface diameter to u, the rigid transformation yields to an average distance of $0.0193u$ when we use the 3d Euclidean norm to compute both the distance and the closest point, whereas the affine transformation (figure 2) yields to an average distance of $0.0152u$. This is a 22% improvement.

3.4   Results

In this section, we present results on skull data (figure 3) and brain data (figure 4). Of course, the two surfaces come from two different patients. The left

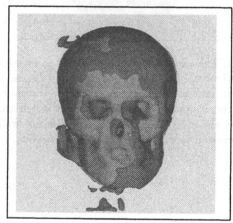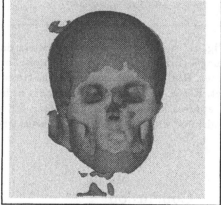

Fig. 3. The superposition of two skulls. The surfaces have been extracted in X-ray scanner images (New-York University Medical Center, Court Cutting). One surface is dark, the other one is bright. **Left** : result using a rigid displacement. **Right** : result using an affine transformation. One can observe that the hole corresponding to the nose and the orbits are not well registered with the rigid displacement, whereas they are with the affine transformation.

images show the rigid displacement found between the two surfaces whereas the right images show the affine transformation. For the skull example, setting the largest surface diameter to u, the error is $0.0120u$ for the rigid displacement and

---

[5] This time could be drastically reduced selecting on the surfaces characteristic points.

0.0098u for the affine transformation. This is a 22% improvement. The affine transformation is found after 8 iterations in about 8 minutes on a DEC 5000 workstation.

For the brain example, the error is 0.011u for the rigid displacement and 0.0091u for the affine transformation. This is a 18% improvement. The affine transformation is found after 12 iterations in about 7 minutes.

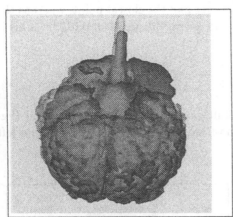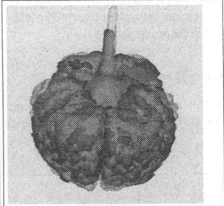

Fig. 4. The superposition of the two brains. The surfaces have been extracted in MRI images (Brigham and Women's Hospital of Boston). **Left** : result using a rigid displacement. **Right** : result using an affine transformation. The brightest surface is transparent. Hence, when the other surface is in front, it appears dark, and when it is behind, it appears less dark. One can observe that the interhemispherical fissure is not well registered with the rigid displacement, whereas it is with the affine transformation.

4   Conclusion

We have described and implemented a complete framework which is fast and robust to find very accurate rigid displacements between smooth surfaces. We have extended this framework to deal with affine transformations. We illustrated that the best affine transformation is generally found and that it brings the surfaces much nearer than a rigid displacement. We believe that this is a good starting point for more local non rigid registration schemes like the ones reviewed in [Bro92]. Moreover, an extension to locally affine transformations is presented in [FA94a].

Acknowledgements

We are very grateful to A. Gourdon, H. Delingette and J.P. Thirion for their help. Thanks are also due to people who gave data to us. This work was supported in part by a grant from **Digital Equipment Corporation** and by the European Basic Research Action **VIVA** (Esprit project).

References

[Aya91] N. Ayache. *Artificial Vision for Mobile Robots — Stereo-Vision and Multisensory Perception*. Mit-Press, 1991.

[Aya93] N. Ayache. Volume image processing. results and research challenges. Technical Report 2050, INRIA, 1993.

[BM92] Paul Besl and Neil McKay. A method for registration of 3−D shapes. *PAMI*, 14(2):239–256, February 1992.

[Bro92] Lisa Gottesfeld Brown. A survey of image registration techniques. *ACM Computing Surveys*, 24(4):325–375, December 1992.

[CAS92] I. Cohen, N. Ayache, and P. Sulger. Tracking points on deformable objects using curvature information. In *ECCV 1992*, Santa Margherita Ligure, Italy, 1992.

[CLSB92] G. Champleboux, S. Lavallée, R. Szeliski, and L. Brunie. From accurate range imaging sensor calibration to accurate model-based 3−D object localization. In *CVPR*, Urbana Champaign, 1992.

[CM92] Y. Chen and G. Medioni. Object modeling by registration of multiple range images. *Image and Vision Computing*, 10(3):145–155, 1992.

[Dan80] P.E. Danielsson. Euclidean distance mapping. *Computer Graphics and Image Processing*, 14:227–248, 1980.

[dC76] Manfredo P. do Carmo. *Differential Geometry of Curves and Surfaces*. Prentice-Hall, Englewood Cliffs, 1976.

[FA94a] J. Feldmar and N. Ayache. Locally affine registration of free-form surfaces. In *CVPR 94*, Seattle, 1994.

[FA94b] J. Feldmar and N. Ayache. Rigid, affine and locally affine registration of free-form surfaces. Technical report, INRIA, 1994.

[FH86] O. Faugeras and M. Hébert. The representation, recognition and locating of 3d objects. *Int. J. Robotics Res*, 5(3):27–52, 1986.

[GA92] A. Guéziec and N. Ayache. Smoothing and matching of 3−D-space curves. In *ECCV 1992*, Santa Margherita Ligure, Italy, 1992.

[Gri90] W. Grimson. *Object Recognition by Computer: The role of geometric constraints*. MIT Press, 1990.

[Gué93] André Guéziec. Large deformable splines, crest lines and matching. In *ICCV 93*, Berlin, 1993.

[ML92] Yau H.-T. Menq, C.-H. and G.-Y. Lai. Automated precision measurement of surface profile in cad-directed inspection. *IEEE Trans. RA*, 8(2):268–278, 1992.

[MR92] G. Malandain and J.M. Rocchisani. Registration of 3−D medical images using a mechanical based method. In *EMBS 92, Satellite Symposium on 3−D Advanced Image Processing in Medicine*, Rennes, France, 1992.

[PS85] Franco P. Preparata and Michael Ian Shamos. *Computational Geometry, an Introduction*. Springer Verlag, 1985.

[TG92] J.P. Thirion and A. Gourdon. The 3−D marching lines algorithm and its application to crest lines extraction. Technical Report 1672, INRIA, 1992.

[Zha93] Zhengyou Zhang. Iterative point matching for registration of free-form curves and surface. *Int. Journal of Computer Vision*, 1993.

The Quadric Reference Surface: Applications in Registering Views of Complex 3D Objects

Amnon Shashua and Sebastian Toelg*

Massachusetts Institute of Technology
Artificial Intelligence Laboratory
Department of Brain and Cognitive Sciences
Cambridge, MA 02139

* University of Maryland at College Park
Computer Vision Laboratory
Center for Automation Research
College Park, MD 20742

Abstract. The theoretical component of this work involves the following question: given any two views of some unknown textured opaque quadric surface in 3D, is there a finite number of corresponding points across the two views that uniquely determine all other correspondences coming from points on the quadric? A constructive answer to this question is then used to propose a transformation, we call a nominal quadratic transformation, that can be used in practice to facilitate the process of achieving full point-to-point correspondence between two grey-level images of the same (arbitrary) object.

1 Introduction

The general problem of achieving correspondence, or optical flow as it is known in the motion literature, is to recover the 2D displacement field between points across two images. Typical applications for which full correspondence (that is correspondence for all image points) is initially required include the measurement of motion, stereopsis, structure from motion, 3D reconstruction from point correspondences, and recently visual recognition, active vision and computer graphics animation.

In this paper we focus on two problems — one theoretical and the other more practical. On the practical side, we address the problem of establishing the full point-wise displacement field between two views (grey-level images) of a general 3D object. We achieve that by first considering a theoretical problem of establishing a quadric surface reference frame on the object. In other words, given any two views of some unknown textured opaque quadric surface in 3D projective space $\mathcal{P}^3$, is there a finite number of corresponding points across the two views that uniquely determine all other correspondences coming from points on the quadric? A constructive answer to this question readily suggests that we can associate a virtual quadric surface with any 3D object (not necessarily a quadric in itself) and use it for describing shape, but more importantly, for achieving full correspondence between the two views.

On the conceptual level we propose combining geometric constraints, captured from knowledge of a small number of corresponding points (manually given, for example), and photometric constraints captured by the instantaneous spatio-temporal changes in image light intensities (conventional optical flow). The geometric constraints we propose, are related to the virtual quadric surface mentioned above. These constraints lead to a transformation (a nominal quadratic transformation) that is applied to one of the views with the result of bringing both views closer together. The remaining displacements (residuals) are recovered by using the spatial and temporal derivatives of image light intensity — either by correlation of image patches or by optical flow techniques.

2 The Quadric Reference Surface

We consider object space to be the 3D projective space $\mathcal{P}^3$, and image space to be the 2D projective space $\mathcal{P}^2$ — both over the field $\mathcal{C}$ of complex numbers. Views are denoted by ψ_i, indexed by i. The epipoles are denoted by $v \in \psi_1$ and $v' \in \psi_2$, and we assume their location is known (for methods, see [6], for example). The symbol $\cong$ denotes equality up to a scale, GL_n stands for the group of $n \times n$ matrices, PGL_n is the group defined up to a scale, and $SPGL_n$ is the symmetric specialization of PGL_n.

Result 1. Given two arbitrary views $\psi_1, \psi_2 \subset \mathcal{P}^2$ of a quadric surface $Q \in \mathcal{P}^3(\mathcal{C})$ with centers of projections at $O, O' \in \mathcal{P}^3$, and $O, O' \in Q$, then five corresponding points across the two views uniquely determine all other correspondences.

Proof. Let (x_0, x_1, x_2) and (x'_0, x'_1, x'_2) be coordinates of ψ_1 and ψ_2, respectively, and $(z_0, ..., z_3)$ be coordinates of Q. Let $O = (0, 0, 0, 1)$, then the quadric surface may be given as the locus $z_0 z_3 - z_1 z_2 = 0$, and ψ_1 as the projection from $O = (0, 0, 0, 1)$ onto the plane $z_3 = 0$. In case where the centers of projections are on Q, the line through O meets Q in exactly one other point, and thus the mapping $\psi_1 \mapsto Q$ is generically one-to-one, and so has a rational inverse: $(x_0, x_1, x_2) \mapsto (x_0^2, x_0 x_1, x_0 x_2, x_1 x_2)$. Because all quadric surfaces of the same rank are projectively equivalent, we can perform a similar blow-up from ψ_2 with the result: $(x_0'^2, x'_0 x'_1, x'_0 x'_2, x'_1 x'_2)$. The projective transformation $A \in PGL_4$ between the two representations of Q can then be recovered from five corresponding points between the two images. $\square$

The result does not hold when the centers of projection are not on the quadric surface. This is because the mapping between Q and $\mathcal{P}^2$ is not one-to-one (a ray through the center of projection meets Q in two points), and therefore, a rational inverse does not exist. We are interested in establishing a more general result that applies when the centers of projection are not on the quadric surface. One way to enforce a one-to-one mapping is by making "opacity" assumptions, defined below.

Definition 2 (Opacity Constraint). Given an object $Q = \{P_1, ..., P_n\}$, we assume there exists a plane through the camera center O that does not intersect any of the cords $P_i P_j$ (i.e., Q is observed from only one "side" of the camera). Secondly, we assume that the surface is opaque, which means that among all the surface points along a ray from O, the closest point to O is the point that also projects to the second view (ψ_2). The first constraint, therefore, is a camera opacity assumption, and the second constraint is a surface opacity assumption — which together we call the opacity constraint.

Together with an appropriate re-parameterization of $\mathcal{P}^3$ we can obtain the following result:

Theorem 3. *Given two arbitrary views $\psi_1, \psi_2 \subset \mathcal{P}^2$ of an opaque quadric surface $Q \in \mathcal{P}^3$, then nine corresponding points across the two views uniquely determine all other correspondences.*

The following auxiliary propositions are used as part of the proof.

Lemma 4 (Relative Affine Parameterization). *Let p_o, p_1, p_2, p_3 and p'_o, p'_1, p'_2, p'_3 be four corresponding points coming from four non-coplanar points in space. Let A be a collineation of $\mathcal{P}^2$ determined by the equations $Ap_j \cong p'_j$, $j = 1, 2, 3$, and $Av \cong v'$. Finally let v' be scaled such that $p'_o \cong Ap_o + v'$. Then, for any point $P \in \mathcal{P}^3$ projecting onto p and p', we have*

$$p' \cong Ap + kv'. \tag{1}$$

The coefficient $k = k(p)$ is independent of ψ_2, i.e., is invariant to the choice of the second view, and the coordinates of P are $(x, y, 1, k)$.

The lemma, its proof and its theoretical and practical implications are discussed in detail in [10]. The scalar k is called a *relative affine invariant* and can be computed with the aid of a second arbitrary view ψ_2. For future reference, let π stand for the plane passing through P_1, P_2, P_3 in space.

Proof of Theorem: From Lemma 4, any point P can be represented by the coordinates $(x, y, 1, k)$ and k can be computed from Equation 1. Since Q is a quadric surface, then there exists $H \in SPGL_4$ such that $P^\top H P = 0$, for all points P of the quadric. Because H is symmetric and determined up to a scale, it contains only nine independent parameters. Therefore, given nine corresponding image points we can solve for H as a solution of a linear system — each corresponding pair p, p' provides one linear equation in H of the form $(x, y, 1, k)H(x, y, 1, k)^\top = 0$.

Given that we have solved for H, the mapping $\psi_1 \mapsto \psi_2$ due to the quadric Q can be determined uniquely (i.e., for every $p \in \psi_1$ we can find the corresponding $p' \in \psi_2$) as follows. The equation $P^\top H P = 0$ gives rise to a second order equation in k of the form $ak^2 + b(p)k + c(p) = 0$, where the coefficient a is constant (depends only on H) and the coefficients b, c depend also on the location of p. Therefore, we have two solutions for k, and by Equation 1, two solutions for p'. The two solutions for k are $k^1, k^2 = \frac{-b \pm r}{2a}$, where $r = \sqrt{b^2 - 4ac}$. The finding, shown in the next auxiliary lemma, is that if the surface Q is opaque, then the sign of r is fixed for all $p \in \psi_1$. Therefore, the sign of r for p_o that leads to a positive root (recall, $k_o = 1$) determines the sign of r for all other $p \in \psi_1$. $\square$

Lemma 5. *Given the opacity constraint, the sign of the term $r = \sqrt{b^2 - 4ac}$ is fixed for all points $p \in \psi_1$.*

Proof. Let P be a point on the quadric projecting onto p in the first image, and let the ray $\overline{OP}$ intersect the quadric at points P^1, P^2, and let k^1, k^2 be the roots of the quadratic equation $ak^2 + b(p)k + c(p) = 0$. The opacity assumption is that the intersection closer to O is the point projecting onto p and p'.

Recall that P_o a point (on the quadric in this case) used for setting the scale of v' (in Equation 1), i.e., $k_o = 1$. Therefore, all points that are on the same side of π as P_o is, have positive k associated with them, and vice versa. There are two cases to be considered: either P_o is between O and π (i.e., $O < P_o < \pi$), or π is between O and P_o (i.e., $O < \pi < P_o$), that is O and P_o are on opposite sides of π. In the first case, if $k^1 k^2 \le 0$ then the non-negative root is closer to O, i.e., $k = \max(k^1, k^2)$. If both roots are negative, the one closer to zero is closer to O, again $k = \max(k^1, k^2)$. Finally, if both roots are positive, then the larger root is closer to O. Similarly, in the second case we have $k = \min(k^1, k^2)$ for all combinations. Because P_o can be either in one of these two cases, then the opacity assumption gives rise to a consistency in picking the right root: either the maximum root should be uniformly chosen for all points, or the minimum root. $\square$

In the next section we will show that Theorem 3 can be used to surround an arbitrary 3D surface by a virtual quadric, i.e., create quadric reference surfaces — which in turn can be used to facilitate the correspondence problem between two views of a general object. The remaining of this section takes Theorem 3 further to quantify certain useful relationships between centers of two cameras and the family of quadrics that pass through arbitrary configurations of eight points whose projections on the two views are known.

Theorem 6. *Given a quadric surface $Q \subset \mathcal{P}^3$ projected onto views $\psi_1, \psi_2 \subset \mathcal{P}^2$, with centers of projection $O, O' \in \mathcal{P}^3$, there exists a parameterization of the image planes ψ_1, ψ_2 that yields a representation $H \in SPGL_4$ of Q such that $h_{44} = 0$ when $O \in Q$, and the sum of elements of H vanishes when $O' \in Q$.*

Proof. The re-parameterization described here was originally introduced in [10] as part of the proof of Lemma 4. We first assign the standard coordinates in $\mathcal{P}^3$ to three points on Q and to the two camera centers O and O' as follows. We assign the coordinates $(1, 0, 0, 0), (0, 1, 0, 0), (0, 0, 1, 0)$ to P_1, P_2, P_3, respectively, and the coordinates $(0, 0, 0, 1), (1, 1, 1, 1)$ to O, O', respectively. By construction, the point of intersection of the line $\overline{OO'}$ with π has the coordinates $(1, 1, 1, 0)$.

Let P be some point on Q projecting onto p, p'. The line $\overline{OP}$ intersects π at the point $(\alpha, \beta, \gamma, 0)$. The coordinates α, β, γ can be recovered (up to a scale) by the mapping $\psi_1 \mapsto \pi$, as follows. Given the epipoles v and v', we have by our choice of coordinates that p_1, p_2, p_3 and v are projectively (in $\mathcal{P}^2$) mapped onto $e_1 = (1,0,0), e_2 = (0,1,0), e_3 = (0,0,1)$ and $e = (1,1,1)$, respectively. Therefore, there exists a unique element $A_1 \in PGL_3$ that satisfies $A_1 p_j \cong e_j$, $j = 1,2,3$, and $A_1 v \cong e$. Denote $A_1 p = (\alpha, \beta, \gamma)$. Similarly, the line $\overline{O'P}$ intersects π at $(\alpha', \beta', \gamma', 0)$. Let $A_2 \in PGL_3$ be defined by $A_2 p'_j \cong e_j$, $j = 1,2,3$, and $A_2 v' \cong e$. Denote $A_2 p' = (\alpha', \beta', \gamma')$.

It is easy to see that $A \cong A_2^{-1} A_1$, where A is the collineation defined in Lemma 4. Likewise, the homogeneous coordinates of P are transformed into $(\alpha, \beta, \gamma, k)$. With this new coordinate representation the assumption of $O \in Q$ translates to the constraint that $h_{44} = 0$ $((0,0,0,1)H(0,0,0,1)^\top = 0)$, and the assumption of $O' \in Q$ translates to the constraint $(1,1,1,1)H(1,1,1,1)^\top = 0$. $\square$

Corollary 7. *Theorem 6 provides a quantitative measure of proximity of a set of eight 3D points, projecting onto two views, to a quadric that contains both centers of projections.*

Proof. Given eight corresponding points we can solve for H with the constraint $(1,1,1,1)H(1,1,1,1)^\top = 0$. This is possible since a unique quadric exists for any set of nine points in general position (the eight points and O'). The value of h_{44} is then indicative to how close the quadric is from the other center of projection O. $\square$

Note that when the camera center O is on the quadric, then the leading term of $ak^2 + b(p)k + c(p) = 0$ vanishes ($a = h_{44} = 0$), and we are left with a linear function of k. We see that it is sufficient to have a bi-rational mapping between Q and only one of the views without employing the opacity constraint. This is because the asymmetry introduced in our method: the parameters of Q are reconstructed with respect to the frame of reference of the first camera (i.e., relative affine reconstruction in the sense of [10]) rather than reconstructed projectively. Also note the importance of obtaining quantitative measures of proximity of an eight-point configuration of 3D points to a quadric that contains both centers of projection — this is a necessary condition for observing a "critical surface". A sufficient condition is that the quadric is a hyperboloid of one sheet [3, 7]. Theorem 6 provides, therefore, a tool for analyzing part of the question of how likely are typical imaging situations within a "critical volume".

3 Achieving Full Correspondence between Views of a General 3D Object

In this section we derive an application of Theorem 3 to the problem of achieving full correspondence between two grey-level images of a general 3D object. The basic idea, similar to [8, 9], is to treat the correspondence problem as composed of two parts: a nominal transformation with the aid of a small number of known correspondences, and a residual displacement field that is recovered using instantaneous spatio-temporal derivatives of image intensity values. along epipolar lines. This paradigm is general in the sense that it applies to any 3D object. However, it is useful if the nominal transformation brings the two views closer together.

Consider, for example, the case where the nominal transformation is a homography of $\mathcal{P}^2$ of some plane π. In that case, the residual field is simply the relative affine invariant k of Equation 1. In other words, if the object is relatively flat, then the k-field is small, and thereby the nominal transformation (which is Ap) brings the two views closer to each other. If the object is not flat, however, then the residual field may be large within regions in the image that correspond to object points that are far away from π. This situation is demonstrated in the second row display in Figure 1. Three points were chosen (two eyes and the right mouth corner) for the computation of the planar nominal transformation. The overlay of the second view and the transformed first view demonstrate that the central region of the face is brought closer on the expense of regions near the boundary (which correspond to object points that are far away from the virtual plane passing through both eyes and the mouth corner).

This example naturally suggests that a nominal transformation based on placing a virtual quadric reference surface on the object would give rise to a smaller residual field (note that the planar transformation is simply a particular case of a quadric transformation). The "nominal quadratic transformation" can be formalized as a corollary of Theorem 3 as follows:

Corollary 8 (of Theorem 3). *A virtual quadric surface can be fitted through any 3D surface, not necessarily a quadric surface, by observing nine corresponding points across two views of the object.*

Proof. First, it is known that there is a unique quadric surface through any nine points in general position. This follows from a *veronese* map of degree two, $v_2 : \mathcal{P}^n \longrightarrow \mathcal{P}^{(n+1)(n+2)/2-1}$, defined by $(x_0, ..., x_n) \mapsto (..., x^I, ...)$, where x^I ranges over all monomials of degree two in $x_0, ..., x_n$. For $n = 3$, this is a mapping from $\mathcal{P}^3$ to $\mathcal{P}^9$ taking hypersurfaces of degree two in $\mathcal{P}^3$ (i.e., quadric surfaces) into hyperplane sections of $\mathcal{P}^9$. Thus, the subset of quadric surfaces passing through a given point in $\mathcal{P}^3$ is a hyperplane in $\mathcal{P}^9$, and since any nine hyperplanes in $\mathcal{P}^9$ must have a common intersection, there exists a quadric surface through any given nine points. If the points are in general position this quadric is smooth (i.e., H is of full rank).

Therefore, by selecting any nine corresponding points across the two views we can apply the construction described in Theorem 3 and represent the displacement between corresponding points p and p' across the two views as follows:

$$p' \cong (Ap + k_q v') + k_r v', \tag{2}$$

where $k = k_q + k_r$, k_q is the relative affine structure of the virtual quadric and k_r is the remaining parallax which we call the residual. The term within parentheses is the nominal quadratic transformation, and the remaining term $k_r v'$ is the unknown displacement along the known direction of the epipolar line. Therefore, Equation 2 is the result of representing the relative affine structure of a 3D object with respect to some reference quadric surface, namely, k_r is a relative affine invariant (because k and k_q are both invariants by Theorem 3). $\square$

Note that the corollary is analogous to describing shape with respect to a reference plane [4, 8, 10] — instead of a plane we use a quadric and use the tools described in the previous section in order to establish a quadric reference surface. The overall algorithm for achieving full correspondence given nine corresponding points $p_o, p_1, ..., p_8$ is summarized below:

1. Determine the epipoles v, v' using eight of the corresponding points, and recover the collineation A from the equations $Ap_j \cong p'_j$, $j = 1, 2, 3$, and $Av \cong v'$. Scale v' to satisfy $p'_o \cong Ap_o + v'$.
2. Compute k_j, $j = 4, ..., 8$ from the equation $p'_j \cong Ap_j + k_j v'$.
3. Compute the quadric parameters from the nine equations
   $(x_j, y_j, 1, k_j)H(x_j, y_j, 1, k_j)^\top = 0$ $(k_o = 1, j = 1, ..., 8)$. Note that $k_1 = k_2 = k_3 = 0$.
4. For every point p compute k_q as the appropriate root of k of $ak^2 + b(p)k + c(p) = 0$, where the coefficients a, b, c follow from $(x_q, y_q, 1, k_q)H(x_q, y_q, 1, k_q)^\top = 0$, and the appropriate root follows from the sign of r for $ak_o^2 + b(p_o)k_o + c(p_o) = 0$ consistent with the root $k_o = 1$.
5. Warp ψ_1 according to the nominal transformation $\bar{p} \cong Ap + k_q v'$.
6. The remaining displacement (residual) between p' and $\bar{p}$ consists of an unknown displacement k_r along the known epipolar line. The spatio-temporal derivatives of image light intensity can be used to recover k_r.

In case (and only then) that the ray $\overline{OP}$ does not intersect the quadric, the solutions for the corresponding k are complex numbers (i.e., p cannot be reprojected onto $\bar{p}$ due to Q). This case can be largely avoided when the nine sample points are spread as apart as possible on the view ψ_1 of the object (see [12] for analytic results and computer simulations on the existence and distribution of "complex pockets").

Also, a tight fit of a quadric surface onto the object can be obtained by using many corresponding points to obtain a least squares solution for H. Note that from a practical point of view we would like the quadric to lie as close as possible to the object — otherwise the algorithm, though correct, would not be useful, i.e., the residuals may be larger than the original displacement field between the two views.

4 Experimental Results on Real Images

We have implemented the method described in the previous section for purposes of computer simulation and for application on a real image situation. The computer simulations are shown in [12], and some of the real image experiments are shown here.

Figure 1, top row, shows two images of a face taken from two distinct viewpoints. Achieving full correspondence between two views of a face is extremely challenging — for two reasons. First, a face is a complex object that is not easily parameterized. Second, the texture of a typical face does not contain enough image structure for obtaining point-to-point correspondence in a reliable manner. There are few points (in the order $10 - 20$) that can be reliably matched, such as

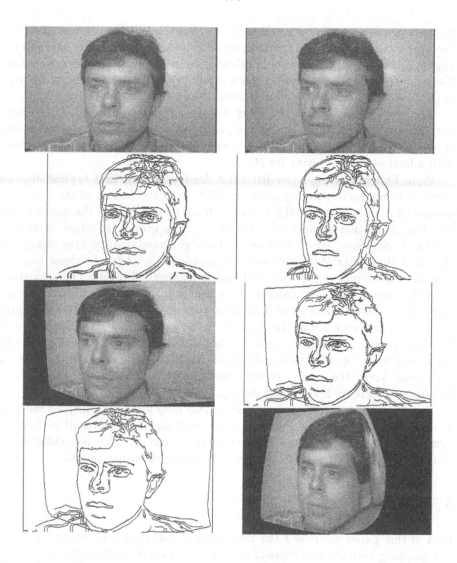

Fig. 1. *Row 1:* Two views of a face, ψ_1 on the left and ψ_2 on the right. *Row 2:* Left-hand display shows the overlayed edges of the two views above. Right-hand display shows the overlay of the affine transformed ψ_1 and ψ_2. The three points chosen were the two eyes and the right mouth corner. Notice that the displacement across the center region of the face was reduced, on the expense of the peripheral regions that were taken farther apart. *Row 3:* Left-hand display shows ψ_1 followed by the nominal quadratic transformation. Right-hand display shows the overlay of edges of the display on the left and ψ_2. Notice that the original displacements between ψ_1 and ψ_2 are reduced to about 1-2 pixels. *Row 4:* The display on the left shows the overlay of the target view ψ_2 with the transformed view ψ_1 (nominal quadratic followed by residual flow). The right-hand display shows the effect of nominal quadric transformation due to a hyperboloid of two sheets. This unintuitive solution due to an unsuccessful choice of sample points creates the mirror image on the right side.

the corners of the eye, mouth and eyebrows. We rely on these few points to perform the quadratic nominal transformation and the epipolar geometry, and then apply optical flow techniques to "finish off" the correspondence everywhere else. The optical flow method we used was a modification on the technique described in [1, 8], which is a coarse-to-fine gradient-based method following [5].

The epipoles were recovered using the algorithm described in [2, 6] using a varying number of points. The results presented here used the minimal number of nine points, but similar performance was obtained using more than nine points with a least squares solution for H.

From Figure 1, second row left-hand display, we see that typical displacements between corresponding points around the center region of the face varies around 20 pixels. Figure 1, third row left-hand display, shows the quadric nominal transformation applied to the view ψ_1. The overlay of edges of view ψ_2 and the transformed view are shown in the right-hand display. One clearly sees that both the center of the face and the boundaries are brought closer together. Typical displacements have been reduced to around 1-2 pixels. The optical flow algorithm restricted along epipolar lines was applied between the transformed view and the second view. The final displacement field (nominal transformation due the quadric plus the residuals recovered by optical flow) was applied to the first view to yield a synthetic image — that if successful, should look much alike the second view. In order to test the similarity between the synthetic image and the second view, the overlay of the edges of the two images are shown in the fourth row of Figure 1, left-hand display.

Finally, to illustrate that a quadric surface may yield unintuitive results, we show in the fourth row of Figure 1, right-hand display, the result of having a hyperboloid of two sheets as a quadric reference surface. This is accidental, but evidently can happen with an unsuccessful choice of sample points.

5 Summary

Part of this paper addressed the theoretical question of establishing a one-to-one mapping between two views of an unknown quadric surface. We have shown that nine corresponding points are sufficient to obtain a unique map, provided we make the assumption that the surface is opaque. We have also shown that an appropriate parameterization of the image planes facilitates certain questions of interest such as the likelihood that eight corresponding points will be coming from a quadric laying in the vicinity of both centers of projection.

On the practical side, we have shown that the tools developed quadrics can be applied to any 3D object by setting up a virtual quadric surface laying in the vicinity of the object. The quadric serves as a reference frame, but also to facilitate the correspondence problem. We have shown that one view can be transformed towards the second view, which is equivalent to first projecting the object onto the quadric and then projecting the quadric onto the second view. For example, in the implementation section we have shown that two views of a face with typical displacements of around 20 pixels are brought closer to around

1-2 pixels displacement by the transformation. Most optical flow methods can deal with such small displacements quite effectively.

Acknowledgments

Thanks to David Beymer for providing the pair of images used for our experiments, and to Long Quan for providing the code necessary for recovering epipoles. A. Shashua is supported by a McDonnell-Pew postdoctoral fellowship from the Department of Brain and Cognitive Sciences. S. Toelg was supported by a postdoctoral fellowship from the Deutsche Forschungsgemeinschaft while he was at MIT.

References

1. J.R. Bergen and R. Hingorani. Hierarchical motion-based frame rate conversion. Technical report, David Sarnoff Research Center, 1990.
2. O.D. Faugeras, Q.T. Luong, and S.J. Maybank. Camera self calibration: Theory and experiments. In *Proceedings of the European Conference on Computer Vision*, pages 321–334, Santa Margherita Ligure, Italy, June 1992.
3. B.K.P. Horn. Relative orientation. *International Journal of Computer Vision*, 4:59–78, 1990.
4. J.J. Koenderink and A.J. Van Doorn. Affine structure from motion. *Journal of the Optical Society of America*, 8:377–385, 1991.
5. B.D. Lucas and T. Kanade. An iterative image registration technique with an application to stereo vision. In *Proceedings IJCAI*, pages 674–679, Vancouver, 1981.
6. Q.T. Luong, R. Deriche, O.D. Faugeras, and T. Papadopoulo. On determining the fundamental matrix: Analysis of different methods and experimental results. Technical Report INRIA, France, 1993.
7. S.J. Maybank. The projective geometry of ambiguous surfaces. *Proceedings of the Royal Society of London*, 332:1–47, 1990.
8. A. Shashua. Correspondence and affine shape from two orthographic views: Motion and Recognition. A.I. Memo No. 1327, Artificial Intelligence Laboratory, Massachusetts Institute of Technology, December 1991.
9. A. Shashua. *Geometry and Photometry in 3D visual recognition*. PhD thesis, M.I.T Artificial Intelligence Laboratory, AI-TR-1401, November 1992.
10. A. Shashua. On geometric and algebraic aspects of 3D affine and projective structures from perspective 2D views. In *The 2nd European Workshop on Invariants*, Azores Islands, Portugal, October 1993. Also in MIT AI memo No. 1405, July 1993.
11. A. Shashua and S. Toelg. Quadric reference surfaces in 3d vision. A.I. Memo No. 1448, Artificial Intelligence Laboratory, Massachusetts Institute of Technology, 1994. Submitted for Publication, Feb. 1994.

Relative 3D Regularized B-spline Surface Reconstruction Through Image Sequences

ChangSheng Zhao and Roger Mohr

LIFIA–INRIA
46 Avenue Félix Viallet 38031 Grenoble cedex, France

Abstract. This paper considers the problem of 3D surface reconstruction using image sequences. We propose a direct method of surface reconstruction which is based on regularized uniform bicubic B-spline surface patches. The reconstruction is achieved by observing the motion of occluding contours [1, 4, 10], i.e., where the view lines graze the surface. It has been shown that reconstruction of such a 3D surface is possible when the camera motion is known, with the exception of those fully concave parts where no view line can be tangential to the surface. This approach differs from previous work, it states directly the problem of regularization on the 3D surface. Experimental results are presented for real data.

1 Introduction

The problem of representing and reconstructing 3D surfaces has received an enormous amount of attention in computer vision research over the past decade. The interest arises at least in part because robust surface reconstruction would have applicability to a wide variety of fields namely, manufacturing automation, terrain mapping, vehicle guidance, surveillance, virtual reality, etc. But aside from any practical applications, the problem has a great deal of scientific and mathematical interest.

From the perspective of classical differential geometry, there are three representations for a surface of an object: explicit, implicit, and parametric [3]. In this paper, we use uniform bicubic B-spline surface patches to give a parametric representation of a surface. Our aim is to reconstruct the 3D surface of an object from the observation of occluding contours [1, 4, 6, 7, 10] together with the knowledge of the motion of the camera mounted on the robot. We assume that the camera is modeled as a pinhole. We suppose that the object is smooth, specifically, that its surface is at least C^2. Our original contributions with respect to these related works are twofold: first, we introduce a direct regularization of the 3D surface to be reconstructed instead of smoothing the contours in the 2D image. This is based on the regularized uniform bicubic B-spline surface patches. Secondly, we propose global surface recovery from small local patches. Previous authors were satisfied with the recovery of only some local properties of the surface such as curvature or normal curvature estimation.

The paper is composed of three parts: in the first part we will introduce the main basic notions used here; i.e., the uniform bicubic B-spline surface patches, the definitions of the occluding contour and the epipolar parameterisation of a surface. The second part describes mathematically our method for B-spline surface patches reconstruction. In the last part, we present experimental results on real data and discuss their accuracy.

2 Definitions and notations

2.1 Uniform bicubic B-spline surface patches

B-spline curves are piecewise polynomial functions. These curves are defined by a sequence of control points, and pass near to those points. For more detail see [2]. In practical applications, cubic B-spline curves are the most frequently used, and play a important role. In this section, we will only concentrate on the uniform bicubic B-spline surface patches, a natural and straightforward generalization of the uniform cubic B-spline curves. The uniform bicubic B-spline surface patches can be expressed by the following double summation:

$$\boldsymbol{X}(s,t) = \sum_{i=-3}^{m-1} \sum_{j=-3}^{n-1} (\alpha_{ij} B_i(s) B_j(t), \beta_{ij} B_i(s) B_j(t), \gamma_{ij} B_i(s) B_j(t)) \qquad (1)$$

where $s, t \in I \times J \subseteq I\!R \times I\!R$, $(\alpha_{ij}, \beta_{ij}, \gamma_{ij})$ are called *control points*, the product $B_i(s) B_j(t)$ is called *tensor-product* B-spline. B_i, B_j are simply the *basis functions* of uniform cubic B-spline curves [8].

They have two following interesting properties: tensor-product B-splines have local compact support. B-spline surface patches transform as their control points under affine transforms.

2.2 Occluding contour

Now we consider an object surface S. The camera model is assumed to be the pinhole, its center of projection is at O. The *occluding contour* w of a surface S, viewed from a point O, is defined to be the projection of the set of points W on the surface S for which $\boldsymbol{n} \cdot \boldsymbol{OW} = 0$, where $\boldsymbol{n}$ is the unit normal vector corresponding to the tangent plane at W.

2.3 Epipolar parameterisation

The parameterisation of the *spatio-temporal* surface and the parameterisation of the object surface are directly linked. We choose two parameters t and s: t is a temporal parameter, i.e., the parameter t is linked to the motion of the camera. The parameter s is spatial, it is imposed by the arc length of the occluding contour in the image, the value of s is linked from one image to the other through the epipolar constraint (see Figure 1). So locally in a sequence each point on a surface is unambiguously parametrised, except for the points where the epipolar lines are tangential to the object surface. The choice we made in our work is the epipolar parameterisation described by Cipolla & Blake [4].

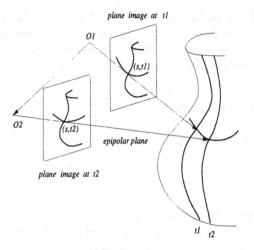

Fig. 1. Epipolar parameterisation

3 Mathematical model

We assume that the parametric representation of a surface is defined by

$$X(s,t) = (X_1(s,t), X_2(s,t), X_3(s,t))$$

$$= \sum_{i=-3}^{m-1} \sum_{j=-3}^{n-1} (\alpha_{ij} B_i(s) B_j(t), \beta_{ij} B_i(s) B_j(t), \gamma_{ij} B_i(s) B_j(t)). \qquad (2)$$

Uniform bicubic B-spline surface patches reconstruction requires then the estimation of $3 \times (m+3) \times (n+3)$ unknowns α_{ij}, β_{ij}, γ_{ij}, $i = -3, ..., m-1$, $j = -3, ..., n-1$ in the formula (2).

3.1 Two linear equations

We suppose that a point w with the coordinates (x, y) is the projection of a point W with the homogeneous coordinates $[X_1(s,t), X_2(s,t), X_3(s,t), 1]$ on the surface S, under the projection matrix $M = (m_{pr})_{p=1,...,3, r=1,...,4}$.

We have for homogeneous coordinates:

$$\begin{cases} x = \frac{m_{11}X_1(s,t) + m_{12}X_2(s,t) + m_{13}X_3(s,t) + m_{14}}{m_{31}X_1(s,t) + m_{32}X_2(s,t) + m_{33}X_3(s,t) + m_{34}} \\[2mm] y = \frac{m_{21}X_1(s,t) + m_{22}X_2(s,t) + m_{23}X_3(s,t) + m_{24}}{m_{31}X_1(s,t) + m_{32}X_2(s,t) + m_{33}X_3(s,t) + m_{34}}. \end{cases} \qquad (3)$$

Trivially, (3) can be rewritten after substituting (2) and multiplying by the appropriate denominator as

$$\begin{cases} P_1(x, s, t, \alpha_{ij}, \beta_{ij}, \gamma_{ij}, m_{pr}) = 0 \\ P_2(y, s, t, \alpha_{ij}, \beta_{ij}, \gamma_{ij}, m_{pr}) = 0. \end{cases} \qquad (4)$$

It is very easy to check that the two equations (4) are linear in the unknowns α_{ij}, β_{ij}, γ_{ij}.

We can compute the view line corresponding to a given point in the image when we know its coordinates and the projection matrix from two equations (3).

3.2 One additional nonlinear equation

From now on, we can write a nonlinear equations system of the surface reconstruction in the following way.

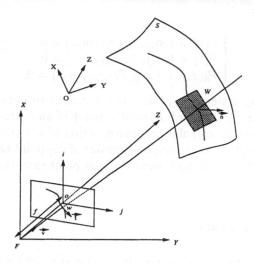

Fig. 2. Property of an occluding contour

Let W be a point on the surface S (see Figure 2). A point $w = (x, y)$ of the occluding contour in the image plane is the projection of the point $W = (X_1(s,t), X_2(s,t), X_3(s,t))$. The optical ray $v = (v_1, v_2, v_3)$ determined by FW is then tangent to the object surface S. The normal vector n to the tangent plane at W is given by

$$\frac{\partial X(s,t)}{\partial s} \times \frac{\partial X(s,t)}{\partial t} \tag{5}$$

where " $\times$ " denotes the cross product.

According to the definition of an occluding contour, we have the following relation:

$$n \cdot v = \left(\frac{\partial X(s,t)}{\partial s} \times \frac{\partial X(s,t)}{\partial t}\right) \cdot v = \begin{vmatrix} \frac{\partial X_1}{\partial s} & \frac{\partial X_2}{\partial s} & \frac{\partial X_3}{\partial s} \\ \frac{\partial X_1}{\partial t} & \frac{\partial X_2}{\partial t} & \frac{\partial X_3}{\partial t} \\ v_1 & v_2 & v_3 \end{vmatrix} = 0. \tag{6}$$

Equation (6) can be rewritten as follows by substituting (2) and (5)

$$P_3(x, y, s, t, \alpha_{ij}, \beta_{ij}, \gamma_{ij}, m_{pr}) = 0. \tag{7}$$

Unfortunately, this equation (7) is not linear in the unknowns α_{ij}, β_{ij}, γ_{ij}.

As the tangent plane to the surface at W is defined by the optical ray v and the tangent t to the occluding contour at w, we have then the following relation:

$$(v \times t) \times n = 0. \tag{8}$$

But this equation (8) gives the same information as equation (6). Indeed, it describes also the orthogonal property between the normal vector and the tangent plane to the surface at W. Therefore, it is omitted.

Finally, we can regroup these equations (4) and (7) into the following system of three equations:

$$\begin{cases} P_1(x, s, t, \alpha_{ij}, \beta_{ij}, \gamma_{ij}, m_{pr}) = 0 \\ P_2(y, s, t, \alpha_{ij}, \beta_{ij}, \gamma_{ij}, m_{pr}) = 0 \\ P_3(x, y, s, t, \alpha_{ij}, \beta_{ij}, \gamma_{ij}, m_{pr}) = 0. \end{cases} \tag{9}$$

From the above system, we notice that s, t are two parameters of B-spline surface patches, (x, y) are coordinates of a point of an occluding contour in an image. According to the epipolar parameterisation of a spatio-temporal surface, s is only the arc length of the occluding contour of the point (x, y) at t time in an image sequence when its origin is chose by first point extracted of the occluding contour.

4 Solving the system

We can generalize the above system for a sequence of images. Let k be the number of image in the sequence. Let l be the number of point extracted from the occluding contour of the kth image of the sequence. We have then the following system of equations:

$$\begin{cases} q_1(x_l^k, s_l^k, t_l^k, \alpha_{ij}, \beta_{ij}, \gamma_{ij}, m_{pr}^k) = 0 \\ q_2(y_l^k, s_l^k, t_l^k, \alpha_{ij}, \beta_{ij}, \gamma_{ij}, m_{pr}^k) = 0 \\ q_3(x_l^k, y_l^k, s_l^k, t_l^k, \alpha_{ij}, \beta_{ij}, \gamma_{ij}, m_{pr}^k) = 0. \end{cases} \tag{10}$$

As there are k_o images and l_o points on each image, this leads us to $3 \times k_o \times l_o$ equations. The unkowns are $3 \times (m+3) \times (n+3)$. So if k_o and l_o are large enough, the system of equations (10) is redundant.

The most direct procedure is to try to solve this system of nonlinear equations. We can hope to solve it by standard least squares technique. The problem can be formulated as minimization over

$$E = \sum_{k=1}^{k_o} \sum_{l=1}^{l_o} \lambda(q_1^2 + q_2^2) + \mu q_3^2$$

where $\lambda, \mu \in I\!R^+$ are two weight parameters.

Since there is some noise, introduced by errors or approximations at the contour detection stage, the above method does not allow the shape of the surface to be easily adjusted. We therefore introduce a regularization term on the surface [8, 11]. The term allows us to minimize the total variation in the local surface orientation. This suggests that the term should measure some factor of the second-order derivatives of the surface.

Finally, the regularized B-spline surface patches functional can be written as

$$E = \sum_{k=1}^{k_o} \sum_{l=1}^{l_o} [\lambda(q_1^2 + q_2^2) + \mu q_3^2] + \tau \int_I \int_J [(\frac{\partial^4 X_1}{\partial^2 s \partial^2 t})^2 + (\frac{\partial^4 X_2}{\partial^2 s \partial^2 t})^2 + (\frac{\partial^4 X_3}{\partial^2 s \partial^2 t})^2] ds dt$$

where $\tau \in IR^+$ is called the tensor of B-spline surface patches. Indeed, the regularization term goes back to minimize the variation of the curvature. This allows to smooth the surface of the regions where there is noise.

Currently, two standard numerical least squares methods, quasi-Newton and Levenberg-Marquardt are implemented in our system. B-spline surface patches are completely determined by a set of control points, and we know that these control points are close to the object surface in space. Therefore we can compute the depth of some points on the surface by a standard triangulation method. The starting values of the system are then provided by the depth points. Experiments show that the Levenberg-Marquardt's algorithm converges better than the quasi-Newton's algorithm.

5 Experimental results

In our experiments we made use of a camera, with a 18 mm lens. The camera is assumed to be a perfect pinhole. In practice, the accuracy of the projection matrix (translation and rotation) does not reach the required precision. We therefore want to use stable points in the scene for computing a reliable projection matrix. We have built a transparent cube and placed a carafe inside (see Figure 3). The polyhedral pieces of paper (white and black) have been added to the scene in order to get accurate epipolar geometry [9]. The contour points were obtained by a standard gradient based edge detector [5], and these contours were approximated with cubic B-splines [8]. The corners of the polyhedral pieces of paper in the scene were detected by a method developed in our laboratory. Then these corners were tracked by the standard correlation operator. The centers of the eight balls were computed as the intersection points of the medians of the bars. Finally, we chose an absolute coordinate frame attached to the cube. The accurate projection matrices of the sequence were thus computed.

Figure 3 shows the first and the last images of the sequence of ten images of a carafe.

Figure 4 shows results of the reconstructed B-spline surface patches of the carafe using a sequence of ten images. The parameters in this process are: $m = 3$, $n = 1$, $k = 10$, $l = 70$. So the number of equations in our redundant system is

Fig. 3. The first (left) and the last (right) images of the sequence

$3 \times k \times l = 2100$, the number of unknowns is $3 \times (m+3) \times (n+3) = 72$, and the number of the control points of the reconstructed B-spline surface patches is 24. The necessary number of iterations of Levenberg-Marquardt's algorithm is only 3. In particular, the total time for 3 iterations is 99 seconds on a SunSparc10. We remark in Figure 4 that the quality of the reconstruction surface is qualitatively good. Our final goal is to reconstruct the whole surface when the camera makes a tour of the carafe.

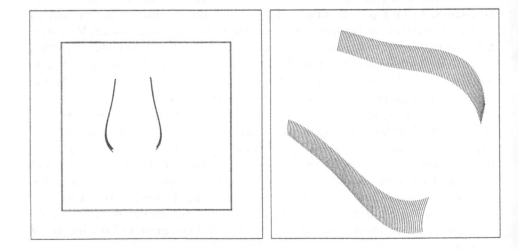

Fig. 4. Two reconstructed B-spline surface patches of the carafe are displayed with the transparent cube (left); A view of two reconstructed B-spline surface patches are displayed without the transparent cube (right)

Figure 5 shows the graphs of Gaussian and mean curvatures for the estimated B-spline surface patches of our carafe. We notice in Figure 5 that the values of the Gaussian curvature of some points on the B-spline surface patches are negative.

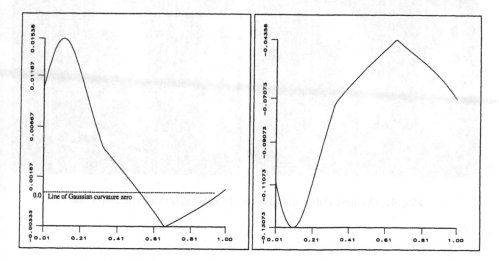

Fig. 5. Graphs of Gaussian (left) and mean (right) curvatures of the reconstructed B-spline surface patches of the carafe

In order to verify the quality of our reconstructed carafe, we compare the real diameter and the measured diameter. Measures of diameter of our carafe are performed with a pair of sliding calipers.

Table 1 gives the diameter of the carafe and the corresponding computed diameter. The maximal error is 5.40 mm. The mean error is 3.83 mm.

Height	Real diameter	Computed diameter	Error
60.0	144.0	139.2	4.8
70.0	148.5	143.1	5.4
80.0	150.2	147.5	2.7
90.0	148.5	149.2	-0.7
100.0	146.0	148.8	-2.8
110.0	142.0	146.6	-4.6
120.0	139.5	143.9	-4.4
130.0	135.0	140.3	-5.3

Table 1. Errors of the diameter of our reconstructed carafe (units are mm)

Figure 6 shows the first and the last images of the sequence of ten images of a tube. Figure 7 shows results of the reconstructed B-spline surface patches of the tube using this images sequence. As the epipolar lines are almost tangential

Fig. 6. The first (left) and the last (right) images of the sequence

to the top surface of the tube, this leads to the poor reconstruction displayed in Figure 7. This is another example of the aperture problem.

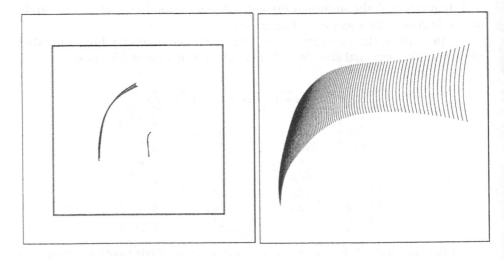

Fig. 7. Reconstructed B-spline surface patches of the tube is displayed with the transparent cube (left); A view of the reconstructed B-spline surface patches is displayed without the transparent cube (right)

6 Conclusion

In this paper we have shown that the reconstruction of a 3D surface is possible when the camera motion is known. The reconstruction process provided good quantitative and qualitative results. We have shown also how the different parameters of B-spline surface patches reconstruction should be conveniently selected according to available data obtained through experiments. The iterative algorithm of Levenberg-Marquard works well, convergence can generally be obtained in two to ten iterations. We have actually tested our algorithm on a large number of real images representing several different shapes of occluding contours.

Once the B-spline surface patches are estimated, the problem of merging the different B-spline surface patches obtained with different motions still remains. This step is presently being completed.

Acknowledgements: We would like to thank Françoise Veillon, Long Quan, David Sinclair, Marie-Odile Berger, Radu Horaud, Boubakeur Boufama and Pascal Brand for their helpful conversations and suggestions. This work was supported by Esprit BRA project Second and by the French national project GDR-PRC.

References

1. Arbogast, E., Mohr R.: 3D structures inference from images sequences. International Journal of Pattern Recognition and Artificial Intelligence. **5(5)** (1991) 749
2. Bartels, R.H., Beatty J.C., Barsky B.A.: An introduction to splines for use in computer graphics and geometric modeling. Morgan Kaufman Pu. Inc., (1987)
3. Do Carmo, M.P.: Differential geometry of curves and surfaces. Prentice Hall, (1976)
4. Cipolla, R., Blake, A.: Surface shape from the deformation of apparent contours. International Journal of Computer Vision. **9(2)** (1992) 83–112
5. Deriche, R.: Using Canny's criteria to derive a recursively implemented optimal edge detector. International Journal of Computer Vision. **1(2)** (1987) 167–187
6. Giblin, P., Weiss, R.: Reconstruction of surfaces from profiles. In Proceedings of the 1st International Conference on Computer Vision. London, England, (1987) 136–144
7. Koenderink, J.J.: What does the occluding contour tell us about solid shape ? Perception, **13** (1984) 321–330
8. Laurent, P.J.: Courbes ouvertes ou fermées par B-splines régularisées. Technical Report RR 652-M-, IMAG, Grenoble, France, (1987)
9. Mohr, R., Quan, L., Veillon, F., Boufama, B.: Relative 3D reconstruction using multiples uncalibrated images. Technical Report RT 84-I-IMAG LIFIA 12, LIFIA-IMAG, (1992)
10. Vaillant, R., Faugeras, O.D.: Using Extremal Boundaries for 3-D Objet Modeling. IEEE Transactions on PAMI, **14(2)** (1992) 157-173
11. Zhao, C.S., Mohr, R.: B-spline patches for surface reconstruction in computer vision. In P. J. Laurent, A. Le Méhauté, and L. L. Schumaker, editors, Curves and Surfaces II, Academic Press, Boston, 1994.

Intrinsic Stabilizers of Planar Curves

H. Delingette

Projet Epidaure, I.N.R.I.A 2004 Route des Lucioles
06902 Sophia-Antipolis, France

Abstract. Regularization offers a powerful framework for signal reconstruction by enforcing weak constraints through the use of stabilizers. Stabilizers are functionals measuring the degree of smoothness of a surface. The nature of those functionals constrains the properties of the reconstructed signal. In this paper, we first analyze the invariance of stabilizers with respect to size, transformation and their ability to control scale at which the smoothness is evaluated. Tikhonov stabilizers are widely used in computer vision, even though they do not incorporate any notion of scale and may result in serious shape distortion. We first introduce an extension of Tikhonov stabilizers that offers natural scale control of regularity. We then introduce the intrinsic stabilizers for planar curves that apply smoothness constraints on the curvature profile instead of the parameter space.

1 Introduction

Most tasks in computer vision can be described as inferring geometric and physical properties of three dimensional objects from two dimensional images. A characteristic of those inverse problems is their *ill-posed* nature[PT84]. Assumptions about the scene, such as *smoothness* or *shape* must be made to retain the "best" solution within the range of prior knowledge. Regularization transforms an ill-posed problem into a well-posed minimization problem by constraining the solution to belong to a set of allowed functions. If the problem is formalized as $A\nu = d$, where A is an operator describing the image formation process and d is a function describing the data extracted from the image, then the regularized problem consists in minimizing a functional of the form[BTT87]:

$$E(\nu) = \lambda \cdot S(\nu) + D(\nu) = \lambda \|P\nu\|_1^2 + \|A\nu - d\|_2^2 \qquad (1)$$

$\|P\nu\|_1^2$ evaluates the smoothness of the solution ν and is called a *stabilizing functional* or *stabilizers*. $\|A\nu - d\|_2^2$ evaluates the distance between the solution to the data. The regularization parameter λ weights the relative importance of smoothness with respect to the closeness of fit.

Variational principles involving smoothness constraints are widely used in computer vision ranging from surface reconstruction[BK86], segmentation with active contours[KWT88] and surfaces[DHI91b]. Geometric modeling primitives such as splines under tension [Sch66], Beta-Spline[BT83] proposed in computer-aided-design are derived from variational principles similar to the interpolation approach of regularization.

In this paper, we first analyze the different smoothness measures with regard to five criteria of invariance. Then, we extend the notion of *stabilizing functionals* to *differential stabilizers* by transforming the variational principle of equation (1) into the problem of solving a differential equation. Finally, we propose a generalization of Tikhonov stabilizers that provides both spatial control of the smoothness constraint and intrinsic shape formulation.

Lecture Notes in Computer Science, Vol. 801
Jan-Olof Eklundh (Ed.)

2 Smoothness Measures

2.1 Invariance

We have retained five criteria that characterize the notion of smoothness as it is generally conceived for the human perception of shape:

- **Invariance with rigid motion**. For all isometries T, a smoothness measure $S(\nu)$ should verify: $S(T\nu) = S(\nu)$.
- **Invariance with size**. The smoothness of an object is independent on how far the viewer is from the object, assuming an infinite perceptual resolution. Therefore, a smoothness measure should verify: $S(l\nu) = S(\nu), \forall l \in \mathbb{R}$.
- **Invariance with respect to parameterization**. Shape is clearly independent of the way a curve or surface is described but relies only on its intrinsic geometric parameters. We would therefore expect for every mapping $\mathcal{M}$ from $\Omega_w \subset \mathbb{R}^d$, $(d = 1$ or $2)$, to $\Omega_u \subset \mathbb{R}^d$, that $S(\nu(u)) = S(\nu(\mathcal{M}(w)))$.
- **Dependance with inner-scale**. Smoothness is clearly relative to the scale at which it is considered. A sensible smoothness measure should therefore be a function of scale.
- **Sphere Invariance**. This criterion states that circles and spheres should be among the curves or surfaces of least energy. Besides that spheres enclose the notion of ideal shape, this criterion ensures natural deformations against external constraints. For instance, if a stabilizer does not accept circles as optimum, the approximating spline minimizing equation 1 would be a circle, generally of smaller radius. Consequently, the spline will tend to consistently deform toward its center of curvature, especially where the curvature is high. This smoothing distortion is known as the "shrinking effect". Several methods have been proposed to overcome this undesirable effect of linear smoothing: Lowe[Low88] and Oliensis[Oli93] studied algorithms for compensating the shrinkage entailed by Gaussian smoothing.

2.2 Quadratic Smoothness Measure

Most regularized problems in computer vision, are based on a quadratic smoothness measure. The first advantage of quadratic measures is that functional analysis provides a solid theoretical framework for studying convexity, stability and convergence. The corresponding Euler-Lagrange equation is a quasi-linear differential equations and in the particular case of the interpolation and approximation surface reconstruction problem, the analytical form of solutions are known explicitly. Let $S(\nu) = \int_{\mathbb{R}^d} (P\nu)^2 du$ be a quadratic functional over a set of multidimensional function $\nu : \mathbb{R}^d \longrightarrow \mathbb{R}^p$. P is a linear, symmetric, and translation invariant operator and therefore the functional may be written as $S(\nu) = \int_{\mathbb{R}^d} |\tilde{p}(s)|^2 |\tilde{\nu}(s)|^2 ds$ where $\tilde{\nu}(s)$ is the Fourier transform of $\nu(u)$. The measure $S(\nu)$ can be interpreted as the power signal of the transformed signal in the frequency domain. When P is a high pass filter, and under unrestrictive conditions, $S(\nu)$ is a semi-norm over a well-defined class of functions $\mathcal{F}$, with a finite dimensional null space[GJP93].

Tikhonov and Arsenin[TA87] used the qth-order weighted Sobolev seminorms restricted on Sobolev spaces as a stabilizing functional for regularizing an ill-posed problem. The qth-order weighted multivariate formulation generalized by Duchon[Duc77] writes as:

$$S(\nu) = \sum_{m=0}^{q} \int_{\mathbb{R}^d} w_m(u) \sum_{j_1+\ldots+j_d=m} \frac{m!}{j_1!\ldots j_d!} \left(\frac{\partial^m \nu(u)}{\partial u_1^{j_1} \ldots \partial u_d^{j_d}} \right)^2 du \qquad (2)$$

where $w_m(u)$ are non negative functions that control the non-homogeneity or the continuity of the surface.

2.3 Harmonic Functions

Curves of surfaces minimizing the Tikhonov stabilizers are harmonic or iterated harmonic functions. Harmonic functions correspond to the "most conservative" interpolation possible in terms of parameterization. Harmonic functions have the unique property that the value at the center of a ball in the parameter space is equal to the mean value taken over the ball :

$$\forall R \in \mathbb{R}^+, \forall u \in \mathbb{R}^d \ \nu(u) = \frac{1}{A(\mathcal{B}_R^u)} \int_{\mathcal{B}_R^u} \nu(v) d\mathcal{B}_R^u \qquad (3)$$

where $\mathcal{B}_R^u$ is the ball of radius R centered on u. This mean value property uniquely characterizes harmonic functions and indeed corresponds to a highly desirable property for solving interpolation problems. The mean value property may be expressed too in terms of mean value over a sphere $\mathcal{S}_R^u$ centered on u rather than over a ball $\mathcal{B}_R^u$.

2.4 Invariance of Tikhonov Stabilizers

Tikhonov stabilizers have the following properties:

- **Invariance with rigid motion.** The multivariate Tikhonov stabilizers have been especially designed for their isometric invariance.
- **Dependence on size.** For all stabilizers $E(l\nu) = l^2 E(\nu)$. However, for a solution ν^* of a given set of data constraints and end conditions, the scaled solution is solution of the scaled problem.
- **Dependence on parameterization.** Tikhonov stabilizers are not posed in terms of intrinsic parameters and consequently fairness of the reconstructed surfaces is not guaranteed.
- **Independence with inner-scale.** The smoothness measure is estimated on infinitely small neighborhood around each point of a surface. The regularization parameter λ weights the smoothing effect on the regularized surface and thereupon controls the scale at which the surface is smoothed. However, it couples both notion of "scale" and "closeness of fit" that are clearly distinct.
- **Spheres are not optimal.** Circles and Spheres do not minimize the Tikhonov smoothness measures. Furthermore, in [DHI91a], we have proved that none of the quadratic stabilizers accept circles as optimal curves. Consequently, shrinkage is inherent to linear filtering.

2.5 Physically-based Smoothness Functionals

Many natural phenomena may be modelled through variational principles and the energy of deformations of physical system may be used as smoothness measures. For instance, an elastic spanned between two points reaches its equilibrium when minimizing its length:

$$S(\nu) = \int_0^{u_0} \|\nu_u\| du$$

The first variation of this first order stabilizing functional is $\delta S(\nu) = \frac{d}{du}\mathbf{T}$ and curves of least energy are lines.

The mechanical spline energy is derived from the physical deformation of a thin beam attached at specified points:

$$S(\nu) = \int_0^{u_0} k^2(u)ds = \int_0^{u_0} \frac{(x_u y_{uu} - y_u x_{uu})^2}{(x_u^2 + y_u^2)^{5/2}} du \tag{4}$$

This energy was proposed by Blake and Zisserman[Bla87] to achieve a viewpoint invariant surface reconstruction. Curves minimizing the sum of their square curvature or *mechanical splines* have been studied by many authors including Horn[Hor83] and they verify the following intrinsic equation:

$$\delta S(\nu) = \frac{d}{du}\left[k^2\mathbf{T} + 2\frac{dk}{ds}\mathbf{N}\right] = \frac{ds}{du}\left(k^3 + 2\frac{d^2k}{ds^2}\right)\mathbf{N} = 0$$

This intrinsic smoothness functional does not accept circles as optimal curves and furthermore is not size invariant.

3 Differential Stabilizer

A *necessary* condition for ν to minimize $E(\nu) = \lambda \cdot S(\nu) + D(\nu)$ is the vanishing of the first variation $\delta E(\nu) = \lambda \cdot \delta S(\nu) + \delta D(\nu) = 0$. Since $E(\nu)$ is formulated as a variational principal, $\delta E(\nu)$ is derived through the Euler-Lagrange equation. In general, solutions of a variational problem are recovered by solving the associated Euler-Lagrange equation, hence making abstraction of the actual minimization problem. In practice, the energy to minimize in non-convex, and the solution of Euler-Lagrange equation leads local minima.

It is therefore natural to extend the framework of regularization by replacing the *necessary* condition $\lambda \cdot \delta S(\nu) + \delta D(\nu) = 0$ by the more general condition

$$\lambda \cdot \sigma(\nu) + \delta D(\nu) = 0 \tag{5}$$

where:

- $\sigma(\nu)$ is an operator from a specified functional space $\mathcal{F}$ into $\mathcal{F}$. We will call $\sigma(\nu)$ a *Differential Stabilizer* (DS).
- $\delta D(\nu)$ is the first variation of $D(\nu) = \|A\nu - d\|^2$.

We will call *stabilization* the transformation of the problem $A\nu = d$ into the following problem:

> Among all $\nu \in \mathcal{F}$, that verify $\lambda \cdot \sigma(\nu) + \delta D(\nu) = 0$
> Find ν^* that minimizes: $\qquad\qquad$ (6)
> $C(\nu) = \int_{\mathbb{R}^d} \sigma(\nu)\nu du + \int_{\mathbb{R}^d} |A\nu(u) - d(u)|^2 du$

Instead of solving a minimization problem , stabilization proposes to solve the differential equation $\lambda \cdot \sigma(\nu) + \delta D(\nu) = 0$, and then to discriminate among solutions by minimizing the cost function $C(\nu)$. In general, stabilization is not equivalent to minimizing the cost function $C(\nu)$. However, when the differential stabilizer $\sigma(\nu)$ is a linear, symmetric and positive operator on a Hilbert space, then $\sigma(\nu)$ corresponds to the first variation of the functional $S(\nu) = \int_{\mathbb{R}^d} \sigma(\nu)\nu du$ and hence stabilization is equivalent to regularization.

The incentive behind stabilization is to provide a wider range of smoothness functional for solving inverse problems. We can justify this approach with an analogy with mechanics theory. The laws of mechanics are based on the minimization of the Lagrangian $L = T - U$ where T is the kinetic energy and U the total potential energy of the system. The Euler-Lagrange equation corresponding to the minimization of L is the law of motion $m\boldsymbol{\Gamma} = \mathbf{F}$. However, some forces do not derived from a potential field such as viscous or friction forces, such that it is not always possible to set the problem in terms of minimization of energy but only in terms of force equilibrium. Hence, the differential stabilizer $\sigma(\nu)$ may be seen as an internal force enforcing shape constraints while $\delta D(\nu)$ may be seen as an external force enforcing accuracy.

Several properties are desirable for a DS to render feasible and computable solutions. In addition to invariance with rigid motion, size, parameterization, we add the notion of sphere invariance as well as stability and convergence.

4 Intrinsic Polynomial Stabilizer

4.1 Controlled-Scale Extensions of Tikhonov Stabilizers

We now propose an extension of the Tikhonov functionals described in section 2.2 by introducing the notion of "scale-sensitive derivatives". For instance, we can evaluate the first derivative on a curve $\nu(u)$ at different scale with the ratio $(\nu(u+r) - \nu(u-r))/2r$ where r controls the scale at which we consider the curve geometry. A smoothness measure of the first order at scale r on closed curves then writes as:

$$S(\nu) = \int_{\Omega} \frac{(\nu(u+r) - \nu(u-r))^2}{4r^2} du$$
$$\delta S(\nu) = \frac{\nu(u)}{2r^2} - \frac{\nu(u+2r) + \nu(u-2r)}{4r^2}$$

The curves of least energy verifying $\nu(u) = \frac{\nu(u+2r)+\nu(u-2r)}{4r}$, are therefore harmonic, i.e. lines for a univariate function. we further extent the Tikhonov stabilizers by allowing the scale parameter r to vary spatially along the curve. In general, the scale parameter should be large at the center of the set Ω where the surface is defined and should be decreasing near the boundary $\partial\Omega$. Table 1 summarizes the different controlled-scale differential stabilizers generalizing Tikhonov functionals.

Controlled-Scale Weak String	$\sigma(\nu) = \dfrac{2}{r^2(u)}\left(\nu(u) - \dfrac{\nu(u+r(u)) + \nu(u-r(u))}{2}\right)$
Controlled-Scale Thin Rod	$\sigma(\nu) = -\dfrac{2}{r^2(u)}\left(\nu_{uu}(u) - \dfrac{\nu_{uu}(u+r(u)) + \nu_{uu}(u-r(u))}{2}\right)$
Controlled-Scale Membrane	$\sigma(\nu) = \dfrac{4}{r(u)}\left(\nu(u) - \dfrac{\int_{S_u^{r(u)}} \nu(u)du}{2\pi r(u)}\right)$
Controlled-Scale Thin Plate	$\sigma(\nu) = -\dfrac{4}{r(u)}\left(\Delta\nu(u) - \dfrac{\int_{S_u^{r(u)}} \Delta\nu(u)du}{2\pi r(u)}\right)$

Table 1. The controlled-scale extensions of Tikhonov stabilizers

Those *controlled-scale differential stabilizers* fully generalizes the Tikhonov stabilizers since they converge toward the Tikhonov stabilizers as $r(u)$ converges toward zero.

Using an analogy with mechanics, those "smoothing forces" can be interpreted as spring forces exerted between a surface point and the centroid of the curve $\nu(v), v \in \mathcal{S}_u^{r(u)}$. Instead of considering the centroid of the curve $\nu(v)$ surrounding a point, we can consider the centroid of the area it encloses. We then obtain another set of smoothing functionals that rely on the same notion of "scaled derivatives", but leads to smoother deformations because it averages over a larger extent. The *uniform controlled-scale differential stabilizers* are defined as:

Uniform Controlled-Scale Weak String	$\sigma(\nu) = \nu(u) - \dfrac{\int_{u-r(u)}^{u+r(u)} \nu(v)dv}{2r(u)}$
Uniform Controlled-Scale Thin Rod	$\sigma(\nu) = -\nu_{uu}(u) + \dfrac{\int_{u-r(u)}^{u+r(u)} \nu_{uu}(v)dv}{2r(u)}$
Uniform Controlled-Scale Membrane	$\sigma(\nu) = \nu(u) - \dfrac{\int_{B_u^{r(u)}} \nu(u)du}{4\pi r^2(u)}$
Uniform Controlled-Scale Thin Plate	$-\sigma(\nu) = \Delta\nu(u) + \dfrac{\int_{B_u^{r(u)}} \Delta\nu(u)du}{\pi r^2(u)}$

Table 2. The uniform controlled-scale extensions of Tikhonov stabilizers

Solutions of the differential equation 5 typically use finite differences or finite elements methods with iterative schemes such as Gauss-Seidel relaxation. Controlled-scale stabilizers involve inverting a banded positive definite matrix whose bandwidth depends on the scale parameter $r(u)$. The computational complexity for solving those systems is the same that for regular Tikhonov stabilizers but the rate of convergence is significantly increased since constraints propagate faster along the curve.

For sparse data approximation, smoothness should not be evaluated over the discontinuity entailed by each data constraint. For appropriate approximation over data points P_i, the scale parameters r_i should be picked such that smoothing does not occur across discontinuities (see Figure (1)).

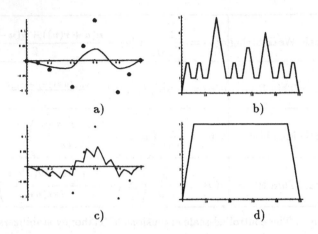

Fig. 1. a) Approximation of data points with the controlled-scale thin rod stabilizers and varying scale parameter; b) Distribution of the scale parameters along the curve. The parameter at each "attached" nodes is one, and vary linearly otherwise; c) Result of the same approximation with almost constant scale parameters ; d) Distribution of the scale parameters corresponding to c): $r_i = Min(5, i, N - i)$

4.2 Intrinsic Polynomial Stabilizer

The Intrinsic Polynomial Stabilizer[DHI91a] (IPS) are differential stabilizers acting on planar curves. They are invariant to rigid motion, parameterization, they are scale sensitive and they accept circles as optimal curves. Another interesting feature is their intrinsic nature which makes them sensitive to shape regardless of the parameterization. Our approach consists in linearly filtering the curvature space instead of linearly filtering the parameter space.

More precisely, given a curve $\nu(u)$, we choose to filter the derivative of the tangent polar angle $\frac{d\phi}{du} = k(u)\frac{ds}{du}$. Given a differential stabilizer $\sigma_1(\frac{d\phi}{du})$ applied on the rate of turn $\frac{d\phi}{du}(u)$, we define a differential stabilizer σ applied on the parametric equation:

$$\sigma(\nu)(u) = \frac{d^2 s}{du^2}\mathbf{T} + \frac{ds}{du}\sigma_1(\frac{d\phi}{du})\mathbf{N} \tag{7}$$

The *Intrinsic Polynomial Stabilizers* are derived directly from equation (7), with σ_1 corresponding to uniform controlled-scale differential stabilizers of different orders:

IPS order zero $$\sigma_{IPS0}(\nu) = \frac{d^2 s}{du^2}\mathbf{T} \tag{8}$$

IPS order one $$\sigma_{IPS1}(\nu) = \frac{d^2 s}{du^2}\mathbf{T} + \frac{ds}{du}\frac{d\phi}{du}\mathbf{N} \tag{9}$$

IPS order two $$\sigma_{IPS2}(\nu) = \frac{d^2 s}{du^2}\mathbf{T} + \frac{ds}{du}\left(\frac{d\phi}{du}(u) - \frac{\int_{u-r(u)}^{u+r(u)} \frac{d\phi}{du}(v)dv}{2r(u)}\right)\mathbf{N} \tag{10}$$

The IPS of order one correspond to the weak string differential stabilizer. The curves that nullify the IPS of order n verify both $\frac{d^2 s}{du^2} = 0$ and $\sigma_1(\frac{d\phi}{du}) = 0$

and therefore are curves whose curvature profile is a polynomial of degree $2n - 3$ of the arc-length. For $n = 0$, the "smoothest" curve verify only $\frac{d^2s}{du^2} = 0$ which does not constraint the shape of a curve, only its parameterization. For second order stabilizers the curve of least energy are *Cornu's Spirals* or *Clothoids*.

Intrinsic Polynomial Stabilizers can be seen as merely scale-sensitive Tikhonov stabilizers regularizing the curvature profile instead of the parametric equation. They are circle-invariant which prevents any "shrinking effect" during filtering.

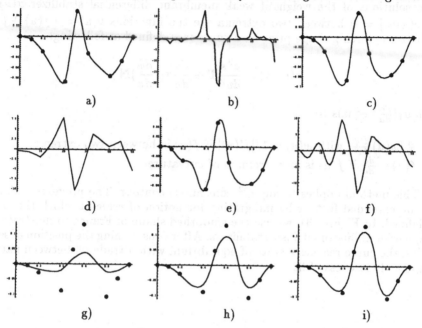

Fig. 2. a) Interpolation with the thin rod stabilizer; b) Its curvature profile; c) Interpolation with IPS of order two; the curve is C^2 continuous; d) Its curvature profile is piecewise linear; e) Interpolation with IPS of order three the curve is C^4; f) Its curvature is piecewise cubic; g) Approximation with a thin rod; h) Approximation with IPS of order one; i) Approximation with IPS of order two (same regularization parameter)

We use an explicit finite difference scheme for solving approximation, interpolation, and segmentation problem. The expression of the stabilizer is simple enough to render real-time deformations of an active contour on a Sun4 workstation. Figure (2) compares the interpolation and approximation solutions for the thin rod, IPS of order two and IPS of order three. The curvature profile shows clearly that IPS release smoother and natural-looking shapes than the linear thin rod stabilizer.

4.3 Shape constraints

Another interesting type of internal constraints for solving computer vision problems, is shape. For instance, in order to track deformable object, one would like to have a template with enough shape constraints for correctly matching the target but with enough flexibility to adapt to perspective distortion and target deformation[BACZ93]. Weighted Intrinsic Polynomial Stabilizers create complex-shaped deformable templates with controlled-rigidity. Those templates naturally converge toward their initial shape when not submitted to any external constraints.

Given a curve and its curvature profile: $k = f(s)$, we first determine the extrema of curvature. If we compute the weight function as $w(u) = 1/|f'(u)|$, then solutions of the weighted weak membrane differential stabilizer $\sigma(\nu) = \frac{d}{du}[w(u)\nu_u] = 0$ between two extrema are the functions $\nu(u) = af(u) + b$. A stabilizer enforcing shape prior on a contour is defined as following:

$$\sigma(\nu)(u) = \frac{d^2 s}{du^2}\mathbf{T} + \frac{ds}{du}\sigma_1(\frac{d\phi}{du})\mathbf{N}$$

with $\sigma_1(\frac{d\phi}{du})$ equals to:

- $-\frac{d}{du}[w(u)\frac{d^2\phi}{du^2}]$ with $w(u) = 1/|f'(u)|$ if $f(u)$ is between two extrema.
- $f(u) - \frac{d\phi}{du}$ if $f(u)$ is an extremum of curvature.

This method applies to any C^2 continuous contour. The previous stabilizer can be extended further by integrating for notion of scale at which the shape is defined. In Figure (3), we use the smoothed shape of France to illustrate the shape prior ability of intrinsic stabilizers. After constraining the position of seven nodes, the curve reaches a state of equilibrium with a trade-off between natural shape and closeness of fit.

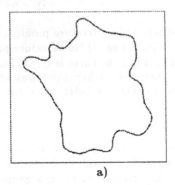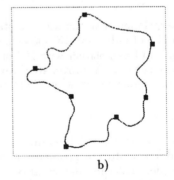

a)   b)

Fig. 3. a)Initial curve with its rest shape; b) Curve solution of an approximation problem under the influence of the weighted intrinsic polynomial stabilizer. The curve is constrained by seven springs attached to the black squares. Under the influence of the stabilizer, the curve shape is similar to its prior shape.

5 Conclusion

The controlled-scale stabilizers, on one hand, provide an additional set of parameters, the scale parameters, that influences both the convergence rate and the smoothness of the reconstructed signal. Intrinsic stabilizers on the other hand, provide a complete control of the curvature profile of a curve and consequently its shape. A promising application of shape-control is the creation of smoothly deformable templates for target tracking. Finally, intrinsic splines for which curvature is a polynomial function of arc-length are of great interest for computer-aided design because of their natural appearance.

Acknowledgments

I would like to thank M. Hèbert, K. Ikeuchi, and N. Ayache for stimulating discussions. This work was supported in part by a grant from **Digital Equipment Corporation**.

References

[BACZ93] R. Blake A.and Curwen and Zisserman. Affine-invariant contour tracking with automatic control of spatiotemporal scale. In *Proc. of the Fourth Int. Conf. on Computer Vision (ICCV'93)*, pages 66–75, Berlin, 1993.

[BK86] T.E. Boult and J.R. Kender. Visual surface reconstruction using sparse depth data. In *Int. Conf. on Computer Vision and Pattern Recognition (CVPR'86)*, pages 68–76, 1986.

[Bla87] A. Blake, A. Zisserman. *Visual Reconstruction*. MIT Press, 1987.

[BT83] H.G. Barsky and J.M. Tenenbaum. Local control of bias and tension in beta-splines. *ACM Trans. on Graphics*, 109–134, 1983.

[BTT87] M. Bertero, Poggio T., and V. Torre. *Ill-Posed Problems in early vision*. Technical Report A.I. Memo 924, M.I.T., A.I. Laboratory, May 1987.

[DHI91a] H. Delingette, M. Hebert, and K. Ikeuchi. Energy functions for regularization algorithm. In *Proc. SPIE., Geometric Methods in Computer Vision*, Vol. 1570, pages 104–115, 1991.

[DHI91b] H. Delingette, M. Hebert, and K. Ikeuchi. Shape representation and image segmentation using deformable surfaces. In *IEEE Computer Vision and Pattern Recognition (CVPR91)*, pages 467–472, June 1991.

[Duc77] J. Duchon. Splines minimizing rotation-invariant semi-norms in sobolev spaces. In *Constructive Theory of Functions of several Variables*, pages 85–100, 1977.

[GJP93] F. Girosi, M. Jones, and T. Poggio. *Priors, Stabilizers and Basis Functions: from regularization to radial, tensor and additive splines*. Technical Report, M.I.T., A.I. Laboratory, 1993.

[Hor83] B.K.P. Horn. The curve of least energy. *ACM Transactions on Mathematical Software*, 1983.

[KWT88] M. Kass, A. Witkin, and D. Terzopoulos. Snakes: Active contour models. *International Journal of Computer Vision*, 1:321–331, 1988.

[Low88] D.G. Lowe. Organization of smooth image curves at multiple scales. In *Proc. of the Second Int. Conf. on Computer Vision*, 1988.

[Oli93] J. Oliensis. Local reproducible smoothing without shrinkage. In *IEEE Transactions on Pattern Analysis and Machine Intelligence*, 1993.

[PT84] T. Poggio and V. Torre. Ill-posed problems and regularization analysis in early vision. In *IUS Workshop*, pages 257–263, 1984.

[PVY85] T. Poggio, H. Voorhees, and A. Yuille. *A Regularized Solution to Edge Detection*. Technical Report, M.I.T., A.I. Laboratory, 1985.

[Sch66] D.G. Schweikert. An interpolation curve using a spline in tension. *Journal of Math. Phys.*, 312–317, 1966.

[TA87] A.N. Tikhonov and V.A. Arsenin. *Solutions of Ill-Posed Problems*. Winston, 1987.

Geometry and Invariants

Affine and Projective Normalization of Planar Curves and Regions *

Kalle Åström

Dept of Mathematics, Lund Institute of Technology, Box 118, S-221 00 Lund, Sweden

Abstract. Recent research has showed that invariant indexing can speed up the recognition process in computer vision. Extraction of invariant features can be done by choosing first a canonical reference frame, and then features in this reference frame. This paper gives methods for extracting invariants for planar curves under affine and projective transformations. The invariants can be used semilocally to recognize occluded objects. For affine transformations, there are methods giving a unique reference frame, with continuity in the Hausdorff metric. This is not possible in the projective case. Continuity can, however, be kept by sacrificing uniqueness.

Keywords: Recognition, planar curves, projective and affine invariants.

1 Introduction

The pinhole camera model is a fairly adequate model of a real camera. Using this model it is straightforward to predict the image of a collection of objects in specified positions. The inverse problem, to identify and to determine the three dimensional positions of possible objects from an image, is however much more difficult. Traditionally recognition has been done by matching each model in a model data base with parts of the image. Model based recognition using viewpoint invariant features of planar curves and point configurations have recently attracted much attention, cf. [MZ1]. Invariant features are computed directly from the image and used as indices in a model data base. This gives algorithms which are significantly faster than the traditional methods. The problem of finding curve invariants have been addressed earlier. Some examples are

1. Differential Invariants, cf. [We1]. Smooth curves can be recognized using differential invariants. These invariant signatures can in theory be used to recognize curves even though almost all of the curve is occluded. Unfortunately such differential invariants under projective transformations require fifth order derivatives, leading to numerical difficulties.

2. Semi-differential Invariants, cf. [GM1]. If distinguished points can be found it is possible to reduce the order of the derivatives needed.

---

* The work has been supported by the Swedish National Board for Technical and Industrial Development (NUTEK). The work is done within the ESPRIT–BRA project VIVA.

3. Distinguished points. If many distinguished points can be found it is possible to use them directly in the construction of invariants.

4. Projectively invariant fitting of algebraic curves, cf. [Ca1]. Invariants can be extracted by fitting ellipses to a curve.

5. Canonical frame, cf. [RZ1]. Four distinguished points at a concavity can be used to transform the concavity into a canonical reference frame. Features are then extracted from the concavity in this reference frame.

In this paper affine and projective invariants of planar curves and regions are discussed. More general normalization ideas have been used. In the affine case robust invariants can be constructed using moments. There are, however, some fundamental limitations in the projective case. This is discussed in Sect. 5. In Sect. 6 we present some ideas on what can be achieved despite these limitations.

2 How to Use Normalization and Invariants

A grayscale image contains a large amount of information. The main idea of invariant based recognition is to throw away information that varies with lighting, occlusion and viewpoint, and to keep invariant features that allow recognition. This can be done by algorithms for edge extraction, segmentation, normalization and feature extraction. Figure 1 illustrates the process of edge extraction and segmentation. The invariant features can be used as indices in a table of known objects. After a recognition hypothesis have been found, it is verified at different levels. Only the problem of normalization and invariant index extraction will be addressed in this paper. The task is thus to extract invariant indices from a configuration, which may constists of one or several points, curve fragments or regions.

3 Using Normalization to Find Invariants

In this section some notations are introduced. The objects i.e. curves and regions are considered as elements in an abstract set Ω. This abstract set may have less structure than R^n but it is still meaningful to talk about invariants and normalization. By adding topology on Ω we can also talk about continuity.

A group G, in this paper the planar affine or projective group, is said to act on a set Ω if there exists a mapping $(G, \Omega) \ni (g, \omega) \longrightarrow g(\omega) \in \Omega$ with properties $1(\omega) = \omega$, $\forall \omega \in \Omega$ and $g_1(g_2(\omega)) = (g_1 g_2)(\omega)$, $\forall \omega \in \Omega$, $\forall g_1, g_2 \in G$. The notation for group action is either $g\omega$ or $g(\omega)$.

Two elements ω_1 and ω_2 are said to have the same shape if $\omega_1 = g\omega_2$ for some transformation $g \in G$. This is an equivalence relation, because of the group structure of G. We write

$$\omega_1 \sim \omega_2 \iff \exists g \in G, \quad \omega_1 = g\omega_2 . \tag{1}$$

The equivalence relation divides Ω into disjoint equivalence classes. Denote the equivalence class containing ω by $G\omega = \{g\omega | g \in G\}$.

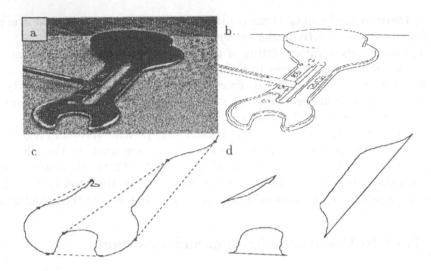

Fig. 1. 1a: A grayscale image of a scene with a roughly planar object. 1b: Edges are extracted using a Canny-Deriche edge detector. 1c: Distinguished points on one edge are used to segment a curve into pieces in a projectively invariant way. 1d: Distinguished points and lines can also be used to extract small regions in a projectively invariant way. Three such regions are shown in the figure.

Let $T : \Omega \longrightarrow W$ be a function defined on Ω with values in some feature set W. This function is called an *invariant* if $\omega_1 \sim \omega_2 \implies T(\omega_1) = T(\omega_2)$ and a *complete invariant* if $\omega_1 \sim \omega_2 \iff T(\omega_1) = T(\omega_2)$.

A normalization schemes is simply a choice of *normal* reference frames. Let Ω_P denote this set of normal elements. One common construction is $\Omega_P = \{\omega | P(\omega) = 0\}$, where $P : \Omega \to R^n$ is some function. For each element ω let the corresponding equivalence class $G\omega$ be represented by its normal elements, i.e. by

$$T(\omega) = G\omega \cap \Omega_P \ . \tag{2}$$

Assume for simplicity that this set-valued function $T(\omega)$ contains only one element for each ω. Any element ω_1 can then be uniquely factorized as $\omega_1 = g_1 \omega_1^{inv}$, with $g_1 \in G$ and $\omega_1^{inv} = T(\omega_1)$.

Isotropy, cf. [Wil, Gål], and maximal compactness, cf. [BY1] are two examples of affine normalization of planar curves. These two ideas give the same normal reference frames.

In our case Ω will be the class of all compact sets $\omega \subset R^2$ with positive area, whose boundary $C = \partial \omega$ is a rectifiable curve, i.e has finite arclength. Digitization errors are typically euclidean, so it is natural to work with the

Hausdorff metric. Two metrics on curves are introduced:

$$d(C_1, C_2) = \max_{z_1 \in C_1} \min_{z_2 \in C_2} ||z_1 - z_2|| + \max_{z_2 \in C_2} \min_{z_1 \in C_1} ||z_1 - z_2|| \ . \qquad (3)$$

and

$$\tilde{d}(C_1, C_2) = \max_{z_1 \in C_1} \min_{z_2 \in C_2} ||z_1 - z_2|| + \max_{z_2 \in C_2} \min_{z_1 \in C_1} ||z_1 - z_2|| + |l(C_1) - l(C_2)| \ . \qquad (4)$$

Here $||z||$ is the euclidean norm and l is arclength. Being close to a given curve in these metrics is a strong restriction. Two curves that are close to each other in the image plane really look alike. They would e.g. produce almost the same image on a CCD screen or on the retina of an eye. All points on one curve are close to some point of the other and with the second metric their arclengths are almost equal. Two elements of Ω are compared using the above metrics on the boundary, i.e. we define $d(\omega_1, \omega_2) = d(\partial\omega_1, \partial\omega_2)$. Let moments be defined as

$$m_0(\omega) = \int_{x \in \omega} dx_1 dx_2$$
$$m_1(\omega)_i = \int_{x \in \omega} x_i \, dx_1 dx_2$$
$$m_2(\omega)_{ij} = \int_{x \in \omega} x_i x_j \, dx_1 dx_2$$
$$m_3(\omega)_{ijk} = \int_{x \in \omega} x_i x_j x_k \, dx_1 dx_2$$

Notice that m_0 is a scalar, m_1 a vector and m_2 a matrix. The moments depend continuously on ω in the metrics above. The area enclosed by a curve C will be denoted $A(C)$, i.e. $m_0(\omega) = A(\partial\omega)$.

The planar affine transformation group G_a and the planar projective transformation group G_p are used. For simplicity we will talk somewhat losely about G_p acting on Ω.

Once in a normal reference frame any feature is invariant. Moments and Fourier coefficients can be used for curves and regions. In our experiments we have divided the plane in sectors and used the area of a region in each sector as a feature, see [Ås3, Ås4]. This has been quite effective.

4 A Continuous Affine Normalization Scheme

One simple example where these ideas work is the following normalization scheme of Ω with respect to G_a, cf. [Ås3, Ås4]. Let I denote the identity matrix. Using ideas from physics, moment of inertia, we define the class of *normal* elements as

$$\Omega_P = \{\omega| \quad m_0(\omega) = 1, m_1(\omega) = 0, m_2(\omega) = aI, a \in R\} \ . \qquad (5)$$

This gives a normalization scheme with the following properties:

- In the factorization $\omega = g\omega^{inv}$, g and ω^{inv} are unique up to rotation.
- Both g and ω^{inv} depend continuously on ω.
- The transformation g can be computed directly from the moments.
- Robust to digitization errors.
- No distinguished points are needed.

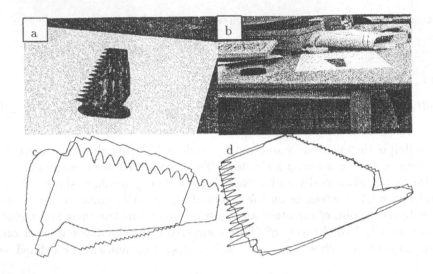

Fig. 2. 2a and 2b: Images of a sawlike planar curve. In 2b, interesting features disappear because of low resolution. 2c: The two curves can be affinely normalized using maximum compactness or weak isotropy, but the normal reference frame depends crucially on how the curve is approximated. 2d: Moment based normalization on the other hand is very robust to these kinds of digitization errors.

This scheme can be useful for recognizing planar curves. The affine approximation works very well for small segmented regions as in Fig. 1d. The method has good robustness properties, also in comparison with maximum compactness and weak isotropy. See Fig. 2. Analogous normalization schemes can be used for point configurations, curve segments and any combination of points, curve segments and regions.

5 Inherent Difficulties with Projective Normalization

It would be nice if it is possible to extend the affine scheme of Sect. 5 to projective transformations. There are fundamental reasons why this is impossible, as will be described below.

5.1 All Smooth Curves Can be Projected Close to a Circle

One idea for projective normalization of curves is to use maximum compactness, i.e. choose

$$\Omega_P = \{\omega \mid \ l^2(\partial\omega)/m_0(\omega) \text{ is minimal in the equivalence class}\} , \qquad (6)$$

cf. [BS1]. One problem with this approach is that optimization is done over a non-compact parameter space. It is therefore possible that the infimum is not attained. In [Ås3] it is shown that this is indeed the case if the convex hull has a part that is smooth and curved. The following theorem is true both in the original Hausdorff metric (3) and in the modified metric (4).

Theorem 1. *Let Γ_0 be the unit circle and let C be a curve with finite arclength which has a smooth curved part on its convex hull, then*

$$\inf_{C' \in G_p C} \tilde{d}(C', \Gamma_0) = 0 \ .$$

The theorem is a simple consequence of the fact that any part of the convex hull, can be magnified to any degree by projective transformations. An immediate corollary is that

$$\inf_{C' \in G_p C} \frac{l(C')^2}{A(C')} = 4\pi \ .$$

The modified metric (4) which includes the arclength is needed here. The projective transformations required when approaching the limit are, however, quite extreme. A proof of the theorem is given in [Ås3].

Theorem 1 has some serious consequences for a scheme based on (6), since most curves can be approximated by smooth curves, If a curve is modeled by a cubic spline the infimum is not attained. If a curve is modeled as a piecewise linear curve then the minimum is attained but the normal reference frame will depend crucially on how the boundary is approximated. This is illustrated in Fig. 3. In this figure the same shape is approximated with polygons to different accuracy. The reference frames in which they have maximal compactness are indeed different.

5.2 Transforming a Rabbit to a Duck

A key feature of Theorem 1 is that the main part of the curve is squeezed into a neighbourhood of a point. Elaborating this idea we obtain the following theorem.

Theorem 2. *Given $\Gamma_1, \ldots \Gamma_m$, closed continuous curves with finite arclength. To every $\epsilon > 0$, there exists a curve C and projective transformations $q_1, \ldots, q_m$ so that*

$$\tilde{d}(q_i(C), \Gamma_i) < \epsilon, \qquad i = 1, \ldots, m \ .$$

A proof is given in [Ås3]. Note that the curves Γ_i do not have to be smooth. The theorem is illustrated by Fig. 4. Notice that the lower four curves are projectively equivalent. The only errors are in plotting, printing, copying and viewing the curves. The theorem is in itself somewhat counterintuitive at first, but it is a simple trick of hiding a shape along the convex hull of another shape. The reason why it works is the use of extreme, but non-singular, projective transformations.

445

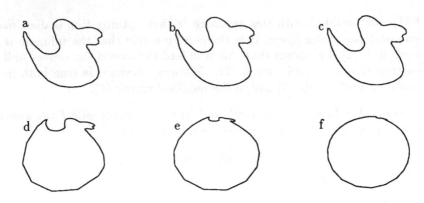

Fig. 3. Three different approximations of a planar curve (a, b and c) and their normal projective reference frames with respect to maximal compactness (d, e and f). Notice how much the normal reference frame depends on the representation of the boundary.

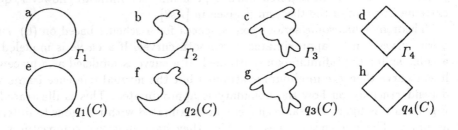

Fig. 4. 4a-d: Four planar curves with different projective shapes. 4e-h: Four planar curves that are projectively equivalent, i.e. have the same shape. Errors in the plotting device, printing, copying and viewing conditions make them look pairwise equal.

The consequences are perhaps more important. Consider a fixed curve ω and all curves in an arbitrary small open neighbourhood O_ω of ω. The theorem says that the orbit of this open set $G_p O_\omega$ is dense in Ω. A corollary is thus.

Corollary 3. Let T be a projectively invariant mapping from the set of closed continuous curves with finite arclength to R^n, then T maps all curves at which it is continuous to the same value.

Another consequence is that projective normalization schemes cannot be continuous and give a unique representative from each equivalence class. Such a scheme would contradict Corollary 3. Either continuity or uniqueness has to be sacrificed. Corollary 3 seems to rule out all attempts to use projective invariants in recognition of planar non-algebraic curves. However, it will be shown in the next section that it is possible to construct something almost as good.

6 Experiments with Projective Normalization

Global projective invariants of curves are tricky. No matter what method you use, distinguished points, fitting ellipses, projective smoothing or maximum compactness, you get non-uniqueness or discontinuity. In this section a normalization scheme is presented which might be useful. Choose the normal reference frames according to

$$\Omega_P = \{\omega| \quad m_0(\omega) = 1, m_2(\omega) = aI, m_3(\omega) = 0, a \in R\} \ . \qquad (7)$$

This gives a normalization scheme with none, one or several representatives from each equivalence class. The number of solutions may vary, but each solution can be continuous in the Hausdorff metric. One way of specifying the rotation is to demand that the maximum distance of a point in ω to the origin occurs at the x_1-axis.

The normalization scheme has been implemented and results from experiments will be presented. Grayscale images of roughly planar objects are taken with a digital camera. Polygon approximations of contours in the image are obtained using a Canny-Deriche edge detector. The curves are then normalized as described above. See Fig. 5. Notice the good performance in Figs. 5c and 5d. The sixteen normalized curves lie practically on top of each other in spite of possible nonlinearities in the camera, errors in segmentation and in edge detection. The normalization scheme is quite general. There are, however, convex curves for which there are no normal reference frames.

7 Conclusions

Projective normalization schemes of planar non-algebraic curves have been discussed in this paper. Such schemes should be continuous, and preferably give a unique representative from each equivalence class. In the affine case, it has been shown that this can be achieved. A canonical frame, that does not depend on ordering of points or choice of affine basis points, can be chosen for general feature configurations such as compact regions, curve fragments, and point configurations. Things are more difficult in the projective case. It has been shown that it is impossible to achieve both uniqueness and continuity for projective normalization of general non-algebraic curves. A normalization scheme is presented, where uniqueness has been sacrificed for robustness. This scheme is applied to closed curves, or to parts that have been segmented in a projectively invariant manner. The resulting invariants have good discriminatory properties and they are robust to digitization errors. The normalization algorithms have to be studied further to become really useful. As an example there exist curves which have no normal reference frame.

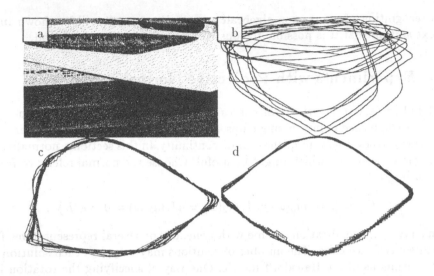

Fig. 5. Figure 5a shows one of 16 images taken of a planar convex curve. All 16 extracted edges are shown in Fig. 5b. In Fig. 5c the edges have been transformed into their unique affine normal reference frame, and in Fig. 5d one of several possible projective normal reference frames have been used.

The work has focused on simple algebraic and topological properties and can be extended in several directions. First, there are several questions on how to use the invariants in a recognition system. There appear to to be curves that are generically difficult to normalize with respect to projective transformations. It may be possible to examine these critical sets. The continuity of the proposed invariants should be investigated further. It would also be interesting to incorporate probabilistic models for image distortions. This could give valuable insight into the effectiveness of the normalization schemes and their use in recognition.

Acknowledgements

I would like to thank my supervisor Gunnar Sparr for inspiration and guidance. I would also like to thank my fellow students Anders Heyden and Carl-Gustav Werner for their help. The paper has been inspired by participation in the ESPRIT-project VIVA, in particular it is heavily influenced by the recognition system that has been developed at Oxford, cf. [RZ1, Ro1].

References

[BM1] Blake, A., Marinos, C.: Shape from Texture: Estimation, Isotropy and Moments. Artificial Intelligence **45** (1990) 332-380

[BS1] Blake, A., Sinclair, D.: On the projective normalisation of planar shape. Technical Report OUEL Oxford Great Britain (1992)

[BY1] Brady, M., Yuille, A.: An Extremum Principle for Shape from Contour. PAMI-6 **3** (1984) 288-301

[BW1] Burns J. B., Weiss R. S., Riseman E. M.: The Non-existence of General-case View-Invariants. in Geometrical Invariance in Computer Vision, Mundy, J. L. and Zisserman, A. editors, MIT Press (1992) 120-131

[Ca1] Carlsson S.: Projectively Invariant Decomposition and Recognition of Planar Shapes, Proc. ICCV4, May, Berlin, Germany (1993) 471-475

[DH1] Duda, R. O. and Hart, P. E.: Pattern Classification and Scene Analysis. Wiley-Interscience (1973)

[GM1] Van Gool, L., Moons, T., Pauwels, E. and Oosterlinck, A.: Semi-differential Invariants. in Geometrical Invariance in Computer Vision, Mundy, J. L. and Zisserman, A. editors, MIT Press (1992) 157-192

[Gå1] Gårding, J.: Shape from Surface Markings. Ph. D. thesis, Dept. of Numerical Analysis and Computer Science, Royal Institute of Technology, Stockholm, Sweden (1991)

[G1] Gros, P., and Quan L.: Projective Invariants for Vision. Technical Report RT 90 IMAG - 15 LIFIA, LIFIA-IRIMAG, Grenoble, France (1992)

[LS1] Lamdan, Y., Schwartz, J. T., and Wolfson, H. J.: Affine Invariant Model-based Object Recognition. IEEE Journal of Robotics and Automation **6** (1990) 578-589

[MZ1] Mundy, J. L., and Zisserman A. (editors): Geometric invariance in Computer Vision. MIT Press, Cambridge Ma, USA (1990)

[RZ1] Rothwell, C. A., Zisserman, A., Forsyth, D. A. and Mundy J. L.: Canonical Frames for Planar Object Recognition. Proc. ECCV92 Genova Italy (1992) 757-772

[Ro1] Rothwell, C. A.: Hierarchical Object Description Using Invariants. Proc. Second ARPA/NSF-ESPRIT Workshop on Invariance, Ponta Delgada, Azores (1993) 287-302

[We1] Weiss, I.: Noise-resistant Invariants of Curves. in Geometrical Invariance in Computer Vision, Mundy, J. L. and Zisserman, A. editors, MIT Press (1992) 135-156

[Wi1] Witkin, A. P.: Recovering Surface Shape and Orientation from Texture. J. of Artificial Intelligence **17** (1981) 17-45

[Ås1] Åström, K.: A Correspondence Problem in Laser-Guided Navigation. Proc. Swedish Society for Automated Image Analysis, Uppsala, Sweden (1992) 141-144

[Ås2] Åström, K.: Affine Invariants of Planar Sets. Proc. SCIA8, Tromsö, Norway (1993) 769-776

[Ås3] Åström, K.: Fundamental Difficulties with Projective Normalization of Planar Curves. Proc. Second ARPA/NSF-ESPRIT Workshop on Invariance, Ponta Delgada, Azores (1993) 377-389

[Ås4] Åström, K.: Object Recognition using Affine and Projective Invariants of Planar Sets. CODEN:LUFTD2/TFMA-3002/5002-SE, Lund, Sweden (1993)

Area and Length Preserving Geometric Invariant Scale-Spaces

Guillermo Sapiro[1] and Allen Tannenbaum[2]

[1] EE&CS Department–LIDS, MIT, Cambridge, Mass. 02139
[2] EE Department, University of Minnesota, Minneapolis, MN 55455

Abstract. In this paper, area preserving geometric multi-scale representations of planar curves are described. This allows *geometric smoothing without shrinkage* at the same time preserving all the scale-space properties. The representations are obtained deforming the curve via invariant geometric heat flows while simultaneously magnifying the plane by a homethety which keeps the enclosed area constant. The flows are geometrically intrinsic to the curve, and exactly satisfy all the basic requirements of scale-space representations. In the case of the Euclidean heat flow for example, it is completely local as well. The same approach is used to define length preserving geometric flows. The geometric scale-spaces are implemented using an efficient numerical algorithm.

1 Introduction

Multi-scale representations and smoothing of signals have been studied now for several years since the basic work of Witkin [30] (see for example [5, 14, 15, 17, 21, 31]). In this work we deal with multi-scale representations of closed planar curves, that is, the boundaries of bounded planar shapes. We show how to derive a smoothing operation which is geometric, sometimes local, and which satisfies all the standard properties of scale-spaces *without shrinkage*.

An important example of a (linear) scale-space is the one obtained filtering the initial curve C_0 with the Gaussian kernel $\mathcal{G}(\cdot, \sigma)$, where σ, the Gaussian-variance, controls the scale [5, 8, 14, 31]. It has a number of interesting properties, one of them being that the family of curves $C(\sigma)$ obtained from it, is the solution of the heat equation (with C_0 as initial condition). From the Gaussian example we see that the scale-space can be obtained as the solution of a partial differential equation called an *evolution equation*. This idea was developed in a number of different papers [1, 2, 13, 21, 23, 25]. We describe below a number of scale-spaces for planar curves which are obtained as solutions of nonlinear evolution equations.

* This work was supported in part by grants from the National Science Foundation DMS-8811084 and ECS-9122106, by the Air Force Office of Scientific Research AFOSR-90-0024 and F49620-94-1-00S8DEF, by the Army Research Office DAAL03-91-G-0019, DAAH04-93-G-0332, and DAAL03-92-G-0115, and by the Rothschild Foundation-Yad Hanadiv.

The Gaussian kernel also has several undesirable properties, principally when applied to planar curves. One of these is that the filter is not intrinsic to the curve. This can be remedied by replacing the linear heat equation by *geometric heat flows*, invariant to a given transformation group [10, 11, 24, 25, 27]. Geometric heat flows are presented in forthcoming sections.

Another problem with the Gaussian kernel is that the smoothed curve shrinks when σ increases. Several approaches, discussed in Section 2.1, have been proposed in order to partially solve this problem for Gaussian-type kernels (or linear filters). These approaches violate basic scale-space properties. In this paper, we show that this problem can be completely solved using a variation of the geometric heat flow methodology, which keeps the area enclosed by the curve constant. The flows which we obtain, precisely satisfy all the basic scale-space requirements. In the Euclidean case for example, the flow is local as well. The same approach can be used for deriving length preserving heat flows. In this case, the similarity flow exhibits locality. In short, *we can get geometric smoothing without shrinkage.*

2 Curve Evolution: The Euclidean Geometric Heat Flow

We consider now planar curves deforming in time, where "time" represents "scale." Let $C(p, t) : S^1 \times [0, \tau) \to \mathbf{R}^2$ denote a family of closed embedded curves, where t parametrizes the family, and p the curves ($C(p, t) = [x(p, t), y(p, t)]^T$). We assume throughout this paper that all of our mappings are periodic and sufficiently smooth. We should add that these results may be generalized to non-smooth curves based on the theory of viscosity solutions or the results in [3, 4].

For the case of the classical heat equation, the curves deform via

$$\begin{cases} \frac{\partial C}{\partial t} = \frac{\partial^2 C}{\partial p^2} = \begin{bmatrix} x_{pp} \\ y_{pp} \end{bmatrix}, \\ C(p, 0) = C_0(p). \end{cases} \tag{1}$$

As pointed out in the Introduction, $C(p, t) = [x(p, t), y(p, t)]^T$, satisfying (1), can be obtained from the convolution of $x(p, 0), y(p, 0)$ with the Gaussian $G(p, t)$.

In order to separate the geometric concept of a planar curve from its formal algebraic description, it is useful to refer to the planar curve described by $C(p, t)$ as the image (trace) of $C(p, t)$, denoted by $\text{Img}[C(p, t)]$ [25]. Therefore, if the curve $C(p, t)$ is parametrized by a new parameter w such that $w = w(p, t)$, $\frac{\partial w}{\partial p} > 0$, we obtain $\text{Img}[C(p, t)] = \text{Img}[C(w, t)]$.

We see that different parametrizations of the curve, will give different results in (1), i.e, different Gaussian multi-scale representations. This is an undesirable property, since parametrizations are in general arbitrary, and may not be connected with the geometry of the curve. We can attempt to solve this problem choosing a parametrization which is intrinsic to the curve, i.e., that can be computed when only $\text{Img}[C]$ is given. A natural parametrization is the

Euclidean arc-length v, which means that the curve is traveled with constant velocity, $\| C_v \| \equiv 1$. The initial curve $C_0(p)$ can be re-parametrized as $C_0(v)$, and the Gaussian filter $\mathcal{G}(v, t)$, or the corresponding heat flow, is applied using this parameter. The problem is that the arc-length is a time-dependent parametrization, i.e., $v(p)$ depends on time. Also, with this kind of re-parametrization, some of the basic properties of scale-spaces are violated. For example, the order between curves is not preserved. Also, the semi-group property, which is one of the most important requirements of a scale-space, can be violated with this kind of re-parametrization. The theory described below solves these problems.

Assume now that the family $C(p, t)$ evolves (changes) according to the following general flow:

$$\frac{\partial C}{\partial t} = \beta \mathcal{N}, \tag{2}$$

where $\mathcal{N}$ is the inward Euclidean unit normal and β the normal curve velocity component. If β is a geometric function of the curve, then the "geometric" curve Img[·] is only affected by this normal component [7]. The tangential component affects only the parametrization. Therefore, (2) is the most general geometric flow.

The evolution (2) was studied by different researchers for different functions β. A key evolution equation is the one obtained for $\beta = \kappa$, where κ is the Euclidean curvature [29]. In this case, the flow is given by

$$\frac{\partial C}{\partial t} = \kappa \mathcal{N}. \tag{3}$$

Equation (3) has its origins in physical phenomena [3, 9]. Gage and Hamilton [10] proved that a planar embedded convex curve converges to a round point when evolving according to (3). Grayson [11] proved that a planar embedded smooth non-convex curve, remains smooth and simple, and converges to a convex one. Next note that if v denotes the Euclidean arc-length, then $\kappa \mathcal{N} = \frac{\partial^2 C}{\partial v^2}$ [29]. Therefore, equation (3) can be written as

$$C_t = C_{vv}. \tag{4}$$

Equation (4) is not linear, since v is a time-dependent parametrization. Equation (4) is called the *(Euclidean) geometric heat flow*. This flow has been proposed for defining a multi-scale representation of closed curves [1, 13, 17]. Note that in contrast with the classical heat flow, the Euclidean geometric one defines an intrinsic, geometric, multi-scale representation. In order to complete the theory, we must prove that all the basic properties required for a scale-space hold for the flow (4). This is obtained directly from [10, 11] on the Euclidean geometric heat flow, and [3] on more general curvature dependent flows [28].

2.1 Euclidean Geometric Heat Flow without Shrinkage

In the previous section, we described the Euclidean geometric heat flow, which can be used to replace the classical heat flow or Gaussian filtering in order to obtain an intrinsic scale-space for planar curves. We show now how to modify this flow in order to keep the area enclosed by the evolving curve constant.

A curve deforming according to the classical heat flow shrinks. This is due to the fact that the Gaussian filter also affects low frequencies of the curve coordinate functions [18]. Oliensis [18] proposed to change the Gaussian kernel by a filter which is closer to the ideal low pass filter. This way, low frequencies are less affected, and less shrinkage is obtained. With this approach, which is also non-intrinsic, the semi-group property holds just approximately. Note that in [1, 5, 31] it was proved that filtering with a Gaussian kernel is the unique linear operation for which the causality criterion holds, i.e., zero-crossings (or maxima) are not created at non-zero scales. Therefore, the approach presented in [18], which is closed related to wavelet approaches, violates this important principle.

Lowe [16] proposes to estimate the amount of shrinkage and to compensate for it. The estimate is based on the amount of smoothing (σ) and the curvature. This approach, which only reduces the shrinkage problem, is again non-intrinsic, since it is based on Gaussian filtering, and works only for small rates of change. The semi-group property is violated as well.

Horn and Weldon [12] also investigated the shrinkage problem, but only for convex curves. In their approach, the curve is represented by its extended circular image, which is the radius of curvature of the given curve as a function of the curve orientation. The scale-space is obtained by filtering this representation.

We now show how to solve the shrinkage problem with the Euclidean geometric heat flow. It is important to know that in the approach proposed below, the enclosed area is conserved exactly.

When a closed curve evolves according to (2), it is easy to prove [9] that the enclosed area $\mathbf{A}$ evolves according to

$$\frac{\partial \mathbf{A}}{\partial t} = - \oint \beta dv. \tag{5}$$

Therefore, in the case of the Euclidean geometric heat flow we obtain ($\beta = \kappa$)

$$\frac{\partial \mathbf{A}}{\partial t} = -2\pi \quad , \quad \mathbf{A}(t) = \mathbf{A}_0 - 2\pi t, \tag{6}$$

where $\mathbf{A}_0$ is the area enclosed by the initial curve $\mathcal{C}_0$. As pointed out in [9, 10, 11], curves evolving according to (3) can be normalized in order to keep constant area. The normalization process is given by a change of the time scale, from t to τ, such that a new curve is obtained via

$$\tilde{\mathcal{C}}(\tau) := \psi(t)\,\mathcal{C}(t), \tag{7}$$

where $\psi(t)$ represents the normalization factor (time scaling). (The equation can be normalized so that the point $\mathcal{P}$ to which $\mathcal{C}(t)$ shrinks is taken as the origin.) In the Euclidean case, $\psi(t)$ is selected such that $\psi^2(t) = \frac{\partial \tau}{\partial t}$.

The new time scale τ must be chosen to obtain $\tilde{\mathbf{A}}_\tau \equiv 0$. Define the collapse time T, such that $\lim_{t \to T} \mathbf{A}(t) \equiv 0$. Then, $T = \frac{\mathbf{A}_0}{2\pi}$. Let

$$\tau(t) = -T \ln(T - t). \tag{8}$$

Then, since the area of $\tilde{C}$ and C are related by the square of the normalization factor $\psi(t) = \left(\frac{\partial \tau}{\partial t}\right)^{1/2}$, $\tilde{\mathbf{A}}_\tau \equiv 0$ for the time scaling given by (8). The evolution of $\tilde{C}$ is obtained from the evolution of C and the time scaling given by (8). Taking partial derivatives in (7) we have

$$\frac{\partial \tilde{C}}{\partial \tau} = \frac{\partial t}{\partial \tau} \frac{\partial \tilde{C}}{\partial t} = \psi^{-2}(\psi_t C + \psi C_t) = \psi^{-2}\psi_t C + \psi^{-1}\kappa\mathcal{N} = \psi^{-3}\psi_t \tilde{C} + \tilde{\kappa}\mathcal{N}.$$

From previous Section we know that the flow above is geometric equivalent to

$$\frac{\partial \tilde{C}}{\partial \tau} = \psi^{-3}\psi_t < \tilde{C}, \mathcal{N} > \mathcal{N} + \tilde{\kappa}\mathcal{N}. \tag{9}$$

Define the *support function* as $\rho := - < C, \mathcal{N} >$. Then, it is easy to show that $\mathbf{A} = \frac{1}{2} \oint \rho \, dv$. Therefore, applying the general area evolution equation (5) to the flow (9), together with the constraint $\tilde{\mathbf{A}}_\tau \equiv 0$ ($\tilde{\mathbf{A}}(\tau) \equiv \mathbf{A}_0$), we obtain

$$\frac{\partial \tilde{C}}{\partial \tau}(p, \tau) = \left(\tilde{\kappa} - \frac{\pi\tilde{\rho}}{\mathbf{A}_0} \right)\mathcal{N}, \tag{10}$$

which gives a local, area preserving, flow. Note that the flow exists for all $0 \leq \tau < \infty$. Since C and $\tilde{C}$ are related by dilations, the flows (3) and (10) have the same geometric properties [9, 10, 11, 28]. In particular, since a curve evolving according to the Euclidean heat flow satisfies all the required properties of a multi-scale representation, so does the normalized flow. See Figure 1, where the flow is implemented using the algorithm proposed in [20] for curve evolution.

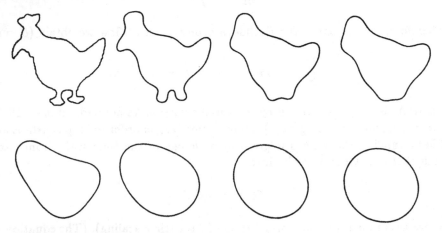

Figure 1. Example of the area preserving Euclidean heat flow.

3 Affine Geometric Heat Flow

We present now the affine invariant evolution analogue of (3) (or (4)). For details see [24, 25, 27].

Following [24], we first consider the affine analogue of the Euclidean heat flow for convex initial curves. Let s be the *affine arc-length* [6], i.e., the simplest affine invariant parametrization. In this case, with C_0 as initial curve, $C(p, t)$ satisfies the following evolution equation (compare with equation (4)):

$$\frac{\partial C(p, t)}{\partial t} = C_{ss}(p, t). \tag{11}$$

Since the affine normal C_{ss} is affine invariant, so is the flow (11). This flow was first presented and analyzed in [24]. We proved that, in analogy with the Euclidean heat flow, any convex curve converges to an elliptical point when evolving according to it (the curve remains convex as well). For other properties of the flow, see [24].

To complete the analogy between the Euclidean geometric heat flow (4), and the affine one given by (11), the theory must be extended to non-convex curves. In order to perform the extension, we have to overcome the problem of the "non-existence" of affine differential geometry for non-convex curves. We carry this out now. See [25, 27] for details. Assume now that the family of curves $C(p, t)$ evolves according to the flow

$$\frac{\partial C(p, t)}{\partial t} = \begin{cases} 0 & p \text{ inflection point,} \\ C_{ss} & p \text{ non-inflection point,} \end{cases} \tag{12}$$

with the corresponding initial condition $C(p, 0) = C_0(p)$. Since C_{ss} exists for all non-inflection points [6], (12) is well defined also for non-convex curves. Also, due to the affine invariance property of the inflection points, (12) is affine invariant.

We already know that if we are interested only in the geometry of the curve, i.e., Img$[C]$, we can consider just the Euclidean normal component of the velocity in (11). In [24], it was proved that the Euclidean normal component of C_{ss} is equal to $\kappa^{1/3}$. Then, for a convex initial curve, Img$[C(p, t)] = $ Img$[\hat{C}(w, t)]$, where $C(p, t)$ is the solution of (11), and $\hat{C}(w, t)$ is the solution of $\hat{C}_t = \kappa^{1/3}\mathcal{N}$. Since for an inflection point $q \in C$, we have $\kappa^{1/3}(q) = 0$, the evolution given by (12) is the natural extension of the affine curve flow of convex curves given by equation (11). Then, equation (12) is transformed into

$$C_t = \kappa^{1/3}\mathcal{N}. \tag{13}$$

If C is the solution of (12) and $\hat{C}$ is the one of (13), Img$[C] = $ Img$[\hat{C}]$, and Img$[\hat{C}]$ is an affine invariant solution of the evolution (13). Note that the image of the curve is affine invariant, not the curve itself.

In [4, 27], we have proved that any smooth and simple non-convex curve evolving according to (13) (or (12)), remains smooth and simple, and becomes convex. From there, it converges into an ellipse from the results described above.

In [1], the authors showed that under certain assumptions, equation (13), when regarded as the flow of the level sets of a 3D image, is unique in its affine invariance property. The uniqueness was also proved by us in [19], based on symmetry groups. In [4], among other results, we also extended the flow to initial Lipschitz curves.

We have showed that the flow given by (12) (or (13)) is the (unique) affine analogue of the Euclidean geometric heat flow given by (4). This evolution is called the *affine geometric heat flow*. It defines an intrinsic, geometric, affine invariant multi-scale representation for planar curves. In [25], we analyzed this flow and showed that the multi-scale representation which we obtained, satisfies all the required scale-space properties. Affine invariant smoothing examples can be found in [25] as well. See also [26] for applications of this flow to image processing.

3.1 Affine Geometric Heat Flow Without Shrinkage

From the general evolution equation for areas (5) we have that when a curve evolves according to (13), the evolution of the enclosed area is given by $A_t = -\oint \kappa^{1/3} dv$. Define the *affine perimeter* as $L := \oint [C_p, C_{pp}]^{1/3} dp$ [6]. Then it is easy to show that $L = \oint \kappa^{1/3} dv$ [24], and

$$A_t = -L. \tag{14}$$

As in the Euclidean case, we define a normalized curve $\tilde{C}(\tau) := \psi(t) C(t)$, such that when C evolves according to (13), $\tilde{C}$ encloses a constant area. In this case, the time scaling is chosen such that

$$\frac{\partial \tau}{\partial t} = \psi^{4/3}. \tag{15}$$

(We see from the Euclidean and affine examples that in general, the exponent λ in $\frac{\partial \tau}{\partial t} = \psi^\lambda$ is chosen such that $\tilde{\beta} = \psi^{1-\lambda}\beta$.) Taking partial derivatives, using the relations (5), (14), and (15), and constraining $\tilde{A}_\tau \equiv 0$ ($\tilde{A}(\tau) \equiv A_0$), we obtain the following geometric affine invariant, area preserving, flow:

$$\frac{\partial \tilde{C}}{\partial \tau} = \left(\tilde{\kappa}^{1/3} - \frac{\tilde{\rho} L}{2 A_0} \right) \mathcal{N}. \tag{16}$$

Note that in contrast with the Euclidean area preserving flow given by equation (10), the affine one is not local. This is due to the fact that the rate of area change in the Euclidean case is constant, but in the affine case it depends on the affine perimeter (which is global).

As in the Euclidean case, the flow (16) satisfies the same geometric properties as the affine geometric heat flow (13). Therefore, it defines a geometric, affine invariant, area preserving multi-scale representation.

Again, based on the theory of viscosity solutions, or in the new results in [4], the flow (13), as well as its normalized version (16), are well defined also for non-smooth curves. Based on the same concepts described above, we showed how to derive invariant geometric heat flows for any Lie group in [27]. In [19] we give the characterization of all invariant flows for subgroups of the projective group and show that the heat flows are the simplest possible. These results are based on classical Lie theory and symmetry groups. The similarity group is also analyzed in detail, including convergence results, in [28].

4 Length Preserving Geometric Flows

Similar techniques to those presented in previous sections, can be used in order to keep fixed other curve characteristics, e.g., the Euclidean length **P**. In this case, when C evolves according to the general geometric flow $\frac{\partial C}{\partial t} = \beta \mathcal{N}$, and $\tilde{C}(\tau) := \psi(t) C(t)$, we obtain the following length preserving geometric flow:

$$\frac{\partial \tilde{C}}{\partial \tau}(p, \tau) = \left(\tilde{\beta} - \frac{\oint \tilde{\beta} \tilde{\kappa}}{\mathbf{P}_0} \tilde{\rho} \right) \mathcal{N}. \tag{17}$$

The computation of (17) is performed again taking partial derivatives and using the relations $\mathbf{P}_t = - \oint \beta \kappa dv$, $\mathbf{P} = \oint \kappa \rho dv$, together with the constraint $\tilde{\mathbf{P}}_\tau \equiv 0$.

Since the similarity flow (scale invariant) is given by $C_t = \kappa^{-1} \mathcal{N}$ [28], its length preserving analogue is $\frac{\partial \tilde{C}}{\partial \tau}(p, \tau) = (\tilde{\kappa}^{-1} - \tilde{\rho}) \mathcal{N}$, and the flow is completely local. Another local, length preserving flow may be obtained for the Euclidean constant motion given by $C_t = \mathcal{N}$. This flow models morphological dilation with a disk [23]. In this case, the rate of change of length is constant and the length preserving flow is given by $\frac{\partial \tilde{C}}{\partial \tau}(p, \tau) = \left(1 - \frac{2\pi \tilde{\rho}}{\mathbf{P}_0} \right) \mathcal{N}$, see Figure 2. A smooth initial curve evolving with constant motion can develop singularities [1, 13, 23, 27], and the physically correct weak solution of the flow is the viscosity (or *entropy*) one [1, 23].

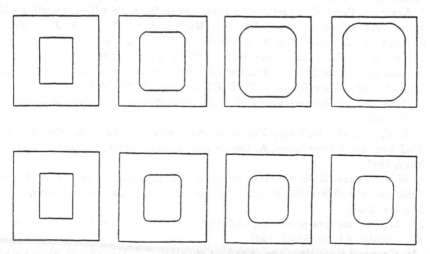

Figure 2. Euclidean constant motion and area preserving form.

5 Concluding Remarks

In this paper, area preserving multi-scale representations for planar shapes were described. The representations are obtained deforming the curve via the invariant geometric heat flows while simultaneously magnifying the plane by a homethety which keeps the enclosed area constant. The flow is geometrically intrinsic to the curve, and exactly satisfies all the required properties of scale-spaces. For the Euclidean case for example, the flow is local as well.

The same approach was used to derive length preserving geometric flows. In this case, locality is obtained for example for the similarity heat flow and the Euclidean constant motion. Similar techniques can be used in order to keep other curve characteristics constant, and to transform other geometric scale-spaces [19, 27], into analogous area or length preserving ones.

Different area or length preserving flows can be proposed. In [9, 22], non-local preserving flows are presented motivated by physical phenomena models. The advantage of the approach here described is that the non-shrinking curve is obtained by a homothety, and the resulting normalized flow keeps all the geometric properties of the original one. The flow is also local in some cases.

In [2], the importance of the Euclidean geometric heat flow for image enhancement was demonstrated. This was extended for the affine geometric heat flow in [1, 26]. We are currently investigating the use of the corresponding area (or length) preserving flows for this application as well.

References

1. L. Alvarez, F. Guichard, P. L. Lions, and J. M. Morel, Axioms and fundamental equations of image processing, to appear in *Arch. for Rational Mechanics*.
2. L. Alvarez, P. L. Lions, and J. M. Morel, Image selective smoothing and edge detection by nonlinear diffusion, *SIAM J. Numer. Anal.* 29, pp. 845-866, 1992.
3. S. Angenent, Parabolic equations for curves on surfaces, Part II. Intersections, blow-up, and generalized solutions, *Annals of Mathematics* 133, pp. 171-215, 1991.
4. S. Angenent, G. Sapiro, and A. Tannenbaum, On the affine heat equation for non-convex curves, *Technical Report MIT – LIDS*, January 1994.
5. J. Babaud, A. P. Witkin, M. Baudin, and R. O. Duda, Uniqueness of the Gaussian kernel for scale-space filtering, *IEEE–PAMI* 8, pp. 26-33, 1986.
6. W. Blaschke, *Vorlesungen über Differentialgeometrie II*, Verlag Von Julius Springer, Berlin, 1923.
7. C. L. Epstein and M. Gage, The curve shortening flow, in *Wave Motion: Theory, Modeling, and Computation*, A. Chorin and A. Majda (Ed.), Springer-Verlag, New York, 1987.
8. L. M. J. Florack, B. M. ter Haar Romeny, J. J. Koenderink, and M. A. Viergever, Scale and the differential structure of images, *Image and Vision Comp.* 10, pp. 376-388, 1992.
9. M. Gage, On an area-preserving evolution equation for plane curves, *Contemporary Mathematics* 51, pp. 51-62, 1986.
10. M. Gage and R. S. Hamilton, The heat equation shrinking convex plane curves, *J. Differential Geometry* 23, pp. 69-96, 1986.

458

11. M. Grayson, The heat equation shrinks embedded plane curves to round points, *J. Differential Geometry* **26**, pp. 285-314, 1987.

12. B. K. P. Horn and E. J. Weldon, Jr., Filtering closed curves, *IEEE–PAMI* **8**, pp. 665-668, 1986.

13. B. B. Kimia, A. Tannenbaum, and S. W. Zucker, Shapes, shocks, and deformations, I, to appear in *International Journal of Compute Vision*.

14. J. J. Koenderink, The structure of images, *Biological Cybernetics* **50**, pp. 363-370, 1984.

15. T. Lindeberg and J. O. Eklundh, On the computation of a scale-space primal sketch, *Journal of Visual Comm. and Image Rep.* **2**, pp. 55-78, 1991.

16. D. G. Lowe, Organization of smooth image curves at multiple scales, *International Journal of Computer Vision* **3**, pp. 119-130, 1989.

17. F. Mokhatarian and A. Mackworth, A theory of multiscale, curvature-based shape representation for planar curves, *IEEE–PAMI* **14**, pp. 789-805, 1992.

18. J. Oliensis, Local reproducible smoothing without shrinkage, *IEEE–PAMI* **15**, pp. 307-312, 1993.

19. P. J. Olver, G. Sapiro, and A. Tannenbaum, Differential invariant signatures and flows in computer vision: A symmetry group approach, *Technical Report MIT – LIDS* , December 1993. Also in *Geometry Driven Diffusion*, B. ter har Romeny Ed., 1994.

20. S. J. Osher and J. A. Sethian, Fronts propagation with curvature dependent speed: Algorithms based on Hamilton-Jacobi formulations, *Journal of Computational Physics* **79**, pp. 12-49, 1988.

21. P. Perona and J. Malik, Scale-space and edge detection using anisotropic diffusion, *IEEE–PAMI* **12**, pp. 629-639, 1990.

22. J. Rubinstein and P. Sternberg, Nonlocal reaction-diffusion equations and nucleation, *IMA Journal of Applied Mathematics* **48** pp. 249-264, 1992.

23. G. Sapiro, R. Kimmel, D. Shaked, B. B. Kimia, and A. M. Bruckstein, Implementing continuous-scale morphology via curve evolution, *Pattern Recognition* **26:9**, pp. 1363-1372, 1993.

24. G. Sapiro and A. Tannenbaum, On affine plane curve evolution, February 1992, to appear in *Journal of Functional Analysis*.

25. G. Sapiro and A. Tannenbaum, Affine invariant scale-space, *International Journal of Computer Vision* **11:1**, pp. 25-44, 1993.

26. G. Sapiro and A. Tannenbaum, Image smoothing based on an affine invariant flow, *Proc. of Conf.on Information Sciences and Systems*, Johns Hopkins University, March 1993.

27. G. Sapiro and A. Tannenbaum, On invariant curve evolution and image analysis, *Indiana University Mathematics Journal* **42:3**, 1993.

28. G. Sapiro and A. Tannenbaum, Area and length preserving geometric invariant scale-spaces, *Technical Report MIT – LIDS* **2200** , September 1993.

29. M. Spivak, *A Comprehensive Introduction to Differential Geometry*, Publish or Perish Inc, Berkeley, California, 1979.

30. A. P. Witkin, Scale-space filtering, *Int. Joint. Conf. Artificial Intelligence*, pp. 1019-1021, 1983.

31. A. L. Yuille and T. A. Poggio, Scaling theorems for zero crossings, *IEEE–PAMI* **8**, pp. 15-25, 1986.

Invariants of 6 Points from 3 Uncalibrated Images

Long QUAN

LIFIA - CNRS - INRIA,
46 avenue Felix Viallet, 38031 Grenoble, France

Abstract. There are three projective invariants of a set of six points in general position in space. It is well known that these invariants cannot be recovered from one image, however an invariant relationship does exist between space invariants and image invariants. This invariant relationship will first be derived for a single image. Then this invariant relationship is used to derive the space invariants, when multiple images are available.

This paper establishes that the minimum number of images for computing these invariants is three, and invariants from three images can have as many as three solutions. Algorithms are presented for computing these invariants in closed form. The accuracy and stability with respect to image noise, selection of the triplets of images and distance between viewing positions are studied both through real and simulated images.

Application of these invariants is also presented, this extends the results of projective reconstruction of Faugeras [6] and Hartley *et al.* [10] and the method of epipolar geometry determination of Sturm [18] for two uncalibrated images to the case of three uncalibrated images.

1 Introduction

Geometric invariants are playing a more and more important role in machine vision applications. A lot of work for recognition and shape description using invariants has already been reported, for instance *cf.* the collection book [13] and [11, 6, 15, 17, 10, 9]. Most of the invariants are derived for planar objects using geometric entities such as points, lines and conics, since in this case, there exists a plane projective transformation between object and image space. Plane projective geometry provides an ideal mathematical tool for describing this. As for general geometric configurations in space, it has been shown that it is not possible to estimate invariants from single images [3]. Therefore, one (cf. [1, 6, 10, 9, 8]) basically deals with space projective invariants from 2 images, provided that the epipolar geometry, or the fundamental matrix [7] of the two images is determined *a priori*. The epipolar geometry may be algebraically determined with at least 7 points by Sturm's method [7, 18] up to 3 solutions. However, Sturm's method is numerically unstable [7]. When more than 8 points are available, numerical minimization methods are used to determine it.

In this paper, we are interested in computing the invariants of sets of 6 points in space from 3 images taken with uncalibrated cameras, given correspondences between image points. The main new results obtained in this paper are that the minimum number of images for computing the invariants of 6 points is three; and the invariants computed from three images can have as many as three solutions. All solutions are given in closed form. As a consequence, we establish that a set of n points ($n \geq 6$) can be projectively reconstructed up to 3 solutions, which extends the results of Faugeras [6] and Hartley *et al.* [10] for 2 uncalibrated images to the case of 3 uncalibrated images.

In comparison with the related work, the method proposed in this paper does not need to estimate the epipolar geometry between images which needs at least 7 points, the minimum of 6 points are enough, however one more image is needed. As a byproduct, the epipolar geometry between pairs of images can be also determined up to 3 solutions from only 6 points instead of 7 points.

The development of this work is largely inspired by the old mathematical work on invariants of Coble [4] and the more recent work of Faugeras [6]. We assume that readers are familiar with elementary projective geometry and invariant theory, as they can be found in [16, 4, 5].

2   Review of invariants of 6 points in space

Given a set of points or other kind of geometric configurations, the number of invariants is roughly speaking the difference of the dimension of the configuration group and the dimension of the transformation group, if the dimension of the isotropy group of the configuration is null. For a set of 6 points in $\mathcal{P}^3$, there are $3 = 3 \times 6 - (16 - 1)$ absolute invariants under the action of general linear group $GL(3)$ in $\mathcal{P}^3$. Since each point in $\mathcal{P}^3$ has 3 degrees of freedom, the dimension of a set of 6 points is $3 \times 6 = 18$. The transformation group $GL(3)$ is represented by a 4×4 matrix up to a scaling factor, its dimension is $4 \times 4 - 1 = 15$.

These 3 invariants can be formed and interpreted differently. For instance, following invariant theory, invariants can be expressed by linear combinations of products of the determinants of 4 by 4 matrix whose columns are the homogeneous coordinates of the points. This is mainly a domain of symmetric functions of the coordinates of the points. The invariants formed this way can be symmetric, therefore independent of the order in which the points are taken. Sometimes, half symmetric functions are also used. Coble [4] has been interested in studying the invariants of point sets using the six half symmetrical Jourbet's functions to define the complete system of the (relative) invariants of 6 points.

Another way is to consider twisted cubics [16], since there is a unique twisted cubic that passes through the given 6 general points in $\mathcal{P}^3$. Any 4 points of a twisted cubic define a cross ratio, therefore a subordinate one-dimensional projective geometry is induced on any twisted cubic. So the 3 invariants of the set of 6 points can be taken as the 3 independent cross ratios of the sets of 4 points on the twisted cubic. Or more algebraically, we can consider the invariants of cubic forms. Cubic forms in $\mathcal{P}^3$ have 5 algebraically independent relative invariants of degree 8, 16, 24, 32, 40 (*cf.* [5]). 3 absolute invariants can be derived from these 5 relative invariants. However the expressions for these invariants are very complex polynomials.

One of the simplest ways to consider these 3 invariants is by considering the 3 non-homogeneous projective coordinates of any sixth point with respect to a projective basis defined by any 5 of them. In the following, we will consider these invariants, since it seems to us that this is the simplest way to deal with them, and also because this methodology has been succeesfully used in [6, 10, 12, 15], particularly by Faugeras in [6]. Obviously, these non homogeneous projective coordinates admit direct cross-ratio interpretation [16].

3 Invariant relationship of 6 points from one image

3.1 Canonical representation of 6 points in space

Given any six points $\{P_i, i = 1, \ldots, 6\}$ in $\mathcal{P}^3$, in view of the fundamental theorem for projective space, any five of them, no 3 of them collinear and no 4 of them coplanar, can be given preassigned coordinates, thus we can assign them the canonical projective coordinates as follows $(1, 0, 0, 0)^T$, $(0, 1, 0, 0)^T$, $(0, 0, 1, 0)^T$, $(0, 0, 0, 1)^T$ and $(1, 1, 1, 1)^T$, this uniquely determines a space collineation $\mathcal{A}_{4 \times 4}$, $det(\mathcal{A}_{4 \times 4}) \neq 0$, which transforms the original 5 points into this canonical basis. And for the sixth point, it is transformed into its projective coordinates $(X, Y, Z, T)^T$ by $\mathcal{A}_{4 \times 4}$.

$X : Y : Z : T$ *gives the three independent absolute invariants of 6 points.*

3.2 Canonical representation of 6 image points

The projections of these six points onto an image $\{p_i, i = 1, \ldots, 6\}$ are usually given in non-homogeneous coordinates $(x_i, y_i)^T, i = 1, \ldots, 6$ take any 4 of them, no 3 of them collinear, and assign them the canonical projective coordinates in $\mathcal{P}^2$ $(1, 0, 0)^T, (0, 1, 0)^T, (0, 0, 1)^T$, and $(1, 1, 1)^T$ and a plane collineation $\mathcal{A}_{3 \times 3}$, $det(\mathcal{A}) \neq 0$, is uniquely determined which transforms the fifth and sixth points into $(u_5, v_5, w_5)^T$ and $(u_6, v_6, w_6)^T$.

$u_5 : v_5 : w_5$ *and* $u_6 : v_6 : w_6$ *give the 4 independent absolute invariants of 6 image points.*

3.3 Projection between space and image plane

If we assume a perspective projection as the camera model, then object space may be considered as embedded in $\mathcal{P}^3$ and image space embedded in $\mathcal{P}^2$. The camera performs the projection between $\mathcal{P}^3$ and $\mathcal{P}^2$, and this projection can be represented by a 3×4 matrix $\mathcal{C}_{3 \times 4}$ of rank 3 whose kernel is the projection center. The relation between the points P_i in $\mathcal{P}^3$ and p_i in $\mathcal{P}^2$ can be written as $\lambda_i\, p_i = C_{3\times 4}\, P_i, i = 1, \ldots, 6$ where p_i and P_i are in homogeneous coordinates. This can be rewritten in ratio form hiding the scaling factor λ_i,

$$
\begin{aligned}
u_i : v_i : w_i = \; & (c_{11}X_i + c_{12}Y_i + c_{13}Z_i + c_{14}T_i) : \\
& (c_{21}X_i + c_{22}Y_i + c_{23}Z_i + c_{24}T_i) : \\
& (c_{31}X_i + c_{32}Y_i + c_{33}Z_i + c_{34}T_i).
\end{aligned}
\tag{1}
$$

For each point, as u_i, v_i and w_i can not all be zero, two independent equations can always be derived from (1). These equations express nothing else than the collinearity of the space points and their corresponding image points. This is a projective property which is preserved by any projective transformation.

3.4   Elimination of camera parameters c_{ij}

For a set of 6 points, when the correspondences are given as

$$(1,0,0)^T \leftrightarrow (1,0,0,0)^T, \quad (0,1,0)^T \leftrightarrow (0,1,0,0)^T, \quad (0,0,1)^T \leftrightarrow (0,0,1,0)^T,$$
$$(1,1,1)^T \leftrightarrow (0,0,0,1)^T, (u_5,v_5,w_5)^T \leftrightarrow (1,1,1,1)^T, (u_6,v_6,w_6)^T \leftrightarrow (X,Y,Z,T)^T,$$

this leads to $12 = 2 \times 6$ equations from (1). All entries c_{ij} of $C_{3\times 4}$ are unknowns, as we assumed that the camera was uncalibrated. Since $C_{3\times 4}$ is defined up to a scaling factor, it counts for $3 \times 4 - 1 = 11$ unknowns. So there still remains one $(1 = 12 - 11)$ independent equation after eliminating all unknown camera parameters.

Substituting all 6 canonical projective coordinates into equations (1) then eliminating c_{ij}, we obtain a homogeneous equation between $(X, Y, Z, T)^T$ and $(u_5, v_5, w_5)^T$ and $(u_6, v_6, w_6)^T$,

$$
\begin{aligned}
& w_6(u_5 - v_5)XY + v_6(w_5 - u_5)XZ + u_5(v_6 - w_6)XT + \\
& u_6(v_5 - w_5)YZ + v_5(w_6 - u_6)YT + w_5(u_6 - v_6)ZT = 0.
\end{aligned}
\tag{2}
$$

3.5   Invariant interpretation of the equation

This equation (2) will be arranged and interpreted as an invariant relationship between the relative invariants of $\mathcal{P}^3$ and those of $\mathcal{P}^2$ as follows.

If i_j and I_j denote respectively

$$i_1 = w_6\,(u_5 - v_5),\; i_2 = v_6\,(w_5 - u_5),\; i_3 = u_5\,(v_6 - w_6),$$
$$i_4 = u_6\,(v_5 - w_5),\; i_5 = v_5\,(w_6 - u_6),\; i_6 = w_5\,(u_6 - v_6),$$

and

$$I_1 = XY,\; I_2 = XZ,\; I_3 = XT,\; I_4 = YZ,\; I_5 = YT,\; I_6 = ZT,$$

then i_j and I_j can be interpreted as respectively the relative invariants of 6 points in $\mathcal{P}^2$ (image) and those of 6 points in $\mathcal{P}^3$ (space).

$\{i_j, j = 1, \ldots, 6\}$ are defined up to a common multiplier, so they are only relative invariants of the 6 points of the image. The 5 ratios $i_1 : i_2 : i_3 : i_4 : i_5 : i_6$

are (absolute) projective invariants. Since (by the arguments of Section 2) for the set of 6 points in $\mathcal{P}^2$, there are $4 = 2 \times 6 - 8$ independent projective invariants therefore the relative invariants set $\{i_j, j = 1, \ldots, 6\}$ are not independent and are subject to one $(1 = 5 - 4)$ additional constraint which is

$$i_1 + i_2 + i_3 + i_4 + i_5 + i_6 = 0.$$

This can be checked from the above definition of i_j.

$\{I_j, j = 1, \ldots, 6\}$ are relative invariants of $\mathcal{P}^3$, only the 5 ratios $I_1 : I_2 : I_3 : I_4 : I_5 : I_6$ are projective invariants in space. Since there are only 3 independent absolute invariants, I_j are subject to two $(2 = 5 - 3)$ additional constraints which are

$$I_1 I_6 = I_2 I_5 = I_3 I_4.$$

An independent set of three absolute invariants could be taken to be

$$\alpha \equiv I_2/I_6 = X/T, \quad \beta \equiv I_4/I_6 = Y/T \text{ and } \gamma \equiv I_2/I_3 = Z/T,$$

the set of invariants $\{\alpha, \beta, \gamma\}$ is equivalent to $X : Y : Z : T$.

Then the invariant relation derived from equations (1) is simply expressed as a bilinear homogeneous relation:

$$i_1 I_1 + i_2 I_2 + i_3 I_3 + i_4 I_4 + i_5 I_5 + i_6 I_6 = 0. \tag{3}$$

This relationship is of course independent of any camera parameters, therefore it can be used for any uncalibrated images. This clearly shows that the 3D invariants can not be computed from one single image, since we have only one invariant relationship for three independent invariants. This invariant relationship can be used in two different ways. First, we can verify whether a given set of points is present in a model base. That means I_j can be computed from the model base and i_j from the image, then the invariant relation can be used to check for the presence of the model in the image. Secondly, to compute 3D invariants from more than one image, this leads to the following section.

4   Computation from 3 images

In this section, we will focus on how to find the absolute invariants of 6 points in space, i.e. $\{\alpha, \beta, \gamma\}$ or equivalently $X : Y : Z : T$ from more than one image. To do this, it is assumed that 6 point correspondence through images have already been established.

So from a six point set in one image, the homogeneous equation (3) can be written in X, Y, Z, T. Therefore if three images of the 6 points set are available, then the three homogeneous quadratic equations in X, Y, Z, T can be written as follows.

$$\mathcal{F}_1 \equiv i_1^{(1)} XY + i_2^{(1)} XZ + i_3^{(1)} XT + i_4^{(1)} YZ + i_5^{(1)} YT + i_6^{(1)} ZT = 0, \tag{4}$$

$$\mathcal{F}_2 \equiv i_1^{(2)} XY + i_2^{(2)} XZ + i_3^{(2)} XT + i_4^{(2)} YZ + i_5^{(2)} YT + i_6^{(2)} ZT = 0, \tag{5}$$

$$\mathcal{F}_3 \equiv i_1^{(3)} XY + i_2^{(3)} XZ + i_3^{(3)} XT + i_4^{(3)} YZ + i_5^{(3)} YT + i_6^{(3)} ZT = 0 \tag{6}$$

here the superscripts (j), $j = 1, 2, 3$, distinguish the invariant quantities of different images.

4.1 Maximum number of possible solutions

Each equation represents a quadratic surface whose rank is of 3. These quadratic forms have no X^2, Y^2, Z^2, T^2 terms. That means that the quadratic surface goes through the vertices of the tetrahedron of reference whose coordinates are $(0,0,0,1)^T$, $(0,0,1,0)^T$, $(0,1,0,0)^T$, $(1,0,0,0)^T$. This is easily verified by substituting these points in the equations. In addition, as the coefficients of the quadratic form $i^{(j)}$ are subject to the following relations,

$$i_1^{(j)} + i_2^{(j)} + i_3^{(j)} + i_4^{(j)} + i_5^{(j)} + i_6^{(j)} = 0, \text{ for } j = 1, 2, 3;$$

so all the equations (4), (5) and (6) necessarily pass through the unit point $(1, 1, 1, 1)^T$.

According to Bezout's Theorem, three quadratic surfaces must meet in $8 = 2 \times 2 \times 2$ points. Since they already pass through the five known points, so only $3 = 8 - 5$ common points remain. Therefore,

The maximum number of solutions for $X : Y : Z : T$ is three.

4.2 Find X/T by solving a cubic equation

Now, let us try to explicit these 3 solutions. For instance, if we want to solve for X/T, the two resultants $\mathcal{G}_1$ and $\mathcal{G}_2$ obtained by eliminating Z between $\mathcal{F}_1$, $\mathcal{F}_2$ and $\mathcal{F}_3$ are homogeneous polynomials in X, Y and T of degree 3:

$$\mathcal{G}_1 \equiv e_1^{(1)} X^2 Y + e_2^{(1)} XY^2 + e_3^{(1)} XYT + e_4^{(1)} X^2 T + e_5^{(1)} XT^2 + e_6^{(1)} Y^2 T + e_7^{(1)} YT^2 = 0,$$

$$\mathcal{G}_2 \equiv e_1^{(2)} X^2 Y + e_2^{(2)} XY^2 + e_3^{(2)} XYT + e_4^{(2)} X^2 T + e_5^{(2)} XT^2 + e_6^{(2)} Y^2 T + e_7^{(2)} YT^2 = 0,$$

whose coefficients are still subject to

$$e_1^{(j)} + e_2^{(j)} + e_3^{(j)} + e_4^{(j)} + e_5^{(j)} + e_6^{(j)} + e_7^{(j)} = 0 \text{ for } j = 1, 2.$$

where

$$e_1^{(j)} = i_4^{(j+1)} i_5^{(j)} - i_4^{(j)} i_5^{(j+1)}, \quad e_2^{(j)} = i_4^{(j+1)} i_6^{(j)} - i_4^{(j)} i_6^{(j+1)}, \quad e_4^{(j)} = i_1^{(j+1)} i_5^{(j)} - i_1^{(j)} i_5^{(j+1)},$$

$$e_5^{(j)} = i_1^{(j+1)} i_3^{(j)} - i_1^{(j)} i_3^{(j+1)}, \quad e_6^{(j)} = i_2^{(j+1)} i_6^{(j)} - i_2^{(j)} i_6^{(j+1)}, \quad e_7^{(j)} = i_2^{(j+1)} i_3^{(j)} - i_2^{(j)} i_3^{(j+1)}.$$

This is due to the fact that the point $(1, 1, 1)^T$ is still on the two cubic curves. The resultant obtained by eliminating Y between $\mathcal{G}_1$ and $\mathcal{G}_2$ is a homogeneous polynomial in X, T of degree 8, which can be factorised as,

$$X T (X - T) (b_1 X^2 + b_2 XT + b_3 T^2)(a_1 X^3 + a_2 X^2 T + a_3 X T^2 + a_4 T^3).$$

It is evident that the linear factors lead to trivial solutions. The solution $X = 0$ corresponds to the common points $(0,0,0,1)^T$, $(0,0,1,0)^T$ and $(0,1,0,0)^T$. The solution $T = 0$ corresponds to the common points $(1,0,0,0)^T$, $(0,1,0,0)^T$ and $(0,0,1,0)^T$. The solution $X = T$ corresponds to the common point $(1,1,1,1)^T$.

Now, let us have a close-look at the coefficients of the quadratic factor,

$$b_1 = i_4^{(2)} i_5^{(2)}, \quad b_2 = i_3^{(2)} i_4^{(2)} + i_2^{(2)} i_5^{(2)} - i_1^{(2)} i_6^{(2)}, \quad b_3 = i_2^{(2)} i_3^{(2)}$$

which depend only on the invariant quantities of the points of the second image, so the zeros of the quadratic factor are the parasite solutions introduced by elimination using resultants, they are not the zeros of $\{\mathcal{F}_1, \mathcal{F}_2, \mathcal{F}_3\}$. Thus, the only nontrivial solutions for X/T are those of the cubic equation,

$$\mathcal{C} \equiv a_1\, X^3 + a_2\, X^2\, T + a_3\, X\, T^2 + a_4\, T^3 = 0.$$

The implicit expressions for a_i (quite long) can be easily obtained with Maple. The cubic equation may be solved algebraically by Cardano's formula, either for X/T or T/X. Since $T = 0$ is allowable, the choice between solving X/T or T/X depends on the estimation of the moduli of the roots. According to Cauchy's Theorem, the moduli of the roots of cubic equations are bounded by the following,

$$(1 + max\{|a_2|, |a_4|\}/|a_1|)^{-1} < |X : T| < 1 + max\{|a_1|, |a_3|\}/|a_4|.$$

If the modulus is large enough, that means T is near to 0, in this case it would be better to solve for its reciprocal T/X instead of X/T.

4.3 Find $Y : Z : T$ linearly for a given X/T

$Y : Z : T$ should be solved for each given X/T. As the equations are symmetric in X, Y, Z and T, we could obtain other similar cubic equations for the other two independent absolute invariants, for instance, Y/T and Z/T or any other ratios if necessary. However, doing this will lead to much more than 3 solution sets which is not desirable. We expect to obtain unique $Y : Z : T$ for each given X/T.

By eliminating Y^2 between $\mathcal{G}_1$ and $\mathcal{G}_2$, we obtain the following homogeneous polynomial

$$\mathcal{H} \equiv (c_1 X^3 + c_2 X^2\, T + c_3 X\, T^2 + c_4 T^3)\, Y + X(d_1 X^2 + d_2 X\, T + d_3 T^2)T,$$

where

$$c_1 = e_2^{(2)} e_1^{(1)} - e_1^{(2)} e_2^{(1)}, \quad c_2 = e_6^{(2)} e_1^{(1)} - e_3^{(2)} e_2^{(1)} + e_2^{(2)} e_3^{(1)} - e_1^{(2)} e_6^{(1)},$$

$$c_4 = e_6^{(2)} e_7^{(1)} - e_7^{(2)} e_6^{(1)}, \quad c_3 = e_6^{(2)} e_3^{(1)} - e_7^{(2)} e_2^{(1)} - e_3^{(2)} e_6^{(1)} + e_2^{(2)} e_7^{(1)},$$

$$d_1 = e_2^{(2)} e_4^{(1)} - e_4^{(2)} e_2^{(1)}, \quad d_2 = e_2^{(2)} e_5^{(1)} + e_6^{(2)} e_4^{(1)} - e_5^{(2)} e_2^{(1)} - e_4^{(2)} e_6^{(1)},$$

$$d_3 = e_6^{(2)} e_5^{(1)} - e_5^{(2)} e_6^{(1)}.$$

Any zero of $\mathcal{H}$ will also be a zero of $\mathcal{G}_1$ and $\mathcal{G}_2$, as $\mathcal{H}$ is a linear combination of $\mathcal{G}_1$ and $\mathcal{G}_2$ with polynomial coefficients, and $\mathcal{H}$ belongs to the ideal generated by $\mathcal{G}_1$ and $\mathcal{G}_2$.

$\mathcal{H}$ can be considered as a linear homogeneous polynomial in Y and T for a given X/T. Therefore a unique Y/T is guaranteed from this equation for each given $\alpha = X/T$,

$$Y : T = -\alpha(d_1\alpha^2 + d_2\alpha + d_3) : (c_1\alpha^3 + c_2\alpha^2 + c_3\alpha + c_4).$$

For a given $X : Y : T$, say $\alpha = X/T$ and $\beta = Y/T$, $Z : T$ is uniquely determined by one of the equations (4), (5) or (6), for instance taking (4), we have

$$Z : T = -(i_1^{(1)}\alpha\beta + i_3^{(1)}\alpha + i_5^{(1)}\beta) : (i_2^{(1)}\alpha + i_4^{(1)}\beta + i_6^{(1)}).$$

In conclusion,

given the correspondences of a set of 6 points for three images taken by un-calibrated cameras, the solutions for the three invariants associated to the set of 6 points in space can have either one or three, all given in closed form.

4.4 Remark

We can note that instead of finding zero sets of $\{\mathcal{F}_1, \mathcal{F}_2, \mathcal{F}_3\}$ for $X : Y : Z : T$, we can equivalently solve for the ratios $I_1 : I_2 : I_3 : I_4 : I_5 : I_6$,

$$\begin{cases} i_1^{(1)} I_1 + i_2^{(1)} I_2 + i_3^{(1)} I_3 + i_4^{(1)} I_4 + i_5^{(1)} I_5 + i_6^{(1)} I_6 = 0 \\ i_1^{(2)} I_1 + i_2^{(2)} I_2 + i_3^{(2)} I_3 + i_4^{(2)} I_4 + i_5^{(2)} I_5 + i_6^{(2)} I_6 = 0 \\ i_1^{(3)} I_1 + i_2^{(3)} I_2 + i_3^{(3)} I_3 + i_4^{(3)} I_4 + i_5^{(3)} I_5 + i_6^{(3)} I_6 = 0 \\ I_1 I_6 = I_2 I_5 = I_3 I_4 . \end{cases}$$

They meet in $4 = 2 \times 2 \times 1 \times 1 \times 1$ intersection points. As the sum of the coefficients is zero, they meet in the common unit point $(1, 1, 1, 1, 1, 1)^T$, so only 3 solutions remain. The same results, cubic equation, can be obtained by a little more symbolic computation.

We can also note that when 5 images are available, a linear solution for the ratios $I_1 : I_2 : I_3 : I_4 : I_5 : I_6$ is possible while ignoring the quadratic constraints $I_1 I_6 = I_2 I_5 = I_3 I_4$.

5 Application of invariants

For the point sets, reconstruction up to a collineation is equivalent to computation of projective invariants. One of the consequences of the above results is that a 3D reconstruction up to a collineation is possible from 3 uncalibrated images as have been achieved by Faugeras [6] and Hartley et al. [10] from two uncalibrated images with epipolar geometry. In [6], Faugeras used epipolar geometry to determine the projection matrix up to projective transformations, here as the projective coordinates of the sixth point was algebraically determined. In return, this projective coordinates of the sixth point can be used to determine the projection matrix $C_{3 \times 4}^{(j)}$ for each camera by solving (1). Then any other point can be projectively reconstructed from these projection matrices. Therefore we establish the following result which can be considered as an extension to that of Faugeras [6] and Hartley et al. [10] for two uncalibrated images.

Given the correspondences of a set of n points (n is at least 6) for three images taken by uncalibrated cameras, the point set can be reconstructed in $\mathcal{P}^3$ up to a collineation. The reconstruction may have as many as three different solutions.

Another consequence of this is that the computation of epipolar geometry of camera pairs can also be achieved with only 6 point correspondences:

Given point-to-point correspondences of 6 points for three images taken by uncalibrated cameras, the epipolar geometries between each pair of images can be determined up to three solutions.

This can be compared with Sturm's method [7, 18] of determining the epipolar geometry from 7 points of two images.

Due to space limitation, more details on application of invariants can be found in the technical report [14].

Image triplet	$\alpha = 0.526421$	d_1	$\beta = 1.880620$	d_2	$\gamma = 0.745762$	d_3
1, 2, 3	0.528183	0.0083	1.877117	-0.018	0.760771	0.0050
4, 5, 6	0.516476*	-0.0034	1.899056*	0.0035	0.747555*	-0.0082
1, 3, 5	0.524387	0.0045	1.889926	-0.0056	0.760802*	0.0051
5, 7, 9	0.514523*	-0.0053	1.899576*	0.0041	0.739840*	-0.016
1, 4, 8	0.520458	-0.00053	1.900477	0.0050	0.763048	0.0073
2, 5, 8	0.516762	-0.0032	1.900178	0.0047	0.751696	-0.0040
1, 5, 9	0.518681	-0.0012	1.902235	0.0067	0.766406	0.011
Ground truth	0.526421		1.880620		0.745762	

Table 1. Table of invariants computed from different triplets of synthetic images. The points of images are noised by ± 1.5 pixel error, the invariants α, β and γ are computed for each different image triplet. d_i are the differences between each computed invariant and its mean value.

6   Experimental results

The theoretical results presented above have been implemented. The accuracy and stability of the invariants with respect to various factors will be studied both for simulated and real images. The application for projective reconstruction is also presented. Due to page limitation, the extended experimental results can be found in [14].

First, a real camera is calibrated at 9 different viewing positions, spaced at 10 degree intervals around the calibration object of about $50cm^3$ in front of the camera. Then, with these 9 calibration matrices as our perfect cameras, we project several sets of 6 known points into these 9 synthetic images. Finally the projected positions of the points in the images are perturbed by varying levels of noise of uniform distribution. As the positions of the 6 simulated points in space are known in advance, their invariants are computed and are compared with those calculated from the simulated image data. The results that will be presented in the following tables are obtained from the set of 6 points whose coordinates are $(2.0, 0.0, 12.0)^T$, $(0.0, 6.0, 0.0)^T$, $(12.0, 0.0, 14.0)^T$, $(0.0, 6.0, 6.0)^T$, $(-1.5, 19.5, 0.0)^T$ and $(0.0, 12.0, 12.0)^T$ (the units are cm).

Table 1 shows the effect of choosing different triplets of images on the stability of the 3 invariants. In the case that the solution is unique, it is marked by a *. In the case of multiple solutions, the one that is the closest to the ground truth value is selected.

For a given triplet of images $\{1, 2, 3\}$, different pixel noise (uniformly distributed) is added to illustrate the influence of the pixel errors. Tables 2 shows that with noise levels up to ± 5.5 pixels, the computed invariants remain numerically stable, so that degradation with the increasing pixel noise is graceful.

The experiment with real images is performed on a sequence of images of a wooden house. Three views covering about a 45° rotation of the camera around the wooden house are taken. The corners marked in Figure 1.a are tracked for the three images. The invariants are computed for different sets of 6 points

Noise	$\alpha = 0.526421$	d_1	$\beta = 1.880620$	d_2	$\gamma = 0.745762$	d_3
±0.5	0.527054	0.00063	1.879408	-0.0012	0.751121	0.0054
±1.5	0.528183	0.0018	1.877117	-0.0035	0.760771	0.015
±2.5	0.529135	0.0027	1.875013	-0.0056	0.769214	0.023
±3.5	0.529938	0.0035	1.873026	-0.0076	0.776658	0.031
±4.5	0.530609	0.0042	1.871119	-0.0095	0.783268	0.038
±5.5	0.531163	0.0047	1.869260	-0.011	0.789171	0.043

Table 2. Table of invariants computed from the triplet of images $\{1, 2, 3\}$. α, β and γ are computed with pixel errors of different levels. d_i is the difference between the computed value and its mean value.

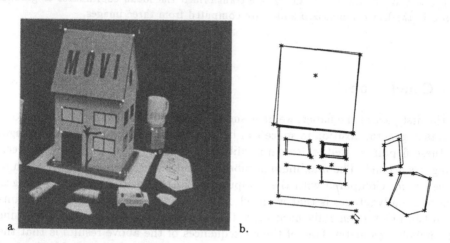

Fig. 1. a. One of the wooden house image sequence. Some points used for the experiment are marked by white circles. b. The rectified projective reconstruction from 3 uncalibrated images: the points are displayed as stars and the line segments as solid lines. Euclidean reconstruction from 5 images: the points are dots and the line segments dashed lines. The 5 reference points used were $\{2, 5, 8, 10, 11\}$ (cf. a.)

and compared with that computed by transforming the estimated Euclidean coordinates (cf. [2]) in Table 3. In the case of unique real solution existing, the computed values are marked by a *. In case of multiple solutions, the one that is the closest to the known value is selected.

Using all tracked 46 points of 3 images of the wooden house (see Figure 1.a), we experimented on the projective reconstruction from 3 uncalibrated images discussed in Section 5. Although the theoretical multiplicity of the projective reconstruction is at most three, in practice often a unique solution is possible. As we can select the sixth point whose projective coordinates are uniquely determined. Further investigation on automatic selection of the sixth point is underway. The sixth point used to compute the projection matrices is point number 1 (see the first raw of Table 3). The projective reconstruction is then transformed into its Euclidean representation (see Fig 1.b) with the known reference points in order to compare the result with direct Euclidean reconstruction from 5 images [2].

Set of points	known $(\alpha', \beta', \gamma')$	computed (α, β, γ)
{1,2,5,8,10,11}	(0.594573, 0.944785, 0.157327)	(0.581565*, 0.925869*, 0.143597*)
{2,3,5,8,10,11}	(0.716795, 0.740667, 0.64426)	(0.714164, 0.739041, 0.662835)
{2,5,7,8,10,11}	(1.68619, 12.7413, 0.970638)	(1.714522, 12.729020, 0.995141)
{2,5,6,8,10,11}	(0.681678, 0.241914, 1.7126)	(0.742775*, 0.325263*, 1.822018*)
{2,5,7,8,10,11}	(-0.22391, 0.225495, 0.858623)	(-0.230072, 0.228533, 0.880303)
{2,5,8,9,10,11}	(0.634079, 0.344556, 3.09316)	(0.705443, 0.448216, 3.303431)
{2,5,8,10,11,12}	(-0.816493, 0.264887, 2.45476)	(-0.849691, 0.233549, 2.523767)

Table 3. Table of invariants computed from the three images of the wooden house for the different sets of 6 points. The first column presents the sets of numbers of 6 points. In the second column, α', β' and γ' are transformed Euclidean coordinates as ground truth. In the last column, α, β and γ are computed from three images.

7 Conclusion

In the first part of the paper, we have shown how the three invariants of a set of 6 points in general position in space can be algebraically computed from 3 images of these 6 points. Neither camera calibration nor epipolar geometry between images is needed. The maximum number of solutions is 3 which are all given in closed form. Compared with the computation of the invariants from 2 images, one of the advantages is that we need only 6 points of the 3 images, invariants from two images generally need more than 7 points in order to first determine the epipolar geometry. One of the consequences of the above results is that the projective reconstruction and epipolar geometry determination can be obtained from 3 uncalibrated images with a multiplicity of at most three. This extends the results of Sturm [18], Faugeras [6] and Hartley et al. [10] from two uncalibrated images.

In the second part of the paper, the stability of the invariants is studied via both simulated and real images with respect to different factors such as pixel errors, selection of the triplet of images and the distance between cameras. The computed invariants are numerically stable both with respect to image noise and to selection of triplet of images if the distance between cameras is not too small. We have also successfully applied the method to perform projective reconstruction of set of points.

Acknowledgements This work is partly supported by European Esprit BRA projects Viva which is gratefully acknowledged. We would also like to thank B. Boufama, P. Gros, R. Horaud, R. Mohr, D. Sinclair, D. Wang and C. Zhao for providing interesting discussion and helps.

References

1. E.B. Barrett, M.H. Brill, N.N. Haag, and P.M. Payton. Invariant linear methods in photogrammetry and model-matching. In J. Mundy and A. Zisserman, editors, *Geometric Invariance in Computer Vision*, pages 277–292. The MIT press, 1992.
2. B. Boufama, R. Mohr, and F. Veillon. Euclidian constraints for uncalibrated reconstruction. In *Proceedings of the 4th International Conference on Computer Vision, Berlin, Germany*, pages 466–470, May 1993.
3. J.B. Burns, R. Weiss, and E.M. Riseman. View variation of point set and line segment features. In *Proceedings of DARPA Image Understanding Workshop, Pittsburgh, Pennsylvania, USA*, pages 650–659, 1990.
4. A.B. Coble. *Algebraic Geometry and Theta Functions*. American Mathematical Society, 1961.
5. J. Dixmier. Quelques aspects de la théorie des invariants. *Gazette des Mathématiciens*, 43:39–64, January 1990.
6. O. Faugeras. What can be seen in three dimensions with an uncalibrated stereo rig? In G. Sandini, editor, *Proceedings of the 2nd European Conference on Computer Vision, Santa Margherita Ligure, Italy*, pages 563–578. Springer-Verlag, May 1992.
7. O.D. Faugeras, Q.T. Luong, and S.J. Maybank. Camera Self-Calibration: Theory and Experiments. In G. Sandini, editor, *Proceedings of the 2nd European Conference on Computer Vision, Santa Margherita Ligure, Italy*, pages 321–334. Springer-Verlag, May 1992.
8. P. Gros and L. Quan. 3D projective invariants from two images. In *Geometric Methods in Computer Vision II, SPIE's 1993 International Symposium on Optical Instrumentation and Applied Science*, pages 75–86, July 1993.
9. R. Hartley. Invariants of Points Seen in Multiple Images. Technical report, G.E. CRD, Schenectady, 1992.
10. R. Hartley, R. Gupta, and T. Chang. Stereo from uncalibrated cameras. In *Proceedings of the Conference on Computer Vision and Pattern Recognition, Urbana-Champaign, Illinois, USA*, pages 761–764, 1992.
11. J.J. Koenderink and A. J. van Doorn. Affine structure from motion. Technical report, Utrecht University, Utrecht, The Netherlands, October 1989.
12. R. Mohr, F. Veillon, and L. Quan. Relative 3D reconstruction using multiple uncalibrated images. In *Proceedings of IEEE Conference on Computer Vision and Pattern Recognition, New York, USA*, pages 543–548, June 1993.
13. J.L. Mundy and A. Zisserman, editors. *Geometric Invariance in Computer Vision*. MIT Press, Cambridge, Massachusetts, USA, 1992.
14. L. Quan. Invariants of 6 Points from 3 Uncalibrated Images. Rapport Technique RT 101 IMAG 19 LIFIA, LIFIA-IMAG, Grenoble, October 1993.
15. L. Quan and R. Mohr. Affine shape representation from motion through reference points. *Journal of Mathematical Imaging and Vision*, 1:145–151, 1992. Also in IEEE Workshop on Visual Motion, New Jersey, pages 249–254, 1991.
16. J.G. Semple and G.T. Kneebone. *Algebraic Projective Geometry*. Oxford Science Publication, 1952.
17. G. Sparr. An algebraic/analytic method for reconstruction from image correspondance. In *Proceedings of the 7th Scandinavian Conference on Image Analysis, Aalborg, Denmark*, pages 274–281, 1991.
18. R. Sturm. Das problem der projektivität und seine anwendung auf die flächen zweiten grades. *Math. Ann.*, 1:533–574, 1869.

A Common Framework for Kinetic Depth, Reconstruction and Motion for Deformable Objects *

Gunnar Sparr

Dept. of Mathematics, Lund University/LTH,
P.O. Box 118, S-22100 Lund, Sweden
email: gunnar@maths.lth.se

Abstract. In this paper, problems related to depth, reconstruction and motion from a pair of projective images are studied under weak assumptions. Only relative information within each image is used, nothing about their interrelations or about camera calibration. Objects in the scene may be deformed between the imaging instants, provided that the deformations can be described locally by affine transformations. It is shown how the problems can be treated by a common method, based on a novel interpretation of a theorem in projective geometry of M. Chasles, and the notion of "affine shape". No epipolar geometry is used. The method also enables the computation of the "depth flow", i.e. a relative velocity in the direction of the ray of sight.
Keywords: Depth, shape, reconstruction, motion, invariants.

1 Introduction

Central problems in computer vision are concerned with reconstruction and recovery of motion from image pairs. A number of algorithms exist, in general based on iterative numerical techniques and known camera calibration. For a survey, see [7]. The problem is ill-posed, both what concerns stability and non-uniqueness, cf. [3], [10]. During the last few years, much interest has been directed on methods that are independent of camera calibration, cf. e.g. [9], [2], [4], [13], [11], [18]. The present paper belongs to this circle. It studies problems related to *depth, reconstruction* and *relative motion*, and what information is attainable by an analyzing system that is "autonomous" in the following sense:

- the only information available is provided by the images, considered as planar geometric objects, and the knowledge that they are formed by projective transformations of a scene, subject to the constraints of the next item. More precisely, we assume that

---

* The work has been done within the ESPRIT-BRA project VIVA, and has been supported by the Swedish National Board for Industrial and Technical Development (NUTEK).

- no quantitative information about the projective transformations is available. Thus nothing is known about camera parameters, focal axis, central point, etc. Different cameras are allowed.
- within each image it is only possible to extract affine information, no metrical. No relation between the image planes is known. Thus each image can be described in an affine coordinate system, where the two systems are independent.
- objects in the scene are allowed to move and even change shape between the imaging instants, provided that, locally, the deformations can be described by affine transformations.

A substantial difficulty is the establishment of correspondences between the two images. In this paper only *point configurations* will be considered, and it is *assumed that a number of point correspondences are known beforehand*.

In spite of the generality of the problem setting, surprisingly much can be said, both qualitatively and quantitatively. Below it will be shown how the three problems of the title can be treated by a common method, originating from a novel interpretation of a theorem in projective geometry. For the reconstruction problem, the results generalise those of [2], [4], both by allowing the objects to deform, and by using fewer basis points in the reconstructions. Moreover a notion of "depth flow" is introduced, enabling a quantitative treatment of the "kinetic depth" effect. Depth-ratio parameters are introduced, enabling a relative motion description that is invariant to e.g. camera calibration and affine transformations of the image planes.

In the literature, the non-calibration reconstruction problem is usually treated by means of epipolar geometry or essential matrices. The approach of this paper is different. The core consists of result about "affine reconstruction and motion" from [17], [18]. However, the objectives in these papers were reconstruction and motion in the case of known camera calibration, and the affine results were only used as computational tools. Here they will be considerably extended and systemised. Also depth properties for compositions of perspective transformations will be used.

In Sect. 2 the fundamental ideas and tools of the approach are summarised. Section 3 is devoted to a description of the central geometric problem, called "the reciprocal Chasles' problem", with some further details postponed to an appendix. In Sect. 4 some applications are discussed, theoretically and computationally, around an example with data from real images.

2 Shape and Depth

Configurations and Transformations. In a series of papers, [17], [19], [18], and in [16], a notion of *shape* has been introduced, and various applications have been described. Here only a brief recapitulation will be given. The objects dealt with are *m-point configurations* $\mathcal{X}$, by which is meant ordered sets of points $\mathcal{X} = (X^1, \ldots, X^m)$ in 3D-space. A point configuration is thus defined in entirely geometric terms, without coordinates. The role of coordinates is discussed below.

The goal is to find efficient tools for studying *perspective transformations*, characterised by mapping every point on a line through a point C onto its point of intersection with a plane π, where $C \notin \pi$. Here C is called the *center* and π the *image plane*. When the domain of P is restricted to some plane, P is called a *perspective isomorphism*. If the point X is mapped onto Y by a perspective transformation with center C, then the factor α in $\overline{CX} = \alpha \overline{CY}$ is called the *depth* of X with respect to Y. If one configuration $\mathcal{X}$ is mapped onto another $\mathcal{Y}$, where the latter is planar, and the depths of X^i with respect to Y^i is α_i, $i = 1, \ldots, m$, then the vector $\alpha = (\alpha_1, \ldots, \alpha_m)$ is called the depth of $\mathcal{X}$ with respect to $\mathcal{Y}$. *Projective transformations* are obtained by composition of perspective transformations.

A central role of the approach is played by the *affine transformations*. These are characterised by mapping parallel lines onto parallel lines, and contain the parallel projections, similarity transformations, and translations. For such transformations all components in the depth vector are equal, i.e. $\alpha \parallel (1, \ldots, 1)$.

Affine Coordinate Invariancy. For computational reasons, coordinates have to be introduced. However, to get truly geometric results, the arguing must be independent of the coordinate systems used, within some convenient class. In chosing this class one has to decide which properties of the configurations are essential for the problem, and which should be filtered away. As has been pointed out above, when studying depth properties for projective transformations, only trivial depth information can be drawn from a pair of affinely equivalent configurations. There is thus no reason to distinguish between them, which leads to a claim on affine coordinate independence. An alternative, often used in computer vision, is to use homogeneous coordinates, with the disadvantage of not being able to distinguish between points on the same ray.

In the references above, it is proved that the linear space

$$s(\mathcal{X}) = \mathcal{N} \begin{pmatrix} 1 & 1 & \cdots & 1 \\ X^1 & X^2 & \cdots & X^m \end{pmatrix} \tag{1}$$

is independent of the coordinate representation used for the points X^i, $i = 1, \ldots, m$, where $\mathcal{N}$ stands for "nullspace". Stated otherwise, this means that

$$s(\mathcal{X}) = s(\mathcal{X}') \iff \text{there exists an affine isomorphism} \quad A : \mathcal{X} \longrightarrow \mathcal{X}' \,.$$

All the affine information is thus contained in the linear space $s(\mathcal{X})$, which is called the *(affine) shape* of $\mathcal{X}$. We write $\mathcal{X}' \overset{s}{=} \mathcal{X}'' \iff s(\mathcal{X}) = s(\mathcal{X}')$. Explicit examples of shape for point configurations were given e.g. in [19]. About the dimension of the linear space $s(\mathcal{X})$, the following can be said:

$$\begin{aligned} &\dim s(\mathcal{X}) = m - 4 \text{ if } \mathcal{X} \text{ is non-planar }, \\ &\dim s(\mathcal{X}) = m - 3 \text{ if } \mathcal{X} \text{ is planar, but not linear }, \\ &\dim s(\mathcal{X}) = m - 2 \text{ if } \mathcal{X} \text{ is linear }. \end{aligned} \tag{2}$$

Remark. For all $\mathcal{X}$ holds $s(\mathcal{X}) \subset \Sigma_0 = \{\xi \mid \sum \xi_i = 0\}$. On the contrary, it is readily verified that for every $S \subset \Sigma_0$, there exist configurations $\mathcal{X}$ such that $s(\mathcal{X}) = S$, cf. [20]. This is an important observation, since it makes it possible to concretise abstract results about shapes in terms of explicit point configurations.

The Shape Transform Theorem and the Depth Theorem. The following theorem completely characterises when two configurations can be mapped onto each other by a perspective transformation. The configurations may be 2D or 3D. For componentwise multiplication on R^m, we use the notation $\alpha \xi = (\alpha_1 \xi_1, \ldots, \alpha_m \xi_m)$ if $\alpha = (\alpha_1, \ldots, \alpha_m)$, $\xi = (\xi_1, \ldots, \xi_m)$.

Theorem 1. Shape transform theorem (STT) *There exists a perspective transformation P such that $P(\mathcal{X}) \stackrel{s}{=} \mathcal{Y}$, where $\mathcal{X}$ has depth α with respect to $P(\mathcal{X})$, if and only if $\alpha s(\mathcal{X}) \subset s(\mathcal{Y})$. P is a perspective isomorphism if and only if $\alpha s(\mathcal{X}) = s(\mathcal{Y})$.*

The advantage of this theorem is that a projective transformation P is transformed into the much simpler *multiplier* operator $s(\mathcal{X}) \longrightarrow \alpha s(\mathcal{X})$. It is possible to characterise the set of α that may appear here for a given $\mathcal{X}$. In fact, with

$$d(\mathcal{X}) = \{\alpha \mid \alpha^T \xi = 0 \text{ for every } \xi \in s(\mathcal{X})\} ,$$

there holds the theorem, cf. [20]:

Theorem 2. Depth theorem (DT). $d(\mathcal{X}) = $ *the set of possible depth values for perspective transformations acting on $\mathcal{X}$.*

Motivated by this theorem, $d(\mathcal{X})$ is called the *depth space* of $\mathcal{X}$. Note that the rows of the matrix in (1) form a basis for $d(\mathcal{X})$. From this observation follows that the i :th component of each vector in $d(\mathcal{X})$ can be obtained by evaluating a function

$$\lambda(x, y) = a + bx + cy \tag{3}$$

in the configuration point X^i, $i = 1, \ldots, m$.

Depth for Projective Transformations. It may seem that the concept of depth is bound to perspective transformations, and has no canonical sense for their compositions, i.e. projective transformations. The following theorem says that it has.

Theorem 3. *If P and Q are perspective transformations, $P : \mathcal{X} \longrightarrow \mathcal{Y}$, $Q : \mathcal{Y} \longrightarrow \mathcal{Z}$, with depths α and β respectively, then there exists a perspective transformation $R : \mathcal{X} \longrightarrow \mathcal{Z}$, of depth $\alpha\beta$, such that $(Q \circ P)\mathcal{X} \stackrel{s}{=} R\mathcal{X}$.*

Qualitatively, Theorem 3 says that by forming a perspective image of a perspective image of a perspective image ..., the last image in the sequence is affinely equivalent to a direct perspective image of the original object. An equivalent formulation is that there exists an affine copy of the object, and a perspective transformation mapping this copy onto the last image in the sequence. The second situation is illustrated in the figure below. The statement may also be reformulated as *modulo affine transformations, the set of perspective transformations is stable under compositions.* This serves as a substitute for the lacking group property of perspective transformations.

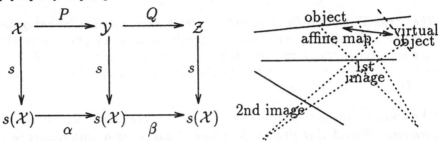

Compensation and Modulation. For humans, the phenomenon of the preceding paragraph is met daily, e.g. when looking at a photograph from any other point than the focal point of the camera. In such situations, it is not evident that what is seen should contain any consistent depth information at all, but that's asserted by the theorem. Moreover, humans seem to have an ability to *compensate* for the distortion, even when the picture is viewed from a very displaced position, see e.g. [14].

The quantitative part of Theorem 3 makes it possible to equip also a machine vision system with a property of compensation, provided that the system has some a priori conception about e.g. a ground plane or points at infinity. More precisely, suppose that an image $\mathcal{Y}$ of a 3D object $\mathcal{X}$ is distorted by a series of planar perspective isomorphisms, resulting in a final image $\mathcal{Z}$. Let α be the depth of $\mathcal{X}$ with respect to $\mathcal{Z}$. From (3) follows that every depth vector of perspective transformations acting on $\mathcal{Z}$ can be written

$$\lambda_{\mathcal{Z}} = (\lambda(Z^1), \ldots, \lambda(Z^m)) \text{ for some function } \lambda(x, y) = a + bx + cy .$$

Then $\alpha\lambda_{\mathcal{Z}}$ the depth of $\mathcal{X}$ with respect to a perspective image of $\mathcal{Z}$, by Theorem 3. This will be called a λ-*modulation* of α. Since λ is uniquely determined by its values in three points, it follows that it is possible to adjust the depth in three given points to any three given values, e.g. on a horizontal or vertical reference plane, and getting consistent depth information in the remaining points. This process will be called *compensation*.

3   The Reciprocal Chasles Problem

It will be seen that the following problem covers the problems addressed in Sect. 1.

RECIPROCAL CHASLES' PROBLEM (RCP). *Given planar configurations $\mathcal{Y}$ and $\overline{\mathcal{Y}}$. Determine all configurations $\mathcal{X}$, $\overline{\mathcal{X}}$, and perspective transformations P, $\overline{P}$, such that*

$$\mathcal{Y} = P(\mathcal{X}), \quad \overline{\mathcal{Y}} = \overline{P}(\overline{\mathcal{X}}), \quad and \quad \mathcal{X} \stackrel{s}{=} \overline{\mathcal{X}} . \tag{4}$$

The problem was first formulated in [17], [18], and has been further studied in [15]. Its name stems from a relationship to a problem, or theorem, of Chasles[2], [1]. In [15] it is shown that Chasles' problem can be formulated in the following way, and a motivation for the prefix "reciprocal" is given.

CHASLES' PROBLEM (CP). *Given two planar configurations $\mathcal{Y}$ and $\overline{\mathcal{Y}}$. Find perspective transformations P and $\overline{P}$ such that the linear configurations $\mathcal{Z} = P(\mathcal{Y})$ and $\overline{\mathcal{Z}} = \overline{P}(\overline{\mathcal{Y}})$ are in affine correspondence.*

In general terms, the relevance of CP and RCP to computer vision is that CP concerns about ways to map two given configurations onto the same linear configuration (modulo affine transformations), while RCP concerns about ways to obtain them as images of the same 3D configuration (modulo affine transformations). Thus CP is related to recognition, and RCP to reconstruction.

STT provides an efficient tool to analyze these problems. It says that (4) holds if and only if there exist $\alpha, \overline{\alpha}$ such that

$$\alpha s(\mathcal{X}) \subset s(\mathcal{Y}) , \quad \overline{\alpha} s(\overline{\mathcal{X}}) \subset s(\overline{\mathcal{Y}}) , \quad s(\mathcal{X}) = s(\overline{\mathcal{X}}) ,$$

or, equivalently,

$$s(\mathcal{X}) \subset \alpha^{-1} s(\mathcal{Y}) \cap \overline{\alpha}^{-1} s(\overline{\mathcal{Y}}) . \tag{5}$$

Here, by (2), the space on the left hand side has dimension $m - 4$ if $\mathcal{X}$ is non-planar, and $m - 3$ if it is planar. Also by (2), both spaces on the right have dimension $m - 3$. Thus two cases may occur: either the two right-hand spaces are identical, with an intersection of dimension $m - 3$, or their intersection has dimension $m - 4$. In the former case there exists a planar configuration $\mathcal{X}$ with shape $s(\mathcal{X}) = \alpha^{-1} s(\mathcal{Y}) = \overline{\alpha}^{-1} s(\overline{\mathcal{Y}})$. Then, by STT, $\mathcal{X}$ can be mapped onto $\mathcal{Y}$ and $\overline{\mathcal{Y}}$ with depths α and $\overline{\alpha}$ respectively. This situation of locally planar objects was treated in [19], cf. also [5]. Here we will concentrate on the other, more complicated case, when the two spaces on the left hand side in (5) intersect in a space of dimension $m - 4$. Then $\mathcal{X}$ is non-planar, and the set inclusion in (5) is in fact an equality.

Forgetting for a moment about the intersection space in (5), which is the one searched for in reconstruction, caring only about the dimensions, it is easy to see that only the *depth ratio* $q = \overline{\alpha}/\alpha$ is of importance. Hence every solution to RCP produces a solution to the following problem WCP. However, more important is that every solution to WCP produces a solution of RCP. This is the content of the reconstruction principle below.

WEAK CHASLES' PROBLEM (WCP). *Given planar m-point configurations $\mathcal{Y}$ and $\overline{\mathcal{Y}}$, find q such that*

$$dim\,(q s(\mathcal{Y}) \cap s(\overline{\mathcal{Y}})) \geq m - 4 . \tag{6}$$

---

[2] Question 296. On donne dans le même plan deux systèmes de sept points chacun et qui se correspondent. Faire passer par chacun de ces systèmes un faisceau de sept rayons, de telle sorte que les deux faisceaux soient homographiques. Démontrer qu'il n'y a que trois solutions.

RECONSTRUCTION PRINCIPLE (RP). Suppose that q is a solution of WCP, satisfying (6). Let $\widetilde{\mathcal{X}}$ be a configuration with shape defined by

$$s(\widetilde{\mathcal{X}}) = qs(\mathcal{Y}) \cap s(\overline{\mathcal{Y}}), \tag{7}$$

where the existence of $\widetilde{\mathcal{X}}$ is guaranteed by the remark of Sect. 2. If the two spaces on the right are identical, $s(\widetilde{\mathcal{X}})$ is obtained from STT as in [19]. Else, if $\widetilde{\mathcal{X}}$ is a non-planar 3D configuration, take $\beta \in d(\widetilde{\mathcal{X}})$. Then $\beta s(\widetilde{\mathcal{X}}) \subset \Sigma_0$, and by the remark of Sect. 2, it is the shape for some 3D configuration $\mathcal{X}$. With this $\mathcal{X}$ and with $\overline{\alpha} = \beta^{-1}$, $\alpha = \overline{\alpha}/q$, (5) is fulfilled, with $\alpha \in d(\mathcal{X})$, $\overline{\alpha} \in d(\overline{\mathcal{X}})$. We thus have found a solution to RCP. Also note that, by STT, $\widetilde{\mathcal{X}}$ and $\mathcal{X}$ are projectively equivalent.

The crucial problem to solve is thus WCP. This is done in [15], with a short summary in the appendix below. It can be shown that the condition (7) can be formulated as a system of second order polynomial equations, having a very particular structure. In the case of 7-point configurations, this structure can be exploited to enable an explicit solution algorithm, with three solutions in general. For less than 7 points, WCP has an infinite set of solutions, while in the case of more than 7 points, it needs not have any solution at all. If there is a solution in this case, it is unique. For 8-point configurations another method to obtain this solution was described in [18]. The results of [15] are summarised in the following theorem.

Theorem 4. Invariants for image pairs. *To every pair $\mathcal{Y}$, $\overline{\mathcal{Y}}$ of planar 7-point configurations are associated three vectors $q = (q_1, \ldots, q_7)$ such that*

- *whenever $\mathcal{Y}, \overline{\mathcal{Y}}$ are projective images of depths $\alpha, \overline{\alpha}$ with respect to some $\mathcal{X}$, $\overline{\mathcal{X}}$, with $\mathcal{X} \stackrel{s}{=} \overline{\mathcal{X}}$, then $\overline{\alpha}/\alpha$ is equal to one of the q-vectors.*
- *given $\alpha, \overline{\alpha}$ such that $\overline{\alpha}/\alpha = $ one of the q-vectors, then there exist $\mathcal{X}, \overline{\mathcal{X}}$, with $\mathcal{X} \stackrel{s}{=} \overline{\mathcal{X}}$, and perspective transformations $\mathcal{X} \longrightarrow \mathcal{Y}$, $\overline{\mathcal{X}} \longrightarrow \overline{\mathcal{Y}}$ with depths α, $\overline{\alpha}$, respectively.*
- *q is a relative invariant for (independent) affine transformation of $\mathcal{Y}$, $\overline{\mathcal{Y}}$. Equivalently, $\frac{\overline{\alpha}_j}{\alpha_j}/\frac{\overline{\alpha}_k}{\alpha_k}$ is an absolute affine invariant, for every $j \neq k$.*
- *The shapes of the possible $\mathcal{X}$ that may appear above are related by a multiplier relation $s(\mathcal{X}') = \beta s(\mathcal{X}'')$. Equivalently this means that $\mathcal{X}'$ and $\mathcal{X}''$ can be mapped onto each other by a projective transformation.*

Large parts of the theory above can be generalised to the case of three or more images, cf. [6].

4 Analysis of Image Pairs

In this section some applications of Theorem 4 will be described, both theoretically and in a numerical example, with data from the image pair of the figure below. The object considered is a "kaleidocycle", built from a kit in [12]. Playing

with it consists in performing local affine deformations. On three adjacent faces, labelled A, B, C, 3+4+3=10 points have been marked. Their pixel coordinates are picked out by hand. The faces have no points in common, which would have been a simplification. As can be seen, the two pictures are taken with different camera adjustments, and the object has been deformed in the meantime.

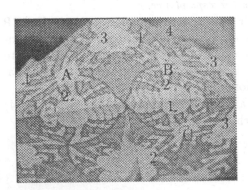 

Reconstruction of Deformable Objects. Generally, let $\mathcal{Y}, \overline{\mathcal{Y}}$ be two planar image configurations. The reconstruction problem, in the sense of this paper, consists in the determination of all $\mathcal{X}, \overline{\mathcal{X}}$, with $\mathcal{X} \stackrel{s}{=} \overline{\mathcal{X}}$, that can be mapped onto $\mathcal{Y}, \overline{\mathcal{Y}}$, respectively, by perspective transformations. About $\mathcal{Y}, \overline{\mathcal{Y}}$, no metrical properties are known, only their affine, represented by the shapes $s(\mathcal{Y}), s(\overline{\mathcal{Y}})$. Hence one can't expect to get a higher precision for the reconstructions, i.e. $\mathcal{X}, \overline{\mathcal{X}}$ can only, at best, be characterised in terms of $s(\mathcal{X}), s(\overline{\mathcal{X}})$. On the other hand, this lack of precision makes it possible to treat also the case of deformable configurations, as long as the deformations can be described by affine transformations.

Suppose the object configuration can be partitioned by overlapping 7-point configurations, such that for each of them the hypothesis about locally affine deformations is met. By gluing reconstructions computed for each subconfiguration separately, according to Theorem 4, a global reconstruction can be obtained. (How to do the gluing will not be discussed in this paper, neither the problem of guaranteeing compatibility of the different solutions for the depth ratios.) After having computed $s(\widetilde{\mathcal{X}})$ an explicit reconstruction $\widetilde{\mathcal{X}}$ is obtained by specifying the location of four points in space, cf. the remark of Sect. 2. From RP follows that every other possible reconstruction has a shape obtained by applying a multiplier β with $\beta \in d(\widetilde{\mathcal{X}})$ to $s(\widetilde{\mathcal{X}})$, where $\beta = \overline{\alpha}^{-1}$ and $\overline{\alpha}$ is the depth of $\mathcal{X}$ with respect to $\overline{\mathcal{Y}}$. By STT, this means that every other possible reconstruction is obtained as a 3D perspective image of $\widetilde{\mathcal{X}}$. In summary, this means that the degrees of freedom in the reconstruction consist in the choices of four points and one perspective transformation. This is a slightly sharper result than in [2], [4], where five points are needed. Another difference is that our results are valid also in the case of deformable objects. Since all theorems above give both necessary and sufficient conditions, it also follows that this reconstruction result can't be sharpened, without adding more a priori information.

By the method described above, the 10-point configuration consisting of the points on the faces A, B, C is covered by two overlapping 7-point configurations, B, A and B, C, respectively. Each of these is affinely deformed between the imaging instants. Applying the algorithm of the appendix, one finds in this case only one real solution for q in each case:

$$q_{ba} : (0.4997 \quad 0.4920 \quad 0.5037 \quad 0.5045 \mid 0.4459 \quad 0.4602 \quad 0.4911)$$
$$q_{bc} : (0.4961 \quad 0.4999 \quad 0.5043 \quad 0.4997 \mid 0.5101 \quad 0.5620 \quad 0.5147) .$$

Here the first four components of q_{AB} and q_{CB} correspond to the same points on face B, and have been normalised to become comparable. As can be seen, they show good agreement. Knowing that B is planar, it is also possible to compute q by the methods of [19], giving the same degree of agreement.

For these q:s, $s(\widetilde{\mathcal{X}})$ in (7) can be computed by linear operations. It can be represented by a matrix S', whose columns form a basis for $s(\widetilde{\mathcal{X}})$. In (8) below, S' is chosen so that the first four rows correspond to points in B, and the last three to points in C. The last four elements in the columns 1, 2 and 3 can be interpreted as the barycentric coordinates of $B1, B2$ and $B3$, respectively, with respect to the points $B4, C1, C2, C3$. By fixation of the latters, $\widetilde{\mathcal{X}}$ is completely determined. Among all possible reconstructions, a configuration $\widetilde{\mathcal{X}}$ constructed this way is characterised by the property that it is mapped onto $\overline{\mathcal{Y}}$ by a parallel projection. Uniqueness can also be achieved by other conditions. For instance, claiming that the face C of the reconstructed object shall be parallel to the second image plane $\overline{\mathcal{Y}}$, i.e. that $\overline{\alpha}_5 = \overline{\alpha}_6 = \overline{\alpha}_7 = 1$, and that e.g. $\overline{\alpha}_4 = 1.2$, by solving the linear system $\beta^T S' = 0$ for $\beta_1, \beta_2, \beta_3$, where $\beta = \overline{\alpha}^{-1}$, and by forming $S'' = \text{diag}(\beta)S'$, another reconstruction is obtained, according to RP. The matrix S'' is given in (8), with elements that again may be interpreted in terms of barycentric coordinates. For images containing three distant points, corresponding to points at infinity, unique reconstruction modulo scale can be achieved by assigning the value $\beta = \overline{\alpha}^{-1} = 0$ to these points, cf. [20].

$$
S' = \begin{pmatrix}
-1.0000 & 0.0000 & 0.0000 \\
0 & -1.0000 & 0 \\
0 & 0.0000 & -1.0000 \\
1.0193 & 0.1857 & 0.5411 \\
0.6752 & 0.9373 & -0.3165 \\
-0.0103 & -0.1861 & -0.0853 \\
-0.6842 & 0.0631 & 0.8607
\end{pmatrix}, \quad
S'' = \begin{pmatrix}
-1.0000 & -0.0000 & 0 \\
0 & -1.0000 & 0 \\
0 & 0 & -1.0000 \\
1.0232 & 0.1597 & 0.4956 \\
0.8133 & 0.9672 & -0.3479 \\
-0.0124 & -0.1920 & -0.0937 \\
-0.8242 & 0.0651 & 0.9460
\end{pmatrix} .
$$

$$(8)$$

Invariant Motion Description. Under the weak assumptions of this paper, with no metrical information at all about $\mathcal{Y}$, $\overline{\mathcal{Y}}$, metrical concepts like orthogonal matrices can't be used to describe motion, as one is used to. Here the q-values enter as invariant substitutes. This can be illustrated by the caleidocycle example.

Since q is determined modulo proportionality, it needs to be normalised, e.g. with respect to the first component. Then e.g. q_3/q_1 quantifies the camera movement relative to $B3$ between the two imaging instants, compared to its movements relative to point $B1$. In case of translatorical motion, a value like $q_3/q_1 = 1.0092$ would mean that $B3$ is that much more distant in the second image than in the first, compared to the corresponding ratio for $B1$. For the two images of this example, the camera motion is more complicated, since also the orientation of the image plane affects the q-values.

Looking at e.g. the three last components of q_{bc} in this way, they describe the motion of the camera relative to the plane C. By the methods of Sect. 2, it is possible to compensate for this motion, by making a λ-modulation with respect to $C1, C2, C3$, to make their q-values equal to 1. After this compensation, we obtain the q-vector (1.0613, 1.0112, 1.0331, 1.0605, 1.0000, 1.0000, 1.0000). This enables a quantitative description of the motion of $B1, B2, B3, B4$ relative the face C. For images with e.g. a ground plane, egomotion can be estimated in this way, and compensated for, cf. [20].

By Theorem 4, q has a number of invariancy properties. Disregarding the 3-fold ambiguity, which doesn't appear for larger configurations, q is invariant with respect to camera calibration and to affine deformations of the image planes. Another non-obvious fact is that it automatically gets the same value for all possible reconstructions with respect to a given image pair $\mathcal{Y}$, $\overline{\mathcal{Y}}$.

Kinetic Depth. Now consider an image pair, taken at two close moments in time. In this case, the q-vector computed from $\mathcal{Y}$, $\overline{\mathcal{Y}}$ can be interpreted as a velocity. More precisely, for real-valued functions of the real parameter t, consider the "multiplicative derivative", defined by

$$Ef(t_0) = \lim_{h \to 0} \left(\frac{f(t_0 + h)}{f(t_0)} \right)^{1/h}.$$

The relation between E and the additive derivative, $Df(t_0) = \lim_{h \to 0} (f(t_0 + h) - f(t_0))/h$, is $Ef = \exp(Df/f)$. Let the E-derivative be applied to a time-dependent depth vector $\alpha(t)$. Since depth vectors are determined modulo multiplicative factors, which may vary with t, $E\alpha$ has no sense in absolute terms, only in relative. It measures *the rate of change with time of the magnitude of the depth at a particular point, relative the corresponding rate at the others*. The vector $E\alpha(X)$ will be called the *depth flow* at the point X, along the ray of sight. With terminology borrowed from psychophysics, the depth flow may be considered as a quantitative description of the *kinetic depth* effect, cf. e.g. [8].

Now put $\alpha = \alpha(t_0)$, $\overline{\alpha} = \alpha(t_0 + h)$, and let $q = \overline{\alpha}/\alpha$. Then $E\alpha \approx q^{1/h}$. In other words, apart from the power, the depth ratio q obtained from the algorithm above, gives an estimate of the strength of the depth flow. In [20] examples are given where the depth flow is computed, also with compensation for egomotion.

Appendix. On the Weak Chasles' Problem

Here the explicit solution formula for WCP, used in Sect. 4, will be described. For a proof, see [15]. Let $\mathcal{Y}$ and $\overline{\mathcal{Y}}$ be two given 7-point configurations, with known shapes $s(\mathcal{Y})$ and $s(\overline{\mathcal{Y}})$. The condition to be investigated in WCP is (6), i.e. in the 3D case for 7-point configurations, $\dim\left(qs(\mathcal{Y}) \cap s(\overline{\mathcal{Y}})\right) = 3$. Let $(a_1, a_2, a_3, 1, 0, 0, 0)$, $(b_1, b_2, b_3, 0, 1, 0, 0)$, $(c_1, c_2, c_3, 0, 0, 1, 0)$, $(d_1, d_2, d_3, 0, 0, 0, 1)$, be a basis for $s(\mathcal{Y})$, and let the corresponding vectors with capitals be a basis for $s(\overline{\mathcal{Y}})$. In (??) the components of the vectors in $s(\mathcal{Y})$ are multiplied by q-factors. Taking this into account, it is convenient to form the following matrix:

$$
\begin{pmatrix}
q_1 a_1 & q_1 b_1 & q_1 c_1 & q_1 d_1 & A_1 & B_1 & C_1 & D_1 \\
q_2 a_2 & q_2 b_2 & q_2 c_2 & q_2 d_2 & A_2 & B_2 & C_2 & D_2 \\
q_3 a_3 & q_3 b_3 & q_3 c_3 & q_3 d_3 & A_3 & B_3 & C_3 & D_1 \\
q_4 & 0 & 0 & 0 & 1 & 0 & 0 & 0 \\
0 & q_5 & 0 & 0 & 0 & 1 & 0 & 0 \\
0 & 0 & q_6 & 0 & 0 & 0 & 1 & 0 \\
0 & 0 & 0 & q_7 & 0 & 0 & 0 & 1
\end{pmatrix}
\tag{9}
$$

It can be shown that in checking (6) for 7-point configurations, it suffices to consider the 5-point subconfigurations with indices $(1, 2, 3, 4, 5)$, $(1, 2, 3, 4, 6)$, $(1, 2, 3, 4, 7)$. This in turn can be formulated in terms of (9), namely that the submatrices formed by columns a, b, A, B, a, c, A, C and a, d, A, D all have rank 3. This in turn can be expressed by the vanishing of a number of subdeterminants. Every such subdeterminant produces a second order polynomial in components of q, containing only mixed terms $q_i q_j$ with $i \neq j$. Thus necessary and sufficient conditions for a solution of WCP is the vanishing of these polynomials.

To investigate this system, start with the three equations only containing q_1, q_2, q_3, q_4. Writing $Q^T = (q_1 q_2 \; q_1 q_3 \; q_1 q_4 \; q_2 q_3 \; q_2 q_4 \; q_3 q_4)$, these equations can be written $GQ = 0$, with an appropriate matrix $G = (g_{ij})$, having components that are 2×2-subdeterminants picked out from (9). Let (ijk) denote the subdeterminant in G, formed by means of the columns i, j, k. Then it can be proved that $GQ = 0$ if and only if $t = q_2/q_1$ obeys the equation

$$
c_4 t^4 + c_3 t^3 + c_2 t^2 + c_1 t + c_0 = 0 , \tag{10}
$$

where

$$
\begin{aligned}
c_4 &= (145)(456) \\
c_3 &= (125)(456) - (134)(456) - (145)(346) + (145)(256) - (146)(156) \\
c_2 &= -(126)(156) + (125)(256) - (125)(346) + (123)(456) - \\
     &\quad - (134)(256) + (134)(346) - (136)(146) + (145)(236) \\
c_1 &= -(123)(346) + (125)(236) + (123)(256) - (134)(236) - (126)(136) \\
c_0 &= (123)(236)
\end{aligned}
$$

However, by construction holds $(q_1, q_2, q_3, q_4) = (A_1, A_2, A_3, A_4)/(a_1, a_2, a_3, a_4)$, which yields one trivial solution of (10). Thus three possible solutions for $t = q_2/q_1$ are obtained as the zeros of

$$
(c_4 t^4 + c_3 t^3 + c_2 t^2 + c_1 t + c_0)/((t - A_2 a_1/A_1 a_2) . \tag{11}
$$

Once q_1 and q_2 are known, q_3 and q_4 can be solved for from $GQ = 0$ by means of linear operations, and thereafter q_5, q_6, q_7 by means of the unused equations obtained by forming subdeterminants in (9). These equations are linear in each indeterminate.

References

1. M. Chasles. Question 296. *Nouv. Ann. Math.*, 14(50), 1855.
2. O.D. Faugeras. What can be seen in three dimensions with an uncalibrated stereo rig? In G. Sandini, editor, *Computer Vision - ECCV92*, pages 563–578. Springer Verlag, jun 1992.
3. O.D. Faugeras and S. Maybanks. Motion from point matches: multiplicity of solutions. *Int. J. Computer vision*, 4(3):225–246, 1990.
4. R. Hartley, R. Gupta, and Tom Chang. Stereo from uncalibrated cameras. In *Proceedings IEEE Conf. on Computer vision and Pattern Recognition*, pages 761–764, 1992.
5. A. Heyden. On the consistency of line drawings, obtained by projections of piecewise planar objects. Technical Report ISSN 0347-8475, Dept of Mathematics, Lund Institute of Technology, may 1993.
6. A. Heyden. Reconstruction from three images of six point objects. In *Proc Swedish Soc. of Automated Image Analysis*, mar 1994.
7. B.P.K. Horn. Relative orientation. *Int. J. Computer Vision*, 4:59–78, 1990.
8. G.W. Humphreys and V. Bruce. *Visual Cognition*. Lawrence Erlbaum Associates, Publishers, 1991.
9. J.J. Koenderink and A.J. Van Doorn. Affine structure from motion. *J. of the Optical Society of America*, 8:377–385, 1991.
10. S.J. Maybank. The projective geometry of ambigous surfaces. *Philosophical Transactions of the Royal Society*, 1990.
11. R. Mohr, L. Quan, F. Veillon, and B. Boufama. Relative 3d reconstruction using multiple uncalibrated images. Technical Report RT 84-IMAG, LIFIA-IRIMAG, jun 1992.
12. D. Schattschneider and W. Walker. *Kalejdocykler*. Benedikt Taschen Verlag, 1990.
13. A. Shashua. Projective depth: A geometric invariant for 3d reconstruction from two rspective/orthographic views and for visual recognitionep e. In International Conference on Computer Vision, pages 583–590. IEEE, IEEE, 1993.
14. R.N. Shepard. *Mind Sights*. W.H. Freeman and Company, New York, 1990.
15. A. Sparr and G. Sparr. On a theorem of m. chasles. Technical Report ISRN LUTFD2/TFMA–7001–SE, Dept. of Mathematics, Lund, 1993.
16. G. Sparr. Depth, shape and invariancy. (Book in preparation, Kluwer Verlag).
17. G. Sparr. Projective invariants for affine shapes of point configurations. In Andrew Zisserman and Joe Mundy, editors, *ESPRIT/DARPA Invariants Workshop*, Reykjavik, apr 1991.
18. G. Sparr. An algebraic/analytic method for reconstruction from image correspondences. In *TheoryApplications of Image Analysis*, volume 2 of *Machine Perception Artificial Intelligence*, pages 87–98. World Scientific Publishing Co, 1992. n.
19. G. Sparr. Depth computations from polyhedral images. *Image and Vision Computing*, 10(10):683–688, dec 1992. Also in Proc. ECCV 92, Springer Lect. Notes in Comp.Sc.
20. G. Sparr. Applications of a theorem of chasles to computer vision. Technical Report ISRN LUTFD2/TFMA–7002–SE, Dept of Mathematics, Lund Institute of Technology, 1994.

Author Index

Lecture Notes in Computer Science

For information about Vols. 1–719
please contact your bookseller or Springer-Verlag

Vol. 756: J. Pieprzyk, B. Sadeghiyan, Design of Hashing Algorithms. XV, 194 pages. 1993.

Vol. 757: U. Banerjee, D. Gelernter, A. Nicolau, D. Padua (Eds.), Languages and Compilers for Parallel Computing. Proceedings, 1992. X, 576 pages. 1993.

Vol. 758: M. Teillaud, Towards Dynamic Randomized Algorithms in Computational Geometry. IX, 157 pages. 1993.

Vol. 759: N. R. Adam, B. K. Bhargava (Eds.), Advanced Database Systems. XV, 451 pages. 1993.

Vol. 760: S. Ceri, K. Tanaka, S. Tsur (Eds.), Deductive and Object-Oriented Databases. Proceedings, 1993. XII, 488 pages. 1993.

Vol. 761: R. K. Shyamasundar (Ed.), Foundations of Software Technology and Theoretical Computer Science. Proceedings, 1993. XIV, 456 pages. 1993.

Vol. 762: K. W. Ng, P. Raghavan, N. V. Balasubramanian, F. Y. L. Chin (Eds.), Algorithms and Computation. Proceedings, 1993. XIII, 542 pages. 1993.

Vol. 763: F. Pichler, R. Moreno Díaz (Eds.), Computer Aided Systems Theory – EUROCAST '93. Proceedings, 1993. IX, 451 pages. 1994.

Vol. 764: G. Wagner, Vivid Logic. XII, 148 pages. 1994. (Subseries LNAI).

Vol. 765: T. Helleseth (Ed.), Advances in Cryptology – EUROCRYPT '93. Proceedings, 1993. X, 467 pages. 1994.

Vol. 766: P. R. Van Loocke, The Dynamics of Concepts. XI, 340 pages. 1994. (Subseries LNAI).

Vol. 767: M. Gogolla, An Extended Entity-Relationship Model. X, 136 pages. 1994.

Vol. 768: U. Banerjee, D. Gelernter, A. Nicolau, D. Padua (Eds.), Languages and Compilers for Parallel Computing. Proceedings, 1993. XI, 655 pages. 1994.

Vol. 769: J. L. Nazareth, The Newton-Cauchy Framework. XII, 101 pages. 1994.

Vol. 770: P. Haddawy (Representing Plans Under Uncertainty. X, 129 pages. 1994. (Subseries LNAI).

Vol. 771: G. Tomas, C. W. Ueberhuber, Visualization of Scientific Parallel Programs. XI, 310 pages. 1994.

Vol. 772: B. C. Warboys (Ed.), Software Process Technology. Proceedings, 1994. IX, 275 pages. 1994.

Vol. 773: D. R. Stinson (Ed.), Advances in Cryptology – CRYPTO '93. Proceedings, 1993. X, 492 pages. 1994.

Vol. 774: M. Banâtre, P. A. Lee (Eds.), Hardware and Software Architectures for Fault Tolerance. XIII, 311 pages. 1994.

Vol. 775: P. Enjalbert, E. W. Mayr, K. W. Wagner (Eds.), STACS 94. Proceedings, 1994. XIV, 782 pages. 1994.

Vol. 776: H. J. Schneider, H. Ehrig (Eds.), Graph Transformations in Computer Science. Proceedings, 1993. VIII, 395 pages. 1994.

Vol. 777: K. von Luck, H. Marburger (Eds.), Management and Processing of Complex Data Structures. Proceedings, 1994. VII, 220 pages. 1994.

Vol. 778: M. Bonuccelli, P. Crescenzi, R. Petreschi (Eds.), Algorithms and Complexity. Proceedings, 1994. VIII, 222 pages. 1994.

Vol. 779: M. Jarke, J. Bubenko, K. Jeffery (Eds.), Advances in Database Technology — EDBT '94. Proceedings, 1994. XII, 406 pages. 1994.

Vol. 780: J. J. Joyce, C.-J. H. Seger (Eds.), Higher Order Logic Theorem Proving and Its Applications. Proceedings, 1993. X, 518 pages. 1994.

Vol. 781: G. Cohen, S. Litsyn, A. Lobstein, G. Zémor (Eds.), Algebraic Coding. Proceedings, 1993. XII, 326 pages. 1994.

Vol. 782: J. Gutknecht (Ed.), Programming Languages and System Architectures. Proceedings, 1994. X, 344 pages. 1994.

Vol. 783: C. G. Günther (Ed.), Mobile Communications. Proceedings, 1994. XVI, 564 pages. 1994.

Vol. 784: F. Bergadano, L. De Raedt (Eds.), Machine Learning: ECML-94. Proceedings, 1994. XI, 439 pages. 1994. (Subseries LNAI).

Vol. 785: H. Ehrig, F. Orejas (Eds.), Recent Trends in Data Type Specification. Proceedings, 1992. VIII, 350 pages. 1994.

Vol. 786: P. A. Fritzson (Ed.), Compiler Construction. Proceedings, 1994. XI, 451 pages. 1994.

Vol. 787: S. Tison (Ed.), Trees in Algebra and Programming – CAAP '94. Proceedings, 1994. X, 351 pages. 1994.

Vol. 788: D. Sannella (Ed.), Programming Languages and Systems – ESOP '94. Proceedings, 1994. VIII, 516 pages. 1994.

Vol. 789: M. Hagiya, J. C. Mitchell (Eds.), Theoretical Aspects of Computer Software. Proceedings, 1994. XI, 887 pages. 1994.

Vol. 790: J. van Leeuwen (Ed.), Graph-Theoretic Concepts in Computer Science. Proceedings, 1993. IX, 431 pages. 1994.

Vol. 791: R. Guerraoui, O. Nierstrasz, M. Riveill (Eds.), Object-Based Distributed Programming. Proceedings, 1993. VII, 262 pages. 1994.

Vol. 792: N. D. Jones, M. Hagiya, M. Sato (Eds.), Logic, Language and Computation. XII, 269 pages. 1994.

Vol. 793: T. A. Gulliver, N. P. Secord (Eds.), Information Theory and Applications. Proceedings, 1993. XI, 394 pages. 1994.

Vol. 796: W. Gentzsch, U. Harms (Eds.), High-Performance Computing and Networking. Proceedings, 1994, Vol. I. XXI, 453 pages. 1994.

Vol. 797: W. Gentzsch, U. Harms (Eds.), High-Performance Computing and Networking. Proceedings, 1994, Vol. II. XXII, 519 pages. 1994.

Vol. 800: J.-O. Eklundh (Ed.), Computer Vision – ECCV '94. Proceedings 1994, Vol. I. XVIII, 603 pages. 1994.

Vol. 801: J.-O. Eklundh (Ed.), Computer Vision – ECCV '94. Proceedings 1994, Vol. II. XV, 485 pages. 1994.